INTERPRETING PRECEDENTS

INTERPRETING PRECEDENTS
A COMPARATIVE STUDY

Edited by
D. NEIL MacCORMICK
Regius Professor of Public Law and the Law of Nature and Nations
University of Edinburgh

and

ROBERT S. SUMMERS
McRoberts Research Professor of Law Cornell University; Arthur L.
Goodhart Visiting Professor of Legal Science, University of Cambridge,
1991–92

Routledge
Taylor & Francis Group

LONDON AND NEW YORK

First published 1997 by Ashgate Publishing

Published 2016 by Routledge
2 Park Square, Milton Park, Abingdon, Oxfordshire OX14 4RN
711 Third Avenue, New York, NY 10017, USA

First issued in paperback 2016

Routledge is an imprint of the Taylor & Francis Group, an informa business

British Library Cataloguing in Publication Data
Interpreting precedents : a comparative study. – (Applied legal philosophy)
  1. Law – Interpretation and construction
  I. MacCormick, Neil   II. Summers, Robert S. (Robert Samuel),
1933–
340. 1'1

Library of Congress Cataloging-in-Publication Data
Interpreting precedents : a comparative study / edited by D. Neil
  MacCormick and Robert S. Summers.
     p. cm. – (Applied legal philosophy)

    1. Stare decisis.   2. Law–Interpretation and construction.
  I. MacCormick, Neil.   II. Summers, Robert S.   III. Series.
  K574.I58   1997
  340–dc21   96–39520
                                                CIP

ISBN 13: 978-1-138-27024-4 (pbk)
ISBN 13: 978-1-85521-686-0 (hbk)

Typeset by Manton Typesetters

Contents

Preface and Acknowledgements

This book on precedent is the second book prepared by a special research group, which calls itself 'The Bielefelder Kreis'. This book, like the first (on statutory interpretation) seeks to advance understanding of fundamentals of law and its methodology through systematic comparative and theoretical analysis. This research group held its founding meeting in Helsinki, Finland in August of 1983 with Prof. Dr Aulis Aarnio as host. The initiative for the formation of the group was taken by Robert Summers of Cornell Law School after some discussions in the Italian Alps during the summer of 1982 with Enrico Pattaro and Aleksander Peczenik.

Participants in this precedent project consist of Professor Aulis Aarnio (University of Helsinki and Tampere, Finland), Professor Robert Alexy (University of Kiel, Germany), Professor Zenon Bankowski (University of Edinburgh, United Kingdom), Professor John J. Barceló (Cornell Law School, USA), Professor Gunnar Bergholtz (University of Lund, Sweden), Professor Ralf Dreier (University of Göttingen, Germany), Dr Svein Eng (University of Oslo, Norway), Professor Ernesto Garzón-Valdés (University of Mainz, Germany), Professor Christophe Grzegorczyk (University of Paris, Nanterre), Professor Francisco J. Laporta (Autonomous University of Madrid, Spain), Professor Massimo La Torre (European University, Florence, Italy), Professor D. Neil MacCormick (University of Edinburgh, United Kingdom), Dr Geoffrey Marshall (University of Oxford, United Kingdom), Professor Alfonso Ruiz Miguel (Autonomous University of Madrid, Spain), Professor Lech Morawski (University of Torun, Poland), Professor Enrico Pattaro (University of Bologna, Italy), Professor Aleksander Peczenik (University of Lund, Sweden), Professor Robert S. Summers (Cornell Law School, USA), Professor Michele Taruffo (University of Pavia, Italy), Professor Michel Troper (University of Paris, Nanterre) and Professor Marek Zirk-Sadowski (University of Łódź, Poland). Professor Neil MacCormick served as co-chair, and Professor Robert Summers as chair.

Since 1983, the research group has met once or more annually in various places in Europe, Britain and the United States, including several times at the Center for Interdisciplinary Studies at the University of Bielefeld, in Germany. The first published effort of this research group, which today calls itself 'The Bielefelder Kreis', consisted of a 567 page work called *Interpreting Statutes – A Comparative Study*, which appeared in 1991. The present work on precedents is, in its methodological orientation, a companion volume, and represents the fruits of work over a five-year period.

The co-authors in the research group for the first volume appear in the table of contents thereof, and the same is true of this second volume. It will be seen that the continuity of membership is considerable, with the exception of new members from Poland, the addition of Spain and Norway and their new members, the addition of a new member from the United Kingdom, and the addition of a scholar concerned with precedent in the European Union. The members met on the precedent project in June 1992 at the Center for Interdisciplinary Studies at the University of Bielefeld, in May 1993 at the Cornell Law School in Ithaca, New York, in June 1994 at Bologna and Florence, in June 1995 at Bologna, and in August 1996 at Tampere, Finland.

The main modes of operation of the research group have been sixfold from the beginning: (1) the formulation of agreed sets of common concepts, terminology and questions to be answered for each country (with the questions printed as appendices to the volumes), (2) the preparation by members from each country of a draft essay for that country addressing the common questions, (3) extensive discussions at annual sessions of the common questions and draft answers, with agreed revisions of both, (4) the assignment and preparation of draft special essays on common topics based on (1), (2) and (3), (5) extensive discussions of the draft special essays on the common topics, and (6) thorough review and editing of the final research effort by the same co-editors of both volumes, Professor Neil MacCormick of the University of Edinburgh, and Professor Robert Summers of Cornell Law School. For each of our annual sessions, all of which lasted several days, a set of minutes was prepared recording the essential understandings and agreed further steps. There have been some differences of emphasis in approach and methodology for the two projects, and these are identified and briefly discussed in the introduction to this second volume.

The members of the research group wish to express their gratitude to a number of persons for various important forms of assistance, or other support including research advice, in the course of the work on the present volume: Dean Russell Osgood of the Cornell Law School, the Cornell Law School, and the Berger International Legal Studies

Program at Cornell Law School, hosts and financial sponsors of the May 1993 annual session of the research group; Professor Enrico Pattaro and Professor Massimo La Torre, hosts of the June 1994 sessions in Bologna and Florence; Professor Enrico Pattaro and CIRFID, co-hosts of the June 1995 session; Professor Dr Aulis Aarnio, Ms. Anja Aarnio Van Aershot, the Finnish Section of the International Association of Social and Legal Philosophy, and the Institute of Social Sciences at the University of Tampere, Finland, co-hosts of the 1996 sessions; Dr Raimo Siltila, University of Helsinki for valuable assistance; Professor Claire Germaine, the Edward Cornell Law Librarian at Cornell Law School, and Mr John Hasko, Associate Law Librarian, Cornell Law School, both for valuable research assistance; Judge Walter Relihan, New York Supreme Court, for valuable information and advice about the workings of the precedent system in New York State; Mr Okko Hendrik Behrends of Göttingen, Germany, for bibliographic assistance and for discussions of what is special about the common law; Dr Svein Eng for various forms of advice both before and after becoming a member of the research group; Professor Dr Ernesto Garzón-Valdés for many forms of participation, advice and information; Professor Michele Taruffo for special contributions from the perspective of the discipline of comparative law; Dorothy Kopp Summers and Elizabeth Anne Summers for various forms of assistance on the final manuscript and on the proofs and index; and to participants in a symposium in 1992 at the Center for Interdisciplinary Studies at the University of Bielefeld who also provided advice directly or indirectly of relevance to our precedent project: Professor Dr Hubert Rottleutner (Free University of Berlin), Professor Dr Niklas Luhmann (University of Bielefeld), Judge David Edward of the European Court of Justice, Justice Hans Linde of the Oregon Supreme Court, Oberlandesgerichtspräsident Gunther Ellscheid of the Saarland High Court and Mr Tony Weir of Trinity College, Cambridge.

The participants are especially indebted to research assistants of Professor Robert S. Summers at the Cornell Law School who provided important services, bibliographical and other, on the final manuscript: Eric Jacobs, Matthew Michaels and Laura McClellan.

All members wish to emphasize their sense of indebtedness to Mrs Sandra Markham and to Mrs Pamela Finnigan, secretaries and assistants at the Cornell Law School who contributed to the work of the research group in countless ways. Special thanks are here recorded to Mrs Finnigan for her remarkable efforts in preparation of the final manuscript for the precedent project.

Again, as with the first book to emerge from the efforts of this research group, the project members wish to record their profound sense of gratitude to the Center for Interdisciplinary Studies of the

University of Bielefeld, and in particular to Dr Gerhard Sprenger, Director; to the Board of Directors of the Center, and to the staff of the Center. The interpretation project of the group was completed under the auspices of the Center, and the precedent project was launched there. The Center also sponsored a symposia on both books emerging from these projects. Without the advice and support of the Center, it is doubtful if either of the books from the research group would have appeared.

Finally, the co-editors wish particularly to express their appreciation to their colleagues in the Bielefelder Kreis for the highly cooperative spirit in which this project was carried out, and for the honour of being invited to act as editors for it. This is very much a joint work, the product of many hands and minds. Especially in the common chapters, 13–18, though individuals or groups had the responsibility for capturing the sense developed through the whole project on one general topic or another, the understandings and advances achieved are of an essentially collective character, the product of contributions to debate by each and every one of our members. We in our role as editors have similarly been very conscious that we act as servants of a group from whose cooperation we have gained the insights that have enabled us to see the project to completion in its present form.

Neil MacCormick insists on adding for his and all his other colleagues' part a special sense of the common debt to Robert Summers for his role in convening and chairing our group, maintaining clear and accurate records of our meetings and regularly prompting us on the timetable of our work. All have contributed much, but he much more than the rest of us.

D.N.M. R.S.S.
October 1996

Series Preface

The objective of the Dartmouth Series in Applied Legal Philosophy is to publish work which adopts a theoretical approach to the study of particular areas or aspects of law or deals with general theories of law in a way which focuses on issues of practical moral and political concern in specific legal contexts.

In recent years there has been an encouraging tendency for legal philosophers to utilize detailed knowledge of the substance and practicalities of law and a noteworthy development in the theoretical sophistication of much legal research. The series seeks to encourage these trends and to make available studies in law which are both genuinely philosophical in approach and at the same time based on appropriate legal knowledge and directed towards issues in the criticism and reform of actual laws and legal systems.

The series will include studies of all the main areas of law, presented in a manner which relates to the concerns of specialist legal academics and practitioners. Each book makes an original contribution to an area of legal study while being comprehensible to those engaged in a wide variety of disciplines. Their legal content is principally Anglo-American, but a wide-ranging comparative approach is encouraged and authors are drawn from a variety of jurisdictions.

TOM D. CAMPBELL
Series Editor
The Faculty of Law
The Australian National University

1 Introduction

D. NEIL MacCORMICK, *EDINBURGH* **AND**
ROBERT S. SUMMERS, *ITHACA*

Precedents are prior decisions that function as models for later decisions. Applying lessons of the past to solve problems of present and future is a basic part of human practical reason. Accordingly, there is no better way for a lawyer to get at the heart of a legal system than to ask how it handles precedent. Precedent represents the law observing itself, in two senses. First, when a lawyer – judge, practitioner or legal scholar – contemplates a legal problem and inquires whether there is any precedent about this problem, what will be produced for scrutiny, should the inquiry succeed, is a record of a prior decision or decisions from the same legal system that solved, well or ill, the same or at least a similar problem. Thus one member of the system observes another member's activity in one of the central tasks of a legal system, the problem-solving, case-deciding task. Second, there may be observance in the stronger sense of compliance; the later decision maker does not merely take note of an earlier solution, but may comply with it as a guiding model for solution of the present problem, and may do so on the ground that present observance of past rulings in like cases is the right or even the obligatory course to follow.

The body of precedents available for consideration in any legal setting represents, at its best, an accumulation of wisdom from the past. There is not always, and there certainly does not have to be, an absolutely perfect match between a new case for decision and any single precedent. More probable is it that, for any new case, a set of prior authorities provides a range of at least persuasively similar patterns which may be either adopted or adapted to solve the present problem. Precedent-based law, 'case law' as it is often called, is a form of law with great antiquity. The establishment of reasonably reliable tribunals for deciding disputed cases is much older than the development of the modern type of legislature. Early legislation is generally an intervention in and superimposition on some form of case law heavily based on the interpretation of general or local custom. Only later does a comprehensive codification of law through carefully designed legislation become possible, and statute law can then very largely supersede case law as the fundamental repository of basic concepts of the law. It does, however, remain necessary to interpret the codes, and they come to be glossed in a body of interpretative precedents. While one can imagine a body of pure case law as a workable legal order, it is difficult so to conceive of statute law, even under the most comprehensive codification.

Precedents, we said, are prior decisions that function as models for later decisions. Authoritative precedents are prior decisions that for some reason one ought to use as governing models for later decisions. The recognition of authoritative precedent has thus a certain backward-looking effect, to the extent that the present must be guided by what was decided in the past. But there is a forward-looking aspect to this as well; for the very existence of a practice of ascribing authority to past decisions means that one who engages in deciding a novel case does so knowing that the decision reached will itself be taken as a guide in later cases. That knowledge sets an important test for the soundness of the present decision: will it be satisfactory as a precedent? Judges are well aware that their decisions contribute to the development of the law, and they do therefore have regard to issues of policy and of principle in working towards their decisions.

As a very broad generalization, this probably holds good everywhere, but there are considerable differences at a level of greater detail. Legal systems differ markedly over the question how, and how far, they require or expect judges and others to observe precedents as governing models for decision. It therefore sheds a penetrating light on the working of a system to consider just where that very system stands on these questions, and from a comparative point of view one achieves a striking set of contrasts by looking together at one or several systems with these questions in mind. To differentiate 'civilian' from 'common law' systems is a commonplace among lawyers. It is trite learning that precedents count for less in civilian legal systems than in those of the common law, and it has sometimes been doubted whether they stand for anything much at all in the civilian systems. The present work shows the doubt to be groundless. Here it is shown that precedent counts for a great deal in civilian systems. The tendency to convergence between systems of the two types is a salient fact of the later twentieth century, although there remain real differences, some of great importance.

Nevertheless, an initial word of warning about the 'civilian/common law' dichotomy is also called for. As shorthand, this is a differentiation that serves a purpose, but it is both unsubtle and to a degree misleading both in terms of history and in terms of present reality. Certainly, the legal systems of Western European countries, except for England (and Wales and Ireland under English dominion), developed as modern systems heavily under the influence of a reception of ideas and even to some extent of actual legal norms from the ancient Roman civil law as that was studied in renaissance and early modern universities. English law was developed in a quite unique way through the Inns of Court and the Chancery and acquired a robust native quality very much less under Roman influence than was common elsewhere, even in neighbouring Scotland, which until the end of the eighteenth century worked much more with the Roman law paradigm than with an English system that was already in full maturity in the eighteenth century. Then, under Napoleon, France adopted codes in the first decade of the nineteenth century and, partly by conquest, partly by their own inherent prestige, the codes, or codes closely modelled on them, were adopted in other places, especially in the European countries of the romance languages, as well as in French or francophone territories beyond Europe. Germany, despite early precocity, rejected codification and sustained that rejection until after the unification of a German Empire under Prussian hegemony at the end of the nineteenth century, and the German codes when introduced were a new production, no mere gloss on the *Code Napoléon*. During the nineteenth century, German legal science as practised in the great university law faculties attained very high prestige, involving deep studies of the *usus modernus Pandectarum*, the modern usage of the body of (Roman) law based on Justinian's *Digest*. This influence was strongly felt in the Nordic countries, which, like the United Kingdom, never produced comprehensive codifications, though most of the modern law on topics of importance has some statutory foundation. The Nordic countries have strongly civilian-influenced systems of mainly statutory law and, if the ultimate basis of the systems lies in the ancient customs of the Scandinavian peoples, these are now almost entirely overlaid by modernizations partly of purely domestic construction, partly imported. Meanwhile, there has been a great growth in both the relative importance and the extensiveness of statutory law in the countries of the common law tradition.

It is thus at best misleading to think that there is a unified 'civilian' type of legal system standing in simple contrast to 'common law' countries like the United Kingdom (along with those countries of the Commonwealth that adopted the English common law and have adapted it to their own preferences over time) and the United States. It is important to remember that the internal legal dualism of the UK leaves Scots law as a system with civilian roots but at the present time a largely 'common law' approach to legal methodology, and that Louisiana has, in important respects, a codified civil law system within the USA, just as that within Canada, Quebec uses the *code civil*. On the other hand, the 'civilian' systems contain several different families and distinct histories, including for some a history of long submersion in a variety of other legal traditions, as has been the fate of Finland and Poland until, and to a degree during, the twentieth century. We do use the 'civilian versus common law' contrast as basic terms of reference throughout much of the rest of this book; but this is acknowledged to be a rather crude distinction taken in gross, and the authors have tried to ensure that more subtle differentiations are used whenever these are required. We hope that no error will have crept in from an unwarranted over usage of the simple dichotomy.

The legal systems of contemporary states and federations are formidably complex and many-faceted. They can be viewed in many perspectives – as adjuncts of the economic system, as frameworks for and products of the political system, as sites of social interaction, as tools in the power play of mighty interests, and so on. One available perspective is that which sees them as quite particularly theatres of practical reason and deliberation. In this perspective they belong, however imperfectly, to the realm of rational order, and they contribute to society a rational system for structuring mutual expectations and interactions. Max Weber (Weber, 1954) and his followers have argued that the emergence of rational legal order is a special feature of commercial and then capitalist societies, so a view of law as participating in rational order and practical reason is not necessarily at odds with some of the other approaches possible – but it is different. And it is the perspective in which the present set of studies belongs.

One conception of legal rationality ties it strongly to statute law and to codification. A modern code is ordered in a rational way into chapters, sections, subsections. The basic ideas of the law are encompassed within well-structured texts written in plain French or plain German or plain Spanish or whatever. Citizens and officials have the same access to the basic rules of the system, and legal certainty and the security of legal subjects in awareness of their rights and confidence about their adequate judicial or administrative protection set a framework for the rational conduct of the business of civil society under the protection of a rationally administered state. This ideal of rational order is then apt to be contrasted with the muddle of the common law, where the rules and principles for the conduct of affairs have to be grasped from a reading of a colossal library of cases that are often intelligible only to people who have already considerable legal learning. Although much law in common law countries is statutory, the statutes are usually built on a foundation of case law, rather than the cases being of significance only as a commentary on the code in which all fundamentals are determined.

The contrast just drawn has real importance, though like all such contrasts it probably exaggerates the two extreme cases contrasted. One way to differentiate the statute law and the case law styles is through the contrast between 'constructivist' and 'critical' rationalism. (See Hayek, 1975.) Statute law requires, of course, a legislature to enact it; there must be a carefully planned project for enactment, followed by debate, and decision laying down all at once a whole scheme of legal norms. For this to work well, the promoters and drafters of a statute have to have foreseen well all manner of possibilities that will arise and be covered by this statute, and have to have worked out how to fit its provisions in alongside the existing law so far as not repealed and superseded by the present enactment. The elaboration of law through precedent is usually a slower, more evolutionary business, in which by an incremental process small adjustments are made case by case, usually never more than necessary for solving the problem in each case, always correctable in the light of experience through overruling of discovered mistakes by highest-level appeal courts, nowadays universally empowered to correct also their own prior errors. The method of statute requires the use of reason to work out a large plan in advance; the method of precedent applies critical intelligence to reasoning out the best new decision in light of the prior ones, in light of what is special about the case at hand, and in light of the need to maintain a coherently principled body of law.

Each of these methods at its best is a general type of rationality in social action, not only in the law. Each is a way of constituting what Summers calls 'authority reasons' for action (Summers, 1978, p.724). In relation to law, it would be beside the point, really, to ask which is 'the best' use of reason, 'the best' kind of rationality. No contemporary legal order is conceivable that does not make large use of both. At most, the issue is how best to balance the two in a well-working system, and that in turn may not admit of any universal answer. Institutions and their history and the legal traditions that have grown up around them will profoundly affect what is possible and desirable as a path of development for any given legal system.

In any event, for the student of practical reason in human affairs, the study of lawyers' use of precedent has a magnetic fascination. Law has in times past been considered a kind of 'written reason' or, by the greatest Scots authority of the early modern law, 'reason itself as it is versant about the rights of man' (cf. Stair, 1995, I.1.1). Neither such view needs be swallowed whole, but each has enough suggestiveness to encourage close inquiry into the questions how and why lawyers reason in relation to their and their peers' past decisions when they come to arguing or deciding new cases, or solving problems in ways that save the labour, anxiety and expense of litigation in court. Is it, and if so in what way or on what ground, rational or reasonable to treat past patterns of decision as supplying a set of convincing reasons for use in later cases? Or as yielding presumptively or even absolutely governing patterns or indeed rules for the present and the future? How close must the resemblance be? Should rules and principles – rules or principles – be explicitly stated in earlier decisions to provide express guidelines for later decisions, or is it enough just to state reasons for the particular case, leaving the later decision maker to figure out the relevance of the old decision, given its factual setting, to the new one, given its facts, untrammelled by such perhaps premature pronouncements? When and by what means can the later decision maker escape the constraints of a decision that seems wrong if applied to the present case? If there are other authoritative (or more authoritative) norms governing decisions – the provisions of a constitution or a code or a statute – how should reasoning with precedents interact with interpreting and applying norms of this kind? Should it fall silent in face of them?

Questions such as these can be multiplied almost infinitely, and they can certainly be set in stricter order, as we shall see. But to ask them even in an initially unstructured way is sufficient for the purpose of pressing home the claim that in them lie strong grounds for thinking the study of precedent essential to grasping the character of law as a rational enterprise, one guided by practical reason. Again, since lawyers carry out their reasoning in quite special institutional settings with quite individual histories and unique contemporary political and social contexts, we expect local differences in the way such matters are handled; tracking a presumptively common rationality through a variety of institutional settings ought to enrich greatly both our comparative insight into differences of institutional rationality and rationale, and our understanding of the fundamentals of reason in law, if there are any.

The present group of authors – the 'Bielefelder Kreis' as we have audaciously called ourselves in gratitude for sponsorship of the Zentrum für interdisziplinäre Forschung ('ZiF') in the University of Bielefeld – have a particular interest in just such an approach from the perspective of practical reason and discourse. For the group comprises legal theorists, philosophers of law and comparatists united by an interest in the comparative and theoretical exploration of aspects of reasoning in different legal systems. There is no single doctrine or set of tenets about legal reasoning or general legal theory to which each of the group subscribes, no 'party line'. But there is a sufficient community of interest and of orientation to make possible a common approach to the task of system comparison.

System
deliberative
process.
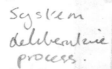

system of courts and their hierarchical interrelationships from first instance courts up to the final instance, either of appeal or of cassation ('cassation' being the concept of having a highest tribunal that supervises the legality of decision making at all lower appellate and trial court levels, and if it finds defects in legality quashes the decision, remitting back to the court below for a correct final decision to be made there); also under this head we sought information about the deliberative process in the courts, the typical form of judgments, and the standard form and content of reports of decisions available to the general public, the profession and the courts themselves. Obviously, it is only possible to understand how precedents are used if one understands the court structure and the way in which earlier decisions can be subsequently made known to courts facing similar questions in later cases. And differences in history, in juridical tradition, and in constitutional and institutional structures may well produce readily understandable differences of practice and approach between different systems.

Answering these institutional questions requires mainly a fairly straightforward descriptive account of matters that are in the main uncontroversial, and not subject to vagaries of interpretation. The same cannot be said of the remaining question topics, which all call in various ways for an interpretation of practice such as is inevitably open to controversy among different interpreters of the system and its practices. To begin with, the second main group of our questions inquires into the binding character that is properly ascribed to precedents in each of the systems, whether they are formally binding or not and, if so, whether there are circumstances in which bindingness can be defeated ('defeasibly binding') or outweighed on the balance of reasons; or whether, even if not formally binding, precedents have an acknowledged normative force in the system such that they ought to be followed, or at least followed except where there are sufficient reasons to justify departure, and so on. The third set of questions concern the rationale, the generally understood justifying and explanatory reasons, for whatever practice of using or ignoring precedent a system has. The fourth turns to the issue of how, from the sometimes considerable bulk of reasoning offered by courts in the judicial opinions that account for the decisions they hand down, later judges, or lawyers with cases to argue, or scholars with legal commentaries to write, are supposed to winnow out the very point of the precedent, the element or elements in it that are specifically binding, or normatively forceful or persuasive or whatever. The fifth group then inquires about departures from precedent. When and on what grounds and by what argumentative methods is it possible to escape or avoid the force of an apparently relevant and putatively binding precedent? How explicit are courts and lawyers in the argu-

2
binding
- ness.

3 -
rationale
justifis-

4
Ratio

5
Evasion

ments they make or expect lawyers or scholars to make in relation to such matters? Finally, in the sixth group we sought generally critical and reflective evaluation of practice from within each system.

Questions of this sort are empirical in a sense, for they refer to the world of experience and require the production and sifting of evidence. They are not, however, essentially quantitative, nor do they demand treatment under the disciplines proper to, for example, sociological or economic description or analysis. They are, as we have stated, 'interpretative' questions, questions of a kind that postulate a good working knowledge of the way the system works and of the corpus of law in the system from a lawyerly point of view, coupled with an ability to argue out the case for a favoured interpretation of the relevant material. The ultimate test of such an interpretation is as much practical as it is theoretical; the issue is whether, guided by such an interpretation, a citizen or a lawyer would reliably be able to operate within the system, making acceptable arguments for claims and responses to the claims of others and, when necessary (if ever), making acceptable and successful arguments before courts.

From another point of view, more scholarly–scientific than directly practical, the method here adopted aims at a 'rational reconstruction' of partial or fragmentary, sometimes in part internally inconsistent, materials, aimed at showing the place they have in a legal system conceived as a complex and well-ordered whole. This calls for a dialectic between assessing the apparent meaning of a part of a system and forming a view of the whole, on the footing that, in its entirety, a legal system is a coherent sum of interacting parts. Almost certainly, of any real legal system in the world, the assumption of holistic coherence is partly false. In the real world, perhaps, there are always conflicts, antinomies, inconsistencies. Yet the very idea of 'system' functions in legal thought as what is sometimes called a 'regulative ideal' (Bengoetxea, 1994). Although inconsistency and partial incoherence keep rising to the surface in the practice of law, the institutions of the law, and particularly the higher courts, have responsibility for the task of trying to purge inconsistency and secure coherence and unity; in this they are guided by a concept of the systematicity of law.

Among the elements in an overall conception of legal system must be included a conception of the norms that govern argumentation, that enable us to discriminate between good and bad, relevant and irrelevant, arguments in the particular context of a given legal system. These include norms about the interpretation of statutes; they include also norms about arguing from, and interpreting, precedents. The task performed in producing each of the country-by-country chapters has been that of 'rationally reconstructing' the often inexplicit norms about the use of precedent in the relevant system. An example

[handwritten marginalia:]
6
critical + reflective

empirical
interpretat-
 ive
operation + basis for advice

2
rational
re-construct
of norms
of use
of precedent
coherence

norms
of argument-
ation
as part of
overall
conception of
a legal system

of the way in which we try to facilitate this is to be found in question
II.1, as listed in the Appendix, a question which was formulated and
reformulated with particular care at the 1994 meeting. What this
question seeks to do is to set a conceptual framework for an account
of the binding character or the normative force of precedent in any
one of various systems; it seeks to differentiate formal bindingness
from a degree of normative force that amounts to less than being
strictly bound to follow a precedent; and both for the formally binding and the merely forceful or persuasive, it frames ways to consider
when these varieties of normative bearing can be defeated, outweighed or overridden. The framework we have constructed here is
terminologically and conceptually more refined ('sophisticated', perhaps) than will be found in the normal discussions of precedent
within present-day systems, common law or civilian (see also Chapter 14, Section II). But the very effort to construct a framework within
which the authoritative character of precedent can be represented in
terms of a continuum rather than purely as all-or-nothing bindingness
gets at something that we take to be an important truth. It provides a
means to reconstruct the criteria of argumentation from precedent in
a way that seems more faithful to underlying realities than a more
simple approach would do.

We discussed this idea of rational reconstruction at greater length
in Chapter 2 of *Interpreting Statutes*, and need say little more of it
here. But there is one point to which attention ought to be drawn, by
way of contrast to our earlier work. In all modern systems of law,
statutes, the subject of our earlier work, play a very large part, even if
there has been no full-scale codification in some of them; hence there
was (and is) much discussion of statutory interpretation in the literature dealing with all legal systems in our earlier study. The same is
not true of precedent, even though the contemporary tendency is
towards increasing significance for precedent even in the civilian
systems. In common law systems, here represented by the United
Kingdom and by the United States of America (with focus on common law precedent in one state – New York), there has long been a
thriving literature on the operation of precedent within the system
and it is a commonplace that quite substantial parts of the law, including the parts that define some of the most fundamental legal
concepts, are made up of case law, a body of legal rules and principles for which no more fundamental authority can be found than
that they have been laid down in or follow from and are implied by
the accumulated precedents of the higher courts. In this there is a
great contrast with other systems reported in this study, most of
which have within the past two hundred years adopted comprehensive codes defining the main parts of at least private law, commercial
law and criminal law, including the most basic concepts deployed in

such areas of law. Under codification, less attention has been paid to precedent than in common law systems, and scholars have had a tendency to omit much discussion of precedent except perhaps in a context of drawing comparisons with the common law systems, pointing up the contrasts between the rational order of codified law and the rather more sprawling organic growth of the common law from precedent to precedent.

One strong message of the present book is that there is here a contrast that has been too often too much exaggerated. There are indeed vital and deep differences between the legal systems of codified law and the legal systems of common law, and some of the deeper differences do relate to the way in which precedents are viewed and used. But the fact remains that also in the systems of codified law precedent has played a great and, it must be said with emphasis, a growing part. Thus the secular movement is towards convergence, not increased differentiation of systems. Moreover, in the system of European Community law that brings together countries from both sides of the divide, the precedents of the European Court of Justice have played a quite decisive part in developing and determining the character of the legal system and indeed its distinct existence as a new legal order independent of those of the member states. The present book engages with a task that participants in our group from civilian systems considered somewhat neglected in scholarly discussion of these systems, namely the task of producing a conceptually helpful and theoretically well-grounded account of the place of precedent and of norms about argument from precedent in these systems. Of particular interest from this point of view are the second, fourth and fifth question topics, concerning respectively the concept of 'binding precedent' including not only formal bindingness but other degrees of normative force as well, the identification of the authoritative element in precedent, and the grounds for and techniques of negating or avoiding or 'distinguishing' that authoritative element in later cases in which, for some reason, departure from, rather than following in line with, the authoritative element of a governing precedent seems preferable.

Among the greatest of the difficulties in the enterprise was to seek out ways of posing the questions that were sufficiently differentiated to cover a body of distinctions well enough known in the common law world without forcing the discussion of the other systems into a mould that would distort the material to be examined. This, we hope, explains what some readers will judge a certain prolixity (or terminological infelicity) in the framing of the questions. Ideally, if we take ordinary talk about precedents in the normal legal discourse of the various systems to be the object of the present inquiry (the 'object language' that we study), what we needed to establish in the questions was a 'metalanguage' in the terms of which we could easily enough discuss each system without importing prejudices or preconceptions from another. This problem is further discussed in Chapter 14, Section II, and will not be discussed extensively here.

Suffice it to say that we remain somewhat concerned about the risk of 'common law bias' in the way the questions are framed. Such a bias could easily arise from the already noted fact that lawyers in the common law tradition have developed a much larger battery of terms and concepts for discussion and analysis of precedents than are in use among civilians, a fact that itself flows from the much more extensive tradition of precedent-based law in the relevant countries. It seems therefore inevitable that a language of interrogation rich enough to match the common law body of discourse will be somewhat overrefined in relation to other systems, and yet may still need to be enhanced in unfamiliar ways to leave open the possibility of fair and meaningful comparison and theoretical analysis. We believe that this work of ours sets an example of an attempt to do this, but that improvement beyond the present achievement remains a challenge, to be taken up either by some of the present writers on later occasions or, better, by other hands altogether.

A different objection might query the use of a single set of common questions as altogether too restrictive and unimaginative a way to approach the topic. One friendly critic of *Interpreting Statutes* animadverted to its character as a 'work by a committee', rather than an extended exploration of comparative–theoretical issues theme by theme. We are fully conscious of the risk implicit in our strategy of pursuing comparison by detailed and, from country to country, repetitive, description and rational reconstruction of each of ten different legal systems, all in exactly the same order with exactly the same subheadings, responding to the promptings of exactly the same list of questions. But we do emphasize that, without the detailed and carefully prepared country-by-country reports dealing with the same issues structured similarly, relevant comparison of functional equivalents would be yet harder. That comparison is carried out fully and faithfully in the set of general chapters, Chapters 13–18, paralleling the sequence of the question topics: one on institutional aspects of precedent, one on its binding character, one on the rationales for justifying and explaining it, one on general approaches to the binding element, one on departures from precedent and a final one on reaching some general conclusions and exploring some value issues about practice concerning precedents. Most of the theoretical and comparative pay-off of our study is to be found in these chapters; but the evidence behind the comparative findings is all gathered from the preceding chapters, and the comparisons would lack validity without them, while any conceptual and other theoretical advances achieved are in a very real sense the collective achievement of the whole Bielefelder Kreis. These shared theoretical insights and the common comparative understanding pervade each of the country-by-country chapters. They are not system-bound essays prepared with blinkered disregard for other systems or in a theoretical vacuum; on the contrary, they are accounts which try to be faithful to local materials in a way that facilitates comparison, because they are prepared in a dialectic of comparative conversations with other authors engaged in the same tasks for their respective systems, and engaged in collectively refining the question topics also.

So far, we have said nothing about the already sizable literature of comparative law and legal theory of relevance to our study of precedent. The foregoing analysis of our methodology is sufficient to indicate its distinctive character. No prior study comparable to this one has occurred. But we have individually and collectively consulted much of the existing literature while doing the current project and, accordingly, acknowledge our general indebtedness to this body of work, much of it of the highest quality. In some instances we have cited particular books and articles that played a role in our thinking. We have not, however, made any effort to cite all of these, and a comprehensive compendium of references to the existing comparative and theoretical literature on precedent is not to be found here.

Perhaps relatively few readers will find it inviting to read the book straight through in order of the table of contents. Some, for example, will wish to proceed straight from this introduction to the general chapters, referring back to relevant sections of the country-by-country chapters for further illumination of the theme, and to check on the evidentiary quality of claims made. Others will want to choose a few particular countries for special reflection before embarking on the general chapters; yet others will read the country-by-country chapters through, with an eye only to a particular section before reading the general chapters, and so on. In relation to each of the countries (and doubtless others) scholars may, we hope they will, take up the challenge of producing a more refined and thorough account of precedent in the national system, transcending the account given here but guided by the underlying approach, and drawing on the data in the various country-by-country chapters. From that point of view, each of the country chapters is an independent and significant starting point for fresh inquiry into legal theory and legal process, informed by a comparative awareness that remains highly beneficial even when only a single system is studied intensively.

We do hope, however, that some readers will indeed take on a study of the whole range of systems before the general chapters. In our far from objective opinion, these essays give strikingly vivid introductions in small bulk to a fascinating array of legal systems in the main European or European-originating families. The confinement to the 'European' in a wide sense may be to a degree regrettable, for other juristic traditions of equal interest and validity are thus left out. This originates more in the coincidences and prior acquaintanceships that led to the initial coming together of the Bielefelder Kreis than in any grand overall plan. But one useful basis for comparison is found where there are relatively strong family resemblances, as there are among the bodies of law we look at here. Already the book is long, already we have problems framing question topics that are viable for all contributors. Obviously, there is much undone work left for other occasions and for other scholars. We shall be content if that which is illuminated here, albeit with a confined beam of light, is found to be illuminated searchingly and with a clarity and accuracy that marks an advance in scholarship and understanding.

References

Bengoetxea, J. (1994), 'Legal System as a Regulative Ideal', *ARSP-Beiheft*, vol. 33, ed. H-J. Koch and U. Neumann, Stuttgart: Franz Steiner Verlag.

Hayek, F.A. (1975), *Law, Legislation and Liberty*, vol. 1, 'Rules and Order', London: Routledge & Kegan Paul.

Kötz, H. and Zweigert, K. (1987), *Introduction to Comparative Law* (trans. J.A. Weir), Oxford: Oxford University Press.

Stair, J. (Viscount) (1995), *Institutions of the Laws of Scotland*, 2nd edn, ed. D.M. Walker, Edinburgh: Edinburgh University Press.

Summers, R. 'Two Types of Substantive Reasons', *Cornell Law Review*, 63, p.707 (1978).

Weber, M. (1954), *Max Weber on Law in Economy and Society*, ed. M. Rheinstein, Cambridge, MA: Harvard University Press.

[illegible]

Follows that if the extent to which formalism applies in an area which is perceived to be the most formalistic is demonstrated to be far less in that area than perceived – this would give rise to doubts about extent of formalism in other areas

– shown in necessary] reciprocity + would be increased if argument that [illegible] knowledge is to be imported.

2 Precedent in the Federal Republic of Germany

ROBERT ALEXY, *KIEL* AND RALF DREIER,
*GÖTTINGEN**

I   Institutional and Systemic

1(a)   Court Hierarchy

In Germany there are – apart from the constitutional jurisdiction and some special exceptions (for example, patent jurisdiction) – five independent jurisdictions. These are (1) the general ('ordinary') jurisdiction which hears civil and criminal cases (ordentliche Gerichtsbarkeit), (2) the administrative jurisdiction (Verwaltungsgerichtsbarkeit), (3) the jurisdiction in labour law cases (Arbeitsgerichtsbarkeit), (4) the jurisdiction in social law cases (Sozialgerichtsbarkeit) and (5) the fiscal jurisdiction (Finanzgerichtsbarkeit) (compare Art. 95 (1) Basic Law (GG)).

In general, each of these five jurisdictions has three levels of courts (exceptions are mentioned below). The levels within the respective jurisdictions are (beginning with the basic trial courts) in the general jurisdiction: the Inferior Court (Amtsgericht), the District Court (Landgericht), the Higher Regional Court of Appeal (Oberlandesgericht) and the Federal Court of Justice (Bundesgerichtshof (BGH)). In spite of these four levels of organization of general courts there is no possibility of a case moving through all of them. The maximum is three. The details are regulated for criminal cases in the General Court Act (Gerichtsverfassungsgesetz (GVG)) and the Code of Criminal Procedure (Strafprozeßordnung (StPO)), and for civil cases in the GVG and in the Code of Civil Procedure (Zivilprozeßordnung (ZPO)). In the administrative jurisdiction the hierarchy of courts is, again beginning with the basic trial court: Administrative Court (Verwaltungsgericht),

* The authors' thanks are due to Mrs Kirsten Bock for help with the translation into English.

Higher Administrative Court (Oberverwaltungsgericht), Federal Administrative Court (Bundesverwaltungsgericht (BVerwG)); in the labour jurisdiction: Labour Court (Arbeitsgericht), Higher Labour Court (Landesarbeitsgericht), Federal Labour Court (Bundesarbeitsgericht (BAG)); in the social jurisdiction: Social Court (Sozialgericht), Higher Social Court (Landessozialgericht), Federal Social Court (Bundessozialgericht (BSG)); and finally in the fiscal jurisdiction: Fiscal Court (Finanzgericht) and Federal Fiscal Court (Bundesfinanzhof (BFH). All jurisdictions are regulated by federal statutes. However, all courts of the five jurisdictions – except for the five supreme federal courts – are institutions of the federal states (Bundesländer).

The constitutional jurisdiction is an extraordinary one, consisting of only one level. In accordance with the federal structure of Germany, there is one federal constitutional court (Bundesverfassungsgericht (BVerfG)) and, in all states except Schleswig-Holstein, a state constitutional court (with different designations: Landesverfassungsgericht, Verfassungsgerichtshof, Staatsgerichtshof).

1(b)   Structural and Procedural Aspects

The numbers of judges of the federal courts are (as of 1991), according to the Statistical Yearbook 1994 for the Federal Republic of Germany (*Statistisches Jahrbuch 1994 für die Bundesrepublik Deutschland*): BGH: 281 (including those of the Federal Patent Court); BVerwG: 65; BAG: 27; BSG: 39; BFH: 60; BVerfG: 16.

The courts of the two highest levels sit in panels. The number of panels of the five supreme federal courts and of the Federal Constitutional Court are (as of 31 December 1993): BVerfG: 2; BGH: 12 for civil cases, 7 for criminal cases, 7 panels with special tasks (for example, anti-trust cases, agricultural cases); BVerwG: 9 for general administrative cases, 2 for disciplinary cases, 2 for cases concerning military service; BAG: 10; BSG: 12; BFH: 11. The number of members who usually sit in a panel is: BVerfG: 8; BGH: 5; BVerwG: 5; BAG: 5 (2 of them are lay judges); BSG: 5 (2 of them are lay judges); BFH: 5.

In 1991, the federal courts decided the following numbers of cases (numbers include all kinds of final decisions on a case, also denials of admission): BVerfG: 3840 (in 1993: 5456); BGH: 4534 civil cases, 3699 criminal cases; BVerwG: 2749; BAG: 1437; BSG: 2022; BFH: 3698 (source: *Statistisches Jahrbuch 1994*).

In general, decisions of the panels require an absolute majority of votes (compare s.15 (3) sentence 2 Code of Constitutional Court Procedure (Bundesverfassungsgerichtsgesetz (BVerfGG)) and s.196 (1) GVG). Special provisions for cases in which a qualified majority is necessary or equality of votes or other problems occur are left aside here. Votes are cast by juniority (compare s.197 GVG). The most junior votes first. The chairperson votes last. If a judge was appointed to report on the case, he or she votes first.

In general, disagreement among the panellists is confidential. Exceptions concern the Federal Constitutional Court. The panels can publish the division of votes (s.30 (2) sentence 2 Code of Constitutional Court Procedure (BVerfGG). Panel members of the Federal Constitutional Court can deliver a dissenting vote, which is published together with the grounds of the decision (s.30 (2) sentence 1 BVerfGG).

1(c)   *Power to Select Cases*

The five supreme federal courts almost exclusively decide appeals based on questions of law, not of fact. Appeals are possible in a twofold manner. The first manner consists in appeals being directly admitted by the law. This applies to criminal cases (compare s.333 Code of Criminal Procedure (Strafprozeßordnung (StPO)) and to fiscal cases above the value of 1000 German Marks in dispute (s.115 Code of Fiscal Court Procedure (Finanzgerichtsordnung (FGO); compare further s.116 FGO). In these cases the courts have no power to select. This is different when the possibility of an appeal depends on an admission by a court. There are two possibilities. The first is chosen when the court of the second level (against whose decision the appeal is filed) has the power to admit or not to admit the appeal to the court of the highest level, that is, to the supreme court of the respective jurisdiction. This applies to administrative cases (compare s.132 Code of Administrative Court Procedure (Verwaltungs-gerichtsordnung (VwGO)), labour law cases (compare s.72 Code of Labour Court Procedure (Arbeitsgerichtsgesetz (ArbGG)), social law cases (compare s.160 Code of Social Court Procedure (Sozial-gerichtsgesetz (SGG)), and fiscal cases up to the value of 1000 German Marks in dispute (s.115 FGO) as well as to many civil cases (s.546 ZPO). The grounds on which an appeal has to be admitted are named by the respective codes of procedure. The most important and interesting grounds are (compare s.546 ZPO, s.132 VwGO, s.72 ArbGG, s.160 SGG, s.115 FGO) that (1) the case is of fundamental importance in principle ('grundsätzliche Bedeutung'), or (2) the decision does not follow a precedent set by the respective supreme federal court, or the Common Panel of the Supreme Federal Courts, or the Federal Constitutional Court.

Regarding the second presupposition, the importance for the discussion of precedents is obvious. But this is also true regarding the first one. The term 'fundamental importance' is interpreted to require that the case offers an opportunity to formulate a general legal thought that furthers the unity of jurisdiction for the future and is relevant for the further development of the law (compare BVerwGE 13, 90 (91)). This is generally assumed to be the case in contested or contestable questions (compare Zöller, 1995, sec. 546, ann. 35) which concern a variety of future cases (Thomas and Putzo, 1995, sec. 546 ann. 19). So this alternative, too, can be used in order to select cases for setting precedents.

If an appeal is admitted by the second-level court, this is binding on the respective supreme federal court. In administrative, labour, social and fiscal, but not in civil, cases a special appeal may be made to the respective supreme federal court against denial of admission (Nichtzulassungsbeschwerde; compare s.133 VwGO, s.72a ArbGG, 160a SGG, s.115 (3) FGO). In this decision, the mentioned possibility of selecting cases 'of fundamental importance' for precedents can be fully brought to bear. The latter is also valid for appeals in civil cases above the value of 60 000 German Marks in dispute. In these cases, no admission by the second-level court (the Higher Regional Court of Appeal) is necessary, but the Federal Court of Justice can reject the appeal for not being of fundamental importance (compare ss.546, 554b ZPO).

The jurisdictional powers of the Federal Constitutional Court are defined in the Basic Law (Grundgesetz), especially in Art. 93 GG, and are exhaustively listed in s.13 BVerfGG. There are 16 different procedures. In most of them the Federal Constitutional Court has no power to select the cases it will decide. This is of special importance in cases which are politically highly controversial. Members of parliament, for example, (a third of them is required for this; compare Art. 93 (1) number 2 GG), can ask for control of statutes made by the parliament. This gives the minority in parliament the power to have the constitutionality of each law made by the majority checked by the Federal Constitutional Court. The Federal Constitutional Court must decide. As there is no political question doctrine in Germany, the Court cannot reject the case on the grounds that it has political implications.

A special admission is required for constitutional complaints which can be raised by anybody ('jedermann': compare s.90 (1) BVerfGG) on the grounds of a violation of basic rights granted by the Basic Law. The complaint has to be admitted if (1) the complaint is of fundamental significance for constitutional law, or (2) admission is indicated to enforce the respective basic right which, for example, can be the case if the complainant would suffer severe detriment from a denial of admission (s.93a BVerfGG).

Admission can be denied by subpanels ('Kammern', consisting of three judges: s.15a, 93b BVerfGG) or by the whole panel. In 1991, 3190 out of 3469 constitutional complaints were denied admission by subpanels (according to the valid law of that time, which permitted denial on procedural grounds or for lack of sufficient prospects of success). If the subpanel neither denies admission (now possible without giving reasons) nor unanimously decides the complaint is justified, the panel as a whole has to decide on the admission (s.93b BVerfGG). A complaint is admitted if at least three out of eight judges vote in favour of the admission (s.93d (3) BVerfGG). This rather complex model of admission gives the Federal Constitutional Court in cases of constitutional complaints a considerable power to select the cases it will decide, but this is not a power to select cases according to political criteria. Nevertheless, it is a very important power, for by far the greatest number of cases before the Federal Constitutional Court are constitutional complaints (in 1993, 5246 out of 5440 new cases).

2   Structure, Content and Style of Judgments

The normal structure and content of court judgments is statutorily regulated in Germany. In s.313 (1) Code of Civil Procedure (ZPO) we find that the decision has to contain (1) the designation of the parties, their representatives and the attorneys of record, (2) the designation of the court and the names of the judges who took part in the decision, (3) the day on which the trial was brought to an end, (4) the operative provisions of the decision, (5) the facts, and (6) the reasons on which the decision is based. Similar listings are contained in other codes of procedure. The Code of Criminal Procedure (StPO) contains specific rules which meet the special needs of criminal law (compare s.267 StPO).

The style of German courts is in principle deductive, legalistic and magisterial, but at the same time to a high degree discursive, substantive and argumentative. All in all, it is somewhere in the middle between the polarities mentioned. The style is deductive, legalistic and magisterial insofar as it is the duty of the courts to apply statutes in case there are any which can be applied. The style becomes more discursive, substantive and argumentative the more problems exist in interpreting the law. It is one of the main tasks of higher and highest courts to solve interpretational questions. Therefore the style of the highest courts is rather discursive, substantive and argumentative. It has all these characteristics, the more controversial the question to be decided. An example of an exceedingly discursive, substantive and argumentative decision is the decision of the Federal Court of Justice on the criminal liability of so-called 'wall guardians' who killed people trying to leave the former GDR (BGHSt 39, 1). According to the self-understanding of the Federal Constitutional Court, its interpretative activities are thoroughly discursive and argumentative:

The interpretation especially of constitutional law has the character of a discourse in which even by methodologically perfect work no absolutely right answers, indisputable by experts, are presented, but reasons and counter reasons are and a decision is finally expected to be brought about by the better reason. (BVerfGE 82, 30 (38 f))

3   Publication of Judgments

The decisions of the two panels of the Federal Constitutional Court are generally published in an official series, which is authorized by the court itself. The proceeding is laid down in the rules of procedure of the court (s.31 (1) GOBVerfG). A comprehensive selection of the other Federal Courts' more important decisions appears in official series edited by members of the courts. Besides, there are some non-official digests of decisions by higher courts as well as by lower courts (compare, for instance, Lindenmaier/Möhring, *Nachschlagewerk des Bundesgerichtshofs*; Buchholz, *Sammel- und Nachschlagewerk der Rechtsprechung des Bundesverwaltungsgerichts*; *Verwaltungsrechtsprechung in Deutschland*). Additionally, many decisions are published in academic journals. These sources are easily accessible in courts' libraries and universities. Moreover, decisions which are of special social or political interest are often reported in newspapers – the better the newspaper, the more extensive and correct the report. Recently, increasing use is being made of legal database systems as media of publication. The most important of these is 'Juris', documenting large parts of the adjudication of German courts since 1976. Judgments by the lower courts are published less often than those by the federal courts or the highest courts of the federal states. Whether or not a low court decision is published depends on many factors, such as deviation from precedent.

4   Contents of Reports

The best available reports of court judgments – those of the official series – allow identification of the decision by giving the name of the deciding court, the date of the court's decision and the file number. In official reports generally no use is made of case names, but in academic or non-academic literature the most prominent cases often are identified by case names. Higher courts customarily preface the decisions selected for publication with headings containing the general rules which have been developed in applying the law and which are regarded as applicable to similar cases. These headnotes play an important part in the decision's function as a precedent.

Reports in series or academic journals usually adopt the structure and content of the judgment. These include the statement of facts.

Judgments of the higher courts state the procedural background of the case as well. Furthermore, if the court took evidence, the result would be given. Many series and academic journals do not print a literal but only an abridged version of the statement of facts, however.

Interpretational problems concerning precedents are rarely the object of a judge's expressed reasoning and therefore rarely part of decision reports. As for interpretational problems concerning statutes, they are less discussed in lower court decisions, but rather often and in great detail in decisions of higher courts. Reports of court judgments usually supply the reasons for the ruling by giving the statement of the grounds for the decision.

Dissenting opinions are admitted only in constitutional adjudication (s.30 (2) BVerfGG). They are published along with the decision in the official series. The higher court decisions published in the official series do not comprise any juristic commentaries. However, decisions as published in academic journals are sometimes accompanied by commentaries by both scholars and practitioners.

5 Meaning of 'Precedent'

'Precedent' (Präjudiz) is usually taken to mean any prior decision possibly relevant to a present case to be decided. The notion presupposes some kind of bindingness, but its use in legal discourse does not imply anything definitive about the nature or the strength of that bindingness. Also it is not necessary that the deciding court expressly adopt or formulate a decision to guide future decision making in order to talk about it as a precedent. Being relevant for any future decision is sufficient.

6 Mode of Citation and Discussion

It is not easy to find a decision in the official series edited by members of the highest courts that does not contain any reference to precedents. If one takes a look into the respective ten latest volumes, it will be recognized that a very high percentage of published decisions refers to precedents: BVerfGE 83–92 (1990–95): 97.02 per cent (228 out of 235 decisions); BGHZ 119–128 (1992–5): 99.29 per cent (417 out of 420 decisions); BGHSt 31–40 (1982–95): 95.94 per cent (686 out of 715 decisions); BVerwGE 87–96 (1990–94): 97.51 per cent (509 out of 522 decisions); BAGE 65–74 (1992–5): 97.6 per cent (406 out of 416 decisions); BSGE 65–74 (1989–94): 98.13 per cent (473 out of 482 decisions); BFHE 168–177 (1993–6): 97.86 per cent (1190 out of 1216 decisions). This picture does not change very much regarding decisions of the other higher courts published in series and academic journals. (A quite lower frequency of citation of precedent by the highest federal courts was found by Roland Wagner-Döbler and Lothar Philipps (Wagner-Döbler and Philipps, 1992, pp.228 ff). The reason for this may be that their investigation was based on different data: that is, the database 'Juris' and not the official series.) Citations of precedents in all jurisdictions are largely self-referential, that is, in most cases the courts cite their own previous decisions. Among the citations of other courts, decisions of the Federal Constitutional Court prevail.

Referring to precedents occurs, indeed, very frequently but in most cases only as a reference and without detailed discussion. A detailed discussion of precedents does not take place in judicial opinions but in scholarly or other juristic treatises in which bodies of precedent law are analysed, explained and synthesized. Often not only scholars and practitioners in general but also judges of the highest courts try to explain and systematize bodies of precedents of their courts in scholarly articles (compare, for instance, Sendler, 1978, pp.581 ff; Grimm, 1995, pp.1697 ff).

Lawyers who argue cases before the courts are expected to know precedents and to cite and discuss them if this is appropriate. This is more often the case in written than in oral argument.

7   Overall Role of Precedent

The relative overall role of precedent in the decision making of courts depends on which other authoritative materials are relevant. If the case can be decided according to the wording of a statute, precedents will play no or nearly no role. If there is no relevant statutory law or if the statutory law needs interpretation, precedents will play an important role. As in the German system most fields of law are regulated by statutory law, interpretative precedents play a much greater role than precedents substituting statutory law. In many decisions interpretative precedents are more important than substantive reasoning and academic writing or professional commentary.

8   Role of Precedent in Different Branches of Law

In Germany, precedents are important in all branches of law but their importance varies. Some areas of labour law are made up primarily of judge-made law. The same was the case in general administrative law before it was codified in 1976 (compare on this Mußgnug, 1986, pp.209 ff). Most precedents interpret statutes, codes and the constitution. Again, there are great differences. Some statutes contain very general clauses which must be concretized by a course of judicial decisions. From a formal point of view, this is statute law interpreted by the judges; from a material point of view, this is precedent-based law camouflaged by statutes. This also applies to all the great codifications. Some parts of it are defined by rather clear and strict regulations, and in some parts not the codification but only the case law determines the content of the codes as written. Due to the great vagueness of those parts of the constitution which regulate the basic rights and the other constitutional principles, precedents play a decisive role in constitutional law. This role has a special character because there is a provision that makes the decisions of the Federal Constitutional Court binding (s.31 (1) BVerfGG) and in some cases even gives them the status of statutes (s.31 (2) BVerfGG).

9 Precedent and 'Gaps in the Law'

The German system is based on the idea of codification. In such a system the non-existence of precedents is, in principle, no problem. The judge has to interpret the law – with the help of precedents or without it. A problem will arise if there is no statute. In penal law a decision against the defendant is excluded in such cases. The rule *nulla poena sine lege* is explicitly incorporated into the constitution (Art. 103 (2) GG). In cases of administrative law the competence of the courts to create law is limited by the rule that infringements of the basic rights presuppose a statute which allows them to do so. The precise content of this rule, however, is contested. The main field of law making without statutes nowadays is labour law (compare BAGE 1, 291; 23, 292; 33, 140; 33, 185; 48, 195). Most decisions against statutes are, perhaps, to be found in civil law. Inspired by the jurisdiction of the Federal Constitutional Court which has, in principle, allowed judge-made law which contradicts the wording of statutes (compare BVerfGE 34, 269 (268 f); 35, 263 (278 ff); 37, 67 (81); 38, 386 (396 f); 49, 304 (318 ff); 65, 182 (190 ff); 71, 354 (362 f); 82, 6 (11 ff)), the Great Panel for Civil Cases of the Federal Court of Justice (which consists of the president of the court and one judge from each of its civil panels (compare s.132 (5) GVG)) has discussed the problem of requirements of judge-made law extensively. One result of its reasoning sounds as follows:

> Such a far-reaching change of circumstances – may it be of technical, social, economical, or (as in this case) legal nature – leads to a loosening of the bindingness of statutes upon the judge because it remains uncertain which regulation 'the legislator' would have chosen if he had knowledge about the subsequently changing circumstances, and because there cannot be confidence in the permanent adjustment of statutes to these circumstances. To help out by judicial improvement of the law very carefully and in accordance with established legal

values in these cases is a legitimate task of the courts. (BGHZ 85, 64 (67 f))

II   The Bindingness of Precedent

1   Kinds and Degrees of Normative Force

The German system is a code system. There are, apart from constitutional adjudication, no strict rules on the binding force of precedents and it is not a common practice to categorize different kinds of precedents according to their bindingness. Rather, it is discussed how strong the binding force of precedents is in general, or if there is any binding force at all. Therefore, the scale of 'formally binding, having force or providing further support' (in quesion II.1) can be applied at best to discuss the overall bindingness of precedents. In this section we will deal with the bindingness of precedent in the practice of the courts. The academic discussion will be reported in Section III.

(a)   The only case of formal bindingness concerns precedents of the Federal Constitutional Court, which are strictly binding. According to s.31 (1) BVerfGG, all decisions of the Federal Constitutional Court are binding for all constitutional organs of the Federation and the states as well as for all courts and authorities. Furthermore, s.31 (2) BVerfGG provides that, in several cases and especially where the court invalidates legal norms, these decisions have the force of statutes ('Gesetzeskraft'). They are published in the Federal Register of Statutes. This extends the bindingness to all citizens. It becomes a bindingness *inter omnes*.

The nature, the scope and the subject matter of strict bindingness of the decisions of the Federal Constitutional Court are contested (compare Kriele, 1976, pp.290 ff; Sachs, 1977, pp.66 ff; Schlüchter, 1986, pp.22 ff). A theoretically as well as practically especially important question is whether the legislature is exempted from the bindingness provided by s.31 BVerfGG (see Schlaich, 1994, pp.275 ff). Even the Federal Constitutional Court has expressed differing opinions concerning this matter. In one of the earliest decisions of the First Panel it was said:

> A decision that declares a law void has not only the force of statutes (s.31 (2) BVerfGG) but, according to s.31 (1) BVerfGG, it is also binding upon all federal constitutional bodies by the reasons supporting the decision (*mit den tragenden Entscheidungsgründen*) insofar as a federal law of the same content can not be enacted once more. (BVerfGE 1, 14 (15))

The Second Panel has quoted this occasionally talking about a 'pro-hibition against repeatedly enacting a norm' ('Normwiederholungs-verbot', BVerfGE 69, 112 (115)). Contrary to this, the First Panel gave up its former holding in 1987 and gave permission to the legislator to re-enact a law that had been declared incompatible with the Consti-tution by the Federal Constitutional Court. Therewith it has exempted the 'democratically legitimate legislator' from the bindingness of its precedents. A very interesting part of its statement of reasons under the aspect of bindingness reads as follows: 'that the Federal Consti-tutional Court has to match acts of the legislative power with the constitution itself and not with precedents' (BVerfGE 77, 84 (104)). This is an exemption from precedents made by a precedent for which reasons are found latterly in the special and tensional relation be-tween the constitutional jurisdiction and the democratic process. The Federal Constitutional Court has decided further that it is not bound by its own precedent itself (BVerfGE 4, 31 (38); 20, 56 (87); 77, 84 (104)). To sum up: the decisions of the Federal Constitutional Court in Germany are formally binding in the sense that, if lower courts do not follow them, their decisions will be unlawful and reversed on appeal (Appendix, question II.1). The legislature and the court itself being exempted from this bindingness forms no exception in the sense of the question, but only a limitation of those to which bindingness applies. The decisions of the Federal Constitutional Court are therefore formally binding without exception and without being subject to overruling or modification except by the Federal Constitu-tional Court itself.

(b)   All other precedents are not formally binding. (In cases of appeal there is a possibility that the higher court confines itself to a reversal of the decision of the lower court and refers the case back for final decision. If this happens, the legal opinion of the higher court is binding upon the lower court (see, for example, s.565 (2) ZPO, s.358 (1) StPO, s.144 (1) VwGO). This is, still, not a case of formal bindingness of precedents because bindingness is restricted to the specific case being decided by both courts.) Nevertheless, precedents play a major role in German law, too. Precedents are cited in most of the published decisions by the highest courts. If there is a deviation from a court's own precedent, it will generally be recognized and substantiated. The lower courts usually follow the precedents of the higher courts, and lawyers and administrative authorities tend to handle precedents in a similar way as legislative decisions.

The question is: how is this practice to be interpreted? One inter-pretation is already excluded because of the aforesaid. The practical use of precedents by German courts cannot be explained by the courts regarding precedents as formally binding. It is therefore ap-propriate to ask whether the other extreme is correct which consists in the assumption that precedents do not have any kind of bindingness. Then, the regular statement and compliance with precedents would not have any normative meaning. Two decisions that hold the same arguments would then always be equally good in every legal respect, even though they differ in one additionally naming and/or following all relevant precedents and the other one naming and following none. If we have regular compliance under this condition we will have what is often – even though misleadingly – called 'de facto validity' (*faktische Geltung*) in the literature (Larenz and Canaris, 1995, p.255). In the sense of question II. 1 (Appendix to this book), this would be something like 'mere illustrativeness'.

To find out whether such a complete non-bindingness or one of the intermediate stages of force or further support exists, there are two possibilities: the first one consists of an examination of explicit statements of the courts concerning the problem of binding force of precedents, the second one in the reconstruction of rules on which the judicial practice is implicitly based.

In Germany there are only a few explicit discussions about the bindingness and the degree of bindingness of precedents in judicial decisions. Normally, judges do not make any general remarks on the binding force of precedent. But there are some decisions in which this has happened. A first group of decisions explicitly discussing the binding force of precedents is formed by decisions of the Federal Constitutional Court. These decisions have a special impact because of the binding force and the general authority of the Federal Constitutional Court.

The most important touchstone for the binding force of precedents is the overruling of judicial opinions, especially those that have been adhered to for a longer time. In a decision of 1964 which dealt with a change of the adjudication of the Federal Fiscal Court (Bundesfinanzhof (BFH)), the Federal Constitutional Court declared that the principle of prohibition of retroaction (Rückwirkungsverbot) and the principle of trust (Vertrauensschutz) which apply to the legislator are not applicable to the courts without further ado: 'This would lead to a binding upon the courts to a once set ruling even though if it proved no longer suitable in the light of refined cognition or in view of changes in social, political or economical situation' (BVerfGE 18, 224 (240 f)). It is of interest that the court talks about 'refined cognition' (*geläuterte Erkenntnis*), here. This hints at one of the main arguments to negate the binding force of principles. It says that all judicial decisions are cognitions, and old cognitions will only influence new ones if they are true. This would be different with an interpretation of judicial acts not as acts of cognition but as decisions. The Federal Constitutional Court is concerned with the question of overruling in a decision from 1991. This decision is interesting because it deals with the ruling of the Federal Labour Court (BAG) in matters of labour law disputes and strikes. This domain belongs to one of the few cases of pure judge-made law in Germany; therefore the question of the binding force of precedent comes up very clearly. The Federal Constitutional Court treats the problem of the binding force of precedent in correspondence with its task as a constitutional problem. The Basic Law (Grundgesetz) binds the judiciary to 'statute and law' (Art. 20 (3) GG). The Federal Constitutional Court does not subsume precedents under this clause. Deviation from them therefore – as a matter of principle – does not violate Art. 20 (3) GG: 'Their claim to validity beyond the single case is solely based on the power of conviction of their reasons as well as on the authority and competence of the court' (BVerfGE 84, 212 (227)).

The formula 'power of conviction of their reasons' (*Überzeugungskraft ihrer Gründe*) follows the line on cognition and correctness that was started by the earlier judgment already mentioned. 'Authority' seems to mean the substantial authority of the court. What is meant by 'competence' remains uncertain. If it is only correctness in its content which gives force to precedent, then plainly better reasons will be necessary for a deviation. Clearly prevailing or compelling reasons are not necessary because the aim is only to replace inferior with superior cognition and not to get rid of an institutional act as well. This corresponds to the courts saying: 'Therefore a proof of a major change of circumstances or general belief is not necessary to enable a court to deviate from its former ruling without violating Art. 20 (3) GG' (BVerfGE 84, 212 (227)). According to this, precedents do not have bindingness because they are not binding law. The court takes into account another reason for precedents having bindingness to some degree: the principle of protection of trust. But it leaves the question unanswered whether or not and to what extent the alteration of adjudication of the highest courts is limited by the protection of trust. In the present case protection of trust is declared inapplicable because the change of judicial opinion was predictable. The latter is said to be the case because only a tendency had been developed further and the former adjudication was heavily criticized (BVerfGE 84, 212 (227); compare further BVerfGE 38, 386 (396)). Altogether it may be stated that the jurisdiction of the Federal Constitutional Court gives only a little force to precedent. In the sense of question II.1 (Appendix), it can perhaps be said that, according to the Federal Constitutional Court, precedent is of the third category, consequently not being formally binding nor having force but still providing some further support. But also a categorizing into the forth category of mere illustrativeness or other value is considerable. The other value would be correctness. But there is the possibility that this picture will change if the protection of trust principle demands something different; as yet, this remains quite unclear.

From the view of the jurisdiction of the Federal Court of Justice (BGH) the situation is different. On the occasion of a disparity of views between two panels of the court the Great Panel of the Federal Court of Justice considered in which cases an overruling of 'established jurisdiction of the highest judges' (*gefestigte höchstrichterliche Rechtsprechung*) is permissible. Its answer is:

> In such cases the legal values of legal certainty and protection of trust come to the fore and generally demand an adherence to the line of legal development that has been chosen. A deviation from continuity of adjudication can only be accepted as an exception if clearly outweighing or even absolutely compelling reasons are in favour of it. (BGHZ 85, 64 (66); compare further BGHZ 87, 150 (155); 125, 218 (222))

This is prima facie binding by precedent. In general, observance of precedent is obligatory. A deviation has to be the exception. A mere better cognition or a mere better reason is not sufficient for this. 'Clearly outweighing' reasons are necessary, and 'absolutely compelling reasons' are most favourable to the court. This amounts to the rule: whoever wishes to depart from a precedent carries the burden of argument (compare Alexy, 1989, p.278). According to the Federal Court of Justice, the reasons for all this do not have anything to do with the concept of law or similar theoretical things. They are normative in kind. They are the principles or values of legal certainty and of protection of trust. These values will lose in importance if a supreme court decision is highly contested. 'Far-reaching legal dogmatical doubts and the incoherence of the achieved results' were declared sufficient by the Federal Court of Justice to justify a change of precedent in such a case (BGHZ 106, 169 (174)). But this may also be interpreted in the sense of the burden of argument just mentioned.

Precedents are therefore, even in correspondence with the opinion of the Federal Court of Justice, not formally binding, which can already be recognized by the ability of substantial reasons to justify their discontinuation. But they do have force in the sense of the second category of question II.1 (Appendix). This force is an outweighable force. Interestingly, the jurisdiction of the Federal Court of Justice refers to an 'established jurisdiction of the highest judges'. This raises the question what will happen if there is a vague, unsteady, or contradicting jurisdiction. There is much in favour of a defeat of the force of a precedent by the proof of vagueness, unsteadiness or contradiction. This would mean that precedents have a defeasible outweighable force according to the decisions of the Federal Court of Justice.

Self-interpretations by the participants of a practice carry a certain assumption of correctness, but they can also be wrong. The criterion for correctness is practice itself. Following this criterion, self-interpretation by the Federal Court of Justice according to which precedents have genuine force is to be given preference over the one by the Federal Constitutional Court according to which this is in principle not the case. German courts who deviate from a precedent set by itself or a higher court in fact usually cite the precedent and name the reasons for the precedent being a substantially wrong decision and explain why its own decision is a better one. Often this is done even in the case of deviation from a precedent set by another court of the same level. The fact that incompatible precedents are usually named and are invalidated by argument is a main reason for the force of precedent.

The force of precedent is shown most clearly in the case of deviation, but it can be recognized in the case of following the precedent, too. The fact that following the precedent usually is not combined with substantial argument – whereas deviating is – shows that precedents have a force of their own. This is underscored by the fact that a lawyer neglecting precedents of higher courts may be liable for damages to his client (BGH NJW 1983, 1665).

In legal doctrine the binding force of precedent is highly contested. In that context it is very controversial whether precedents are to be recognized as a source of law. At the centre of this controversy is the question whether precedents have any binding force at all. But the problem of degrees of bindingness already arises because many authors hold the opinion that precedents have a binding force which is allocated in between formal bindingness and mere illustrativeness. These questions shall be dealt with below. It is worth noticing that the academic discussion has not been reflected in court practice to a significant extent.

2   *Law Concerning Precedent*

(a)   There is no legislation requiring the use of precedent except s.31 BVerfGG concerning the constitutional jurisdiction (see Appendix, question II.1). There are some provisions, though, that regulate procedure in case of a deviation from certain precedents. A first group of such regulations provides duties of presentation (Vorlagepflichten). So, for instance, a constitutional court of one of the federal states which wants to deviate from a precedent set by the constitutional court of another federal state or by the Federal Constitutional Court has to present this intention to the Federal Constitutional Court (Art. 100 (3) GG). Similarly, if one of the five supreme federal courts (BGH, BVerwG, BAG, BSG, BFH) wants to deviate from a decision of another supreme federal court, it has to present the divergence to the Common Panel of the Supreme Federal Courts (Gemeinsamer Senat der obersten Gerichte des Bundes; Art. 100 (3) GG, s.2 (1) RsprEinhG). Finally, if one of the panels of a supreme federal court wants to deviate from a decision of another panel of that court, the divergence will have to be presented to the so-called 'Great Panel' (Großer Senat; compare s. 132 (2) ZPO, s.11 (2) VwGO, s.45 (2) ArbGG, s.41 (2) SGG, s.11 (2) FGO; for divergence between the two panels of the Federal Constitutional Court, compare s.16 (1) BVerfGG). All these procedures apply to constitutional or supreme courts. There are similar procedures which apply to some cases in which a lower court has the final decision (compare, for example s.121 (2) GVG, s.12 VwGO). The second group of procedural regulations aiming at the unity and the coherence of the legal system provides an obligation for higher courts which want to deviate from a precedent of the respective supreme court (or of the Common Panel of the Supreme Federal Courts or of the Federal Constitutional Court) to allow appeal to the supreme court (compare s.546 (1) ZPO, s.132 (2) VwGO, s.72 (2) ArbGG, s.160 (2) SGG, s.115 (2) FGO).

These procedural regulations show that precedents – in spite of their missing formal bindingness – are taken rather seriously in Germany under the aspect of unity or coherence in the administration of justice. This is an argument for a certain degree of binding power below the level of strict formal bindingness. For why should coherence of precedent be taken seriously if it were merely illustrative (compare Kriele, 1976, p.249; Koch and Rüßmann, 1982, p.188)?

In Austria there is a special, yet only negative, provision on the binding force of precedents (s.12 ABGB (1811)). The provision reads: 'The rulings issued in particular cases and the judgments passed by judges in particular lawsuits never have the force of a law, they cannot be extended to other cases or to other persons.' It is controversial whether this provision states a prohibition against the use of precedent (see Bydlinski, 1991, pp.501 ff).

It may be worth mentioning that in Germany there have been attempts by legislation to make precedent binding. A very interesting one took place in 1838 in the Kingdom of Hanover where a statute was enacted which provided for a procedure to make the precedents of the Supreme Court of the Kingdom in Celle formally binding. Two purposes are explicitly mentioned in the statute: legal certainty and equal application of the law (compare the collection of Statutes, Decrees, and Announcements of the Kingdom of Hanover 1838, p.213). But only ten years later this regulation was repealed. It was said that legal uncertainty had not been reduced but increased by it (Gunkel, 1911, p.295; compare further Weller, 1979, pp.82 ff).

(b)   It is not common in German judicial opinions to find different kinds of precedents, categorized into those that are binding de jure, and those that are binding only de facto. But these terms play a certain role in the academic discussion on the binding force of precedent in general (compare, for example, Larenz and Canaris, 1995, 255). The term 'de facto bindingness' is sometimes used in a negative sense to express that precedents have not the same binding force as statutes and other formal sources of law. Sometimes it is used in a positive sense in order to explain the power precedents have below the level of strict formal bindingness. But this is an explanation easy to misunderstand, for it is not true that binding de jure can only be strict formal bindingness. Weaker or softer kinds of bindingness can be legal bindingness as well. In addition, the weaker bindingness of precedents is conceived by the participants in the legal system as something normative in character and not only as a kind of empirical regularity.

(c) As mentioned before, the jurisprudence of the courts does not treat precedents as sources of law independent of statute and custom. (In academic writings this question is contested.) The power or force of precedents is therefore mainly an indirect one. A precedent has the power it has because it is an interpretation of a certain statute and this statute is used in the interpretation given by the precedent. In this sense precedents in Germany derive their power from the power of the formal source of law they interpret. Formally, it is the statute which binds; substantially, the precedent.

Things become difficult in fields of law in which the main substance of the contemporary governing law derives from precedent. In Germany the most important example is the collective labour law, especially the law of industrial action. The Federal Constitutional Court has decided that it is, in principle, the task of the legislature to regulate the freedom of association (BVerfGE 50, 290 (368 f); 57, 220 (245 ff); 84, 212 (226)). But if the legislator remains inactive, the judge will have to become active:

> In case of insufficient legislative provisions the courts are to derive the substantive law by the acknowledged methods of finding the law from general foundations of law relevant to the legal relationship concerned. This is also true where a legal provision, for instance, because of a constitutional guarantee of protection is necessary ... Only in this way are the courts able to fulfil their duty imposed by the Basic Law to decide every legal dispute brought before them appropriately. (BVerfGE 84, 212 (226))

This statement shows that in Germany neither precedent as such nor a basic formal power of courts to create law is a sufficient basis or foundation of judge-made law. If precedents cannot be related to formal sources of law (especially statutes), they will have to be based on general foundations of law (allgemeine Rechtsgrundlagen), that is, on general legal principles and general legal rules, from which they have to be derived by recognized methods of finding the law (anerkannte Methoden der Rechtsfindung). The basis of precedent even in areas not regulated by statutes or custom is not an undefined pure power of courts to create them but legal principles and legal method.

In the decision of the Federal Constitutional Court just quoted, the court stresses that the competence of courts to create law where the legislature has not made any is limited to the relation of coordinated subjects of law, that is, mainly to civil law. In the relation between state and citizens, where the state interferes with the freedom of the citizens, the state may only become active on the basis of a statute made by parliament (Vorbehalt des Gesetzes; BVerfGE 84, 212 (226)). The same is a fortiori sound wherever the maxim *nulla poena sine lege* applies (Art. 103 (2) GG). Interpretations of provisions of criminal law must not exceed the semantic latitude left open by the text. Though this limits the possibility of setting precedents, they nevertheless play an important role in criminal law as interpretation of statutory law.

3   *Factors Determining Degrees of Normative Force*

As pointed out above, there is no explicit categorization of precedents according to the degree of their bindingness, either in court practice or in legal doctrine. Therefore the following has to be read as an attempt to elaborate what might influence a court's decision to follow or not to follow a precedent or its argument for doing or not doing so.

(a)   The hierarchical rank of the court setting the precedent certainly is an important factor. It can be said that rulings of the five supreme federal courts are considered far weightier than those of other courts. Decisions of the Federal Constitutional Court are not only formally binding (s.31 BVerfGG), they are also considered especially important from a substantive point of view.

(b)   It might be considered as relevant whether the decision is made by a normal panel, or by a Great Panel (Großer Senat), or a Common Panel (Gemeinsamer Senat) on a presentment of divergence. In constitutional adjudication, the decision of a panel (Senat) is much more important than the decision of a subpanel (Kammer).

(c)   Since it is not made public which judge wrote the opinion, his or her reputation is generally not relevant. The reputation of the court does not play an important role either, even though it has a certain effect.

(d)   Changes in the political, economic or social background can be of great importance for the change of an 'established body of precedent set by the highest judges'. As said before, the Federal Court of Justice calls for 'clearly outweighing reasons' to admit such a change in jurisdiction (BGHZ 85, 64 (66)). Such reasons could exist if a change of political, economical or social background since the prior decision took place. Such a change is after all a sufficient reason for the Federal Court of Justice even to decide against the letter of a statute (BGHZ 85, 64 (67 f)).

(e) The soundness of the supporting arguments in the opinion is of greatest importance for subsequent decisions. According to the opinion of the Federal Constitutional Court already quoted, the soundness of the supporting arguments is the main reason for following a precedent (BVerfGE 84, 212 (227)).

(f) The age of a precedent as such is of minor weight for its significance, as is exemplified by decisions of the former 'Reichsgericht' and the former 'Prussian Higher Administrative Court' (Preußisches Oberverwaltungsgericht) which are still accepted and cited in fields of law where there are no new statutes or more recent divergent precedents.

(g) A dissent is published only in constitutional law (s.30 (2) BVerfGG). Therefore the presence or absence of dissent could be of influence only for decisions of the Federal Constitutional Court. But they are strictly binding anyway (s.31 BVerfGG). What can be influenced is the critical discussion of the decision which may end in its revision by the Federal Constitutional Court itself.

(h) The branch of law involved seems not to be of importance.

(i) Whether the precedent represents a trend is significant insofar as those decisions which represent an established line of decision (ständige Rechtsprechung) are considered to be especially weighty (compare BGHZ 85, 64 (66 ff)). In particular, if a supreme federal court cites its own prior decision and deems it to be an established adjudication, this is a clear indication that it will not alter its adjudication. Decisions representing an established line of decision making are the main case where precedent is weighty. But there are also trends of adjudication which are adduced for justifying a change in the line of decision. So the Federal Constitutional Court observes that there has been a tendency by the Federal Labour Court (BAG) for some time to change its line of decision as an argument for its opinion that the confidence in continuance of the previously established line does not deserve protection (BVerfGE 38, 386 (397)).

(j) According to the Federal Constitutional Court the academic critique of a decision is important for the question whether the confidence of the citizen in the continuance of an adjudication is protected: 'Moreover, the decision of the Great Panel was so heavily criticized that the unchanged continuance of this line of decision could not seem secured' (BVerfGE 84, 212 (227)).

The Federal Court of Justice as well has, as mentioned, regarded highly contested precedents as being of lower value. To overrule them, 'far-reaching legal dogmatical doubts and the incoherence of the achieved results' (BGHZ 106, 169 (174)) are sufficient. 'Clearly outweighing or even absolutely compelling reasons' as they are demanded for the alteration of an established jurisdiction of the highest judges are not required in this case. By this, academic critics are able to weaken the power of precedent.

(k)   Legal change in related areas is often considered relevant. Treating the non-conjugal life companionship as equivalent to the marriage relationship in tenancy law by judicial decision making was held admissible beyond other reasons because the legislator had already gone in this direction in fields of law such as social and labour law (BVerfGE 82, 6 (14)).

(l)   Courts may have a factual tendency to adhere to their own precedents more strictly than to precedents of other courts.

Summing up, the most important factors seem to be whether the precedent represents an established line of decision, the hierarchical rank of the court and the soundness of arguments. The tendency of courts to adhere to their own precedents might be considered weighty, too.

4   Factors that Weaken Precedent

As pointed out, in the German system only the decisions of the Federal Constitutional Court are formally binding. There are no factors which deprive them of the formal bindingness they normally have. The same applies to the weaker binding force of the precedents of other courts. There is no distinction drawn in the degree of bindingness between precedents dealing with statute law and precedents of other kinds.

5   Vertical and Horizontal Bindingness

(a)   A vertical formal bindingness exists only regarding rulings of the Federal Constitutional Court (s.31 BVerfGG). Apart from this, there is no legal rule which establishes a general formal bindingness of precedents of higher courts on lower courts. Naturally, the lower court bears the risk that its departing decision may be reversed by the higher court. This is a major reason why a lower court generally follows the precedent of the higher court. Still, this does not imply formal bindingness. If a lower court follows the precedent of a higher court *solely* because it wants to avoid being reversed, one will not be able to say that it was guided by normative reasons. This is rather a case of mere de facto bindingness which can be based on very different motives. The spectrum reaches from a mere wish not to be criticized to the intention to work one's way up.

A downright classic case of a decision in which a lower court follows the precedent of a higher court because of very respectable normative reasons was formed by a decision of the Higher Administrative Court of North Rhine–Westphalia in 1986. The Higher Administrative Court argued that members of the Tamil minority in Sri Lanka are persecutees on political grounds in the sense of the German right of asylum and therefore have a right to asylum. The Federal Administrative Court, on the contrary, held that the Tamil dispute is a matter of civil war concerning separation rather than persecution on political grounds. For some time the Higher Administrative Court of North Rhine–Westphalia adhered to its opinion and refused to follow the higher court. But once the Federal Administrative Court had reversed the decisions of the lower court in more than 160 proceedings, the Higher Administrative Court gave up its opinion:

> In view of the fact that the Federal Administrative Court as the appropriate court of appeal has, after repeated thorough reconsideration of the actual and legal circumstances to be decided upon in numerous fundamental judgments, come to a decision unfavourable to the Tamils affected and has reviewed judgments and orders in a multitude of similar proceedings of the adjudging panel and dismissed the respective actions for asylum, the panel is of the opinion that it is no longer defensible in respect of the uniformity in adjudication to continue to object to this practice of adjudication of the highest judges. (OVG NW, decision of 27 June 1986 – file number 19 A 10005/85, p.18)

'Uniformity in adjudication' forms the crucial argument. It is instructive how the principle of uniformity is substantiated. The court first of all states that it is only bound by 'statute and law' and not also by precedent:

> Certainly, the rule-of-law principle embodied in Art. 20 (3) GG binds the adjudging panel only to statute and law so that the right of asylum as embodied in Art. 16 (2) sentence 2 GG as well as the principle of substantive justice, which must be observed in its application, have to be in the fore of its decision regarding legal asylum.

The 'principle of substantive justice' can be understood as a command to substantial correctness. The court therefore declares that what matters principally is to interpret and to apply the norm in point in a substantively correct way. This corresponds with the adjudication of the Federal Constitutional Court (BVerfGE 84, 212 (221)) stated in question II.1 (Appendix). Yet subsequently the Higher Administrative Court introduces a counterweight to material justice and substantive correctness:

Not only material justice but also legal certainty belongs to the rule-of-law principle. Yet legal uniformity serves to guarantee legal certainty. It is the task of the courts of appeal and not that of the trial courts to ensure these. (OVG NW, decision of 27 June 1986 – file number 19 A 10005/85, p.19)

Herewith the court shows that it latterly was formal justice that caused it to submit its opinion about material justice to that of the higher instance after more than 160 attempts failed to convince the higher court of its opinion. Complementarily, the interest of all concerning a final decision as soon as possible is mentioned. This is indeed an extreme case but still a case which shows how the lower courts ought to treat the precedents of higher courts: they are to be critical and ought to risk deviation for reasons of substantive correctness, but they ought to respect the authority of the higher instance in the case of an unsuccessful critique for reasons of formal correctness.

A certain vertical bindingness exists, as already mentioned, in some cases in which a lower court passes a final judgment and wants to deviate from a precedent: the inferior court needs to lay the case before the superior court. This is, for example, the case in specific decisions of the Higher Regional Courts of Appeal (Oberlandesgerichte) in penal cases (s.121 (2) GVG; compare further s.28 (2) FGG, s.47 (5) VwGO). Such an obligation of explicit presentation in case of deviation from decisions of the higher courts does not exist, however, in all cases in which lower courts have final decision. There are numerous cases in which the District Courts (Landgerichte) have final decision without the possibility to control the observance of precedents set by higher courts. These cases are regarded as petty for the little pecuniary value of the subject-matter in dispute. Summing up, it can be said that in general the hierarchy of courts has a de facto impact, so that the precedents of the higher courts are followed by the lower courts, but there are exceptions because not every case is granted the legal possibility to go through all the successive stages of appeal. That the hierarchy of the courts promotes unity of jurisdiction is not only a de facto aspect of the situation, but is indeed designed to bring this about, as can be recognized by the various codes of procedure prescribing that in case of a judgment of a higher court not respecting a precedent of the supreme court of the respective judiciary, the higher court has to admit the appeal to this supreme court (compare s.546 ZPO, s.132 (2) VwGO, s.72 (2) ArbGG, s.160 (2) SGG, s.115 (2) FGO). Sometimes similar provisions occur in the relationship between the first and the second instance (compare s.131 (3) VwGO, s.78 (3) AsylVfg). The lower court's ability to depart from precedent of the higher courts serves as a permanent control and therefore contributes to correctness of adjudication; the higher court's ability to check deviation and to reverse if necessary serves legal unity and certainty. This is how a hierarchy of courts not vested with formal bindingness tries to meet the value of correctness as well as the value of legal certainty.

(b)   There is no general rule of horizontal formal bindingness. Courts are not formally obliged to follow precedents of courts of the same level. But there are some procedures which secure unity and coherence between the decisions of the different panels of the different federal supreme courts (s.132 (2) GVG, s.11 (2) VwGO, s.45 (2) ArbGG, s.41 (2) SGG, s.11 (2) FGO) and the two panels of the Federal Constitutional Court (s.16 (1) BVerfGG), and between the decisions of the different federal supreme courts (Art. 95 (5) GG, s.2 (1) RsprEinhG). These procedures concern only the highest judiciary. In the higher and lower judiciary such procedures are lacking (for an exemption, see s.12 (1) VwGO). The only possibility to enforce uniformity is for a higher court to reverse one or the other of two contradicting decisions because of substantive incorrectness. But since an appeal to a higher court is not always possible and also because an appeal is not always taken even though it might be, many contradicting precedents by lower courts exist.

(c)   There is no general rule that courts must follow their own precedents, nor a special one that the highest courts must do so. Even the strict bindingness of the decisions of the Federal Constitutional Court is not considered to apply to the court itself. In practice, the highest courts have a strong tendency to follow their precedents. If there is a deviation, it will generally be grounded in countervailing reasons demanding a change. This corresponds to the normative force of precedent already stated.

6   Analysis of Force, Support and Illustrative Role

The German courts do not differentiate explicitly between the possibilities that precedents (a) may have justificatory force, (b) provide further support or (c) merely have illustrative value, but there are factors which contribute to the impact a precedent or a chain of precedents has. It has already been mentioned that in the case of an 'established line of decision of the highest judges' according to the Federal Court of Justice deviation is only correct where there are 'clearly outweighing reasons' (BGHZ 85, 64 (66)). This means that precedents are not formally binding if they are an 'established line of decision of the highest judges', but that they still have a strong justifying force. According to the adjudication of the Federal Constitutional Court already mentioned, the protection of confidence principle will not be applicable in any case if a ruling meets 'strong criticism' and if tendencies towards a change are already recognizable (BVerfGE 84,

212 (227)). There is no legislation in the German system about these matters and little discussion in scholarly works.

7   Excess of Precedents?

There is no explicit view that there are too many precedents in some fields. In practice the presence of numerous precedents is handled by concentrating on the leading rulings (Leitentscheidungen) of the supreme courts as well as on the decisions which have attracted attention in commentaries. Commentaries are an important filter. The entry of a precedent into a leading commentary makes it stand out amidst the immense mass of precedents and emphasizes its practical importance. How much will change in this respect because of the growth of electronic database systems remains an open question.

III   The Rationale of Precedent

In Section II we have discussed the bindingness of precedent in the practice of courts. In this section we will deal with the *academic debate* on the bindingness of precedent (including Austrian and Swiss authors so far as they are part of the German debate). We will begin with a short look at the historical background (in general, see Wieacker, 1967; Larenz, 1991, part 1; Ogorek, 1986; Weller, 1979).

1   General Rationales for Formal Bindingness

(a)   As already mentioned, the German system is a code system. This feature can be traced back to the reception of the Roman Law in the late Middle Ages. However, this reception itself was the result of the practice of lawyers, and the ensuing challenge to adapt and apply Roman Law to German ways of life (in case there was no special German statute) gave considerable power to the courts. So, within the *usus modernus pandectarum* (seventeenth and eighteen centuries) precedents played a remarkable role. Collections of judgments were published, and in the nineteenth century it was a common topic to denounce the 'cult of precedents' of the foregoing century. Absolute monarchs, supported by natural law theorists, tried to reduce the power of judges, not least by enacting natural law-inspired codifications (for example, in Prussia in 1794). Yet, with respect to the role of courts, their efforts had little success.

(b)   At the beginning of the nineteenth century, after the defeat of Napoleon, a debate arose in Germany on the question of whether a common, nationwide German civil code would be worth striving for. The most prominent opponent of this project was Friedrich Carl von

Savigny, whose scholarly authority formed one of the reasons for the fact that the project was not realized until the end of the century. Savigny's famous book 'On the Vocation of Our Time for Legislation and Jurisprudence' (*Vom Beruf unserer Zeit für Gesetzgebung und Rechtswissenschaft*, 1814), in which he denies this vocation with regard to legislation, was at the same time the founding document of the Historical School of Law. The theory of sources of law, first developed in this monograph, provided the frame in which the problem of precedent and judge-made law was discussed for a long time. The influence of this theory is still felt today.

According to Savigny, the supreme source of the entire law is the common convictions of a nation or, in the case of international law, of the community of nations. These convictions, in Savigny's view, are manifested directly in customary law and indirectly, insofar as the legislator and the jurists may be regarded as representatives of the people, in statutory law and in what he calls 'scholarly law' (*wissenschaftliches Recht*) or 'law of science' (*Recht der Wissenschaft* – 'science' in the broader sense, including the humanities) (Savigny, 1814, pp.8 ff; 1840, s.14, 19, 20). More common, then, became the term 'law of jurists' (*Juristenrecht*), coined by Georg Friedrich Puchta, Savigny's scholar and successor at his professorship in Berlin (Puchta, 1828, pp.161 ff; 1837a, pp.14 ff; 1837b, s.11). Savigny used the terms 'scholarly law' and 'law of science' synonymously with 'practical law' (*praktisches Recht*) and Puchta called the law of jurists also 'law of practice' (*Recht der Praxis*). The underlying idea of both is that the practice of courts should be oriented towards scholarly criteria, just as the scholarly research should be oriented towards the needs of practice. At the same time, the terms 'practical law' and 'law of practice' indicate that the concept of scholarly law or law of jurists includes 'scholar-made' law as well as judge-made law. That Savigny prefers the term 'scholarly law' may be explained by the fact that his ideal was the 'learned judge'.

Savigny as well as Puchta (concerning the difference between their views see Jakobs, 1992) hold that the law of jurists originates in two ways: first, by finding the guiding principles of the law and deducing consequences from them, thus producing 'new' norms by elaborating the latent content of positive law, and second, by establishing leading scholarly opinions (*communis opinio doctorum*) and established usages of the court (*usus fori*, Gerichtsgebrauch). It is obvious, and was stressed by both authors, that a single precedent, based on norms the court has arrived at in the first way, owes its binding force exclusively to its 'inner truth', that is its being a correct elaboration of the law. The same holds true for leading opinions and established adjudications – as long as they do not qualify as customary law. So the theory of precedent and judge-made law, as presented by the Historical School, is a classical form of a declaratory theory. The underlying concept of law considers law as a body of convictions and principles, embedded in legal relationships and institutes, prior to statutory, customary and established scholarly law.

(c)   The further development of the theory of precedent and judge-made law in the second half of the nineteenth and the first half of the twentieth century shows a rich variety of positions. We shall specify only some tendencies and characteristic theories.

(1)   In general, the theory of law of jurists as a third source of law steadily declined. Positivist theorists denounced it as a hidden form of natural law (for example, Bergbohm, 1892, pp.480 ff). At the same time, the term 'law of jurists' began to be replaced by the term 'judge-made law' (Richterrecht), though until the end of the nineteenth century only sporadically.

Highly influential, in particular for the practice of courts (and as the drafter of the German Civil Code, set in force 1 January 1900), was the theory of Bernhard Windscheid, representative of the late phase of the Historical School and of the Conceptual Jurisprudence (Begriffsjurisprudenz). His theory formed the leading opinion for decades, especially in the textbooks of civil law. The main features of his theory are the following. There are only two sources of law: statutory and customary law. An established adjudication qualifies as source of law only if it satisfies the requirements of customary law (*longa consuetudo, opinio necessitatis*). The method of receiving norms by drawing consequences from principles is part of legal methodology, more precisely, of the theory of gap filling. The authority and practical force of a single precedent depends on the quality of its reasons (Windscheid, 1891, s.16, 22).

Concerning the bindingness of precedent, an exceptional position was held by Heinrich Thöl (1875, s.14). Contrary to the leading opinion, Thöl maintains that a sentence will become a legal sentence already by being applied in one single judgment. In this sense he affirms the formal bindingness of precedent. As a rationale, he names the principle that equal cases should be treated equally. It is worth mentioning that this theory was presented in a textbook on commercial law, that is, in a rapidly developing field of law.

(2)   Positivist theories, defining the law by the will of the state, increasingly gained in importance. Within their frame, the judicial judgment qualifies as an authoritative declaration of the will of the state, and the judge was regarded as being empowered to create law in cases of vague statutes and gaps. However, the leading positivists of that period (Binding, Laband, Bergbohm, Kelsen) did not elaborate a theory of the binding force of precedent or judge-made law. (Kelsen added a chapter on this in the second edition of his 'Pure Theory of Law' (1960, pp.255 ff)). A forward-looking conception, frequently re-

ferred to in the contemporary debate, was presented by Oscar Bülow (1885). In his view, statutory law is only an attempt to create law, which always needs to be realized and completed by the judge. Thus valid law, according to Bülow, originates by the cooperation of legislature and judiciary. In this sense, he argues in favour of a theory of judge-made law. Often quoted, to the present day, is the last sentence of his essay: 'Not statutes, but statutes and the judge together create their law for the people ('Denn nicht das Gesetz, sondern Gesetz und Richteramt schafft dem Volke sein Recht')'. (Bülow, 1885, p.48)

(3)   Besides Savigny, Rudolf von Jhering was the most important German lawyer in the nineteenth century. The early Jhering represented the classical form of Conceptual Jurisprudence ('The system is an inexhaustible source of law': Jhering, 1898, p.386), the late Jhering represented the turning point to a jurisprudence of purpose ('The end is the creator of all law': Jhering, 1893, motto). In both phases, Jhering stressed the creative role of jurists and, notwithstanding the mentioned break, there are good reasons to underline the continuity of his work. Yet he was reserved about the bindingness of precedent (see Jhering, 1893, pp.387 ff).

In general, emphasis on the active and creative role of judges was a characteristic feature in the period in question. In particular, it was an essential concern of the Free Law Movement and the Sociological Jurisprudence in the first decades of the twentieth century. But neither the main representatives of these movements nor Philipp Heck, founder of the Jurisprudence of Interests (Interessenjurisprudenz) and most influential methodologist of those days, paid much attention to the authority of a single precedent. However, there was a tendency towards recognizing judge-made law as a source of law from the sociological point of view, and as a subsidiary and defeasible source from the juristic point of view (Ehrlich, 1913, pp.275 ff; 1925, pp.169 ff; Huber, 1921, p.445; Isay, 1929, pp.240 ff).

2   Rationales for Force, Further Support, and so on

(a)   As to the contemporary debate, the outstanding role played by precedents in the practice of courts is generally acknowledged. Highly disputed is the question of how this phenomenon should be classified and evaluated in terms of the theory of sources, of legal methodology and under the aspect of constitutional law. Converging tendencies between code law and common law systems are often noticed (as comparative studies see, for example, Schlüchter, 1986; Pilny, 1993). But there is no doubt that essential differences between the systems still exist.

There are three main areas of the debate. The first concerns the problem of bindingness of one single precedent (or some few precedents). This problem is usually dealt with in legal methodology. The second area regards the problem of bindingness of lines of precedents. This problem is discussed not only in legal methodology but also, and with special impact, in the theory of sources. A rather new point of emphasis forms the debate on the constitutional admissibility and significance of judge-made law. Of course these topics are overlapping, and in many contributions those distinctions are not drawn. A detailed discussion would go beyond the scope of this chapter. We confine ourselves to outlining the most significant positions and to addressing some problems connected with them.

(b)   Concerning the bindingness of single precedents, there are two main groups of theories. The first, representing the leading opinion, continues the tradition founded by the Historical School. The theories belonging here, which may be labelled 'classical' ones, hold that (except s.31 BVerfGG) the authority of precedent depends exclusively on its being a correct interpretation of the valid law or, in other words, on the quality of its reasons (Enneccerus and Nipperdey, 1959, pp.254 ff; Esser, 1974, pp.267 ff; 1967, pp.116 ff; 1970, pp.184 ff; 1976, pp.68; Larenz, 1991, pp.429 ff; 1974, pp.32 ff; Larenz and Canaris, 1995, pp.525 ff; Flume, 1967, pp.17 ff; Fischer, 1971, pp.25 ff).

The second group comprises, so to speak, 'modern' theories. Their common feature is the effort to give stronger weight to precedent than the classical theories do. The most discussed theses are the following:

- in favour of precedent there is a presumption of its reasonableness (Kriele, 1976, pp.243 ff);
- a precedent sets a burden of argumentation for those intending to deviate from it (Alexy, 1989, pp.274 ff; Koch and Rüßmann, 1982, pp.186 ff; Raisch, 1995, p.192);
- a precedent is binding in 'non-liquet' cases, that is, in cases in which, if the precedent were not taken into account, more than one decision would be substantively and methodologically admissible (Bydlinski, 1985, pp.151 ff; 1991, pp.501 ff; compare Pawlowski, 1991, pp.229 ff emphasizing the principle of equally treating equal cases).

A particular position is held by Fikentscher (1977, pp.313 ff, 336 ff). According to him, the 'case norm' (Fallnorm) of a precedent is strictly binding. In this sense, he affirms the principle of *stare decisis* with respect to the German system. However, his concept of case norm is not identical with the Anglo-American concept of case rule. Case norms, in his view, are rules, arrived at by a correct and justice-oriented interpretation of the positive law and being directly applicable to the case in question. So his theory of precedent is essentially a declaratory one.

Leaving aside the conceptual framework of Fikentscher's approach, there is good reason to assume that the theories of the second group are equivalent in their result. As to their status, they are recommendations in favour of methodological rules (though at the same time describing the overall practice of courts). Taking careful account of methodological rules may be regarded as a constitutional requirement, based on Art. 20 (3) GG according to which the jurisdiction is bound 'to statutes *and law*' (compare Esser, 1976, p.86). In this sense, a decision which does not satisfy those rules is legally faulty in a broader sense which, however, does not imply that it is voidable after appeal or even *ipso jure* void. Whether it is voidable or void depends on the question of how far the methodological defect has an impact on the actual decision.

(c)   Concerning the bindingness of a line of precedents, two main groups of theories should be distinguished, too. The first one, again, is formed by 'classical' theories. These theories regard a permanent or established adjudication, as such, to be a mere fact, having weight only by virtue of its underlying reasons, and being binding only if it fulfils the requirements of customary law in a strict sense, that is, by expressing a longlasting custom based on the common conviction of its being right, not only for the judiciary but for the people. However, within this frame it is widely acknowledged that the argumentative weight of lines of precedents increases the longer they last, and by support of a dogmatic consensus (Enneccerus and Nipperdey, 1959, pp.254 ff; Mayer-Ladewig, 1962, pp.107 ff, 125 ff; Larenz, 1991, pp.433 ff; Hübner, 1996, s.3 IV; Flume, 1967, pp.17 ff; Picker, 1988, pp.72 ff).

A variant of this group is formed by theories which are in the tradition of Oscar Bülow. They argue that all statutory law has to be understood under the proviso that it needs to be concretized by the judiciary. In this sense judge-made law qualifies as the 'prolonged arm' of statutory law (Esser, 1967, pp.113 ff; 1976, pp.75 f; Adomeit, 1969, pp.37 ff).

According to the theories of the second group, an established line of decision, even below the threshold of customary law, qualifies as a source of law of its own standing, though subordinate to statutory and customary law. The character of this source is expressed by terms like 'informal', 'subsidiary' and 'defeasible' (Less, 1954, pp.59 ff; Germann, 1969, pp.227 ff; Kruse, 1971, pp.9 ff; Wolff *et al.*, 1994, s. 25 IV; Ossenbühl, 1992, s.7 VIII; Raisch, 1995, pp.193 ff).

Fikentscher's theory has a particular status in this respect, too. He holds that judge-made law qualifies as a source of law ranking equally with statutory law (Fikentscher, 1977, p.323). However, this thesis again is to be understood on the basis of his theory of case norm which cannot be discussed here in detail.

In general, the debate suffers from the ambiguity and vagueness of the term 'source'. Two overlapping distinctions are frequently used. The first one distinguishes between formal sources, that is, those that validate norms as legal by virtue of pedigree (especially legislation and custom) and material sources, that is the entirety of all other legitimate reasons for judicial decision making. In this sense, precedents and permanent or established lines of decision may qualify as material sources, but not necessarily as formal ones. The second distinction is to be traced back to the Historical School and differentiates between sources from which law originates (Rechtsentstehungsquellen), sources of the recognition of law (Rechtserkenntnisquellen) and sources of validation of law (Rechtsgeltungsquellen) (see Savigny, 1840, s.11; Puchta, 1828, pp.143 ff, 180 ff; 1837, pp.3 ff, 120 ff; compare Ross, 1929, pp.128 ff). In this sense, precedents and permanent or established lines of decision are sources from which law originates. Whether they are sources of the recognition of law depends not least on the perspective from which the problem is discussed. In German legal theory, the perspective of the judge is dominant, and the question of whether lines of precedents qualify as sources of the recognition of law depends on the question of how much weight should be given them (see (d) below). In the perspective of lawyers, administrative authorities and citizens different answers might be suitable (compare, for example, Mayer-Ladewig, 1962, pp.113 ff). Sources of validation of law are always principles and not lines of precedents.

(d)   The constitutional basis of the legitimacy as well as of the binding force of judge-made law, according to an increasing opinion, is found in Art. 20 (3) GG (Stern, 1984, pp.581 ff; Fikentscher, 1977, pp.325 ff; Benda, 1995, pp.733 ff; Heyde, 1995, pp.1629 ff). As already mentioned, under this article the courts and the executive are bound to 'statutes *and law*'. Indeed (and in spite of BVerfGE 84, 212 (227), quoted above – see Appendix, II.1), on the basis of a concept of law which includes the reasons for norms as well as the reasons for decisions, one may argue that the term 'law' in this provision comprises judge-made law. However, a clear distinction should be drawn between the question of which elements are included in the concept of law and the question of how these elements rank in case of conflicts between them. In this respect, there is no doubt that in the German constitutional system priority in law making rests with the legislature. So, even if one includes judge-made law in the concept of law, there remains the question of its ranking and its constitutional limits. This question, according to unanimous opinion, has to be answered by weighing colliding constitutional principles (see Ipsen,

1975; 1984, pp.1103 ff; Stern, 1984, pp.583 ff; Wank, 1978, pp.154 ff; compare further Neuner, 1992).

Reconstructing the debate, one has to distinguish between two quite different problems. The first one concerns the reasons in favour of and against the *power of courts to create precedent and judge-made law*. The second one concerns the reasons in favour and against the *bindingness of precedent and judge-made law*. As to the first problem, the most significant reason for giving courts such power is Art. 20 (3) GG, in the sense that the law to which the judge is bound includes constitutional principles like fundamental rights (Art. 1-19 GG) and the requirements of democracy, the rule of law and the social state (Art. 20, 28 [1] GG). Being bound to these principles, at the same time means empowered to interpret, weigh and apply them, thus completing, improving and developing the law. Supporting analytical and empirical arguments refer to the openness of written law, the obsolescence of codifications and statutes by reason of their age, the rapidity of social change, the complexity of modern societies and, not least, the deficiencies of the parliamentary legislator (see Schmitt, 1923; Hedemann, 1934; Diederichsen, 1974; Grimm, 1990). The main counter-argument, as already mentioned, holds that the priority of law making rests with the legislature, in other words, that a too active role of courts infringes the principles of balancing separate powers and of democratically legitimized law making by the parliament. Supporting empirical arguments in this respect refer to the danger of ossification or petrification of judge-made law, and to the limited capacity of courts, as compared with the parliament, to explore the relevant empirical facts and take due account of the possible consequences of new regulations. A particular position is held by Friedrich Müller. In his view, constitutionally admissible judge-made law, that is decisions remaining *intra legem*, does not deserve the name, and judge-made law deserving the name, that is decisions that are *praeter, extra* and *contra legem*, is constitutionally inadmissible (Müller, 1986, p.126; compare Sendler, 1987, criticizing Müller; Christensen, 1989, defending Müller).

Concerning the second problem, three constitutional principles in favour of the bindingness of precedents or lines of precedents generally are acknowledged: the principle of legal certainty (deriving from the rule of law or more particularly the principle of state legality (Rechtsstaatsprinzip), as laid down in Arts 20 and 28 (1) GG), the principle of equality (Art. 3 (1) GG) and the principle of the protection of trust (also deriving from the principle of the constitutional state). Supporting arguments refer to the requirements of limiting litigation and securing the uniformity of the legal system. The main counter-arguments are taken from the principles of democracy, of the separation of powers and of the principle of substantive correctness or rightness of judicial judgment.

IV   Precedents: What They Stand for and How They Apply

1   *What Counts as Binding or Having Force?*

(a)   German courts usually refer to precedents without explicitly stating what elements are considered as binding, having force or providing other support. If the subject is touched upon at all, it is treated somewhat vaguely. Rather precise and extensive considerations can be found in the decisions of the Federal Constitutional Court. The reason for this is that the question of 'what is binding' is of special importance in constitutional jurisdiction because it is the only adjudication in which strict formal bindingness occurs (compare s.31 (1) BVerfGG). The basic formula of the Federal Constitutional Court says that the 'supporting reasons' (*tragende Gründe*) are binding (BVerfGE 1, 14 (37); 19, 377 (392); 20, 56 (87); 40, 88 (93)). This is disputed in academic writing; compare Kriele, 1976, pp.290 ff, Sachs, 1977, pp.66 ff, Schlüchter 1986, pp.25 ff). By using this formula reference is made to the classical distinction between *rationes decidendi* and *obiter dicta* (compare Schlüter, 1973, pp.77 ff). But this formula does not yet hold any criterion for differentiating between *rationes decidendi* and *obiter dicta*. Such a criterion cannot be found in the cases. The Federal Constitutional Court has occasionally used the radical method of declaring the whole text of substantiation as supporting: 'All statements of the opinion ... are necessary, and therefore, in the sense of the adjudication of the Federal Constitutional Court, part of the reasons supporting the decision' (BVerfGE 36, 1 (36)). This was heavily criticized and remains an exception. It becomes obvious, though, that everything that is 'necessary' counts as supporting. Nevertheless, it still remains open what indeed is necessary.

   In relation to precedents of other courts, the distinction between *rationes decidendi* and *obiter dicta* does not play a very important part. This is due to the fact that precedents, except those of the Federal Constitutional Court, are not formally binding. If precedents are formally binding, it will be worth trying to classify a ruling that one is not willing to follow as an *obiter dictum*, even if this needs extensive argumentation. If, on the other hand, the precedent is not formally binding, it will usually be easier to present substantive reasons for not following it. This does not exclude that there are cases in which formerly held opinions one does not want to follow any more are declared 'non-supporting' (compare BGHSt 40, 218 (234)). But this is rather an exception; thus the aforementioned decision dealt with the special case of a synthesizing reconstruction of their own case law. The distinction between *ratio decidendi* and *obiter dictum* is of much greater significance, however, in the case of a question such as whether a panel of a supreme federal court which wants to deviate from a decision of another panel of that court has to present the divergence to the so-called 'Great Panel' (compare, on this and further cases, Appendix, question II. 2, and Lilie, 1993).

(b)   As a matter of principle, everything from a prior decision can be put forward as long as it is relevant. Of special importance are explicit rules formulated with the help of numbers. The Federal Court of Justice, for example, fixed the term of complete unfitness to drive, which is not defined by law, at 1.3 per cent blood alcohol concentration (BGHSt 21, 157). The Higher Regional Court of Appeal of Brunswick considered this too high and presented to the Federal Court of Justice the question whether or not it may be allowed to lower the blood alcohol concentration to 1.1 per cent (compare s.121 (2) GVG). The latter overruled its former jurisdiction and fixed the concentration at 1.1 per cent because of a change of scientific cognition (BGH, NStZ 1990, 491 (492)). A subpanel of the Federal Constitutional Court did not interpret this as a violation either of the prohibition of retroactivity (Rückwirkungsverbot) or of the protection of trust principle, and therefore approved of the change in ruling (BVerfGE, NStZ 1990, 537). The lower courts now follow this ruling as they followed the former 1.3 per cent limit. Rules that are formulated with the help of numbers and percentages can be found to quite a great extent in the jurisdiction of the Federal Labour Court and the Federal Social Court as well as in maintenance law. But they form an exception despite the multitude of rules formulated with the help of numbers and percentages. Most of the rules, even if they are very specific, can do without numbers.

Besides specifically formulated rules, abstract principles play a major part. A famous example is formed by the general constitutional right to personality (allgemeines verfassungsrechtliches Persönlichkeitsrecht). The Federal Constitutional Court has constantly added new subprinciples to this main principle (compare, for example, BVerfGE 65, 1 (42)) which play an important role in decision making. In between rules formulated with the help of numbers and principles of the highest degree of abstractness, rules and principles of all degrees of generality may be of importance as parts of prior decisions. Since correctness of a decision always matters, the substantive reasons stated for those rules and principles are of relevance, too.

2   Reasoning about Applicability

There is but scarce judicial and scholarly practice of giving arguments for and against the applicability of a precedent, and it is difficult to recognize determinate types of arguments that are used in the practice of applying precedents. Yet there have been a few attempts in academic discussion about legal methodology to analyse the applicability of a precedent more closely (compare, for example, Kriele, 1976, pp.269 ff; Fikentscher, 1977, pp.343 ff), but these, as is apparent so far, have been of little influence on the judicial or scholarly practices of applying precedents.

3   *Juristic Discussion*

There are only a few judicial discussions about methods for defining and finding what a precedent stands for. The reasons for this have already been given in Section IV.1. There are more comprehensive discussions about this matter in academic writings. It is a characteristic that on this occasion theories of the Anglo-Saxon sphere of law are discussed to a great extent (compare, for example, Schlüter, 1973, pp.81 ff; Kriele, 1976, pp.243 ff; Schlüchter, 1986, pp.58 ff).

4   *Illustrative or Analogical Precedent*

Precedents not regarded as strictly in point and therefore not applicable are more often used in arguments *e contrario* than in illustrative examples. If a precedent is considered as being sufficiently similar to the case to be decided, it will not be utilized to draw an analogy; instead, it will simply be applied. If it is considered as not being sufficiently similar, it will not be applied. If a court wishes to refer to a precedent only vaguely resembling the case to be decided, its policy will be to adopt the principles underlying the *ratio decidendi* of the precedent, not the *ratio* itself.

5   *Single Precedents or Lines of Decision?*

(a)   There is a distinction between the force or further support of single precedents on the one hand and lines of precedents on the other. A line of precedent has a much greater weight than a single case. A line of precedent that has been established for some time is called 'permanent adjudication' (*ständige Rechtsprechung*). The reference to permanent adjudication often appears as follows: 'The Federal Constitutional Court is in permanent adjudication (since BVerfGE 1, 109 (110 f.)) of the opinion that ...' (BVerfGE 92, 122 (123)). Frequently, the abbreviation 'st. Rspr.' (permanent adjudication) is used and often more than the first decision of a line is named: 'According to the principles developed in the adjudication of the Federal Constitutional Court, Art. 2 (1) GG guarantees general freedom of action in an extensive sense (permanent adjudication since BVerfGE 6, 32 (36); more recently BVerfGE 74, 129 (151); 75, 108 (154 f)). (BVerfGE 80, 137 (152)).'

The Federal Court of Justice does not, as mentioned, talk only about a 'permanent adjudication' but also about an 'established adjudication of the highest judges' from which deviation is only permitted exceptionally (BGHZ 85, 64 (66)). It is not quite clear how a distinction can be made between an 'established' and a 'permanent' adjudication. One of the criteria may be length of time. The Federal Court of Justice designates an established adjudication as a 'permanent adjudication lasting for decades' (BGHZ 125, 218 (222)). A second criterion may be that this adjudication resisted the critique by science and the check by jurisdiction. Under these two circumstances permanent adjudication has a special weight.

(b)   The following distinction can be made between lines of precedents, but the broader lines are often fluid.

(1)   A first kind consists of 'merely repetitive' precedents. An example is presented by the adjudication of the Federal Constitutional Court saying that political parties in a dispute about their constitutional status are not allowed to apply for a constitutional complaint, which is open to everyone, but can only initiate a proceeding reserved to constitutional organs, only which is labelled an *Organstreit* proceeding (a constitutional dispute between the highest organs of the Federal Republic). In a decision of 1991 the Federal Constitutional Court plainly declared, without a single statement about the academic critique raised in the literature:

> According to the permanent adjudication of the Federal Constitutional Court, political parties may assert and charge an encroachment on their constitutional status – as described in Art. 21 (1) GG – by a constitutional organ with the help of an *Organstreit* proceeding (compare most recently BVerfGE 82, 322 (335)). (BVerfGE 84, 290 (298); compare further BVerfGE 85, 264 (284); 92, 80 (90))

Here the court does not even make the effort to trace the line of precedents back to the leading ruling of 1954 (BVerfGE 4, 27 (31)). To find the leading ruling one has to look it up in the cited decision (BVerfGE 82, 322 (335)). This can be called an indirect reference to the leading decision. Viewing such a very established adjudication, academic critics become resigned: 'This adjudication concerning the ability of political parties to be a party to *Organstreit* proceedings one has to put up with for this time. But it is wrong because ...' (Schlaich, 1994, p.62).

(2)   There is a distinction between the merely repetitive use of precedents and the continuation of a line after an explicit confirmation. A typical example is presented by a decision of the Federal Constitutional Court of 1989 which deals with the question whether or not riding in the woods is protected by 'the right to the free development

of one's personality' (Art. 2 (1) GG). This is the case corresponding to the permanent adjudication of the Federal Constitutional Court:

> According to the principles developed in the adjudication of the Federal Constitutional Court, Art. 2 (1) GG guarantees general freedom of action in an extensive sense (permanent adjudication since BVerfGE 6, 32 (36); more recently BVerfGE 74, 129 (151); 75, 108 (154 f)). This does not only protect a limited scope of development of personality but every kind of human action regardless of the weight it has for the development of personality (compare e.g., the decision of a sub-panel in BVerfGE 54, 143 (146) – Dove Feeding Case). (BVerfGE 80, 137 (152 f))

This interpretation has been heavily contested in academic writing. The Federal Constitutional Court names two critiques and some arguments and confirms its adjudication thereupon with the following statement: 'A limitation of the scope (Schutzbereich) of Art. 2 (1) GG deviating from former adjudication is not justified' (BVerfGE 80, 137 (154)). Then this is substantiated briefly.

In the judgment of the Federal Constitutional Court just mentioned, the arguments pro and con to keep the permanent adjudication are stated very shortly. Two critics but no defenders are named. Only the line of precedent, a critique, and its rejection by the court exist. An instructive example for a decision in which a court defends its line of precedent quite extensively and also names its critics as well as its defenders is a decision of the Federal Court of Justice of 1995 concerning the criminal responsibility of the so-called 'Mauerschützen' (guardians who shot people at the Berlin Wall). Here, an explicit confirmation takes place as well: 'The panel adheres to the principles of its adjudication' (BGH, NJW 1995, 2728 (2730)). Differing from the decision on riding in the woods, the court presented itself in this decision as a participant in a comprehensive discourse.

Explicit confirmation provides a special kind of weight to lines of precedent. A sudden change of a merely repetitive line of precedents would perhaps cause surprise; a sudden change following an explicit confirmation would cause astonishment.

(3) An interesting example for a 'synthesizing' or reconstructive line of precedent (that is, for a line in which the precedents are taken to stand for a legal point not explicitly formulated in the prior precedents considered individually) is the decision of the Federal Court of Justice on criminal responsibility of members of the National Defence Committee of the former GDR for wilful slaying of refugees by soldiers of the former GDR. It deals with the question whether members of the highest military command of the GDR can be regarded as indirect perpetrators, that is as perpetrators behind the common soldier active as a direct perpetrator, or whether only a weaker kind

of participation is suitable. The adjudication of the Federal Court of Justice so far concerning this problem, which was not totally stringent and rather ambiguous, held that this leads to an affirmation of indirect perpetratorship of the highest military commander of the former GDR. This is reduced to a basic rule and to a clear exceptional clause (BGHSt 40, 218 (236)), so that now the line of precedents shows an explicit and relatively clear direction. Out of all precedents of the line, this synthesizing precedent now bears the greatest weight. (4) 'Conflicting' (zigzag) lines of precedents appear relatively seldom but they do exist. The adjudication of the Federal Court of Justice just mentioned concerning indirect perpetratorship serves as an example. Contradicting tendencies were brought into a single line only by synthesization in this decision. A certain zigzag character can also be found in the adjudication of the Federal Constitutional Court concerning religious symbols and actions in public facilities. In 1973, the court held that the basic right of freedom of religion of a Jewish lawyer would be violated if a crucifix were not removed from the court room despite his protest (BVerfGE 35, 366 (373)). A judgment in the year 1979 concerning school prayers leads, to a certain extent, in the opposite direction. The court held that a school prayer is admissible in public schools even if parents or children protest against it under the provision that participation is voluntary and non-participation does not lead to discrimination. But an encroachment to a certain degree is understood as reasonable: 'The rest of the exceptional position, which still remains because of his non-participation, has to be and can be endured by the differently minded pupil' (BVerfGE 52, 223 (252)). By this, positive freedom of religion of those who want to pray in school is given priority over the negative freedom of religion of those who reject a school prayer.

The latter is held differently in the decision of the Federal Constitutional Court in 1995 concerning crucifixes and crosses in classrooms of public schools. The court declares in this decision that the order of the state to fix crosses or crucifixes in classrooms of public schools to which all school children have to go to is constitutionally void (BVerfG, EuGRZ 1995, 359 (363)). In this decision negative freedom of religion is, contrary to the case of school prayer, given priority over positive freedom. This decision has been one of the most criticized decisions of the Federal Constitutional Court. Only five out of eight judges of the first panel approved of the decision; three of them wrote a dissenting opinion. If only one additional judge had not approved of the decision, the constitutional complaint would have failed (s.15 (3) sentence 3 BVerfGG). It is an interesting question whether the line started by this decision will be developed further or whether a movement back to the ruling in the school prayer decision will take place. Anyhow, such a contested and zigzag course of decision carried by a bare majority bears relatively little precedential weight.

6   The Concept of a 'Leading Case'

The concept of a 'leading case' plays an important role in the German system's approach to precedent. The lines of precedent stated in question VI.5 (Appendix) are often started by a leading case. Leading cases that start a line keep their importance if the line does not change fundamentally, most often in cases of a merely repetitive line. These may be designated 'line-starting leading cases'. Cases in which a line is given up or changed can be referred to as 'line-closing' and 'line-changing cases'. If they form the beginning of a new line of precedents, they will at the same time be line-starting leading cases.

Cases that synthesize a line which has been cloudy up to this point are of special importance. The decision of the Federal Court of Justice concerning the question of criminal responsibility of members of the National Defence Committee of the former GDR which has been mentioned above represents such a case (BGHSt 40, 218). Here, we can speak about a 'line-synthesizing leading case'.

Whether a case becomes a leading case or not depends not only on its substantial importance but also on the community of lawyers who contribute to the interpretation and application of the law. From the mass of cases only a few are able to attract attention and be memorized. Drawing a case from the permanent flow of decisions as a leading case includes on the one hand an understanding about what is important and on the other hand an act of reduction of complexity.

V   Distinguishing, Explaining, Modifying, Overruling

1   Distinguishing

Due to the minor importance of precedents as a formal source of law, German courts do not have a highly developed practice of distinguishing. Apart from the decisions of the Federal Constitutional Court and apart from procedures like those of presenting a divergence to a Great Panel (see Appendix, question II.2) there is, besides distinguishing, always the possibility of an overruling. Still, distinguishing is not unusual, owing to the fact that precedents have force in the sense of question II.1 (Appendix). Especially if the precedent is a decision of the same court or a higher court which is ostensibly or arguably applicable, deviation from precedent will sometimes be supported by explicitly stating differences between the precedential case and the case to be decided. A typical prelude is the following statement: 'The panel is thereby not at variance with the decision BGHZ 25, 217, 225 referred to by the court of appeal' (BGH LM § 123 BGB, Nr. 28, p.3). An elaboration of a relevant distinction of the case in hand follows. As a second example, a decision of the Federal Constitutional Court may be mentioned in which distinguishing from a similar prior decision is started by the words: 'But there are serious doubts whether a case comparable with the former situation lies before the court' (BVerfGE 79, 1 (19)).

2   Juristic Commentary

Scholarly and other juristic commentators often discuss the coherence of established lines of precedents and try to extract principles underlying the decisions. But the discussion of points of difference between reported precedents plays none or only a minor role. Commentators concentrate on the questions whether there have been changes, whether inconsistencies exist and how they can be overcome.

3   Excessive Distinguishing?

In German law distinguishing – in contrast to overruling – is not an established or even an obligatory method of dealing with precedents when wishing to make a seemingly deviating decision. Therefore abuse of distinguishing by drawing excessively fine or unreal distinctions is a rare occurrence. The same applies to reformulating precedents as regards their factual and legal aspects in order to reconcile them with the present decision. Overruling is the easier way of dealing with an unwelcome precedent. It might be the case, though, that an adjustment of a present judgment and a precedent is unavoidable (for example, because the precedent is a decision of the Federal Constitutional Court or because the panel does not want to present a divergence to the respective Great Panel (see question II.2, Appendix)). In this case, courts attempt to harmonize the precedent and the seemingly deviating decision they wish to make by applying the traditional methods of interpretation in restating the precedent, especially by semantic and systemic arguments (compare Larenz and Canaris, 1995, pp.178 f). This way of dealing with the problem is usually restricted to judicial practice, it occurs seldom if at all in scholarly or other juristic commentaries.

4   Types of Overruling

(a)   It is not a common practice to differentiate between different types of overruling in the German legal system. But some of the differences formulated in the question can be applied to the German system, too.

(1)   Overruling in the strict sense – an explicit judicial act of overturning a *binding* precedent or a line of precedent – can only exist where there are binding precedents as well. In Germany, as stated above in Section II.1, only precedents by the Federal Constitutional Court are formally binding (s.31 (1) BVerfGG). But this bindingness does not apply to the Federal Constitutional Court itself. This is why the Federal Constitutional Court is only able to practise overruling in the strict sense insofar as it can overturn a precedent being binding upon all authorities except upon itself. Due to the relation between the Federal Constitutional Court and its own precedents there is only an overruling in a broader sense, for its own precedents only have force but are not binding upon itself strictly or formally. It still seems to be adequate to classify this case as a special variant of overruling in the strict sense.

During the first decades of jurisdiction of the Federal Constitutional Court there were only relatively few cases of overruling. This number has increased lately. This is probably due to the increasing age of decisions, a change of circumstances and a revised constitutional cognition.

One of the most important cases of an overruling in the strict sense is the alteration of adjudication of the Federal Constitutional Court concerning the financing of political parties. The Federal Constitutional Court held in 1966 that it will be unconstitutional if the political parties receive subsidies for all their activities in the field of 'political opinion and will formation' from the federal state budget. According to this decision, only the necessary expenses of election campaigns can be restituted (BVerfGE 20, 56 (96 ff)). In 1992, the court repealed this rule along with a few others concerning the financing of political parties and established a new set of rules. This was done in the form of an explicit overruling:

> In opposition to the opinion held by the panel up to this point the state is not constitutionally debarred from giving resources to the political parties for financing their *general* activities incumbent on them by the Basic Law ... Therefore – in opposition to the former adjudication of the panel (compare for the first time BVerfGE 20, 56 (113 f)) – it is not obligatory to search for the limits of public financing of political parties on grounds of the constitution in the restitution of 'necessary expenses of an appropriate election campaign'. (BVerfGE 85, 264 (285 f)

Cases of such an overruling are possible within all areas of constitutional law. They can be found, for example, in the area of basic rights (BVerfGE 85, 191 (206)) and in the Maastricht judgment (BVerfGE 89, 155 (175)).

(2)   Overruling in a broader sense – an explicit judicial act of reject-ing a precedent (or line of precedent) only having force – can be found in the jurisdiction of all courts. Outstanding examples are BGHZ 56, 97 (100), BGHSt 40, 138 (145 ff) and BVerwGE 84, 361 (365).
(3)   Silent overruling – not following a precedent (or line of pre-cedent) and not explicitly acknowledging this – occurs sometimes, but not very often. Courts have no reason to proceed in this way, for they have the power of explicit overruling. Silent overruling might well be criticized by legal scholars as not meeting appropriate standards of juristic rationality, which includes consideration of precedent.
(4)   Overruling whereby a precedent is explicitly or implicitly cut down so severely in scope that it no longer exists as a precedent is not a common practice in Germany. Within the German system there is no reason for such a procedure. The desired result can be obtained more easily by a simple overruling.
(b)   In a few cases there is a special procedure to comply with. The details have been stated in Section II.2 above. Of special importance is the presentation of divergence before the Common Panel of the Supreme Federal Courts (Art. 100 (3) GG, s.2 (1) RsprEinhG), before the Great Panels of the different supreme courts (s.132 (2) ZPO, s.11 (2) VwGO, s.45 (2) ArbGG, s.41 (2) SGG, s.11 (2) FGO) and before the Plenum of the Federal Constitutional Court (s.16 (1) BVerfGG). All this is completed by the obligation for higher courts wanting to deviate from a precedent of the respective supreme court to allow appeal to the supreme court (s.546 (1) ZPO, s.132 (2) VwGO, s.72 (2) ArbGG, s.160 (2) SGG, s.115 (2) FGO).

Special reasons to justify an overruling are not necessary. It is necessary, though, for the reasons to be strong enough to comply with the burden of argument in favour of following the precedent. This is valid for all fields of law. Very strong reasons have to be put forward in case of an 'established line of decision of the highest judges' (BGHZ 85, 64 (66); compare Section II.1 above). Precedents of the Federal Constitutional Court can only be overruled by the court itself.

5   Prospective Overruling

There is no common practice of prospective overruling in Germany. Such a practice has sometimes been demanded in academic writing (compare, for example, Knittel, 1965, pp.50 ff) but has never become the ruling opinion. Overruling of a precedent with an effect only on future cases and therefore having no effect on the case being decided has remained an exception in reported cases. A famous example of such an exception is formed by a decision of the Federal Labour Court (BAG) in 1981 in which the court imparted that it 'would take into consideration' to change its adjudication in the future (BAG NJW 1982, 788 ff). This decision was harshly criticized (compare Picker, 1984, pp.153 ff; Larenz and Canaris, 1995, p.260). More often remarks and hints are given that stay below the threshold of an explicit prospective overruling, but on the other side drop a hint that a line of decisions could be changed in the future.

6   Anticipatory Overruling by Lower Courts

Anticipatory overruling is, indeed, practised in the German system. There is the possibility that a lower court refuses to follow a precedent of a higher court in anticipation of the likelihood that the higher court when hearing on appeal will overrule it as well, that is, will uphold the overruling decision of the lower court. One could say that one of the main reasons for precedents not being strictly and formally binding in the German system consists in keeping the opportunity of review still open. The lower courts are not supposed to follow the higher courts mechanically but are expected also to take a critical line where reason exists. A certainly extreme but still instructive example of this is given by the Higher Administrative Court of North Rhine–Westphalia as introduced above in Section II.5, which tried more than 160 times to push through its opinion concerning political asylum for Tamils, until it finally submitted to the authority of the Federal Administrative Court (OVG NW, decision of 27 June 1986 – file number 19 A 10005/85).

7   Precedent and Legislative Practice

In legislative practice drafters of legislation and the legislature do take account of case law and precedent. In a considerable number of cases the legislature adopts what courts have developed as an established adjudication. For example, the rules that govern the withdrawal of acts of administration, ss. 48 and 49 of the Federal Administration Procedure Act (Verwaltungsverfahrensgesetz (VwVfG)) of 1976 largely reflect what the courts had ruled as case law before codification.

In other cases the legislature has overturned precedents. One example concerns a provision of the German Civil Code (Bürgerliches Gesetzbuch (BGB)). Section 181 BGB prohibits an agent (representative) of another person entering into an agreement for himself personally if the agreement entails obligations for the party being represented by the agent. This provision is meant to exclude possible conflicts of interest. But the Federal Court of Justice ruled that this provision should not be applicable in the case of a managing director and only partner of a private limited liability company (Gesellschaft mit beschränkter Haftung (GmbH)) making an agreement with himself as a private person (BGHZ 56, 97 (102 ff)). The judges felt that a conflict of interest could not occur in this constellation. In 1980, however, the legislature inserted a provision into the Limited Company Act (GmbH-Gesetz (GmbHG)) according to which s.181 BGB is applicable in this case (s.35 (4) GmbHG).

The adjudication of the Federal Constitutional Court plays a special role. There are many examples of legislation repeating what the court said. One example is the Political Party Act (Parteiengesetz (PartG)) which is in its major parts a codification of the rulings of the Federal Constitutional Court.

A confirmation of case law by the legislature is seen as a reason for the bindingness of this case law. For example, the German Civil Code of 1900 (BGB) does not comprise general rules concerning breach of contract ('positive Vertragsverletzung', meaning the violation of duties regarding protected interests of the other party). The law of breach of contract has been developed by the courts. Nowadays, it is deemed customary law. As a confirmation of its bindingness, it is sometimes cited that the legislator mentions the term 'breach of contract' in s.11 no. 7 of the Exemption Clauses Act (AGB-Gesetz (AGBG)) of 1976 (compare Jauernig, 1994, s.276 ann. V.1).

8   Conflicts of Precedents

There are, as mentioned in the answer in Section II.2 above, procedures to prevent the development of conflicts of precedents. But in case a conflict still arises, there are no firm rules. It could be said that the generally recognized rules of posteriority, speciality and superiority (compare Alexy and Dreier, 1991, p.99) have a certain prima facie force not only on statutes but also on precedents. Yet, in contrast to statutes, precedents are always capable of being subverted by a change in the balance of substantive reasons on a given point.

9   Hypothetical Cases

There are no firm rules about the use of hypothetical cases in reasoning about the creation and application of precedent. Hypothetical cases may be used in *reductio ad absurdum* argumentation (compare Diederichsen, 1973, pp.155 ff). Also a usage of extreme hypothetical cases does occur (BGHSt 8, 263 (267); 11, 74 (78); 14, 116 (121)). Nevertheless, there is no substantive difference in the use of hypothetical cases between the creation and application of precedent and the interpretation and application of statutes.

VI   Matters of General Perspective, Evaluation and Other

1   'Saying and Doing'

There may be a gap between saying and doing in the use of precedent in that courts claim to interpret the law and to give reasons for the correct interpretation but in fact simply follow the precedent without much reflection, or after reflection not so much on interpretation of the law as on the interpretation of precedent. Thus the importance of precedent in the process of judicial decision making is perhaps not always adequately reflected in the reported decisions. However, this is not a gap between saying one is free, while de facto following precedent, but a gap between the presentation of the argument as an interpretation of statutes, and its true nature as a use of precedent. This gap is not very big, though. It is more of a tendency which is almost to be expected in a codified system. This tendency is opposed to a tendency to an open and reflective use of precedent.

2   Recent Change or Evolution

There has been a change in the use of precedents within the past decades in which the creation and use of precedents was more reflected in legal doctrine and legal methodology (compare especially Kriele, 1976) and in which the courts became more aware of their creative role in the process of making and applying the law. The adjudication of the Federal Constitutional Court concerning the admissibility of judge-made development of the law caused far-reaching effects, starting with the Soraya decision in which the Federal Constitutional Court declared a line of precedent of the Federal Court of Justice as constitutional despite its contradicting the wording of a statute (BVerfGE 34, 269 (286 ff)). The Federal Court of Justice took up this affirmation of its adjudication by the Federal Constitutional Court again. It cited one of the rulings from the Soraya decision by letter: 'The judge is, according to the Basic Law, not obligated to apply legislative orders within the limits of the literal sense in an individual case (BVerfGE 34, 269, 287)' (BGHZ 85, 64 (66); compare further BGHZ 87, 150 (155)).

By creating precedent against the wording of a statute, the Federal Labour Court went so far that the Federal Constitutional Court set restraints on it. The Federal Constitutional Court accused the Federal Labour Court in a famous case of having made the decision for 'reasons of social politics' and not for legal reasons (BVerfGE 65, 182 (194)). Since the 1970s, the discussion about constitutional problems of creation and use of precedent has increased (compare Ipsen, 1975). The result is a broad critical consciousness that has only had relatively little force against a commonly spread judicial activism.

3 Changes in International Environment

Remarkable new approaches to precedents due to changes in the legal environment have not occurred. However, the requirement to follow prior decisions of the EC Court in Luxembourg in Art. 177 EC Treaty on the interpretation of this treaty as well as of some other questions has created a new form of binding precedent.

4 Juristic or Other Criticism

In Germany the courts are often accused of overstepping their competences and being active in areas that are reserved to the legislature. This critique aims most of all at the Federal Constitutional Court but also concerns the other higher courts. The weightiest criticism is that the courts often try to establish general rules or principles as *rationes decidendi* although this is not necessary in order to decide the case. An extraordinary case is the decision of the Federal Constitutional Court on the Fundamental Treaty (Grundlagenvertrag) between the Federal Republic of Germany and the former German Democratic Republic entered into in 1973. In this decision the court declared, as already mentioned above (Section IV.1), that all the reasons for its decision to be *rationes decidendi* are binding according to s.31 (1) BVerfGG: 'All statements of the opinion, including those that do not explicitly refer to the content of the Treaty, are necessary, and therefore, in the sense of the adjudication of the Federal Constitutional Court, part of the reasons supporting the decision' (BVerfGE 36, 1 (36)). This decision remained an exception, though.

It is considered problematical when the courts in particular decisions lay down general rules with the help of numbers or percentages which serve as an orientation to practice just as if the decisions were being made by the legislature. Many are of the opinion that, because of the high degree of discretion in fixing the data and also because of the general character of the provision, this should be left to the legislature (compare Larenz and Canaris, 1995, pp.260 f).

The defenders of the current practice of creating precedent in Germany stress that this practice is brought about by the insufficiencies of legislation. Often, the legislator does not provide clear provisions but flees to a general clause (compare Hedemann, 1934). Then the courts have to do the creative part: 'This is the only way the courts are able to fulfil their task imposed on them by the Basic Law to decide correctly every legal dispute laid before them' (BVerfGE 84, 221 (227)). If one adds that equal treatment is a fundamental principle of justice as well as a fundamental constitutional principle (Art. 3 (1) GG), the courts will have no choice left but to create precedential rules.

The critique as well as the defence of the current practice of creating legal precedents in Germany concerns a problem necessarily occurring in every system that knows the separation of powers: the delimitation of competences between courts and legislature. This problem cannot be solved once and for all by a formula comprising all possible cases but only by a continuation of practice duly aware of this problem. Hitherto, the German practice, can be considered a reasonable effort to strike an appropriate balance, even though some significant criticisms have been put forward.

References

Adomeit, K. (1969), *Rechtsquellenfragen im Arbeitsrecht*, Munich: Beck.

Alexy, R. (1989), *A Theory of Legal Argumentation*, Oxford: Clarendon Press (translation of *Theorie der juristischen Argumentation*, 1978).

Alexy, R. and Dreier, R. (1991), 'Statutory Interpretation in the Federal Republic of Germany', in MacCormick, D. Neil and R. Summers (eds), *Interpreting Statutes*, Aldershot/Brookfield USA/Hong Kong/Singapore/Sydney: Dartmouth.

Benda, E. (1995), 'Der soziale Rechtsstaat', in Benda, Ernst, Maihofer, Werner *et al.* (eds), *Handbuch des Verfassungsrechts*, 2nd edn, Berlin/New York: de Gruyter.

Bergbohm, K. (1892), *Jurisprudenz und Rechtsphilosophie*, Leipzig: Duncker & Humblot.

Bülow, O. (1885), *Gesetz und Richteramt*, Leipzig: Duncker & Humblot.

Bydlinski, F. 'Hauptpositionen zum Richterrecht', *Juristenzeitung*, 40, p.149 (1985).

Bydlinski, F. (1991), *Juristische Methodenlehre und Rechtsbegriff*, 2nd edn, Vienna/New York: Springer.

Christensen, 'Richterrecht – rechtsstaatlich oder rechtspraktisch?', *Neue Juristische Wochenschrift*, 42, p.3194 (1989).

Diederichsen, U. (1973), 'Die "reductio ad absurdum" in der Jurisprudenz', in Paulus, Gotthard, Diederichsen, Uwe and Canaris, Claus-Wilhelm (eds), *Festschrift für Karl Larenz zum 70, Geburtstag*, p.155, Munich: Beck.

Diederichsen, U. (1974), *Die Flucht des Gesetzgebers aus der politischen Verantwortung im Zivilrecht*, Karlsruhe: C.F. Müller.

Ehrlich, E. (1913), *Grundlegung der Soziologie des Rechts*, Munich/Leipzig: Duncker & Humblot.

Ehrlich, E. (1925), *Die juristische Logik*, Tübingen: J.C.B. Mohr (Paul Siebeck).

Enneccerus, L. and Nipperdey, H. (1959), *Lehrbuch des Bürgerlichen Rechts*, vol. I.1, 15th edn, Tübingen: J.C.B. Mohr (Paul Siebeck).

Esser, J. (1967), 'Richterrecht, Gerichtsgebrauch und Gewohnheitsrecht', in *Festschrift für Fritz von Hippel*, Tübingen: J.C.B. Mohr (Paul Siebeck).

Esser, J. (1970), *Vorverständnis und Methodenwahl in derRechtsfindung*, Frankfurt a.M.: Athenäum.

Esser, J. (1974), *Grundsatz und Norm in der richterlichen Fortbildung des Privatrechts*, 3rd edn, Tübingen: J.C.B. Mohr (Paul Siebeck).

Esser, J. 'In welchem Ausmaß bilden Rechtsprechung und Lehre Rechtsquellen?', *Zeitschrift für vergleichende Rechtswissenschaft* (1976).

Fikentscher, W. (1977), *Methoden des Rechts in vergleichender Darstellung*, vol. IV, Tübingen: J.C.B. Mohr (Paul Siebeck).

Fischer, R. (1971), *Die Weiterbildung des Rechts durch die Rechtsprechung*, Karlsruhe: C.R. Müller.

Flume, W. (1967), 'Richter und Recht', in *Verhandlungen des 46, Deutschen Juristentages 1966*, vol. II, part K, p.5, Munich/Berlin: Beck.

Germann, O. (1969), *Probleme und Methoden der Rechtsfindung*, Bern: Stämpfli & Cie.

Grimm, D. (ed.) (1990), *Wachsende Staatsaufgaben – sinkende Steuerungsfähigkeit des Rechts*, Baden-Baden: Nomos.

Grimm, 'Die Meinungsfreiheit in der Rechtsprechung des Bundesverfassungsgerichts', *Neue Juristische Wochenschrift*, 48, p.1697 (1995).

Gunkel, K. (1911), *Zweihundert Jahre Rechtsleben in Hannover, Festschrift zur Erinnerung an die Gründung des kurhannoverischen Oberappellationsgerichts in Celle am 14, Oktober 1711*, Hanover: Helwigsche Verlagsbuchhandlung.

Hedemann, J. (1934), *Die Flucht in die Generalklauseln*, Tübingen: J.C.B. Mohr (Paul Siebeck).

Heyde, W. (1995), 'Rechtsprechung', in Benda, Ernst, Maihofer, Werner *et al.* (eds), *Handbuch des Verfassungsrechts*, vol. 2, 2nd edn, Berlin/New York: de Gruyter.

Huber, E. (1921), *Recht und Rechtsverwirklichung*, Basle: Helbing & Lichtenhahn.

Hübner, H. (1996), *Allgemeiner Teil des Bürgerlichen Gesetzbuches*, 2nd edn, Berlin/New York: de Gruyter.

Ipsen, J. (1975), *Richterrecht und Verfassung*, Berlin: Duncker & Humblot.

Ipsen, J. 'Verfassungsrechtliche Schranken des Richterechts', *Deutsches Verwaltungsblatt*, 99, p.1102 (1984).

Isay, H. (1929), *Rechtsnorm und Entscheidung*, Berlin: Franz Vahlen.

Jakobs, H. (1992), *Die Begründung der geschichtlichen Rechtswissenschaft*, Paderborn: Ferdinand Schöningh.

Jauernig, O. (ed.) (1994), *Bürgerliches Gesetzbuch*, Munich: Beck.

von Jhering, R. (1898), *Geist des römischen Rechts auf den verschiedenen Stufen seiner Entwicklung*, part II 2, 5th edn, Leipzig (reprint 1968, Aalen: Scientia).

von Jhering, R. (1893), *Der Zweck im Recht*, vol. 2, 3rd edn, Leipzig: Breitkopf & Härtel.

Kelsen, H. (1960), *Reine Rechtslehre*, 2nd edn, Vienna: Franz Deuticke.

Knittel, W. (1965), *Zum Problem der Rückwirkung bei einer Änderung der Rechtsprechung*, Bielefeld: Gieseking.

Koch, H. and Rüßmann, H. (1982), *Juristische Begründungslehre*, Munich: Beck.

Kriele, M. (1976), *Theorie der Rechtsgewinnung*, 2nd edn, Berlin: Duncker & Humblot.

Kruse, H. (1971), *Das Richterrecht als Rechtsquelle des innerstaatlichen Rechts*, Tübingen: J.C.B. Mohr (Paul Siebeck).

Larenz, K. (1974), 'Der Richter als Gesetzgeber', in *Festschrift für Heinrich Henkek*, Berlin/New York: de Gruyter.

Larenz, K. (1991), *Methodenlehre der Rechtswissenschaft*, 6th edn, Berlin: Springer.

Larenz, K. and Canaris, C. (1995), *Methodenlehre der Rechtswissenschaft*, 3rd edn, Berlin/Heidelberg/New York: Springer.

Less, G. (1954), *Vom Wesen und Wert des Richterrechts*, Erlangen: Palm & Enke.

Lilie, H. (1993), *Obiter dictum und Divergenzausgleich in Strafsachen*, Cologne: Carl Heymanns.

Mayer-Ladewig, 'Justizstaat und Richterrecht', *Archiv für civilistische Praxis*, 161 p. 97 (1962).

Müller, F. (1986), *Richterrecht*, Berlin: Duncker & Humblot.

Mußgnug, R. (1986), 'Das allgemeine Verwaltungsrecht zwischen Richterrecht und Gesetzesrecht', in *Richterliche Rechtsfortbildung, Festschrift der Juristischen Fakultat zur 600-Jahr-Feier der Ruprecht-Karls – Universitat Heidelberg*, p.203, Heidelberg: C.F. Müller.

Neuner, J. (1992), *Rechtsfindung contra legem*, Munich: Beck.

Ogorek, R. (1986), *Richterkönig oder Subsumtionsautomat, Zur Justiztheorie im 19, Jahrhundert*, Frankfurt a.M.: Vittorio Klostermann.

Ossenbühl, F. (1992), 'Die Quellen des Verwaltungsrechts', in Erichsen, Hans-Uwe and Martens, Wolfgang (eds), *Allgemeines Verwaltungsrecht*, 9th edn, Berlin/New York: de Gruyter.

Pawlowski, H. (1991), *Methodenlehre für Juristen*, 2nd edn, Heidelberg: C.F. Müller.

Picker, 'Richterrecht und Rechtsprechung', *Juristenzeitung*, 39, p.153 (1984).

Picker, 'Richterrecht oder Rechtsdogmatik – Alternativen der Rechtsgewinnung?,' *Juristenzeitung*, 43, pp.1–12, 62–75 (1988).

Pilny, K. (1993), *Präjudizienrecht im anglo-amerikanischen und im deutschen Recht*, Baden-Baden: Nomos.

Puchta, G. (1828), *Das Gewohnheitsrecht*, part I, Erlangen: Palm'sche Verlagsbuchhandlung (reprint 1965, Darmstadt: Wissenschaftliche Buchgesellschaft).

Puchta, G. (1837a), Das *Gewohnheitsrecht*, part II, Erlangen (reprint 1965, Darmstadt: Wissenschaftliche Buchgesellschaft).

Puchta, G. (1837b), *Lehrbuch der Pandekten*, Leipzig: Johann Ambrosius Barth.

Raisch, P. (1995), *Juristische Methodenlehre*, Heidelberg: C.F. Müller.

Ross, A. (1929), *Theorie der Rechtsquellen*, Leipzig/Vienna: Franz Deuticke.

Sachs, M. (1977), *Die Bindung des Bundesverfassungsgerichts an seine Entscheidungen*, Munich: Vahlen.

von Savigny, F. (1814), *Vom Beruf unserer Zeit für Gesetzgebung und Rechtswissenschaft*, Heidelberg: Mohr und Zimmer (reprint 1967, Hildesheim: Georg Olms).

von Savigny, F. (1840), *System des heutigen römischen Rechts*, vol. I, Berlin: Veit.

Schlaich, K. (1994), *Das Bundesverfassungsgericht*, 3rd edn, Munich: Beck.

Schlüchter, E. (1986), *Mittlerfunktion der Präjudizien*, Berlin/New York: de Gruyter.

Schlüter, W. (1973), *Das obiter dictum*, Munich: Beck.

Schmitt, C. (1923), *Die geistesgeschichtliche Lage des heutigen Parlamentarismus*, Berlin: Duncker & Humblot.

Sendler, 'Teilhaberrecht in der Rechtsprechung des Bundesverwaltungsgerichts', *Die Öffentliche Verwaltung*, 31, p.581 (1978).

Sendler, 'Richterrecht – rechtstheoretisch und rechtspraktisch', *Neue Juristische Wochenschrift*, 40, p.3240 (1987).

Stern, K. (1984), *Das Staatsrecht der Bundesrepublik Deutschland*, vol. II, 2nd edn, Munich: Beck.

Thöl, H. (1875), *Das Handelsrecht*, vol. I, 5th edn, Leipzig: Fues.

Thomas, H. and Putzo, H. (1995), *Zivilprozeßordnung*, 19th edn, Munich: Beck.

Wagner-Döbler and Philipps, 'Präjudizien in der Rechtsprechung: Statistische Untersuchungen anhand der Zitierpraxis deutscher Gerichte', *Rechtstheorie*, 23, p.228 (1992).

Wank, R. (1978), *Grenzen richterlicher Rechtsfortbildung*, Berlin: Duncker & Humblot.

Weller, H. (1979), *Die Bedeutung der Präjudizien im Verständnis der deutschen Rechtswissenschaft*, Berlin: Duncker & Humblot.

Wieacker, F. (1967), *Privatrechtsgeschichte der Neuzeit*, 2nd edn, Göttingen: Vandenhoeck & Ruprecht.

Windscheid, B. (1891), *Lehrbuch des Pandektenrechts*, vol. I, 7th edn, Frankfurt a.M.: Rütten & Loenig.

Wolff, H., Bachof, O. and Stober, R. (1994), *Verwaltungsrecht*, I, 10th edn, Munich: Beck.

Zöller, R. (1995), *Zivilprozeßordnung*, 19th edn, Cologne: Schmidt.

3 Precedent in Finland

AULIS AARNIO, *TAMPERE**

I Institutional and Systemic

1(a) Court Hierarchy

According to the Constitution of Finland (Constitution Act, Art. 2), independent courts exercise the judicial function. The court system consists of two *separate* branches, the general courts and the administrative courts, each of these two having three levels.

The general courts are divided into the lower courts of general jurisdiction (the district courts), the six Courts of Appeal and the Supreme Court. The district courts, when operating, are chaired by a professional judge or by junior lawyers undergoing court training. In addition to the judicially trained chairman, the district courts have in their basic composition professional judges and lay judges. The lay members of the court are elected for a four-year term by the municipal council. In both questions of law and questions of evidence, the lay judges have, formally, the same position as the professional judge. Actually, however, the opinion of the professional judge is in most cases decisive. The so-called 'non-contentious' civil cases, such as cases of insolvency and the registering of the ownership of a real estate, are decided by the professional judge.

The Court of Appeal is the appellate level from the lower courts. The Court of Appeal is the first instance in cases involving treason or high treason, and in certain cases involving charges for an offence committed in office and all charges against judges.

The highest court in civil and criminal cases and certain administrative cases including the nomination of judges is the Supreme Court.

* I am grateful to the High Justice of the Supreme Court, Olavi E. Heinonen, Jukka Kemppinen and Raimo Siltala for the valuable help that I have received in the form of constructive criticism.

In principle, only the decisions of the Supreme Court have a precedential value in the strict sense. As will be seen later on, the precedential value is prospective as to its nature, which is a special feature of the Finnish precedential system.

In administrative cases, a citizen who finds the decision of an authority to violate his or her right may appeal the decision as high as the Supreme Administrative Court unless the law stipulates another way of appeal, such as a ministry, the rector of a university or another authority. The decisions of senior administrative authorities, such as national boards, are subject to appeal either to the Council of State (in cases involving an appointment or questions of policy) or in legal matters to the Supreme Administrative Court.

The first level of appeal for most decisions of lower administrative authorities is the county administrative court which, in administrative issues, corresponds to the Court of Appeal. This is the case in, for instance, zoning and taxation cases and decisions of the municipal council. The normal channel of appeal from the decisions of the county administrative court goes to the Supreme Administrative Court, which consists of a chief justice and at least 13 justices. The cases are presented for decision by judicial secretaries and senior secretaries. Special experts may, on the basis of certain special provisions, participate in the hearing of a case as extraordinary members.

The competence of the Supreme Administrative Court is limited to questions of law. If an appeal concerns an issue that primarily requires consideration of questions of expediency (policy), the Supreme Administrative Court must transfer the case to the Council of State for a decision. This happens in about one per cent of the appeals made to the Supreme Administrative Court.

The Supreme Court has the competence to revoke a decision both of the Supreme Administrative Court and of the Council of State. According to the modern theory, the two Supreme Courts may take up the question of constitutionality of a (statute) law enacted by the parliament.

Finland *does not have* a separate constitutional court that would consider the constitutionality of an act of parliament or interpret the constitution. The responsibility for the constitutionality of acts is held not only by the President of the Republic but also by the Constitutional Committee of Parliament (Committee for Constitutional Law), which exercises *advance control* of constitutionality during the legislative procedure. If a legislative bill is inconsistent with the constitution, a special, qualified legislative procedure must be followed. A directive given by the European Union must be followed even in conflict with national law. A court may on that ground review the validity of an act or a part thereof.

For particular purposes, there are special channels of trial. Hence, in the litigation concerning insurance, the Insurance Court corresponds to the Court of Appeal in general cases. To the courts of the same hierarchical level belong also the Land Rights Court as well as the High Water Court. The former deals, for example, with the partition of land and real estate as well as interpreting the legislation concerning private roads, whereas the latter is entitled, for example, to decide cases concerning the use of water power, the building of waterways and the pollution of waters.

Due to the limited space available, the questions will in the following be answered exclusively as concerns the general courts. Thus, from among the highest courts, only the Supreme Court will be considered more closely. The Supreme Administrative Court follows in its activities mainly the same principles as the Supreme Court.

1(b) Structural and Procedural Aspects

Each Court of Appeal has a president and ordinary or extraordinary justices as well as legal clerks to prepare the cases for decision. All of them are judicially trained. Some of the law clerks in the two Supreme Courts are highly specialized. In principle, they are appointed for a lifetime. In practice, however, the clerks or referendaries are often promoted to be judges in the Court of Appeal or other courts. Many of justices of the Supreme Court have worked as referendaries in their time.

According to the Supreme Court Act (1918), the minimum number of members in this court is 15 (the chief justice and 14 members). At present (1996), the Supreme Court consists of 21 (one plus 20) members, but the number will probably decrease in future years. The docket has ceased to be excessive (see the statistics below).

The Supreme Court is divided into sections. According to the Working Order of the Supreme Court (WO, Art. 22), a case that will be published as a precedent shall be decided in a section consisting of at least five members. This means that at the minimum the Supreme Court consists of three sections (divisions), and the quorum is five justices. However, the Supreme Court is at present (1996) divided only into two sections (one plus nine) so that the first one deals with the leaves to appeal and the second one with the appeals (substantial decisions). Every second month the sections rotate.

The Supreme Court assembles for a plenary session in which all the justices take part. The chief justice invites the justices to the plenum, and he also acts as the chairman of it. The plenary session deals not only with certain administrative issues as nominations, but also, which is important here, with questions, that according to WO, Art. 21, have to be decided in a plenum. WO, Art. 21 prescribes as follows: if the prevalent opinion of the section in a given case deviates from a principle, or an interpretation, previously accepted by the Supreme Court, the section has to inform the chief justice who may order the case or a certain question connected to it to be decided in a plenum. The chief justice also has the right to order a case to be decided in a plenum in view of its far-reaching consequences or its significance in principle.

In this way, using the plenary session, the Supreme Court has a possibility to develop and to create the law, deviating from its own earlier practice. Hence WO, Art. 21 manifests that the Supreme Court is not legally bound to its previous decisions. The degree of bindingness depends upon the deliberation of the Supreme Court itself (discussed later).

The total number of cases coming to the Supreme Court has been quite balanced. This can be seen in Table 3.1, which shows the statistics of the Supreme Court practice.

Table 3.1   Cases at the Supreme Court, 1992–5, divided into subgroups

Year	Criminal	Civil	Others*	Total
1992	883	1 796	1 454	4 133
1993	887	2 108	1 492	4 487
1994	1 073	2 264	1 486	4 833
1995	1 460	2 662	1 061	5 183

* Cases from the Insurance Court, the Land Rights Court and the High Water Court.

The corresponding statistics of the Supreme Administrative Court are shown in Table 3.2.

It is possible to perceive from the statistics that the workload of the Supreme Administrative Court has decreased. This can be seen also in the shortening of the average duration of proceedings, which is nowadays less than nine months. Especially during the years 1991–3, the work of the Supreme Administrative Court was burdened by a backlog of cases. It was then possible to resolve fewer matters than were arriving. Now the backlog problem has been overcome. In 1995, approximately 1000 more matters were solved than arrived.

The referendary always presents his report that is written as a completed decision of the court. After this, the justices of the Supreme Court give their votes in order of seniority, from the youngest

Table 3.2 Cases at the Supreme Administrative Court, 1992–5, divided into subgroups

Year	Taxation	Pensions	Construction and planning	Others	Total
1992	29%	13%	11%	48%	6 827
1993	30%	13%	9%	48%	6 698
1994	28%	15%	9%	48%	6 157
1995	34%	4%	12%	50%	4 475

Note: In addition, there are 300–400 so-called non-contentious civil cases (petitions) annually. The column 'others' comprises, for example, matters related to labour and those related to foreigners and the environment, municipal matters and matters related to traffic and roads as well as matters related to water.

to the oldest. The finding of the majority is the decision of the SC. If the votes are divided and two opinions that have received the most votes receive equal support, the opinion of the chairman prevails in civil cases and in criminal cases the opinion that is most lenient to the defendant prevails. There are very many kinds of complex situations. For instance, if in a criminal case two members take a stand for the dismissal of the indictment, two sentence the accused to imprisonment and one to pay a fine, the final result is the fine, that is, the majority passes the judgment, but the standpoint of a two plus one majority is that there is to be no sentence to imprisonment. There are also precedents concerning the voting, see, for example, SC 1973 II 37.

All the opinions are part of the decision. Both dissenting and concurring opinions are common. In the last mentioned case, the short résumé of the decision is marked with a 'Diss' meaning that the decision was not unanimous. However, the discussions and deliberations of the judges remain secret, as well as all written memoranda, both those of the justices and that of the referendary.

The entire file of the case, the memoranda excluded, is available to the public in the registry of the Supreme Court, and can be freely copied and quoted. The documents include, for example, the briefs of the lawyers as well as, in a criminal case, the minutes and records on hearings prepared by police and given to the court by the prosecutor. Certain documents as well as records in special cases (rape, child molesting and so on) may be kept secret. However, the decision is seldom proclaimed utterly secret (as with high treason).

1(c)   *Power to Select Cases*

Except where the Court of Appeal has to decide the case at first instance, a decision of the Court of Appeal can be appealed to the Supreme Court if and only if the latter grants *leave to appeal*. In this way, the Supreme Court can select cases of importance for a substantial hearing and direct its resources to the most important questions.

According to the Code of Judicial Procedure s.30, Art. 3 (1980), leave to appeal can be granted in three cases: (1) if the hearing of the appeal is important for other similar cases (the so-called *precedential argument*), or if the decision of the Supreme Court would increase the uniformity of legal practice (*uniformity argument*); (2) if there are special reasons for granting leave to appeal due to a procedural (or other) error in the lower court's decision (*rescission argument*); or (3) if there are other grave reasons for granting the leave to appeal (the case is *of special importance for the party*). Only on these grounds can the Supreme Court take the case in a further (substantial) hearing. In other cases, the hearing ends in rejecting the application or in leaving the application unheard owing to, for example, a formal deficiency.

The system of leave to appeal does not cover all groups of cases. For instance, in some cases of the Land Rights Court a party can appeal directly to the Supreme Court. In some cases of extraordinary appeal the Supreme Court may hear the case and publish its decision as a precedent. In general, however, the statistics are as shown in Table 3.3.

Table 3.3   Leave to appeal

Year	Total cases	Leave granted	Per cent
1991	1 599	168	10.5
1992	1 785	165	9.2
1993	2 091	178	8.5
1994	2 254	206	9.1
1995	2 643	187	7.1

In criminal cases, the percentage shares of leaves to appeal granted during 1991–5 have been a little lower than in civil cases: 7.3, 7.9, 8.2, 7.2 and 5.1.

In the Supreme Administrative Court, the system of leave to appeal is not of similar significance to that of the Supreme Court. The number of rejected petitions for leave to appeal is around 10 per cent.

In the cases of leave to appeal, the Supreme Court can also prescribe a prohibition to execute the decision of the lower court, or interrupt an execution already begun. This possibility increases an individual's legal protection to a remarkable degree and is therefore used in cases where, for example, the economic losses may be significant. The frequency with which execution is interrupted is indicated by the number of instances in the following years: 1988 (46), 1989 (27), 1990 (35), 1991 (35) and 1992 (50).

The decision to grant the leave to appeal is *not* reasoned. The Supreme Court simply grants leave without taking any stand on the substantial questions of the case. The same holds true when the application for leave to appeal is rejected. The party will never know why he or she did not get leave. The Supreme Court argues for this practice, referring to the rationales of the system. The main goal of the leave to appeal system is to make it possible for the Supreme Court to clear the backlog of cases, and this could not be attained if also the decisions to grant or reject the leave to appeal were to be reasoned. The arguments presented by the Supreme Court are not, however, widely accepted outside of the court. Several authors have criticized the leave to appeal practice, saying that at least some reasoning would be necessary in order to guarantee legal certainty. However, no change in this regard is in view.

The practice of not stating reasons for granting or refusing leave to appeal does not thus indicate the true criteria on the basis of which the Supreme Court selects the cases for substantial hearing. There is no material available to argue, for instance, that a certain case has been thought to have precedential value. The economic, social or political consequences of the case do not seem to be decisive, maybe not significant at all. If the case has precedential value, it has it because of its significance for the interpretation of statutes or for gap filling only. This means that a number of cases without any exceptional economic or social value get leave to appeal only because they are of *legal* importance.

For the same reason, the proportion of merely procedural questions, and of cases dealing with the interpretation of a single provision, is relatively high compared to the cases in which systemic issues or the application of legal principles (weighing and balancing) are the core of the decision. The chief justice of the Supreme Court has admitted that the court should in future take into account – more than hitherto – the needs of barristers, prosecutors and other authorities in selecting the precedents. The clarification of new legislation is also important, because in the application of new statutes the need for precedents is especially urgent.

2   Structure, Content and Style of Judgments

Traditionally, the Finnish courts have been very terse in their style of formulating the opinions (see MacCormick and Summers, 1991, p. 490). The reasoning has often been abstract and the information included in it quite insignificant. Over the past 15 years, a clear development in the style of reasoning can be identified. However, the internal structure of reasoning is still more deductive than discursive as to its nature. The style and the internal structure of reasoning can be described as follows. The Supreme Court does not usually argue *in* syllogisms, yet it very often argues *syllogistically*; that is, it does not set out all the steps of the logic in each case, despite the syllogistic internal structure of thinking.

In its decisions, the Supreme Court normally gives 'universalizations': it formulates the information in general rather than in concrete terms. The addressee of this information, for instance a district court, has then to interpret the message and to clarify the *ratio decidendi* (see also question I.5).

There is one feature in the decision making of the Supreme Court which leads the guiding information in an abstract direction. The Supreme Court's decision is *collective*, so that the names of those judges who formed the majority are published in the case report, but their opinion is collective. It is impossible for an outsider to know who actually had the major influence on the opinion. The collective opinion is formulated in discussions based on the referendary's memorandum. Therefore it is more than understandable that the discourse procedure eliminates all such opinions that do not fit the collective whole. If there is a vote, which is quite often the case, the dissenting opinions are written down separately and identified individually.

As a result of the legalistic attitude towards the application of the law, dating from the last part of the nineteenth century, and the peculiar political atmosphere of passive resistance directed towards Imperial Russial and channelled via courts of justice, the style of reasoning in the Finnish courts, the Supreme Court included, is still legalistic and formal rather than substantial, although the substantial arguments are more often an integral part of reasoning. The more substantial attitude also means that in several cases the reasoning is nowadays quite extended and elaborate. However, there are still (in 1996) totally unreasoned Supreme Court decisions and decisions in which the reasoning is extremely terse. Parallel to the above-mentioned, the style of opinions has for a long time been typically magisterial. From the end of the 1970s, a more argumentative style has gradually been accepted by the Supreme Court and, following it, by the Courts of Appeal. Differences between the six Courts of Appeal are, however, remarkably large. In connection with the recent renewal of the procedural order, the district courts have recently begun to use discursive argumentation, in some minor cases even to excess.

The entire structure of Finnish court decisions has, however, developed remarkably over the past 15 years. This concerns all court decisions independently of the court's status in the organizational hierarchy: the decisions of the district courts, of the Courts of Appeal, as well as of the Supreme Courts.

In some routine cases (such as divorce, the custody of children, the maintenance of a child born out of wedlock), the district courts (at town and municipal level) use special *formulae* to be filled in by the court. In the formula, there is a space for the identification of the decision (the record number, date and the court) and of the parties, the facts of the case, the claims of the parties, the decision and the statutes on which the decision is based, as well as the directions about how to apply them.

In other than routine cases and in other than district courts, the formulae are not used. However, the decisions are *structured* so that their internal logic can easily be identified. Before we go into this structure in detail, let us have a look at the hearing procedure of the Supreme Court, because it gives some background for the later presentation. The hearing procedure follows a certain single scheme from which there are some exceptions depending on whether the hearing concerns the leave to appeal or the full appeal. These differences are not taken into account here.

The refendary preparing the case at issue writes a memorandum on the basis of which he or she introduces the case orally to the section of the Supreme Court. In the introduction, the refendary uses the documents of the case and the memorandum. After a discussion in the section on the memorandum, the senior secretary presents his proposal for solution. In giving the proposal, he can change his opinion presented in the memorandum if the preceding discussion gives cause. Thereafter, all the justices express their opinions in the order of seniority in service. On this basis, the chairman pronounces a conclusion on the *collective opinion* of the Supreme Court. If there is voting, the majority of the justices share the collective opinion and the minority have to give the dissenting opinions individually. Quite often the refendary prepares drafts for the opinion of both the majority and the minority.

3   Publication of Judgments

Except for the leave to appeal system, the Supreme Court has another, and a relatively effective, means to select a precedent. As was mentioned above, only a part of all decisions will be published in the yearbook of the Supreme Court. The main source of information is nowadays the electronic database. In it those decisions that will be published are included in full. Other decisions are referred to by short résumé.

When a final decision is given (for example, 7 April 1993), it will be surrendered to the record office of the Supreme Court. The registrar informs the parties that the decision is available in his office. When the decision is recorded (for example, April 1993), it is *public* according to the Act of the Publicity of Documents in Finland. The Supreme Court deliberates separately whether the decision should also be published or not. If so, it is available, as was mentioned above, in the databased expert systems within four weeks of the decision being made. The decisions published in this way will later on be published also in the yearbook of the Supreme Court. Only a minority of all Supreme Court decisions will be published in this way; others are public but only available at the record office of the Supreme Court or in the form of a résumé (see below, question I.6). If a decision is *not* published, the decision may be written without reasons in the form of the so-called 'appendage decision' (a short decision plus the decisions of the lower courts as an appendage to the decision).

When a decision is to be published, the Supreme Court writes the decision according to either a long or a short pattern. In the former, the Supreme Court reports the entire hearing, beginning from the claims in the district court. This pattern is used, for example, when the application of leave to appeal is presented by the plaintiff whose action was dismissed by the Court of Appeal. The short pattern begins with a report about the decision of the district court.

The selection of published decisions is very restrictive, as the following statistics indicate the number of published decisions is given in parentheses): 1988 (140), 1989 (157), 1990 (181), 1991 (189), 1992 (197). For example, in 1992, the Supreme Court published 185 leave to appeal cases and 12 other decisions (197 in all). At the same time, the Supreme Court gave 293 decisions, which means that 108 decisions were left unpublished. Due to the system of publication, the unpublished cases are only exceptionally used in legal reasoning, for example by the lower courts or by scholars. The Supreme Court seldom refers to its own unpublished decisions.

The Supreme Court does not publicly explain the criteria according to which it selects the decisions for publication. The selection seems again to be based only on the legal importance of a case: that is, on its significance in the interpretation of statutes or in gap filling. Hence the publishing of a case indicates that the Supreme Court considers it to be of importance. Only the *published* cases can have, and actually do have, a guiding function. Lower courts seldom use or cite unpublished decisions. However, in scholarly works (doctrinal opinions) unpublished decisions are quite commonly referred to. Referring to this, only published Supreme Court decisions can thus be called *precedents* in the Finnish system. They and only they have the guiding function that is typical of precedential decisions in the Finnish system. Therefore in the following only the role, function and significance of the published Supreme Court decisions will be dealt with.

In principle, all decisions are catalogued in legal publications. Some cases are also reported in the law journals, *Lakimies* (Lawyer), *Defensor Legis* (Journal of the Bar Association) and *Tidskrift utgiven av den Juridiska Föreningen i Finland* (Journal of the Swedish Law Association in Finland). There are two types of law reports. Most of the reports are short headlines indicating the essential content of the decision. The report also includes all data making it possible to find the case in the registers and documents pertaining thereto. The other type is a case review written by a scholar (sometimes by a judge). It includes the description of the case as well as the reasoning of the Finnish Supreme Court (FSC). In addition to that, the author gives background material (previous cases, scholarly opinions, and so on) in order to make the decision understandable. Sometimes the case reviews are quite critical, too.

There are also collections of important (leading) cases introducing a *reconstructed headline* of precedents (Miettinen, 1970). They give first-hand information about the *ratio decidendi* but only in an abstract and a general form; that is, in the form of rules and principles. The book, *Precedents in Scholarly Opinions*, and the electronic database (FOKI) list and identify those cases which are referred to in the doctrinal opinions of professors or other authors. Normally, textbooks and monographs include an index of the precedents (and other court decisions) cited and/or analysed in the treatise.

What has been said above also holds true as far as the Supreme Administrative Court is concerned.

4   Contents of Reports

The Supreme Court decision is never pronounced in session. It is available as a document. One copy of the document is signed by the five justices as well as by the referendary and is archived. The litigants get their own copies signed by the referendary. In most civil cases, a fee is collected (about 200–500 $US). Copies are sent to certain officials and in criminal cases copies or specific documents for execution (imprisonment, fine and so on).

The Supreme Court decision is divided into parts, each of them having their own caption. In general, the structure of the Supreme Court decision (normally) looks as follows:

(1)   The rubrication (headline) of the case includes a summary of the legal question solved in the decision and, if needed, other information about the case and the reasons for the decision (holding of an issue). References to the statutes and previous precedents, if there are such, are written at the end of the rubrication. On the top left of the rubrication text there are entries which make it easier to find the precedent in the registers.

The rubrication is formulated after the substantial decision is ready. The referendary outlines a proposal for the rubrication for the section or the plenum which made the decision. The wording of the rubrication is confirmed by the chairman of the session. The names of the parties are never mentioned in the rubrication. In the published report, names may be mentioned in civil cases.

Finland is a bilingual country, the official languages being Finnish and Swedish. Therefore the rubrication and the entries are written in both languages. In addition, all the rubrications are recorded once a month in the databased expert system (KKO and FHDR) in Finnish and Swedish. The rubrication is recorded in the expert system of the language in which the decision was given, and in the other register there is a reference to that case.

In general, the rubrication indicates an abstract (normative) description of the decision. For instance:

Supreme Court 1991:143
Marriage – The Matrimonial Property Relations – The Division of Property – Title to Property Registration.
The spouse (B) of a person A had died before the reforms of the Marriage Act (1.1.1988) came into force. A and B had common minor children. A had after 1.1.1988 but before the division of the matrimonial property sold unseparated parcels of real estate owned by him. The spouse B had a matrimonial right to this real estate. The buyer's application to get title to a property registration was rejected because according to the Marriage Act, Art. 86.2, valid at the time of B's death, a court's leave for the sale was necessary.

Sometimes, especially in somewhat older cases, the rubrication is even more terse in expression, indicating only the reformulation of the norms applied to the case. For instance: 'The last will was null and void because the testator was under the influence of drugs and he could thus not understand the significance of his action.' In this case, the rubrication gives only a specific interpretation of an unclear statute, or it formulates a norm filling a gap.

(2)   The hearing in the district court includes a description of facts and the claims of the parties. Traditionally, the fact description has been long and elaborate, often the best formulated part of the decision. Recently, the Supreme Court has begun to rewrite the description

about the hearing in the district court in order to avoid inaccuracies. This part contains even explicit summary of the hearing of witnesses and documents referred to as evidence.

(3)   The description of the district court's decision, giving the basis for understanding the hearing in the higher courts.

(4)   The decision of the Court of Appeal with information of eventual dissent.

(5)   The appeal to the Supreme Court and other parties' answers to the writ of appeal.

(6)   The decision of the Supreme Court. This chapter includes:

(a)   The reasons for the decision. According to the tradition accepted by the Supreme Court, only reasons for the solution, not conter-arguments, are written down. This holds true as far as the proof of evidence and the interpretation of statutes are concerned. This tradition is, however, at present changing, possibly because of the critique of legal authors and the example of the Swedish courts.

(b)   The resolution, which may include the following alternatives:

- the decision of the Court of Appeal is upheld, as it is or with added or amended grounds,
- the case is remitted to a lower instance, or
- the case is solved by the Supreme Court itself changing,
- the decision of the Court of Appeal.

(c)   Normally, but not always, the Supreme Court lists the statutes on which the decision is based.

(7)   The names of the judges who took part in the hearing, with dissenting or concurring opinions.

(8)   The memorandum of the referendary and the dissenting opinions written as a proposition for a decision so that a consenting justice may only state: 'I accept the proposition.'

All the above-mentioned parts of the decision are public, although only a certain number of the Supreme Court decisions are published.

The reasons for the Supreme Court decision indicate the *ratio decidendi* of the case as well as the facts relevant to the case. In both respects, the precedent has value as guiding information. It tells us which norms should be applied to the fact combination in hand. In this regard, one can speak about the precedential function of the Supreme Court decisions.

It is useful to grade guiding information on two scales: open versus closed and abstract versus concrete. It is open if and only if the written reasons correspond to the real reasoning procedure. A closed reasoning, in its turn, consists of so-called 'facade' arguments without revealing anything, or revealing only partially, about the action argumentation.

The distinction abstract/concrete indicates the way in which the normative information is related to the facts of the case. The information is abstract if it has only a loose connection or no connection at all to the actual fact combination. In this case, the guiding information expresses only abstract norms or guidelines to be followed in the same type of cases in the future. Perfectly concrete information tells us about a unique case: the decision was A in this single combination of facts.

The effect of the guiding information can now be analysed using these distinctions. If the information is abstract, it manifests the fact that the Supreme Court has an *intention to guide* future practice, that is, the task of the Supreme Court is understood to be to formulate general norms comparable to the statutes (the legislature) and applicable to a certain type of (future) cases. From the addressee's point of view, there is always a need to interpret this kind of abstract information as occurs in the case of statutes, too. This can thus be called a *prospective precedential relation* between the Supreme Court and the addressee of the information. The addressee can be either a lower court or the Supreme Court itself.

The information being concrete, the Supreme Court does not formulate a general norm or other normative information but simply tells us how it has solved a single case. The addressee of concrete information has to formulate the rule or principle that it is possible to apply to the facts at issue. The precedential relation is *retrospective*, and here it is the task of the addressee to find the *ratio decidendi*.

Against this background, four different ways of guiding the adjudication are possible: (1) abstract and open information gives to the addressee the best possible basis for understanding the *ratio decidendi* from the prospective point of view; (2) abstract and closed information is, on the contrary, very ineffective as a guiding instrument due to the difficulties of understanding the proper content of the information; (3) a concrete and open reasoning, in turn, reveals the real reasoning procedure and is optimal from the retrospective point of view; whereas (4) a concrete and closed reasoning includes the least possible amount of information and is therefore ineffective also retrospectively.

As far as the Finnish Supreme Court is concerned, the type of guiding information has traditionally been more abstract and closed than concrete and open. This means that the *ratio decidendi* is not openly expressed in the rubrication and reasoning, but it must be *reconstructed* by the instance that wants to refer to the case. The role of the Supreme Court in Finland can thus be understood especially from the *prospective* point of view. It belongs specifically to the role of the Supreme Court to decide which case is a precedent and which is not. A true precedent can only be the decision of the highest instance; only it can have guiding force in the system. The Supreme Court produces mainly general norm information applicable to future cases and, doing this, the Supreme Court also intends to be a guiding instance in the adjudication. In some cases this guiding may be quite dramatic, as with overruling an established doctrine. This might be the case in Finnish adjudicature in questions concerning volition and *mens rea* in homicide. On the other hand, the effectiveness of the prospective guiding information depends on the degree of openness of this information. Until the 1970s, the terse reasoning of the Supreme Court decisions made their effectiveness very limited, and thus the significance of the Supreme Court practice was in many cases and in many branches of law at least questionable. In order to increase the effectiveness of the prospective guiding information, the decisions must be properly reasoned. In this respect, the Finnish precedents are now (1996) closer to the ideal (abstract and open information) than they were 15 years ago.

5   Meaning of 'Precedent'

According to the Constitution of Finland, the task of the courts of law is to give a legally binding solution in individual cases. This concerns also the highest courts of law. Thus the courts of law in Finland have an obvious decision-making function.

This means that in legal argumentation not even the solutions of the highest courts of law have the position of an independent source of law. This also comes out indirectly in the Code of Judicial Procedure, s.24, Art. 3. According to it, each judicial decision must be based on a statute or, if there is no statute, 'on the custom of the land' (the phrasing of the article is ancient). The condition made by the provision can be called a formal statutory precondition. If the filling of a gap and interpretation *contra legem* are excluded, a precedent is of significance in the interpretation of statutes in particular.

Actually, there are quite wide areas even in central private law that are uncodified, so that no statute exists as the firm basis for decision making. This is the reason why the relation between the statute and the precedent is more complicated than is often acknowledged. There are several areas where the decisions *contra legem* have been more a rule than an exception (warranties, collaterals and so on). On the other hand, it is impossible according to Finnish law to say that any prior decision possibly relevant to a present case to be decided is a precedent. The concept 'precedent' has a special position in the Finnish system of the application of law. This special position can best be described by distinguishing the prospective and the retrospective guiding function of the solutions of the Supreme Court from one another.

In the first mentioned case, one aims by a precedent at directing the subsequent application of the law. This feature can be called a 'prospective prejudicial relation'. The court of justice is keeping an eye on the future and trying to give effective guiding information. It is characteristic of it that the one giving the solution decides which decision is a real *pre*judgment and which is not. In other words, a precedent is expressly a decision preceding the solutions to be given subsequently.

The situation may, however, be also the other way around. Then the starting point is a case B that is to be solved and the task is to find, in accordance with the doctrine of *stare decisis*, a kind of previous decision (precedent) A that can be considered binding when solving a new case. Jääskinen aptly calls this a 'regressive prejudicial relation'. A judge looks back, into the past, and seeks an authoritative (or a material) direction there. He himself does not consciously direct, or try to direct, the subsequent solutions. He just solves the problem in hand and, for this reason, the prejudgments, for him, are previous decisions, though as such of a normative value.

The Supreme Court of Finland has adopted a clearly prospective function. It aims, by the published solutions it has defined as precedents, to guide the application of the law of the lower courts of justice – and, on certain conditions, also its own subsequent decision-making activity. Thus one tries to create legal uniformity covering the entire country. In the Finnish system, the meaning of 'precedent' is thus best taken as a decision which the deciding court expressly adopts or formulates to guide future decision making (see Appendix, question I.5).

The lower courts of justice are not, however, legally bound by the guiding information given by the Supreme Court in its precedents. Seen retrospectively, the ultimate meaning of a precedent as guiding information thus remains dependent on how justified the lower courts of justice determine the precedent of the Supreme Court to have been. A precedent thus has retrospective value above all as a legal argument. In practice, precedents are followed to quite a high degree; that is, their argumentative value is high, but following them is not an absolute rule.

In scholarly works, precedents nowadays have an increasing value. They are used as a weakly binding source of law always when there is a case applicable to the problem. Due to the abstract nature of the guiding information, the precedents are often easy to use as normative interpretational material in typical cases. The scholars, then, normally read the rubrication and the reasoning together, as a whole, trying to clarify the core of the information (the *ratio decidendi*).

6   Mode of Citation and Discussion

In regard to the Supreme Court, the *use* of precedents must be differentiated from *citing* them. As was mentioned before, the hearing in the Supreme Court is based on a memorandum written by the referendary. According to the manual of secretaries in the Supreme Court (fifth revised edition, 1992, pp.75 ff), the memorandum must include a report on all statutes, *precedents* and scholarly opinions dealing with the case. Actually, the memorandum is normally a complete and a well-written essay on the case and the legal data concerning it. In this very sense, it is evident that the Supreme Court is in most cases well-informed about the prior practice.

On the other hand, the Supreme Court does not very often publicly *cite* the previous decisions except in the above-mentioned way in the rubrications. If reference is made to previous practice, the court may refer only abstractly to the lines of a precedent without identifying individual cases. Sometimes the number of the precedent is mentioned, as follows: 'In the Finnish judicial practice, it has been regarded (SC 1971 II 89) that...'. Then a short description of the abstract norm applied in the precedent is formulated.

If an individual precedent is cited, the Supreme Court may discuss the following issues:

1   General (and abstract) principles adopted in the precedent referred to. Typically, what this gives is rather abstract and relatively closed guiding information, and, therefore, also the references to prior precedents almost inevitably include only general principles, or general statements of law.
2   Factual differences between cases. This is often a means to identify the case at issue in order to deviate from the prior practice. Because the Supreme Court gives a new precedent in similar cases only when it intends to change the practice, it is rare to refer to factual *analogies*. Of course, when the change of practice is consciously intended, the references to such analogies may be found in reasoning.
3   Sometimes, but seldom, the Supreme Court analyses the arguments or reasons given in the prior precedent. Then the Supreme Court intends to make clear the difference or the similarity of the case at issue compared to the previous precedent. Lately, the Supreme Court has sometimes openly discussed questions of legal policy (*de lege ferenda*) in choosing between alternative arguments. For example, the justices may note that the previous precedents at issue are not satisfactory but the question has to be solved by the legislature, not by the court setting a precedent.

What has been said above concerns the *explicit* references. The discussions, as well as other written material, such as the published memorandum of the secretary, are *secret* independently of whether they deal with a normative or a tactical question. Even scholars cannot get to know them. Hence other information than that explicitly expressed in the precedent cannot be given here. Therefore the other (lower) courts and scholars using or citing the precedent meet a problem. The guiding information given by the Supreme Court is partially included in the rubrication (see question I.4 above) and partially in the reasoning of the case. It is usual to refer only to the former, that is to the general normative information expressed in the rubrication.

There is a practical reason for that: the computerized expert systems include the headlines (the rubrication of the case) and the decision of the Supreme Court as well as the relevant parts of the decisions given by the lower courts. In practice, it is normal to use the information given in the expert systems. Therefore the rubrication has actually – independently of the intentions of the Supreme Court – an essential role in legal practice. The headlines (rubrications) begin to 'live their own life' after acquiring the status of official information in the public registers. It is also worth mentioning that these headlines are, until now, taken as part of legal information in the collection of statutes (the law book, *Finnish Law*). This information can be compared to a general norm given by the legislator. The reasoning is material to interpret the rubrication. However, if the reasoning is scanty, as it often still is, the possibilities of specifying the general information of the rubrication are quite limited.

The sloppy tradition valid in the days of printed material is now vanishing. Formerly, not even the complete text of the precedent was available to the judges in the district courts. Only the registers containing the rubrication were in use. According to this old tradition, it is still possible that a judge reads the rubrication as if it were a statute (when the correct method would, of course, be to analyse the reasoning itself).

7   Overall Role of Precedent

In Finland, a matter cannot, in principle, be solved on the basis of a precedent alone. Finland belongs to the system of statutory law in which a solution has ultimately to be based on a statute (the Code of Judicial Procedure, Art. 24, s.3). In practice, precedents do, however, have a significant argumentative value in the interpretation of statutes. They have been characterized as so-called 'should' sources (weakly binding): a precedent must be referred to if the decision maker wants to avoid the decision being changed in a higher instance.

However, no special order of preference is, included in the Finnish law or in the principles guiding the decision-making activity of the courts of law. This means that a weighty substantive reasoning can, as an argument, supersede a precedent.

8   Role of Precedent in Different Branches of Law

Since in Finland the constitutional court is replaced by a preliminary control in parliament, the problems of the interpretation of the constitution have not arisen much in the courts. However, especially in the case of human rights, a tentative attempt to change the interpretation is in the offing. Due to the binding nature of EU directives that supersede national laws, the superior courts have begun to take an analogical standing on questions concerning the constitutional liberties found to conflict with other statutes to that which they have taken in cases of other laws.

Otherwise, it can generally be said that the practical relevance of precedents depends on how the interaction between the legislator and the courts of law as the developers of the legal order is realized. The value of precedents is the greatest in areas in which the pace of change of the statutes is slow (for instance, family law, law of contract, torts, criminal law, law of property). The precedents mean an elastic adaptation of provisions to the changing social conditions by means of interpretations. No legislation can react to change as quickly as a court of law.

For these reasons, the solutions given by the Supreme Court do not differ according to which field of law they are concerned with. As a general rule, the Supreme Court interprets the statutes undergoing a transformation relatively slowly. There are, however, also exceptions. The Supreme Court has taken an active role to develop ('create') law, for instance, in cases of fraudulent acts in connection with bankruptcy.

However, the guiding function of the solutions of the Supreme Administrative Court varies to some extent according to the fields of law. In addition to what was said above, this is partly due also to the fact that the Supreme Administrative Court gives solutions in administrative matters coming up frequently. In them, the need for precedents is notable owing to the bulk of litigation that arises in practice and regardless of what the pace of transformation of the statutes is. Taxation cases are a typical example. The fiscal authorities have traditionally without exception followed the line of decision formulated by the Supreme Administrative Court. To those applying the law, precedents have been sources of law equal to a general norm.

On the other hand, where the pace of transformation of statutes is rapid, legislation eats into the value of precedents. This is nowadays evident even in the matters of taxation. In the area of the law of taxation, the pace of reform of legislation has been so great that a solution previously significant as a precedent may quickly lose its weight after new provisions have come into force.

9   Precedent and 'Gaps in the Law'

In the case referred to by the question (Appendix, I.9), one often speaks about a gap. Traditionally, it has been customary to distinguish between a gap in the statutes and a gap in the legal system. It has to do with the former when a matter has been regulated by statute but the statute fails to provide a solution for a certain problem. In the latter case, the incompleteness of the body of statute law is filled, for instance, by a legal principle.

The application of the law recognizes in Finland the incompleteness of the statutes. As was previously stated, the Code of Judicial Procedure, Art. 24, S.3 presupposes that every solution should be based on a statute or, should there be no statute, on the custom of the land.

In the Finnish system, one speaks about a gap in all the senses described above. Most particularly, however, the question can be answered by defining, in the manner of Alchourrón and Bulygin, the lack of a statute as a normative gap: it is known that there is no solution to the case. A normative gap can sometimes be recognized by a mere linguistic consideration of a statute (on the basis of the wording). In the literature one speaks in this case about an 'open gap'. The custom of the land is nowadays a very rare source of law so, when an open gap occurs, the cases can in practice hardly be solved by referring to the custom of the land.

The recognizing of a normative gap thus most often presupposes the interpretation of the statute in order to know that the statute provides no answer to the legal issue in hand. The result is 'wrong' according to what is known about the circumstances having an effect on the interpretation. A normative gap has at this point been filled.

A solution has to be given to every case also when dealing with a 'filled gap'. If a normative gap has on some grounds mentioned above been identified, it has to be filled by a court of law. Since every court decision has, on the other hand, to be justified by referring to a statute or the custom of the land (the Code of Judicial Procedure, Art. 24, s.3), the filling of a normative gap mainly means that the solution is to be based on legal principles, which, in turn, have to be connected to some statute or statutes. The incompleteness of statutes is filled by the completeness of law. A court of law then has a law-creating, law-constituting role (judge-made law: Richterrecht).

Due to the legalistic tradition of the Finnish application of the law, the courts of law have been extremely cautious in explicitly declaring that they have to do with filling a normative gap. Most often, one has tried to cope with the situation through argumentation by analogy or *e contrario,* in which case the formal support of the statutes is available. The filling of a gap shows up in practice perhaps most clearly in the justifications of a judgment, which in the case of a gap tend to be more circumstantial than usual, even if the reason for the circumstantiality is not stated in the justifications of the solution.

II   The Bindingness of Precedent

1   Kinds and Degrees of Normative Force

We may usefully differentiate bindingness, force, further support and illustrativeness or other value of a precedent as follows:

1   Formal bindingness: a judgment not respecting a precedent's bindingness is not lawful and so is subject to reversal on appeal. Distinguish:
    (a)   formal bindingness not subject to overruling:
        (i)   'strictly binding' – must be applied in every case;
        (ii)   defeasibly binding – must be applied in every case unless exceptions apply (exceptions may be well defined or not);
    (b)   formal bindingness (with or without exceptions) that is subject to overruling or modification.
2   Not formally binding but having force: a judgment not respecting a precedent's force, though lawful, is subject to criticism on this ground, and may be subject to reversal on this ground. Distinguish:
    (a)   defeasible force – should be applied unless exceptions come into play (exceptions may or may not be well defined);
    (b)   outweighable force – should be applied unless countervailing reasons apply.
3   Not formally binding and not having force, but providing further support: a judgment lacking this is still lawful and may still be justified, but not as well justified as it would be if the precedent were invoked, for example, to show that the decision being reached harmonizes with the precedent.
4   Mere illustrativeness or other value.

In relation to the Finnish legal system, a discussion of the bindingness of precedents in the terms set by the present work requires certain conceptual specifications. The first of these concerns the distinction between horizontal and vertical bindingness. 'Horizontal' bindingness means that a certain court, for instance the Supreme Court, is bound by its own former decisions, whereas 'vertical' bindingness refers to the hierarchical order of courts (a Court of Appeal/the Supreme Court). In principle, every court decision can have a binding effect, either horizontally or vertically. Hence the decision of a Court of Appeal may bind the local courts, and a decision made, for instance, by a city court can be interpreted as binding by the same court or other courts of the same level. However, in the following only the binding effect of the Supreme Court decisions will be analysed, and only they will be called precedents.

According to the Working Order (WO), Art. 21, the Supreme Court is in principle required to follow its own former decisions. However, if a panel of the Supreme Court wants to deviate from a principle, or an interpretation, previously accepted by the Supreme Court, the case can be transferred to a plenum session. WO, Art. 21 thus indicates that a panel of the Supreme Court is formally bound by the prior practice, but opens at the same time the gate to the change of practice. Bindingness is formal but, on certain preconditions, subject to overruling or modification. In this very respect, not even the Supreme Court is subject to the strict horizontal formal bindingness of the prior interpretive precedents.

Instead, the published Supreme Court decisions, that is precedents, are not formally binding but have force both horizontally and vertically. The precedent is an authoritative reason which should be taken into account in subsequent reasoning. This means that the precedents are followed if the guiding information is well-formulated, that is if the reasoning is acceptable. Also when the guiding information is in need of interpretation, the precedents are often used as arguments supporting the other reasoning. In a case where the reasoning is no longer acceptable, the precedent will easily be overruled. As a matter of fact, practically all precedents seem to become obsolete in this very sense due to the changes in society and in the legal order.

The Supreme Court follows its previous practice mainly by not accepting an application for leave to appeal if there is no reason to change the prevalent line. The low number of leaves to appeal indicates that the selection of the leaves is an effective tool to control legal development. However, the Supreme Court is not perfectly consistent in this control. First, the internal catalogue of precedents is partially ineffective, so that a panel simply does not always know the prior precedent, especially when it is not recent. It may thus happen that there are two or more decisions deviating from each other without anybody outside of the court knowing if there is a change of the decision line at issue or not. Second, the Supreme Court sometimes uses in the rubrications of the decisions notes like 'see' and 'cf.' when a reference to the prior precedents has been regarded as necessary.

However, especially the note 'cf.' is ambiguous. It does not clearly reveal if the case at issue *deviates* from a previous one, or if the Supreme Court has changed the line. This ambiguous way of referring has been strongly criticized by scholars.

2 Law Concerning Precedent

In Finland there are no general statutes concerning the use of precedents. The only norms are the provisions of the Working Order of the Supreme Court mentioned above. Neither has any case law concerning the precedents been formed.

The distinction between the concepts of bindingness de jure and de facto has been described above, in Section II.1. Bindingness de facto means that precedents are more or less followed regardless of the fact that there is no legal bindingness. Factually, bindingness de facto means that a precedent forms for a judge a part of his motivation basis when solving a case. Using the terminology adopted by Alf Ross, one could say that the case is included in the normative ideology internalized by the judge. It has thus to do with psychological bindingness.

In certain areas, such as the legal regulation of a guarantee, the interpretation of legal acts related to law of property, contractual liability in the area of services (immaterial services) and building contracts, arrangements are to a large extent based on precedents. The trade in movables was, in practical terms, entirely based on precedents until 1988. In the law concerning compensation for damage, the tort liability has to a large extent been determined in precedents only, and the so-called 'strict liability' for damages has consciously been left completely unregulated in statute law. In incorporeal property law, the principle of the obligation to use a certain form (enumeration) has been accepted, but one has had to solve in precedents, for instance, the question of the material content of some right (for instance, what 'work' means).

According to the legalistic tradition adopted in Finland, law developed from precedent has often led to legislative measures, and principles based on precedents have been transformed into statutory law.

In criminal law, the legalistic tradition means that the principle of *nulla poena sine lege* requires a statute to support criminal charges or convictions. Culpability cannot in Finland be entirely based on precedents. As far as culpability is concerned, statutory law is interpreted, not replaced, by precedents.

3   *Factors Determining Degrees of Normative Force*

In Finland only the solutions of the Supreme Court (and of the Supreme Administrative Court) have a guiding function as precedents. Other solutions can be of only a factual (de facto) relevance.

In general, the following circumstances are relevant when considering the guiding effect of precedents in Finnish law: that the decision rules by a full bench rather than by a panel; that the social and economic background has changed since the decision; that the arguments supporting the prior decision are sound ones; that the precedent is of more or less recent vintage; that there was no or there was some dissent; that the decision represents a trend; that it has been favourably received or not in academic writings; that there has been legal change in related areas. But the significance of a precedent is influenced in particular by how great a need for interpretation is experienced in practice as concerns a statute. The need generally shows itself in an unsteadiness in the practice of the Courts of Appeal that the Supreme Court wants to remove.

The weight of a precedent is at its greatest when it is based on a published plenum decision (full bench). Usually, it has then to do with a case in which the Supreme Court wants emphatically to interfere in the interpretation of the law (legal non-uniformity) or to change its own previous practice. Except for the changes having taken place in society, this may also be due to reforms elsewhere than in the statute being interpreted. The system changes when a part of it is changed.

It is also possible that the precedent is based on a legal principle or a theory of law that has ceased to be valid. The same holds true as far as the *value basis* of the precedent is concerned. The entire value code may have been changed, so that the precedent can no longer be applied to the new case. This is obsolescence of the norm (or value information). Independent of the reason for this obsolescence, the guiding information indicated in the precedent is at least problematic or even without any value, and the precedent has no justificatory force in this situation.

In all cases, however, the final significance even of a (Supreme Court) decision, that is, of a precedent, is highly dependent on its reasoning. A scanty argumentation forces the lower court itself to interpret the *ratio decidendi* and, this being so, the guiding force of the precedent is weak whereas a well-founded decision has a more convincing effect. The decision is acceptable due to the weight of its arguments.

Sometimes the Supreme Court tries to fulfil its role as a guiding instance giving a precedent which confirms the prior practice. In such a case, the confirmed trend naturally increases the justificatory force of the precedents. In the practice of the Supreme Court one can, however, find decisions which only confirm a well-known rule or principle accepted for a long time, for example, by the scholars.

The age of a precedent is decisive in several respects. In some cases, the economic, social, technical and other development makes it impossible to identify a correlation between the facts of a precedent and the facts of the case at issue. The world has taken a different turn and the former fact combination no longer exists. This can be called obsolescence of the facts.

Factually, the value of a unanimous solution is greater than that of a decision by a vote (a divided judgment). Jurisprudence especially takes up a relatively careful – sometimes even critical – attitude towards narrow voting majorities (a three to two majority). In jurisprudence, cases often come up in which a well-justified position of a minority is considered more enduring than the opinion of the majority that won in the voting.

In the formation of practices, jurisprudence has in Finland a strong position also in the negative sense. It often 'filters' the precedents into practice, equipping them with comments and connecting the solutions to other arguments clarifying the system.

The bindingness of precedents is of a somewhat similar degree in different branches of law, excepting the matters belonging to the jurisdiction of the Supreme Administrative Court discussed previously (for instance, taxation).

4 Factors that Weaken Precedent

In socially normal conditions, it does not seem possible for a precedent to lose the formal bindingness normally belonging to it. In the event of sudden social–political changes, a decision, though binding on the parties, is bypassed by events and so never achieves the status of a precedent. In Finland the matter is not current, save perhaps in questions of obscene publications (pornography), where there are several even quite recent strict statutes but the courts actually never deem 'customary' pornography as violating the law. Therefore old precedents concerning, for instance, a novel deemed to be obscene, are tacitly considered to be overruled.

No essential distinction can be drawn between a precedent interpreting a statute and one filling a normative gap. In both cases, it has only to do with how strong a guiding information a precedent gives, and this is exclusively based on factors mentioned in II.3 above.

5   *Vertical and Horizontal Bindingness*

So far as concerns 'horizontal' and 'vertical' bindingness of precedents, this is fully discussed, in Section II.1 above.

6   *Analysis of Force, Support and Illustrative Role*

Due to the prospective function of the precedents of the Supreme Court in Finland, the distinctions mentioned in question II.6 (see Appendix) are not dealt with in the discussion about precedents. The Supreme Court itself does not differentiate between different precedents according to whether the guiding influence is of type (a), (b), or (c).

7   *Excess of Precedents?*

There is no discussion concerning this matter in Finland except as a problem about whether the Supreme Court's line of decision must be considered to have changed when the latest precedent deviates from a line that has prevailed for a long time previously. In a case where there are in some area several precedents that seem to conflict with one another, the conflict generally disappears when cases are analysed into their contributory factors and the distinctive characteristics of each solution are clarified.

The judges sometimes feel that, for example, precedents on undue gain (approximately 350 published cases) as well as various cases concerning guarantee (more than 500 cases published) create confusion. There is no clear idea which cases are really relevant and which not. Even formally obsolete precedents, when the law has been changed, remain retrievable in the electronic database. Therefore the clearing of the register has been discussed. However, the Supreme Court does not regard this task as belonging to it but, for instance, to the doctrinal study of law.

III   The Rationale of Precedent

1 and 2   General Rationales for Formal Bindingness; Force, Further Support, and so on

The general rationale for precedent may be either explanatory or justificatory. In the former case, the rationale explains why a certain decision is accepted as a precedent and why it is followed by the FSC and/or other courts. The justificatory rationales indicate how the court itself reasons in favour of the establishing or following of the precedent.

In Finland the *justificatory* rationales of precedents are only exceptionally stated in judicial opinions, very seldom also in the texts of
respected writers following the precedents. It is almost unknown for
the FSC to express general rationales justifying why a certain decision is a precedent. The decisions are, to some extent, reasoned, but
not by reference to the rationales mentioned above. On the other
hand, there are some *explanatory* rationales which indicate the main
ideas of the precedent system. They can be identified in the general
scholarly discussion about the role and function of the Supreme
Court. The problem is often traced back to the system of leave to
appeal as well as to the division of labour between the legislator and
the independent courts. According to the Finnish constitution, the
task of the courts is to solve individual cases applying general norms
to the concrete facts at issue. In other words, the task is simply to
apply the law, whereas the legislator has to give the general norms to
be applied. This dichotomy has in recent years changed radically.

First, the Supreme Court is no longer only the third appeal instance but, due to the system of leave to appeal, a true precedential
court. It can radically limit the number of the cases to be dealt with.
The main rationale can thus be found here: the central task of the
Supreme Court is to produce prospective guiding information for
other courts. This is important in order to guarantee the stability of
legal relations, and to produce for that as high a degree of predictability as possible. The stability eases the social integration and
coexistence, making the planning of social activities possible. This
can be called the rule-of-law rationale.

In accordance with the Code of Judicial Procedure (s.30, Art. 3), the
Supreme Court has to take care of the uniformity of the adjudication.
The system of leave to appeal makes this possible. Hence the unifying policy is the second main rationale for the precedential system. It
promotes equality among people living in different parts of the
country. Some Court of Appeal may deviate from the decision line
accepted by other courts of the same level. The Supreme Court can
eliminate the possible confusion by a precedent.

Third, the prevalent legislative style tends to transfer the legal
power from the legislator to the hands of the court system. This is
due to the general clauses and statutes of an open texture. As an
example, Art. 36 in the Finnish Contracts Act can be mentioned
according to which the court has the competence to adjust the unreasonable terms of a contract. In other words, it has to weigh and
balance the interests of the parties in order to reach a reasonable
solution. This means that the decision can no longer be read directly
in the statutes but is based on the deliberation of the court. The task
of developing the legal order is thus the third of the main rationales.
The legislative procedure is too inflexible to react to the often quite

quick changes in society, especially typical of the welfare state. That task is naturally left to the courts.

Finally, the traditional goal, typical of all court systems, viz. to guarantee a legal and just solution in every single case, is still an important (fourth) rationale of the Finnish precedential system, although this goal is realized in the majority of cases on the basis of two appeal instances only. The background of this rationale is the need to guarantee the maximal legal protection in each individual case.

The intention of the Supreme Court is not only to solve the individual cases but to give abstract and general guiding information for the future. Therefore all the rationales mentioned in this answer are emphasized by the Supreme Court, especially when determining the scope and weight of a precedent. The lower courts do not, due to the prospective nature of the precedents, explicitly express their opinions on the rationales.

IV   Precedents: What They Stand for and How They Apply

1   *What Counts as Binding or Having Force?*

In Finland the decisive guiding information of a precedent is included in the so-called 'rubrication'. It includes a description of the legal norm (a rule or a principle) that has to be applied to the facts described in the case. A rubrication is thus not exclusively a description about a solution, but one wants, by its means, to influence the subsequent application of the law. It is thus a normative instruction. A rubrication contains an indication of the relevant facts as decided on; an explicit holding on an issue of law, or *ratio decidendi*; an explicitly formulated (or implicit) rule; and, sometimes, an explicitly formulated (or implicit) principle. It is the *ratio decidendi*, whether in the form of a rule or a principle.

Consequently, a judge solving a subsequent case receives the guiding information expressly from the rubrication. In many cases, the normative guiding information is, however, expressed only implicitly and has to be rationally reconstructed on the basis of the rubrication and the other parts of the precedent. In this regard, the rubrication must be interpreted in a similar way as statutes have to be interpreted in cases of ambiguity and so on. The very content of the 'rubrication norm' cannot be understood without taking into account, for example, the previous hearing of the case (in the district court and in the Court of Appeal) and/or the reasoning of the decision.

Whether the norm expressed by the rubrication is applicable to the case being solved depends, in turn, on whether the fact description of the precedent and the description of the case to be solved are sufficiently analogical. Discretion is in this respect similar to that used in drawing conclusions by analogy in relation to other legal norms.

A special problem is in practice created by the fact that the rubrications of precedents are recorded in the FINLEX database and its derivatives. Then it often happens that a lawyer or a lower court judge calls up from the database only the wording of the rubrication recorded there without working out the interpretation of the rubrication in the light of the facts of the case and the arguments in the court's opinion. The rubrication has, thus used, begun to live an 'independent life' in the same way as a general norm issued by the legislator. In fact, the rubrication itself has become a general norm.

Referring to this, it is possible to speak about a certain kind of a 'case positivism' as the modern version of legal positivism. The statutes have been replaced by the rubrications of the precedents recorded in the database; the rubrications that, interpreted according to their wording, are used as valid norms of law. Then the critical attitude disappears and the practice slavishly drifts in the direction of the guiding information given by the rubrications. This is what has to some extent happened in Finland, especially where the statutes have left areas of law open to interpretation through precedents.

2 Reasoning about applicability

Discussions of precedent in Finland have focused on the process of setting precedents and thereby providing guiding information for the future. There has been much less discussion of the process of application, or of the problems of applicability or inapplicability of precedents to current cases. The theory and practice concerning the applicability of a precedent are only now beginning to be developed in Finland.

3 Juristic Discussion

The doctrine about the bindingness of the precedent is relatively new in Finland because it was only in the 1980s that the Supreme Court determined the guiding function of precedents. Until then, the role of precedents was to some extent unclear both in the application of the law and in jurisprudence. This was partly due to the fact that, in the Finnish legalistic tradition, the wording of the law and the legislative drafts had a relatively significant role when clarifying the content of the legal order. The second reason has been the previously mentioned scanty justifications of a judicial decision and the bureaucratic language of the decisions. It has been difficult to determine the argumentative weight of the court solutions.

Over the past few years, primarily three principles have been established in the doctrine of the precedent (compare Section IV.1 above). It is decisive to clarify the content as based on the wording of the guiding norm in the rubrication. In case there are problems in interpreting it, the rubrication must be interpreted in the light of the other elements of the solution. Finally, one has to clarify the compatibility of the facts of the case to be solved with the facts of the precedent.

In general, legal literature dealing with precedents from the substantive point of view has increased in a marked way in the 1990s.

4   *Illustrative or Analogical Precedent*

The published decisions of the Supreme Court have a binding guiding effect to a certain degree, as described previously. The unpublished decisions (that are thus not precedents according to the concept of the Supreme Court) as well as the obsolete precedents may be of an illustrative meaning in several different situations:

1   A decision may identify the legal question at issue. The decision thus helps the other courts to analyse similar cases except in scholarly work in which their role is more illustrative than argumentative.
2   A decision gives an example about how a certain type of a case can be solved. It may thus open the way to reasoning pro and contra in a similar configuration of facts.
3   Sometimes, a decision is used as an argument or it is even followed as a guideline without the decision being binding in any sense of the word. The lower courts, for instance, have no time or interest to argue against the solution or to use distinctions. The scholars, too, sometimes use appellate court decisions in this way, at least to give support to arguments in the legal reasoning.

The same concerns the Court of Appeal solutions. They are not considered to have actual binding guiding effect even in cases in which (a) a judgment has not been appealed to the Supreme Court or (b) no leave to appeal has been granted and the Court of Appeal solution has remained final.

5   *Single Precedents or Lines of Decision?*

The courts of law draw no explicit distinction between the guiding effect of an individual precedent and that of a certain line of decision. In jurisprudence, instead, the line of decision has been considered, even if often implicitly.

It has then often to do with a reconstructive line that jurisprudence formulates on the basis of arguments built up from the precedents. In

Finland 'merely repetitive' precedents come up only exceptionally. A line arises, if one exists, most often from a certain subsequent precedent strengthening a previously prevailing position in a situation in which uncertainty has arisen as regards whether the previous position is still valid.

In the Finnish statute-centred and legalistic system, no doctrine has developed in the courts about how one is to respond to precedents that reinforce or conflict with one another. The prospective guiding function adopted by the Supreme Court means that the Supreme Court either simply reinforces the continuance of a certain line or removes the conflict. If there is uncertainty as regards the line, or the conflict is implicit, reconstruction remains the task of jurisprudence. Recommendations of interpretation, in fact, very often arise expressly as outputs of jurisprudence, and go over from there into practice, and through it possibly to the Supreme Court, which revises its line, and so on.

In litigation, of course, it is quite common that the attorneys have different opinions about the correct meaning of the precedents in question.

6   The Concept of a 'Leading Case'

In Finland, the concept of a 'leading case' is of no significance due to the reasons mentioned in IV.5 above. However, even here the situation is slowly changing. Some 'leading cases' could be pointed out, for instance, in the borderline between contractual liability and a tort, where there are no clear statutes concerning the problem.

V   Distinguishing, Explaining, Modifying, Overruling

1   Distinguishing

In Finland the doctrine of 'distinguishing' has gained no footing because, in the theory of precedent, the prospective guiding function of precedents has received the main attention. Of course, the courts do not follow guiding precedents that they consider inapplicable, but there is no special practice of adducing arguments to show why a particular precedent is inapplicable.

2   Juristic Commentary

Juristic discussion of precedure in Finland has concentrated on the use of the prospective power of precedent setting. As yet there has been little discussion of the distinguishability of precedents.

3   *Excessive distinguishing?*

See V.1 above. In addition, it can be stated that artificial conclusions may be drawn in jurisprudence from the rubrications of precedents and one may, then, also arrive at excessively fine or unreal distinctions. Most often, it is the other way around: one makes no distinction at all between different types of cases, but one generalizes past the wording of the rubrication of an individual precedent.

False conclusions are most often due to those engaged in jurisprudence not sufficiently taking into consideration the procedural provisions. It may have been impossible in a precedent to take a stand on a certain question for the reason, for instance, that it has not been brought into focus by the pleadings in the action. In the Finnish process, the procedural development of an action plays an important part, and deficiencies in that respect may have the result that nothing can be stated in a judgment about a circumstance otherwise typical of the matter. Procedural rules thus restrict the content of a judgment in such a way that it cannot be generalized without great caution.

The fault of juridical commentaries in Finland often lies in the very fact that one draws hasty conclusions from the precedents. This may be due, for instance, to precedents being used only to legitimate an opinion already formed on other grounds.

4   *Types of Overruling*

Overruling in the strict sense can in the Finnish system only take place in the Supreme Court. Only the Supreme Court can give guiding information and only this instance can annul or amend guiding information once given. If it has to do with amending in the Supreme Court a decision given by the Supreme Court itself (horizontal bindingness), the matter is settled by the Working Order of the Supreme Court previously described. In other cases, the Supreme Court may simply amend its position.

When it has to do with an amendment of any importance, the solution is generally properly justified. However, in the rubrication no more than in the justifications is it explicitly made known that an amendment is being undertaken, even if the Supreme Court may in the justifications refer to the overruled decision, in which case the reference indirectly indicates that amendment is intended. When this is not the case, the amendment can generally easily be inferred from a previous precedent or precedent line.

Overruling in the weak sense of the word can also take place in the lower courts. A precedent is disregarded because (a) it is not considered to concern the case in hand (the facts and circumstances are not analogical); (b) the justifications of the precedent are not considered legally enduring; (c) the *ratio decidendi* does not correspond to the prevailing social or social–moral situation; or (d) the statutes on which the precedent is based have been amended (the system is not the same as it was at the time the precedent was given).

5 Prospective Overruling

In the light of the foregoing, it is easy to infer that prospective overruling is effectively unknown in Finland, although in all cases this prospective aspect of precedent attracts attention far greater than that attaching to its retrospective aspect.

6 Anticipatory Overruling by Lower Courts

To the extent that lower courts are free to 'overrule' in the weak sense mentioned in Section V.4 above, we may indeed say that the Finnish system allows of (weak) anticipatory overruling.

7 Precedent and Legislative Practice

In a statutory law system, a precedent or precedent line is one, but only one, basis for changing statutes. A conflict between precedents, for instance, is an extremely rare reason for legislative reform. Generally, the basis for changing a statute is found in society. For instance, the provisions of the Marriage Act relating to law of property have been amended in order to strengthen the position of the woman (to protect the weaker party), not because of the ambiguity, faultiness or lack of a clear line of previous legal practice.

When preparing statutes, precedents are likewise only one basis among many others. In some areas, such as the trade in movables at the end of the 1980s, a part of the precedents is recorded in the texts of the law, but normally, for the legislative draftsmen, they are merely indications as regards the direction in which statutes should be developed.

In a statutory law system, it is not possible to even doubt, at least in Finland, that the confirmation of a solution by legislation is a basis for evaluating the bindingness of a precedent. When a statute changes, the matter is assessed on a new basis. Previous precedents may be of an argumentative value also in a new situation, but only through their justifications. If the justifications are in line with the objective on which a new statute is based, it is possible to refer to the precedent for an interpretation in accordance with the wording and the legislative drafts of the statute. Mostly, however, old precedents are, of no more than illustrative force.

In Finland judges often take part in drafting laws. Therefore it is quite evident that the bulk of precedents is well known and the draft for a statute is, among other things, the judges' comment on an existing societal problem.

8   *Conflicts of Precedents*

Conflict between precedents can be either apparent or actual. In the former case, the conflict can be solved by interpreting either the normative content of the decision or the facts of the case. On closer inspection, one finds that *the question of law* solved in the precedents is not the same. The first precedent answers to another question than the second one. In some cases, the procedural requirements explain the final solutions and cause the difference between the precedents. Most often the scrutiny of the facts reveals that there is an essential difference as far as the fact combination is concerned or in the way the Supreme Court has weighed the single state of affairs of the precedents.

The actual conflict is an internal (built-in) contradiction of the entire legal system. It cannot be solved by means of interpretation. The origin of such a conflict points out how it can be and is solved in practice.

1   The first precedent may be so old that the case will be settled in favour of the later one. The decisive factor, however, is not the mere age of the precedent but the out-of-date principles, theories or values backing it. The Supreme Court itself solves the conflict by simply omitting the precedent from the registers.

2   If two (or more) precedents conflict with each other, there can be, despite the age of the precedents, a change of decision line in question. The conflict must be solved in favour of the latest one if the reasoning reveals that the change has been conscious (intended). Sometimes the Supreme Court really gives a precedent only in order to indicate the change of its standpoint in that legal question.

3   In case the actual conflict cannot be settled in either of the above-mentioned ways, it is the quality of the reasons that is decisive. The better reasoned precedent (A) is prior to that (B) in which the reasoning is closed or worse than in A.

4   If the conflict is not ostensible only, and if networks (1)–(3) are not available, the precedents (A and B) do not have a special value in legal reasoning. The problems of interpretation and gap filling must be solved by means of other reasons.

In recent times, this kind of a conflict has been extremely rare due to the improved recording systems for precedents.

9   Hypothetical Cases

The use of hypothetical cases in *reductio ad absurdum* argumentation, the use of hypothetical cases as paradigms of the applicability of a rule or principle in a precedent, the use of extreme hypothetical cases to test the appropriateness of formulations of a rule or principle in a precedent, and the use of extreme hypothetical cases to test the limits of the scope of a precedent are all known in Finnish law. The use of such arguments is common both in jurisprudence and in the activity of the courts. Primarily the use of hypothetical cases is, however, actual in situations referred to in questions V.9 (b) and (c) (Appendix). For example, the prevailing doctrine on *mens rea* in criminal law is often founded on the basis of certain hypothetical tests (whether the accused would have committed his act even if he had known what was going to happen).

VI   Matters of General Perspective, Evaluation and Other

1   'Saying and Doing'

In the Finnish system, again due to its prospective nature, the gap between saying and doing is not a problem. In the application of the law, the Supreme Court mainly uses what was called 'open' reasoning at the present time.

2   Recent Change or Evolution

A significant change of the doctrine of the precedent took place in Finland in the 1980s, at which time the Supreme Court itself defined certain of its (published) solutions as precedents. On the level of statutes, no other change took place than the reform of the Working Order of the Supreme Court described previously. It defined the ways in which a Supreme Court section may deviate from a previously reinforced position.

The then president of the Supreme Court, Curt Olsson, presented the reform as a radical change of the doctrine of the precedent. Since the position and the tasks of the Supreme Court are defined in the constitution, a lively discussion arose about whether the Supreme Court can by a mere reform of the Working Order change the doctrine of the precedent and, through that, the constitutional position of the Supreme Court as the highest decision-making instance for individual cases.

The discussion primarily concerned three matters: (1) whether it is possible, by a reform of the Working Order, to influence the degree of normative force of precedents; (2) should the claimed change have been enforced in the order of procedure required for the enactment of constitutional legislation, because it has to do with the changing of the role of the Supreme Court solutions; (3) to which element in a precedent can the possible bindingness refer?

The results of the discussion can be read in the pages of this report. The arrangement is moderate. Precedents have within the Supreme Court a horizontal bindingness de jure. For this change, no amendment of the constitution is needed, and no other essential change has been made in the previously accepted doctrine of precedent. The conceived guiding function of precedents is realized the better the more exhaustively the decisions are justified. Precedents are followed because they are well argued for, and, as such, convincing, not because of mandatory authority.

3   Changes in International Environment

As far as the Supreme Court of Finland is concerned, above all the question concerning all the EU member countries has become a problem about the extent to which a national Supreme Court is bound to the solutions of the Court of Human Rights and, on the other hand, those of the European Court of Justice. Generally speaking, the EU arrangements have given rise to a situation in which part of the judicial power has been transferred from the judicial organs of a national state to a supranational court machinery.

The highest judicial organs have accepted this fact, and no mentionable discussion about the matter is any longer going on in Finland. What is considered more essential is the question about the extent to which the solutions of supranational courts are binding in Finland. The arrangement is somewhat the same as within a national state in the vertical respect (the Supreme Court/the lower courts). The Supreme Court has the same possibility, as it considers the applicability of a solution of the European Court of Justice to a case being solved in Finland, that the lower courts have to deviate from a precedent.

Besides, it has to be remembered that the harmonizing effect of the EU application of the law only extends to the area of the EU regulations. All other application of the law still follows the principles adopted within a national state.

4   Juristic or Other Criticism

Academic criticism was decisive in opposing the attempt to make the Supreme Court a precedential court *sensu stricto*. Now, the next step is to open a discussion about the theory of distinction, overruling and so on.

In a system maintaining the idea of the prospective function of precedents, the body of judicial or scholarly discussion of methods for defining and finding what a precedent stands for is necessarily undeveloped. In the recent scholarly discussion, however, some weak signs about the increasing interest in these methods can be identified.

The actual work of courts was previously virtually unknown. Therefore well-grounded criticism was often difficult, if not impossible. Now legal research has gone so far as to study the work of judges and even their biographies. The former segregation of legal writers, attorneys and judges is tending to crumble.

Bibliography

Aarnio, A. (1987), *The Rational as Reasonable*, D. Reidel, Dordrecht.
Aarnio, A. (1989), *Laintulkinnan teoria*, Helsinki.
Kekkonen, J. (1996), *Kriisit, valta ja oikeus*, Helsinki.
Kemppinen, J. (1990), *Oikeus kulttuuri-ilmiönä*, Helsinki.
Kemppinen, J. (1990), *Tätä kaikki asianomaiset noudattakoot*, Helsinki.
Klami, H.T. (1983), *Ihmisen säännöt*, Turku.
Klami, H.T. (1987), *Oikeustaistelijat*, Porvoo.
MacCormick, D.N. and R.S. Summers (eds) (1991), *Interpreting Statutes – A Comparative Study*, Dartmouth: Aldershot.
Makkonen, K. (1965), *Zur Problematik der juridischen Entscheidung*, Turku.
Miettinen, M. (1970), *Prejudikaateista ja niiden merkityksestä. Suomen Lakimiesliiton XXI lakimiespäivät*, p. 250, Pöytäkirja.

4 Precedent in France

MICHEL TROPER, *PARIS* AND
CHRISTOPHE GRZEGORCZYK, *PARIS*

I Institutional and Systemic

1(a) Court Hierarchy

The main feature of the French system of courts is the existence of two distinct and separate hierarchies of courts: the judicial and the administrative. This is usually explained by reference to the French interpretation of the separation of powers, which prohibits traditional, that is, ordinary, judges from creating general rules, thereby invading the provinces of other branches. From the time of the Revolution, a court has not been allowed to decide a case involving an administrative body, because this would be to exercise the administrative function. At the time of the Revolution, the judicial function was conceived as a mere application of statutes, by way of syllogisms. Since administrative bodies necessarily enjoy a large degree of discretion in the exercise of their function, there is usually no statute that can serve as a major premise when deciding a case. If courts were permitted to decide these administrative cases, they would be in a position to produce their own rules to serve as major premises and they would therefore invade at the same time the legislative and the administrative functions.

Cases involving administrative bodies were thus decided by other, higher, administrative bodies, under the authority of the executive. It became rapidly necessary to form, within the executive, special bodies to act as courts here. The most important of these bodies was, at the beginning of the nineteenth century, the Conseil d'Etat. At the beginning of the Third Republic (1870–1945), these bodies were made independent of the executive, but remained separate from the ordinary courts, which are headed by the Court of Cassation.

103

The two systems of courts still differ in many respects. Judges are not recruited and trained in the same manner, rules of procedure are different and, above all, the substantive rules to be applied are not the same. This is due to the fact, already mentioned, that there is no codified law applicable in administrative matters. Therefore the administrative courts to a very large extent have had to produce their own law and it is nowadays frequently said that French administrative law is judge-made law, thus comparable to Anglo-American common law. This is partly an exaggeration, especially because administrative courts are still limited by the principles stated in Article 5 of the Civil Code which declares: 'it is prohibited for judges to decide by way of general provisions and rules on the cases that are brought before them'.

In both the judicial and administrative courts, there are three levels of courts, but only two levels of adjudication. In other words, a decision by a lower court can only be appealed once. In both, above the lowest courts, there are courts of appeal. The decisions of the courts of appeal can be brought to the highest court in the hierarchy, but, in principle, this is not an appeal, (it is called a *pourvoi en cassation*) because the highest court does not examine the whole case for a third time. It is not supposed to examine the facts, but only the legal issues. Naturally, the difference between issues of fact and legal issues is a difficult question, and there are many ways in which the highest court does consider the facts. The most important is the *qualification juridique des faits*: in order to decide whether some facts can be subsumed under certain legal categories, these facts have to be examined: this is considered a legal issue. Thus to say that the highest court does not examine the facts means only that it leaves to the lower courts the question of the material existence of facts. This has a formal consequence: once a decision of a court of appeal has been invalidated by the Court of Cassation, it is sent to another court of appeal, which will make a new decision, both on the legal issue and on the issue of fact, normally applying the rule mentioned in the Court of Cassation's decision.

In practice however, the highest courts function as courts of a third level, because of two factors. The first lies in the difficulty of differentiating between issues of fact and issues of law. The second is that the Conseil d'Etat and the Court of Cassation may not select cases, which explains the very large number of appeals. In 1994, a bill was introduced to allow selection of cases in the Court of Cassation. Nevertheless, the purpose of that bill was not to enable the Court of Cassation to select the most important and significant cases, in order to create precedents, but simply to dismiss the less serious ones. This bill has not been adopted as of August 1996. It may be submitted again to parliament by the new minister of justice.

Outside the two court systems is the Conseil Constitutionnel, established by the 1958 constitution, mainly to settle electoral disputes and to control the constitutionality of the statutes enacted by parliament. In 1971, the Conseil Constitutionnel decided that the constitution, to which laws must conform, includes the preamble and all the principles which are referred to in the preamble. This decision has led to a considerable development of the role of the Conseil Constitutionnel, and after a long scholarly discussion about the nature, judicial or political, of that body it is now generally agreed that it is truly a court. Nevertheless, there are some important particularities: first, its members are appointed, for nine years each, one-third by the president of the Republic, one-third by the president of the National Assembly and one-third by the president of the Senate. Secondly, it is only competent a priori, immediately after a new law has been passed in parliament, prior to its promulgation (hence before it could be applied). Therefore nothing can be done, in the French Conseil Constitutionnel, to a statute after it has been promulgated, even if it violates the most fundamental principles. Thirdly, a statute can only be brought to the Conseil Constitutionnel by one of the following authorities: the president of the Republic, the prime minister, the presidents of the two houses, 60 deputies or 60 senators. Fourthly, even though the decisions of the Conseil Constitutionnel are binding on other courts, no appeal can be made from the other courts to the Conseil Constitutionnel. Finally, no public sessions are held, and lawyers may not appear before it.

It is also necessary to mention the fact that, according to the constitution, international treaties have a value superior to that of statutes. This has been interpreted to mean (1) that a law which violates a treaty is not contrary to the constitution and cannot be annulled by the Conseil Constitutionnel; (2) that an ordinary court ought to refuse to apply a law contrary to a treaty. Among the treaties binding in France are the European treaties that establish international courts: the European Court of Justice and the European Court of Human Rights. When a problem arises about the meaning of the treaties, the courts ought to resort to the European courts. In that respect, they are considered as elements of a European court system.

1(b)   Structural and Procedural Aspects

In the Court of Cassation, there are 84 judges, not counting state attorneys. They decide a very large number of cases. In 1991, there were more than 26 000. At that time, there were 33 000 waiting to be decided. The situation has not improved: in 1993, 25 000 cases were decided, but 26 000 new ones had been filed and the cases to be decided had increased to between 36 000 and 37 000 on 31 December

1994. It is estimated that, if the purpose of the Court of Cassation were only to create precedents, only about 120 decisions a year in civil law would be necessary and 206 in criminal matters (*Rapport annuel de la Cour de Cassation*).

The same is largely true of the Conseil d'Etat: it is difficult to determine the number of judges, because there are approximately 270 members of the Conseil d'Etat, but the majority of them have administrative functions and do not take part in adjudication. Cases are decided by the Section du contentieux (about 60 members). The Conseil d'Etat decided 11 000 cases in 1991.

Both courts are organized in sections. The Court of Cassation is divided into six sections (chambres), five civil and one criminal. Decisions can be made by each of these sections separately. Important cases are decided by a mixed section, composed of members belonging to two or more sections, or by a plenary assembly, in the case of a resistance by the Court of Appeal, to which a case has been sent back.

A similar organization can be found in the Conseil d'Etat. Less important cases are examined by subsections (there are ten), by a union of two subsections, or by the whole adjudication section (section du contentieux).

1(c)   Power to Select Cases

As mentioned before, the courts have so far had no power to select cases, but the presidents of the courts have some discretion to allocate cases either to a section or, in hard cases, to a mixed section, or to the largest assembly. This explains the very large number of cases the courts have to decide each year, and the very long time it takes before a case is decided in the last instance.

2   Structure, Content and Style of Judgments

The basic prescription regarding the form and content of judgments is Article 455 of the Code of Civil Procedure, which reads: 'The judgment must describe briefly the claims of the parties and their arguments; it must be motivated. That is, it must include justifying arguments. The judgment expresses the decision in the form of a disposition.' This provision only applies to the ordinary courts, but the law binding on administrative courts is similar.

Any judgment is composed of five elements:

1   *mentions*: the judgment mentions whether it has been read in public, the names of the parties, the fact that a report has been read and the composition of the court;

2 *visas*, which are the list of documents which have been examined by the court: summary of briefs, documents presented by the parties and statutes;
3 *motifs*: they are the most important and (relatively) longest part of the judgment. The obligation to motivate, prescribed by Article 455, is currently justified by two arguments: it is the proof that the arguments of the parties have been examined, and it allows higher courts to exercise control over the judgment. It normally consists of a brief statement of facts and a discussion of arguments justifying the decision.

The main justifying argument is usually a statement of the general rule to be applied to the case. This general rule can be simply a formulation of the provisions of the statute or an interpretation of the 'true content' of the statute or the statement of a principle. Thus this formulation is clearly precedent-oriented, because, with this statute, interpretation or principle, the court intends to resolve, not only the single case to be decided, but a class of similar cases. This is the reason why French scholars use the expression *'cour régulatrice'* (ruling court);
4 *dispositif*: this is the decision proper, the ruling on the issue, the command emanating from the court. It is usually composed of one or two articles, a form similar to that of statutes. It is important to stress that the *dispositif* is the only part of the judgment that in principle enjoys the authority of *res judicata*, although that authority has been extended by the courts to the *motifs* that are the necessary basis of the *dispositif*.
5 *formule exécutoire*, which is an order, addressed to some public authority to execute the judgment.

The character of the style of the opinions follows from the general conception of the French judge, who is supposed to exercise not 'judicial power', but only a 'judicial function'. The only legitimate source of law is 'the law', which is equated with statutory law because, as stated in the Declaration of the Rights of Man of 1789, 'the Law is the expression of the general will'. Therefore (a) it is deductive, because the judgment is conceived as a syllogism; (b) it is principally legalistic, but it should be noted that, because of the importance of the *'qualification juridique des faits'*, courts tend to discuss, not the meaning of the statute, but the nature of the facts, in order to establish whether they can be subsumed under the categories of the law; this discussion tends to be substantive, although it is usually concise; (c) opinions are magisterial. French court decisions are extremely brief: sometimes no more than a few lines. The magisterial style can be explained partly by the large number of cases to be decided each year, and partly by the authoritative character of the courts, which derives from a tradition going back to the Ancien Régime, when the parlements exercised the power of the king himself. Today, in spite of the idea that courts are but instruments of the law, procedural rules and tradition evoke the idea of a third 'power' of the state, endowed with majesty. Each decision starts with the formula, 'Au nom du Peuple Français'.

Some French scholars have been advocating for several years more elaborate and substantiated justifications of court decisions, especially by judicial courts. There is a recent and slight tendency to move in that direction, because of the influence on the one hand of European courts and on the other of the Conseil Constitutionnel. Since the Conseil Constitutionnel, when reviewing statutes concerning various fields of the law, decides the constitutional basis of private or administrative law and issues directives for the interpretation of statutes, judicial and administrative courts are sometimes forced to go into a more detailed and substantive discussion of arguments, in order to demonstrate the coherence of their decisions with the jurisprudence of the Conseil Constitutionnel.

3   Publication of Judgments

A large proportion of the decisions of the highest courts (Court of Cassation and Conseil d'Etat) are published in official bulletins. The court itself decides what decisions will be published. Sometimes, for very important decisions, an opinion of a reporting judge (commissaire du gouvernement) is published, together with the decision itself. Since the decision itself is brief, this opinion is very helpful to interpret the case.

The most important decisions of administrative tribunals and courts of appeal appear in law journals. It is exceptional that decisions of the lowest courts are published. Those decisions that are not published are nevertheless sometimes referred to in doctrinal articles. These cases can then be cited and used in a legal argument and, in principle, photocopies can then be obtained from the courts.

When court decisions are published in an official bulletin, they comprise, first, a short list of related topics or key words (for example, liability, contracts, leasing), which correspond to the general index of the volume, reproduced in electronic data banks. The choice of items in this list is usually made by junior members of the courts. They also include a short summary of the *ratio decidendi*. The same thing is done by law journals (Jobard-Bachellier and Bachellier, 1994, p.35.)

In academic journals, cases to be published are selected by the editorial board, but the most important cases are published accompanied by a commentary (note d'arrêt), usually written by a law professor. Law professors receive a typed copy of all the decisions of the Court of Cassation or the Conseil d'Etat relating to their speciality, before they are published in the official bulletin, and they select the cases worthy of a commentary. Practising lawyers and judges rely heavily on these commentaries, which are often regarded as a contribution to the shaping of precedents and are globally referred to as '*la doctrine*'.

Few newspapers report judgments by higher courts and those who do only do so exceptionally. There are several electronic media. The most widely used is Lexis. It is also possible to read a summary of recent decisions of the Conseil d'Etat or Court of Cassation on the MINITEL and to order Fax copies.

4   Contents of Reports

Since the decisions are brief, they are normally published in unabridged form in the official bulletins. In the law journals, it is not always considered necessary to publish the 'visas' and the 'ruling itself', because what is considered of interest to the public is the 'motifs'. In a typical law journal, the reports of court judgments will normally contain the following, in addition to the decision itself:

a   the name of the case;
b   the name of the deciding court;
c   a headnote with key words (decided by the editors of the bulletin or the law journal and therefore very diverse);
d   a brief statement of the facts will be found in the decision. When there is a commentary, it will normally contain a more developed and detailed statement of the facts. This is particularly important whenever the issue depends on a 'legal qualification' (characterization of the facts);
e   a discussion of prior decisions in this very case will also be found in the decision of the highest court, and will be discussed again at length in the commentary;
f   a statement of the legal issue is not always overtly made in the decision, but will be an essential part of the commentary;
g   a discussion of interpretational problems will not normally be found as such in the decision because there is a legal presumption that the text of the statute is clear and *intepretatio cessat in claris*. Therefore one finds interpretations in the opinions, but there is only exceptionally a discussion of interpretational problems. But such discussions, naturally, are found in commentaries;
h   as mentioned before, the ruling is not always published, because (1) it is only a consequence of the *motifs* and (2) it consists of only one or two sentences, which only concern the parties to the case and are of no interest to the public;

i   reasons for the ruling are the essential part of the decision. When the decision is published, the reports invariably include the reasons for the ruling. These reasons will be exposed at length by the commentator, drawing from other sources of information, for example opinions of a reporting judge;

j   there is a statement of the final decision. This part of the judgment is called the *'dispositif'* and it is followed by the *'formule exécutoire'*, ordering every public authority to enforce the decision;

k–l   there are no concurring or dissenting opinions in any French court. Moreover, the results of the vote are never made public and there is a presumption that the decision was taken unanimously. Some scholars recommend that dissenting opinions be introduced, but this idea is very strongly opposed by the judges. It is generally thought that such opinions would weaken the legitimacy of the courts, because their decisions would be seen, not as the expression of the truth, but as the mere private opinion of a majority of the court.

m   arguments by counsel are sometimes mentioned, more frequently by judicial than by administrative courts, but they are only mentioned in the form of a very short summary;

n   in administrative courts one official is called the *'commissaire du gouvernement'*. In spite of this name, he or she is supposed to represent the interest of the law, as distinct from that of both parties, even that of the 'executive'. His or her report states what the law requires and proposes the substance of a decision. These suggestions are followed most of the time and these reports in important cases are published both in official bulletins and in law journals. They are considered the best source for analysing the reasoning of the courts, both because they are so influential and because they compensate for the brevity of the decision.

There are no opinions on the decision by legal officials, writing in their official capacity, but it happens that some officials write commentaries in law journals. It is, for example, considered an important step in the career of a young member of the Conseil d'Etat (an *auditeur*) to write commentaries which regularly appear as part of *la doctrine*;

o   law journals but not official bulletins follow the publication of the most important court decisions with scholarly commentaries. These commentaries are considered a typical expression of the jurisprudential work of *'la doctrine'* and are written according to regular canonical style, which is an essential part of legal education in France (Mendegris and Vermelle, 1995).

5 Meaning of 'Precedent'

In the French legal language, the word 'precedent' never means a binding decision, because courts are never bound by precedents. As one author justly writes, 'the very idea that a judge could search for the base of his decision in a prior judgment is literally unthinkable in a legal system based on statutory Law' (Zenati, 1991, p.102). It cannot mean a decision expressly adopted by a court to guide future decision making, for two reasons:

1   The only situation when a court expressly guides future decision making is that in which the Court of Cassation rules in plenary session, after a previous ruling has been disregarded by a Court of Appeal. This decision by the Court of Cassation is binding on the new Court of Appeal, but in principle it is binding only for the particular case and not for future similar ones. Moreover, its binding force derives only from the statute which institutes the Court of Cassation.
2   A court decision only has 'relative binding force' (*autorité relative de la chose jugée*): it is binding only on the parties and in the same case.

The word 'precedent' therefore only means in French, according to the most widely used legal dictionary, 'in a decision-making situation, a decision taken in the past in similar circumstances or in a similar case' (Cornu, 1990). It is used with two different meanings:

1   in a strong sense, referring to a decision of a higher court, not as a legal, but as an authoritative argument, implying that this decision, without being binding, ought to be followed by the lower court; the lower court has no legal obligation to follow that argument, but nearly always does, for practical reasons;
2   in a weak sense, referring to a decision in a similar case by any court, even by a lower one, which could serve as a positive or a negative model; following this kind of precedent saves the court an extensive analysis of the facts and of the legal issue and is justified by the assumed principle of equality before the law.

We must nevertheless mention an important institutional change introduced by a statute of 15 May 1991 (Article L 151-1 et s. du code de l'organisation judiciaire). Any judge in the judicial system of courts can ask the Court of Cassation for advice on the interpretation of a statute on a new and difficult legal issue arising frequently. That advice, given in a similar form to that of a decision in 'Assemblée pleinière', is not legally binding, even for the judge who asked for it, but in fact it obviously has considerable force. It can even be assimilated to a leading case, because the purpose of the statute is to prevent future litigation (Jobard-Bachellier and Bachellier, 1994, pp. 17–18).

6   Mode of Citation and Discussion

Judges do not cite precedents in their written decisions, but practitioners and scholars do. The importance of these citations varies according to the type of court and the type of law. They are more frequent when the statutes are few, or not codified, as in administrative law, or have been subject to interpretation by the courts. These citations refer to the published text of the precedent and the reasons given for the ruling, but mostly to commentaries. The role of these juristic writings is of capital importance, for several reasons: (1) it has already been mentioned that law professors select the cases worthy of a commentary, which will then be cited as precedents; (2) they provide practitioners and other scholars with an interpretation of the very brief and sometimes unclear text of the decisions; (3) they place the decision in the context of previous and related decisions; (4) they shape the concepts with which precedents and also statutes will be cited and interpreted; (5) they sometimes suggest new principles on which decisions could be based or show the existence of hidden assumptions, thus exercising an influence on future court decisions. This explains that '*la doctrine*' is sometimes considered in France an auxiliary source of law.

7   Overall Role of Precedent

One ought to draw a distinction between the role of precedents as a whole (jurisprudence in the French sense) which is considered in the current legal culture as a source of law, albeit secondary, and the role of the single precedent on a particular issue. The sources of law are ranked in the following order: constitution (including constitutional principles), European law, statutes (including statutory principles), precedents.

Precedent cannot be compared with codes, statutes or the constitution, in terms of superiority or inferiority, because precedents are not binding, but their relative authority can only derive from that of the formal source of law, which the precedent applies and interprets. In that respect, the role of precedents in the French system can be considered either very small or very important, according to whether one looks at the justificatory material that is cited or to the material that is in fact used by the courts. The courts very rarely cite precedents and must not base their decisions on them, because the only legitimate source of law consists of statutes. On the contrary, if one looks at the material that is in fact used, one realizes that precedents are the most important. One could even say that other materials are relevant only to the extent that they have been mentioned and interpreted by precedent – at least for lower courts and courts of appeal. The Civil Code itself only plays a role through the interpretation that has been given by a precedent. One famous example is that of Article 1384 of the Civil Code, stating that one is liable for damages caused by 'things that one has to guard'. This provision was very rarely used by the courts until the Court of Cassation decided that these 'things' meant machines which caused injuries to factory workers, thus making the proprietor, the 'guardian' of the machine, liable for these injuries. Hence Article 1384 became one of the main bases of the law of torts. The same can be said a fortiori for principles or academic writings. They have no authority per se, but only to the extent that they are embodied in precedents. This can be explained simply by the hierarchy of the courts. The decision of a lower court will be confirmed if it applies statutes or principles as they have been interpreted by the precedent of a higher court. The highest courts, however, are not in any way bound by precedents, not even by their own, so that they can be cited, not for their value per se, but only for the value of the interpretive arguments or of the principles that they embody.

8   Role of Precedent in Different Branches of Law

The differences rest not so much in the role of precedent as in the manner in which precedents are created and the way in which each branch of law is systematized and represented.

It is generally said that French administrative law is mainly based on precedents. This does not mean that there are not any statutes regulating the activity of public administration. On the contrary, there is an enormous number of statutes. But they do not form a systematic body of rules, as in a code, and they do not state general principles. Therefore a systematic exposition of administrative law can only be made by stating the principles that are expressed in the decisions of the Conseil d'Etat. Conversely, one says that civil law is mainly statutory, because it is expressed in the Civil Code yet, as mentioned, the provisions of the code are constantly interpreted by the decisions of the Court of Cassation.

Thus one could say that, in both cases, the role of precedent is capital. The difference is mainly ideological: the Court of Cassation is seen as transparent, its jurisprudence being considered as an interpretation in the classical meaning of the word, viz. a revelation of the meaning of the statute. On the basis of that conception, it can be said that the only source is the statute, as interpreted by the court. In the case of the Conseil d'Etat, on the contrary, it is impossible, in the context of French legal culture, to admit that the principles expressed in the 'jurisprudence' exist in the same way that statutes exist and are only 'revealed' by the courts. Even if the Conseil d'Etat itself sticks to that terminology, scholars have for a long time accepted the idea that these principles have been created and not discovered or revealed.

On the other hand, any scholarly treatise on civil law can at least approximately follow the order of the code, whereas a treatise on administrative law will be divided according to the great principles shaped by the Conseil d'Etat. Constitutional law is an intermediate case. On the one hand, the Conseil Constitutionnel is a relatively recent institution and it has not been given the power to establish new principles, but only to apply the constitution. In that respect it resembles the Court of Cassation, because its decisions are presented, not as the creation of new principles, but as the interpretation of the text of the constitution. But, on the other hand, the text of the constitution is extremely vague, so that it is impossible to write a treatise of constitutional law without using the concepts, the principles and the distinctions of the Conseil Constitutionnel.

One example can be taken from the 1971 decision already mentioned. The Conseil Constitutionnel decided that reviewing the constitutionality of statutes amounted to reviewing their conformity not only to the numbered articles of the constitution, as was done previously, but also to the preamble. The preamble of the Constitution of 1958 refers to the Declaration of the Rights of Man of 1789 and also to the preamble of the previous constitution of 1946. Now the latter mentions the 'fundamental principles recognized by the laws of the Republic', without listing those principles. The Conseil Constitutionnel therefore is empowered, on the basis of its own interpretation of the constitution, to list and define the fundamental principles. But, so far, when the constitutional court has mentioned one of the principles, it has not done so without citing the particular statutes previously recognizing the principle. It follows that, although the description of French constitutional law is nothing but the 'jurisprudence' of the Conseil Constitutionnel, it is still possible to defend the ideological thesis that, much as the Court of Cassation applies the code, the Conseil Constitutionnel has applied the text of the preamble and expressed principles that were enacted before it by the legislature. But it remains true that in fact the Conseil Constitutionnel has, as the Conseil d'Etat has, complete discretion to determine what these principles are.

9   Precedent and 'Gaps in the Law'

As mentioned above, courts never expressly acknowledge that they create precedents. Precedents always appear as the expression of a previously existing rule, be it a statute or a principle, 'valid even in the absence of a legal text' (v. arrêt Arramu oct. 1945). The reason is that the court decision is only supposed to reveal the 'true' meaning of the statute or the previous existence of a principle. The ideological assumption is that the legal system is complete. Nevertheless, one can speak of a precedent when there is a new interpretation of a statute or the revelation of a new principle.

The legal community will be aware that a new precedent has been created, either because the decision has been rendered in a particularly solemn form (*assemblée pleinière de la Cour de Cassation* or *assemblée générale du Conseil d'Etat*) or because scholars, analysing the *ratio decidendi*, find that (1) a lacuna has been filled, (2) a new interpretation of some legal text has been provided, (3) that some new principle has been constructed or (4) that a previous line of decisions has been overruled (revirement de jurisprudence).

II   The Bindingness of Precedent

1   Kinds and Degrees of Normative Force

(1)   There is no formal bindingness of previous judicial decisions in France. One might even argue that there is an opposite rule: that it is forbidden to follow a precedent only because it is a precedent. One can understand the rule of formally binding precedent as meaning 'a court decision that does not treat an applicable precedent as binding is void and will be reversed on appeal'. The French system, on the contrary, contains a rule: 'a court decision that treats a precedent as binding is void'. This rule is expressed by Article 455 of the Code of Civil Procedure, which reads: 'The judgment must describe briefly the claims of the parties and their arguments; It must be motivated.' This provision only binds the courts in the judicial hierarchy, but the law binding on courts in the administrative hierarchy is similar in substance. This is the reason why any judicial decision making exclusive reference to a precedent, even that of the Court of Cassation, is considered not motivated and therefore illegal, because it violates Article 455 of the Code of Civil Procedure (Cass. civ. II, 4 mai 1961, Bull. civ. II, n. 314; Cass. com. 13 avril 1964: Bull. civ. III, n. 179). In the same manner, it is illegal if it mentions 'jurisprudence' or judge-made law, without examining the specificity of the case (Cass. civ. III, 6 février 1969, Bull. civ. III, n. 119).

Two possibly exceptional types of cases must be analysed. The first is procedural and occurs very rarely: once the Court of Cassation has invalidated the decision of a Court of Appeal, the case is sent to a second Court of Appeal. If the latter decides in the same manner as the first Court of Appeal, and if the case is brought once more to the Court of Cassation, on the basis of the same arguments, the Court of Cassation will decide the case finally in a plenary assembly. If the case is then sent to a third Court of Appeal, that court is under obligation to follow the decision made by the highest court. Only in this special context may one speak about the 'formal' or 'strict' bindingness of precedent, but still in an improper way, because we have not a new case, similar to a previous one, but one decision that must be followed by the Court of Appeal in the same case. Therefore the decision by the Court of Cassation is not a real precedent, but a directive given by one court to a lower one.

The justification for this legal mechanism lies in the distinction, very important in French legal culture, between facts and law. The Court of Cassation has been established for one purpose only: to make sure that the law, viz. statutes, is correctly and uniformly applied by the courts. Therefore what is brought before the Court of Cassation is not the claims of the parties, but only the decision of the Court of Appeal. Once it has decided that this decision is illegal, a new decision correctly applying the law can only be taken by a new Court of Appeal, having full jurisdiction: that is, not only in regard to the legal issue, but also in regard to the facts. But the Court of Cassation has no jurisdiction to decide on the facts of the case or to give an order to the parties.

The second type of case arises under Article 62 of the constitution: 'The decisions of the Constitutional Council shall not be subject to review. They are binding on governmental, administrative and judicial authorities.' This provision may be interpreted in two ways. Some scholars write, that because of Article 62, precedents from the Conseil Constitutionnel are formally binding on other courts. This interpretation is based on the attitude of the Conseil Constitutionnel itself which states that its decisions enjoy the authority of *res judicata* and, moreover, that this authority extends, not only to the *dispositif*, but also to the *motifs* (Decision 62-18 L 16.1.1962, GDCC, p.158 and 92-312 DC 2.09.92, Rec. p.76). Moreover, when a statute has been declared constitutional on the condition that it be interpreted in a specific way, other courts, when applying that statute, are bound to follow the Council's interpretation. (DC 69-58 L 24.10.1969, Rec. p.34 and TA Dijon, 12.07.1988, *Abdekader*, RFDA, 1989, p.155).

Nevertheless, one should not confuse *res judicata*, which is only relative to the issues decided, in this case the validity and sense of the statute, on the one hand, with the authority of precedents, on the other. The latter is not relative to the particular issues decided but to a class of strongly analogous decisions. If the Conseil Constitutionnel has decided that a statute must be interpreted in a certain way, in order to be constitutional, other courts must indeed interpret the statute in the way prescribed. But, in doing so, they do not follow any precedent because they do not deal with another statute of the same class or follow interpretive methods established by the Conseil Constitutionnel. What they do is merely apply a judicial decision in the precise situation described by the Council. Any other distinction between several species of formal bindingness is irrelevant.

(2) Precedents, without being formally binding, may have force if created by a court superior to that where the case is pending. This simply reflects the hierarchical structure of the courts. A lower court is conscious of the fact that, in disregarding a precedent emanating from another court, it runs the risk of being reversed. Therefore, if 'defeasible' means that a precedent can be overruled only when it is affected by certain specific flaws, predetermined by a formal rule, one cannot speak of defeasible force since precedents are never formally binding. They have always only outweighable force.

(3) Precedents, without being formally binding and without having force, can in some cases provide further support either for an interpretive decision or for some substantive decision. For example, courts may follow their own precedents or precedents of other courts of the same level, or even of a lower level whenever not following them would mean not treating like cases alike. Thus the amount of damages given in liability cases is published in tables for every Court of Appeal. There is no obligation to follow them and no risk of being overruled. Yet, in spite of the fact that the court will always justify its decision by the statement of the rule applied in the case, this is merely a matter of practice.

(4) In some cases, precedents will be used as illustrative legal arguments for the *ratio decidendi* of the pending case either by analogy or *a contrario*.

The general principle at the basis of the French legal system, deriving from the French interpretation of the separation of powers, is that statutes are the only source of law. This principle was formerly established by the law of 16–24 August 1790, forbidding the courts to make rules or interfere with legislation. This principle has two consequences: the first is a prohibition on courts enacting general rules, which was stated first at the beginning of the French Revolution (loi des 16–24 août 1790) and again in Article 5 of the Civil Code (1804): 'it is prohibited for judges to decide by way of general provisions and rules on the cases that are brought before them'.

The second consequence is a prohibition against applying any rule other than a statutory one. This is the reason why, according to a

prevailing interpretation of Article 455 of the Code of Civil Procedure, a court decision only applying a precedent is not considered
sufficiently motivated. Applying a precedent is considered essentially different from applying the law (Cass. civ. II, 4 mai 1961, Bull.
civ. II, n. 314; Cass. com. 13 avril 1964: Bull. civ. III, n. 179). The
application of this Article extends beyond private law, and is considered a general principle of the French legal system.

Nevertheless, while this is true de jure, it is generally understood,
not only that it is possible for courts to follow precedents, but that
there is a de facto obligation to do so, which simply derives from the
hierarchy of courts already mentioned above. Because a lower court's
decision can be overturned if it contradicts the mode of interpretation
and application of the statute established by the Court of Cassation, it
will be bound to follow it (Van de Kerchove, 1985, p.232).

The expression 'de facto obligation' could be seen as a *contradictio
in adjecto*. We can understand it in the following way. That a precedent is formally binding usually means (1) that there is a formal
rule requiring courts to follow precedents and (2) that, if the court
does not comply with this formal rule, its decisions ought to be
reversed. In the French legal system, no such formal rule exists but, if
a court does not follow a precedent, its decision ought still to be
reversed.

Therefore one should distinguish between factual and normative
constraints. Normative constraints are those constraints that result,
not from norms themselves, but from the normative system and from
behaviour according to norms. One example is the birth of government responsibility. Originally, there was no formal norm prescribing
the cabinet to resign at the request of a parliamentary majority. Nevertheless, there were norms enabling the majority to impeach ministers
or to refuse to adopt the budget, thus forcing the cabinet to resign
and creating the general feeling that, when the majority requires it,
the cabinet ought to resign. This type of normative constraints we
can call 'de facto bindingness'.

A de facto obligation can be partly formalized as with Article 604
of the new Code of Civil Procedure, which reads: 'the purpose of the
pourvoi en cassation is to let the Court of Cassation sanction the non-
conformity of the attacked decision with legal rules'. This is a
significant evolution from the previous theory, formed at the time of
the Revolution, which accepted only one motive for the invalidation
of a judgment by the Tribunal of Cassation, namely the violation of a
statute (*loi*). From now on, the 'law' is not only the statute, but the
statute as interpreted and applied by the courts, that is in conjunction with precedents. To use the term 'legal rule' instead of *loi* means
that one accepts the idea that there can be a creation of legal rules by
way of precedents.

Today, French scholars recognize the fact that 'jurisprudence' is a source of law and therefore that a reversal inflicted by a higher court on a lower court's decision can be based on the violation by the latter of a rule based on precedent. Lawyers looking for a substantive rule will obviously today not be content with statutes, but will have to look for precedents.

The same can be said of Administrative law, where the basic principle, namely that the only source of law is the statute, was the same principle of legality and where the hierarchy enabled the highest court to impose its mode of interpretation and application of statutes. Nevertheless, because the number and scope of statutes regarding administrative activities were extremely restricted and not codified, the Conseil d'Etat, still pretending to apply statutes, had to produce the vast majority of substantive rules. Consequently, it is sometimes asserted that French administrative law is judge-made law, thus comparable to the common law. This is partly an exaggeration, especially because precedents cannot be cited in administrative courts any more than in the civil or criminal courts.

We can conclude by saying that the bindingness of 'precedent' in the French system is a question of normative constraints in the sense defined above, and if precedent is deemed a source of law, it is always in conjunction with statutes, which is the ultimate basis of its validity, even in the field of administrative law.

2   Law Concerning Precedent

As noted above, the provisions of Article 455 of the Code of Civil Procedure (also Article 5 of the Code Civil) have been interpreted to exclude formal bindingness of precedents. Their normative force depends on custom.

3   Factors Determining Degrees of Normative Force

Since there is no formal bindingness, the following are only factors of de facto bindingness or of normative force of precedents.

a   The hierarchical rank of the court   We have already explained the role of the hierarchy of courts in the task of the formation of precedents, and especially the role of the Court of Cassation (and of the Conseil d'Etat). It could also be said that Courts of Appeal are, in this respect, more closely bound by the jurisprudence of the Court of Cassation than Courts of First Instance are bound by Courts of Appeal. It is a well known fact that the Paris Court of Appeal follows carefully the precedents of the Court of Cassation.

As regards the lower courts (Courts of First Instance and Courts of Appeal), a first instance court acts independently and often declares that it does not fear an appeal when disregarding a precedent of the Court of Appeal above it. Yet this independence is only apparent for, according to a well-known psychological and sociological pattern, there is a considerable amount of self-restraint among lower judges regarding the higher courts. This amounts to a sort of discipline of the judges, especially vis-à-vis the Court of Cassation. This demonstrates the authority of the decisions of the court which, according to Van de Kerchove 'alone possesses a power of unification that other courts can only acquire by the repetition of identical decisions, without any guarantee of stability' (Van de Kerchove, 1985, p.259.) The same scholar adds: 'This is also what leads to the idea that the binding force of the jurisprudential rule depends on its unification through the highest court. This explains in particular the stance of the Court of Cassation towards a lower court, which bases its decision on its own precedents. The Court of Cassation will normally accept that the lower court bases its decisions on a 'jurisprudence constance' (a series of precedents of any court) or the jurisprudence of the Court of Cassation itself' (ibid.).

Some scholars go so far as to assert that this mechanism functions both ways: there is a self-restraint on the part of the receiver (the lower court) but, on the other hand, there is pedagogy on the part of the sender (the higher court). Substantive self-restraint on the part of judges thus seems to be a general principle of the production of precedents, when disciplinary sanctions are an element of constraint (Serverin, 1985, p.264).

b   Decision taken by a panel or by a full bench   French scholars make a distinction, in regard to decisions of the Court of Cassation, between leading cases where the decision states important principles (arrêts de principes) and specific decisions (arrêts d'espèces). Only the former can be considered similar to a precedent. Among the criteria currently used to classify decisions in one or the other category is the composition of the court making the decisions.

Naturally, those decisions of the Court of Cassation that have been rendered by the plenary assembly are easy to identify and label as decisions of principle, because that assembly is only convened for particularly important cases. Moreover, the Act of 3 January 1979 has increased that power of the Court of Cassation to impose a decision, since the plenary assembly can be convened as soon as the first *pourvoi*, when the case poses a question of principle, for example if there is contradiction between substantive decisions by Courts of Appeal.

It is also possible to identify decisions of principle, in a negative way. By an Act of 6 August 1981 reforming the Court of Cassation, a decision can be taken by a smaller, restricted, panel for the purpose 'of applying a permanent jurisprudence in cases the solution of which does not raise any difficulty'. It is then perfectly clear that the decision rendered is not a precedent, but only a specific decision. Therefore the decision to give the case to the smaller panel can be interpreted as the will of the Court of Cassation to stick to its jurisprudence and not to create a new precedent. But the Court of Cassation can also make decisions of principle in a normal panel and, in that case, it is only the substance or a more imposing style that enables one to classify them as precedents.

In the same way, a decision taken by the Conseil d'Etat as a whole (arrêt d'assemblée) has more force than a decision taken by a subsection.

c   The reputation of the court   In France the reputation of the court is proportional to its hierarchical rank. This fact is tied to the manner of recruitment of judges, and their career progress, from lower to higher courts. On the other hand, the Court of Appeal of Paris has a special prestige, higher than the other courts of the same rank. One may observe the tentative development of the original 'jurisprudence' of some Courts of Appeal, achieving some special reputation (the Court of Aix-en-Provence, for example), but, as was said previously, the Court of Cassation does not formally recognize it.

d   Changes in the political, economic and social background   It is often the case that change is used as an argument to support the idea that the force of a precedent has been weakened or even lost. The type of change used in that way can be economic, social or technological.

Political change affects the force of precedents in the following way. Since the basic principle is the pre-eminence of statutory law, statutes are interpreted according to the hypothetical will of the present law giver, because the latter has always the power to overrule precedents by the passing of a new statute. This submission to the present law giver does not normally take place when there is a mere change of majority in parliament, but only in case of a radical political change in the history of the country, such as at the end of the Vichy regime. On those occasions, precedents established during the earlier period can be disregarded by lower courts.

e   Soundness of the supporting arguments in the opinion   Regarding the soundness or the quality of the court's opinion as a possible factor of its bindingness, several distinctions should be made and several difficulties underlined. A concrete decision can become a precedent by way of two different mechanisms. First, a decision may be the first interpretation of a new statute, so that it does not matter what court it comes from. Second, the decision may be an interpretation by the Court of Cassation (whether the statutory text is ancient or new). In that case, the argument from authority plays an important role, especially when the decision has been issued by the plenary assembly.

Thus the quality of arguments can help in identifying a judgment as a precedent. It is often said that a rejection of the appeal concerns only the plaintiff, but that a decision to invalidate is aimed at the lower court's decision. There are thus more precedents in decisions to invalidate than in decisions to confirm. French scholars also discover precedents by deciphering decisions, as will be discussed below.

f   Age of precedent   There is some tension between, on the one hand, the force of an ancient precedent, because it has been constantly applied over a long period of time, and, on the other hand, the idea that an old precedent which has not been frequently applied since it was established lacks force. In the latter case, a more recent one is better adapted to present circumstances. Thus one author writes that 'a precedent has not an unlimited lifetime; its influence decreases with time and this is the reason why there is from time to time a new decision, that shows that the rule is still in force. Past and future are thus united in the jurisprudential rule. The norm is made up of all judgments, which crystallize in it. Yet it can be changed' (Saluden, 1985, p.197).

g   The presence or absence of dissent   There are no dissenting opinions in the French system.

h   The branch of law involved   We cannot say that the weight of decision as precedent depends upon the character of the branch of law involved. All we can observe is some specific importance of precedents in French administrative law, explained above by the historical reasons of its case law formation.

i   Whether the precedent represents a trend   The fact that the decision represents a trend is an important factor of its bindingness as precedent. We have already mentioned the fact that the character of being a precedent depends to a certain extent on the adherence of lower courts. This can be seen most clearly when a new statute is promulgated, for, in that case, the Court of Cassation often waits to be enlightened by the decisions of the Courts of Appeal, before deciding between various possible interpretations of the new text. It is the Court of Cassation that will follow a trend revealed or set by the lower courts.

Naturally, courts making use of precedents do not use that word, but mention a 'persisting jurisprudence' (*jurisprudence constante*), not-

withstanding the fact that one single decision of the Court of Cassation can be considered persisting jurisprudence. This is what leads
many scholars to write that a jurisprudential rule can arise from one
decision by the Court of Cassation. The Court of Cassation itself
accepts that idea, on the condition that the lower court's decision
restates the arguments supporting the precedent and states the analogy between the facts of the precedent and the facts of the case it has
to decide. (Serverin, 1985, p.259).

But the 'trend' can also have the reverse effect: it may happen that
the Court of Appeal decides in a way contrary to what the Court of
Cassation has decided up to now: 'the resistance by the courts of
appeal can also enlighten the Court of Cassation. What might seem
to be a rebellion of the lower judge also gives the Court of Cassation
the opportunity to re-examine its position, and change the jurisprudential rule' (Saluden, 1985, p.196).

j   Acceptance in academic writings   In our view, the quality of being a
precedent does not arise only from the character of the decision
itself, but from a collection of decisions and from their interpretation
by legal dogmatics. Naturally, this classification will often depend on
the appreciation of commentators, especially of law professors, but
sometimes the attitude of practising lawyers may be more revealing,
especially that of the 'avocats à la Cour de Cassation et au Conseil
d'Etat', who hold a monopoly of representing clients before these
highest courts. This is the reason why, as a scholar writes, 'The reading of the production of the court tends to become selective, partial,
normative' (Serverin, 1985, pp.267–8).

The question of precedents being, to a large extent, as mentioned,
related to the authority of some judicial practice, this character is not
linked to a formal rule, nor even to the rank of the court. As has been
cogently stated, 'It is the interpreter, the lawyer, who will translate
into a set of prescriptions, prohibitions or permissions, the conclusion that emerges from the decision' (Serverin, 1985, p.275).

Nevertheless, one may not assert that the influence of legal dogmatics on the courts (including the Court of Cassation) is direct and
immediately operating. Rather it is a 'long-term' trend representing
the progressive penetration of the most influential ideas and dogmatic constructions in judicial practice.

k   The effect of legal change in related areas   This effect can be better
observed between fields within one branch, rather than between
branches. The new trend in this matter – after decades of mutual
isolationism – is the new and interesting question of the use by the
Conseil d'Etat of precedents emanating from the Court of Cassation.
The Conseil d'Etat is the highest court in the administrative realm,

and is not bound to apply the same rules as the Court of Cassation, and vice versa. This sometimes results in differences in the substantive law applied by the various courts. For example, unlike judicial courts under the Court of Cassation, administrative courts did not, for a long time, give compensation for moral damages. Nevertheless, there is often, after a few years, an adoption by the Conseil d'Etat of the rules set down by the Court of Cassation. This never takes the form of the citation of a precedent, however.

On the other hand, there is a growing influence of precedents of the Conseil Constitutionnel in all other branches of law, including even private law. This new phenomenon penetrates the whole French legal system, and is widely discussed nowadays in legal dogmatics.

As stated before, precedents are never binding and one can only speak of factors which deprive them of force. This is why these factors are the same as the factors which determine their force, and which were analysed in Section II.1.

One can simply add that the question of precedents being, in the French system, closely related to the actual adherence of other courts to the decisions of a given judge, the principal factor which might deprive a decision of precedential force is the refusal of these other courts to follow it. The resistance of the courts can of course be overcome by the highest court, but the procedure is long and the Court of Cassation will hesitate. The second possible reason is the 'reversals of jurisprudence' (revirements) mentioned above and which will be discussed below.

As for the influence of a distinction drawn between precedents dealing with statutory law and precedents of other kinds, this distinction is especially important in administrative law. The Conseil d'Etat asserted, in a decision considered as an important precedent, the existence of 'general principles of law valid even in absence of the legal text' (Arrêt Aramu, oct. 1945). This decision introduced formally a new kind of precedent 'revealing' principles of law, not necessarily related to the statute law. Recently, the growing 'constitutionalization' of all branches of law has resulted in the multiplication of decisions of this kind, stating new general principles of constitutional value, but 'revealed' by the courts of justice. Precedents dealing with these principles seem to carry more weight, for two reasons. The first is that precedents dealing with statutes appear as mere interpretations of the texts of the statutes. A new interpretation can always be tried and be considered acceptable, if social and economic conditions have changed or if the court wishes to conform to the intention, not of the original law maker, but to that of the present legislature. But the principles affirmed in court decisions can only be presented as being permanent and independent of social and economic circumstances as well as the intention of the law maker, so that it is more difficult to challenge them. The second reason is related to the development of judicial review. It was believed, until the Fifth Republic, that these principles rank in the hierarchy of norms above government regulations, but immediately below statutes, because a statute could always, at least in principle, change or abrogate them (Chapus, 1966, p.99). But the constitutionalization of these principles by way of precedents emanating from the Conseil Constitutionnel has changed this situation: if these principles rank among constitutional norms, they cannot be altered by the legislature, and the highest courts, especially the Conseil d'Etat, will strike down lower court decisions that depart from such precedents.

4 Factors that Weaken Precedent

In the French context, factors weakening precedent are simply the negation or absence of the factors contributing to the normative force of precedent.

5 Vertical and Horizontal Bindingness

We have already discussed the effects of the hierarchy of courts. As regards the highest courts, they have no obligation to follow their own precedent, but almost always do so in practice. This is justified by the idea that the precedent has revealed the 'true' meaning of the law, by the principle of equality before the law and by the requirement of coherence as a precondition of efficacy. By following their own precedents, the highest courts regulate the activity of the lower courts much more efficiently than if there were frequent and random overruling.

6 Analysis of Force, Support and Illustrative Role

The distinction is not used by French scholarly writings and neither these terms nor the corresponding concepts appear in the decisions. The only legislation regarding this matter is the already mentioned law about the effects of the second cassation.

7 Excess of Precedents?

This is irrelevant in the French context.

III   The Rationale of Precedent

In the French system, official rationales for treating precedents as formally binding do not exist. It seems that the most recognized rationales for treating precedent as having force or the like are, in some way contradictory: on one hand, there is a well-established general principle that statutes are the principal source of law. The use of the term 'persisting jurisprudence' makes precedents appear as interpretations of statutes and thus expresses the ideal of fidelity to statutes. Yet, in spite of the lack of binding force of precedents, some decisions use the phrase 'it has already been judged that...'. This can be explained through a distinction devised by some French scholars between the authority of *res judicata* and the authority of *res interpretata*. According to this view, the system of codified law has two different types of precedents, which could be called 'precedent of solution' and 'precedent of interpretation'. Clearly, the latter is more easily accepted in this system, where the official function of the Court of Cassation is to unify the application of statutes – and thus their interpretation – than the 'precedent of solution' because France has no binding rule of precedent. This explains why the courts never discuss the facts of prior decisions and why they generally mention, not the precedents themselves nor the authority of another court, but the substance of these precedents, that is the *ratio juris*.

In legal dogmatics, the argument which French scholars often mention in order to justify the bindingness of precedents is the necessary unification of judge-made law, reflected on an institutional level through the hierarchy of courts. Some writers also cite the principle of justice, which demands not only a solution adapted to the specificity of the case, but also equal treatment of similar cases. This is particularly important for what we call 'precedent of interpretation', because the primacy of the statute, which is a standing principle in France, also demands uniformity of interpretation (Boré, 1980, p.249).

In other words, one may speak, in this context, of the use of 'universalization' argument, which is considered very important. Scholars agree that it is even constitutive, because of the identification of 'precedent' with 'decisions of principle', decisions capable of being generalized. In the above-mentioned distinction between 'precedent of solution' and 'precedent of interpretation', this is particularly clear for the latter, because an interpretation of a statute, held to be correct for one case, is necessarily correct for a large number of cases (Bellet, 1980, p.293). Bellet speaks of the individualizing and the generalizing function of the Cour de Cassation. According to Marty, the essential character of a 'decision of principle' is its 'aptitude to generalization ... in such manner that the solution can acquire a general value by serving as precedent in solving future similar difficulties' (Marty, 1929).

Therefore it is perfectly safe to say that, in France, what is really a precedent is the formulation of a principle. The power to formulate principles can depend either on the institutional situation of the court or the quality of the decision, appearing as a particularly well-suited reading of the statute or a particularly good solution to a hard case.

The identity of 'precedent' with the 'generalizable' solution seems self-evident and even analytical; one can only call 'precedent' something that can be used in future cases and is therefore generalizable. A non-generalizable solution can only be an *'arrêt d'espèce'* (a specific decision). But the argument of generalization is, to our knowledge, not formulated as such by judges, who most often cite 'principles' or 'general principles of law'.

Some scholars also mention self-restraint on the part of lower courts and the fear of being overruled by a higher court, or a natural tendency for a court overburdened with cases to operate more rapidly by reproducing decisions or the main rulings on legal issues. Nevertheless, these are only psychological explanations and cannot be considered rationales. Moreover, they are naturally never stated in judicial opinions.

Finally, some authors explain the creation of precedents by the pedagogical disposition of higher courts toward lower ones. According to this view, the statutory law system would seem closer to the common law and would appear contrary to the idea, related to the primacy of the statute, that the Court of Cassation has a disciplinary function (Serverin, 1985, p.260). But others are critical of this theory. They think that the recognition of the legal validity of a judge-made rule is not only based on formal criteria (that the rule should emanate from an organ exercising adjudication) or empirical criteria (the existence of a unified practice of the courts), but also on axiological criteria (adaptation to the evolution of law and society, 'rightness' of the decision, capacity of the decision to provoke adherence of other courts and so on) (ibid.). Such rationales are never discussed in judicial opinions, which are written in a deductive, legalistic and magisterial form (see above).

IV   Precedents: What They Stand for and How They Apply

1   *What Counts as Binding or Having Force?*

Precedent is never officially binding. The obligation of the court is to apply, not the precedent, but the rule behind the precedent. A court will never expressly discuss a similarity of facts between the case pending and the precedent, but will necessarily take it into account before deciding that the same statute (interpreted in the same way) or the same principle applies.

Therefore, to discover what elements are binding, one must look at the reasons that a superior court will use to justify reversing a decision, if the lower court has wrongly disregarded some element in a precedent. The justification of such a decision to reverse will never be drawn from a similarity of facts, but always from a violation by the lower court of some rule or principle expressed or implicit in the precedent. It is, however, impossible to distinguish between the elements of a precedent and to isolate the rule from the facts, because of one particularity of French adjudication, *'qualification juridique des faits'*: the court decides whether the facts of the case can be subsumed under the categories of the rule. This is done by examining simultaneously the facts and the substance of the rule.

2   *Reasoning about Applicability*

There is no judicial practice of discussing arguments for or against the applicability of a precedent, because there is no judicial practice of citing or expressly referring to a specific precedent, but at the most to a continuous and permanent practice of the courts (*jurisprudence constante*). But naturally counsel and commentators do enter into such discussions. Because of the theory of qualification juridique , they can indifferently argue from the facts or from the rules.

They will argue, for example, that the facts are different and cannot be subsumed under the category, so that the rule does not apply to the case. Or, conversely, they can argue that the meaning of the rule, particularly the words used in the formulation of the rule in the precedent, have a meaning which prevents applying that rule to the facts of the case. This is the reason why scholarly writings often take the form of a long list of cases deciding which qualification juridique was given.

It sometimes happens that counsel or scholars refer to substantive reasons in a precedent to argue that these reasons do not apply to the case at hand. They may try to demonstrate that application would lead to absurd or socially undesirable consequences. It is impossible to tell what the effect of this type of argument can be, but no court will discuss it in its decision and it will usually not be mentioned in the opinion, with a notable exception. The substantive reasons may be part of the rule. This is the case in administrative law, when the rule empowers an authority to make a decision, if the advantages are greater than the costs. In such cases, a court will have to follow precedents in three different ways:

1 as the empowering rule itself has been formulated not by statute, but, expressly, by the Conseil d'Etat, the lower court will apply the precedent according to the following pattern, that is, argument from rules;
2 the lower court must balance advantages and costs for the case at hand (substantive reasons);
3 as the Conseil d'Etat itself has applied the rule and decided, for example, that the taking of a particular parcel of land has advantages greater than the costs, the lower court must analyse the facts of the case at hand to weigh advantages against costs in the same manner as the Conseil d'Etat (factual analysis). (Jurisprudence, 'Lille ville nouvelle est'.)

3 Juristic Discussion

A precedent is binding to the extent that a decision by a lower court contrary to a precedent by a superior court can be reversed by that superior court. But, as already mentioned, French courts have no obligation to follow a precedent as such, but only to the extent that it is considered by the superior courts as the 'correct' application of a rule. What the precedent stands for is the rule. But the rule is not always expressly stated, the decision appears as particular and not general and the authority of *res judicata* is only relative to the parties (Article 1351 of the Civil Code). The function of constructing a large number of precedents into a coherent system is, in the French tradition, performed by legal scholars, collectively referred to as 'la doctrine' (Zenati, 1991). This is mainly done by law professors and the role of the doctrine is sometimes said to be analogous to codification. Because these writings often have an evaluative and prescriptive dimension, they may have an influence on the courts and even on the law giver. It is sometimes the case, for example, that a commentator reveals that a series of precedents is based on a principle that was expressed in the decision, and of which the courts themselves had been unaware. After the publication of the commentary, the principle is officially ratified and expressed in court decisions. Thus the concept of the public service as the fundamental principle of administrative law and the autonomy of the will as the fundamental principle of civil law is the result of such constructions. This is the reason why the 'doctrine' is sometimes called a 'source of law'.

While the commentaries on precedents are written in law journals by scholars, because of the brevity of the decisions, a similar task must be performed by every jurist when reading a case. One of the main types of exercise practised in law schools is the writing of commentaries. The form of these academic commentaries is standardized: they first state the facts of the case, then the legal issue, thirdly the legal ruling and fourthly the principle on which the decision is based.

Since this type of exercise has been practised by many generations of lawyers, it is the subject of textbooks, but there is no discussion of the methods used in the commentaries. (See, for example, Mendegris and Vermelle, 1995.)

4   *Illustrative or Analogical Precedent*

It follows from all that has been said that all precedents in France merely illustrate legal principles or work as analogies. There is no contrast between illustrative or analogical precedents and other precedents.

5   *Single Precedents or Lines of Decision?*

As far as bindingness is concerned, such a distinction cannot be made in the French system, because no precedent is formally binding. What is binding is the obligation to follow the principle or the rule on which the precedent is based, and it is therefore of no importance that the principle is applied in a long line of precedents or in a single precedent.

In spite of the fact that a new principle or rule can be formulated in a single precedent, courts as well as scholars tend to recognize the existence of that rule and the character of '*arrêt de principe*' of the precedent when it has been followed by a line of others. To that extent, the line of precedents plays the role of an implicit confirmation of a single decision. It can also happen that, in the first decision, the rule or principle is not explicitly stated, and therefore it will be only clearly be expressed in subsequent decisions, thus giving the impression that a long line of precedents is necessary to implicitly confirm the first.

Because of the technique of deciding on the *qualification juridique des faits*, it is often the case that the judge gives successive qualifications, not actually conflicting, but without any apparent coherence. It is then the function of scholars and also of the reporting judge to reinterpret a long line of cases and show that they all follow a common trend.

In fact, the idea that 'jurisprudence' in the French sense can only result from a long line of precedents is an ideological construction which, in a democratic system, justifies the creation of general norms by an authority different from parliament, an authority, moreover, which is expressly denied that power by Article 5 of the Civil Code. By stressing that a great number of precedents are necessary to create a 'jurisprudence', scholars make it a subcategory of a legal custom (Zenati, 1991, p.103).

But if the authority of a precedent derives mainly from the hierarchical position of the Court of Cassation or the Conseil d'Etat, a single precedent can suffice. It is often said that one decision, *'fait jurisprudence'*, establishes a principle that is binding. On the other hand, even a long line of precedents can be overruled by a single decision of the highest court.

6   The Concept of a 'Leading Case'

As already mentioned, among decisions of the Court of Cassation, commentators distinguish between decisions of principle and specific decisions (arrêts d'espèces). Only in the case of the 'arrêt de principe' do French scholars speak of the jurisprudential activity of the Court of Cassation. Marty defines this as 'every intervention of the Court of Cassation susceptible of serving as precedent for the ruling of similar difficulties in the future' (Marty, 1929, p.256). Other scholars are of the opinion that this activity takes place whenever the Court of Cassation poses a rule regarding a new or controversial matter. On the other hand, an 'arrêt d'espèce' only gives a concrete solution, without any bearing on future decisions.

Naturally, the difficulty is to indicate clearly which, among the decisions of the Court of Cassation (and the same is true of the Conseil d'Etat), must be considered decisions of principle and which specific decisions. Their 'bindingness as precedent' is precisely the problematic question discussed by scholars, and French dogmatics uses the expression 'evaluation of the positivity of jurisprudential rule' to describe the degree of their bindingness. This character does not emerge from the text of the decision. 'It is the interpreter, the lawyer, who will translate it into a set of prescriptions, prohibitions or permissions, a conclusion that emerges from the decision' (Serverin, 1985, p.275). Sometimes the behaviour of the practising lawyer will be enlightening, particularly that of the avocats aux Conseils, who in France have a legal monopoly to bring appeals to the supreme courts.

There are several ways in which to identify a case having the character of a precedent. There is a saying to the effect that 'a rejection of the appeal only concerns the plaintiff, while a cassation concerns the ruling'. This means that it is easier to find precedents in decisions of cassation than in decisions which reject the appeal. One can also consider that the Court of Cassation acts as a disciplinary court every time it upholds its own precedents.

French scholars decipher the linguistic style in which the opinion has been written, to see if it can be considered as a precedent:

> Arguments [justifying a decision of cassation] which are mostly formal (for example, if the appealed decision has refrained from answering

the arguments of the parties; or if it is not sufficiently justified) are considered to be a purely disciplinary means of control of the appealed decision. On the contrary, the lack of legal base and the erroneous qualification are considered to produce rules, to the extent that they are at the border of law and fact. The argument of erroneous interpretation (or application) of the law forces the Cour of Cassation to take sides on the interpretation to be given to a text, and constrains it therefore to give to the concept in question a more elaborate legal definition... . The reunion of these signs enables the lawyer to assert the existence of a ruling within a decision and therefore to distinguish 'important' cases, which create a general principle, from specific decisions (arrêts d'espèces). The reading of the jurisprudence of the Court of Cassation tends to become selective, partial, normative...'). (Ibid. p. 276–7)

This means that the character of a precedent is not implied by the character of the decision of the court, but follows both from the decisions themselves and from their interpretation in legal dogmatics.

V   Distinguishing, Explaining, Modifying, Overruling

1   *Distinguishing*

It seems that this practice is necessary only in a system where courts have an obligation to follow a precedent and must therefore give a justification when they do not follow it. In the French system, this obligation does not exist as such and the courts in their decisions do not distinguish any more than they cite precedents. However, in the reasoning that leads to the decision, the argument that a precedent is applicable to the case will normally be discussed by the parties and the court will take it into account.

2   *Juristic Commentary*

Commentaries in law journals are constructed to discuss points of difference between precedents in order to explain and justify a particular decision. Commentators will stress that the difference in the facts justifies a decision different from some arguably applicable precedent.

3   *Excessive Distinguishing?*

This practice exists, not in the courts, but in scholarly commentaries. In fact, it is a typical academic exercise to reinterpret leading cases of the past, in order to show that their 'real' *ratio decidendi* was different from that which everyone believed, so that the application of the precedent to a new case, or to a hypothetical one, would lead to a given result. For example, professors of administrative law have been discussing for generations the existence of a simple criterion that could explain the allocation of cases to one or the other order of courts judicial or administrative. Some scholars hold that administrative courts have jurisdiction over all cases related to the public service (service public) even if the public service is run by private persons. Another group of scholars teaches that only cases involving the exercise of a power, essentially different from the power of private persons (puissance publique) fall under the competence of administrative courts. In order to prove their respective theories, scholars currently interpret whole lines of cases from a sometimes very ancient past, to show that the criterion of the service public or that of puissance publique has always been the real criterion used by the courts in deciding on their jurisdiction.

4   Types of Overruling

There are no special courts with power to overrule precedents and no special procedures because no precedents are officially recognized as binding. Since precedents are a matter of practice and since it is mainly the Court of Cassation, because of its hierarchical position, that establishes precedents, the problem is when and how does the Court of Cassation overrule its own precedents? Overruling is very hard to identify, because neither the precedent nor the decision to overrule are mentioned in the opinion. It is often an object of debate between scholars whether a particular decision has in fact overruled a precedent.

There are some departures from precedents by legislation, which we shall conventionally not call 'overruling' and which will be discussed in V.7 below.

5   Prospective Overruling

No prospective overruling is conceivable in the French system, because it would amount to the statement of a general rule applicable to future cases, a practice that would be considered a violation of Article 5 of the Civil Code: 'it is prohibited for judges to decide by way of general provisions and rules on the cases that are brought before them'. This provision derives from the French interpretation of the separation of powers, forbidding judges to make law. Its aim was to prohibit the practice of the highest courts of the Ancien Régime which had power to enact general rules. It was expressed first in a statute enacted at the beginning of the French Revolution, on 16–24 August 1790 before being restated by Article 5 of the Civil Code (1804). Nowadays, Article 5 is viewed as a general principle binding for every kind of court. In tort law, for example, the French system considers that all decisions – all case law – are really derived from three provisions of the civil code.

Nevertheless, it often happens that scholars, in commenting on important decisions of the highest courts, are able to foresee some possible overruling. They can do this because they notice a trend in 'jurisprudence' from which they can extrapolate a prospective over-ruling. In this task they are helped by the opinions of reporting judges and by the annual report of the Court of Cassation.

6   Anticipatory Overruling by Lower Courts

Anticipatory overruling by lower courts is obviously permitted, since no precedent is officially binding and in practice they are very frequent. This can be explained by the very hierarchy of the courts and the procedure before the Court of Cassation. The highest court is not, in principle, a third degree of appeal and *a pourvoi* can only be made because there is a legal issue and never on a purely factual issue. The Court of Cassation will therefore only deal with cases where it is argued that a Court of Appeal has violated the law. Frequently, that violation is conscious and deliberate, because the lower courts make an attempt to change the rule, by disregarding a precedent of the Court of Cassation, with the hope that the highest court will overrule its own precedent. ('Lower courts' here includes the trial courts of general jurisdiction.)

This can also be explained by social and political factors. French judges are trained in the Ecole Nationale de la Magistrature after they graduate from law school. They start their career at a very young age on lower courts and receive promotions to higher courts when they have more experience. The younger judges, sitting on the lower courts, belong in higher proportions to trade unions. These unions take positions on important legal issues and encourage their members to make certain types of decisions, sometimes by attempting to change precedents.

7   Precedent and Legislative Practice

One characteristic of the French system must be stressed here: one of the most frequent justifications for the power of the courts to produce general norms is the tacit consent of the legislature, because it is in principle always possible to pass a statute to overrule judge-made law. This is the reason why the Court of Cassation and the Conseil d'Etat write an annual report, outlining their most important decisions and sometimes suggesting new legislation. It sometimes happens that the Court of Cassation, in its annual report, regrets its own decision and explains it by the existence of statutes, which it had to apply, thus calling for statutory reform. In fact new legislation is very frequently presented as a necessity, because case law is not satisfactory. Sometimes the courts use a particular strategy to incite the legislature to enact new statutes by making radical decisions, showing undesirable and secondary effects (perverse effects) of the statute in force.

The intervention of the legislature can in fact occur for two symmetrically different purposes, either to confirm or to overrule a precedent:

(a)   Sometimes, the legislature enacts a statute that confirms a precedent. (Cass. 21.7.82 (Bull.II, n°111) and loi du 5 janvier 1985, cf. Jobard-Bachellier and Bachellier, 1994.) One example is that of a precedent regarding the interpretation of Article 1384 of the Civil Code. Until 1982, the Court of Cassation interpreted Article 1384 of the Civil Code as allowing a tortfeasor to claim *partial* exoneration of liability whenever the victim was negligent. In 1982, a precedent decided that no partial exoneration was possible, but only a total exoneration when the negligence of the victim had been unforeseeable and irresistible. A law of 1985 simply confirms this principle. We can think of five explanations for this kind of attitude. First of all, the legislature may fear that lower courts will resist or will be slow in following the precedent. Secondly, the statute is binding on all courts and all court systems and not only on the court system in which the precedent has been issued. Thirdly, some drafters of the bill may wish to appear as the true inventors of the policy involved in the rule. Fourthly, when it is not clear whether the rule involved in the precedent extends to another subject matter, the legislature may wish to extend it explicitly, so that there is no need to wait for new cases. Fifthly, if new systematic legislation is enacted, it will necessarily take into account the rules established by the court and reproduce their substance.

(b)   More often, the legislature enacts a statute to depart from the precedent. It sometimes happens that the courts resist this new legislation, by way of a new precedent. Thus the Tribunal des Conflits, a mixed court deciding conflicts of jurisdiction between the administrative and the judicial order, gave what was considered an interpretation *contra legem* of a 1933 statute, and decided that not judicial but administrative courts have jurisdiction when the victim of arbitrary arrest and detention seeks damages from the state and when the arbitrary arrest has taken place under exceptional circumstances (T.C. 27 mars 1952, Dame de la Murette, Rec. 626, D./1954.291, note Eisenmann). After this decision had been criticized by legal scholars, parliament adopted a more liberal statute: in every case where someone's personal liberty had been attacked, only judicial courts have jurisdiction (Article 136 du code de procédure pénale, modifié par la loi du 31 décembre 1957). Nevertheless, both the Conseil d'Etat and the Tribunal des Conflits gave very strict interpretation to this law and decided that judicial courts have no jurisdiction to decide on the validity or the meaning of the administrative acts which had led to arbitrary arrest (T.C. 16 nov. 1964, Clément, Rec. 796, D. 1965.668, note Demichel).

It even happens that the Court of Cassation departs from its own precedent when that precedent has been confirmed by a statute. In the case cited above of the law of 1985, the Court of Cassation decided two years after the law that a partial exoneration was possible, thus overruling its own precedent of 1982 and restating a precedent of 1976.

8   Conflicts of Precedents

The role of the Court of Cassation is to unify the jurisprudence of the courts, which means precisely the solution of conflicts. In that case, we will normally find a leading case. The same is true for the Conseil d'Etat in the administrative order. In the event of a conflict of precedents between the two jurisdictional orders, the Tribunal des Conflits is competent to find a solution. More difficult is the case of conflicting decisions in the same court. This can happen first between two sections (chambres) of the Court of Cassation (14.3.1984, Cass. 2è ch.civile, n°49, et 5.11 85, Cass. Comm. n° 260, cité par Jobard-Bachellier and Bachellier, 1994, p.114). Solutions can be found either by a mixed section or by a plenary assembly summoned by the president of the court. But this does not necessary mean that the conflicting sections will follow the decision of the plenary assembly (Cass. civ. 1, of 8 déc. 1987, Bull. I. 342 did not follow, but another section did : 21.1.1987, Cass. civ. II, Bull. II, n°23).

Finally, the worst contradiction is that between two decisions of the same court or same section of the court (Cass. civ. I, 24 fév. 1987 and 24 nov. 1987, interpreting Article 832 of the Civil Code; cf. Jobard-Bachellier and Bachellier, 1994, p.115). This is only explicable according to scholars by the overload of the court, which is deeply regretted, but without any solution, institutional or doctrinal.

9   Hypothetical Cases

The style of French court decisions and of their justification forbids judges to envisage hypothetical cases when reasoning about precedents. As mentioned previously, this style is very concise, magisterial and legalistic. It does not leave room for a detailed and elaborate justification.

The use of hypothetical cases is no doubt frequent with scholars commenting on court decisions or lawyers. A scholar, for instance, will often use a *reductio ad absurdum* argument, when commenting on a court decision, in order to prove that the decision would be unsuitable for similar cases and would lead to unacceptable or irrational consequences. On the other hand, if he approves of the decision, he will try to prove that it can be generalized to similar cases, even hypothetical ones. But this type of reasoning is not limited to precedents and can be applied to a decision applying a statute.

The same is true for lawyers' reasoning: they also can use this type of argument, in order to criticize the reasoning of their opponents. Whenever they are confronted with a rule – be it written or precedent – which is not in favour of their client, they will naturally try to show that it does not apply to the case. Again, we find here nothing specific about precedents. This type of reasoning, both in its general hypothetical form and in the particular form of a *reductio ad absurdum*, is one of the topical forms of legal argumentation.

VI   Matters of General Perspective, Evaluation and Other

1   'Saying and Doing'

There is a very big gap between saying and doing in the French system, at least in its official legalistic version, which still does not admit the real justificatory role of precedents, yet accepts the role of precedent in developing the content of judicial decisions and the law.

The method of the Court of Cassation is significant in this respect. In order to reach its real goal, adherence of lower courts to new solutions, the court imposes its jurisprudential views. Once it has established a principle, it never ceases making it more and more sophisticated from case to case. The principle is thus stabilized, then exceptions and distinctions are made that determine its scope. This method is described by scholars as that of proceeding by 'small paces' (Saluden, 1985, p.197).

In this manner, the fiction of the exclusivity of the statute as source of law is preserved and, at the same time, the unification and stability of judicial activity are secured, for a precedent is very rarely an isolated decision. It is the result of an evolution. (See Breton, 1975, p.26: 'Once the principle has been accepted, the Cour de Cassation will proceed by way of continuous formulation of rules, related together and gradually forming a coherent system. This is what practising lawyers call the method of small paces.') This method therefore consists mainly in the formulation of a generalizable principle, flexible enough to allow adaptations to a large number of specific cases. But by means of a fiction, it is still affirmed (officially), that this principle is stated in the positive, written statute.

2   Recent Change or Evolution

One can definitely say that the proportion of judge-made law has increased in this century, in spite of and perhaps because of the fact that the absolute number of statutes has also increased. This can be explained by several factors. Firstly, the large number of statutes, often badly written, leads to interpretational difficulties which have to be decided by way of precedents. Secondly, the growing complexity of economic and social policies has led the law maker to leave a large amount of discretion to administrative authorities and government agencies. Courts exercise control over the exercise of these discretionary powers. They set limits and establish rules by way of precedents. Thirdly, in many fields, the pace of new legislation cannot keep up with social needs, thus generating a feeling that there are gaps in the law to be filled by precedents. Fourthly, the development of judicial review has had a great influence. The Conseil Constitutionnel has established precedents which have to be taken into account by the other courts and cannot be challenged by the legislature. Fifthly, because of the new role of the Conseil Constitutionnel, partly because of better knowledge of the role and prestige of courts in other countries, partly because of changes in the international, especially European, environment, judges are gradually changing their views about the nature of adjudication.

3   Changes in International Environment

We have already mentioned the provision of the French constitution giving treaties an authority superior to that of statutes. It follows that, in case of a contradiction between a treaty and a statute, in spite of the fact that the Conseil Constitutionnel refuses to declare the statute ipso facto unconstitutional, the treaty must prevail. It was the Court of Cassation which first decided, in an important precedent followed by the Conseil d'Etat, that a statute contrary to a treaty cannot be applied to the case at hand (Café Jacques Vabres). This naturally gave to all the courts a very important scope to examine statutes. The existence of this power is an important argument for those who wish to extend judicial review of legislation in France. But, what is more significant for our purpose, in exercising that power, the courts are bound by treaties to follow precedents established by the two European courts.

Another factor is the enormous development of judicial review of constitutionality of legislation in continental Europe. The fundamental conceptions of judicial review are quite different from the American conception but very similar between European countries. The various courts keep informed on the precedents of the others and on adjudicating techniques. There are regular meetings and conferences between constitutional judges. Scholars can assert substantive similarities in the decisions and some even go so far as to speak of a development of a 'Constitutional Common Law in Europe' (Favoreu, 1984, pp.1147ff).

4   Juristic or Other Criticism

The use of precedents is sometimes criticized. Some French scholars fear that this tendency to imitate the examples of higher jurisdictions could even, if exaggerated, be dangerous, if it leads to the simple mechanical repetition of the solution in every more or less similar case. The danger is due not only to the fact that lower courts tend to mimic the higher courts, but also to the working habits of the Court of Cassation itself. The first task of a reporting judge, writes Saluden,

> is to search for precedents. The *conseillers référendaires* also work with files, thus also looking for precedents.... It is probable that the generalization of computerized data will encourage these habits.... A government regulation (décret n°84-134 du 20 février 1984) even prescribes that the documentation service analyses and stores data regarding arguments in appeals filed by plaintiffs, in order to bring together cases in store.... It is easy to imagine what consequences such a programme will have. It could even be said that adjudication might degenerate into administration. (Saluden, 1985, p.193ff)

Nevertheless, that danger should not be overestimated, because 'the court is between two alternative objectives: that of justice and that of the exemplary character of its decision. The latter leads to set general rules. But the court hesitates to make an unjust decision and to make other unjust decisions possible, because of the generality of the principle it is about to establish. The court's decision is therefore a compromise between these two objectives' (Breton, quoted by Serverin, 1985, p.263).

References

Bellet, T. 'Grandeur et servitude de la Cour de Cassation', *Rev. internat. de dr. comp.*, p.293ff (1980).
Boré, R. *'La cassation en matière civile'*, Sirey, 12° 2129, p.249 (1980).

Breton, A. 'L'arrêt de la Cour de Cassation', *Annales de l'Univ. de Toulouse,* vol. XXIII, p. 26 (1975).

Chapus, R. (1966), *De la valeur juridique des principes généraux du droit et des autres règles jurisprudentielles,* Paris: Dalloz, pp.99ff.

Cornu, G. (ed.) (1990), *Vocabulaire Juridique,* 2nd edn, Paris: PUF.

Favoreu, J. 'Actualité et légitimite du contrôle juridictionnel des lois en Europe Occidentale', *RDP,* 5, pp.1147ff (1984).

Jobard-Bachellier, M.-N. and Bachellier, X. (1994), *La Technique de cassation,* 3rd edn, Paris: Dalloz.

Marty, G. (1929), 'La distinction du fait et du droit', doctoral thesis, Toulouse.

Mendegris, R. and Vermelle, G. (1995), *Le commentaire d'arrêt en droit privé. Méthodes et exemples,* 5th edn, Paris: Dalloz.

Saluden, M. (1985) 'La jurisprudence, phénomène sociologique', *Archives de Philosophie du Droit,* Paris: Sirey, p.197.

Serverin, E. (1985), *De la jurisprudence en droit privé, Théorie d'une pratique,* Lyons: Presses Universitaires de Lyon, p.264.

Van de Kerchove, M. (1985) 'Jurisprudence et rationalité juridiques', *Archives de Philosophie du Droit,* Paris: Sirey, p.236.

Zenati, F. (1991), *La jurisprudence,* Paris: Dalloz, p.102.

5 Precedent in Italy

MICHELE TARUFFO, *PAVIA* AND
MASSIMO LA TORRE, *FLORENCE*

I Institutional and Systemic

1(a) Court Hierarchy

The system of courts in Italy is divided into two main parts: one is the system of ordinary jurisdiction; the second includes several special jurisdictions, among which the most important is the administrative jurisdiction. Moreover, an extremely important court, that is placed outside the ordinary system of courts, is the Constitutional Court. In its turn, the ordinary jurisdiction plays two different roles: civil justice and criminal justice. The distinction between civil and criminal justice is not really a distinction affecting the hierarchy of courts, because it often happens that both functions are performed by the same court. Only in the largest courts, in big cities, are there chambers or panels dealing only with civil cases, and other chambers or panels dealing only with criminal cases.

The hierarchy of ordinary courts, in principle administering both civil and criminal justice, starts from the bottom with first-level courts of three different types. A justice of the peace *(giudice di pace)* was introduced by a statute enacted in 1991. The justice of the peace has a limited civil jurisdiction and will probably have in future (but not as yet) a criminal jurisdiction concerning minor offences. He is a lay judge serving for periods of four years. He is selected by means of complex procedures and finally by the national committee which controls and administers the judiciary (the Consiglio Superiore della Magistratura). The second judge of first instance is the *pretore*. He is an ordinary professional judge, that is, a member of the ordinary judiciary. He has a civil and criminal jurisdiction that is higher than the jurisdiction of the justice of the peace but that is limited to given matters and to limited amounts of money. The third first instance court is the Tribunale. It has a general civil and criminal jurisdiction, except for matters belonging to the jurisdiction of the justice of the peace and of the *pretore*. The Tribunale works usually in panels of three professional judges; however, a statute of 1991 introduced a new system according to which the Tribunale works with a single judge in most civil matters, and in panels only in a few civil matters (and in criminal matters). A special criminal court of first instance is the Corte d'Assise, sitting in mixed panels composed of professional and lay judges, with jurisdiction over most important crimes. Special panels, composed also of lay members, are provided for the decision of special matters (land tribunals, juvenile courts).

The second level of courts includes the Courts of Appeal (Corte d'Appello). They work in panels of three professional judges. They have a general appellate jurisdiction in civil and criminal matters. However, appeals against a judgment of a justice of the peace or of the *pretore* are usually brought to the Tribunale instead of the Corte d'Appello. Appeals against judgments delivered by the criminal Corte d'Assise are decided by a Corte d'Assise d'Appello, sitting with a mixed panel of professional and lay judges.

At the top level of the hierarchy of ordinary courts there is a supreme court, the Corte di Cassazione. It has a general civil and criminal jurisdiction of last resort. Generally, the supreme court deals only with issues of law, both procedural and substantive, and never with issues of fact. Moreover, it is the supreme court dealing with issues concerning the jurisdiction of every court of the system. According to a constitutional provision (Art. lll al.2), every judgment delivered by any court can be appealed to the supreme court, as a matter of right. The appeal to the Corte di Cassazione is conceived as a general guarantee of lawfulness.

The supreme court sits usually in chambers composed of five judges (three chambers deal with general civil matters, one with labour matters, and six with criminal matters). A special panel of seven judges, the Sezioni Unite, decides matters of jurisdiction, cases decided in conflicting ways by the ordinary chambers and cases of special importance. The supreme court is composed of about 400 professional judges who reach the court at the top of their bureaucratic career inside the hierarchy of the judiciary. They are neither chosen nor elected: they are appointed on the basis of the rank they have reached in their career.

Usually only judgments delivered by the Courts of Appeal can be appealed to the Corte di Cassazione; first-level judgments may be directly appealed to the supreme court if the parties agree to it, but this very seldom happens. Appeals can be brought to the supreme court only on the basis of grounds specifically provided for by the law; these grounds deal only with errors of law concerning the application of procedural or substantive law made by the court below. A special ground for appeal to the supreme court arises when the opinion delivered by the court below is lacking, or it is insufficient or inconsistent.

We now turn to the system of special administrative justice, which is based upon a two-level hierarchy of courts. Such courts deal only with administrative matters, that is matters that are regulated by special administrative rules dealing with the role and powers of the government in civil affairs and transactions. In principle, when the government has some regulatory or controlling power on any matter, litigation stemming from such a matter is administrative in nature, and decided by special administrative courts.

There are administrative courts of first instance, called Tribunali Administrativi Regionali (TAR). They sit in chambers composed of three professional judges. Their territorial jurisdiction corresponds roughly to the regional organization of the state. A TAR sitting in Rome has a general jurisdiction concerning matters affected by the acts of the central national government. The TAR have a general first instance jurisdiction in administrative matters. At the level of second instance there is a central court called the Consiglio di Stato. This court sits in chambers composed of five judges; a special panel called the Adunanza Plenaria, composed of seven judges, decides cases that are especially important, or deals with matters that were decided in conflicting ways by the ordinary chambers. The Consiglio di Stato is the appellate court in administrative matters, and it is also the court of last resort in such matters. Its judgment may be appealed to the Corte di Cassazione, but only on jurisdictional grounds.

An extremely important special court is the Constitutional Court (Corte Costituzionale) introduced by the 1948 Republican constitution and which began to operate in 1957. The Constitutional Court does not belong to the ordinary hierarchy of courts; it is a constitutional body performing a very special function. Its function is to check the constitutional legitimacy of ordinary statutes: when a statutory rule conflicts with a constitutional rule or principle, the court delivers a judgment eliminating this rule. As a consequence, this rule will never be applied in any subsequent case. The court performs this function only when an issue as to the constitutional validity of an ordinary statute arises in the course of a judicial proceeding before a court. When this occurs, the judge stops the proceedings and sends the issue to the Constitutional Court, asking for its judgment.

The Constitutional Court is composed of 15 members that are appointed for nine years. Five of them are elected by the parliament according to special voting procedures, five of them are appointed directly by the president of the Republic, and five are elected by the ordinary judges. Usually the constitutional judges are professional lawyers (judges, law professors and advocates), but this is not formally required. The function performed by the Constitutional Court inside the Italian legal system has become more and more important in the last decades, because a lot of crucial legal issues have been decided by the court, and its judgments are more and more important as guidelines in the interpretation of the law, even when they do not invalidate the statute involved.

In sum, it may be said that the Italian system is now based upon two supreme courts, each playing a different role, but both being extremely important from the point of view of analysing precedent. The first is the Corte di Cassazione, whose judgments determine the final legal outcome in a wide number of civil and criminal cases; the second is the Corte Costituzionale, whose judgments determine the main standards for the constitutional interpretation of any statute included in the legal system.

1(b)   Structural and Procedural Aspects

The Corte di Cassazione is composed of about 400 judges. The Corte Costituzionale is composed of 15 judges. The Consiglio di Stato is also composed of several hundred judges. It should be stressed, however, that only three chambers of this body act as a court performing the judicial functions described in Section 1a above; the other three chambers act as an advisory body giving opinions and advice to the most important branches of the government.

The Corte Costituzionale decides 300–400 cases a year. Its workload has grown progressively. The Corte di Cassazione now decides about 12 000 civil cases (including labour cases) and about 35 000 criminal cases (including special issues concerning the personal freedom of criminal defendants) a year. Also the Consiglio di Stato decides several thousand administrative cases a year.

The Corte Costituzionale always sits as one court and never works in panels. A judge is charged with preparation of the case, but the whole court decides it. The Corte di Cassazione and the Consiglio di Stato sit in panels of five judges in ordinary cases, and in panels of seven judges in cases of special importance, or concerning matters that were decided in conflicting ways by the ordinary chambers.

In all courts, decisions are made according to majority vote. However, votes are always made in secret. The judgment is, therefore, the judgment of the whole court; it can never be ascribed to this or that judge, or to this or that majority inside the court. It is also impossible to know whether the decision was unanimous or only by majority. Correspondingly, if differences occurred in the decision making among the members of the court, these can never be known outside. There is only one limited exception to this rigid rule of secrecy concerning decision making: in ordinary courts the dissenting judge may state his own dissent and write it on a paper that will be sealed in an envelope. This paper will be kept secret until such time when the judge is sued under the rule of civil liability of judges for damages caused by their errors in performing their job; only in such a case is the judge entitled to use his dissent to show that he did not concur in the judgment involved, and then that he is not liable for damages. In any other case the dissent of a judge cannot be made public.

A feature of decision making that is actually very significant in relation to precedent concerns the justification of judgments by means of written judicial opinions. As a rule, and on the basis of a constitutional principle (Art. 111 al.1), every judgment delivered by any court must include an opinion stating the reasons which justify the decision. Such a rule holds obviously also for the supreme courts. Their judgments are stated in written form and include a part that is devoted to developing the arguments supporting the final judgment.

In the Corte di Cassazione and in the Consiglio di Stato, and both in ordinary chambers and in special panels, after the decision has been made a member of the court is charged by its chairman with the task of writing the opinion *for the court*. This judge will write the opinion stating the arguments that he believes show that the judgment is founded upon good and lawful reasons. Then the judgment will be signed by him and by the chairman of the chamber or of the panel. *Dissenting opinions* are never admitted. The official opinion of the court is the one that has been written by the judge charged with it.

The system of writing opinions is different in the Constitutional Court. According to a statute dealing with the court's procedure, the opinion is viewed as made not only by a judge 'in the name of the court', but by *the court as a whole*. It means that, after the decision is made, a member of the court is charged with the task of preparing a draft of the opinion; this draft is examined and discussed by the other members, and only when the agreement of the whole court is reached does the draft become the opinion of the court. Even in the Constitutional Court *dissenting* or *concurring opinions* are not allowed, since the governing principle is that of strict secrecy concerning decision making. Such a principle has been discussed and criticized, and some scholars are in favour of permitting dissenting and concurring opinions at least in the Constitutional Court, but rules concerning this matter have never been changed.

1(c)   Power to Select Cases

The higher courts that in the Italian system create precedents do not have any power to select the cases they decide. On the one side, the Corte Costituzionale will decide every issue of constitutional legitimacy that arises and is duly sent to the court. The court will check whether the issue is admissible and whether it is relevant for the decision of the case, and will decide the issue on the merits. Likewise, both the Corte di Cassazione and the Consiglio di Stato are expected to decide every case the parties bring to them by way of appeal against judgments delivered by the civil and criminal Courts of Appeal and by the TAR. Art. lll al.2 of the constitution quoted above is construed as obligating the Corte di Cassazione to decide every case on its merits, and giving a subjective right of every citizen to have his own case decided on the merits by the supreme court. This constitutional rule is often used as the main argument to reject proposals to allow some forms of selection of the cases that are to be decided by the supreme court.

Thus there is no machinery aimed at letting the supreme court choose the cases to decide in order to review precedents or to set new ones. It should be stressed, however, that in the Corte di Cassazione and in the Consiglio di Stato there is a special institution that may be used for this purpose. As we have already seen, in both courts a case may be decided by a special panel of seven judges, when the chairman of the court finds that the case deals with especially important issues of law, or when the same issue has been decided differently by different chambers of the court. The case of the 'especially important legal issue' is clearly related to the problem of setting an authoritative precedent. Also the case of conflicting judgments delivered by different chambers is related to the problem of setting or reviewing precedents, since conflicting or inconsistent judgments on the same issue cannot represent an effective precedent. The special panel is expected to solve the conflict with a judgment that, being uniform and authoritative, may actually be a precedent for future cases. No judge, and not even the single chamber of the court, is formally obliged to comply with the judgment delivered by the Sezioni Unite of the Corte di Cassazione or by the Adunanza Plenaria of the Consiglio di Stato in these situations. However, their judgments are usually considered as especially authoritative and they are normally used as precedents.

2   Structure, content and style of judgments

The normal structure of the higher court judgment is deductive, since the opinion aims at showing that the final decision is a conclusion stemming from a chain of consistent logical steps, moving from given premises and arriving at a 'necessary' end. The theoretical model that inspires the logical structure of the judgment is that of syllogistic deduction. Even when the actual structure of the judgment is more complex and less pure than a logical syllogism, the prevailing tendency is to shape the justification of the judgment as a series of logically stringent passages. At least, this is the ideal scheme often in the minds of judges writing opinions in the supreme courts. However, an argumentative factor is often present because of the prevailing conception of what a judgment delivered by the Corte di Cassazione should be. Such a conception is that the court should state its judgment in response to the 'grounds of appeal' that the party has stated in order to support his or her own attack on the judgment being appealed. Therefore the judgment is structured also as a sequence of answers that the court gives to the issues raised by the parties. This is a significant argumentative dimension of the supreme court judgment, that is combined in several ways with the deductive dimension of the justificatory opinion. Note, however, that this argumentative dimension is normally present only in judgments delivered by the Corte di Cassazione and the Consiglio di Stato, since they decide cases that are brought to them by the parties. Such a dimension does not appear in the judgment of the Constitutional Court, because it is not a Court of Appeal in a strict sense. Sometimes, however, the court answers arguments of the judge who raised the issue of constitutional legitimacy.

The prevailing style of higher court judgments is legalistic. The legal professional jargon is normally used, even when common language would do. Legal technicalities are never avoided; on the contrary, they are often invoked, even when they are not especially useful or significant. The opinion is often written as if it were a doctrinal essay, and the writing judge aims at showing his legal and scientific culture. Substantive arguments and value judgments, choices of policy and discretionary evaluations are usually hidden behind technical legal arguments and formal reasoning concerning the meaning of the statutory rules involved. Sometimes the judgments delivered by the Constitutional Court are more substantive and less formal, and deal more openly with policy arguments, value judgments and general principles. This is easily understood, considering that the court deals with the interpretation of principles and standards that are often stated in broad constitutional rules.

The prevailing style is also magisterial. The judgment is presented as a Staatsakt that is delivered by an official body vested with the state power and speaking 'in the name of the people'. It is the court that formally delivers a judgment; there are no single judges expressing their own personal opinions about the case. The opinion is not written in a discursive style. Rather, its model is that of a bureaucratic and official state act, where the person of the author is completely obscured by forms and special technical language.

The content of the supreme court judgments is defined by their institutional function. The Corte di Cassazione and the Consiglio di Stato decide cases on the basis of the grounds of appeal stated by the attacking party, and they answer to stated grounds by means of legal arguments. The main part of their judgment is the opinion justifying their final judgment by means of arguments supporting the answers given by the court to the attacking party, and thus also supporting the final judgment on the case. The content of judgments delivered by the Constitutional Court is somehow simpler, although in many cases its merits are extremely important. The court states whether a statutory rule is or is not in conflict with a constitutional provision. The arguments supporting such a judgment deal with interpretation of constitutional rules and principles, and with the interpretation of the statutory rule involved. In many cases the court states what in its opinion is the 'proper and correct' interpretation of such a statutory rule, from the viewpoint of constitutional principles.

3   Publication of Judgments

The judgments of the Constitutional Court are regularly published in the official journal of the State, the *Gazzetta Ufficiale*. They are published in their entirety.

The judgments of the Corte di Cassazione are not regularly published in their full text. In Italy there is a rather peculiar institution that was created in 1941 and is annexed to the Corte di Cassazione. It is called the Ufficio del Massimario and is composed of judges. Its main function is to analyse all the judgments delivered by the court in order to extract from them the so-called *massima*. This is a short statement (usually five to ten lines) concerning the legal rule that has been used in the decision considered: it is stated in very general terms, usually without any express reference to the facts of the specific case, and it takes into account only the legal side of the decision. It may contain a restatement of the statutory rule that was applied in the decision, or a statement concerning an interpretation of a rule, or a legal principle used by the court. The *massima* is extracted from the opinion included in the judgment; it concerns every general statement of law that may be found in the opinion. Therefore several *massime* can be derived from the same judgment, when it touches several legal problems. Perhaps the most important feature of such a system is that the *massime* are usually stated without any effective connection with the facts in issue and with the peculiar aspects of the single case. Correspondingly, it cannot be said that a *massima* contains the *ratio decidendi* of the case. It may happen, of course, but it is not certain in every case. It often happens, in fact, that legal *obiter dicta* are included in a *massima*, just because they are legal statements. Therefore a *massima* expresses a legal rule or principle that was stated in the judgment considered, but such a rule or principle does not necessarily correspond to the *ratio decidendi* of the case.

The *massime* that are extracted from the judgments of the Corte di Cassazione are not published in an official series. They are published in a semi-official series by the most important legal journals. The *massime* are stored by the Ufficio del Massimario, now also by means of computer systems. They are accessible by electronic media: every court and many legal firms have terminals connected with the data bank of the court (called CED), and then they have a direct access to all of the *massime*.

The whole judgments of the Corte di Cassazione are not regularly reported, nor are they regularly published in official or private series. The main reason for this is the exceedingly large number of such judgments. If somebody wants to have the text of a judgment, he or she may obtain it from the clerk offices of the court simply by asking for it.

Judgments are published by the many legal journals existing in Italy: some of them are general in scope and cover every area of the legal system, but there are dozens of legal journals concerning special areas, such as commercial law, bankruptcy, criminal law and procedure, civil procedure, tort law, family law, and so on. 'Generalist' legal journals publish the most important judgments in the several fields; 'specialized' journals publish a broader choice of judgments concerning the specific matter. In every case the choice is made by lawyers acting as members of the scientific board of the journal. The selection is made according to the importance of the judgment in the evolution of the case law in that field. Legal journals are the usual source for knowledge of the *Corte di Cassazione's* judgments, especially when the whole judgment is needed. The analysis of the court's case law usually starts from the *massime* as the first means to know what the court says; a second step is searching to see whether the significant judgment has been published in a legal journal. When not, the only source is the *massima* of the case.

Judgments delivered by appellate courts or by first instance courts are not regularly recorded or published. Sometimes they are published in legal journals, when they are especially significant in a given area. The choice is made by the scientific advisers of the journal.

4   Contents of Reports

As we have seen above, only the judgments delivered by the Constitutional Court are published in their whole text by an official journal. They are often published also by legal journals, usually with notes and comments by legal scholars.

The judgments of the Corte di Cassazione are regularly recorded and published only under the form of the *massime*. This means that the judgment is identified by the name of the court (determining when it has been delivered by the special panel called the Sezioni Unite), by the number it has in the official record of the court, by its date and by the name of the parties. As we have seen, the text of the *massima* is a short statement, made in very general and abstract terms, of a legal rule of principle. Facts are not stated, except in extremely rare cases and in a very short form. Arguments supporting or contrasting with the statement are not reproduced: sometimes, but rather infrequently, a very short reference to a supporting argument is included in the *massima*. Procedural features of the specific case are not included. Other elements of the original judgments are not referred to.

Things are different when a judgment is published in a legal journal. In such a case the report includes the name of the court and of judges signing the judgment, a headnote concerning the main topics decided by it, a short statement of the main holdings included in the judgment (sometimes the official *massima* is reproduced; sometimes a different *massima* is stated by a scientific adviser of the journal) and the main parts of the judgment. Usually such parts deal with the legal issues involved, the discussion of interpretational problems as to statutes and precedents, the holdings concerning the legal issues, the reasons for these rulings and the final dictum.

No concurring or dissenting opinions are published, since they are not allowed in Italy. Some parts of the arguments developed by counsel are published, but only when they are referred to in the text of the judgment, and when they are useful in order to define a legal issue. No quotations are made from the pleadings of the parties. Statements concerning the facts of the case and the procedural background of the judgment are sometimes published, but only when they are deemed to be absolutely necessary to understand the judgment. Very frequently, they are omitted (and you find one or more *omissis* in the text that is published), because the prevailing attitude is in favour of selecting for publication only the legal parts of the judgment. In such a case there is no possibility of knowing anything concerning the facts of the case. Therefore the reported text has the form of a puzzle. It consists only of parts of the judgment dealing with the legal issues and the arguments of the court to support its resolution of these issues. Except the data that are needed to identify the judgment, every other element of the original judgment, concerning the specific features of the case, is usually omitted. The main reason for this way of reporting is that the judgments are taken into account only with reference to the legal issues and legal arguments, from the point of view of their general meaning. The specific facts of the case are not relevant from this point of view.

Rather frequently, the judgment is published with a note of comment: sometimes the note is a synthetic summary of precedents and academic opinions concerning the legal issue; sometimes the note is a broad academic essay discussing the issue, the significant precedents, the relevant legal dogmatics and the arguments supporting or contrasting the solution that was adopted in the judgment.

5 Meaning of 'Precedent'

In the Italian system 'precedent' is mainly used in a very broad sense, that is, to mean any prior decision possibly relevant to a case to be decided. More strictly, a precedent is any prior decision dealing with the same legal issue. There is, however, a more proper use of the word, although this use is sometimes vague and uncertain. In such a use, 'precedent' means a decision that is taken as somehow significant or possibly influencing the decision of a following case. There is some reference to the 'authority' of precedent, although in Italy the precedent has no formally binding force. In some sense, a precedent is a decision that may or should be taken as a model or a reference point in the following decision. Then, for instance, the judgments delivered by the Sezioni Unite of the supreme court and by the Constitutional Court are usually considered as precedents in the proper sense, that is, as judgments that should be taken into account in a later case. More broadly, the judgments of the Corte di Cassazione are often considered as precedents, at least in the sense that they should be considered while deciding a subsequent case dealing with the same legal issue. Sometimes, but much less frequently, judgments delivered by appellate courts are also considered as precedents.

Besides that, there is also another sense of 'precedent' that is sometimes used in Italy. In such a sense a precedent is either the judgment that decides a new legal issue for the first time, or a judgment that decides a legal issue in a new way or in an especially thorough and original way. In these cases, the type of court which delivered the judgment is relatively unimportant (although judgments of higher courts are preferred), because the 'authority' of the precedent is based mainly on the specific quality of the decision.

It may happen that a court prepares a judgment with the aim of setting a precedent, but the intention of the court is unimportant (even when setting a precedent is institutionally inherent in delivering a judgment, as in judgments of the Sezioni Unite of the supreme court). In fact a judgment is a precedent only when it is considered as a precedent by the judges deciding the following cases. Rather frequently, judgments delivered with the aim of influencing decisions in future cases are rejected or set aside.

6   Mode of Citation and Discussion

When a precedent is cited by judges, practitioners or scholars, the reference is often made to the *massime* that are extracted from the judgments of the Corte di Cassazione. The obvious reason is that in many cases the *massima* is the only thing that can be used. When a judgment has been published in some legal journals, then it is cited by reference to its specific contents.

Judicial opinions, judicial papers written by counsel and academic legal writings very often devote much space and detailed analyses to the discussion of precedents. Rather frequently, the main part of a judicial opinion consists only of the discussion of precedents, and the same happens in notes and comments that are published in legal journals. Lawyers arguing cases before courts are expected to cite and discuss the relevant precedents, and they usually do so in fact. The main part of their pleadings concerning legal issues is often devoted to the discussion of precedents.

Scholarly treatises and essays have a very important role in the synthesis, rational reconstruction, explanation and critical analysis of the case law in the several areas of the legal system. A major part of the legal literature in Italy is devoted to the analysis of the case law; there are several legal journals that are exclusively devoted to this task.

7   Overall Role of Precedent

In the practice of judicial opinions, the use of precedents is now certainly major. The last decades have seen a great expansion in the use of precedents, and they are now employed as one of the main bases of every judicial decision. The reference to precedent is not an alternative to reference to codes, statutes or constitution. On the contrary, precedent is very often a sort of *medium* for the reference to codes, statutory provisions and constitution. Judges rather infrequently refer to a 'pure' rule, in its original textual terms. In fact this happens only when 'literal argument' is used, or when the statute is new and no case law yet exists. But very frequently the rule is considered, analysed and interpreted *by means of* the discussion of precedents concerning it. The same happens for interpretive arguments, policies, principles and substantive reasons: rather infrequently, such justificatory materials are used 'by themselves'; much more frequently, they are used because or insofar as they are embodied in one or several precedents.

However, even if precedents are treated as 'materials' to be compared with other materials, the outcome is that in Italian judicial practice they play a major and growing role. Such a role is clearly much more frequent and important than the role that is played by academic or professional writings. There is no doubt that precedents are now by far *the most important* justificatory material used in judicial opinions.

8 Role of Precedent in Different Branches of Law

From the historical point of view, the expansion of the use of precedents and case law in Italy started becoming important mainly in the area of civil law. At present, however, no significant distinction can be made among several areas of the legal system, as to the frequency and importance of the use of precedents. The important role that is played by precedents in judicial practice is roughly the same in every legal branch, and in every court of the Italian system. The use of precedent may depend on such factors as the 'age' of a statute or the difficulty of an issue, or the uniformity or inconsistency of the case law concerning a legal problem, but these variations may occur inside every legal area.

An important factor is whether a given area of the legal system is completely or mainly 'covered' by statutory regulations, because one may think that, where statutory rules are lacking, precedents play a more important role. However, precedents are normally relied on even when the legal issue is 'covered' by statutory rules, since such rules are usually interpreted and applied by means of the reference to precedents. Then the problem is not whether precedents are frequently used, but whether they are the *only basis* of the judgment, or they are used to interpret statutory rules governing the case.

The only difference that may be sometimes perceived in the use of precedents by Italian courts is among the different levels of the administration of justice. Trial courts often devote their main attention to the issues of fact; therefore the use of precedents, being limited to the decision of the issues of law, seems to be less overwhelming. In contrast, since appellate courts and supreme courts deal mainly with legal issues, they make daily use of precedents and precedents play a prominent role in the justification of their judgments.

9   Precedent and 'Gaps in the Law'

The case in which on a given issue there are neither statutes nor precedents is rather infrequent in the Italian system at present, since the system includes thousands of statutes and thousands of precedents. However, the completely 'new' case does sometimes arise. In such a case judges do create new precedents, since they are obliged to decide every case submitted to a court, and must find a legal basis to decide any case. Sometimes they expressly say that the case or the issue is new and that therefore they must look for a new solution. However, the decision concerning the new issue is not created *ex nihilo* or directly based upon substantive reasons or policy and value judgments, or on reasons of justice related to the facts of the case. Since the general principle is that every judgment should be based upon legal rules, the courts always look for arguments supporting the new precedent. Then the new judgment never is 'naked' or grounded barely on policy arguments. It is usually supported by arguments connecting it, by means of more or less long and loose chains of passages, to a statutory rule or to a general or a constitutional principle, or at least to another precedent concerning a similar or related matter.

Judges do perceive the 'novelty' of a case or of an issue, and sometimes they even stress this. However, they try to demonstrate that their decision, although dealing with a new topic, is consistent with the existing statutory, constitutional or case law. They present their decision as a rationally justified and coherent development of the existing legal system rather than as a break or a jump.

II   The Bindingness of Precedent

1   Kinds and Degrees of Normative Force

In the Italian legal system no precedent may be considered as strictly binding: the main reason for this is that it is not a system based upon the principle of formally binding precedent. Precedents are not listed among the 'sources of law', although sometimes they are defined as de facto sources. Therefore it never happens that a precedent *must* be applied as a rule for a subsequent decision. Every Italian precedent is therefore a de facto or *persuasive* precedent, lacking any formally binding effect.

There is only one type of case where a precedent is formally and strictly binding, not subject to overruling, and must be followed in every subsequent case: when the Constitutional Court finds that a statutory rule is contrary to a constitutional provision, and therefore the court declares that such a rule is 'unconstitutional'. It should be stressed, however, that such a judgment is not a precedent in the proper sense: rather, it has the same effect as an abrogation, since after it the statutory rule involved is no longer deemed to 'exist' in the legal system. This is the reason why the judgment cannot be overruled and must be applied in every case. But this is not 'force of precedent' in the proper sense. Consider, moreover, that when the Constitutional Court finds that a statutory rule is not in conflict with a constitutional provision, such a judgment has no special effect. It may be overruled by the same court, and it is not formally binding, but it is a de facto precedent.

Since in the Italian system no precedent in the proper sense is formally and binding, there are no defeasibly binding precedents. Again, for the same reason, the Italian system does not include formal binding precedents subject to formal overruling or modification. (Italian precedents can be de facto overruled or modified, but they are not binding.)

The typical Italian precedent is not formally binding, but it has force. A judgment not applying a relevant precedent may be lawful in itself, since its lawfulness depends on its consistency with statutory and constitutional provisions, not on its coherence with precedents. Such a judgment may be *legally valid*, although it does not follow any existing and relevant precedent. However, judgments not following the relevant precedents are usually criticized, especially when they do not even consider relevant precedents. A court may decide not to follow a precedent but, in such a case, the court is expected to discuss the issue and to state arguments supporting the choice not to follow the precedent. When a higher court decides not to follow its own precedents, this is a sort of non-formal overruling of such precedents. The court should give good and sound arguments supporting its new and different choice. When a lower court does not follow a relevant precedent of a higher court, its judgment is subject to reversal on this ground. Probably it will be reversed, unless the lower court shows – by means of detailed arguments – that the precedent did not properly apply to the specific case, or that there were good substantive reasons not to apply it in that case.

Since there is no formal bindingness, the Italian precedent has outweighable force and defeasible force. It is defeasible because exceptions may be invoked in order not to apply the precedent. Also the precedent may be too old; it may be contradicted by other judgments; it may be based on inconsistent or badly stated reasons; it may have been strongly criticized by authoritative legal scholars; it may have been overruled or implicitly abandoned. Also, it may be outweighable because a court may adduce several countervailing reasons in order to show, for example, that it would lead to unjust outcomes in subsequent cases, that it is contrary to a new policy or to some general value or principle, that it is doubtful from a legal point of view or that it does not properly fit the features of the following case.

The general attitude is that a precedent should be applied, at least when no good reasons can be found not to follow it. When such reasons exist, every court is expected to state them using proper arguments and justifying its own decision. Moreover, lower courts should follow the precedents of higher courts, and each court should follow its own precedents, unless good reasons exist not to do this. However, Italian courts exercise broad discretion in deciding to follow or not to follow a precedent.

In many cases the Italian courts refer to other judgments, not as precedents in the proper (although non-formal) sense, but only as materials supporting a decision that is grounded on statutory provisions and/or also on proper precedents directly applied. Of course a decision lacking this kind of basis is lawful, and it may also be well justified by arguments based upon legal rules or principles. However, rather frequently judgments are quoted, not as justifying authorities directly dealing with the legal issues of the case, but as 'surrounding' materials. For example, some judgments may be referred to just in order to show that the decision in the concrete case is consistent with other judgments, or with trends existing in the case law or in some areas of it.

Sometimes judgments are quoted only with the aim of illustrating a possible interpretation or application of a provision, but not to support the subsequent judgment. In such cases the reference is made to judgments being used as mere *examples*, even without saying that the example should be followed. Their function is just to show that there is another interpretive possibility, without choosing or supporting this possibility. An example may be a judgment concerning a different subject matter, or a judgment of a court lacking any authority in the legal system (as a foreign court) or the deciding court (as a lower court or a court belonging to the same rank). An example may also be *negative,* as when it is quoted just to show that it should not be followed.

It happens rather infrequently that the degree of force or bindingness of a precedent is explicitly discussed in judicial opinions. Most often, the situation is that precedents are referred to merely to support the decision. In such a case the court does not explain why it is or it should be so. The court merely quotes the precedent without any further argument applying it to the case. Just by being quoted, a precedent is implicitly assumed to have some force or influence on the decision. Precedents are explicitly discussed only when there are several conflicting or different precedents concerning the same topic, and when the court decides not to follow some precedent. In such cases, arguments supporting precedents are discussed and compared, and a decision rejecting a precedent is justified on the basis of countervailing reasons.

Precedents are usually discussed, sometimes very broadly, in commentaries, treatises, comments and notes published by legal journals. In most cases the subject matter of scholarly discussion is the substantive merits of the decision. However, the force of precedents is also considered and analysed, as well as the possible exceptions and countervailing arguments, and the existence, consistency and development of a corpus of case law concerning a topic or an area of the law. Conflicts among precedents and changes in the case law are a frequent subject matter of the Italian legal literature.

A rather widespread opinion favours a more strict and consistent use of precedents by Italian courts. An attempt is being made to develop a clear theory of precedents and to persuade the courts, and especially the higher courts, to make better use of precedents. The main aim is to reduce the breadth of free discretion of courts in the use of precedents, to ascribe a stronger force to precedents (at least of the highest courts) and to state some rules or principles that the courts should comply with while overruling or rejecting relevant precedents. In fact many scholars believe that a strong and clear system of precedents would be a great advantage for the Italian legal system.

2   Law Concerning Precedent

In Italy there is no legislation requiring or forbidding the use of precedent, or otherwise regulating it. Some scholars believe that a statutory basis for the precedents of the Corte di Cassazione may be found in rules concerning the function of the supreme court in securing uniformity of case law (Art. 65 of the basic law about the judiciary). It is true that such a function may be better performed if some bindingness is ascribed to the precedents of the supreme court, but such a rule is probably not a clear statutory basis for the force of precedent.

There is no case law about the formally binding character of precedent: such a character is not admitted at all in the Italian system. The value and role of precedents are not frequently discussed in judicial opinions. Precedents are frequently used, even without any explicit justification, but when this issue is explicitly considered, the formally binding value of precedents is denied.

In Italy there is no de jure precedent. Precedents are de facto. This means that precedent has some persuasive or supporting function and that it may influence the decision of subsequent cases, but only on the basis of the choices made case by case by the courts, without any legal rule or standard governing the matter.

Precedents are not considered true sources of law. Some scholars define precedents as 'de facto sources of law', but such a definition sounds self-contradictory: it is difficult to imagine something that is de facto legally binding.

Theoretically, therefore, precedents should be used only in connection with statute or custom, or any other formal source of law, such as constitutional provisions. In fact, however, there are several very important branches of the law that are *for the most part* based upon precedents instead of upon written or customary rules. Examples may be found in constitutional law, since a rich body of precedent exists in many areas of constitutional matters; in tort law, since several standards determining the amount of damages (biological damages, moral damages) are stated in the case law instead of in statutory rules; in administrative law, since for instance the concept of 'acts *ultra vires*' is based upon case law created by administrative courts. Other examples may be found in commercial law, in family law, in transport law, in bankruptcy law and in civil procedure. However, even when the basis of the legal regulation of a matter can be found in precedents, a reference to some statutory provision is required. In many instances such a reference is weak and vague, but nevertheless the prevailing opinion is that precedents cannot be *the only* basis of a judicial decision. In fact, precedents are often the only basis because the actual *ratio decidendi* is derived from the case law rather than from some statutory provision. Then a further reference to a statutory provision is often a kind of justification ex post for the use of precedents, rather than the true picture of the decision making.

The maxim, *nulla poena sine lege,* is applied in criminal law, and it is interpreted as forbidding the use of *analogy* in criminal judgments. However, this does not prevent use of precedents, since precedents are used as a means to interpret statutory provisions. Criminal provisions need to be interpreted in order to be applied and precedents are actually used in the interpretation of criminal provisions. Here the problem arises of distinguishing the argument by analogy from interpretation on the basis of precedents. In practice such a distinction may be uncertain and puzzling. Theoretically, it may be said that the argument by analogy leads to the application of a rule to a situation that is somehow different from the one that is directly regulated by the rule, while a precedent is used to specify and determine the proper meaning of the rule itself. From this viewpoint, precedent does not raise any problem in criminal law.

3   Factors Determining Degrees of Normative Force

(a)   The hierarchical rank of the court is by far the most important factor influencing the degree of force of precedents in Italy. Precedents having the highest degree of effectiveness are those of the Constitutional Court in any matter, of the Corte di Cassazione in civil and criminal matters, and of the Consiglio di Stato in administrative matters. Every lower court is expected to take into due account precedents of the higher courts. Although lower courts are not legally bound to apply such precedents, they should be considered while deciding matters already decided by one of the higher courts. If a judge does not apply these precedents, he or she should justify his/ her own decision with good arguments. Correspondingly, a decision of a lower court is deemed to be properly justified if it applies clear precedents of the higher courts.

The hierarchical factor works also in other ways. For instance, a precedent of a court belonging to the same rank is considered less effective than a precedent of a higher court. A precedent of a court of appeal is deemed influential by trial judges, particularly when the precedent is of the same appellate court that would review the judgment on appeal. On the other hand, a precedent of a lower court is not considered a true precedent: when a judgment of a lower court is cited, it is an example rather than a precedent.

(b)   A decision of the higher court is considered more influential when it has been delivered by a special panel of the Corte di Cassazione or of the Consiglio di Stato (the Constitutional Court always sits in full bench). One reason is that these courts deal with especially important issues of law, and resolve conflicts among the ordinary chambers. In such situations the court is expected to deliver a judgment that should influence subsequent cases. At any rate, these are the situations in which the higher courts deliver judgments that are clearly intended to serve as precedents.

(c)   The reputation of the court or of the judge writing the opinion may sometimes affect the value and authority of the precedent, but this happens infrequently, and it is at any rate only an additional factor. Some appellate courts, or some chambers of an appellate court or of a supreme court, are sometimes considered to be especially authoritative on given matters, but this is not a decisive factor in determining the degree of force of a precedent. The same happens, but even more infrequently, with individual judges that are known as especially wise in some matters.

(d)   Changes in the political, economic or social background since the prior decision are usually considered good reasons not to apply the precedent. Such changes are frequently invoked by courts as a justification for not following the precedent. On the other hand, when the background of the prior decision has changed, there is the possibility of setting a new precedent. The new precedent may be considered especially influential when it reflects effectively the new political, economical or social situation.

(e)   Soundness of the supporting arguments is a relevant factor influencing the force of the precedent. It is so especially when a new precedent has to be applied, or when there are conflicting precedents, because in these situations the precedent does not hold 'in itself', but only according to the persuasiveness of its supporting arguments. The same happens, for similar reasons, when a precedent is discussed in order to decide whether to overrule it or not. This factor is less important when precedents are cited automatically and formally, that is without reference to their actual content.

(f)   The age of precedent is sometimes a significant factor, but it works in different ways in different contexts. A *new* precedent may be influential when it provides a solution to a new legal issue, if it is supported by persuasive arguments. But a new precedent may also be considered with caution and uncertainty just because it is new. A common opinion about the issue will not yet exist.

An *old* precedent may be considered highly influential because of its age, but this happens when the background has not changed substantially and the legal basis of the issue of law is still the same. The old precedent is also influential when it has been followed by a coherent and continuous case law repeating the same solution of the same issue. On the other hand, an old precedent may be considered 'weak' or negligible just because it is old, when the social and economic context has changed, and especially when the legal basis of the issue has changed. Obviously no value at all is ascribed to old precedents that have been overruled or superseded by newer ones.

(g)   Dissent is never explicitly stated in judicial decisions.

(h)   The branch of law involved is not significant for the degree of force of precedents. Precedent is a general phenomenon that does not seem to vary according to the several branches of law. There are branches where precedents are more frequent, or where precedents are the true legal basis of many judgments, but this does not affect directly the force of precedents.

(i)   A very important factor concerning precedents in the Italian system is whether there is a *trend* in the case law. A single precedent is effective only in special situations, mainly when it is a new precedent concerning a new legal issue. Apart from this case, the value of the isolated precedent is doubtful and uncertain. In contrast, trends in the case law concerning a given legal issue are extremely influential for the decision of subsequent cases (consider that, in a system where high numbers of judgments are delivered by higher courts every year, trends in the case law are frequent. One may even say that the highest degree of bindingness of precedents is reached by trends composed of several precedents on the same matter. This is the case of the so-called *giurisprudenza costante* or *consolidata*, which is usually considered a sufficient and binding basis (except for very good countervailing reasons) for a subsequent decision.

It should be stressed, however, that this happens only when the trend in the case law, or the series or chain of precedents, is *uniform, coherent* and *consistent,* that is when the several judgments compos-ing the trend decide the same legal issue in exactly the same way. In the Italian system such a situation occurs rather frequently, but there are also many cases in which there are several judgments (even delivered by the same court) that are inconsistent or even in open and sharp contrast (see Section II.7).

(j)   The acceptance of a precedent by academicians is sometimes a significant factor influencing its degree of force, but certainly it is not a decisive factor. When the precedent is approved by legal scholars it has more of a chance to be applied in subsequent cases. But academic criticism provides arguments for the judge who does not agree with the precedent.

(k)   Legal change affecting related areas may influence the value of a precedent insofar as it entails also some change in the legal context concerning the issue involved. The real problem, however, seems to be whether such a change affects the conditions under which the precedent can be applied in the given case. Changes in the legal context may or may not affect the legal issue involved: if not, the value of the precedent remains the same; if so, the precedent prob-ably cannot any longer be applied to that issue (but this is not a problem of degree of bindingness).

4   Factors that Weaken Precedent

A precedent is deprived of its weight when it is counterbalanced by a contrary precedent, as often happens in Italy (see Section II.7), espec-ially when the conflicting precedent is a judgment delivered by the same court in the same period. In such a case it cannot be said that an actual precedent exists, since both conflicting judgments could be invoked as precedents.

A second situation arises when a precedent is overruled or super-seded by following judgments, especially when they form a consistent trend supporting a different solution of the same legal issue.

A third situation occurs when statutes concerning the legal issues are changed, or when a matter is regulated by new statutory pro-visions, or when a judgment of the Constitutional Court invalidates the provision concerning the case. It is clear, that when the legal basis of the case changes substantially, every precedent that was founded upon the prior legal situation is deprived of its force or weight.

A fourth situation is when a judgment is declared null and void, or is modified, by a subsequent judgment delivered by a higher court by way of appeal (as in the case of a judgment of an appellate court that is appealed to the supreme court and is declared void).

There are no formal reasons why a judgment cannot achieve the status of precedent, if the judgment is valid and legally effective. In Italy precedents do not have any special status depending on formal conditions; therefore every valid judgment may be used, at least theoretically, as a precedent. No distinctions are usually made between precedents dealing with statute law and precedents of other kinds: the main idea is that precedents always deal with statute or constitutional law, although such a relationship may be indirect and weak.

5   Vertical and Horizontal Bindingness

Lower courts are generally expected to take into account precedents set by higher courts. Since in Italy there is no formal bindingness of precedents, this is only a matter of persuasive effectiveness. (But, quite obviously, the rule stated by the Corte di Cassazione on a specific case is strictly binding on the lower court which is called to decide on the merits of the case according to the directives given by the supreme court concerning the legal side of the case at hand.) Precedents set by higher courts, and especially by their special panels, are considered particularly persuasive, at least until there are good reasons not to apply them. Also precedents set by appellate courts have some persuasiveness from the viewpoint of lower courts.

Decisions of courts of the same level are never considered binding on each other. Sometimes a judgment may be taken into account by a court of the same level; this happens when it is a new precedent, based upon new arguments, or a decision on a new legal issue, or when the arguments used are especially sound and interesting. 'Horizontal' precedents usually have a rather weak persuasive force, and they are often cited only as examples, rather than as precedents.

According to a reasonable and widely shared theory, the highest courts in the system, and especially the Corte di Cassazione, should follow their own precedents. It is a matter of equal treatment of all citizens under the law, of properly performing the institutional functions of the supreme court, and of reasonable consistency and coherence in the case law. Moreover, it seems that precedents set by the court would be much more effective and useful if they were followed by the court itself. According to this theory, the court should change its own precedents only when relevant changes occur in the legal situation or in the social or economic background. In such a case the court should openly overrule its own precedents, adducing good reasons for doing so.

However, this is nothing but a theory concerning what the supreme court *should* do in order to be a proper supreme court. Such a theory is evidently contradicted by practice. The supreme court does not follow its own precedents, except when it seems that repeating the same solution of the same legal issue is just and correct, or even comfortable. The court does not feel bound to follow, or even to take into due account, its own precedents. Conflicts in the case law of the court are extremely frequent; conflicts among different chambers of the court are frequent; even conflicts among different panels of the same chamber exist. Sometimes, the special panel of the court tries to solve such conflicts, but the judgments delivered by the special panel cannot be formally binding even for the chambers of the court itself. Therefore it happens sometimes that a precedent set by the Sezioni Unite is not followed by the ordinary chambers of the court. On the other hand, even the Sezioni Unite do not feel bound by their own precedents, and these often change orientation. Something similar happens also in the highest administrative court, that is the Consiglio di Stato.

The Constitutional Court does not feel bound to follow its own precedents, and frequently changes its approach to legal issues. When the court finds that an issue of constitutional legitimacy is well founded, it invalidates the provision. Correspondingly, the same issue cannot be raised in a subsequent case. Only when the court does not wipe off the provision involved may the issue be raised again, and in such a case the court is not bound by its prior decision.

There is a type of decision by the Constitutional Court which has been called 'double pronouncement' *(doppia pronuncia)*, by which the court declares that it will draw all legal consequences from a principle established in the decision if the legislator or the judiciary do not comply with the instructions given by the court. In this case, the court is supposed to be bound by its decision, that is, to the general constitutional principle settled in it. Nevertheless, the practice of the court reveals that it does not in all cases feel bound to that previous assessment of a general principle.

6   Analysis of Force, Support and Illustrative Role

Italian courts do not differentiate clearly, as far as precedents are concerned, between (a) justifying force, (b) providing further support and (c) merely illustrative value. They simply use precedents very frequently in their opinions, making several kinds of references to them, but avoiding any clear and rational analysis of this topic. Differences in the types of reference made by the courts to precedents may be detected case by case, but the courts infrequently state these explicitly.

Such differences do not depend on clear and rationalized factors. Courts tend to quote precedents in every case when a precedent can be found. The precedent is used as a justifying argument or as an illustrative example according to the kind of concrete situation in which it is used. It is the starting point of a justifying argument, or a mere example when no direct connection exists. It plays only the role of further support of the judgment when the decision is mainly based upon a direct reference to a statutory rule or to another precedent directly applied.

In Italy there is no legislation dealing with these matters. There are discussions of these matters in the legal literature, because the analysis of the use of precedents made by the courts often concerns the force of the precedents used or the function they play. However, this kind of analysis usually deals with specific problems and with the force or function of precedents concerning specific topics. The main aim of the legal literature usually is to reconstruct the 'state of the law' concerning a legal issue, partly on the basis of the relevant precedents and examples used by the courts. A general and theoretical approach to the different uses of precedents is rather uncommon.

7   Excess of Precedents?

The Italian system is characterized by an excessive amount of precedents, mainly of precedents of the Corte di Cassazione. Thousands of judgments are delivered by this court every year, and each of these judgments may be used as a precedent. Actually, many of them are referred to in subsequent judgments of the same court and of lower courts. Accordingly, one precedent or a few precedents on the same legal issue are rather uncommon. Several consequences derive from this. One is that 'precedent' may be very different in the different situations. Sometimes it is one judgment or a little group of judgments, but quite often there are 'strings', 'series' or 'groups' of precedents clustering about the same legal issue.

Another consequence is that the force of precedent varies according to these differences. If a single judgment is considered, its force as a precedent may be very different in the several cases. If it is the only precedent, its force may be the highest inside the system, and it may be extremely influential and authoritative. But if a judgment is no more than one precedent in a string of many precedents, its specific force is very low. It may even be impossible to establish which specific force may be ascribed to a judgment included in a list of dozens of judgments concerning the same issue. As a rule, the higher the number of precedents included in a string, the lower the force of each single precedent. But when the chain of precedents is uniform and consistent, and it is taken as a whole, its force may be extremely high.

A further consequence stemming from the 'overproduction' of judgments by Italian higher courts is that the probability increases of having conflicts in the case law concerning the same topic. This is a very common phenomenon in Italy, and it has been studied in recent legal literature. *Diachronic* conflicts have been distinguished from *synchronic* conflicts. The former ones derive from quick and often unjustified changes in the approach to the same legal issue. When an issue is decided many times, the chance that solutions will change is higher. Different chambers and panels of the same higher court may deal with the same issue at the same time, deciding it in different ways. Conflicts may arise among single precedents, but there are also rather frequent conflicts among chains or strings of precedents. It often occurs that a legal issue has several solutions, and each solution is supported by a group of precedents. This actually happens even within the case law produced by the same court: the Corte di Cassazione is a significant example of this. A recent essay concerning conflicts in civil matters, which considers only five years and only the judgments published by 12 legal journals, shows that the court has fallen into contradiction no less than 864 times. That is, genuine inconsistencies arose in all of these cases.

When the case law includes several trends on the same issue, or conflicting groups of judgments, or many judgments that do not combine to produce a coherent trend, the degree of authoritative force of such case law is very uncertain and doubtful. Moreover, the precise force of a single judgment in such a complex and chaotic situation may be impossible to establish. And it can only be extremely low.

III The Rationale of Precedent

In Italy there are no generally recognized rationales for treating precedents as formally binding, since the precedent is not ascribed any formal binding force.

According to common opinion about the rationale of precedent in Italy, the main reasons supporting the use of precedents are (a) equal treatment under the law, (b) certainty of legal standards in decision making, (c) predictability of judicial decisions, and (d) uniformity of the case law as a fundamental feature of the legal system.

Equal treatment under the law is a basic principle of the system, and it is also required by a constitutional provision (Art. 3 of the Italian constitution). A widespread opinion holds that equality should be assured also in judicial decisions, so that the same legal issue should always be solved in the same way. Correspondingly, a system of precedent is considered as a means to produce a reasonable degree of equality in the interpretation and application of the law inside the legal process.

Certainty of the law is also a fundamental principle of the legal system. The law is 'certain' if legal provisions are applied in a reasonably clear and unchanging way to the same sets of facts. A varying application of the law, if not justified by relevant differences in factual situations, would impair the principle of certainty and would introduce a high degree of doubt into the legal system.

Predictability of judicial decisions is considered a fundamental need for the parties and for any subject of the legal system. Predictability is extremely important in every legal transaction, and it may also be useful to prevent or to reduce litigation. This is one of the main reasons adduced to support rational use of precedent in Italy. Predictability can be considered a development of the principle of legal certainty, since legal certainty means, as we have seen, certainty in legal application through judicial decisions.

Uniformity of the case law is a sort of instrumental value, since it is a means to ensure equality, certainty and predictability. If the case law is uniform about any legal issue, then it may be said that citizens are treated equally, that the law is certain and that judicial decisions are predictable. This is the main reason why the function of ensuring the uniformity of the case law is one of the main jobs of the Corte di Cassazione, according to Article 65 of the basic law concerning the judiciary. Correspondingly, this function is sometimes considered to be one of the legal foundations of precedent in the Italian legal system. Moreover, uniformity in the administration of justice is often considered a necessary condition of a rational, clear and consistent legal system, especially by those legal theorists who maintain that the legal system should be rational, clear and consistent. In this sense uniformity can be considered a value in itself, not merely instrumental to other fundamental values.

Apart from all this, a very important rationale may be that Italian courts *actually* make daily use of precedents, although the features of it are somehow vague and uncertain. Since precedents are used, and the tendency to use them is growing and growing, its seems quite unreasonable to cast doubt upon the foundation of such a reality, or simply to deny it. Therefore the existence of precedents and their growing importance are plainly acknowledged. Moreover, it is also clear that referring to precedents may be useful in solving issues deriving from gaps and indeterminacies in statute law, and in finding guidelines for the evolution of the case law and for adapting the interpretation of the law to changing social and economic conditions. In a word, even if theoretical or 'principled' rationales are not considered, an important practical rationale is that precedents are actually useful as suggestions, examples and reference points, and also as supporting materials and justificatory arguments, when a decision must be made inside a complex, inconsistent, varying and vague legal system.

Although there are no rules or principles expressly vesting the courts with the power to create and develop the law through precedents, such development nevertheless occurs. The main reason for this is that legislatures are not able to follow the developments of the society and corresponding legal needs. Then it is up to the courts to amend obsolete statutes, to adapt the law to changing conditions and to fill gaps stemming from new issues and problems.

These rationales are not usually discussed in judicial opinions. The practice of the courts is just to create and use precedents as if this were the normal institutional function of the judiciary, without discussing it and submitting it to critical scrutiny or to scientific rationalization. This may not be necessary, anyway, since the Italian system of precedent is only a de facto system lacking any formal bindingness. The discussion of the rationales supporting the use of precedent in Italy is a task performed by legal scholars, when they try to understand the real nature of the Italian legal system and of the sources of law in this system. The main tendency in the Italian legal literature is in favour of a clear system of precedents, with some sort of formal bindingness in vertical and horizontal dimensions, and allowing overruling only when good reasons arise that are well stated in judicial opinions. Such a system is widely considered as a necessary means of improving the Italian legal system.

IV   Precedents: What They Stand for and How They Apply

1   *What Counts as Binding or Having Force?*

Since in most cases the precedent is actually a *massima* representing a short and abstract statement of a legal rule, the consequence is that the binding element in a precedent is often seen as an *explicit* ruling or principle. If and when the maxim is not merely repeated, and is analysed in order to elicit its meaning in broader terms, then it happens that the binding element of the precedent is an *implicit* rule or principle; however the maxim often consists of the explicit statement of a rule or principle, so that such a rule or principle is the actual content of the precedent. Sometimes the *massima* states something that was merely *obiter dictum* in the prior judgment, but without specifying that this was the case: the consequence is that the *obiter dictum* is taken as a precedent by the subsequent judge, who does not know the real nature of the statement expressed in the *massima*.

When the precedent is a judgment that has been published in a legal journal, things are different. Legal journals usually publish the whole opinion concerning the legal issues involved, or at least a broad selection of the legal arguments which were used to justify the decision of the legal issues involved. Correspondingly, the precedent may consist of the explicit or constructed holding on the issue of law, and also of the reasons stated for the holding, both substantive and formal or procedural. When the whole opinion or significant parts of it are at hand, it is possible to derive from it rules and principles, implicitly or explicitly formulated, but also holdings and supporting arguments. In such a case, the subsequent decision often includes broad discussions concerning the holding of the precedent and the arguments adduced to justify the solution given to the legal issues involved. Not infrequently, however, the mere dictum or the maxim are derived from published judgments without paying any attention to the arguments used in the opinions.

The same happens when the precedent is a judgment delivered by the Constitutional Court. The judgment is always published in its whole text, and the binding part of the precedent is often the holding and the arguments stated in support of it. Sometimes even the *obiter dicta* are taken into account, if it seems that the court ascribes a special importance to them. Very often, however, even the judgments of the Constitutional Court are used only as abstract maxims.

The factor that is usually lacking in the use of precedents by Italian courts is the thorough analysis of facts and the emphasis on the similarity between the facts of the prior and of the subsequent decision. The 'facts' of the precedent are not known, nor are they knowable, when the precedent is used in decision making. There is also a habit of reasoning by legal abstract situations or by legal issues, rather than by factual situations. Therefore the only similarity that can justify the use of a precedent concerns the legal issues involved, not the facts of the cases. Notwithstanding all this, rather frequently, and when it is actually possible, the court in the subsequent case takes into account the substantive reasons adduced by the precedent to support the interpretation of a rule or the application of a principle.

As we have already seen, in the Italian system it is improper to ascribe any past legal decision a formally binding force in the sense that the judge would be bound in issuing the decision for the question at stake to conform to past legal decisions, subject to reversal. The Italian judge has no such obligation. Nevertheless, precedent in its various forms (as one single authoritative past legal decision, as a coherent set of past decisions constantly solving similar issues in a certain uniform way, a 'maxim' extrapolated either from the *ratio decidendi* or from *obiter dicta* of a legal decision by a special public agency) is quite relevant to justify decisions taken by judges, insofar as precedent serves as an interpretative argument, as a means of interpreting a legal rule (a statute) or a legal principle. An Italian judge is not allowed to justify decisions solely with reference to precedents. The judge ought to refer to legal rules, or to principles of the legal order, that is, to principles internal to the system. Now, in order for precedent to play its supplementary role as interpretive argument, it is necessary to know or to establish what counts as a precedent, or what part of a precedent has to be taken into account as an argument for the present decision. This varies according to the different kind of precedent we are confronted with. As regards the so-called *'massime'*, there is not so much to discuss. A *massima* is already drafted as a general rule or principle, deprived of its previous contextual qualities. In this case the binding – so to speak – element quite obviously is an explicitly formulated rule or principle. The problem is more complicated where the precedent at hand is a complete concrete decision (one, for example, published in a legal journal because of its novelty and relevance). In this second case, the 'binding' element is a combination of two elements: on the one side a similarity of material facts, and on the other an explicit or a constructed holding on an issue of law.

Another element of 'bindingness' of precedents is held to be their age. For instance, the Constitutional Court is used to distinguish between (a) recent, (b) less recent and (c) old precedents, ascribing a higher binding value to the 'recent' rather than to the 'less recent' or to the 'old' precedent. Behind this view there is a conception of judicial activity centred around the idea of evolutionary or progressive interpretation. We might conclude, then, that with regard to precedent Italian judges have a *right* to use precedent, not an *obligation*. The same holds as far as precedents of the Constitutional Court are concerned.

In Italy precedents are adduced as authoritative examples in order to support a particular interpretation of a statute or of a general principle of law. We are here very close to a typical argument *ex auctoritate*, that is, to that argument by which a normative sentence is given that meaning which had already been attributed to it by someone and by this mere fact. Indeed, we are here in between a mere authoritative argument (based on the authority of the court or of the judge issuing a ruling, as is the case with judges and courts at the top of the institutional judicial hierarchy, for instance the Italian Corte di Cassazione) and an argument based on examples, where the latter represents a bridge between a plurality of previous cases decided in a uniform and coherent way and the present case. The precedent is therefore one among many other possible examples used to certify a regularity in the judicial activity, which by this very fact acquires an element of bindingness.

2　Reasoning about Applicability

Generally, the applicability of a precedent is justified by arguments stated for and against it. This is especially true in scholarly writings devoted to the analysis and discussion of the case law concerning specific legal issues. Something similar happens rather frequently also in judgments based upon precedents. In such cases the prevailing form of argument consists in determining what is the rule or principle stated by the precedent, and in applying it as the legal premise of the decision. This happens mainly when the precedent is in fact a trend or chain of consistent and conforming precedents: the precedent is clear and undoubted, and then the maxim may be used easily as the legal standard for the following decision. There are, however, many situations in which precedents are unclear, inconsistent or conflicting. Correspondingly, the choice of the precedent to follow is complex and difficult. In such a situation the judge in the following case cannot avoid a critical analysis of the precedents at hand, in order to choose the one he or she considers as the 'true' precedent to apply. Then the reasoning of the judge about the precedents must deal with the substantive reasons supporting the several precedents, and with a critical examination of them. Consider, however, that in most cases this critical examination deals with the legal and technical arguments supporting the different precedents, and that the discussion is often theoretical and abstract.

It should be stressed that in many cases the precedent is merely referred to, simply by citing (with date and number) the judgment(s) invoked as precedent(s). Then a maxim concerning a legal rule or principle is stated, and a precedent or a list of precedents are cited in support of it. Rather frequently, conflicting maxims are stated, and lists of precedents are cited in support of each of them. In such cases, the substantive reasons that were stated in the precedent are not taken into account, nor are they discussed. The precedents are cited just to show that a legal maxim has been used in other judgments. Moreover, the mere citation of some precedents is usually considered to be a fair and sufficient justification of the statement of a legal rule or principle. Close factual analysis is normally absent from arguments adduced to justify the use of precedents.

Reasoning from general rationales for following precedent does not occur. Following precedent is something *in re ipsa* in judicial practice. The real problem is to find a precedent to follow among a chaotic and complex case law.

3 Juristic Discussion

Until quite recently, in Italian legal doctrine obsessed by supremacy of legislation and by a principle of the rule of law interpreted in a strict formalist and positivist way, there was no room for discussion about the value of precedents. Precedents as such were considered irrelevant for a valid justification of judicial decisions: judges should decide only with reference to legislative acts of parliament. Thanks to studies by a few scholars, reflecting the emerging reality of a widespread use of precedents in legal argumentation, there is now an interest in precedents. Since the 1960s there has been discussion about whether the Italian legal order, in spite of being a 'civilian' system, does have a doctrine of precedents. Thanks also to the increasing power and scope of action of the Italian judiciary, there is now a growing tendency to use past legal decisions to justify present judicial work. A sign of a modified attitude towards precedents may be seen in the recent reform of the exams required for admission to the bar. Now the law (see Article 4 of the law of 27 June 1988, n. 242) allows candidates to use codes containing commentaries of past judicial decisions when they are publicly called to write their exam papers.

In particular, given the peculiar system of *massime* elaborated by the Ufficio del Massimario of the supreme court (Corte di Cassazione), there has been a debate about the rational structure of the *massime* themselves. Three problems at least have been singled out: should a *massima* contain only a *ratio decidendi*, or could it reproduce an *obiter dictum*; what is the normative value of *obiter dicta* for the decision of future cases; and what are the methods for distinguishing an *obiter dictum* from the *ratio decidendi*? There is also a discussion of what conditions are required in order that the principle which justifies its solution could be considered a *ratio decidendi*. The character of the *ratio decidendi* for a principle or ruling does not depend, it has been argued, only on its being material for the reasoning which has led to the decision. In order to understand this point we should remember that precedents in the Italian system usually are *massime*, that *massime* usually are taken from decisions by the Corte di Cassazione, and finally that these decisions deal with 'formal' cases, that is, mainly points of law. Thus, the *ratio decidendi* adopted for the solution of a 'formal' case by the supreme court (Corte di Cassazione) can be different from the *ratio decidendi* which justifies the decision on the merits of the concrete case by the lower court to which the case has been remitted. Some scholars have also underlined the extreme difficulty in distinguishing between *ratio decidendi* and *obiter dictum* in those cases in which a decision is taken by moving from a rule or principle established as generally valid, except for the case at hand, which must be decided on the basis of a different standard because of its 'exceptional' features. What here is the *ratio decidendi* of the case – the ruling explicitly formulated as generally valid except for the case at hand, or the more particular considerations which justify the 'exception' and then the concrete decision?

4 Illustrative or Analogical Precedent

Precedents are very frequently used as mere examples rather than as binding standards of decision making. They are often referred to just in order to show that a rule or principle may be and has been interpreted in a given way and applied to a given factual situation. In such cases they are used in order to clarify the meaning of a provision or of a principle, and to stress that they may be applied to some situations. Precedents are often cited also as *negative* examples, that is as examples of wrong or disputable and doubtful solutions of a legal issue. Also in these cases, the example is used to clarify *e contrario* the meaning of a provision or principle. Generally, when a statutory or constitutional rule is interpreted, and its meaning has to be completely explored, examples given by precedents are used as interpretive tools, just to show that certain meanings have been adopted in prior decisions. Of course, in such cases the precedent has no binding effect.

The same may happen when there is an analogy between the prior decision and the case at hand, but it is not strictly in point: the reference to precedents may be useful to show that there is a trend in the case law, concerning cases or issues *roughly similar* to the case at hand. Also in such a situation the precedent does not have any really binding effect: its actual function is to provide knowledge concerning the case law in a given area, and is not to be applied as the governing *ratio decidendi* in the subsequent case. In such cases, examples are referred to with the aim of harmonizing the decision with the case law existing on the topic or in that area of the law.

5 Single Precedents or Lines of Decision?

In the Italian system there is a sharp distinction between the single precedent and the line or chain of precedent. The single precedent may be persuasive, but only when it is a new precedent on a new legal issue, or it is the only precedent concerning a legal issue. But the persuasive effectiveness of a coherent line of precedent is much higher and is almost binding, or at least weakly binding. It means that the line of precedent should be used as a standard for decision making, unless good countervailing reasons apply. In fact, when a coherent line of precedents exists, it is almost as if there were a corresponding legal principle saying what the precedents say. Of course, the line of precedents is not formally binding, but it is usually considered as strongly influential in the subsequent decisions. Once again, however, it should be stressed that this happens only when the line of precedent is clear and consistent; things are much more complex and doubtful when the line of precedent is uncertain or when there are conflicting lines of precedents.

In fact the Italian judicial practice has several types of lines, chains or strings of precedents. Lines consisting of merely repetitive precedents are frequent, and they are often used as a basis for a subsequent judgment. A line of repetitive precedents is considered as a clear and sure standard for decision making. It is used as a sort of deductive major premise in judicial reasoning. Its effect and function is similar to that of a legal rule or principle. Lines of precedents are often explicitly confirmed by following judgments. Frequently, the Corte di Cassazione quotes a line of its own precedents about a legal issue, stating expressly that such a line is confirmed.

Sometimes this confirmation is not only a repetition of the exact terms of the precedents confirmed. The subsequent confirmation may add something to such terms: it may restate the meaning of precedents in a more explicit way, or even reinterpret the precedents so as to reconstruct their global meaning. Then the following confirming judgment may 'synthetize' the prior line of precedents, and restate their ratio in new and clear terms, with some possible additions.

Conflicting and zigzag lines of precedents are a quite common phenomenon in the Italian system. The overproduction of precedents by the higher courts is the obvious main reason for this. When thousands of judgments are delivered every year, and the same legal issues are dealt with dozens of times, such a phenomenon is almost unavoidable.

Scholars and commentators often deal with lines of precedents. Actually, an important part of the Italian legal literature is made up of essays, books and commentaries entirely devoted to the analysis of the case law in the several areas of the legal system. Sometimes these books or essays do not use any critical or systematic approach: they are mere compilations simply listing the precedents about a topic in reverse chronological order; sometimes the only original contribution is in choosing the most important judgments among a mass of precedents concerning the same issue. There are, however, also more interesting and sophisticated analyses of lines of precedents and of the case law in general. Scholars and commentators deal with precedents using systematic conceptual frameworks, with the aim of clarifying the meaning of a line of precedents, of making more explicit such a meaning, and of reconstructing it when it is not clear enough in the terms of precedents themselves. This work of analytic reconstruction may go very far: the author often reconstructs the meaning of the case law using his own concepts and theories in order to determine the 'proper' meaning of precedents. Sometimes it may be impossible to detect whether it is a critical and systematic reconstruction of the case law, or a dogmatic theory that is built up by a scholar using references to precedents merely as a support for his own theory. At any rate, the work of scholars and commentators is very useful: they research and study the lines of precedents, eliciting their proper meaning; they stress conflicts among precedents and lines of precedents, trying to identify the just way to overcome the conflict; they tend to reconcile diverging precedents and to put some coherence and consistency into the mass of precedents; they also suggest further developments of the case law, stressing the gaps in the system, and urge new approaches. Sometimes these efforts have some influence in the courts, but usually this takes a long time. The influence is more direct when legal scholars suggest new solutions for new issues, because the courts may use the ideas in legal literature as comfortable 'ready-made' solutions. The influence is more indirect and slow when there is already a complex mass of precedents on uncertain and doubtful legal issues.

6   The Concept of a 'Leading Case'

A leading case usually has significant importance in the Italian practice concerning precedents. Leading cases are frequently cited just as precedents that opened the way for a solution of a legal issue. The arguments that were used in leading cases are often discussed and followed in subsequent decisions, sometimes for decades later. Consider, however, that a leading case is not important in itself, but just because it is a 'leading case', that is because it has been followed by a consistent line of precedents. Then it may be said that the actual function of precedent is not performed by the leading case alone, but by the line of precedents that it started. On the other hand, it is clear that a leading case can be identified as such only ex post, that is only by checking whether it has 'led' a coherent line of precedents. Ex ante, every judgment stating a new solution of a legal issue, or solving a new legal issue, may eventually become a leading case, but this will actually happen only if such a judgment is followed by a series of subsequent decisions applying the same legal standard. The leading case is significant, therefore, but only because it is the first link in a chain of coherent precedents.

V Distinguishing, Explaining, Modifying, Overruling

1 Distinguishing

In the Italian system it is quite difficult to conceive a practice of 'distinguishing', since the precedent considered most of the time is actually a kind of principle *(massima)* and not a case. What judges and lawyers find are not cases with the specification of the facts on which the decision was taken, but general principles (without reference to cases, to facts) expressed as general formulations of the contents of rules. There is then no need for 'distinguishing', since there is no factual point on which to base distinguishing, since what is considered is not a 'case' which, in order to be relevant for the present case, we hold similar to the case in question.

Nevertheless, there have been changes due to the evolving role of the Corte di Cassazione. Since this court is more and more oriented to serving as a higher court of appeal deciding not only questions of legitimacy but also the merits of the case, its decisions have an increasingly smaller scope. The present practice of the court is directed to making effective, not a *jus constitutonis*, that is a uniform interpretation of the law (as it was conceived in its 'pure' theoretical formulation), but to satisfy a *jus litigatoris*, that is, the parties' specific claim dealing with their particular interests – questions of substantive justice rather than issues of coherence in law. Thus a decision by the Corte di Cassazione might serve as precedent only for cases which are 'identical' (very similar) to the one covered by the precedent.

2 Juristic Commentary

For the reason explained above, scholarly or other juristic commentators do not discuss points of difference (distinguishing) between reported precedents in a way that could give rise to a technique of 'distinguishing' along lines similar to the technique developed in common law systems. Nevertheless, it is a matter of course that a precedent in order to be used should be considered relevant for the case at hand, that is, showed concern facts similar to those of the case to be decided. And in order to ascertain such similarity there must be some practice, be it even unreflective, of distinguishing between cases which are not similar and between precedents which do not deal with similar cases.

The technique of 'distinguishing' has been seen as fundamental on the one side in order to evaluate the contrast between two decisions and their respective *rationes decidendi,* which after a scrutiny of the material facts would appear compatible, and on the other side in order to appreciate the similarity of two decisions which would in the end be only literary (as similar only in their respective linguistic formulation) without correspondence in the supportive justification, once the material facts of the cases have been considered. Given the structure and editing of our collections of 'maxims', it is even possible that a contrast of abstract rules ('maxims') does not correspond to a real contrast of views concerning the *ratio decidendi,* since one of the contrasting maxims might well be based on some *obiter dicta* rather than on the *ratio decidendi.*

3   Excessive Distinguishing?

In common law systems, 'distinguishing', 'explaining' or 'restating' a precedent is more or less equivalent to what in civilian systems is represented by statutory interpretation. Indeed, one interprets a statute by 'restating' or 'explaining' and, in a sense, 'distinguishing' between the abstract state of affairs or conduct provided for in the written law and the case at hand to be decided. Italian courts did not develop any practice of 'distinguishing' a precedent as a special legal technique. If they do not intend to refer to a precedent, they either ignore it or abruptly say that they do not agree with the precedent in question, and that they consider it a piece of wrong statutory interpretation. Fine or even unreal distinctions are used in the interpretation of a statute (for instance, in the case of 'extensive' or 'progressive' interpretation).

'Distinguishing', in the moderate form it takes in Italian judicial practice due to the non-bindingness of precedent, might be related to the hierarchical rank of the court. Precedents of the supreme court or of higher courts are more weighty than precedents by lower courts. They cover, at the same time, a more general area of cases. Distinguishing between precedents of the supreme court requires special consideration of the legal issues at stake rather more than the merits of the case. Special care is required if one distinguishes a precedent issued by the full bench (Sezioni Riunite) of the Corte di Cassazione. The reputation of the court or of the judge writing the opinion is not so relevant since the precedent, as we have seen, often takes the form of a 'maxim' extrapolated from the concrete opinion by some other subject.

Changes in the political economic or social background since the prior decision are fundamental, especially so far as decisions of the Constitutional Court are concerned. This court has explicitly manifested an attitude according to which the constitutional judge has to consider whether the previous decision of the court does correspond to the new social, economic and political situation. Quite important is the 'age' of a precedent. As has been remarked, as a matter of fact the criterion of equality between different facts which directs the application of a precedent holds only if the facts to be compared are not so distant in time that their similarity could be called into question by this very distance. This attitude might be due to the legalist ideology which lies at the bottom of a statutory system such as the Italian. According to the modern doctrine of public law, one of the features of the law, or of statutory law, is the fact that it introduces a modification of (legal) reality. Law is such insofar as it changes a previous state of affairs. This view contrasts strongly with the pre-modern concept of law as something 'old'. This radical turn of the concept of law brought about by modernity has an impact on the concept of precedent itself, that is on something which as a matter of course should have an age, and be somewhat *old*. But in our modern legal systems, and especially in statutory codified systems, for a precedent to be 'valid' it must not be *too* old. If it is, it will be considered to be deprived of its normative force, connected as this is to some capacity of representing or causing a change, a *modification*, in the legal sphere. In modern civilian systems, past legal decisions have validity in future cases insofar as they are open to some procedure of distinguishing and restating, since the law (and that dictated by the judge is no exception) is seen as constitutive of a new state of affairs.

4 Types of Overruling

In the Italian system there is no formal machinery to overrule precedents, since there are no formally binding precedents. There are no special procedures to follow when overruling is under consideration. For the same reason, the power of overruling precedents is not vested in a given court. Such a system may be better understood by considering that a precedent is not formally overruled or set aside, or declared null or void, or cancelled and erased from the legal system. Instead of that, the precedent is merely not followed any more as a legal basis for deciding subsequent cases. It simply stops being considered as persuasive, and then it is no longer taken into account. However, it should be stressed that a sort of institutionalized overruling may be an outcome of special procedures existing in the Corte di Cassazione and in the Consiglio di Stato. There are special panels in these courts whose function is to decide cases of special importance or cases that have been already decided in contrasting ways by the ordinary chambers of the court. When these special panels decide a case, it may happen that such a judgment actually overrules some precedents.

Sometimes a precedent is overruled implicitly, simply because the judges in the subsequent cases ignore it. Sometimes, on the contrary, precedent is explicitly rejected or set aside. Generally, this peculiar kind of overruling is used by the same court that set the precedent, when the court reconsiders the case and chooses a different solution for the same legal issue. This happens rather frequently because the highest courts, and especially the Corte di Cassazione, have several opportunities to decide the same issue, in many cases also in the same year or in the same month. Since, moreover, different chambers or different panels may deal with the same legal issue in different cases, one may easily understand that occasions for changing approaches and solutions to the same problem are very frequent.

When the precedent is openly set aside by the same court that set it, this sometimes happens on the basis of arguments concerning changes that have occurred in the legal context that affects the specific issue, or in the political, social or economic background of the issue. In a word, the precedent is superseded when it appears *obsolete* and no longer sound as a basis for deciding a subsequent case. This often happens with precedents of the Constitutional Court: the court changes its mind when the legal context or some other background conditions have changed, and also when the evolution of the legal culture or of the general conscience leads to stating the problem in a new and different or more developed and sophisticated way. Then a statute that was 'saved' in the past may be found unconstitutional because the social or cultural context concerning its constitutional legitimacy has changed.

More often, however, a precedent is set aside because a different solution of the same legal issue is considered more sound or more proper and correct from the legal technical point of view. Sometimes this happens because something has changed in the context of the provisions concerning the case. But often it happens only because the evolution of the technical analysis or of the dogmatics concerning the legal issue yields a new solution that is preferred because of its theoretical or technical advantage. Then a new solution is adopted just because it is legally more sophisticated than the prior one. When this is the case, the arguments used to justify the choice of the new solution and the overruling of the precedent are based upon the legal and conceptual analysis of the reasons why the new solution is technically 'correct'.

It is worth stressing that, in the Italian system, even in the trial courts of general jurisdiction, precedents are frequently abandoned or set aside or overruled, both implicitly and explicitly. This is probably a symptom of a rapid evolution, at least in some areas of the law, but it is also the source of conflicts, uncertainties and vagueness of the case law. Generally, there are no significant differences depending on the kind of precedent or the area of the law involved.

When a precedent is explicitly overruled, the court usually gives some reasons for this, although no special reasons are required to justify an overruling. Such reasons are usually more complex and detailed when a line of precedent is set aside and the court chooses a new and different standard of decision making. A single precedent is more often implicitly overruled. Overruling a line of precedent usually requires an explicit holding and a justificatory argument supporting the decision to overrule.

In the Italian system the precedent is not even defeasibly binding. Nevertheless, precedents are often followed in fact, especially precedents of the supreme court (Corte di Cassazione). If in the judicial ruling we distinguish two different moments or contexts, that of the decision making and that of the justification, we could say that precedents are effective as far as the mere moment of decision is concerned. The same does not hold for the justification. A decision may be justified also without reference or mention of any particular precedent, although such a reference or mention can be used as supportive or persuasive argument.

That is why there is no normative practice or procedure for 'overruling'. Nonetheless, a judge who does not intend to follow an established precedent by the supreme court (Corte di Cassazione) will pay special attention to the argumentation employed. The lower court judge is even expected to mention the precedent which that judge is not willing to follow.

5   Prospective Overruling

The power of prospectively overruling a precedent is not vested in any court. Moreover, the technique of 'prospective overruling' is not used. The main reason is probably that every judgment of higher courts is delivered about a specific and concrete case, and what is said in the decision, and in arguments supporting the judgment, refers only to the decision of that case. Therefore either the court overrules the precedent while deciding the case in issue or it does not overrule the precedent and applies it in the decision of the concrete case. Sometimes it happens that, examining the arguments used and paying attention to the *obiter dicta*, one may guess that the court is probably going to change its orientation in future cases. But it is a matter of interpreting signs and symptoms in a judgment, not a prospective overruling in the proper sense.

Something similar to prospective overruling occurs sometimes in judgments delivered by the Constitutional Court. The court may believe that the statute involved is actually in conflict with a constitutional principle, but also that it is better not to invalidate it immediately, in order to avoid relevant gaps in the legal system. But the court sometimes invites parliament to change the statute according to the requirements of the constitution, threatening to abrogate that statute in the future if it is not changed. In most cases, however, parliament does not react to the court, and the court does not dare to nullify the statute.

6   Anticipatory Overruling by Lower Courts

Anticipatory overruling is not specifically conceptualized as such in Italy. Correspondingly, there is no legal problem concerning whether it is permitted or not. What happens in practice is that, rather frequently, lower courts refuse to follow precedents set by higher courts. It may depend on the foresight that the higher court will probably overrule the precedent, but this is not the only situation. Quite often, in fact, lower courts 'rebel against precedents' of higher courts just because they do not agree with the solutions adopted by the precedents (independently of any prediction of the future behaviour of the higher court). The reason for such a rebellion is simply that the lower court believes that a different decision is more proper and just, or more legally correct, for the case at hand. Then the precedent is set aside as 'not fit' for the case, or as legally wrong. When this happens, the lower court usually delivers an opinion containing the arguments supporting its decision and justifying the choice not to apply the precedent.

7   Precedent and Legislative Practice

In legislative practice, Italian drafters of legislation or members of government do take account of case law and precedent as well of prior statute law. In particular they (should) take account of the decisions of the Constitutional Court which, although only abrogative of prior legislation, do often issue directives the legislator should follow in future practice in order to comply with constitutional rules and principles. But the same is generally true so far as matters not covered by decisions by the Constitutional Court are concerned. A consistent interpretation of a statute, especially by the supreme court (Corte di Cassazione), is taken into account as a basis for the legislative reformulation of the statute.

Since in the Italian legal system one might seek 'bindingness' of precedents only from a sociological (external) perspective, by the ascertainment of regularities in the behaviour of judges, and not from a legal (internal) point of view, there is no need for legislative confirmation or reversal of case law through legislation.

8 Conflicts of Precedents

Conflicts of precedents and of lines of precedents are rather common in Italy. We have already dealt with this situation and its reasons above (Section II.7). Conflicts often last several years, although the higher courts may deal several times with the same issue. The consequence may be that lines of precedent support every possible solution of the same issue.

Sometimes conflicts are solved because one of the conflicting precedents, or one of the conflicting lines of precedent, is abandoned or overruled, and the other precedent or line of precedents finally prevails. It may also happen that a new solution, different from all prior conflicting solutions, is adopted, and this solution becomes authoritative and is uniformly followed in subsequent judgments. All these possibilities may occur inside the slow and complex development of the case law concerning a legal issue. Changes in the orientation of courts may even produce the solution of conflicts among precedents. Sometimes conflicts among precedents are solved because scholars and commentators suggest a solution that is accepted and followed by the courts.

There are, however, special procedures that are aimed at solving conflicts of precedents in peculiar situations. When the same legal issue has been solved in conflicting ways by the ordinary chambers of the Corte di Cassazione or of the Consiglio di Stato, and it seems clear that such conflicts cannot be eliminated through normal development of the case law, the conflict can be submitted (by the chief chairmen of the courts) to the decision of special panels. The special panel of the Corte di Cassazione is called the Sezioni Unite and is composed of nine judges of the court; the special panel of the Consiglio di Stato is called the Adunanza Plenaria and is composed of seven judges of the court. These special panels decide the case submitted to them with a judgment that *should* be followed by the ordinary chambers of the court while deciding subsequent cases dealing with the same legal issue. However, the ordinary chambers are not formally bound by the precedent of the special panel; they are allowed to decide new cases not following such a precedent. In such a case, the ordinary sections are only expected to state good justificatory arguments supporting their choice not to follow the precedents of the special panel. Therefore the decision of the special panels is just *aimed at* solving the conflict, but the conflict may last even after such a decision, or it may arise again afterwards. Such decisions have in fact only a persuasive force: they may influence the following of judgments of the ordinary sections of the court, and also of any other court, but they do not have any formal bindingness.

9   *Hypothetical Cases*

The use of hypothetical cases is a rather frequent type of argument in legal reasoning in general and in the creation and application of precedents. Probably the most frequent way of using hypothetical cases is in the form of *reductio ad absurdum* argument: a hypothetical case is imagined just to show that a precedent or a legal rule cannot be interpreted and applied to that case without producing absurd and unacceptable consequences.

However, a positive use of hypothetical cases seems also to be rather frequent. The hypothetical case has then the same function as a real decision used as an example: it is useful to show that a precedent or a rule can be interpreted and applied in that way; that is, also covering that case. Extreme hypothetical cases are also used sometimes, although much less frequently, in order to test the meaning and the scope of a precedent.

VI   Matters of General Perspective, Evaluation and Other

1   *'Saying and Doing'*

Reported decisions fail to reflect the real justificatory use of precedent, since they are drafted and edited in a too abstract and general way. Although the style of the Italian judge is more deductive than inductive, still he has to take into account the peculiarity of the case, and this is not revealed in legal reports and collections of *massime.*

There is a lively discussion going on now among scholars about the inadequateness of our collections of reported decisions, especially of collections of *massime.* These, as we know, are abstract rules and principles derived from the legal decision and laid down by a special agency sitting in the Corte di Cassazione (Ufficio del Massimario) or else they are 'extracted' by the editorial boards of the private publishers collecting these general rules. These collections are criticized from many angles. First of all, they do not mention the facts on which the decision has been taken. This happens often in the case of decisions reported in legal journals, which reproduce only the legal points of the decisions and omit any reference to facts. Collections of 'maxims' in legal journals report abstract rules without even mentioning the case involved. This practice – as has been remarked by one of the most influential Italian comparative lawyers, Gino Gorla – does not help Italian judges and lawyers develop a justificatory style based on some sort of inductive or analogical procedure (drawing a solution for a case from the solution adopted for a similar case). Instead, the style is deductive: first having a general rule, and then applying it to the case. The 'maxim' is a general rule in a way which is quite close to the statutory rule. It is even, sometimes, more general than the latter. The 'maxim' is also very often no more than a restatement of the statutory provision without any addition to it.

But there is a further problem concerning the 'maxim'. The reader of the report cannot be sure that it is the *ratio decidendi*, let alone the nucleus of the *ratio decidendi*. The maxim might have been derived from an *obiter dictum* without any special relevance for the decision of the case. Moreover, the omission of any reference to the facts means that maxims of two or more decisions can appear contradictory when, all things considered, they are quite coherent.

For all these reasons, there have been proposals to change the way of reporting decisions. In particular, it has been proposed that the 'maxim' should be laid down by the same judge who writes the decision. This innovation would limit the possibility of having a 'maxim' taken from an *obiter dictum*. Some scholars have also proposed changing the style of Italian legal reports by the introduction of a short version of the facts for each case.

2 Recent Change or Evolution

We may divide the evolution of the use of legal precedent in Italy into three main stages. In a first stage, which began around the sixteenth century with the establishment of the so-called 'Grandi tribunali', that is of supreme courts, in the various Italian states, precedents had a binding character, since they were seen as a formal source of law. Article 9, Title 22, of Book 3 of the 'Regie Costituzioni' of the State of Piedmont, issued in 1729, reads as follows:

> Voulons que dans la décision des procès on observe uniquement: en premier lieu nos Constitutions; secondement les Statuts des lieux, pourvu qu'ils soient par nous approuvés, ou par nos Royaux Prédecesseurs, et qu'ils soient en observance; troisièmement les décisions de nos magistrats, et finalement le texte du droit commun.

Judges thus were bound, first, by the laws issued by the prince, secondly by local statutes approved by the prince himself or by his predecessors, thirdly by judicial decisions taken by the courts, and finally by the *jus commune*.

The second stage of this evolution began with the enactment of the codes of the nineteenth century. In particular, Article 73 of 'Statuto albertino' of 1848, which later became the constitution of the new Italian kingdom, ascribed the power of interpreting the law with general validity only to the legislator. By virtue of this article, which embodied a rigid conception of the separation of powers, any judicial decision was deprived of binding force, that is, of any validity going beyond the case in question.

A third stage began with the establishment of a unique Corte di Cassazione in 1924 dealing with private law cases and in particular with the new codes (Civil Code and Code of Civil Procedure) enacted on 21 April 1942. A very important role is also played by the Act on the Organization of the Judiciary of 30 January 1941. In this act we find a provision (Article 65) which prescribes that the supreme court (Corte di Cassazione) ought to guarantee 'the uniform interpretation of the law, the unity of national law'. Furthermore, Article 118 of 'Disposizioni di attuazione' of the Code of Civil Procedure prescribes how the Italian judge has to justify formally his decisions, forbidding any reference to particular legal scholars but not forbidding the use of precedent, which therefore might be considered as permitted. It has been argued that, because of these two articles, the decisions issued by the Corte di Cassazione, though not binding, nevertheless have a legal, normative force. They are not only factually relevant; they have legal authority, insofar as they should be respected in order to secure the uniform application of the law. This normative force prevails unless there are good reasons based on values which are considered stronger than coherence of the legal system and formal equality. Any decision to deviate from the precedent should be explicit and properly justified.

In recent decades the Corte di Cassazione has indeed been more concerned with deciding correctly (justly) the single case rather than with establishing a coherent interpretation of the law. The court has been looking more often backwards, not forwards. Its behaviour has not been especially different from that of lower courts. This means that the precedent is not established as such by the court itself, but rather the decision is 'constructed' by a later judge as a precedent. This, of course, allows for manipulation and arbitrariness.

3   Changes in International Environment

The quite high degree of unawareness about precedents in legal adjudication among Italian judges and lawyers has not changed despite the increasing intertwining between the national legal order and a supranational one (deriving from international treaties and covenants, and especially from the emergence of European Community law). The development of transnational institutions such as the EC, now the European Union, or special human rights agencies, such as the European Court of Human Rights, has not, in Italy, contributed to new approaches to the doctrine of precedent. Nonetheless, as regards the practice of precedent, there has been an important development through decisions of the European Court of Justice taken according to Article 177 of the EC treaty. As is well known, such decisions deal with issues of interpretation of European Community law; these are reserved to the European Court of Justice which is required to see to it that European Community law be uniformly interpreted and applied. A lower court of a member state *may* and a court of last instance *should*, refer to the European Court of Justice, if an interpretive question is raised and is relevant while dealing with an issue of domestic law. The European Court of Justice decisions taken according to Article 177 are binding as far as the case at hand is concerned. That means that the national court should adopt the interpretation of the rule of EC law by the European Court of Justice for solving the particular issue which has been brought before the national court itself. The question then arises whether the decision taken by the European Court of Justice ex Article 177 on a specific case can claim to bind national judges beyond the case for which it was laid down. In an important decision, *International Chemical Corporation* v. *Amministrazione dello Stato* ([1981] ECR 1191), the European Court of Justice has affirmed that its interpretive decision, establishing an act of a European Institution as legally void, is a sufficient reason for any national court of a member state to consider that act as void as well, unless the national court thinks it necessary to reconsider the case (that is, the nullity of the act), as when there is a controversy concerning the grounds, the scope and the consequences of the nullity of that act.

Now this declaration of the European Court of Justice in the *International Chemical Corporation* case seems to introduce a doctrine of *stare decisis* even within systems where this doctrine has never been accepted. It obliges national courts first of all to feel bound by the precedent established by the European Court of Justice – which can already be a dramatic change in an internal domestic legal order and in the doctrine of judicial application adopted within it. The *stare decisis* doctrine affirmed by the court also obliges courts of member states to acquire and develop methods for assessing precedents (their scope, for instance). The national court should first take into account the precedent established by the European Court of Justice, then consider to what extent it covers the issue at hand and, if it does not, the court should raise a new interpretive issue for the same case before the European Court of Justice. All this implies that domestic courts should somehow acquire some familiarity with techniques of 'distinguishing' precedents. This new development introduces an explicit doctrine of precedent even in legal systems, such as the Italian, quite hostile to it.

4   *Juristic or other criticism*

In the last decades a large body of academic literature has been devoted in Italy to a critical analysis of the way precedents are created and used. It is generally acknowledged that the use of precedents is by now a daily practice in every court, that precedents are an essential factor in the evolution of the legal system, that they are actually a source of law (even if not formally or legally recognized) and that they are an extremely useful means of filling gaps, interpreting statutes and determining just decisions for concrete cases.

Yet the common opinion is strongly critical of the way precedents are created and used in the Italian system. The higher courts, and especially the Corte di Cassazione, decide an enormous mass of cases each year, and they annually decide the same legal issue several times. The enormous workload requires that hundreds of judges and several chambers with different panels are employed to deal with all the cases brought to the court. This is the main cause of an inconsistent, varying and uncertain body of case law in almost every area of the legal system. Moreover, the court makes its decisions with the main aim of deciding concrete cases, and shapes its judgments mainly on the basis of the specific features of the cases and of the arguments adduced by the parties. Its decisions are thus oriented much more 'to the past', that is to the case that must be finally decided, than 'to the future', that is, to subsequent cases. Usually, therefore, the court does not decide in order to set a precedent, but only in order to solve a concrete case. The only exception to this is when a special panel (the Sezioni Unite of the Corte di Cassazione and the Adunanza Plenaria of the Consiglio di Stato) is charged with the task of 'showing the way' in an especially important case, or with resolving a conflict in the case law produced by single chambers.

A consequence is that there are far too many precedents in most areas of the law. Moreover, they are often inconsistent, uncertain and conflicting. In a way, the case law set by higher courts is like a sort of department store where every litigant may find anything he needs, if he searches carefully. Since precedents are shaped according to the features of concrete cases, it is obvious that they are not coherent as a body of legal rules.

Paradoxically, the Italian precedent, which usually – as we already know – has the form of a *massima*, may lack any real connection to the case about which the judgment was delivered. Therefore using precedents frequently becomes a play of abstract maxims rather than the search for a just and proper *ratio decidendi* governing the case at hand.

A further defect of the system is that many features of precedents and of their use are vague and uncertain. Vertical precedents exist, but their effective way of functioning is often unclear. The degree of bindingness of precedents may be defined mainly 'by exclusion' in comparison with the binding precedent of the common law systems, but it is extremely difficult to determine positively. In fact, precedents are used in very different ways according to the various situations, and the practice concerning precedents is extremely uncertain and varies from case to case. The overruling of a precedent is very common, but it happens in different ways, for very different reasons and without any rational framework. In fact, changes and variations are too frequent, and often they seem devoid of any sound justification. Therefore the precedent is too often an uncertain and unreliable point of reference for the decision of subsequent cases.

The creation and the use of precedents ought to be strongly and clearly rationalized. The higher courts should consciously create precedents, and should do this consistently and clearly. In order to do so, their workload should be reduced to, at most, 20 per cent of the present size, and other machinery should be introduced in order to rationalize this activity. Precedents should be recorded in a different way: the *massime* should be abolished, and the real *ratio decidendi* of the case should be elicited and reported, together with the main facts of the case. The problem of bindingness of precedent should be framed in rational terms defining what, when and under what conditions precedent should be binding. Correspondingly, the requirements of proper and justified overruling (even prospective or anticipatory, if deemed necessary) should also be clearly stated.

In a word, in the Italian system precedents have become essential and unavoidable in the daily practice of law and in the administration of justice. But they are badly created and even worse used, so that a deep and complete rationalization of the whole matter is necessary. The difficulty is that this requires important reforms concerning the functions and the organization of the higher courts and the role they perform in the system. But important changes are needed also in the daily practice of judges and counsel, and in the current legal culture.

Bibliography

Galgano, G. 'L'interpretazione del precedente guidiziario', *Contratto e impresa*, p.701 (1985).

Gorla, G. (1990), 'Precedente Giudiziale', in *Enciclopedia Giuridica*, vol. XXIII, Rome.

La dottrina del precedente nella giurisprudenza della Corte costituzionale (1971), Turin: UTET.

La giurisprudenza forense e dottrinale come fonte di diritto (1985), Milan: Giuffrè.

La giurisprudenza per massime e il valore del precedente (1988), Padua: CEDAM.

Taruffo, M. (1994), 'Giurisprudenza', in *Enciclopedia delle Scienae Sociali*, vol. IV, Rome: Istituto Della Enciclopedia Italiana, p.348.

6 Precedent in Norway

SVEIN ENG, *OSLO*

I   Institutional and Systemic

1(a)   Court Hierarchy

There are three main levels of courts in Norway, and these are the same both in civil and criminal cases. At the first level there are numerous local courts. When referring to this level in the abstract, or collectively to the individual courts at this level, one uses the common nouns *'byrett'* or *'herredsrett'*, for towns and rural areas respectively. A particular court at this level is referred to by prefixing the name of the place where the court is located or of the geographic area in which the court has power, for example, 'the decision of Oslo byrett'.

At the middle level there are six regional appeal courts. When referring to this level in the abstract, or collectively to the six courts at this level, one uses the common noun *'lagmannsrett'*. A particular court at this level is referred to by prefixing a proper name of Old Norwegian origin ('Borgarting', 'Eidsivating', 'Agder', 'Gulating', 'Frostating' and 'Hålogaland'), for example 'the decision of Borgarting lagmannsrett'.

At the highest level there is *one Supreme Court* (on scepticism towards specialized courts, see below). When referring to this level in the abstract, or collectively to the institutional forms in which decisions are made at this level, one uses the proper name *'Høyesterett'* (this is the wide sense of this name).

The Supreme Court carries out its work in three different institutional forms. The daily work is carried out in panels of five judges, called *'Høyesterett'* (this is the restricted sense of this name), or in panels of three judges, called 'Høyesteretts kjæremålsutvalg'. In some cases of a more exceptional kind (see Section I.1(b) below) all the

189

judges take part. This is called the 'Høyesterett i plenum' ('plenary session of the Supreme Court').

The three-judge panels of the Supreme Court decide several hundred cases each year, mostly on procedural matters or substantive matters of lesser importance; the court's decisions are based on the written pleadings and it gives a single collective, rather summary opinion. However, some of its decisions concern matters of more general legal importance, in which case the three judges themselves or the chief justice may transfer the case to a panel of five judges, thereby giving the case a full hearing, resulting in a full-fledged judgment (see Act Amending the Law Relating to Høyesterett of 25 June 1926, no. 2 § 6; and, for applications, for example Rt. 1994/1244, 1994/1036, 1994/732, 1994/729, 1994/721, 1994/610).

The main emphasis in the answers to this questionnaire is on panels of five judges, since it is through this institutional form that the Supreme Court produces most of its precedents. When nothing else is said or appears from the context, 'the Supreme Court' is used to refer to this form.

Norwegian lawyers traditionally entertain a sceptical attitude towards specialized courts, that is, courts whose competence is limited to particular areas of the law. (The term '*lawyer*' is used as a translation of the Norwegian 'jurist', that is, as denoting persons using their law degree professionally, be it in public or private positions or as self-employed persons). For example, the Norwegian system does not have courts with exclusive jurisdiction in constitutional matters or administrative matters.

1(b)   Structural and Procedural Aspects

There are 19 judges in the Supreme Court, which is the only court producing formally binding precedents (see Section II.1 below). In 1994 (figures for 1993 in brackets) the Supreme Court decided 337 (325) cases which may be termed 'possible full-fledged precedents'; that is, cases given a full hearing before an ordinary panel of five judges (see Section I.1(a) above; see also below) and with the opinions of all five judges (see below; also Section I.4). In 1994, this category of cases consisted of 68 (67) civil and 268 (258) criminal cases. In addition, the three-judge panels of the Supreme Court decided several hundred cases (mostly on procedural matters or substantive matters of lesser importance, as explained in Section I.1(a) above).

Usually the Supreme Court sits in panels of five judges (Courts of Justice Act of 13 August 1915, no. 5 § 5). The judges circulate according to internally instituted routine rules, that is, randomly in relation to the issues raised in the cases and the legal ability of the judges in relation to these issues (Sandene, 1989, p.300).

The Supreme Court *must* (according to the Act Amending the Law Relating to Høyesterett of 25 June 1926, no. 2 §§ 1–2) decide in *plenary session* when (a) two or more members of an ordinary panel wish to overrule a previous decision by the Supreme Court (whether this previous decision is one of an ordinary panel or one of a plenary session) *and* one of the members of the panel demands a plenary session; or (b) two or more members of an ordinary panel wish to invalidate a statute or a decision of the parliament, on constitutional grounds. In addition, the Supreme Court *may* (according to the said Act of 1926 § 3) decide in plenary session when special reasons make it desirable to do so.

The final decision of the Supreme Court consists of the opinion of each judge; that is, each and every judge has *a right and a duty* to voice his own opinion (the Civil Procedure Act of 13 August 1915, no. 6 § 149 compared with § 141, the Criminal Procedure Act of 22 May 1981, no. 25 § 41 compared with § 32).

The order of presenting one's opinion is fixed by routine rules, that is, without any consideration of the issues raised by the concrete case or the legal ability of the judges in relation to these issues. The chief justice is always the last to present his opinion (the Courts of Justice Act of 13 August 1915, no. 5 § 5 compared with the Civil Procedure Act of 13 August 1915, no. 6 § 141 and the Criminal Procedure Act of 22 May 1981, no. 25 § 32). When the chief justice does not take part in the adjudication of a case, the judge of senior age is the last to present his opinion (see the immediately preceding references). These statutory routine rules are supplemented by internally instituted routine rules according to which the judges alternate in presenting the first opinion (Sandene, 1989, pp.300–301).

During the discussions preceding the final decision, the judge writing the first opinion will try to incorporate the views of the other judges. If he succeeds, the other four will just concur in the first opinion. If he does not succeed, the first judge thereafter to disagree will voice his *dissenting opinion*. And so on, until each of the five judges in the panel has either concurred to a preceding opinion or voiced his own opinion. The final outcome of the case is then a function of the votes so cast (five to nil, four to one or three to two).

The constellation of votes, the opinions and the name of the judge giving each individual opinion, are all published in the law report for the decisions of the Supreme Court (see Section I.3 below). The constellation of votes and the quality of the opinions are regarded as important factors when deciding on the bindingness (weight) of the decision (see Section II.3 below, and factors (g) and (j) in the corresponding question in the Appendix).

1(c)   Power to Select Cases

The Civil Procedure Act of 13 August 1915, no. 6 § 373 says that the three-judge panels of the Supreme Court (see Section I.1(a) above) have power to deny leave of appeal when a panel unanimously finds that neither does the case have such *general significance* nor are any such other reasons present as to warrant the decision of the Supreme Court. On 1 August 1995 there came into force a procedural reform transforming the Supreme Court from first to second level appellate court in criminal cases (Act of 11 June 1993, no. 80). The Criminal Procedure Act of 22 May 1981, no. 25 § 323 was part of that reform; § 323 says that the three-judge panels of the Supreme Court only have power to grant leave of appeal when the case has *general significance* or when other reasons make it especially important to see the decision of the Supreme Court; however, a denial of leave must be unanimous.

These statutory provisions confer a *discretionary* power, the use of which is not followed by any reasons and is not itself appealable. How the power is used depends, among other factors, on how keen the judges are on making new law. This varies with the personality of the judge and with the mood of the time. At present, there seems to be a certain movement in Norwegian legal culture away from viewing the Supreme Court as a body only passively applying national rules, towards viewing it as a body with more active tasks, among others the task of incorporating and enforcing in the national system rules from international law on human rights (see also Section VI.2 and 3 below).

2   Structure, Content and Style of Judgments

The content of judgments must meet the statutory requirements laid down in the Civil Procedure Act of 13 August 1915, no. 6 §§ 141 (second paragraph, second sentence) and 144–9, and the Criminal Procedure Act of 22 May 1981, no. 25 §§ 32 (last sentence) and 39–41. A higher court judgment in a civil case contains the following, usually in this order:

1   name of the deciding court (one of the six 'lagmannsretter' or 'Høyesterett'; see Section I.1(a) above);
2   time and place of the judgment;
3   identification of the case in relation to the journal system of the court;
4   names of the litigants and their counsel;
5   names of the judges;
6   a brief statement of the legal issue(s), including a sketch of the factual background;

7   a brief procedural history of the case, including the final conclu-
    sions of prior judgments in the case;
8   a summary of arguments by counsel;
9   the reasoning of the judges (see immediately below on a differ-
    ence between judgments of 'lagmannsretter' and of the Supreme
    Court), including a statement of the facts upon which the decis-
    ion is grounded and discussions of legal questions actualized by
    the case;
10 the final conclusion.

In a judgment of a *lagmannsrett* this structure and content is presented as a joint product, signed by all the judges. In the case of a
disagreement, the part of the judgment presenting the reasoning of
the judges is split into a majority opinion and a (or several) minority
opinion(s). These are still presented as the joint product of those who
agree, that is, of the majority and of the minority (or minorities)
respectively. A Supreme Court judgment is presented as the product
of five separate opinions, so there the material part of the said structure and content (from and including the brief statement of legal
issue(s)) is presented as the first opinion, the other four judges concurring or dissenting; for details, see Section I.1(b) above. On the
statement of facts in a judgment of the Supreme Court, see Section I.4
below.

When the principle of legality is not deemed to apply, the opinion
style of the Supreme Court tends towards a middle ground in relation
to all of the polarities mentioned in question I.2 in the Appendix. In
criminal law, and in other cases where the principle of legality is
deemed to apply, the opinion style turns more towards the deductive,
legalistic and magisterial end of the spectrum. Perhaps there has occured
over the last few years a certain more general movement in the opinion style of the Supreme Court, towards a more discursive, substantive
and argumentative style. See, for example, Rt. 1994/1244 at pp.1251–6;
1994/1089 at pp.1095–6; 1994/813 at pp.820–21; and 1994/721 at pp.724
ff. If there has occurred such a movement, it is probably connected
with the movement mentioned in Section I.1(c) above.

3   Publication of Judgments

The leading general law report series in Norway is called 'Norsk
Retstidende', usually abbreviated to 'Rt.'. It is published on a commercial basis by The Norwegian Bar Association. *Norsk Retstidende*
contains *all* the decisions of the Supreme Court, either in full: today,
in all civil cases and in about two-thirds of the criminal cases, or in
the form of a short summary (Stenberg-Nilsen, 1986, p.6; Selmer,
1986, p.15). The recent reduction in the number of criminal cases

which the Supreme Court has to decide (see Section I.1(c) above), will most certainly lead to a greater proportion of the Supreme Court's decisions in criminal cases being reported in full.

Today *Norsk Retstidende* contains *only* decisions from the Supreme Court. Previously it sometimes, although rarely, contained decisions from other courts; the most cited among these decisions is probably Rt. 1951/371 (*'Vedbolaget'*, an arbitrament on what in Scandinavian law is called *'bristende forutsetninger'* ('failed contractual assumption')).

The Norwegian Bar Association also publishes a series called *'Rettens Gang'*, usually abbreviated *'RG'*. This contains decisions from courts other than the Supreme Court, from the middle as well as from the first level in the hierarchy of courts. However, these decisions are not collected in any systematic way, but selected among decisions received at random from the judges in the various lower courts or from counsel. This may help to explain why many Norwegian lawyers would hesitate to confer authority on (would not qualify as precedents) decisions from courts other than the Supreme Court.

In the mid-1970s, *Rettens Gang* received some 180–200 decisions each year from the two court levels below the Supreme Court. The total number of decisions from these two levels was at the time about 12 000–12 500 a year. In percentages, the journal received about 0.5–0.6 per cent and published about 0.3–0.4 per cent of the decisions from the first level ('byrettene'/'herredsrettene'). It received about 5–6 per cent and published about 3 per cent of the decisions from the level next to the Supreme Court ('lagmannsrettene') (Bråthen, 1978, p.8). These figures also give a rough indication of the current situation. On scholarly opinions about whether authority is or should be conferred on decisions from courts other than the Supreme Court, see Section II.1(b) below.

In addition to the general series just mentioned, there are published several *special series*, for example in labour law, tax law and maritime law. *Norsk Retstidende* is easily accessible for most lawyers, and is often referred to in decisions of the Supreme Court. The other series are seldom at hand for others than those with a special interest, and are very seldom referred to in decisions of the Supreme Court. Increasing numbers of judgments are stored in a database provided by *Lovdata*, which is a private body with a monopoly (factual, not legal) in this area. The cost of access to its database is so high that it makes electronic retrieval of judicial decisions an alternative only for firms and bodies such as universities.

Reports are not authenticated by judges. There is no tradition in Norway of publishing judgments in academic journals or in newspapers. Regarding questions I.3 and I.4 (Appendix), see also Eng (1994, section 3.2).

4   *Contents of Reports*

Norsk Retstidende and *Rettens Gang* usually contain all of the elements listed in question I.4 (Appendix) except (n) and (o). Concerning (d), the Supreme Court refers in its decision to the statements of facts given in the decisions from the lower courts. These statements are not part of the decision of the Supreme Court. They are nonetheless regularly published in *Norsk Retstidende*, as appendices to the judgment of the Supreme Court, with a view to giving background information on this judgment. However, the editors of *Norsk Retstidende* are steadily cutting down on these appendices. A calculation concerning the number of pages allotted to excerpts from the decisions of the lower courts in the years 1964, 1974, 1984, 1994 and 1995 shows a steady and marked decrease, both absolutely and as a percentage of the total number of pages of the annual volume: 1964, 600 pages (41 per cent); 1974, 560 pages (39 per cent); 1984, 440 pages (29 per cent); 1994, 200 pages (12 per cent); 1995, 178 pages (9 per cent). Although these figures must be read with several provisos, they appear to support the following hypothesis: the lawyer today will typically get a narrower picture of the facts of a Supreme Court case than he did 30 years ago; consequently, there is a weaker basis for discussions of the facts that have been or ought to be legally relevant.

It is not obvious what effect, if any, this development will have on the use of the decisions of the Supreme Court as precedents. One possible consequence is that, the less one knows about the facts that have been decided upon, the more leeway there will be in the interpretation and application of the judgment *qua* argument in later cases. Another possible consequence is that lawyers, in generating arguments from a previous judicial decision, will shift from methods of generating arguments which presuppose knowledge of the facts of the case to methods which do not presuppose such knowledge (on methods of generating arguments from a previous judicial decision, see Section IV below).

Concerning (n), there are no legal officials other than judges who suggest, draft or make an opinion. In particular, there is no person summarizing the facts, going through arguments, and/or suggesting a decision, such as for example the Advocate General in the EC system.

Concerning (o), juristic commentary is not published in *Norsk Retstidende* or *Rettens Gang*, but legal periodicals regularly present articles which take particular judicial decisions as their subject.

5   Meaning of 'Precedent'

Norwegian lawyers use *'prejudikat'* ('precedent') in several senses. Partly it is used in an *ex ante* sense, that is, about a judicial decision independently of whether the decision is in fact used as a guide in later cases. Most often the *ex ante* sense is *restricted* by some further criteria, especially whether the decision concerns a question of law or is given by the Supreme Court (then it is viewed as in some degree binding) or concerns a question of fact or is given by a lower court (then it is not viewed as binding in any degree or to the same extent). See, for example, Knoph (1948, p.43; 1949 p.16); Andenæs (1994, pp.113–14); Boe (1993, pp.228–9). More rarely the *ex ante* sense is *not* restricted by further criteria, which means that 'prejudikat' is used synonymously with 'a previous judicial decision'. (Fleischer, 1995, pp.160–61, says that he will adhere to this usage; however, his discussions are based upon the citerion that the decision is given by Høyesterett: see, for example, p.173). Partly 'prejudikat' is used in an *ex post* sense, that is, about a judicial decision which is in fact used as a guide in later cases.

A problem in discussions of precedent is that the sense of the key term 'prejudikat' is left undetermined or that the term is used in more than one of the senses mentioned without this being registered. Symptomatically, the two leading textbooks on sources of law in Norwegian jurisprudence use 'prejudikat' in a rather undetermined manner (Eckhoff, 1993, p.134; Augdahl, 1973, p.244).

6   Mode of Citation and Discussion

Norwegian lawyers identify the precedent by referring to the pages in the law report, for example 'Rt. 1994, p. ...' (see Section I.3 above, on the law reports). For the rest, they often refer to the parts of the decision mentioned in question I.4 (d)–(l) in the Appendix.

Precedents are used and discussed in a variety of ways, both in judicial opinions and in juristic legal writing (see Sections IV and V below). Most often the discussions in judicial opinions are more summary than the discussions in juristic legal writing. It is usually said that a main function of scholarly writings is to make sensible patterns out of the mass of individual judicial decisions (Gaarder, 1967, p.238; Eckhoff, 1993, p.231). See Section IV.5 below.

When arguing before the Supreme Court, the lawyers are expected to know and cite *all* the relevant cases from this court, irrespective of whether or not they are mentioned in scholarly writings. When arguing before lower courts, the expectations are not set so high; it is accepted that lawyers confine themselves to citing the most important cases mentioned in scholarly writings; they do not have to do independent research in the law reports. These rules apply to the oral argument in court. In the documents preparing the case, counsel should not argue the law, just sketch the outlines of their legal argument (see the Civil Procedure Act of 13 August 1915, no. 6 § 122).

7 Overall Role of Precedent

In relation to the Norwegian legal system, the types of arguments specified in question I.7 in the Appendix, with the exception of academic writings and other professional commentary, are in the context of the question most adequately seen as on a par with each other. All of them are quite often cited (with the possible exception of 'codes', which we do not have in Norway if one defines the concept strictly enough). All of them can be given considerable weight in the individual case. At the same time, none of them could in general be said to determine the result in any type of case; all of them can in principle be outweighed in the individual case by other arguments. This also holds good for constitutional rules; they may in case of conflict have to yield, for example, to rules in international law on human rights (see Section VI.3 below).

8 Role of Precedent in Different Branches of Law

There probably are some differences between various branches of law as regards the factors that determine the weight of precedents (see Section II.3 below on these factors). However, it is difficult to pinpoint these differences. For example, is foreseeability viewed as more important in private law than in administrative law?

Given that there are some differences in emphasis in the policies behind precedent in the different branches of law, they do not seem significantly to affect the end result as to the weight of precedents. In Norwegian law one cannot say, for example, that precedents in private law have systematically more or less weight than precedents in administrative law. The explanation probably is that the end result is a net result (the product of a process of weighing and balancing a manifold of arguments), so that possible differences in policies behind precedent are balanced against other differences in and between the different branches of law.

See also the last part of Section II.4 below, on the import of the principle of legality.

9 Precedent and 'Gaps in the Law'

If there is no statute or precedent, Norwegian judges tend to avoid the formulation of general rules. There are two reasons for this. First,

Norwegian judges do not like to demonstrate publicly that they create law. Second, they prefer to create law in small steps, because they feel that they lack the factual information and the time for deliberation, which they deem necessary for formulation of an adequate general rule. Consequently, the reasons given are often explicitly tailored to the particular facts of the case, with standard formulations such as 'given these facts (in the case at hand) I find ...', or 'with this I have not meant to say anything on how the solution should be, given other facts'.

However, there are perhaps signs of a certain change in the attitude of the judges in the Supreme Court: see Sections I.1(c) and I.2 above; VI.2 and VI.3 below.

II   The Bindingness of Precedent

1   *Kinds and Degrees of Normative Force*

We differentiate bindingness, force, further support and illustrativeness or other value of a precedent as follows.

1   *Formal bindingness*: a judgment not respecting a precedent's bindingness is not lawful and so is subject to reversal on appeal. Distinguish
   (a)   formal bindingness not subject to overruling: (i) 'strictly binding' – must be applied in every case; (ii) defeasibly binding – must be applied in every case unless exceptions apply (exceptions may be well defined or not);
   (b)   formal bindingness (with or without exceptions) that is subject to overruling or modification.
2   *Not formally binding but having force*: a judgment not respecting a precedent's force, though lawful, is subject to criticism on this ground, and may be subject to reversal on this ground. Distinguish
   (a)   defeasible force – should be applied unless exceptions come into play (exceptions may or may not be well defined);
   (b)   outweighable force – should be applied unless countervailing reasons apply.
3   *Not formally binding and not having force (as defined in (2) above) but providing further support*: a judgment lacking this is still lawful and may still be justified, but not as well justified as it would be if the precedent were invoked, for example, to show that the decision being reached harmonizes with the precedent.
4   *Mere illustrativeness or other value*.

The relevance of these distinctions for an understanding of the Norwegian legal system is as follows:

(a)   Given that the previous decision duly interpreted (that is, treated according to norms on how to generate arguments from previous decisions – see Section IV below) furnishes arguments relevant to the case at hand (for the sake of simplicity I often speak of the previous decision itself as an 'argument', instead of speaking of 'arguments furnished by the previous decision'), the following patterns emerge.

(1)   The Supreme Court treats its own previous decisions as arguments that *must be taken into consideration*, without, however, determining the result in the case at hand; that is, the previous decisions can be outweighed by reasons pulling in the direction of another result ('the weak sense of bindingness'; see Eng, 1994, section 4.1.2 (2)). This practice corresponds to not being formally binding, yet having (outweighable) force (Eckhoff, 1993, pp.136, 149–52).

(2)   Lower courts treat a previous decision from the Supreme Court as an argument that, with virtually no exceptions, *determines the result* in the case at hand ('the strong sense of bindingness'; see Eng, 1994, section 4.1.2 (2)). This practice corresponds to formal bindingness not subject to overruling (Eckhoff, 1993, pp.135–6; Andenæs, 1994, p.87; probably in the same direction, Augdahl, 1973, p.266).

With regard to (1) and (2), it has been maintained in the literature that the foregoing distinction between the Supreme Court and the lower courts in relation to the precedent weight of a previous decision from the Supreme Court is unsound from a normative perspective, the main argument being that the distinction makes the law dependent upon which court makes the decision and that this again depends on such accidental features as whether a party to the case has time and money to wait for a decision in the Supreme Court (Fleischer, 1995, pp.178–9). However, the descriptive correctness of the distinction in relation to the practice of the Norwegian courts does not seem to be contested.

(3)   The Supreme Court very seldom mentions decisions from the lower courts. Whether they are mentioned or not, the Supreme Court treats them as *merely illustrative*.

(4)   Courts at the intermediate and regional level in the hierarchy ('lagmannsrettene' – see Section I.1 above) probably treat previous decisions from the same level as arguments that must be taken into consideration, without, however, determining the result in the case at hand; that is, the previous decision can be outweighed by reasons pulling in the direction of another result ('the weak sense of bindingness'; see (1) above). This practice corresponds, as does the practice of the Supreme Court with regard to its own previous decisions, to not being formally binding yet having (outweighable) force. However, one should note an important factual difference influenc-

ing the practice of precedent: while all the decisions of the Supreme Court are reported, only a small fraction from the intermediate court level are reported, and then only in an arbitrary manner – see Section I.3 above.

(5)   Courts at the intermediate level in the hierarchy of courts probably treat decisions from the lowest level ('byrettene'/ 'herredsrettene' – see Section I.1 above) as merely illustrative.

(6)   Courts at the lowest level in the hierarchy of courts ('byrettene'/ 'herredsrettene') probably treat previous decisions from the intermediate level ('lagmannsrettene') as supportive in the sense of not being formally binding, yet having (outweighable) force. However, see the proviso in (4) above concerning law reporting and the practice of precedent.

(7)   Courts at the lowest level in the hierarchy of courts ('byrettene'/ 'herredsrettene') probably treat their own previous decisions as merely illustrative.

With regard to 3–7, see also (b) below on jurisprudential and legal literature concerning which, if any, precedent weight ought to be accorded to decisions from the lower courts.

(8)   When speaking above of decisions of the Supreme Court, I have presupposed the usual situation: that the case at hand is decided by, and that the previous decision is the decision of, an ordinary panel of the Supreme Court. I now add some remarks on *plenary decisions*. In relation to the lower courts, the plenary aspect will of course serve to strengthen the bindingness of the decision (see (2) above), leaving the lower courts with the alternative of strict bindingness. In relation to the Supreme Court itself, the plenary aspect has significance in three relations. The main points (all of them in contrast to what holds good in the relation between ordinary panels, see (1) above) are as follows.

On the one hand, there is no example yet of an ordinary panel explicitly saying that a previous plenary decision is outweighed by reasons pulling in the direction of another result. (Rt. 1993/409 at p.413 is no exception: an ordinary panel interprets two plenary decisions in such a way that the later decision (Rt. 1977/24) silently overrules the earlier decision (Rt. 1976/1); that is, the panel does not claim a competence for itself to overrule a plenary decision.) An ordinary panel will probably reserve for extreme situations the option of overruling a plenary decision, because, if the panel cannot bring itself to respect the plenary decision, it has the much more legitimate option of demanding a new plenary decision (see the first part of Section II.2 below). On the other hand, plenary decisions have treated previous decisions from ordinary panels more freely than the panels themselves do (Vislie, 1957, pp.299, 300–302; and, as a recent example, Rt. 1996/ 521 at p.532). Finally, there is no example yet of a plenary decision explicitly saying that a previous plenary decision is outweighed by reasons pulling in the direction of another result. But a plenary session will surely find it less hard to say so than an ordinary panel.

(b)   Judicial opinions seldom discuss the different concepts of kinds or degrees of bindingness presented above at the beginning of Section II.1, or whether certain types of previous decisions should be seen as binding. What does occur with a certain regularity is discussion of whether a *particular* previous decision should be seen as binding in the case at hand, most often in the form of adducing reasons for *not* following the earlier decision. Whether the question is discussed in this or some other form, it is usually touched upon only very sketchily (Eng, 1994, section 3.1).

The different concepts of kinds or degrees of bindingness are more often discussed in jurisprudential and legal literature than in judicial opinions, and then usually in a somewhat more detailed manner, although still often at a rather elementary level (see however, Sundby, 1974, pp.252–4).

The question whether certain types of previous decisions should be seen as binding has been debated in the following form: should decisions *from the lower courts* be given any precedent weight at all, in scholarly literature or by the courts themselves? It is a fact that many scholars refer to decisions from the lower courts. However, it is not always clear what argumentative status they confer on these decisions, that is, where they would place lower court decisions in a conceptual scheme of kinds or degrees of bindingness. In jurisprudential and legal discussions of the subject, most authors who have expressed an opinion argue *for* conferring *some* precedent weight on decisions from lower courts (for example, Smith, 1963, pp.12–13; 1975, pp.311–15; Frihagen, 1966, pp.191–2; Lødrup, 1966, pp.70–71; Sandvik, 1966, p.78 compared with pp.70–79 (on arbitration); Andenæs, 1994, p.89). Some authors refrain from taking a position (Eckhoff, 1993, pp.136–7) and some argue against conferring any precedent weight at all on decisions from the lower courts (Fleischer, 1968, pp.186–91; 1995, pp.172–4).

2   *Law Concerning Precedent*

The Act of 25 June 1926, no. 2 (Act Amending the Law Relating to Høyesterett) § 1 requires a *plenary session* in the Supreme Court when two or more members of an ordinary panel (consisting of five judges) wish to overrule a previous decision by the Supreme Court (whether this previous decision is one of an ordinary panel or one of a plenary session) *and* one of the members of the panel demands a plenary session. This provision *presupposes* both that the Supreme Court as a rule follows its own previous decisions and that it has the competence to overrule the same decisions. The Act does not constitute the basis for a duty to follow or for a competence to overrule, and it does not place any restraints on the competence of the Supreme Court to delimit its own competence to overrule, that is, on the competence of the Supreme Court to create a doctrine of precedent addressed to itself.

The Act of 25 June 1926, no. 2 instituted plenary decisions as a means of unifying the practice of the judges in ordinary panels when they were in disagreement about whether to follow a previous decision of the Supreme Court: unifying, not by a plenary decision on the doctrine of precedent, but by a plenary decision on the *substantive* question of law, taking it for granted that *this* plenary decision would be treated as a formally binding precedent by the panels.

Previous to the Act of 1926 the Supreme Court had experienced much disagreement in ordinary panels about whether to follow a previous decision of an ordinary panel. This situation incited some of the judges to explicitly state their opinion on the binding character of a previous decision from an ordinary panel (Vislie, 1957, pp.289–94). However, neither these nor later judicial statements of an *explicit* kind have been treated as constituting case law about the binding character of precedent – neither by the judges themselves nor by scholars. If they are mentioned or cited, it is more as curiosities than as arguments regarding the binding character of precedent (see, for example, Eckhoff, 1993, p.16).

Today, one rarely comes across judicial statements of an explicit kind concerning the binding character of precedent (Eng, 1994, section 3.1.2), but every judicial decision using an earlier judicial decision as an argument, is thereby *instantiating* the rules of precedent, and in that way implicitly confirming or changing the rules (Eng, 1994, section 2.2). Norwegian lawyers do not differentiate precedent as binding de jure or only de facto. During the twentieth century Norwegian lawyers have come to see precedent as a source of law *independent* of statute or custom. Before that a different view held sway: case law was seen as evidence of custom, that is, not as in itself constitutive of the law (Eckhoff, 1993, pp.227–8).

Important parts of Norwegian law, such as law of torts, law of contract, administrative law and constitutional law, *derive mainly from precedent* (Gaarder, 1967; Eckhoff, 1994, chs 11, 15 III, 17 III, 20 X, 29; Hiorthøy, 1967). There is no requirement for an ultimate basis or foundation in custom. Nor is there any requirement for an ultimate basis or foundation in statute law, as long as the principle of legality is not deemed to apply.

Criminal liability is at the centre of the principle of legality. According to the Constitution of 17 May 1814, § 96 no one can be punished without statutory authority (Andenæs, 1990, pp.421–4). This provision is taken to imply that precedent is never alone sufficient authority for criminal liability. However, the application of a statute of course requires interpretation of its words, and in this process of interpretation precedent often plays a central role. For example, the Supreme Court has taken the word 'ship' ('*skip*') in the Criminal Code of 22 May 1902 § 422 (a provision against 'drunken boating') to cover a cabin-cruiser; see Rt. 1973/433. And the court has subsequently included vessels of decreasing size and engine power, see Rt. 1980/1154, 1982/808, 1986/823, 1995/901, 1995/1734.

3   Factors Determining Degrees of Normative Force

All the factors mentioned in question II.3 of the Appendix are considered relevant by Norwegian lawyers when they decide the weight of a previous judicial decision in relation to other arguments in the case at hand (but, of course, a weighing process only takes place when other arguments speak in favour of another result than the previous decision, so that a balancing of the arguments is necessary). The factors motivate across the distinctions presented above at the beginning of II.1.

Concerning the first factor, see the analysis of practice and doctrine in Section II.1 above. See also Eng (1994, section 4.1, esp. section 4.1.3) where mention is made of a couple of other factors. First, does the statement in the previous decision lead to a *reasonable result in the case at hand*? This is probably the most important factor when lawyers assess the relevance and weight of previous judicial decisions. Second, *how clear* is the statement in the previous decision? Does it, for example, choose between two precise alternative interpretations of a given statute? Or does it characterize some fact with a value-laden legal term, as for example 'negligence'? The former type of statement typically gives more information as to the content of the law than the latter type, and is therefore given correspondingly more weight. (See also Section IV.4 below.)

4   Factors that Weaken Precedent

Except for cases of nullity there are no factors which can cause Norwegian lawyers *absolutely* to preclude a class of judicial decisions from becoming precedents. In times of 'politics as usual' it is very impractical that a judicial decision be considered a *nullity* (Eckhoff, 1945, pp.35–8). In politically more extreme situations, it is not so impractical: the decisions from the court which the Germans appointed in 1940 to replace the Supreme Court, and which held office until the end of the war, are not used as legal arguments by Norwegian lawyers.

In the literature it is quite common to separate discussions of precedents into two parts: one part concerned with judicial decisions dealing with statute law, and another part concerned with the argumentative role of judicial decisions in general (see, for example, Andenæs, 1994, ch. 6 IV, contrasted with ch. 9; Fleischer, 1995, pp.112–14 contrasted with pp.159–79). However, this separation seems to be meant more as a pedagogical device than as the expression of a distinction of substance. And this is probably representative of the view of most Norwegian lawyers: they do not draw a distinction of substance between precedents dealing with statute law and precedents of other kinds when deciding upon the weight of a previous judicial decision.

Within the area of the principle of legality (especially criminal law and administrative law; see also the last part of Section II.2 above) the statutory text gains in importance relative to other types of legal arguments, including previous judicial decisions. This may be seen as a modification of the view just stated: inside the area of the principle of legality, judicial decisions depend upon a statutory text to have any precedent weight; outside the area of the principle of legality, judicial decisions can have precedent weight independently of any statutory texts. In this way, Norwegian lawyers draw a distinction of substance between precedents dealing with statute law and precedents of other kinds, when deciding upon the weight of a previous judicial decision.

5   Vertical and Horizontal Bindingness

See Section II.1 above for an exhaustive mapping of vertical and horizontal bindingness, for the meaning of the terms 'strong or weak sense of bindingness' and for further references. Here we recapitulate only the main points. In the day-to-day work of the courts in the Norwegian legal system there are two important cases of vertical bindingness. First, the decisions from the Supreme Court, and they only, are spoken of and used as binding in the *strong* sense. Second, the decisions from the intermediate and regional level in the hierarchy of courts are seen as binding in the *weak* sense by and on the courts at the lowest level. Further, there are two important cases of horizontal bindingness, both in the form of *weak* bindingness: the persuasive bindingness between the panels within the Supreme Court, and the persuasive bindingness between the courts at the intermediate and regional level in the hierarchy of courts.

The plenary decisions of the Supreme Court have a more remote relation to the day-to-day work of the courts, including the panels of the Supreme Court. On the significance of these decisions, see (8) in Section II.1(a) above.

6   *Analysis of Force, Support and Illustrative Role*

Judicial opinions seldom discuss the different concepts of kinds or degrees of bindingness presented above at the beginning of Section II.1, including the concepts of force, support and illustrative value. On the major factors considered relevant by Norwegian lawyers, including judges, when they decide the weight of a previous judicial decision in relation to other arguments, see Section II.3 above. These factors motivate across the distinctions presented above at the beginning of Section II.1, that is, also across the distinctions between force, support and illustrative value. There is no legislation directly referring to the distinctions between force, support and illustrative value.

Most authors recognize that previous judicial decisions have at least illustrative value. The main question discussed is whether judicial decisions should also be used as authoritative arguments, and, if so, according to which principles. Norwegian authors do not distinguish between the different kinds or degrees of bindingness mentioned above. Instead they usually discuss one or more of the following: (a) arguments for and against conferring precedent weight on judicial decisions (see Section III.2 below); (b) aspects of judicial decisions which are seen as typically relevant in determining the precedent weight of a particular decision (see Section II.3 above); and (c) whether certain types of judicial decisions are barred in principle from having precedent weight (see Section II.1(b) above).

These discussions do not appear significantly to have influenced or to influence Norwegian courts: the practices and attitudes of the courts concerning kinds or degrees of bindingness have in the main come into being independently of the scholarly literature.

7   *Excess of Precedents?*

We do not know of any view that there are too many precedents in particular fields of the Norwegian legal system. (But of course, one regularly faces constellations of legal arguments where two or more previous judicial decisions seem hard to reconcile, which in one sense may be said to be a case of too many precedents.)

Different previous judicial decisions can reinforce each other by pulling in the same direction, or weaken each other by pulling in different directions. Apart from this (in practice, very important) fact, there is no significant connection between the number of previous judicial decisions and their formal bindingness, force and so on in the case at hand.

III   The Rationale of Precedent

1   *General Rationales for Formal Bindingness*

In the Norwegian legal system, there is no well-developed theory or view of legal precedent (Eng, 1994, sections 3.1–3.2.2). If rationales are given, they most often consist of justificatory grounds for granting power to courts to create and develop law or justificatory theories for requiring courts to follow previous decisions. These rationales are most often stated independently of distinctions between formal bindingness, force, further support and so on. See the more detailed presentation in Section III.2 below.

Judges surely consider rationales when they decide upon the degree of bindingness of previous judicial decisions, but the rationales are seldom discussed in judicial opinions (Eng, 1994, section 3.1.2; see also Sections II.1(b), II.2 and II.6 above).

2   *Rationales for Force, Further Support, and so on*

In the Norwegian legal system, the weight of previous judicial decisions often takes on the character of justifying force, further support or mere illustrative value: see Section II.1 above. The arguments adduced in favour of conferring some precedent weight on judicial decisions can be sorted into three groups: first, the need for *certainty and reliability* (predictability) (Augdahl, 1973, p.265; Eckhoff, 1993, p.153; Andenæs, 1994, p.89; Fleischer, 1995, p.166); second, the value of *equality* before the law (formal justice); herein is included the dislike of the retroactivity of judicial legislation (judge-made law) (Augdahl, 1973, pp.263–4; Eckhoff, 1993, p.153); third, *reduction of litigation* (Augdahl, 1973, p.264; Eckhoff, 1993, p.153; Andenæs, 1994, p.89; Fleischer, 1995, pp.166–7).

The main arguments adduced against conferring precedent weight on judicial decisions, especially against formal bindingness not subject to overruling, are the need for *flexibility* at the general level of the *rule* (for example, to change the rule with changing social conditions) and the need for flexibility in the *application* of the rule, so that one can reach reasonable results in the particular case (substantive justice) (Augdahl, 1973, p.263; Eckhoff, 1993, p.152; Andenæs, 1994, p.114; Fleischer, 1995, pp.165–6).

IV Precedents: What They Stand for and How They Apply

1 What Counts as Binding or Having Force?

In the Norwegian legal system, all of the following can, without violating any norms on what is to qualify as good argumentation, be taken as the binding element in a previous judicial decision: the relevant facts as decided on; explicit or constructed 'holding' on an issue of law or *ratio decidendi*; explicitly formulated (or implicit) rule; explicitly formulated (or implicit) principle; substantive reasons stated for any of the above; and carefully formulated *obiter dicta* dealing authoritatively with a point of law not ultimately resolved by the court. The most common types of arguments are probably the first four. Concerning the present Section IV, see in general Eng (1994, sections 2.3–2.4).

2 Reasoning about Applicability

In the Norwegian legal system, all of the following can qualify as good argumentation concerning the applicability of a previous judicial decision to the case at hand: close factual analysis or characterization of the facts of judicial decisions, often in the form of a comparison of the facts in the previous case with the facts in the case at hand; isolating rules or principles in the previous decision and reasoning from the language of those; argument in terms of the applicability of substantive reasons in the previous decision to the case at hand; and reasoning from general rationales for following previous judicial decisions.

3 Juristic Discussion

Current legal theory, when stating how the Norwegian courts identify the binding part of a previous judicial decision, enumerates three alternative ways (Eckhoff, 1993, pp.138–44; Fleischer, 1981, pp.39–50; 1995, p.171): first, to search for a rule both expressly stated in the opinion of the previous decision and necessary for the outcome of the decision ('the stated *ratio decidendi*'); second, to construct a rule that one thinks the previous decision 'must' be seen as an instance of ('the constructed *ratio decidendi*'); and third, to compare as to similarity the facts of the previous case with the facts of the case at hand. In judicial opinions the subject is seldom explicitly reflected upon.

4   Illustrative or Analogical Precedent

In Norwegian law, the most adequate perspective on the distinction between 'strictly in point' and 'analogy', in relation to previous judicial decisions as (sources of) arguments, is the following. In the argumentative practice of Norwegian lawyers, previous judicial decisions are treated as lending support in varying degrees. One of the factors determining this degree is how clear is the guidance which the previous decision is claimed to give; see the last part of Section II.3 above. In relation to the argumentative practice of Norwegian lawyers, terms such as 'strictly in point' or 'analogy' would most often in effect just be tags for conclusions as to clarity of guidance.

So previous judicial decisions are used as arguments even when not strictly in point. However, it is rather unusual for Norwegian practising lawyers to use the term 'analogy' in relation to judicial decisions; most of them reserve that term for the interpretation and application of statutory texts. In scholarly writings the term is sometimes used also in relation to judicial decisions (see, for example, Eckhoff, 1993, p.145).

The use of constructed *ratio decidendi* (see Section IV.3 above) can illustrate what has just been said: in Norwegian law, the acceptability of a constructed *ratio decidendi* depends upon the extent to which the construction fits the constellations of facts and results in the relevant previous cases; that is, to what extent the constructed *ratio decidendi* can argumentatively generate the same results which were reached in the previous cases, given the facts of those cases (Eng, 1996, section V.2.4). Such a structure of reasoning allows for many nuances in several gradual dimensions. And it may be used to clarify, to harmonize or to show relevance or non-relevance.

5   Single Precedents or Lines of Decision?

Norwegian lawyers do not draw an explicit and sharp distinction between the bindingness or force or further support of a single judicial decision on the one hand and lines of judicial decisions on the other. Instead the distinction shows itself in a gradual way, according to whether the previous decision represents a trend: the more so, the greater the weight (see Sections II.3 and II.7 above).

If a line of previous decisions is available, the courts will often take this line as their starting point (see, for example, Rt. 1994/721 at p.727; 1964/197 at p.200 (opinion for the majority) and 201 (dissenting opinion)). However, when one particular previous decision is regarded as the first, the latest, the most important or the most typical in the line, the reasoning of the courts may mention only this decision ('leading case').

When lines of previous decisions are used in judicial opinions, lines consisting of 'merely repetitive' decisions and explicit confirmation of lines of decisions are the (relatively) most common (see, for example, Rt. 1996/385; 1994/912). 'Synthesizing' or reconstructive lines (the decisions are taken to stand for a legal point not explicitly formulated in the decisions considered individually) are more a scholarly phenomenon. 'Conflicting' (zigzag) lines of previous decisions are seldom acknowledged in judicial opinions. In contrast, scholars may discuss what they see as conflicts between decisions and suggest solutions. The influence of such suggestions on the practice of the courts depends, among other things, on what authority the author has.

Norwegian lawyers do not *speak* of any generally accepted methods of synthesis. On the basis of their *practice,* another work (Eng, 1996, section V, 2.4) has shown the existence of a distinctive and practically important pattern: see the outline of this in the last part of Section IV.4 above.

Examples of synthesis are many and their occurrence is often important, as with strict liability in the law of torts and judicial review in administrative law. Synthesis is most often the result of an interaction between scholarly works and judicial practice: the scholar points to a possible pattern in the cases; the judges seize his suggestion and give it their authority, either by directly referring to the work of the scholar or by referring to some of the cases that he has connected; against this background the scholar further refines his suggestion; and so on (Eckhoff, 1993, pp.232–6).

6   The Concept of a 'Leading Case'

Norwegian lawyers may speak of a 'leading case' in the sense of the first, the latest, the most important or the most typical case in a line of cases. Usage is most often intuitive and indeterminate in relation to these senses; equivalent Norwegian terms have no precise role to play in the doctrine of precedent. It is difficult to say anything in general about when a precedent will start a 'line of precedent', not least because this is the ordinary course of events: on the whole, questions of the same type tend to be solved in the same way. In this perspective, the first decision on a new question will often be seen in retrospect to have started a 'line of precedent'.

V   Distinguishing, Explaining, Modifying, Overruling

1   *Distinguishing*

One cannot say that Norwegian courts consistently follow a practice of expressly distinguishing. Sometimes they just ignore the adduced decision or simply say that it is not in point or not decisive, without any further explanation: see, for example, Rt. 1978/1001 at p.1006. At other times they draw attention to some dimensions in which the cases differ without trying to formulate any general rule: see, for example, Rt. 1994/1617 at p.1623; 1994/1288 at p.1293; 1994/748 at p.751. And at still other times they expressly distinguish, in the sense that they draw attention to a dimension in which the cases differ, nail this dimension down as being in general legally relevant and, as a consequence, use it as a justification for a different result in the case at hand: see, for example, Rt. 1995/1422 at pp.1425–6.

One factor explaining this variation is the degree of confidence which the court has in the legal viability of a distinction: the less confidence, the less outspoken will the court be as to the relevance of the distinction; and the more confidence, the greater is the chance that the court will draw attention to the distinction and use it as a justification for reaching a different result in the case at hand from the one in the previous case.

2   *Juristic Commentary*

It is a regular part of legal literature to discuss points of difference (distinguishing) between reported precedents. On the conceptual framework within which such discussions take place, see Sections IV. 3–5 above.

3   *Excessive Distinguishing?*

Since, and to the same degree as, Norwegian lawyers do not entertain a generally strict doctrine of (bindingness of) precedent (see Section II.1 above), they are not always forced to distinguish; they may instead ignore. And since, and to the same degree as, Norwegian lawyers entertain a doctrine of *some* bindingness of precedent (see Section II.1 above), distinguishing is one way of circumventing a precedent. (Two others are overruling and adjusting the facts in the case at hand: see Eng, 1994, section 4.3). However, Norwegian lawyers tend to avoid finer distinctions and restatings when applying precedents. This holds especially for judges, but also for scholars and practising lawyers.

4 Types of Overruling

The types of overruling possibly recognized are:

a. Overruling in the strict sense: an explicit judicial act of overturning a *binding* precedent or a line of precedent;
b. Overruling in a broader sense: an explicit judicial act of rejecting
   a precedent (or line of precedent) having only *force*, or other
   possible support;
c. Silent overruling: not following a precedent (or line of precedent)
   and not explicitly acknowledging this;
d. Overruling whereby a precedent is explicitly or implicitly cut
   down so severely in scope that it no longer exists as a precedent,
   e.g., is 'confined to its facts' as common law judges say.

Alternative (a) is very rare. The Supreme Court is not formally bound by
its own previous decisions (see (1) in Section II.1(a) above) and the lower
courts, which consider themselves formally bound by the decisions of the
Supreme Court (see (2) in Section II.1(a) above), in practice very rarely
explicitly overrule those decisions (Eckhoff, 1993, pp.135–6).

The most important instances of alternatives (b) and (c) are cases
in which the Supreme Court (in plenary session, in ordinary panels
or in three-judge panels – on these forms, see Section I.1 above)
overrules its own previous decisions (in ordinary panels or in three-
judge panels; on the bindingness of plenary decisions, see (8) in
Section II.1(a) above). For the period 1916–70, Augdahl found 17
examples of *explicit* overrulings of this kind (Augdahl, 1973, pp.248–
53). An example from the period after his investigation is Rt. 1987/80
(a plenary decision overruling Rt. 1978/442).

Silent overruling can take place in relation to a single previous decision. For example, concerning the question of whether the waiver of a
claim imposes a tax liability on the debtor, the decision in Rt. 1978/
1001 (tax liability affirmed) may be seen as a silent overruling of the
decision in Rt. 1956/1323 (tax liability denied). More often, however,
silent overruling takes place in relation to a line of previous decisions;
more specifically, in the form of incremental changes over longer periods of time, often many years (Eckhoff, 1993, pp.155–9) – especially
changes in the area of application of indeterminate criteria, such as
good faith, *culpa* (negligence) or frustration of contract, but also changes
in the subsumption area of seemingly determinate criteria (see the last
part of Section II.2 above, on the decreasing size that the Supreme
Court deems necessary for subsuming a boat under the term '*skip*'
('ship')). Alternative (d) occurs more rarely than (b) and (c).

As regards procedure, a case to be decided by the Supreme Court
is usually transferred to a plenary session when an ordinary panel

considers overruling a previous decision or line of decisions from the Supreme Court (on the criteria for plenary sessions, see Section I.1(b) above). No special reasons are required for overruling; the factors mentioned in Section II.3 above are considered sufficient.

There are no differences concerning procedures or types of reasons as between overruling precedent dealing with a constitution, with a code, with a non-codified statute or with mere case law area; or as between overruling a single precedent or a line of precedent.

5   Prospective Overruling

The technique of prospective overruling is unknown in the Norwegian legal system (Eng, 1994, section 3.4). Examples of statements with some similarity to prospective overruling are found in Rt. 1980/52 (especially pp.58–9) and Rt. 1979/572 (especially pp.585–6). In the decision from 1980, the Supreme Court said that they thought it doubtful whether a statutory provision in procedural labour law, which declared the Supreme Court incompetent to try certain cases, was in accordance with the Constitution (§ 88). In part as a consequence of this, the provision was later abrogated. The statements of the Supreme Court differed from prospective overruling in two respects. First, they did leave it an open question whether the disputed provision was to be considered in conflict with the Constitution (p.59). Second, it was not necessary to pass judgment on this point in that particular case, since the plaintiff had not yet reached the level in the hierarchy of courts where he was blocked from appeal to the Supreme Court. But apart from these differences, the statements approximated prospective overruling in that they gave a warning as to how the Supreme Court would view the law in the future.

6   Anticipatory Overruling by Lower Courts

Anticipatory overruling may be said to be formally permitted in the Norwegian legal system. However, it very seldom occurs (Eckhoff, 1993, p.135; see also (2) in Section II.1(a), and Sections II.5 and V.4 above).

7   Precedent and Legislative Practice

It is quite often the case that a new statute is said by the drafters to be only a formalization of a particular line of case law, not being aimed at any changes in substance. However, the case law is not seen as having any authority in itself (*qua* case law); the decisive factor in the respect that the drafters pay to case law is the force of good reasons which in the estimation of the drafters support the case law rules.

Apparent legislative confirmation or reversal of case law through statute does not count as a reason for or against the bindingness of precedent in general, but of course it counts as a reason for or against the bindingness of the particular line of case law being confirmed or reversed. For example, when, as just mentioned, the statute is said to be only a formalization of a particular line of case law, this gives additional weight to that line; or, when the statute is said to be a reversal of a particular line of case law, this makes irrelevant that line.

8   Conflicts of Precedents

Conflicting precedents are rather unusual in the Norwegian legal system, since the main source of precedent is the Supreme Court and since the output of this court is manageable (one does not easily overlook a previous and clearly relevant decision).

However, given that precedents may conflict, for example as a consequence of a court consciously evading a precedent (see Section VI.1 below) or through oversight by counsel and court, Norwegian judges seldom acknowledge such conflicts. Instead of qualifying the relation between the decisions as a conflict, they prefer to see it as a question of *interpretation*, that is, to treat the relation as only a seeming conflict. Because of this, no stable patterns exist concerning resolution of acknowledged conflicts.

9   Hypothetical Cases

The reasons given by Norwegian judges are often explicitly wedded to the particular facts in the case at hand (see Section I.9 above). In this there is an element of hypothetical thinking of a denying kind, as in standard formulations such as 'With this I have not [the denying element] meant to say anything on how the solution should be if [the hypothetical element] the facts a, b, c ... n, had been otherwise' (see, for example, Rt. 1983/1052 at p.1056; 1972/965 at p.969). Hypothetical thinking of a more affirming kind is very unusual in the opinions of Norwegian judges. Lawyers other than judges, for example scholars in treatises or in books for students, or counsel during oral proceedings, use hypothetical cases of all varieties.

VI   Matters of General Perspective, Evaluation and Other

1   'Saying and Doing'

Some Norwegian lawyers hold the opinion that the real justificatory use of legal arguments, not only of precedent but of legal arguments in general, is not very well reflected in the public opinions of the judges (whether reported or not). However, one could not speak of a general opinion on this point, since most lawyers have not reflected much upon it. The discrepancy between saying and doing varies with a lot of factors. With regard to overruling or modifying a precedent, an important factor is *the cause* of the overruling or modification: very often the cause is the evaluations of the judge, and this cause is seldom given its appropriate place in the public opinions of the judges (Eng, 1994, sections 2.4.2, 4.2 and 4.3.4; 1996, section IV).

Instead of an open discussion of the reasons for and against following a previous judicial decision, judges often choose one of the following alternatives: first, to omit any reference to the precedent; second, just to say that the facts are different, without specifying the assumed relevant differences (see Sections V.1 and V.4 above; Zimmer, 1986, pp.766–71 exemplifies the uncertainty that this way of handling precedents has led to in tax law); third, to interpret the precedent in a new way (distinguishing); fourth, to adjust the facts of the case at hand, so that any contradiction or disharmony in relation to the precedent vanishes (Eng, 1994, section 4.3); and fifth, to give the description of the facts in the case at hand which the judge thinks most probable, without discussing the relationship to the precedent, leaving it to judges of later cases to harmonize the precedent and the decision in the case at hand by interpretation (distinguishing) (see Section V.8 above).

2   Recent Change or Evolution

The present chief justice of the Supreme Court has, both before and after his appointment in 1991, expressly stated a wish for the court to participate more actively in evolution of the law (Smith, 1975; 1992–3, esp. at pp.785, 787, 789, 790–91). Such a change in the role of the Supreme Court implies a more outspoken and principled way of writing judicial opinions, which may mean that the Norwegian style of opinion writing will draw nearer to the discursive English style. See also Section I.9 above, last paragraph, with further references.

3   Changes in International Environment

Since some prominent Norwegian lawyers (among them, three chief justices of the Supreme Court: see Wold, 1963, p.358; Smith, 1964, pp.87–8; Ryssdal, 1981, p.534–5) have considered that treaties and/or international customs on human rights rank above national legislation, and since infringements of human rights are more often pleaded in Norwegian courts today than they were some years ago (Dolva, 1993, pp.45–6, 51–5; NOU 1993:18, pp.51–68), the Norwegian Supreme Court quite often discusses the treaties, especially the European Convention on Human Rights of 1950 and the decisions of the European Court of Human Rights. Through Norway's participation in the EEA (European Economic Area), a similar legal situation arises in relation to some parts of EC law and the decisions of the European Court of Justice.

Arguments from human rights and from European Community law pull in the direction of unity in legal thinking throughout Europe; not only as regards substantive law, but also as regards rules about how to generate substantive law, including the various national doctrines of precedent. And probably the said arguments will also tend to unify the way European lawyers express themselves. But, of course, other factors can pull in the direction of diversity, and many parts of the law develop independently of arguments from human rights or European Community law.

4   Juristic or Other Criticism

We end by drawing attention to four subjects which have been discussed in the Norwegian literature on precedent and which have been touched upon in this chapter. First, should precedent weight be conferred on decisions from courts other than the Supreme Court? See Section II.1(b) above, with further references. Second, does the Supreme Court too often overrule its own decisions? See Section V. 4 above. There is a certain disagreement in the literature on this point: see, on the one hand, the critique of the practice of the Supreme Court in Augdahl (1973, p.259) and, on the other hand, the defence of the same practice in Eckhoff (1993, pp.154–5). Third, should the Supreme Court say more openly when and on what points it overrules a precedent? See Section VI.1 above and the reference there to Zimmer (1986). Fourth, should the Supreme Court take a more active part in the evolution of the law? See Section VI.2 above and the references there to Smith. A more cautious view on the role of the courts is expressed in Eckhoff (1993, pp.172–3).

References

Andenæs, J. (1990), *Statsforfatningen i Norge* (Norwegian Constitutional Law), 7th edn, Oslo: Tano.
Andenæs, J. (1994), *Innføring i rettsstudiet* (Introduction to the Study of Law), 4th edn, Oslo: Grøndahl Dreyer.
Augdahl, P. (1973), *Rettskilder* (Sources of Law), 3rd edn, Oslo: Aschehoug.
Boe, E. (1993), *Innføring i juss: Juridisk tenkning og rettskildelære* (Introduction to Law: Legal Reasoning and Sources of Law), Oslo: Tano.
Bråthen, B. (1978), *Underinstansavgjørelser som rettskilde* (Decisions from Courts other than the Supreme Court as a Source of Law), Oslo: Institutt for privatrett, Jus og EDB no. 27.
Dolva, T. (1993), 'Den europeiske menneskerettighetskonvensjon og Norges Høyesterett' (The European Convention on Human Rights and the Norwegian Supreme Court), in E. Nerep and W. Warnling-Nerep (eds), *Homage Volume for J.W.F. Sundberg*, Stockholm: Juristförlaget, pp.45–56.
Eckhoff, T. (1945), *Rettskraft* (Res Judicata), Oslo: Johan Grundt Tanum.
Eckhoff, T. (1993), *Rettskildelære* (The Doctrine of the Sources of Law), 3rd edn, Oslo: Tano.
Eckhoff, T. (1994), *Forvaltningsrett* (Administrative Law), 5th edn, Oslo: Tano.
Eng, S. 'The Doctrine of Precedent in English and Norwegian Law – Some Common and Specific Features', *Scandinavian Studies in Law* (1994).
Eng, S. (1996), Dissertation, University of Oslo. To be published as *U/enighetsanalyse – med særlig sikte på jus og allmenn rettsteori* (Analysis of dis/agreement – with particular reference to law and legal theory), by Universitetsforlaget, Oslo, in January 1998. Also to be translated into English and published by Kluwer, Dordrecht.
Fleischer, C.A. (1968), *Grunnlovens grenser* (The Limits of the Constitution). Oslo: Universitetsforlaget.
Fleischer, C.A. (1981), *Anvendelse og fortolkning av dommer* (Application and Interpretation of Judicial Decisions), Oslo: Universitetsforlaget.
Fleischer, C.A. (1995), *Rettskilder* (Sources of Law), Oslo: Ad Notam Gyldendal.
Frihagen, A. (1966), *Villfarelse og ugyldighet i forvaltningsretten* (Mistake, Misrepresentation and Invalidity in Administrative Law), Oslo: Universitetsforlaget.
Gaarder, K. (1967), 'Domstolene og den allminnelige rettsutvikling' (The Courts and the Evolution of the Law), in G. Nissen, F. Hiorthøy and K. Gaarder (eds) *Den dømmende makt*, Oslo: Universitetsforlaget, pp.223–90.
Hiorthøy, F. (1967), 'Domstolene og forfatningsutviklingen' (The Courts and the Evolution of Constitutional Law), in G. Nissen, F. Hiorthøy and K. Gaarder (eds) *Den dømmende makt*, Oslo: Universitetsforlaget, pp.69–222.
Knoph, R. (1948), *Rettslige standarder* (Legal Standards), Oslo: Grøndahl & Søn.
Knoph, R. (1949), *Oversikt over Norges rett* (A Survey of Norwegian Law), 3rd edn edited by S. Grette, Oslo: Nationaltrykkeriet.
Lødrup, P. (1966), *Luftfart og ansvar* (Aviation and Responsibility), Oslo: Johan Grundt Tanum.
NOU (Norwegian Public Reports) (1993:18), *Lovgivning om menneskerettigheter* (Legislation on Human Rights), Oslo: Statens Forvaltningstjeneste.
Ryssdal, R. 'The Relation between the Judiciary and the Legislative and Executive Branches of the Government in Norway', *North Dakota Law Review*, p.527 (1981).
Sandene, E. (1989), 'Norges Høyesterett – organisering og arbeidsordning' (The Norwegian Supreme Court – Organization and Working Procedures), in E. Andersson *et al.* (eds), *Homage Volume for Curt Olsson*, Helsingfors: Juristförbundets Förlag, pp.297–304.

Sandvik, T. (1966), *Entreprenørrisikoen* (The Risk of the Building Contractor), Oslo: Johan Grundt Tanum.

Selmer, K. 'Norsk Retstidende i data-alderen' (*Norsk Retstidende* in the Age of the Computer), *Norsk Retstidende*, p.14 (1986).

Smith, C. (1963), *Studier i garantiretten* (Studies in the Law of Guarantees and Bonds), Oslo: Universitetsforlaget.

Smith, C. (1964), *Folkerettens stilling ved norske domstoler* (International Law in Norwegian Courts). Here cited from *Statsliv og rettsteori*, Oslo, 1978, pp.71–89. (Originally published in *Tidsskrift for rettsvitenskap*, 1964, pp.356 ff.)

Smith, C. 'Domstolene og rettsutviklingen' (The Courts and the Evolution of the Law), *Lov og Rett*, p.292 (1975).

Smith, C. 'Høyesteretts stilling i samfunnet' (The Supreme Court and Society), *Juridisk Tidskrift*, p.781 (1992–3).

Stenberg-Nilsen, H. 'Norsk Retstidende 1836–1986', *Norsk Retstidende*, p.1 (1986).

Sundby, N.Kr. (1974), *Om normer* (On Norms), Oslo: Universitetsforlaget.

Vislie, A. 'Om prejudikater i Høyesteretts plenum' (On Precedents from the Supreme Court in Plenary Session'), *Tidsskrift for rettsvitenskap*, p.284 (1957).

Wold, T. (1963), 'Den europeiske menneskerettighetskonvensjon og Norge' (The European Convention on Human Rights and Norway), in *Homage Volume for Frede Castberg*, Oslo: Universitetsforlaget, pp.353–74.

Zimmer, F. (1986), 'Noe om prejudikater og andre høyesterettsdommer i skatteretten' (Some Remarks on Precedents and other Decisions in Tax Law from the Supreme Court), in A. Bratholm *et al.* (eds), *Homage Volume for Torstein Eckhoff*, Oslo: Tano, pp.757–73.

7 Precedent in Poland

LECH MORAWSKI, TORUŃ AND MAREK ZIRK-SADOWSKI, ŁÓDŹ

I Institutional and Systemic

1(a) Court Hierarchy

At present three types of courts administer justice in Poland: the Supreme Court (SC), courts of ordinary jurisdiction and special courts. The Supreme Administrative Court (SAC) is most important among the special courts. The Constitutional Tribunal (CT) and The Tribunal of State function outside the system of courts.

Courts of ordinary justice are divided into courts of appeal, regional (wojewod) and district courts. Judicial decisions of the courts of ordinary justice are divided into two fundamental groups: civil justice and criminal justice. However, the hierarchy is the same for all types of justice since they are carried out by the same courts which are internally divided into chambers dealing with a specific type of case.

The cases belonging to the courts of ordinary justice are usually considered by district courts in the first instance, except for cases handed over by statute to the competence of regional courts. Regional courts also examine appeals against judgments of district courts. In cases of greater importance, regional courts are the courts of first instance. Appeals against their decisions made in the first instance are examined by the Court of Appeal.

It is the principle of the courts of ordinary justice that the panels of first instance are composed of professional and lay judges. Only in some more difficult cases does the statute incorporate in the first instance courts a panel composed of professional judges exclusively. In the second instance courts, the panel consists of professional judges. Thus the courts of appeal are composed of professional judges.

The Supreme Court supervises the functioning of all other courts (of ordinary justice and special courts) over the whole range of their decisions. According to the Act on The Supreme Court, it also provides for the correctness and uniformity of the interpretation of law and judicial practice. The Supreme Court may also pronounce opinions on drafts of proposed statutes. The Supreme Court is divided into four chambers: the Administrative, Labour Law and Social Insurance Chamber, the Civil Chamber, the Criminal Chamber and the Military Chamber. The Supreme Court performs its functions by means of:

1   examining appeals against judicial decisions pursuant to the rules of procedure,
2   examining extraordinary appeals against judicial decisions and by force of special provisions against decisions of other bodies,
3   resolutions aiming at explanation of legal norms which raise doubts or whose application has resulted in divergences in judicial decisions (abstract resolutions),
4   resolutions which contain solutions of legal problems raising serious doubts in a concrete case (concrete resolutions).

From the point of view of precedent, functions (3) and (4) have the greatest significance, though since 1989 these resolutions have not been binding. Resolutions aiming at explanation of legal norms which raise doubts (abstract resolutions) are pronounced by a panel of seven judges, one chamber, combined chambers or by the full panel of the judges of the Supreme Court. Such resolutions are proposed by the presidents of the Supreme Court, the minister of justice, public prosecutor general or the ombudsman. In labour law cases, they are proposed by the Minister of Labour, and in administrative law cases by the president of SAC.

The SAC and panels of SC may propose that SC should pronounce a resolution of legal problems raising serious doubts in a concrete case (concrete resolutions). If such a legal problem has been submitted by a panel of three or five judges of the SC, the resolution is pronounced by a panel of seven judges, and when the problem has been presented by seven judges, the resolution is pronounced by the full panel of the whole chamber. A legal question submitted by SAC is examined by the panel of five judges of the SC. This panel may present the question to the panel of seven judges.

The general principle is that resolutions of the full panel of the SC, the panel of combined chambers and the panel of the whole chamber gain the force of legal principles at the moment they are pronounced. The panel of seven judges may also grant the force of legal principle to its resolution. Until 1989, legal principles bound all the panels of the SC. They were published by the first president of the SC. At present, legal principles are not binding. The SAC is a court of cassation. It consists only of professional judges. The court is divided into two chambers: administrative and financial. It decides on complaints which concern final administrative sentences and it also settles legal disputes between authorities of state administration and authorities of local administration. As a rule, the SAC decides as a panel of three judges. The panel of three judges may apply to the president of the court for resolution of legal doubts by a panel of seven judges, or by a chamber or combined chambers because of important legal doubts occurring in the case. Also some authorities of local administration may address SAC with their legal questions. The court examines them in a panel of five judges. The resolutions of SAC are binding only in a given case.

The Constitutional Tribunal decides on the accordance of statutes with the constitution and on the accordance of normative acts lower than a statute with the constitution and statutes. The motion may be put forward by the president, the prime minister, the ombudsman, the president of the SC, the president of SAC, the public prosecutor general and other leading state agencies mentioned in the Act on the Constitutional Tribunal. Decisions of the Constitutional Tribunal on discordance of the statutes with the constitution must be confirmed by the parliament (Seym).

The CT also answers legal questions connected with current proceedings, administrative or judicial, for example, which are posed by the first president of the SC, the president of SAC, the panels of the SC, of SAC and of the courts of the second instance and the leading organs of state administration. The CT also establishes the binding interpretation of statutes on motion of the president, the prime minister, the first president of the SC, the president of SAC, the ombudsman and the public prosecutor general.

The CT examines the motions in panels of three or five judges and in particularly complex cases in the full panel. Decisions of the CT are published.

The Tribunal of State decides on responsibility of persons who hold the highest posts in the state, mentioned in the Act on The Tribunal. Evidently, its competence to decide on the president's impeachment is most important. The Tribunal also decides on who has responsibility for violating the constitution and statutes.

1(b)   Structural and Procedural Aspects

The number of judges in Poland (basing on the *Statistic Data Yearbook 1994*) is as follows: in the SC, 72 judges; in the SAC, 134 judges; in the courts of appeal, 219 judges; in the regional and district courts, 6896 judges. In 1991–4, 57 800 lay judges were selected. A total of 4 568 000 cases were submitted to the courts of ordinary justice in 1993. In 1993, SAC examined about 24 000 complaints.

In all courts, decisions are made according to the majority rule. Deliberations take place in secret and the course of discussion among judges, and the results of voting, are not revealed. Only a case of the so-called *'votum separatum'* is revealed: the judge may state his own dissent, which is disclosed. The judgment is always a sentence of the court and not the judges and is passed in the name of the Republic.

From the point of view of the problem of precedent, it is important that the judgments are always in writing and the written justification of judgments is always issued in the second instance. SAC, CT and the SC always prepare the written justifications of judgments and most of them are published. However, this depends on the agreement of the panel and of the so-called 'Office of Judicial Decisions' which selects the cases to be published. The Office of Judicial Decisions consists of the judges of the court.

1(c)   Power to Select Cases

'Precedent' is a term which appears in everyday Polish as well as in the language of jurisprudence and in the language of legal acts. In everyday speech, it denotes 'a case preceding another similar one; binding force possessed by a decision of a state agency (e.g. judicial decision) for application of law in similar cases' (Kopaliński, 1985, p.339). In the language of jurisprudence there are two conceptions known, one connected with Wróblewski's name and the other with Ziembiński's name. Wróblewski understood precedent as 'a decision which normatively or factually influences the making of other decisions' (Wróblewski, 1971, p.525) so he attempted to follow the natural understanding of this term. Ziembiński, on the other hand, is of the opinion that two meanings of the term 'precedent' ought to be distinguished. In the affirmative sense, precedent is the recognition of some social norm as a legal norm in the state agency's decision making (Ziembiński, 1980, p.262). A law-making precedent, in turn, is a situation in which the authority gives a decision without clear legal sources and this decision is treated jurisprudentially as expressing a binding general and abstract norm, not yet distinctly formulated.

For a short time now, precedent has occurred as a legal term of acts in the Code of Civil Procedure, Art. 479 § 3, which allows an economic case to be presented to a panel of three judges for examination if its precedent-setting character calls for this. It is emphasized in the commentaries to this provision that 'the precedent-setting character of a case' means that the case refers to a new, vague phrase in the

legal text, or explains problems not yet explained in earlier precedents, and thus will have influence on future decisions.

The role of precedent began to be discussed as early as the 1950s
when, in Poland just as in the other communist countries, guidelines
for administration of justice and judicial practice were introduced.
According to the constitution of that time (Article 56) those were the
SC, regional courts, district courts and special courts that administered justice. At the same time, the system of two instances was
adopted, in which the great majority of civil and criminal cases were
examined in the first instance in the district court, and appeals against
those judgments were examined by regional courts. As a consequence,
in the normal course cases never reached the SC. Competence of the
SC as a court of the second instance was either entirely eliminated or
limited to a small number of exceptionally important cases.

In order to achieve uniformity in judicial decisions, there was an
extension of methods for supervising the courts outside of the ordinary judicial process. The SC performed this with the help of some
institutions of which these guidelines for administration of justice
and judicial practice were the most powerful tool. The Act on The
Supreme Court of 1962 determined the function of the guidelines as
a tool for securing correct application of law and uniformity of judicial decisions.

However, they were not established in connection with examining
a concrete case; they contained general norms and bound all courts
like legal norms and were published in the official publication, *Moni-
tor Polski*. Hence the opinion arose that the guidelines have
characteristics of legal norms. Finally, the guidelines were recognized as being 'law-making decisions' since they contained general
norms, while other forms of judicial supervision of the SC were
ranked among the so-called 'precedent decisions' which were never
more than individual norms connected with examining a concrete
case.

Other forms of judicial supervision were (a) resolutions containing
answers to legal questions in order to explain doubtful regulations;
(b) decisions made by a panel of seven judges of SC, in the form of a
resolution, on legal problems which were introduced by the ordinary
panel of the SC (three judges) as doubtful; and (c) examination of
extraordinary appeals against valid judicial decisions. However, the
guidelines were for about 40 years the fundamental means of securing uniformity in the judicial process.

The turning point came in 1989 when the SC lost the right to issue
them. Since 1989, the resolutions and legal principles issued by SC
have also lost their binding force. The institutional separation of the
court from the executive authority and the legislature has greatly
influenced the Polish model of adjudication. The year 1989 is obvi-

ously a conventional date in the domain which we are considering here. Changes in the judicial system began earlier. The SAC was created in 1980 and the CT in 1985. Both these courts changed the previous conception of the judicial power by introducing the institutions of cassation and judicial review.

The *stare decisis* principle is not accepted in Polish law and, as will be further considered in detail, judicial decisions are not formally regarded as a source of law. However, we may safely say that many decisions function de facto in a way similar to precedents. These are in most cases decisions of the supreme courts. The decisions of the CT, the SC and the SAC should be included here first of all.

Asking the question whether courts have any possibility to select cases with regard to the function of precedent, we should state that judicial proceedings are nearly always instituted on the motion of other subjects (for example, the parties, lower courts) and not of the court which decides the case, and therefore the court cannot in principle make its own selection of cases to examine. However, there exist certain categories of judicial decisions which are particularly predestined to become precedents. In the first place we should mention the following:

1 Resolutions of the CT, establishing generally binding interpretations of statutes (pursuant to Article 5 of the Act on CT of 1985, this court makes the generally binding interpretation of statutes. Resolutions of CT in this matter are published in the *Journal of Law*, similarly to the statutes).

2 Resolutions of the SC, and especially those which enunciate legal principles. (The Act on SC of 1984 imposes the duty to provide for correctness and uniformity in the interpretation of law and in court practice (Art. 2). Accordingly, SC on the motion of certain organs (among others, the president of SC, the minister of justice and the ombudsman) may pronounce a resolution aiming at interpreting legal rules which raise doubts in practice or whose application has caused divergences in jurisdiction (abstract resolutions) or, on the motion of lower courts, may pass a resolution including the decision concerning legal problems raising serious doubts in a concrete case (concrete resolutions). Some of these resolutions automatically gain the status of legal principles (resolutions passed by at least one Chamber of SC), the others may be recognized as legal principles only on the motion of the bench. Though legal principles lack a formally binding force, their abrogation requires the application of special procedure (resolution of the full panel of a Chamber of SC – Art. 22 of the Act on SC).)

3 The fact that the decision has been published in the official collection of decisions of CT, SC or SAC. (All the above-mentioned

courts publish their decisions (all or only some of them) in official journals and in practice a judicial decision has a chance of becoming a precedent only when it is placed in such a journal (this is emphasized by the resolution of CT of 7 March 1995, W 9/94). Of course, it does sometimes happen that courts and the doctrine also refer to decisions which have not been officially published, but their role is undoubtedly smaller.)

2 Structure, Content and Style of Judgments

Making a general evaluation of the way of justifying judicial decisions in Poland, we may formulate the thesis that the prevailing style of opinions is deductive, legalistic and magisterial in style.

(a) The domination of the deductive style over the discursive one is quite visible in judicial decisions of SC and SAC. These courts first of all present their point of view and give the reasons for it by referring to the content of legal rules. In this approach the attitude of courts is to represent a conclusion derived from the content of legal rules. The domination of arguments pro over arguments contra is one of the characteristic features of this style. The court submits arguments confirming its thesis in the first place and pays less attention to analysing arguments which could shake it. The discursive and polemic elements are manifested in the strongest way in those fragments of the justification of the decision in which the court criticizes the position of a lower court or arguments of the defeated party.

In comparison with judicial decisions of SC and SAC, those of CT undoubtedly show most features of the discursive style. First of all, this results from the fact that in the practice of CT the presentation of its own standpoint and arguments and the evaluation by CT of the standpoint and arguments of the participants in the proceedings are inseparable elements. Consequently, the result of considerations of CT is very often presented as the result of cumulative evaluation of the arguments which confirm, or which question, the decision handed down.

However, it can be noticed that the scope of deductivity and discursivity of judicial decisions is at all levels clearly correlated to the degree of controversiality of the case before the court. The degree of discursivity of the reasons for the decision visibly grows in highly controversial cases where a number of competing views and opinions occur, and also in the cases which are controversial from the point of view of public opinion (for example, teaching religion in public schools or the problems of medical ethics).

(b) In the justifications of all the courts, the domination of the legalistic style over the substantive one is clear. The reasons are formulated in professional legal language, and legal arguments predominate in them. In the case of some fields of law (financial law and civil building regulations) they may be even incomprehensible to laymen. However, it would be misleading to say that courts formulate their reasons only on the basis of legal arguments and give up substantive arguments. Referring to ethical and to economic reasons, and to the rules of rationality or social consequences, is a popular practice in the jurisdiction of Polish courts. To a great extent this practice follows from the fact that legal texts, especially those of statutory rank, very often refer to general clauses and evaluative terms.

(c)   Judicial opinions stated by Polish courts, as in other countries of civil law, clearly prefer the magisterial style of justification. Judicial decisions are presented as authoritative acts of state and not as decisions of a concrete person. The fact that higher courts act collegiately and bear collegial responsibility for the content of their decisions partly contributes to this. In any case, the legal doctrine, commentators and the courts themselves never argue with the person of a concrete judge, but with the standpoint of court as an institution. Of course, the institution of *votum separatum*, in which an individual judge may submit his own point of view when it strays from the attitude assumed by the majority of judges, is an exception to the principle of impersonality.

The tendency to regard judicial decisions rather as the only correct solution than as the choice of the best alternative is also clearly visible, which seems to be connected with the domination of the deductive style over the discursive in the jurisdiction of Polish courts. This attitude also finds its justification in the ideology of the rule of law, accepted in Poland, which seems to assume that the law should give only one correct answer for every situation.

3   Publication of Judgments

According to Polish law, CT, SC and SAC are bound to publish their decisions. CT publishes all its decisions in full, while SC and SAC publish most of their decisions usually also in full. The so-called 'Offices of Judicial Decisions' are attached to all the mentioned courts; it is their task to elaborate and store the decisions of these courts, and in the case of SC and SAC also to select decisions to be published.

The following practice of selecting decisions has developed in SC. If the judge drawing up the reasons considers that the legal view contained in the decision ought to be published, he marks the relevant section of the justification and signs. If the rest of the bench shares his opinion, they also give their signatures. The Office of Judicial Decisions debates once a month; it consists, besides the judges of SC, of representatives of the Ministry of Justice and prominent academic lawyers, and they make the final decision as to what decis-

ions and what fragments of them are to be published. A similar mode
of publishing decisions has also developed in the practice of SAC.
Apart from the official promulgating journals, jurisdictional activity
of supreme courts is a subject of many elaborations (commentaries,
glosses, articles) in literature and academic periodicals.

We may venture the hypothesis that statute law in Poland functions in very strict symbiosis with the jurisdiction of courts. Though
most judicial decisions are not formally binding, referring to judicial
precedent makes up a very important argument in litigation before a
court. For this very reason the jurisdiction of higher courts is a subject of many elaborations and analyses.

Unlike the case of higher courts, the law does not require that
decisions of lower courts be published. They are also rarely a subject
of elaborations and doctrinal analyses. Collections of decisions of
lower courts which sometimes appear are of a private character and
are published in some legal periodicals.

4   Contents of Reports

The content of judicial decisions and the way of giving reasons for
them are to a great extent determined by the binding law. The rules
of civil and penal law procedure may serve as an example; they
determine quite precisely what content should be included in judicial decisions. Attempting to make a generalization, we may say
that in a typical case a judicial decision is composed of the conclusion and the reasons for it (the justification) except that obviously
not all judicial decisions are subject to justification. The following
elements are contained in the conclusion of a decision: type of a
decision (judgment, resolution and so on), the date of adoption,
number (signature), mark of the bench in a given case specifying
the names of the presiding judge and the reporting judge, determination of the parties or participants in the proceedings and their
claims, and the content of the decision of the court. In the justification of a decision we may essentially distinguish three parts: the
historical part, the factual basis and the legal basis. In the historical
part the court presents the course of proceedings, that is the claims
of the parties and the reasons for the claims. In the factual basis
part, the court presents facts of the case and the evidence on which
it has based its decision. In the legal basis, the court mentions legal
rules on which it has based its decision and, if necessary, it interprets them and submits legal arguments which constitute the reasons
for the decision (arguments pro) and refutes the arguments against.
Of course, the content of both the conclusion and the reason may
more or less depart from the given scheme according to the character of a decision.

When we compare decisions of the different supreme courts from this point of view, the decisions of CT are undoubtedly the most developed and comprehensive. CT principally passes two types of decisions: the decisions about (non-) constitutionality of statutes and other normative acts, and resolutions determining the generally binding interpretation of statute (interpretative resolutions). In the so called 'historical part' of justification of decisions, CT presents in detail the standpoint of the applicant and other participants of the proceedings and the reasons for them. In the further part of the justification, CT presents not only its own point of view but also its position towards arguments of the participants in the proceedings, and this part of the justification gives a visibly discursive and argumentatitve character to the reasons. It is also worth mentioning that, as compared to other courts, CT refers to doctrinal views and decisions of the other courts in a notably broad way. Sometimes it even refers to foreign literature and case law; sometimes it even draws on Polish and foreign literature on philosophy of law. As it seems, this practice results mostly from the fact that CT deals in its decisions with the basic principles of the legal system. As has been said, the decisions of CT are published in full and, if there is a *votum separatum* in the case, this also is published in full, together with its justification.

As far as the decisions of SC are concerned, we should distinguish two kinds: resolutions (cf. Section I.1) and judgments. Resolutions and judgments are published as a whole on principle. In the case of judgments, a partial publication is also possible, if the reasons are very detailed or contain fragments which are irrelevant from the point of view of the thesis taken from the decision. In the case of resolutions, a thesis or a legal rule resolved by the court is the main element of the sentence (it is displayed by special type). This thesis is extracted from the justification of the judgment and presents the court's point of view on a determined legal problem.

Publication of the decisions of SAC is based on the same rules as publication of the decisions of SC. Both SC and SAC refer first of all to legal regulations and their own decisions and they less frequently go into the decisions of other courts and the doctrinal views.

5   Meaning of 'Precedent'

Speaking about understanding the term 'precedent' in Polish jurisprudence, we should say in advance that this term is rather rarely used in Polish jurisprudence. This is connected with the fact that, in Polish law, precedent is not considered to be an official source of law. However, the problems of precedents are a subject of vivid interest for legal doctrine, which is generally aware of the fact that many judicial decisions function in a similar way as classical precedents.

The definition proposed by Wróblewski may be a typical example of the definition of a precedent which suits the content connected with this notion in Polish judicial decision making and doctrine. This author has defined precedent as a decision of a court which de facto or de jure influences the making of other decisions (Wróblewski, 1973, p.133). The mentioned definition should of course be specified by pointing out that a whole decision of a court (for example, a judgment) is not a precedent but only a general norm contained in the sentence or in the reasons for the decision. As we can see, it is a very wide definition and it comprises all the understanding of this notion distinguished in the guidelines, and so it refers to both the formally binding decisions and the non-binding ones provided they influence the making of decisions in similar cases in the future.

Talking about the fact that some judicial decisions function in Polish law in a way similar to classical precedents, we should carefully distinguish between two entirely different types of judicial decisions: the decisions made in concrete cases and the decisions made *in abstracto* without connection with any concrete civil or penal law proceedings. Ordinary judicial judgments are examples of decisions of the former kind, the interpretative resolutions of CT and abstract resolutions of SC (cf. Section I.1) (Sanetra, 1992) are examples of the latter. Seeing that the procedure of proclaiming resolutions of this type is not connected with settling individual cases and has many features resembling classical legislative procedures, the latter kind of decision is quite popularly included in judicial legislation. This type of legislation is a widespread phenomenon in some countries (Bodenheimer, 1962, p.231; Pomorski, 1974, p.352).

It seems obvious that precedents may be created on the basis of both kinds of decision. In any case, it is quite a general opinion in Polish jurisprudence that both the ordinary judicial decisions in individual cases and the abstract resolutions of SC or CT play the role of precedents (Stelmachowski, 1984, p.434). Accordingly, we may distinguish precedents *in concreto* and precedents *in abstracto*. The way of formulating and justifying both the types of precedents is similar, although the precedents *in concreto* appear in connection with concrete judicial proceedings in an individual civil or criminal case while the precedents *in abstracto* are without such connection but are a reaction of the court to the occurrence of general legal problems in practice. Both the types of resolutions may gain the status of legal principles. The fact that the precedents *in concreto* become similar to the precedents *in abstracto* is undoubtedly promoted by the way of publishing them. When an ordinary judgment in an individual case is published in an official promulgating journal, this judgment is preceded by a general thesis extracted from the justification of this judgment (cf. Section I.3), and this thesis does not differ in character from the abstract resolutions of SC or CT.

Incidentally, we could remark that the phenomenon of judicial legislation seems to prove the fact that the courts gradually take over the legislative functions in the classical understanding of this term. The rigid borderlines between statute law or, as Frank (1972) has put it somewhat paradoxically, legislative legislation and the traditional case law start to become obliterated.

It should also be stressed that, in some Polish legal terminology, the term 'precedent' is used with reference to decisions which contain an element of normative novelty (Zirk-Sadowski, 1980a and 1980b), that is to decisions which either depart from the former line of decision making or modify it or introduce entirely new rules and principles.The term 'precedent' is not applied in general to the decisions which only confirm in an authoritative way the past line of jurisdiction or the existence of determined rules, principles or customs (for example, constitutional customs). So the notion of precedent firstly refers to constitutive or even law-making decisions. However, this view is rightly questioned and it seems that the notion of precedent may be given a wider interpretation. And so the following categories of precedents may be distinguished in the doctrine: (a) constitutive and declaratory (cf. Section III.1), (b) law making and non-law making (Resolution of CT of 2 October 1991, Wróblewski, 1973, p.133; Zirk-Sadowski, 1980b, p.73), (c) *contra, praeter* and *secundum legem* (Stelmachowski, 1984, p.444).

The constitutive precedents create new rules or change the rules that have existed until now, while the declaratory precedent only confirms the existence of determined rules or principles. The law-making precedent is a general norm embodied in a judicial decision. It introduces new obligations and permissions into a legal system. If a decision does not entail such consequences, its character is not that of a law-making decision (Ziembiński, 1993a, p.50). The *secundum legem* precedent is a precedent consistent with the binding law. The decisions which authoritatively determine how to understand expressions contained in evaluative notions or in general clauses (Gudowski, 1993, p.197) are usually called the *secundum legem* precedent. The *praeter legem* precedent is a decision which enters the sphere which has not been regulated yet, while the *contra legem* precedent is a decision contradictory to the binding law. The distinguished categories of precedents may remain in very complex logical relations with one another. Here we shall only indicate that, pursuant to the standpoint of CT, the precedents created by this court should not be of a law-making nature and *secundum legem*. They should only signal a proper direction of the interpretation of the law and aim at achieving uniformity in the practice of application of law (Decision of CT of 20 January 1988, U1/87).

6   Mode of Citation and Discussion

At the moment when a judicial decision acquires the force of a precedent, it begins to function like an abstract rule, separate from concrete
facts on whose basis it has been formulated. In the case of the precedents *in abstracto*, this comes as a natural consequence of the fact
that such precedents are created without a connection to concrete
facts of a case. However, the precedents *in concreto* typically function
in a very similar way, despite the fact that they are formulated in the
context of concrete facts of cases established in civil, criminal or
administrative proceedings. As we have said, this practice is partly
justified by the rules on publication of judicial decisions and it may
partly be explained by the tradition typical of the countries of civil
law. First, the conclusion of a decision is preceded by a legal thesis
formulated in an abstract way even in the publication of ordinary
judgments of SC or SAC. Second, normative acts (statutes and governmental acts) are the main source of law in the countries of civil
law. Consequently, even when a court or lawyers refer to judicial
decisions, they are accustomed to treating them in a way similar to
the abstract rules of statute law.

No doubt, precedents in Poland and other countries of civil law
are only subsidiary sources of the law in relation to statutory norms,
so it is no wonder that analyses of precedents are subject to the
analysis of statutes and mainly serve to explain and exemplify their
content. A great number of judicial decisions is published every year
and only those decisions which are of interest for legal practice and
doctrine have a chance of getting into the legal relations and becoming precedents, and especially the ones which are often quoted in
justification of judicial decisions and in legal literature (glosses, commentaries, manuals, academic articles). Although judges and lawyers
are not formally bound to cite judicial decisions, however, it is a fact
that they do so on a wide scale. We should also pay attention to the
circumstance that the trainees preparing for the barrister's or judge's
examination are obliged to know, not only the text of statutes, but
also precedents of higher courts.

7   Overall Role of Precedent

Comparing precedent with other rules and legal materials, we should
start with the following remark. The extremely dispersed conception
of the sources of law was one of the basic faults of the communist
system of law. In particular, the administrative institutions laid down
a whole number of normative acts without any statutory authorization. In like manner, the status of some decisions of SC raised many
doubts, especially as concerns the guidelines. The guidelines of SC

not only had the character of general norms but their violation could also be a basis for appeal proceedings. No wonder, therefore, that they were regarded by many people as an official source of law.

In a number of its decisions (dec. of CT of 28 May 1986, U 1/1986; dec. of CT of 7 September 1988, Uw 3/88, dec. of CT of 9 May 1989, Kw 1/89; see also K. Działocha, 1992) CT has attempted to define which normative acts were ranked among the sources of law in Polish law. CT has said that the following are included in the binding sources of law: the constitution, statutes and governmental acts passed with statutory authorization. After some hesitation, CT also included the norms of international law (dec. of CT of 7 January 1992, K.19/91; dec. of CT 30 November 1994, W 10/94; see also Skubiszewski, 1994). Thus we can say that CT has definitely declared itself for the positivistic conception of the system of law according to which only the rules contained in the official legal texts may be the source of law.

However, the decisions of CT did not dispel all the doubts connected with the conception of sources of law. It had been long recognized that Polish law had no clear line concerning the status of legal customs, or the status of the so-called 'rules of exegesis' including rules of interpretation, rules of legal reasoning and the rules determining the criteria of the binding force of legal norms. Similarly, a lot of doubt had been raised by the character of judicial decisions creating general norms. Rival theoretical constructions were applied to solve the problems connected with this. Thus Ziembiński pointed out that a developed conception of the sources of law should comprise also the rules of exegesis, although the majority of them had not been recorded in the official legal texts (Ziembiński, 1993b, p.82). Wróblewski and many others rightly maintained that not only legal norms were mentioned in justification of a judicial decision but also the rules of interpretation and numerous extralegal principles and rules (Wróblewski, 1972, p.82). However, the status of judicial decisions in particular caused a lot of controversy.

Different arguments were used in the dispute between those who advocated and those who opposed including judicial decisions among the official sources of law. The advocates first of all referred to the fact that the general rules formulated by courts often functioned analogously to the rules contained in legal texts. They also maintained that neither the constitution nor the statutes contained provisions from which the prohibition of law making by courts would follow (Stelmachowski, 1967). It is hard to recognize a reference to the principle of separation of powers (Stelmachowski, 1984, p.436) as such an argument, since this principle functions also in the countries (such as the USA or England) where making law by courts is a widely recognized fact. The opponents of judicial law making in turn derive the prohibition of making law by courts in the first place from the principle of independence of the judiciary (K. Działocha, 1993, p.7; Murzynowski and Zieliński, 1992, p.6). This principle says that courts are subject only to statutes and so they cannot be subject to any general norms contained in judicial decisions. This view is also questioned. The principle of independence of the court of law only excludes creation by courts of norms contradictory to statutes, and the same applies to administrative acts, but it cannot be interpreted as the basis for the general prohibition of law making by courts and other organs (Stelmachowski, 1967, p.614). However, the point that in their judicial opinions the courts themselves do not claim the law-making functions seems to be decisive Wróblewski, 1967, p.869). This is proved by numerous decisions of the highest courts. And so, for example, SC and then CT have many times stressed that, even when the law is wrong or outdated, judicial decisions cannot change the content of legal norms or provide new rules (Wróblewski, 1967, p.870; see also dec. of SC of 19 March 1962, dec. of SC of 29 May 1961 and dec. of SC of 12 June 1968). On the other hand, it is an undisputable fact that judicial decisions are very often cited in the reasons for judge's decisions and play an essential role in them.

Therefore the question arises about what role is played by judicial decisions in the justification of judges' decisions and about their relation to the rules contained in the official legal texts and other rules and principles which are mentioned in justifications of legal decisions. In our view, in order to answer this question, it is worth introducing a distinction between autonomous and non-autonomous sources of law. Any norm or rule which may constitute an independent basis of a judge's decision shall be called an autonomous source of law, that is, such a norm or rule which may be an independent source of our rights and duties. Such norms and rules, in turn, which cannot constitute an independent basis of judicial decisions, and from which we cannot directly derive our rights and duties, shall be called a non-autonomous source of law. Doubtless in Polish law only the norms contained in the official legal texts, that is in the constitution, statutes and normative acts based on them, and in international agreements, have the status of autonomous sources of law. All the remaining rules and principles which are specified as the reasons for the judicial decision should be included among the non-autonomous sources of law. We should mention here, in particular, the following:

1   precedents and other judicial decisions;
2   the rules of exegesis, for example the rules of interpretation and the rules of legal reasoning, (such as analogy, *argumentum a contrario, a fortiori etc*);
3   the opinions of the legal doctrine;

4   extra legal rules and principles (the principles of equity, moral norms);
5   the jurisdiction and the opinions of foreign doctrine (Wróblewski, 1988, p.309; Zieliński, 1984; cf. dec. of CT of 19 June 1992, U 6/92; dec. of CT of 9 October 1993, K 11/93).

The necessity of including judicial precedents in the category of non-autonomous sources of law follows explicitly from both the jurisdiction and the doctrinal views. Lack of autonomy of precedents as sources of law is expressed first in the fact that a precedent is an element giving additional reasons for a decision made, and precedent cannot occur as the decision's independent and only basis (Leszczyński, 1994, p.4; Radwański, 1994). It is also manifested in the fact that it is the main function of precedents in Polish law to uniformize the application and interpretation of the existing law and not to create new rules or correct the existing ones (dec. of CT of 20 January 1988). Another symptom of the lack of autonomy of precedent as a source of law is that precedent loses its validity when the statute related to the precedent has been abrogated. And finally it is also characteristic of the lack of autonomy that, even when courts create brand new rules, they try to present their decisions as following from the binding law or constituting an act of interpretation of it (Morawski, 1994; Stelmachowski, 1967, p.612; Sanetra, 1992, p.17; cf. also, in common law countries, Pound, 1961, p.51; Dworkin, 1986a, p.38). Although the former guidelines of SC could be an autonomous basis for appeal proceedings and at present CT is considering the same problem in relation to its interpretative resolutions (res. of CT of 7 March 1995, W 9/94), this is an exceptional situation which only shows that the borderline between the autonomous and non-autonomous sources of law is not ultimately sharply defined.

Here we may ask what role is played by precedent in relation to other principles and rules distinguished here. From the very inclusion of precedent among the non-autonomous sources of law, the thesis obviously follows that precedent is a subordinate and auxiliary source of law in relation to statutes and other official legal texts (the same as in other civil law countries: see Coing, 1969, p.337). Of course, in Poland delegated legislation must take into account the interpretation of statutes established by CT (res. of CT of 7 March 1995, W 9/94). However, among the non-autonomous sources of law, precedents play the leading role. Precedent functions in the strictest connection with statute law since in practice these are judicial decisions which determine the interpretation of this law.

It is apposite here to add a few observations. The change of political system in Poland of the end of the 1980s has led to deep changes in the system of law. The category of autonomous sources of law has been broadened by the norms of international law. The importance of the non-autonomous sources of law has also increased very considerably. The courts show a greater tendency to quote judicial decisions and doctrinal views. It even happens that Polish courts call upon judicial decisions of foreign courts and views of foreign jurisprudence which is an entirely new phenomenon in Poland, resulting not only from the integrating trends in Europe (Walker, 1988, p.140; Habscheid and Schlosser, 1987, p.35) but also from the growing sense of intellectual independence of the Polish legal culture.

8 Role of Precedent in Different Branches of Law

As it seems, the activity of courts in creating precedential decisions depends mostly on two factors, one having universal meaning and seeming to refer to a majority of legal systems, while the other has a regional character and concerns the countries which, like Poland, find themselves at the stage of profound transformation of their political and economic systems.

The universal factor refers to a type of a branch of law. It has been pointed out for a long time in the theory of law that, from the point of view of completeness of regulation by law (see Lang, Wróblewski and S.Zawadzki, 1979, p.365), we may distinguish two different types of legal system: open systems and closed systems. An open system is a system in which it is not excluded that the regulation by law may be incomplete and, hence, the application of analogy and other argumentative operations is admitted in order to complete the legal regulation. On the other hand, a closed system is a system in which it is assumed that the regulation by law is complete and in principle does not require any complements. Civil law is an open system, while penal law seems to be a closed system.

Talking about the influence of the openness or closeness of a system on creating precedents, we should consider the problem of law-making and non-law-making precedents in a different way. Although there is a general prohibition on law making by the courts, the openness of the civil law seems to be the factor which justifies greater tolerance towards such law-making precedents than in the case of the criminal law. Indeed, also in the latter we come across the law-making precedents, but it is generally held that such precedents cannot violate the *nullum crimen, nulla poena sine lege* principle (Fuller, 1993, p.153). On the other hand, there are no obstacles in the civil law or in the penal law to creating the non-law-making precedents which aim only at achieving uniformity in the practice of application and interpretation of law. Having regard to the circumstance that in Polish law this very category of precedents definitely dominates, we may formulate the thesis that there are not essential differences between civil and penal law in respect of the degree of their being saturated with precedents.

The other factor which motivates courts to make precedential decisions is regional in character. Poland and other post-communist states are at the stage of deep political and economic reforms. The legal systems of these countries are axiologically incoherent, legislation often lags behind the rate of change and the courts carry the burden of making decisions on how to adjust the law to the new political and economic reality. Let us take Polish constitutional law as an example. As is well known, Poland has not had a new constitution yet, and on many weighty questions must continue to base itself upon the communist law, which did not respect a number of principles fundamental to democratic societies. In this situation, it is CT which, using the constitutional clause of the rule of law, has derived from it a whole number of explicit principles of fundamental significance for the political system, such as the principle of separation of powers and the right to a fair trial (dec. of CT of 22 August 1990, K 7/90, see also Morawski, 1994, p.11). Similar manifestations of the activity of courts may also be found in different branches of law, and particularly in the ones where the difference between the old communist law and the new reality is so deep that it simply forces the courts to make precedential decisions. Property law, financial law and labour law are the main examples here.

9   Precedent and 'Gaps in the Law'

If a judicial decision creates a rule for cases and matters previously unregulated (legal gap), this is called a *praeter legem* precedent in Polish jurisprudence (see Section I.5). Precedents *praeter legem* are in principle admissible in civil law and inadmissible in criminal law (because of the *nullum crimen, nulla poena sine lege* principle). It is disputable in Polish legal doctrine whether precedents *praeter legem* have a law-making or non-law-making character. Hence, when courts make *praeter legem* decisions, they try to present them either as a result of the interpretation of law, or as rules following from the existing law, or as possibly derived from this law at least by way of analogy. Putting it in a different way, the courts usually hide the fact that their decisions are *praeter legem* and do not openly present them as acts of creating new law. Nonetheless, the more realistically oriented representatives of the legal doctrine are aware of the fact that, precisely in such situations when there are lacunae in the law, the courts de facto make the law and, according to the opinion of many people, they should make it (Stelmachowski, 1967, p.613; Łętowski, 1990, p.28; J.Małecki, 1993).

II The Bindingness of Precedent

1 *Kinds and Degrees of Normative Force*

Speaking about the binding force of precedents, we should note that there is a general tendency in Polish law to limit all kinds of formally binding judicial decisions which in this or another way create general norms. Here we mean in particular various signs of judicial legislation (precedents *in abstracto*). This tendency has become significantly firmer since the fall of communism. It is justified by the necessity of abolishing all limitations and restraints on the principle of the independence of the judiciary. Abolition of the institution of the guidelines of SC in 1989, which had all the features of a classical legislative act (general norms, publication in the official law journal, generally binding force, autonomous basis of appeal proceedings – see Nowacki, 1974; Włodyka, 1971; similar institutions were known in all socialist countries – on this subject, see *Studia Prawnicze*, 1987/ 2) was a spectacular expression of this. Also legal principles passed by SC have been deprived of formally binding force.

In contemporary Polish law the resolutions of CT establishing the generally binding interpretation of statutes (interpretative resolutions), introduced in 1989, that is in the year of the abolition of the guidelines of SC, are the only candidates for the role of formally binding precedents. These resolutions are a source of general norms, their character is abstract, they are published in the law journal and their generally binding force lies in the fact that they bind not only the courts but also all the addressees of legal norms (res. of CT of 7 March 1995, W 9/94). The interpretative resolutions of CT fall into the category of precedents which are subject to overruling since CT may reverse or change its resolution (res. of CT of 7 March 1995).

Contemporary Polish law does not recognize any other judicial decisions which could be regarded as a source of formally binding precedents. The character of the qualified decisions of SC is not such. As SC has explained: 'Legal principles do not formally bind the courts. There is no provision which would impose the obligation to decide according to these rules [res. of CT of 5 May 1992, Kw Pr P/ 92].' However, the sequel of the quoted decision is significant: 'This does not mean that the resolutions passed by SC will not affect the decisions of lower courts. Lower courts should derive the authority of precedent primarily from the great weight of courts' argumentation and not only from its hierarchical rank.' Similar opinions are also pronounced by the doctrine. Let us cite one of them: 'The decisions of SC, although they bind other courts and organs only in a given case, affect the practice of application of the law in a much wider way that follows from the scope of their formal and legal bindingness.' Thus we may assume that, although all the remaining categories of judicial decisions must be included in the category of the formally non-binding precedents, they do have some justifying force. It is not easy to classify them accurately. In particular, neither Polish law nor Polish doctrine uses the notions of precedents 'having force', 'providing further support' or 'being merely illustrative'. The relevance of precedents cannot be determined on the basis of statutes, since their decisions in this matter are extremely terse. So the position of precedents first of all follows from the vague doctrinal paradigm. It is doubtful, and both the practice and doctrine so indicate, that non-binding precedents differ in justifying force and they may be arranged in a determined way from this point of view.

In our opinion, legal views expressed in the reasons for the decisions of CT should be placed at the top of this hierarchy, and the resolutions of SC should be the next, particularly those which have the status of legal principles. They seem to be closest to the category of precedents which are not formally binding but having force. From a formal point of view, only the conclusion of a decision has binding force (Wróblewski, 1989, p.4), but often the justification pronounces legal views and formulates rules and principles which then play an enormous role in the practice. Many fundamental constitutional principles (cf. Section I.8) originate from the justifications of CT decisions. CT is aware of the importance and significance of the opinions formulated by itself. This was expressed in the decision of 20 January 1988 (U 1/87) where, having in mind its justification, CT expressed the view that 'all the state authorities must take into account the standpoint of CT, expressed in justification of its decision'. The resolutions of SC also seem to fall into the category of precedents which are not formally binding but have force. This concerns particularly the resolutions which have gained the status of legal principles. Legal principles differ from ordinary resolutions of SC in the special mode of establishing and special procedure of abrogating them. SC cannot depart from a legal principle simply so that it passes a judgment contradictory to the content of a given principle, but it must make an adequate resolution (Article 22 of the Act on SC).

The next group in the category of precedents which are not formally binding is composed of ordinary judgments of SC and SAC, passed by these courts in individual cases. It seems that this category of precedents is closest to the category of precedents 'providing further support'. We should also pay attention to the fact that the wide acceptance of a given precedent by the courts and by doctrine may give it a higher status than it would have merely because it is contained in an ordinary judgment of SC or SAC.

The lowest category of precedents with mere illustrative meaning should include the precedents which come from the decisions of lower courts (dec. of CT of 19 June 1992, U 6/92, see also Stelmachowski, 1984, p.441 and, for common law countries, Frank, 1985, p.XIII). As it seems, we should treat the no longer binding guidelines of SC in a similar way. As SC has pointed out, the guidelines, although they have been abrogated, 'may still be a source of inspiration for the lower courts' (res. of SC of 5 May 1992, Kw Pr/92).

2 Law Concerning Precedent

Most of the problems connected with the question of the binding force of precedents and their relation to other sources of law have already been considered (cf. Sections I.5 and I.7), so here we can limit ourselves to the following remarks. Polish law in principle does not deal with the problems of precedents. The law, if it prohibits law making by courts, does so at most indirectly and by implication from the principles of the independence of the courts and the separation of powers. Statute law, on the other hand, distinguishes certain qualified categories of judicial decisions (such as resolutions of CT and SC) and partly determines their functions and binding force. In short, the position of precedent in Polish law results rather from the doctrinal paradigm and practice of courts than from statute law. Polish courts and doctrine rarely use the notion of precedent de jure and de facto and, if they do so, the decisions which are formally binding are usually regarded as precedents de jure while the decisions which are not formally binding but are taken into account while passing a judgment as precedents de facto (Włodyka, 1971, p.29).

Precedent is not considered to be an autonomous source of law and cannot be called independently of a statute as an exclusive basis for a judicial decision. For the same reason, in Polish law there is no branch of law that consists mainly of precedents. As we have already indicated, the role of precedents grows very considerably in those branches of law which are most deeply affected by the problems of political and economic transformations (see Section I.6). As to relation between the *nullum crimen, nulla poena sine lege* principle and precedent, compare Section I.8.

3 Factors Determining Degrees of Normative Force

The question whether and when a rule contained in a judicial decision has formally binding force is entirely determined by the provisions of statute law. It is in this sense that Article 5 of the Act on CT states that 'CT establishes the generally binding interpretation of statutes.' In this context all other factors must be recognized to be irrelevant as the sources of precedents which are formally binding.

4 Factors that Weaken Precedent

Pursuant to the attitude of CT, its interpretative resolutions may lose their formally binding force in two cases. First, CT may change such a resolution or abrogate it (res. of CT of 7 March 1995, W 9/94). Second, the resolutions of CT as a non-autonomous source of law lose their binding force at the moment of reversal of a statute which has undergone interpretation (the same rule refers to precedents which are not formally binding). However, it is not quite clear what will happen when the old law has indeed been abrogated but new regulations do not differ from the ones that CT has made subject to interpretation. The most probable assumption is that in this situation the resolution of CT loses its formally binding force and may be regarded at most as a source of precedent de facto (which is not formally binding).

5 Vertical and Horizontal Bindingness

CT is the supreme court and its interpretative resolutions are binding for all other courts, but not vice versa. Because of this, we may assume that Polish law is based on the principle of vertical formal bindingness. It was explicitly stated by CT in the resolution of 7 March 1995 (W 9.94): 'In case of divergences between the interpretation of CT and the interpretation by other organs, all the organs applying the law are bound to assume the primacy of the interpretation (…) made by CT. This means that no subject may refer to different understanding of a provision than the one which has been indicated in the resolution of CT.' Of course, CT is bound by its resolutions only as long as it does not abrogate them (for more details, cf. Section II.4).

6 Analysis of Force, Support and Illustrative Role

Posing the problem of the factors the justifying force of precedents which are formally not binding depends on, we should recall that Polish practice and doctrine, being fully aware of the fact that such precedents differ in their justifying force, do not categorize them so as to take this justifying force into consideration. The most important factors which affect the justifying force of precedents are (a) hierarchy of the court, (b) character of decisions, (c) composition of the bench in a court, (d) fact that precedent represents a determined line of jurisdiction, (e) support of the doctrine, (f) importance of argumentation and (g) origin of decision (before or after the fall of communism).

The hierarchy of the court doubtless determines the importance of precedent in the first place. From this point of view, the precedents derived from the decisions of CT should go first, then those of SC and then of SAC. The next factor in the sequence is the character of a decision. This particularly concerns the decisions of SC. As we have already said, this court has the power to pass resolutions as well as ordinary judgments, and among resolutions legal principles take a distinguished position. Composition of the bench in a court is another factor which determines the justifying force of a precedent. Sometimes the SC even repeats a view expressed earlier while passing a resolution with an enlarged bench in order to strengthen its influence on practice (for example, the resolution of the bench of seven judges of 6 December 1991, III CZP repeats the view expressed in the resolution of three judges of 25 June 1991, III CZP). Similarly, legal doctrine often mentions the fact that a judicial decision was passed by an increased panel in order to emphasize its importance and significance. And finally, the fact that precedent represents a standing line of decision and not a single standpoint of the court is of great importance for its justifying force as well as the fact that it has the support of the doctrine. The wide consensus in judicature and the doctrine without a doubt greatly strengthens the position of precedent. It even seems that, in relation to decisions which are not formally binding, in a situation where we meet divergent judicial decisions, it is the wide support of doctrine that may determine which decisions will gain the status of precedents.

In our opinion the influence of the weight on the justifying force of precedent of argumentations expressed in the decision should not be overestimated, since in many cases this feature has a subjective character, difficult to define, especially when highly controversial views and opinions come into play. However, it is worth stressing that, in the opinion of SC, this very factor, the importance of argumentation and not (only) the hierarchical rank of the court, should determine the influence of a decision of SC on lower courts (res. of SC of 5 May 1992, Kw Pr 5/92).

In view of the fact that Poland is now in a period of profound changes in its political system, we should also emphasize the influence of the political context on the justifying force of precedents, and in this sense SC has formulated the opinion that the courts, using precedents from the period of the communist state, should 'with particular care and scrupulousness approach the application of law of that period since very often it was especially restrictive and painful for the citizens' (judgment of SC of 14 June 1991, I PRN 23/91).

As we have already said, most of the factors determining the justifying force and status of precedents which are not binding follow in the first place from the doctrinal paradigm, since statutory regulations in this matter are rather scarce.

7   *Excess of Precedents?*

As we have said above, many judicial decisions are published every year. Most of them, exclusive of interpretative resolutions of CT, belong to the category of precedents which are not formally binding. Such precedents function in practice like typical argumentative *topoi* (*loci*) (Perelman and Olbrechts-Tyteca, 1969, p.84; Viehweg, 1974) which may or may not be employed by parties in the argumentative game before the court according to whether it is profitable for them or not.

On the other hand, criticism aimed at the institution of precedents which are formally binding is often met. Formerly, it concerned the guidelines of SC; now it relates to the interpretative resolutions of CT. In both cases, as we have already stated, the same kind of objections were raised against these precedents, for it was maintained that this institution was contradictory to the principles of independence of the courts and separation of powers and that it may lead to petrification of law, hindering its development (Strzembosz, 1995, p.10).

III   The Rationale of Precedent

1   *General Rationales for Formal Bindingness*

Except for literature referring to common law, the differentiation of declaratory and authoritative or constitutive theories (Frank, 1972, p.263; Fuller, 1993, p.128; Pomorski, 1974, p.357) has not been applied in Polish jurisprudence. Before the resolution of 7 March 1995 (W9/94) CT did not take up this problem directly. Although CT has explicitly advocated the declaratory theory it is hard to say that there is an entire uniformity of views in this matter. We may only say that the declaratory theory seems to have more advocates in Poland than the authoritative theory. The arguments of the advocates of this theory are usually based on the statement that precedent is not a formal source of law and so it cannot create new rules and its role is reduced to determining the correct meaning of legal provisions. The above-mentioned resolution of CT undoubtedly settles this matter when it states explicitly: 'In its interpretation CT neither takes away nor adds anything to the system of binding legal norms but it states what the content of these norms is. Therefore we may speak about the declaratory and not law-making character of the interpretation made by CT.' For the reason that interpretative resolutions of CT only determine the correct meaning of the existing rules and do not create any new rules, CT in the quoted decision comes to the conclusion that these resolutions have retroactive force (Walker, 1988, pp.134, 142;

Frankowski, 1969, p.373); that is, they are binding from the moment a statute interpreted by CT comes into force and not from the moment of passing an interpretative resolution by CT. Of course, the attitude of CT may raise doubts, especially when retroactive force is given to resolutions passed in matters raising such controversies. The CT may also raise doubts that the view assumed by CT cannot have been regarded by participants in legal relations as the only one admissible interpretation. However, this is a subject for separate elaboration. It is only worth adding that CT has created certain possibilities for preventing negative consequences of the retroactive force of its resolutions.

On the other hand, it must be emphasized that, at least in the doctrine, the declaratory theory is not accepted univocally. Many representatives insist on the fact that a number of judicial decisions have a distinctly law-making character and that these decisions often create even *contra legem* entirely new rules which cannot be reduced to the acts of interpretation of the existing law, which suggests that they take the position of law-making theories.

We shall consider the problem of reasons justifying the making and observance of precedents together since these problems are strictly connected with each other. The reasons quoted in favour of precedents in Polish doctrine are very similar to the ones that we meet in other countries (Walker, 1988, p.134; Coing, 1976, p.337; Wróblewski, 1973, p.148). At the same time, many of these reasons refer both to precedents which are formally binding and to those which are not.

All precedents are first of all regarded as instruments providing uniformity and correctness of application of the law, adjusting it to changing social contexts and even eliminating its most blatant defects (Nowacki, 1974). Especially in the sphere of judicial discretion, in particular where we have to do with general clauses, vague notions and evaluations, the law functions mainly by means of precedents (Leszczyński, 1994, p.5; Włodyka, 1971, p.68; Stelmachowski, 1967, p.617; cf. Davis, 1969, p.20). It is thanks to precedents that in the discretionary sphere similar cases should be determined in a similar way. So the precedent ensures a foreseeability of judicial decisions and the just application of the law (Cardozo, 1949, p.33).

However, an objection raised against precedents which are formally binding is that, although they provide for uniformity of the application of law, they very often hinder its development and restrict the necessary elasticity (for more detail on this, see Section II.7).

2 Rationales for Force, Further Support, and so on

Negative evaluation of precedents which are formally binding, or of some aspects of their functioning, does not exclude a generally friendly attitude of most of the legal doctrine and judicial opinions towards the institution of precedent as such. This concerns particularly the precedents which are formally not binding, because they ensure the necessary level of uniformity of jurisdiction and at the same time do not restrict the courts too much. Such an attitude is convincingly represented by the resolution of SC of 5 May 1992 (Kw Pr 5/92) in which it is stated: 'it is necessary to reject all these formalized methods which are to ensure uniformity of jurisdiction, which are contradictory to the requirements of just adjudgment, and particularly to independence of judiciary, to the right to institutionally free interpretation of legal provisions and their application conformably to circumstances of a given case'. Further, in its decision SC indicates that the uniformity of the application of law should not be a fetish because uniform decision making does not necessarily mean correct decision making. From this point of view, precedents which are formally not binding perhaps offer greater possibilities of shaping both uniform and correct decision making than precedents which are formally binding, because the possibilities for correcting erroneous decisions are greater. For the same reason, in the resolution of 7 March 1995, CT acknowledged that CT ought not to determine the generally binding interpretation of general clauses since such interpretation could petrify interpretative errors and thus impede development of law. Precedents which are not formally binding cannot be accused of limiting the principle of independence of the courts either.

As we have indicated, the reasons justifying the creation and observance of precedents which are not formally binding are in many aspects similar to the reasons in the case of precedents which are formally binding. The most important of them undoubtedly refer to the principle of the uniform, foreseeable, right and just application of law (for example, Wróblewski, 1971). We can also mention the following additional reasons:

1   Legal systems are neither complete not infallible and therefore precedent often occurs as an instrument of making up for gaps in a legal regulation, or of correction of its most obvious mistakes (Larenz, 1979, p.350).
2   It is also to be mentioned that legislation, and particularly parliaments, are not always able to keep pace with the rate of social transformations and must be supported by case law (Stelmachowski, 1984, p.452; Trocker, 1978, p.224). This is manifested in a forcible way in Poland undergoing the period of deep constitutional changes (cf. Section I.8, see also Stelmachowski, 1967, p.4; 1984, p.455). So Fuller is only partly right when he says that case law is not a suitable instrument for societies which experience rapid changes

(Fuller, 1993, pp.162–3). Although for technical reasons precedents cannot be instruments of a global and systematic reform of law, they are an invaluable and often indispensable tool of its partial correction.

3 Finally, precedent facilitates the making of decisions by lower courts and in this sense it improves their work because, orienting themselves to the decisions of higher courts, they take less risk of abrogating their decisions.

J. Frank mentioned two basical weaknesses of a legal order: uncertainty of law and uncertainty of facts (1983, p.XIII). We would like to remark here that almost all of us see in precedents an instrument first of all for reducing uncertainty of law (for example, interpretative precedents) and we quite wrongly forget about the function of precedent which lies in reducing uncertainty of facts. Yet such a function is fulfilled by presumptions, rules of prima facie evidence or other evidential rules, created by different courts (Morawski, 1980; 1981). It is also a task of these rules to tell courts that they should draw similar conclusions from similar facts in cases where there are various possibilities of interpretation of facts. This type of precedent, as distinct from precedents of law, could be called a precedent of fact.

IV Precedents: What They Stand for and How They Apply

1 What Counts as Binding or Having Force?

Speaking about the function of precedents and the ways they are applied, we should call to mind that in an enormous number of cases (resolutions of CT and SC), not excluding ordinary decisions of SC and SAC, in the conclusion of a decision a general thesis is published. In reality the thesis is reduced to a rule or principle expressing the point of view of the court concerning a determined legal problem. It is this rule or principle which is regarded as a precedent and courts refer to it in their decisions (cf. Sections I.3 and I.4). Legal opinions and views expressed only in justification of a judicial decision in respect of their importance are distinctly subordinate to the thesis contained in the conclusion.

However, we should not underestimate the function of justifications since in many cases the courts formulate legal views in a justification. This particularly concerns the resolutions of CT in which this court determines the constitutionality of certain normative acts, since then in the conclusion of a decision this court does not formulate any rules or views, and then the justification of the decision is used for reconstructing precedents. CT itself states it distinctly: 'in most cases (...) first of all the reasons for decisions (per obiter dicta)

assume an autonomous character acting on the direction of develop-
ment of legislation in agreement with the principles of the
Constitution' (Dec. of CT of 20 January 1988, U 1/87) (also cf. Section
II.1.).

Here it is worth noting that in Polish law there are no rules comparable, for instance, with English law, which would at least
approximately determine which elements of the reasons for a judicial
decision may be *ratio decidendi* and which may be treated as *obiter
dicta* (Walker, 1988, p.135) and in this matter both courts and doctrine
have full liberty.

2   Reasoning about Applicability

The rules of publication of judicial decisions determine the fact that
in many cases precedent assumes the form of an abstract rule or
principle which functions in a way similar to the rules and principles
of statute law (examined more precisely in Section I.6.). However,
seeing that the majority of precedents in Polish law are precedents
which are not formally binding, the reference to a precedent must be
frequently supported by substantive reasons and factual analysis.

3   Juristic Discussion

Precedent functions in Polish law (exclusive of the binding resolutions of CT) similarly to classical argumentative *topoi*. The practice of
justifying and applying precedents is thus of a non-formalized character and cannot be compared with the rules binding in this range in,
for example, English law (Walker, 1988, p.135). So it is hard to say
that there are any precise methods for defining what a precedent
stands for.

4   Illustrative or Analogical Precedent

Like any other argumentative topos, a precedent is used as an argument illustrating a definite thesis, explaining it or showing the
relevance of a determined point of view. We meet examples of this
kind both in jurisdiction and in the literature.

5   Single Precedents or Lines of Decision?

It is clear that both a single decision and a collection of such decisions representing a definite line of jurisdiction may have the character
of a precedent (Wróblewski, 1971, p.531; 1973, p.142).

In the case of precedents which are formally binding, this distinction is not so important since courts are obliged to apply a binding

precedent even when it would be based on a single decision. The mentioned distinction, however, plays a large role in relation to non-binding precedents. Generally, we may state that the justifying force of a precedent which is not binding clearly increases when it is supported by an established and steady line of precedents and not only a single decision (cf. Section II.6) and probably for this reason reference to a precedent in Poland most often takes the form of reference to a line of precedents (Leszczyński, 1994, p.4).

Moreover, in the practice of the courts we meet all the characteristic types of lines of precedents. So we have both decisions which only repeat a determined line of cases (merely repetitive precedents) and decisions which explicitly confirm a former line of cases. We meet the latter situation especially when in doctrine or court practice counter-arguments are presented against a determined line of precedent and in spite of that the court chooses to continue it (Garlicki, 1991, p.63; Zieliński, 1985, p.22). We also sometimes meet a confirmative precedent when, in given proceedings, one of the parties tries to shake the former line of precedent.

In complex cases with many aspects, courts sometimes make a number of partial decisions which explain some aspects of a definite problem and only after that do they pass a resolution, often in the increased panel, synthesizing the particular points of view (Gudowska, 1992, p.77).

A situation of shaping a definite line of cases and at the same time depicting the situation in which conflicting (zigzag) lines of precedents coexist for some time is described by one author in the following way: initially, cases on the matter are inconsistent, and it is only against the background of the experience gained that one of the lines begins to dominate over the rest and consequently the law-making practice crystallizes in a way that achieves widely respected stability (Małecki, 1993, p.39). In a situation of this kind, quite often occurring in Polish practice, the support of doctrine plays a very important role. It may decide which line of precedents will dominate in practice. Another way of solving the problem of conflicting lines of precedents is to pass a resolution in an enlarged panel.

However, speaking about a precedent in the case of a single non-binding decision is quite risky if a court does not confirm this decision in future decisions. It seems that, if a single case does not give a start to a constant line of decisions, there is no basis for regarding it as a precedent. In this sense, Wróblewski was right when he said that, in relation to single decisions, it is possible to determine whether single decisions are precedents only ex post factum (Wróblewski, 1973, p.138).

6   The Concept of a 'Leading Case'

Although the terminology of the leading case is not generally used in Polish jurisprudence, we quite often find it said of a given decision that it 'started a determined line of decisionmaking', 'opened the way to solving a definite problem', was a 'classic', or simply is 'precedential' in the sense of formulating a new rule or principle (cf. Section I.5. on normative novelty; also Garlicki, 1991).

V   Distinguishing, Explaining, Modifying, Overruling

1–3   *Distinguishing, Juristic Commentary, and Excessive Distinguishing?*

On the matter of modification of a precedent, as in many previous issues, we come across terminological problems. Polish legal terminology does not employ terms like 'distinguishing', 'overruling' or, say, 'statement reached per incuriam' (Walker, 1988, p.143; Raz, 1979, p.185) which, of course, does not mean that the problem of modification does not exist in Polish law.

We ought to remember that in the majority of cases precedents function in practice like typical argumentative *topoi*, whose use is determined by courts and parties, which in principle are entirely free to follow them in a concrete case. A substantially informal character is a distinctive feature of this practice. However, it is a fact that courts generally do not depart from a precedent by simply ignoring it but, in rejecting or modifying it, they usually give reasons for their decision.

The attitude of Polish courts thus seems to fall into this ideology of applying a precedent which was called by Dworkin 'the relaxed doctrine of precedent'. And for the reason that the courts have great freedom of modifying precedents, if a court wants to depart from a definite rule, it need not draw excessively fine or unreal distinctions in order to prove that it does not apply to a given case. So we can say that the practice of using mostly precedent which is not formally binding gives Polish courts the advantage that distinguishing does not have to be abused and it does not have to lead to consequences described by Walker in the following way: 'The law reports are full of strained distinctions where the court was evidently anxious not to follow an apparently binding precedent' (1988, p.43).

We have said that the term 'distinguishing' does not occur in Polish legal language, which, of course, does not mean that the practice covered by this term does not occur either. Let us use the decisions of CT constituting the so-called 'principle of the protection of acquired rights' as an example (for example dec. of CT of 4 November 1989, K

3/89). In accordance with this principle, in a great simplification, a citizen cannot lose the legally acquired rights for the reason of a change of the political and economic system. The principle of acquired rights, however, from the very beginning caused some controversies in the domain of the widely understood social rights. Having them in mind, CT has introduced a point of difference and distinguished situations in which definite rights were acquired justly from those in which acquired rights were a form of privilege for certain social groups and in this sense were the unjust acquisition of a definite right. Following this distinction, CT has deprived the employees of the Communist Party, functionaries of the security service and some employees of public administration of their right to a special pension (dec. of CT of 22 August 1990, K 7/90). Similarly, in many decisions CT has defined in what situations it is admissible to depart from the *lex retro non agit* principle (dec. of CT of 29 January 1992, K 15/91). 'The method of giving a wholly new or modified meaning to the words of an old rule is another measure often applied by courts to modify a precedent' (Frank, 1971, p.288).

4   Types of Overruling

Discussing the types of overruling, we must say that the formalized methods of overruling (in the strict sense) refer exclusively to precedents which are formally binding (interpretative resolutions of CT) and precedents which, although they are not formally binding, have the form of qualified decisions of SC, namely resolutions or legal principles. In both situations it is necessary to pass a special resolution in order to abrogate the precedent, and in the case of legal principles additional procedural conditions defined in Article 22 of the Act on SC concerning the composition of the bench must be met. When we take into consideration Walker's distinction between 'reversing', which concerns the whole decision, and 'overruling', which refers only to the precedent contained in the decision (see Walker, 1988, pp.141–2), we may say that the procedures described above refer to situations in which a precedent is overruled by formal reversing of the whole resolution of CT or SC. All the remaining non-binding precedents are overruled in such a way that the court departs from a former precedent or line of precedents, formulating a new rule or principle. As we have already mentioned, a practice has developed of specifying the judicial decision from which the court is departing and of justifying the new standpoint. For these reasons, the institution of silent overruling does not seem to play much of a part in Polish practice. The courts depart in a silent way usually only from those decisions which are weakly based on practice so that it is possible to doubt whether they have even reached the status of a precedent. There is one important exception to this rule. Each precedent may be silently overruled by a statute since a statute does not, of course, specify judicial decisions which lose their validity as a result of a change of law (Walker, 1988, p.142).

5–6   *Prospective Overruling and Anticipatory Overruling by Lower Courts*

The institution of prospective overruling has not been known in Poland up to now. It is a general opinion that it serves in the first place to avoid negative consequences which may result from the retroactive operation of a precedent (Lévy, 1971, p.309). In one of its recent resolutions (of 7 March 1995, W 9/94) CT also takes up this problem and formulates the principle that CT may settle a different date of coming into force of an interpretative resolution than the date of coming into force of the interpreted statute. Perhaps on the basis of this principle, the institution of prospective overruling will develop in Poland. At present it is obviously too early to make any forecasts (also cf. Section II.1).

The institution of anticipatory overruling as a separate notion has not been known in Polish jurisprudence either. However, in the face of the fact that most of precedents are not binding, it sometimes happens that the lower courts differ from the opinion expressed by a higher court, and the latter assumes their point of view subsequently.

7   *Precedent and Legislative Practice*

Speaking about mutual interactions between statute law and precedent, it must be emphasized that they function in strict symbiosis and cases of one influencing the other are very numerous. In many situations, courts create rules and those rules are next taken over by the legislator. Thus, for example, the admissible threshold of the content of alcohol for drivers was first determined by SC and only then was it registered in statute (Frankowski, 1969, p.371; for other examples, see Stelmachowski, 1967). On the other hand, reversal or change of a statute influences the importance of a precedent in an obvious way. Generally, we may say that in Polish law there is the principle of overruling by statute (Walker, 1988, p.142).

8   *Conflicts of Precedents*

We wrote about ways of removing conflicts between conflicting lines of precedents in Section IV.5. Conflict of single legal opinions is usually regarded as proof that a precedent has not yet been formed, unless these are the formally binding precedents (interpretative resolutions of CT). In the latter situation, CT ought to reverse the resolution which is contradictory to the attitude represented now. In case of a conflict of a resolution of CT with a resolution of SC, the former is regarded as binding since it comes from the court higher in rank (res. of CT of 7 March 1995, W 9/94).

9 Hypothetical Cases

The problem of hypothetical cases in the creation and application of a precedent seems to play a minor role in Polish law. Using the Anglo-Saxon terminology, we should say that reasoning of this kind is treated as *obiter dictum* with only illustrative or persuasive meaning. They usually appear in the situation when the court rejects argumentation of one of the parties but states in what hypothetical conditions it could be deemed right.

VI Matters of General Perspective, Evaluation and Other

1 'Saying and Doing'

We have throughout emphasized that the paradigm accepted by courts and jurisprudence in Poland definitely declares against law making by courts. As a consequence, even when the courts engage in the law-making decisions they try to present them either as a consequence of binding norms or as acts of interpretation of the law (cf. Section I.9). It has been rightly noted that such a practice may lead to dangerous consequences since it leaves this type of activity of courts out of the reach of any control (Frankowski, 1969). This *sui generis* crypto-law making is undoubtedly favoured by the fact that, in the case of legal texts using a lot of general clauses, vague or evaluative terms, it is difficult to find sharp criteria which would make it possible to separate accurately law making from interpretation (Zirk-Sadowski, 1980a). As a consequence, as Pound noticed long ago, genuine interpretation and law making run into one another (Pound, 1961, p.91; Frank, 1971, p.263). However, we should strongly emphasize that, contrary to official declaration, public opinion in a considerable part of the legal community is fully aware of the fact that in many cases the courts participate in some way in law making. As an example, let us use the sharp and decided reaction of journalists against one of the decisions of SC in which this court expressed the view that, under some circumstances, a journalist may be obliged by the court to reveal the name of his informer. The explanation by the press spokesman of SC that this view did not bind other courts and was related only to a concrete criminal case was recognized as not entirely convincing because of the factual role played by decisions of SC.

2   Recent Change or Evolution

In comparative legal studies it is sometimes mentioned that the systems of common law and civil law gradually become more convergent. The growing role of statute law in Anglo-Saxon countries and of 'case law' in the countries of continental Europe is one of the symptoms of this tendency. In this context, Aarnio even speaks about 'silent revolution' (*eine stille Revolution*: Aarnio, 1988, p.33, see also Wróblewski, 1971, p.524; 1988, p.378) taking place in the countries of civil law. In the case of Poland and other countries of Eastern Europe, this tendency has undoubtedly been intensified by the fall of communism. It is rightly indicated that progressing judicialization of the law, which began as early as the 1980s, is one of the most visible consequences of constitutional transformations. At this time in Poland administrative courts were created and the Constitutional Tribunal, the Tribunal of State and economic courts were founded (Wasilewski, 1992; Piotrowski, 1994). CT recognizes the right to a fair trial as one of the fundamental civil rights (Działocha and Gromski, 1995, p.12). As a consequence, many cases which were decided in administrative proceedings have now become the subject of judicial proceedings. Significant growth in the importance of courts' jurisdiction is an obvious consequence of these changes. Two facts no doubt contribute to this growth: (a) the dynamics of social transformations and the fact that legislation could not cope with these changes, and (b) the axiological incoherence of the Polish legal system, which partly consists of norms originated under communism and partly of norms created after 1989.

Using Dworkin's terminology, we could say that the Polish system of adjudication evolves from the doctrine of judicial restraint, where courts play an essentially passive role, which is limited to application of the law, to the doctrine of judicial activism, where courts actively participate in formation of the law, although they usually hide the fact that they are doing so (cf. Section VI.1).

3   Changes in International Environment

Poland's opening to the West after the collapse of communism has also undoubtedly opened the Polish legal system to ideas and values characteristic of the political and legal culture of the West. As we have emphasized, the very fact that the norms of international law have been recognized as an autonomous source of law greatly influences the Polish legal system. However, it is too early at present to say whether this turning point will have a significant influence on the attitude of Polish courts and jurisprudence towards precedents. In our opinion, Poland, though opening to the West, will still remain in the circle of legal culture of the countries of civil law and, despite the considerable growth of the role and activity of courts, it will continue to accept Justinian's principle: *Non exemplis sed legibus judicandum est.*

4 Juristic or Other Criticism

Referring to Dworkin once again, we may distinguish two opposite pairs of ideologies describing the role of courts and precedents in the legal system, namely the programme of judicial restraint and the programme of judicial activism, and the strict doctrine of precedent and the relaxed doctrine of precedent (Dworkin, 1980, p.137; 1986a, p.24). We may generally say that the Polish legal system evolves towards judicial activism and carries it out by means proper to the relaxed doctrine of precedent.

When we separate three basic categories of precedents, precedents *secundum, praeter* and *contra legem*, we may also say that they correspond to three basical functions fulfilled by precedent in Polish law:

1 precedent is an instrument providing for uniform and right application and interpretation of law (precedent *secundum legem*) and this is its basic function in Polish law;
2 precedent is an instrument filling gaps in legal regulations (precedent *praeter legem*);
3 precedent is an instrument for correcting the law, especially in the case of obvious and flagrant legislative errors (precedent *contra legem*). The latter function, of course, raises most controversies because of the official prohibition against law making by courts.

Realizing these functions, Polish courts and jurisprudence have declared definitely for the relaxed doctrine of precedent, reducing the institution of precedent which is formally binding to interpretative resolutions of CT. These resolutions are subject to severe criticism (cf. Section II.7), though CT employs them relatively rarely. Thus, in 1993, for example, CT passed only 14 such resolutions (Garlicki, 1994). This new philosophy of precedent, which clearly prefers the precedent which is not formally binding, is most emphatically manifested by the resolution of CT of 10 April 1995 (W 9/94):

> Striving for a consensus of opinions in legal community and for uniform understanding of regulations (...) ought to be connected with making the law open to different rational arguments, with readiness

to revise views under the influence of such arguments or in connection with the evolution of social and cultural context. So it is natural that, in a democratic state, legal thought develops in conditions which cannot be subject to determination by means of acts of interpretation whose binding force would extend beyond the case being decided by the court.

Let us, however, note that the mentioned tendency is no peculiarity of the Polish legal system and has its equivalence in gradual weakening or loosening of the *stare decisis* principle in Anglo-Saxon countries (Reynolds, 1971; Szyszkowski, 1969). The courts in these countries also cease to accept the principle that, no matter how absurd or unwise or unjust a rule once announced by a court may turn out to be, the court must not, cannot properly, change it, but must go on endlessly applying it until the legislature, by a statute, intervenes (Frank, 1971, p.266). Both these tendencies, as it seems, constitute in turn the expression of instrumentalization of law which is in the making all over the world (Morawski and Molter, 1993; Morawski, 1993). Since, if the law becomes an instrument of social policy (interventionism, welfare state), that is an instrument serving the realization of different objectives and social programmes, then slavish sticking to rules in the situation when they do not bring about the expected results loses any sense. As Frank rightly remarks: 'The judicial practice of adhering to a rule embodying an unjust policy seems itself to be a policy – a policy of doing injustice' (1971, p.270). To describe the mentioned tendency on a higher level of abstraction, it should be said that it is an expression of evolution of modern legal system from fundamentalistic systems, that is the systems treated as sets of absolutely binding and incorrectible rules and principles to anti-fundamentalistic systems understood as sets of rules and principles open to correction and revision in situations when they turn out to be erroneous (Morawski, 1988, p.212). Let us note that, as the complexity of social systems grows, so does the fallibility of decisional structures used by the law (Morawski, 1995). This is an additional argument in favour of the anti-fundamentalistic option. Although the opponents of precedents in the countries of civil law maintain that the correction of law ought to be made through parliamentary procedures, which of course is advisable, and the function of courts should be limited only to signalization of legislative errors, it has turned out in practice that parliaments very often are not able to react quickly enough to such signals (Frank, 1971, p.226; Dworkin, 1986b, p.18).

However, at present one of the most important reasons for 'taking precedent into account in judicial decisions', which consists in the fact that precedents provide for uniformity of decisions, seems largely to have lost its force. It is a commonplace to say that Polish law is undergoing a process of fundamental change. The quantity of new normative material exceeds the perceptive capacity not only of the law maker himself but also of any lawyer (this is proved by the size of the annuals of the *Journal of Law* of the 1990s). The system of administration of justice has become complicated through the intro- duction of the courts of appeal (see the statute of 13 July 1990, *Journal of Law*, no. 53, p.306). Besides the SC, courts of appeal pass an ad- ditional number of final sentences and in some cases they amplify divergences in judicial decisions.

So the view that 'in any case of referring to precedent decisions, precedent functions as a factor which fosters uniformity of jurisdic- tion (Wróblewski, 1967, p.542) seems to be exaggerated. More and more often decisions of the SC are variable, more and more often it departs from the 'established line of decision'. At present there ap- pears the characteristic formula, connected with changeability of law itself, in the decisions of the SC: 'in the new legal situation created by the amendment (...), the resolution [the former decision of the SC] has become out of date (...)'(res. of SC of 4 February 1993, III AZP 37/92). The departure from the established line of decision has also been caused by the change of the social and economic situation of Poland. This argument entails breaking lines of precedent going back many years (particularly in the case of labour law). The resolution of the Full Panel of the Supreme Court's Civil Law, Administrative, Labour Law and Social Insurance Chamber of 11 March 1993 (I PZP 68/92), concerning Article 41 of the labour code, is characteristic of this kind of decision. Thus the court broke its previous judicial deci- sions, creating a new legal situation. Similarly, it did so in the resolution of seven judges of the SC of 16 April 1991(III PZP 22/90). Other reasons for departing from the adopted line of judicial de- cisions lie in the lack of support for the decisions in the binding legal regulations (res. of SC, 01.1992, I PZP 37/92) or in the conflict between the decision and the adopted principles of the construc- tion of the system of law (for example, the principle of equal treatment of all the subjects of law: see res. of SC of 27 May 1993, III AZP 36/92).

Thus it seems that the above-mentioned reasons for departing from the definite, constant line of judicial decisions (and the chosen de- cisions to support them) underline the growing creative role of the courts in the Polish system of law. This is often exposed and stressed in the legal literature of the 1990s. It is pointed out that the court, deciding on a concrete case, first of all aims at the 'situational adap- tation to the binding law', 'harmonization and integration of the rules of this law', at its 'development and completion', and finally it fills gaps in it. The elements of the law-making role of the court occur also while applying *analogia juris*. Sometimes the doctrine goes still further, emphasizing that, in the present system of law (first of all in the constitutional provisions), such norms are missing as would distinctly exclude the law making of courts.

So the 1990s have become the period of a certain laxity of the rigid division into the making and the application of law. Sometimes it is very difficult to separate them from each other.

Thus the question, fundamental not only for Poland but also for all the countries of civil law, arises: if judicial law making is an unavoidable phenomenon, should situations be tolerated in the name of loyalty to official ideology in which the courts under cover of interpretation create the law, or should the courts rather be allowed to make this law openly, at least in exceptional circumstances? Our opinion is that the latter solution is more justified, as the gulf between the official ideology and practice, between 'saying' and 'doing' (cf. Section VI.1), seems to favour neither functional properties of the law, which as a consequence of legislators' indolence sometimes become absurd, nor its prestige. Opinions in favour of such a solution appear more and more often in Polish jurisprudence (Łetowski, 1990; Małecki, 1993; Leszczyński, 1994; Morawski, 1994), although for now one still should have doubts about whether it is possible to break the official paradigm.

Abbreviations

ARSP	Archiv für Rechts- und Sozialphilosophie
CT	Constitutional Tribunal
dec.	decision
NSA	Naczelny Sąd Administracyjny (Supreme Administrative Court)
PiP	Państwo i Prawo (State and Law)
PS	Przegląd Sądowy (Judicial Review)
res.	resolution
RPEiS	Ruch Prawniczy, Ekonomiczny i Socjologiczny (Legal, Economic and Sociological Studies)
SAC	Supreme Administrative Court
SC	Supreme Court
SN	Sąd Najwyższy (Supreme Court)
TK	Trybunał Konstytucyjny (Constitutional Tribunal)

References

Aarnio, A. (1988), *Wegen Recht und Billigkeit*, Berlin: Duncker & Humblot.
Bodenheimer, E. (1962), *Jurisprudence*, Cambridge, MA: Harvard University Press.
Cardozo, B. (1949), *The Nature of Judicial Process*, New Haven/London: Yale University Press.
Coing, H. (1969), *Grundzüge der Rechtsphilosophie*, Berlin/New York: de Gruyter.

Davis, K. (1969), *Discretionary Justice*, Urbana: University of Illinois Press.
Dworkin, R. (1978), *Taking Rights Seriously*, London: Duckworth/Cambridge Ma: Harvard University Press.
Dworkin, R. (1986a), *Law's Empire*, London: Fontana/Cambridge Ma: Harvard University Press.
Dworkin, R. (1986b), *A Matter of Principle*, Oxford: Clarendon Press.
Działocha, K. (1992), 'Państwo prawa w warunkach zmian zasadniczych systemu prawa', *PiP*, 1.
Działocha, K. (1993), 'Model ustrojowy TK de lege ferenda', *PiP*, 2.
Działocha, K. and Gromski, W. (1995), 'Niepozytywistyczna koncepcja państwa prawa a TK', *PiP*, 3.
Frank, J. (1963), *Courts on Trial*, New York: Atheneum.
Frank, J. (1985), *Law and Modern Mind*, Birmingham Ala: Legal Classics Library.
Frank, S. (1971), 'Wytyczne SN w zakresie prawa karnego materialnego', *PiP*, 10.
Frankowski, S. (1969), 'Z problematyki tzw. Normotwórczej działalności sądów w prawie karnym', *PiP*, 8–9.
Fuller, L. (1993), *Anatomia prawa*, Lublin.
Garlicki, L. (1991), 'Przegląd orzecznictwa TK za 1990', *PS*, 3.
Garlicki, L. (1994), 'Przegląd orzecznictwa TK za 1993', *PS*, 3.
Gudowska, B. (1992), 'Przegląd orzecznictwa NSA w sprawach podatkowych', *PS*, 11–12.
Gudowski, B. (1993), 'Przegląd orzecznictwa SN', *PS*, 4.
Habscheid, W. and Schlosser, P. (1987), 'Improvement of Civil Litigation', *Justice and Efficiency*, 8th World Conference on Procedural Law, Utrecht.
Kopaliński, W. (1985), *Słownik wyrazów obcych*, Warsaw.
Lang, W., Wróblewski, J. and Zawadzki S. (1979), *Teoria państwa i prawa*, Warsaw.
Larenz, K. (1979), *Methodenlehre der Rechtswissenschaft*, Berlin/Heidelberg.
Leszczyński, L. (1994, 'Precedent and the Judge's Axiological Choices' in Sawczuk, M. (ed.), *Unity of Civil Procedure and its National Divergencies*, Lublin.
Łętowski, J. (1990), 'Prawotwórstwo w czasach konfliktów', *PiP*, 5.
Lévy, H. (1971), 'On Justifications of Judicial Decisions', *Logique et Analyse*, 53–4.
Małecki, J. (1993), 'Prawotwórcza rola orzecznictwa w sprawach podatkowych', *RPEiS*, 4.
Morawski, L. (1980), 'Domniemania faktyczne i reguły dowodu prima facie', *Studia Prawnicze*, 1–2.
Morawski, L. (1981), *Domniemania a dowody prawnicze*, Toruń.
Morawski, L. (1988), *Argumentacje, racjonalność prawa i postępowanie dowodwe*, Toruń.
Morawski, L. (1993), 'Instrumentalizacja prawa', *PiP*, 6.
Morawski, L. (1994), 'Spór o pojecie państwa prawnego', *PiP*, 3.
Morawski, L. (1995), *The Rule of Law in the Welfare State*, 17th World Congress IVR, vol. III, Bologna.
Morawski, L. and Molter, A. (1993), 'Autopoiese und reflexives Recht', *ARSP, Beiheft* 52.
Murzynowski, A. and Zieliński, A., (1992), 'Ustrój wymiaru sprawiedliwości w przyszłej konstytucji', *PiP*, 2.
Nowacki, J. (1974), 'Kryteria obowiązywania norm prawnych a wytyczne SN', *Studia Prawno-Ekonomiczne*, 3.
Perelman, Ch. and Olbrechts-Tyteca, L. (1969), *The New Rhetoric. Treatise on Argumentation*, Notre Dame, Notre Dame University Press.
Piotrowski, A. (1994), 'Precedens w systemie polskiego prawa ustawowego', *RPEiS*, 4.
Pomorski, S. (1974), 'Z zagadnień prawotwórczej funkcji sądów amerykańskich' in Sokolewicz, W. (ed.), *Instytucje i doktryny prawno-polityczne USA*, Ossolineum.

Pound, R. (1961), *An Introduction to the Philosophy of Law*, New Haven: Yale University Press.

Radwański, Z. (1994), 'Rola prawników w tworzeniu prawa', *PiP*, 3.

Raz, J. (1979), *The Authority of Law*, Oxford: Clarendon Press.

Reynolds, B. (1971), 'A Formal Model for Judicial Discretion', *Logique et Analyse*, 53.

Sanetra, W. (1992), 'Wyjasnianie przepisów prawnych przez SN a zagadnienie powszechnej wykładni prawa', *PS*, 4.

Skubiszewski, K. (1994), 'Przyszła konstytucja Polski a miejsce prawa międzynarodowego w krajowym porzadku prawnym', *PiP*, 3.

Stelmachowski, A. (1967), 'Prawotwórcza rola sądów', *PiP*, 4–5.

Stelmachowski, A. (1984), *Wstęp do teorii prawa cywilnego*, Warsaw.

Strzembosz, A. (1995), 'Władza sądownicza w przyszłej Konstytucji w świetle stanowiska Zgromadzenia Ogólnego sedziów SN', *PS*, 2.

Szyszkowski, W. (1969), *SN w USA*, Warsaw.

Trocker, N. (1978), 'Gegenwartsprobleme der italienischen Zivilrechtspflege', *Zeitschrift für Zivilprozess*.

Viehweg, T. (1974), *Topik und Jurisprudenz*, Munich: Manz Verlag.

Walker, R. (1988), *The English Legal System*, London: Sweet & Maxwell.

Wasilewski, A. (1992), *Problem aktualizacji porządku prawnego, (w) Sadownictwo a obowiazujący system prawa*, Warsaw.

Włodyka, S. (1971), *Wiążąca wykładnia sądowa*, Warsaw.

Wróblewski, J. (1967), 'Sądowe stosowanie prawa a prawotwórstwo', *PiP*, 6.

Wróblewski, J. (1971), 'Precedens i jednolitość sądowego stosowania prawa', *PiP*, 10.

Wróblewski, J. (1972), *Sądowe stosowanie prawa*, Warsaw.

Wróblewski, J. (1973), *Wartość a decyzja sądowa*, Ossolineum.

Wróblewski, J. (1988), *Sądowe stosowanie prawa*, Warsaw.

Wróblewski, J. (1989), 'System prawa, tworzenie i wykładnia prawa w orzecznictwie TK', *PiP*, 2.

Zieliński, A. (1984), 'Podstawa prawna decyzji administracyjnej', *PiP*, 3.

Zieliński, A. (1985), 'Współdziałanie NSA z TK', *PiP*, 5.

Ziembiński, Z. (1980), *Problemy podstawowe prawoznawstwa*, Warsaw.

Ziembiński, Z. (1993a), 'Tworzenie a stanowienie i stosowanie prawa', *RPEiS*, 4.

Ziembiński, Z. (1993b), *O pojmowaniu pozytywizmu oraz prawa natury*, Warsaw.

Zirk-Sadowski, M. (1980a), 'Tzw. Prawotwórcza decyzja sądowego stosowania prawa', *Studia Prawnicze*, 1–2.

Zirk-Sadowski, M. (1980b), 'Precedens a tzw. decyzja prawotwórcza', *PiP*, 6.

8 Precedent in Spain

ALFONSO RUIZ MIGUEL, *MADRID* AND
FRANCISCO J. LAPORTA, *MADRID* *

I Institutional and Systemic

1(a) Court Hierarchy

The Spanish constitution (1978) in Article 117.1 states: 'Justice emanates from the people and is administered on behalf of the King by Judges and magistrates of the Judiciary who shall be independent, irremovable, and liable and subject only to the rule of law'; in Article 117.3: 'The exercise of judicial authority in any kind of action, both in passing judgment and having judgments executed, lies exclusively within the competence of Courts and Tribunals laid down by the law'. These statements are unanimously interpreted as giving the exclusiveness of adjudication to a single set of courts, implying that no special court (such as military or administrative ones) can be constitutionally allowed, at least in the sense that none of them has separate powers to judge without ultimate control of the Supreme Court, which is the unifying court of final instance in ordinary jurisdiction (as distinct from constitutional jurisdiction); the statements are also interpreted as giving to the judicial power its independence, understood in a double sense: first, as a whole body that has its own system of self-government, by means of the *General Council of the Judicial Power (Consejo General del Poder Judicial)*, which is competent

*   The authors have many debts to acknowledge. Particular thanks are due to our colleagues at the Faculty of Law, Javier Matía (Labour Law), Blanca Mendoza (Criminal Law), Angel Menéndez (Administrative Law) and Jose María Miquel (Civil Law), who gave us important information and insights. Emilio Jiménez Aparicio, former Director of the Legal Service of the State, provided us with data and intuitions hard to find elsewhere. Justice Pascual Sala, former President of the Supreme Court, encouraged us to go ahead in the vindication of a unified and binding doctrine of the Supreme Court.

to decide in all matters regarding judges' selection, appointments, promotion, disciplinary (that is, administrative) sanctions, and so on; the Council acts also as a consultative body whenever a new bill or statutory reform is proposed concerning some of the most important branches of the legal system (procedural code reforms, criminal or civil code reforms and so on); second, the independence is especially and chiefly understood as the power every judge has to perform the activity of passing judgment. This individual sense of independence has often been conceived of as including a certain degree of formal independence from the previous decisions of other judges or courts, even if they are higher in the judicial hierarchy (an exception to this, as we will see, is the special position of the sentences (rulings) of the Constitutional Court).

In the Spanish ordinary jurisdiction there are five types of courts: civil, criminal, labour, administrative and military. The hierarchy and competencies of each vary according to the type of adjudication involved and, thus, the following outline is of necessity a simplification of an organization which is in reality much more complex.

Juzgados form the lowest level of courts, with different denominations according to the jurisdiction of each: *de primera instancia*, first instance courts for cases involving civil matters; *de lo penal*, dealing with criminal cases; *de lo social*, for social cases, and *de lo militar*, for military offences (administrative juzgados are legally envisaged, but they are not functioning yet). These first instance courts are in the charge of one judge, who rules in all first instance civil and social cases. In criminal matters the judge is either in charge of the inquiry in the case (this is the 'instruccion' stage, that has an inquisitorial character and is meant to prepare the oral trial before a court composed by, at least, three judges) or decides when the offence is a minor one.

At a second level, there are two types of intermediate courts usually formed by panels of three judges: (a) Audiencias Provinciales (provincial courts) one for each of the 52 Spanish provinces, which may have either first instance jurisdiction (for severe crimes) or appellate jurisdiction. They may sometimes even have final ordinary jurisdiction (for misdemeanors and minor civil cases like house renting conflicts); (b) Tribunales Superiores de las Comunidades Autonomas (Superior Courts of the Autonomous Communities) which correspond to the quasi federal division of the Spanish state into 17 autonomous communities. These courts act as the ordinary courts of appeal, especially in criminal, civil and labour cases, have first instance jurisdiction in administrative cases, and can even have final jurisdiction in civil cases involving legislation of an autonomous region. There is also an atypical court, the Audiencia Nacional, with jurisdiction in the first instance in matters of national relevance in criminal, administrative and labour cases and in matters involving terrorism and organized drug dealing.

At a higher level, the Tribunal Supremo (Supreme Court) acts as the court of last instance in ordinary jurisdiction in appeals on important matters (most of them about legal interpretation (*casación*). It is divided into five chambers, corresponding to the five types of courts previously mentioned: civil, criminal, administrative, military and labour; each of them, in turn, is divided into different sections with five judges each. The decisions made by the Supreme Court are unappealable except on a constitutional basis, as explained next.

The Tribunal Constitucional (Constitutional Court), although not strictly considered as part of the ordinary jurisdiction and judiciary power, has important competencies which affect the decisions of ordinary courts. It is composed of 12 judges, the majority of whom are law professors and, in smaller number, former judges of the Supreme Court. The Constitutional Court rules on (a) appeals of unconstitutionality *(recursos de inconstitucionalidad)* which may be brought against a law under limited conditions (on petition of 50 parliamentary deputies or 50 senators, the president of the government and so on); (b) conflicts of competencies *(conflictos de competencias)* between organs of the state or between the state and the autonomous communities; (c) questions of constitutionality *(cuestiones de constitucionalidad)* which all judges must present when they have a doubt about the constitutionality of a law they must apply when deciding a case, and (d) individual complaints *(recursos de amparo)* which any citizen may lodge alleging that one of his fundamental rights guaranteed in the constitution has been violated by acts of the administration, by decisions of a court, or by parliament in one of its non-legislative acts.

Because Spain is a member state of the European Union, all Spanish courts are subject to the 'reference procedure' of the Court of Justice of the European Communities sitting in Luxembourg, according to which every court of a member state of the EU is bound to refer to this European court any aspect of community law that requires interpretation, meanwhile suspending its own decision. For similar reasons of international treaty law, all the Spanish authorities' acts, including courts' are subject to scrutiny of the European Court of Human Rights sitting in Strasbourg, which has the power to review the observance of the European Convention of Human Rights.

The courts most relevant to a discussion of precedent are the Supreme Court and the Constitutional Court, as we will see in the following paragraphs.

1(b)   Structural and Procedural Aspects

The Supreme Court is at present composed of 94 judges divided into five chambers, each of which is divided into sections (or panels) of five judges. The court hands down more than 25 000 decisions a year. Deliberation is confidential and, as in the French system, used to result in a unique collective decision with the eventual dissenting opinions unpublished. This tradition of external unanimity was discontinued after the constitution of 1978, which stated in its Article 164.1 that the decisions of the Constitutional Court, including the dissenting opinions, shall be published in the official gazette. Thereafter, this rule has been made applicable to the rest of the courts by means of new statutory regulations (Article 260 of the Organic Statute of the Judicial Power, hereinafter OSJP). However, it is still scarcely used by the Supreme Court and other ordinary courts.

The Constitutional Court is divided into four sections of three judges each for the process of admitting individual complaints, and into two chambers of six judges each for passing judgments on the individual complaints admitted; it sits in plenary session to resolve appeals and questions of unconstitutionality, as well as when 'a chamber considers it necessary to deviate from any point of previous constitutional doctrine which has been established by the Court' (Article 13 of the Organic Statute of the Constitutional Court, hereinafter OSCC). Although not as rare as in the rest of the courts, the dissenting opinions seldom appear, especially when the Constitutional Court resolves individual complaints. Their frequency is higher when the court deals with appeals and questions of constitutionality. The reason for this disparity lies in part in the greater importance of the latter cases, and in part in the more repetitive character of the decisions regarding individual complaints: after years of rulings, the court has reached a settled jurisprudence (case law). This firm doctrine is more likely to be lacking when approaching the constitutionality of statutory rules. The 'concurring opinions' are even rarer. Only 20 concurring opinions had been registered up to 1995.

The number of cases decided has been nearly 300 a year (excluding minor court orders – *autos* – and procedural orders – *providencias*). Decisions in every court are taken by majority. If there is a tie, the vote of the court's president or chief justice decides. Every judgment is studied and prepared by a reporter (*ponente*), who is selected by turn and presents a project of resolution for discussion and vote by all the panel and, finally, writes the resolution according to the arguments and criteria of the majority, usually including cumulative, subsidiary and even alternative arguments, so avoiding the likelihood of concurring opinions (and furthermore, lessening the chances for dissent). The higher the court, the more complex and articulated the discussion and the writing of the resolution.

1(c)   Power to Select Cases

The Spanish constitution confers on everybody a general right to obtain effective judicial protection. This is meant to include a wide access to a system of appeals (*recursos*) which on all important issues ends in the Supreme Court. Moreover, with regard to matters of fundamental rights guaranteed by the constitution, every citizen (or every person as regards the most basic rights) has a right to lodge an individual complaint (*recurso de amparo*) before the Constitutional Court. In addition to this, in the preliminary chapter of the Civil Code (which is considered a very important although not constitutional body of norms) there is an explicit prohibition for the courts to refuse to pass judgment on any ground. This legal framework provides that the power of Spanish courts to select the cases is very limited. In general terms, only those cases with grave and irreparable formal defects, or petitions, incidents and exceptions which are formulated with 'evident disregard for the law or which involve legal or procedural fraud' (Article 11, OSJP) can be excluded *a limine* and, even then, only by means of a reasoned resolution.

However, an exceptional faculty has recently been given to the Constitutional Court. It consists in the possibility of rejecting any individual complaint with almost no express justification if a section of the court (composed of three judges) considers unanimously that, among other causes, a precedent exists which would be ground to dismiss the appeal. In this case, the law requires that the order 'cite expressly the judgment or judgments on which the dismissal is based' (Article 50.1.d, OSCC). This is a prerogative which serves, not to select cases in order to review or to set precedents, but to reject ill-founded claims and so to confirm a line of precedents. It is obvious that this power of case selection is quite different from the use of *certiorari*.

Following this same path, a new redaction of Article 885 of the Criminal Procedure Act confers on the Supreme Court the power to reject, in criminal appeals of cassation, those appeals which manifestly lack any foundation and those substantially equal to others already rejected.

2   Structure, Content and Style of Judgments

The structure of the judgments in all Spanish courts is very similar, being divided into four parts. First is the heading (*encabezamiento*), with the date, the name of the court and, if applicable, chamber and section, the names of the judges and the 'reporter' (*ponente*), the names of the parties and their advocates, and finally the type of lawsuit, appeal and legal claim laid down. This is followed by the statement of facts (*Antecedentes* or *Resultando de hechos probados*), where the court declares as 'proven' the relevant facts that have been considered; in appellate judgments, the court reports an outline of the proceedings in the lower courts and relates more or less concisely the arguments of the parties in the claim or appeal.

The third part is the legal justification (*Fundamentos jurídicos*), where the court lays down the legal arguments relevant in the case, usually by commenting on the meaning of the words of the applicable statute or other legal rule and sometimes also considering the judicial doctrine – jurisprudence of the Supreme Court and precedents of the Constitutional Court – in similar cases. Very rarely, the arguments of the parties are expressly discussed here, although they can be implicitly accepted or rejected, and the same is to be said as to the arguments laid down by the inferior courts (except when the case is a complaint before the Constitutional Court against a direct violation of the Bill of Rights by the judgment of a court). This part varies not only with the legal importance and complexity of the case, but also with the rank of the court, the rule being that, the higher the court, the longer and richer is the reasoning: the judgments of the Constitutional Court are usually the richest and most articulate.

Finally, there is the decision or ruling, strictly speaking (*fallo*), where the court states the judgment, setting the matters in issue between the parties, upholding or reversing the decision of the court below or, in the judgments of the Constitutional Court, declaring the constitutionality or unconstitutionality of the statute or (in the individual complaints) of the administrative or judicial act affecting the Bill of Rights, as well as all other measures the court considers as required.

These four parts are the judgment *sensu stricto*. It must be signed by all the members of the panel, even if they disagree with it; in this case they can give a 'particular vote' (dissenting or concurring opinion) which is added to the judgment and published with it, although it is not strictly considered as part of the judgment.

The style of opinions in all the Spanish courts is deductive rather than discursive. Leaving out the heading, the structure of judgments follows a syllogistic mode of presentation with the minor premise in the first term. This structure is a historical consequence of the influence of the nineteenth-century theory of judicial activity as a syllogistic operation, a theory which was even included in Article 142 of the old Criminal Procedure Act of 1882, which stipulated that judgments had to be drafted indicating, first, the proven facts, then the legal criteria applicable to them and, finally, the specific decision deducible from both. The statute that regulates the structure of the judicial power contains nowadays a general statement saying that 'judgments shall be formulated expressing, after a heading, in different and numbered paragraphs, the factual record, or the proven facts, the legal foundations and, finally, the ruling (*fallo*)' (Article 248.3, OSJP). This article, nevertheless, does not claim to advance any particular conception of judicial adjudication.

The reasoning style is almost exclusively legalistic. The parties generally plead their cases alleging explicitly written rules of different rank and the courts also follow this. Although judicial interpretation of statutory rules can often raise matters of principle, these are usually dealt with in a rather legalistic manner too, resorting more to constitutional rules assumed to be clear-cut – that is, once more, interpreted in a legalistic manner – than to any kind of moral, political or policy criteria, which tend to be omitted, at least in explicit discourse. And this is also the prevailing style of the Constitutional Court when interpreting the constitutional rules (for instance, in the ruling that reviewed the constitutionality of some forms of abortion, the Constitutional Court asserted from the very beginning that it was going to settle the matter using legal and not moral arguments: see Constitutional Court Ruling 53/1986).

The style, finally, is strictly magisterial in all courts (including the Constitutional Court), usually expeditious and even dogmatic in tone. This is evidenced even in the writing of the dissenting opinions, where one could expect a more personalized way of reflection (we can cite as an exception the emotive dissenting opinion of Justice Mendizabal against the affirmative judgment of the majority of the court in the case concerning the constitutionality of a statute that decriminalized a certain kind of controlled sterilization of mentally disabled people). The arguments of advocates or lower courts are taken into account, if they are at all, as if they came from outside the procedure, like abstract reasoning that fits or does not fit the case but about which it is assumed not to be necessary to argue explicitly, and still less to enter into any kind of dialogue.

The Constitutional Court has adopted from its first decisions a didactic (although impersonal) style in the expression. In this aspect, the Constitutional Court was from the beginning especially concerned with the need for clarity in its linguistic expressions. The court expressly decided to abandon the use and abuse of gerundive forms in judicial language, forms that traditionally allowed and accompanied an archaic, long-winded and obscure jargon. Contrary to this, the court tried to express itself in common terms, in order to make its decisions as understandable as possible to a cultivated but not legally skilled person (with that aim, according to the testimony of the present chief justice, Rodriguez Bereijo, the court sometimes discusses even the linguistic form of the project of a judgment prepared by the reporter). This new trend is beginning to influence the rest of the courts.

3   Publication of Judgments

The final judgments (not the minor orders, that is *'autos'* and *'providencias'*) of the Constitutional Court are published promptly (never more than a month later) and in their entirety, including dissenting opinions, in the official gazette of the state (*Boletin Oficial del Estado*, hereinafter OGS). Moreover, other collections of jurisprudence exist. The OGS itself (lacking in this case its official character) annually publishes a book with all the Constitutional Court judgments (plus the text of the most significant *'autos'*) including some abridged references before each of them (see Section 1.4). There is also a private collection of constitutional jurisprudence on CD-ROM, but it is not complete.

There is an official publication of the judgments of the Supreme Court. There are also private collections and journals which publish these decisions, not in a complete form but merely including, selected by the editor, the legal justification and the final ruling. However, the most promptly published and most used series, especially by the private counsel, is one of these private collections (known by the publisher's name, Aranzadi). There are available also different collections of the jurisprudence of the Supreme Court on CD-ROM, none of them complete.

Selections and summaries of judgments of the Superior Courts of Justice of the Autonomous Communities, the National Court (Audiencia Nacional) and the Provincial Courts (Audiencias Provinciales) are published by public agencies (General Council of the Judicial Power) and by private journals and, eventually, commented on in specialized legal periodicals.

4   Content of Reports

The official report of the Constitutional Court's judgments contains the full text of them, with the dissenting or concurring opinions if they exist, beginning with a serial number – annually counted and correlated to the successive dates – and the date of the decision (for instance: 'Sentencia del Tribunal Constitucional 2/1983, de 24 de Enero'). This is the usual way to identify constitutional judgments (sometimes without the date), personal names not being used as names of the case. The annual reports collected by the OGS, after the serial number and the date of decision and before the full text, include the following paragraphs: (a) the number and date of the official gazette in which the text was first and officially published; (b) in abstract judgments of constitutionality (that is, appeals of unconstitutionality, conflicts of competencies and questions of constitutionality: see above, I.1(a)), a reference indicating that the judgment is made by the full bench, mentioning the name of all judges that have participated in the decision; in judgments of individual complaints (*recursos de amparo*) there is included the chamber that has decided the judgment and the names of the judges that have participated in it; in the case of the orders (*autos*), there is indicated the section number and the names of the judges that have decided the case; and (c) the register number of the case in the Constitutional Court (an annual and date-correlated number followed by the day of the year when the case was brought into the court) and the kind of appeal (appeal of unconstitutionality, for example). Finally, and before the judgment, in the following paragraphs the editors, at their own discretion, provide summaries or abstracts of the most significant doctrinal and legal arguments contained in the judgment, including precedents quoted and, in some cases, a summary of the dissenting or concurring opinions; such summaries can be longer or shorter according to the complexity of the decision, but usually do not fill more than one or two pages.

The judgments of the Supreme Court published by the OGS (but in this case acting as a private publisher) are collected by subject matter (civil, criminal, administrative, social and military) and reproduced in their full text. As in the case of the Constitutional Court judgments, every report begins with a serial number, annually counted, and with the date of the decision (although judgments, except those of the Constitutional Court, are usually identified by their date, the court and, if contextually required, the number of the chamber). Below this line, the following data always appear: (a) Reporter (*Ponente*), that is, the name of the judge who has written the opinion of the Court; (b) Procedure (*Procedimiento*), that is, the type of appeal (they are essentially of two types: substantive law infraction and procedural infraction, the main difference between them being that, in the former, if accepted, the case is to be completely and definitively resolved by the Supreme Court, whereas in the latter, if accepted, the case is sent back to the procedural moment when the infraction occurred; (c) Content (*Materia*) or the editor's reference to the legal rules of the judgment, generally expressed in technical terms (for instance, 'Drug dealing: intent; notorious importance'); (d) Applied rules (*Normas aplicadas*), that is, the editor's reference to the legal rules applied in the case; and (e) Doctrine (*Doctrina*), that seeks to identify in short terms (two or three lines) the criteria that, in the eyes of the editor, have founded the decision of the court (for instance: the 'notorious importance as aggravating circumstance; crime consummated when the first act of execution was accomplished');

sometimes an additional item may be found: (f) Quoted jurisprudence (*Jurisprudencia citada*), when the judgment expressly refers to previous decisions, generally of the same court, in support of the present decision.

Summarizing, the main contents of the best available reports of the Constitutional Court and the Supreme Court include the following items (ordered as in question I.4 of the Appendix):

(a)   The serial and annual number and the date of decision.

(b)   The name of the deciding court, including the chamber and section, and the names of the sitting judges.

(c)   (i)   The editor's headnote, which summarizes the legal and doctrinal foundations of the case, and that can also include the type of appeal, the rules applied and the jurisprudence or precedents quoted in the judgment. (ii)   The headnote with which every judgment begins, where is indicated the type of appeal and its essential content, the names of the parties and of their counsel, and the name of the judge that has acted as reporter.

(d)   The statement of the facts of the case are usually included as a part of the judgment (*antecedentes*).

(e)   The '*antecedentes*' also contains a reference to the procedural background and the prior decisions in the case.

(f)   The legal justification (*fundamentos jurídicos*) of the judgment usually begins, especially in the Constitutional Court's judgments, with a short and ordered statement of the legal issues relevant in the case, announcing more or less explicitly the order in which these will be dealt with in the rest of the judgment.

(g)   The specific discussion of the legal issues in the Supreme Court and the Constitutional Court deals almost always with interpretational problems of statutes (including the constitution). Only occasionally are precedents discussed, although they can be quoted or mentioned.

(h)   The judgments normally lay down propositions about the correct interpretation of a statute or of the Constitution which are to be taken as the *rationale* of the decision. These propositions are not necessary brief or expressed in an axiomatic or canonical form. Although not always quoted expressly, they can be consolidated in future decisions, so constituting a jurisprudential trend.

(i)   The prevailing legalistic and magisterial style does not always leave much space for a deep elaboration of the reasons that justify the interpretations adopted by the court, which usually are asserted rather than argued. In this setting, however, the richness of the Constitutional Court's argumentation compared to the rest of the Spanish courts is worth pointing out.

(j)   There is always a statement of the final decision (*fallo*), that has a quasi-canonical form, being the part of the judgment properly mandatory in the case.

(k)   Concurring opinions are very rare in the Spanish legal system, but if there were one in a given case, it would be published.

(l)   Dissenting opinions are also published.

(m)   The part of the judgment called '*antecedentes*' can contain a summary of the arguments by counsel. The report of the judgments of the Constitutional Court always contains it.

(n)   Apart from the public counsel – public prosecutor or '*ministerio fiscal*', and State's counsel or '*abogado del Estado*'– whose arguments can be summarized as in (m) above, no other legal opinions are usually considered in a judgment.

(o)   The report does not contain commentaries other than the mentioned summaries and references of the editor's headnote.

5   Meaning of 'Precedent'

In Spanish judicial doctrine and legal dogmatics, the expression 'system of precedent' or 'doctrine of precedent' generally tends to be understood as referring to the (assumed) formally binding *stare decisis* of the common law system; that is, a system in which the lower courts and judges are bound by the rulings of the higher courts. So a precedent is usually understood as a prior judicial decision that has to do with a similar case and binds other courts to a similar decision.

In the cultural framework of the Spanish legal mind, the fundamental principle, ratified on many occasions by the Constitutional Court, is that 'the judge is bound by (statutory) law and not by precedent' (Constitutional Court ruling 49/1985). In this tradition, 'jurisprudence' has only been considered a 'complement' of the legal system of sources. The central problem was that the 'bindingness' of a norm had traditionally been linked to its membership as one of the formal sources of law, and as the Civil Code did not include 'jurisprudence' as one of these formal sources, 'jurisprudence' could not have, strictly speaking, formally binding force. However, the constitution of 1978 and some subsequent statutes have introduced some new procedural devices, together with partial references to the concept of precedent, which are making their way into the Spanish legal literature and even into judicial doctrine (see below, Section II.2).

6   Mode of Citation and Discussion

In theoretical legal doctrine, the 'jurisprudence' related to the legal interpretation of the law under analysis is cited and considered in greater or lesser detail depending, of course, on the type of study (in more detail in technical monographs or essays). References to jurisprudence or precedent made by judges, practitioners or scholars do not focus so much on the specific factual features of the previous case or cases as on the legal doctrine, that is on the standard followed by the previous decisions in interpreting the legal rules considered applicable to the present case.

Anyway, in judicial opinions there has not usually been any detailed discussion of precedents, but rather a simple reference (or, at times, a direct quotation of the text) when this proves to be of interest. But now, the discussion of the judicial interpreting standards is becoming in academic legal writing more and more accurate and rich. Detailed commentaries on the judicial opinions of both the Constitutional and the Supreme Court are commonly found in journals in different fields of Spanish legal science. So, after a few years of activity of the Constitutional Court, several studies have appeared analysing its jurisprudence on specific topics such as equality, personal liberty, freedom of expression, due process and the like. But only among scholars is it usual to find open discussion of the quality and timeliness of precedents and legal interpretations. The courts and the judiciary almost never debate them, either in the body of the sentences or in journals and periodicals.

Lawyers who argue cases before the courts sometimes cite jurisprudence to support their arguments. Counsel, either private or public (in administrative, civil and labour cases), are not required to mention the relevant precedents, because the institution of reversal of a decision taken *per incuriam* does not exist in Spain.

7   Overall Role of Precedent

The overall role of precedent in the Spanish legal system is difficult to establish. If we understand the question to be what role does precedent play in legal argumentation, we could say that it depends on the type of process. The jurisprudence of the Constitutional Court may be considered as a strong argument for a given legal solution. The jurisprudence of the Supreme Court, although usually followed, does not play a major role in the day-to-day legal adjudication, but displays its force in the different kinds of appeals in *cassation* (as considered in Section II.2). Open deviation from some clear and firm precedents of the Supreme Court may be a source of criticism, but a good bit of weight is given to legislative materials and to the classical criteria of interpreting them. The interplay between formal rules and interpretative criteria may at times serve to support decisions different from those set by precedent. Only certain Supreme Court's decisions are deemed as plainly authoritative. In any case, precedent never takes priority over the constitution, codes, statutes or bylaws, and its usual role is as an interpretation of these normative materials.

8 Role of Precedent in Different Branches of Law

In the Spanish legal system a very important distinction can be made between constitutional matters and the other types of adjudication. In constitutional affairs, the doctrine of the Constitutional Court is very influential, with a high degree of unity, and is much respected. It is influential because it is, as we will see later, plainly binding. The respectability comes from the technical quality of its rulings and from the significant activist role it has played in the interpretation of the constitution in order to adapt the old legislation to the new democratic scenario. Sometimes (as in the development of the due process clause or freedom of expression), the court has produced a very dense and articulated body of rules, some of them following the American inspiration in cases, for instance, of unlawfully obtained evidence or of the public officer/private citizen difference in freedom of expression affairs, cases that have heavily affected both the procedures and the decisions of other courts.

In ordinary jurisdiction, the value of the Supreme Court jurisprudence as precedent varies among the different branches of law. The Supreme Court demonstrates a rather high degree of unity of criteria in general civil law cases, and its rulings are very influential and considered as practically binding, although some deviation from them is not unthinkable. In criminal cases, there are sometimes discrepancies between jurisprudence of the different provincial courts (which are the last instance for minor offences) as well as between the different sections of the same provincial court. There used to be also a few discrepancies among the rulings handed down by the different sections of the Criminal Law Chamber of the Supreme Court, but a short time ago this chamber decided to use a legal procedure to unify criteria. In taxation matters, although there is a degree of unity in administrative decisions, there are abundant discrepancies in the jurisprudence of the different superior courts of justice (which in some cases are the last instance of appeal), as well as in the different sections of the Supreme Court. In social or labour law, the doctrine is more influential and unitary, due to some features of this branch of the law: first, because there does exist an 'appeal for unification of doctrine' before the Supreme Court which is used very often, and second, because the principle of equality of treatment has great weight in these matters. In administrative law, the Supreme Court pays lipservice to the principle of the unity of doctrine and, as we will see, there are procedural mechanisms to achieve unified jurisprudence, but reality still may show another face.

9   Precedent and 'Gaps in the Law'

All Spanish courts are reluctant to recognize they are creating a new rule when they fill a statutory gap. Even more, they very rarely recognize that there exists a real gap in the law that has to be filled, considering that the general principles of law and what they call 'interpretation according to the legal order' are good enough to manage the problem. The usual pattern in the rare cases when a legal loophole is expressly recognized is rather the tendency to dismiss the lawsuit. Naturally, the self-consciousness of the courts cannot be the only and final proof of their role in the creation of new patterns when the law is unclear or lacking, although this attitude of the judiciary makes it difficult to measure the scope of the creative dimension of the judgments. Nevertheless, as a general consideration, it could be said that the Spanish judiciary as a body does not look upon creativity as a correct attitude of judges. There are some called 'activist' or 'creativist' judges, but they are a clear minority.

II   The Bindingness of Precedent

1   Kinds and Degrees of Normative Force

In the Spanish legal system, there are some judicial decisions that have some sort of formal bindingness as precedents. First, precedents of the Constitutional Court tend to be considered as formally and strictly binding for all other courts, as a consequence of a legal precept of the OSJP that states the duty of all judges and courts of interpreting the law according to the interpretation of the constitution laid down in the judgments of the Constitutional Court (for a literal translation, see below, Section II.2). However, although the influence of the decisions of the Constitutional Court is in practice quite effective and hardly disputed by public authorities, the scope of this precept has been widely debated in theoretical doctrine. Some authors admit that this precept effectively initiates a Constitutional Court system of formally binding precedents, while others deny this on the basis that the constitution guarantees the independence of all judges and courts, binding them only to statutory law. Nevertheless, the Constitutional Court itself has interpreted this precept at least on one occasion as a 'binding rule' (*regla vinculante*) (Constitutional Court Ruling 6/1991). And it can really be concluded that a judgment contrary to a settled interpretation of the Constitutional Court is to be considered unlawful and liable to reversal on appeal.

Second, according to the doctrine of the Constitutional Court, the precedents set by a judicial organ must be followed by the same

organ unless it gives a sufficient reason for changing its own criterion. The last ruling of the court summarizing this doctrine (20
September 1993) states that, for a change of doctrinal criteria to be
unconstitutional, it is necessary that decisions come from the same
judicial organ, that the basic facts and the applicable norms be substantially equal and that the foundation of the change be not express.
That is to say, these precedents have a formal bindingness subject to
easy overruling or modification. Otherwise, the decision is subject to
reversal as unconstitutional through an individual complaint (*recurso
de amparo*) before the Constitutional Court on the basis that it may be
a breach of Article 14 of the constitution that declares the equality of
citizens before the law. This doctrine of formal bindingness subject to
plain overruling or modification has been created by the Constitutional Court, although some limited indication of it can be found in
the statute that regulates the organization of the Constitutional Court
itself (see below, Section II.2). However, the extent of the doctrine has
been even more weakened not only by reducing the duty to follow
the court's own precedents through an unrestricted understanding
of the term 'the same organ' (two sections of a court are *not* the same
organ), but also by other arguments such as the refusal of the Constitutional Court to examine the adequacy of the legal grounds of the
court's decision and even the approval of the possibility of departure
from precedent based merely on implicit reasoning.

Third, the jurisprudence of the Supreme Court has traditionally
been given particular consideration within the Spanish legal system,
to the extent that the Civil Procedure Act of 1881 (Ley de
Enjuiciamiento Civil) established 'infraction of law or of *legal doctrine*' as grounds for cassation (quashing) decisions of other courts.
The Supreme Court, for a long time now, has been interpreting the
expression 'legal doctrine' as the criteria established by the court on
a given subject in more than one decision, thus understanding that a
minimum of two judgments with the same criterion made jurisprudence. This position is still in force. But at the same time, the
self-perception and the practice of the Supreme Court have always
made plain that the criteria established as jurisprudence do not bind
the court itself, considering, as we will see, that it was entitled to
overrule its own precedents when advisable.

An old and never-ending dispute has always been alive among
legal scholars as to whether all this implied that the so-called 'jurisprudence' is or is not a source of law. The dominant doctrine has
been that jurisprudence is not a *formal* source of the Spanish law, a
position reinforced by a reform of the Civil Code (1974, Art. 1) that,
as we mentioned before, introduced a specific mention of 'jurisprudence' (instead of the old expression, 'legal doctrine') but placed it,
not among the 'sources of law', but as 'a complement of the legal

order'. One of the main reasons supporting this doctrine of jurisprudence as a mere subsidiary inspiration has been a rather bizarre
understanding of the independence of judges and courts (an understanding that, from 1985 on, even has a legal basis in Article 12 of the
OSJP, which confers such independence even 'with regard to every
other judicial or ruling organ of the judiciary'). Because of this, and
although the literal statutory expression of most procedural acts (civil,
administrative and social) establishes 'infraction of jurisprudence' as
a motive of reversal in appeals of cassation, the Spanish judiciary
tends to reject the proposition that jurisprudence be considered formally and strictly binding. A judgment ignoring or not respecting
jurisprudence is not considered properly unlawful, but simply subject to discussion and only to a possible reversal by the Supreme
Court.

Nevertheless, and despite those conceptions of the judicial role,
the force of jurisprudence has increased as a consequence of the
division of the state into 17 'autonomous communities', each of them
with its own institutionalized judiciary and its own structure of judicial adjudication (see Section I.1 (a)). As a natural consequence of
this, the Superior Courts of the Autonomous Communities have final
jurisdiction in several matters, and this multiplicity of courts could
have as an outcome the possible coexistence of contradictory judgments in cases relevantly similar. To avoid this perverse effect, the
new acts of procedure have extended to some branches of the legal
system a new appeal in cassation (called 'appeal for the unification
of doctrine') before the Supreme Court. Whenever two final decisions on similar cases, arising from those courts, are in contradiction,
the Supreme Court, on appeal, has the competence to issue a judgment establishing *the* jurisprudence to be followed. Starting from this
type of appeal, which is becoming more and more frequent, the force
of the doctrine of the Supreme Court, that is to say, the force of
jurisprudence, is coming closer to 'formal bindingness' (see Section
I.1(b)) than to mere 'having force'. If a judgment of a lower court
violated the doctrine emanating from one of these unifying decisions, this judgment would be quashed (*cassé*) by the Supreme Court,
that is to say, it would be reversed on appeal.

Leaving aside the formal mechanisms which determine the 'official' bindingness or force of jurisprudence, we deem worthy of mention
some other features of the Spanish judiciary which, although rarely
discussed, are of some importance, namely, the hierarchical structure
of the judicial career and the traditions of the judiciary as a body.
Although career promotion is often automatic (mere seniority), all
posts of president of the different kinds of courts are selected by the
General Council of the Judicial Power, which is a board influenced
by those judges and magistrates who belong to the highest levels of

judicial career. This circumstance might implicitly compel the members of the judiciary towards an attitude of observance of the higher courts' doctrine. The other factor to take into account is the tradition of respect for this doctrine, and the usual resort to it as a source of information that almost every judicial organ requires in Spain. This is due to such tradition of respect or to the more crude consideration that it is easier and faster to pass judgment appealing to known and routine criteria. Together with the element of reflection, the foregoing leads to the conclusion that, all things considered and from an empirical point of view, the Spanish judge, as a matter of fact, follows more than he ignores the jurisprudence of the higher courts, and that the few cases of clear and explicit departure or of plain ignorance that can be found should be considered exceptions.

As to the academic discussion about the formally binding character of precedents in general and precedents of the Constitutional Court in particular, it is relatively recent and its influence in the complex and entire practice of the courts' adjudication is not yet clear.

2   Law Concerning Precedent

As regards legislation referring to formal bindingness of precedent, a few remarks may summarize the core of the subject in Spanish law. First, the formal bindingness of the precedent established by the Constitutional Court seems to be statutorily deducible from Article 5.1 of the OSJP, which states, 'the Constitution is the supreme norm of the legal system and is binding for all judges and courts, who shall interpret and apply laws and administrative norms according to constitutional precepts and principles, in accordance with the interpretation of them resulting from the decisions handed down by the Constitutional Court'.

Secondly, with regard to the duty of following their own precedents on the part of the same courts, two statutory norms can be found in the Spanish legislation. On the one hand, the OSCC states: 'when a Chamber of the [Constitutional] Court considers it necessary to deviate in any way from previous constitutional doctrine, the matter will be submitted to the decision of the entire Court in plenary session' (Article 13). On the other hand, Article 264 of the OSJP states: '1. The judges of the different Sections of a same Chamber should meet in order to unify criteria and to coordinate procedural practices. The meetings should be convoked by the Chief Justice of the Chamber, on its behalf, on request of a majority of the Judges as well as in the cases established by the laws. The Chief of the Chamber will be the chairman. 2. Anyway, Sections will be independent in the judgment and resolution of the different cases submitted to them.'

It is not common in Spain to differentiate precedent as binding de jure or de facto. As we have seen, doctrinal debate has traditionally centred on whether or not jurisprudence constitutes a formal source of law. Although this attitude is changing, a majority of scholars still think that jurisprudence is not formally binding. Thus jurisprudence is considered both in character and in hierarchy as inferior to legal norms (be they constitutional, legislative or administrative) as well as to custom and to general principles of law, that is, the three sources of law expressly mentioned in the preamble of the Spanish Civil Code. As we have said before, the relevant legal text here is Article 1 of this Civil Code, which in its first paragraph enumerates those sources: 'the sources of the Spanish legal order are the statutes, the custom and the general principles of law'. And the sixth paragraph of Article 1 states: 'Jurisprudence shall complement the legal order with the doctrine which in a reiterated way the Supreme Court establishes when interpreting and applying statutes, custom and general principles of law.' It is this 'reiterated doctrine' (which, as seen, the Supreme Court understands as two or more judgments) which is called 'jurisprudence' in the Spanish legal culture; and it is the infraction of this doctrine that constitutes a motive to appeal in 'cassation' in the civil, labour and administrative branches of law, but not also in the criminal law, where the principle *'nulla poena sine lege'* (Article 25.1 of the constitution) determines that the cassation be only established by 'breach of the law' and not of 'jurisprudence'.

Precedents in Spain are mainly settled and used in conjunction with the interpretation of statutory (including constitutional) rules, there not being branches of law, as in the Anglo-Saxon counterpart of tort and contract law, which may be rightly referred to as developed by the judges. In Spanish law, which is fundamentally codified, only a few concrete rules have been created by jurisprudence (the doctrine of abuse of rights, which from 1944 on moves away from the previous application of the principle *qui suo iure utitur neminem laedit*, or the so-called 'accident *in itinere*' of the social law, which includes in the insurance compensations the harms suffered in accidents while going to the place of work, or the so called 'continuous crime', which determines the duration of some punishments). Even in the case of precedents arising from the constitutional interpretation, one could say they are not independent of the written source of the constitution, especially of the Bill of Rights included as its Title I. In fact the Constitutional Court's precedents are never appealed to without citing also the relevant text of the constitution. Thus any arguments based on precedent are almost always accompanied by a specific interpretation of a law or of the constitution.

3   Factors Determining Degrees of Normative Force

The relevant factors for the formal bindingness of precedents are in Spain the hierarchical rank of the court (question II.3(a) of Appendix). This is significantly related both to the reputation of the court (3(c)) and, in regard to the precedents of the Constitutional Court, to the branch of the law involved (3(h)), the changes in the social, political and economic background (3(d)), which is a factor greatly related to the age of the precedents in the sense that the older they are, the less tends to be their force (3(f)), and the soundness of the supporting arguments in the opinion (3(e)). As to jurisprudence of the Supreme Court, the relevant fact is that precedents represent a trend (3(i)): although there have to be at least two decisions in which similar criteria were used to reach the final judgment in order to raise an appeal, the more repeated the solution the stronger it is as a precedent.

Three more factors can be mentioned for their significant importance in determining the force and, perhaps, the relevance of any precedent, in light of the fact that they are discussed among scholars (we therefore assume that their evaluation is more likely to be an objective one): first, the size of the sitting court question II.3(b) can sometimes be related to the quality of the decision; second, although theoretically a judgment bears the same legal force if it is agreed unanimously by the court or only by simple majority, the existence of dissenting opinions can weaken the force of the precedent; and third, either by statutory reforms or by departure by the courts from their own judicial precedents, legal change in proximate areas to the norms interpreted in a case can be a reason to exclude, or at least to severely qualify, the force of the precedent, since the argument by analogy and principles (*analogia legis* and *analogia juris*) is a familiar argument among Spanish lawyers.

4   Factors that Weaken Precedent

The most important factor that weakens a binding precedent is probably the obsolescence of its rationale due to changes in the 'social reality of the time when they (the norms) have to be applied', as this is one of the general criteria of interpretation included in the Civil Code (Article 3) and often used by the Supreme Court to change a line of precedents.

A factor that automatically deprives a precedent of its force is the enactment of statutory norms, or even of a bylaw, contrary to this precedent. As we have remarked several times, the bindingness or force of precedent is in Spain generally dependent on the pre-existence of enacted norms which the precedent interprets.

5   *Vertical and Horizontal Bindingness*

As has been said before, vertical formal bindingness can be considered the rule with regard to Constitutional Court precedents which are in fact nearly always followed by the other courts, and in a weaker sense the 'reiterated doctrine' or 'unified doctrine' of the Supreme Court.

In the Spanish system, there is no trace of 'horizontal formal bindingness', neither de facto nor de jure, if we understand this as the bindingness of decisions of courts of the same level on each other. As to the bindingness of the decisions of the same court, there is a weak duty to follow its own precedents, as we have seen. Concerning the Constitutional Court, we recall that it is statutorily required to summon a full bench when one of the two chambers 'considers it necessary to deviate in any way from previous constitutional doctrine' (Article 13, OSCC); as a matter of fact, the Constitutional Court follows its own precedents with a few exceptions. The Supreme Court is not so stable.

6   *Analysis of Force, Support and Illustrative Role*

It has been suggested in Section II.1 that the Spanish system of precedent is changing to a stronger and more formal bindingness due to a new system of appeals focused on the unification of doctrine. But the consciousness of this change is not so clear among the very members of the judiciary, and many still think that jurisprudence, to use the expression of the questions, is 'not formally binding but has force'. An example of the ambivalence and lack of precision of judicial attitude here is the most recent judgment of the Supreme Court on the 'value of jurisprudence' (Sentence, 18 April 1995):

> as to the value of jurisprudence, the sentence of January the 3rd and December the 12th, 1990, have declared that 'the jurisprudential doctrine does not consist either in a *disposition* or in a *norm*, but rather in some *criteria of applicability* consubstantial with the exercise of the function' and that 'jurisprudence, although it cannot be considered in principle as a strict source of the legal order, according to the first paragraph of Article 1 of the Civil Code, does nevertheless evidently come to complete and redesign the legal order through the reiterated doctrine, as is recognized in the sixth paragraph of the same rule, this being the reason why it is not possible to ignore the real *normative transcendence* of jurisprudence...'; the Supreme Court having also declared that a function of it is, in the abstract, 'to look after the exactness and the uniformity in the application of the valid legal order, because otherwise it would not be possible to reach the unity in the interpretation of norms, a unity on which certainty and legal security rest'.

The text of the judgment is illustrative of the ambiguous predicament of jurisprudence in Spain between *criteria of applicability* (nobody knows what sort of thing these are) and *normative transcendence* (something really hard to distinguish from a rule or norm). Apart from this statement of the Supreme Court, the status of jurisprudence is not discussed in judicial opinions and the majority of the debates take place in the academic field, dealing traditionally with the aforementioned character of jurisprudence as a source of law.

7   Excess of Precedents?

There is no view on the existence of too many precedents, but the common opinion of the legal community is that the existence of many coincident – and preferably not too old – precedents reinforces the doctrine developed therein and the existence of non-coincident precedents weakens it. This opinion is, nevertheless, implicit and informally expressed through topical phrases and commonplaces as 'firm jurisprudence' or 'erratic jurisprudence', the former being a solid ground to argue, the latter being not reliable.

III   The Rationale of Precedent

1   General Rationales for Formal Bindingness

The formal bindingness of Constitutional Court precedents arises from the idea of the 'normativity of the constitution' together with the proviso of the first article of the Organic Statute of the Constitutional Court, which states that the Constitutional Court is the 'supreme interpreter of the constitution'. By 'normativity' or 'normative force' of the constitution it is usually understood that the constitution is not merely 'programmatic', as the historical constitutions in Spain used to be, but directly applicable by judges and authorities without intermediation of the legislature. But 'normativity' also means the rule or empire of the constitution, that is to say, 'constitutionalism' as an expression of the general idea of the rule of law. In this sense 'normativity' means that all political, administrative and judicial powers are subject to the constitution. These two ideas, combined with the central interpretative role of the Constitutional Court, result in the binding force of its judgments. It is worth remarking here that it is not impossible that all this construction implies a theory of the precedent as 'declaratory' of the real and true meaning of the constitutional norms, a theory, however, that the Spanish jurists are not aware of tacitly promoting.

Theoretical discussion of the rationale and scope of precedents with binding force is fairly generic and therefore no settled doctrine actually exists. Authors in favour of giving more weight to precedents use arguments based on the size and reputation of the court, as well as the criteria of equal treatment before the law and the moral criterion of universalization. Judicial opinions only assert, and never discuss those rationales.

2   Rationales for Force, Further Support and so on

As to the rather weaker bindingness of ordinary jurisprudence, the main rationale to justify the force of the 'unity of doctrine' is clearly 'certainty' and the classical notion of 'legal security' (*seguridad jurídica*). The 'uniformity in the application of the legal order' is seen as a means to achieve, through the predictability and the certainty of law, the actual guarantee of the rights in question.

In what concerns the courts' own precedents, which carry a weak and overridable justifying force, the rationale is always the same: the principle of equality before the law seen from the point of view of equality in the application of the same rules to similar cases.

IV   Precedents: What They Stand for and How They Apply

1   What Counts as Binding or Having Force?

Theoretically, only the *ratio decidendi*, understood as the reasoning on which a decision is grounded, is the basis for the bindingness of precedents and, consequently, for the justifying force of jurisprudence (question IV.1(b) of Appendix). In practice, the reasons cited by the Constitutional Court as *obiter dicta* may be considered as authorized criteria, not binding but with some (not clearly determined) force, and are sometimes used as judicial and doctrinal arguments (IV.1(f)). This is the pattern that appears in the only statement (as far as we know) made by the Constitutional Court about the bindingness of its own precedents: in a case where it was discussed whether the raised point had force of *res judicata* or not, the Constitutional Court said,

> a different matter is the incidence that the reflections and estimations of the legal foundations (*fundamentos jurídicos*) can bear, as we will say straight away; because it cannot be ignored that the internal opinions or considerations that express a legal decision on the specific problem raised have a relevance by no means negligible. Indeed, through the technique of the judicial application of law it is necessary to make the pertinent distinctions as to the so-called *obiter dictum* or *dicta*. These refer to the collateral arguments that, to a greater or a lesser extent, contribute to the constructing of the main foundation (*fundamento*) or

ratio of the final decision or ruling (*fallo*). One thing is the simple *dictum* – assertion *en passant* that is not transcendent even as a complementary argument – and another thing is the argumentative *dictum* related more or less incidentally to the decisive reasons of the ruling (*fallo*). In that case, these *dicta* are judge's or court's opinions with proper efficacy, and if they do not integrate the *res judicata* (which is framed in the ruling and its determinant ground), they count as legal evaluations of the Court and constitute, in a certain way and to a significant extent, antecedents with *auctoritas*. Therefore, this interpretation of the Court, in the fields of its concrete competence, constitutes a mandatory rule (Articles 164 of Constitution, and 38 of OSCC) that, specifically, all judges and courts should follow according to the statement of Article 5.1 of the OSJP. (Constitutional Court Ruling 6/1991)

And, in fact, it can be maintained that this same ruling is an example of this very doctrine, for the Constitutional Court applied the same criteria which it had previously held, arguably as *dicta*, in other rulings.

Moreover, the interpretative style of all Spanish courts allows one to add that both the *ratio decidendi* and the *obiter dicta* formulate criteria (principles or rules, according to their variable nature and function) that are either paraphrases of constitutional or statutory rules or developments made by the court of these legislative rules (questions IV.1(c) and (d)). Although these criteria are not usually taken as canonical formulations by other courts or by scholars, they are not amply discussed with reference to the substantive reasons behind them (see question IV.1(e)), but, frequently, simply cited or quoted if considered relevant to the actual case.

2 Reasoning about Applicability

As has been said before, the prevailing style of interpretation in the Spanish legal doctrine and practice is mainly based on express invocation of legislation. This does not mean that courts, scholars and counsel do not cite or comment on precedents, but generally they do so only in support of an argument already grounded in legislation. However, a significant part of the work of scholars consists in commenting on and discussing difficult points or problems in relation to which precedents or jurisprudence can be a richer source of ideas than the legislation itself. In such works, arguments about the applicability of a precedent or a jurisprudential line are invoked but they again take the form of reflections on the appropriateness of the authoritative reasons behind the criteria used in the precedent or jurisprudence, and nearly all of these reasons are once again the invocation of statutes, norms of the constitution, principles or analogy (*analogia juris* and *analogia legis*) and the appeal to the different criteria of interpretation (intention of parliament, systematic coherence, purpose of law, social needs, and so on).

Nevertheless, there is a difference between, on the one hand, courts and counsel and, on the other hand, scholars. Courts and counsel tend to be formally respectful towards jurisprudence and precedents, although they may depart from them on a variety of grounds. Scholars, by contrast, even in the case of mandatory and clear precedents of the Constitutional Court, sometimes adopt an especially critical and detached perspective, contemplating the matter discussed in a prescriptive way, as giving the better legal interpretation at hand and, therefore, assuming that, eventually, it is the court which should change its criteria.

3   *Juristic Discussion*

In general, the answer would be that there is no substantial discussion, either judicial or scholarly, of methods for defining and finding what a precedent stands for. Although in some general discussions about jurisprudence or precedent the distinction between *ratio decidendi* and *obiter dicta* is considered and discussed, this scarcely transfers to the interpretation of concrete matters (only two exceptions can be found: the Constitutional Court Ruling 6/1991 quoted above (Section IV.1) and a dissenting opinion, in the Constitutional Court Ruling 222/1992, '*Voto particular del Magistrado Rodriguez Bereijo*': see below, Section IV.6).

4   *Illustrative or Analogical Precedent*

In using analogy as a typical means of interpreting legislation, lawyers always have been able to include the jurisprudential hermeneutic of the relevant legal rules. In this technique of analogy, argument by precedent is used, then, as a component of an argument not merely illustrative but as a means to extend the meaning of a rule or principle employed in a certain type of case to others which appear similar in kind.

The use of precedents as mere illustrative examples is, as far as we know, much more unusual.

5   *Single Precedents or Lines of Decision?*

As has been said before, in the Spanish system a distinction can be drawn between the bindingness of a single precedent of the Constitutional Court and the force of reiterated jurisprudence of the Supreme Court. However, even in the case of the binding Constitutional Court doctrine, a distinction may be drawn between the force of a single precedent and the force of a line of consistent precedents. This applies both to lines consisting of 'merely repetitive precedents' and to lines that at a given moment aré explicitly confirmed by the court. There are examples of both cases in the constitutional jurisprudence. Actually, the Constitutional Court usually makes reference to its precedents, reformulating the significance and scope of its doctrine, but it does not do so using any pre-established formulas, and this sometimes allows the court to qualify its doctrine without stating expressly that this qualification constitutes a distinguishing or an implicit partial overruling of a previous precedent. The Supreme Court follows similar practices.

As far as we know, there are no 'synthesizing' or reconstructive lines of precedents in the sense formulated in question IV.5(c) of the Appendix (extending the meaning of precedents to different particular cases), but courts reformulate precedents rather in order to avoid their application to a specific type of case. There are, however, relevant examples of 'conflicting' (or zigzag) lines of precedents in constitutional matters (freedom of expression, for example) as in other branches (administrative law, civil law and so on). Academic commentators and scholars nowadays examine the lines of the Constitutional Court jurisprudence (because of its importance) and organize, synthesize and try to reconstruct it, and sometimes uncover its contradictions and gaps. So they sometimes speak of 'sinuous jurisprudence'. On the other hand, there is a remarkable contrast between the attention scholars pay to the Constitutional Court and the almost non-existent studies on the jurisprudence of the Supreme Court on many matters. It is just in recent years that academic jurists are beginning to focus their attention on the doctrine of the non-constitutional courts.

6   The Concept of a 'Leading Case'

The concept of a 'leading case' does not play a significant part in the Spanish approach to precedent. Especially when there is abundant jurisprudence on the same matter, both the Constitutional and the Supreme Courts tend to cite more recent decisions rather than the first judgment which established the criterion. This may be due to the fact that the precedent has been 'fine-tuned' with time, making the later formulation more precise, as well as to the fact that no special importance is given to the concept of 'leading case', but rather to the application of a criterion of, so to speak, *sententia posterior*, so important in statutory law (as *lex posterior*).

Nevertheless, perhaps as the result of the expanding influence of some Anglo-Saxon legal practices and notions, the concept of 'leading case' has been employed in a recent dissenting opinion related to a case before the Constitutional Court. The problem was this: a judge presented a question of constitutionality, asking whether a woman had a right to continue living in the rented house of the deceased tenant, with whom she had been living *more uxurio*, since a statute allowed the legal widow to continue renting the house on the same, usually highly advantageous, contractual conditions. The Constitutional Court, grounding its decision upon the principle of equal treatment by the law, declared the unconstitutionality of the legal norm because it limited the right of substitution to legal wives or husbands, stating in the judgment that the statute should be interpreted as including the real, although not legally married, cohabiting partner. The court did so in spite of having previously denied in several judgments that the members of cohabiting couples (de facto unions) were entitled to receive the widower's pension, except in those cases where marriage was not legally possible because, at the time, divorce was not permitted. The dissenting opinion of Justice Rodriguez Bereijo (present chief justice) was that the majority of the court had contradicted itself and departed from 'the former doctrine of the court, and significantly from what can be considered the "leading case", the Constitutional Court Ruling 184/1990', with the result that there was an unacknowledged conflict between the present decision and the leading case, which would be a source of future disputes and a risk of this precedent being overruled (dissenting opinion to the Constitutional Court Ruling 222/1992).

V   Distinguishing, Explaining, Modifying, Overruling

1   Distinguishing

There is no firm practice of expressly 'distinguishing' precedents. Courts tend rather to ignore those which might be applied but are considered not in point, or cite them, but affirm without much discussion that this case is different. The ruling commented on in Section IV.6 is in Spanish terms unusually careful in considering (although in this case not respecting) the previous line of precedents.

2   Juristic Commentary

There has been no significant development of this type. Only limited criticism by scholars of some judicial decisions occurs.

3   Excessive Distinguishing?

Given the fact that there is no firm practice of expressly 'distinguishing' or 'explaining' precedents, changes in judicial doctrine tend to come about without discussion or express consideration of previous criteria. The usual way of modification or revision of precedents is the reformulation of the criteria of the previous judgments in order to restrict or extend its meaning to the present case.

The criticism raised by scholars can sometimes have influence in these 'fine-tuning' changes, but it is never expressly cited *nominatim* nor is it mentioned that the academic doctrine had suggested the change.

4 Types of Overruling

In general, overruling in the Spanish legal system most often consists of silent overruling simply through not following a precedent or a line of precedents; and it is so even when dealing with a formally binding precedent. The Constitutional Court has a practice of changing its precedents through almost unnoticed remarks and interpretations without acknowledging it. The Supreme Court, without mentioning it, changes its own precedents. It sometimes even mentions and transcribes the former decision and then proceeds to reinterpret it in a different way. And in very particular circumstances it changes them expressly, as when a sentence of 28 March 1994 declared that the court abandoned an old jurisprudential line on matters of parricide when the victim was a husband or a wife factually separated from the other. The 'factual separation' – so argued the court changing its previous doctrine – excludes the crime of parricide: 'The form in which this sentence was gestated, the very ruling explains, provoked, due to the importance of the question therein posed, a general meeting of the chamber, which took place on February the 18th, 1994, in which meeting, after a wide deliberation and exposition of the positions of every Magistrate of the Chamber it was agreed by a majority not to apply Article 405 of the Criminal Code in those cases of "factual" destruction of the marital relationship between the active and the passive subjects of the crime against life.'

The Supreme Court has declared (by a sentence of 3 January 1990) that within the function of interpreting and applying statutes is included the function of 'evolving the hermeneutic criteria in relationship to the historical data and the social reality of the time when the rules are to be applied. Thus it is possible to change orientation, provided the change is grounded in a new non arbitrary and reasonable interpretation. Such constant revision of the Court's own doctrine to keep pace with the evolution of the society is "salutary" (*saludable*).'

This means that, although as a matter of fact Spanish courts usually follow their own precedents, they are nevertheless not very respectful towards the institution as such and they do not always pay much attention to the formal requirements of the legal system about changing precedents. These requirements are, as we know, the obligation to submit the case to the full bench (Constitutional Court) and the weak duty of backing the new decision with sufficient argumentation (the rest of the courts). The first requirement has not always been observed in significant cases: in point of fact, it has scarcely been employed. As to the second requirement, the justification to be given is so general and weak that it would be an exaggeration to call it 'special'.

Nevertheless, there are two types of cases where the Supreme Court has explicitly overruled a line of precedent: when an important change in the legislation backing the line of precedent has taken place (which has been common in Spain since the constitution of 1978) and when a deep change in the social and cultural values of the people has been detected by the court (which has been frequent from the 1960s on in matters of so called 'private morality', as the example of the crime of parricide shows).

5   Prospective Overruling

There is neither authority nor practice of prospective overruling in Spain. All the decisions of the courts have effect on the case under scrutiny and on the future ones. Nevertheless, there is a procedural exception to this rule: the so-called appeal in cassation 'in the interest of the law', which can be posed before the Supreme Court in civil and administrative matters. When the decisions of some lower courts are reputed 'harmful to the general interest', the state's counsel in administrative procedures or the public prosecutor in civil matters is empowered to appeal in cassation against them. The judgment of the Supreme Court 'will have effect only to form jurisprudence on the questions legally discussed and solved in the case, *leaving intact the particular legal situations created by the resolution appealed*' (Article 1718, Civil Procedure Act, emphasis added). The significance of these appeals is evident: they can change a former precedent and, in so doing, constitute a genuine prospective overruling. They deserve the characterization of 'formally binding', because without any doubt they must be followed by the lower courts. In fact, the existence of this appeal is the strongest argument in favour of the bindingness of precedents in Spain, because a procedural device which concludes in a decision which does not apply to the facts of the case under scrutiny would be a sort of joke had it no binding force *pro futuro*.

6   Anticipatory Overruling by Lower Courts

As a consequence of the principle of direct applicability of the constitution by all authorities and judges, there have been cases during the
last 15 years where a judge, even a judge of a lower level, has refused
to follow precedents because they were based on preconstitutional
legislation, so anticipating the likelihood that a superior court or the
Constitutional Court itself would overrule these precedents by declaring the legislation unconstitutional. However, the usual way to
achieve the same result is for the judge to put the 'question of
unconstitutionality' before the Constitutional Court, whenever a
legal rule he or she must apply and 'on the validity of which the
decision depends' (Article 163 of the constitution) could be deemed
unconstitutional. Naturally, the unconstitutionality of the rule entails
the overruling of all the precedents based on it.

7   Precedent and Legislative Practice

The legislature often takes into account the existing precedents, especially in the case of Constitutional Court decisions, towards which
there is a complete and diligent respect. Several statutory rules have
expressly included criteria previously applied by the Constitutional
Court in individual complaint judgments. The criteria of other courts
have traditionally been taken into account, especially those of the
Supreme Court (thus the parliament reformed the Civil Code, accepting the criteria of the Supreme Court's jurisprudence about the
abuse of rights and the social statutes included immediately the
'accident *in itinere*').

In the event that legislation confirms or reverses a precedent in
non-constitutional matters, the precedent loses all its weight and
interpretation comes to rest completely on the new legislation. In
constitutional matters, although the hypothesis is by now merely
theoretical, the Constitutional Court would maintain the power to
review that legislation and could not only declare it unconstitutional
but also interpret it on the basis of criteria previously settled in its
own precedents.

8   Conflicts of Precedents

If there are conflicts between precedents of different courts, Constitutional Court jurisprudence prevails over all others, and Supreme
Court jurisprudence over the lower courts. When precedents of the
same court conflict, the more recent decisions tend to prevail over
the earlier ones, but sometimes opposite trends of jurisprudence can
coexist for a long time. Fortunately, the existence of the new 'appeals

in cassation for the unification of doctrine' (in the scope they have) are means to relieve these situations. Nevertheless, there still exist living precedents and lines of precedents which are plainly contradictory. If conflicts are resolved through one of the aforesaid appeals, unified doctrine acquires a heightened influence.

9   *Hypothetical Cases*

Neither judges nor lawyers utilize hypothetical cases in reasoning about the creation or application of precedents, still less when they are arguing or deciding a case. The prevalent deductive, legalistic and magisterial style of opinions and argumentations in the Spanish courts does not facilitate the presence of *'reductio ad absurdum'* or similar argumentative devices. Only scholars when teaching (and not very often) have a practice of reasoning around some hypothetical cases to show, for example, the probable consequences of a certain interpretation of a rule or principle, or how a judgment fits into a line of precedents or a set of legal norms. What Spanish lawyers call 'consequences unwanted by the legal order' (*consecuencias no queridas por el ordenamiento*) are particular norms or decisions that do not coherently fit into the legal order or into some subset of norms thereof. And sometimes lawyers illuminate this idea by projecting hypothetical cases or decisions which would presumptively produce this type of consequence. Nevertheless, it would not be accurate to think that this didactic practice has much to do with a sound and constructed vision of precedents.

VI   Matters of General Perspective, Evaluation and Other

1   *'Saying and Doing'*

The effective weight of precedents is probably greater than that which is reflected in the more traditional official doctrine. The traditional legal mind of judges can be described as follows: in the case of the Supreme Court's jurisprudence, maybe lower courts say they are free, yet de facto their practice is to consider and follow the jurisprudence; in the case of precedents of the Constitutional Court, ordinary judges probably *accept* that they are bound, yet they do not normally admit the loss of their traditional (assumed) independence and, perhaps, there may be cases where they do not follow them in fact. Hence, some gap between saying and doing could exist in Spanish legal practice.

2   *Recent Change or Evolution*

As has been said before (see above, Section II.2) the explicit bindingness of precedents of the Constitutional Court is practically as recent as the present court, which has operated since 1980, the subjection to its doctrine having been statutory and expressly established in 1985. The special horizontal bindingness of precedents of the same court for itself has been settled recently too, being a consequence of the constitutional interpretation of the Constitutional Court. The same constitutional changes have produced the new structure of the Spanish jurisdictions which has brought about the existence of a 'Superior Court of Justice' in each autonomous community. And this sort of 'federalization' of justice has been considered as demanding a system of appeals designed to unify the 'doctrine'. This unification gives to the law which produces it a special force.

3   *Changes in International Environment*

The Constitutional Court itself takes into account the doctrine of the European Court of Human Rights (and, less frequently, that of the European Court of Justice) and this fact could be interpreted in two ways which are not really in conflict with each other: (1) in order to avoid having its decisions overruled by the European Court of Human Rights and (2) in order to comply with Article 10.2 of the Spanish constitution, which states, 'The principles relating to the fundamental right and liberties recognized by the Constitution will be interpreted in conformity with the Universal Declaration of Human Rights and the international treaties and agreements thereon ratified by Spain.'
   As already said, all Spanish Courts are subject to the procedure of reference to the Court of Justice of the European Communities. This seems to imply that, by virtue of a treaty, precedents of this court are formally binding over the Spanish courts, but it does not appear that this fact has changed the overall view on judicial application of law, although that institution has effectively changed the practice of the courts.

4   *Juristic or Other Criticism*

There are no firm and established theoretical currents of analysis and criticism of precedent in the strict sense and its manner of creation in Spain. The bibliography to this chapter, which is not exhaustive but is very full, vividly demonstrates this. This is in part due to the recent evolution of the legal system, together with the traditional and rather palaeo-positivistic mentality in which the judges used to be socialized for years. The traditional judge imagined his own role as depending on two *'idées-forces'*: the principle of legality (or of the binding force of the law) and the classical requirement of independence of the judiciary (although under Francoism this independence was severely distorted). As a consequence of both ideas, jurisprudence got very little room in the Spanish system of sources of law (only as a complement of the legal order) and the individual judge did not feel strictly bound to the precedent. If judges used to follow the doctrine of the Supreme Court it was because the French device of *cassation* included the breach of 'doctrine' as a motive for appeal (what is now called infraction or breach of jurisprudence) and because there were some features of the judiciary (hierarchical structure) and the legal tradition (with respect to the higher courts) apt to produce that attitude. Nevertheless, these features were not able to bring about a theoretical account of precedents. Discussions centred on the old question of sources of law.

But the deep evolution of the system starting from the constitution and the new establishment of the constitutional jurisdiction suddenly introduces the formally binding character (*ope legis*) of the jurisprudence of the court and the implicit binding character of the decisions on questions of unification of doctrine. The academic debate has centred on the former (as shown in the bibliography), but it would not be an arbitrary conjecture to predict that the latter (the bindingness of 'ordinary' jurisprudence) will be an important innovation in the Spanish legal landscape. Actually, the majority of scholars recognize nowadays the growing importance of the role of jurisprudence in the articulation of the different branches of law and in the creation of concepts. Most of them have told us, in effect: 'It is more difficult to understand now my field of studies without having resort to jurisprudence.' And most of them acknowledge nowadays that, despite the existence of ambiguities and contradictions, the force of jurisprudence is more intense now than it used to be. A certain discrediting of the legislature (due, of course, to hastiness, carelessness and even frivolity in the making of new statutes, but also to the ever growing and demanding requests of the society undergoing change) has brought a new and more extended prestige to judges, as the main controllers of political powers, but giving rise at the same time and once again to the old and everlasting question, *quis qustodiet ipsos custodes?*

Bibliography

Diez Picazo y Ponce de León, L. (1983), 'La Jurisprudencia' in Instituto de Estudios Fiscales, *El Poder Judicial*.

García de Enterría, E. (1981), *La Constitución como Norma y el Tribunal Constitucional*, Madrid: Ed. Civitas.

Gascón Abellán, M. (1993), *La Técnica del Precedente y la Argumentación Racional*, Madrid: Tecnos.

Instituto de Estudios Fiscales (1979), *La Constitución Española y las Fuentes del Derecho*, 3 vols.

Instituto de Estudois Fiscales (1993), *El Poder Judicial*, 3 vols.

Lafuente Suárez, J.L. (1991), *La Vinculación al Precedente: inconvenientes para su aplicación en el ámbito del sistema jurídico español*, Madrid: Tapia.

López Guerra, L. (1981), 'El Tribunal Constitucional y el principio "stare decisis"', *El Tribunal Constitucional*, vol. II, Madrid: I.E.F.

Ministerio de Justicia (1991), *El Principio de Igualdad en la Constitución Española. XI Jornadas de Estudio de la Dirección General del Servicio Jurídico del Estado*, 2 vols, Madrid.

Nieto, A. (1990) 'El Precedente Judicial en la doctrina del Tribunal Constitucional', *Estudios Jurídicos en honor de José Gabaldón López*, Madrid: Trivium.

Ollero Tassara, A. (1989), *Igualdad en la Aplicación de la Ley y Precedente Judicial*, Madrid: C.E.C.

Otto, I. de (1987), *Derecho Constitucional. Sistema de Fuentes*. Madrid: Ed. Ariel.

Requejo Pajés, 'Juridicidad, Precedente y Jurisprudencia', *Revista Española de Derecho Constitucional*, X, no. 29 (1990).

Roca Trías, 'Jurisprudencia, Precedente y Principio de Igualdad', *Revista Jurídica de Cataluña*, 4 (1986).

Sala Sánchez, P. (1993), *La Unificación de Doctrina, Tarea Fundamental del Tribunal Supremo*, Madrid: Consejo General del Poder Judicial.

Xiol Rius, 'El Precedente judicial en nuestro Derecho: una creación del Tribunal Constitucional', *Poder Judicial*, 3 (1986).

9 Precedent in Sweden

GUNNAR BERGHOLTZ, *LUND* AND
ALEKSANDER PECZENIK, *LUND*

Introduction

It is possible that Scandinavian law, including Swedish law, constitutes a legal family of its own (cf. Bergholtz, 1993, pp.489–90). On the
other hand, most comparatists would place it in the Romano-Ger-
manic (continental) family. Nevertheless, Swedish law may be seen
as having a tradition of its own. It has many properties of a civil law
system with codifications, but it also includes less codified areas
where precedents are very important. Even if statutes exist in a certain area, precedents play an important role. Indeed, the influence of
precedent in Sweden is even greater than in England, where there
are rules that state when a court is not bound by precedents. In
Sweden, in the absence of such rules, precedents have a very strong
influence. Despite this, precedents are not binding de jure; but they
are regularly followed by the courts (binding de facto).

I Institutional and Systemic

1(a)   Court Hierarchy

Sweden has courts of first instance, six courts of appeal and the Supreme Court. Since Sweden is not a federal state, it has – apart from
administrative courts and the like – only one court organization.

1(b)   Structural and Procedural Aspects

The Supreme Court consists of 16 judges, each year producing about
130–160 precedents. The six courts of appeal decide a lot of cases, but

not more than 200 each year appear in the special law report from the appellate courts. Note that cases appealed from the appellate courts, given *certiorari* to the Supreme Court, do not appear in the special appellate law report. The cases reported from the appellate courts have, of course, much less persuasive effect than precedents from the Supreme Court. Both the Supreme Court and the appellate courts work in panels and the Supreme Court, when changing a legal principle, may have plenary sessions or a panel consisting of 12 judges. In the Supreme Court, a panel consists of at least five judges or, in some cases, for example when granting or denying *certiorari*, three or just one. The courts of appeal sit in panels of three or four judges and in more serious criminal cases with three judges and two lay assessors. The judge–rapporteur casts his vote first and then the youngest of the remaining judges and so on. The point is not to allow the younger judges to be influenced by the votes of the older ones. Last to vote is the chief justice or chairman of the court. If lay assessors are members of the court, as in some cases in the courts of appeal, they are the last to vote. The voting takes place in camera, but differences are made public through concurring and dissenting opinions.

1(c)   Power to Select Cases

The Supreme Court can grant *certiorari* much as it likes, but one must also take into account the 1971 amendments of the procedural law. According to Ch. 54, s.10 of the Code of Judicial Procedure, the Supreme Court is only to give *certiorari* in cases in which (a) it is important that a general ruling be given by way of precedent for judicial practice or (b) special reasons exist, such as a grave mistake made by the lower court. The preparatory materials to these provisions support the conclusion that the law givers intended to strengthen the role of the court in creating precedents (cf. Government Bill 1971, no. 45 for amendment of the Code of Judicial Procedure, especially p.88). It is not certain whether the amendments caused the increase in the role of precedents (as for example, Professor Stig Strömholm claimed) or vice versa. A reasonable hypothesis is that of feedback: the increased role of precedents caused the amendments, and then the latter amplified the former (cf. Bergholtz, 1987, p.429). Sometimes meetings of judges are held to discuss court-related problems. On such occasions, the chairman (the president) of the Supreme Court may ask the judges in which areas they want precedents. The main road to creating precedents is through reporting in the *Nytt Juridiskt Arkiv* (NJA – the 'Supreme Court Reporter'). The court itself chooses which cases to report with full opinion (including dissenting and concurring opinions). Those are the important precedents. The other cases decided by the Supreme Court are published with just a short *per curiam* opinion. The Supreme Court creates precedents in areas of law requiring elaboration or clarification. Most of the time, there is a consensus on the need for precedents. It may be needless to say that the parties themselves must take an appeal to the Supreme Court. No public authority can do so in their place. Thus the making of precedents depends on the parties going to the Supreme Court and on the court ruling that a precedent is necessary.

2 Structure, Content and Style of Judgments

The style of the opinions of Swedish higher courts has changed continually since the end of the nineteenth century. The following methods of justifying judicial decisions can be distinguished (cf. Peczenik *et al.*, 1990, pp.136 ff).

1   A pseudo-deductive, legalistic, brief and magisterial justification dominated in Sweden at the end of the nineteenth century. In many cases, the court forced the whole reasoning into one sentence with many subordinate clauses and the decision as a consequence ('since... and since... inasmuch as...', then' and so on). Stig Strömholm cites the following examples: NJA 1875, p.489; 1876, p.458; 1877, p.487; 1877, p.334. (Strömholm, 1988, p.336).

2   Later on, the pseudo-deductive style was abandoned, but the legalistic, brief and magisterial way of writing was preserved for a while. This kind of 'justification' dominated in Sweden in the first half of the twentieth century. As an example, one may cite NJA 1947, p.299. An association was held responsible for damage negligently caused by the supervisor of a shooting range owned by the association. The Supreme Court majority expressed itself so obscurely that it was not clear whether it considered the association liable because the supervisor's position was considered to be equivalent to one of management; or because his position was judged as connected with particular risk; or because a contract-like relation was considered to exist between the association and the injured person.

A decision might also be justified with the use of unclear expressions of the type, 'must be assumed' and so on. For example, in the case NJA 1954, p.268 a person having a significant connection with Bulgaria made an application to collect an amount which had been deposited in Sweden for his account. The Bulgarian state contested his right to collect the amount personally and stated that the payment should take place through a Swedish–Bulgarian clearing account and be made to him in Bulgaria. The Supreme Court majority recognized the Bulgarian state's right to plead in the case but without giving any reason other than that the members of the majority 'found no hindrance to exist to the consideration of the Bulgarian state's plea', after which the case was decided in a way favourable to that state.

3   Subsequently, the dominant method became discursive, elaborate and argumentative. The way of reasoning, however, was rather fact-stating than principled. In the decision there were statements concerning facts, but neither value judgments nor norms. The interpreter of such a decision must himself guess which statutory rules, norms for statutory construction, moral value judgments and other premises, together with the proffered facts, logically implied the conclusion. In Sweden this method is still used in lower courts today and even in the courts of appeal, albeit there to a decreasing extent. See also NJA 1952, p.184, the Supreme Court.

4   In other cases, the discursive, elaborate and argumentative method is used in a more coherent manner. The court proffers clearly both the reasons for and against the decision, including facts, norms and, often general, value judgments; then it concludes that the former weigh more in the case at bar; see NJA 1984, p.693, where the Supreme Court performed weighing and balancing of reasons for and against the principle that security transfer according to foreign law should have an effect against the transferor's creditors in Sweden.

This method was frequently used, for example, by the former Housing Court: compare case RB 1978 38:78, for example, where the court completed an extensive reasoning with the following statement: 'A reasonable weighing of the reasons proffered above leads, according to the Housing Court, to the result that the tenancy relation ought to expire, unless particular reasons tell against this conclusion.' The method, influenced by the Common Law jurisdiction, is frequently used also in Norway (cf., for example, the case RB 1978 38:78).

5   The deductive, substantive, elaborate and discursive method is also used. The court proffers clearly both the reasons for and against the decision, including facts, norms and value judgments; then it modifies these reasons in such a way that the decision becomes a logical conclusion of them. The proffered norms and value judgments are often general. *Inter alia*, one aims at formulating a clear precedent norm. The method, influenced by the German practice, also occurs in Sweden, especially in some courts of appeal; see also NJA 1983, p.487.

3   Publication of Judgments

Cases are reported in semi-official series published by a commercial publisher. Selection and editing are done by the judges themselves, so there are no law reporters in Sweden. The law reports are very easily accessible. You can find them in every major public library. All legal preparatory materials including case law can be found in either of two national databases: *Rättsbanken* or *RIKSLEX*. In the court hierarchy, cases are regularly reported from the Supreme Court and from

the courts of appeal. Important precedents are also regularly reported, discussed and criticized in academic journals.

4 Contents of Reports

The cases reported in NJA (*Nytt Juridiskt Arkiv*/the 'Supreme Court
Reporter') have a headnote, running from a few lines up to half a
page, stating in a nutshell the important issue(s) of the case. The case
itself then follows in full account (verbatim) as written and decided
by the district court, the Court of Appeal and the Supreme Court. As
said, the courts' judgments and opinions are published verbatim, so
all details are there. You find a full account of all the tricky questions
in line with the style of opinions as they are written in Sweden.
Concurring and dissenting opinions are published from all the courts,
along with the opinion of the secretary of the Supreme Court. A
summary of arguments by counsel may be published as a part of the
judgment or opinion if of importance, which is not always the case,
since you can infer the arguments by counsel from reading the opinion. Juristic comments on cases can be found in scholarly journals,
but not in the law reports.

5 Meaning of 'Precedent'

In Sweden a 'precedent' is a case reported in NJA. The main rationale
behind this publishing is to guide future decision making by the
courts in three ways: according to justice, utility and as a contribution to a coherent and well-designed body of law, utility probably
being the strongest drive behind the rationale.

6 Mode of Citation and Discussion

Precedents are, as a rule, just cited in the court's opinion as follows:
'(See NJA 19…p..) or (Cf. NJA 19…p..)'. Sometimes such a reference
is preceded or followed by some explanatory sentences stating the
ruling. But from time to time, if the court finds it important, the
opinion can include a more discursive discussion of previous precedents. In juristic legal writing, detailed discussion of precedents is
very common. Precedents are often criticized in detail. Explaining,
synthesizing and criticizing precedents is an important part of legal
science. Lawyers who argue cases often invoke precedents in both
written and oral argument, but they do it as the courts do, in short
and condensed fashion.

7   Overall Role of Precedent

The most important source of law is, of course, the statute or code itself. Second to that comes legislative preparatory materials, and thirdly we have the precedents. So in Sweden, compared to most countries, *travaux préparatoires* are a more important source of law than precedents and second only to the law text itself. Things are changing, however. It has been predicted that, in the future, legislative preparatory materials will fall back as a source of law and precedents will take their place. This prediction of a change is due to Sweden joining the European Union.

8   Role of Precedent in Different Branches of Law

The most important single factors to take into account are the following: is there legislation and, if so, how old is this legislation? This is the leading perspective. Generally speaking, precedents are seen as a complement to legislation and also as giving it full force. When it comes to constitutional law, precedents are rare. In commercial law, this is also the case due to most commercial cases being solved through arbitration (see Bergholtz, 1993, p.486). Criminal law statutes do not have such a wide range of possibilities of interpretation, so here the statutes are of overriding importance, even so, precedents are important.

9   Precedent and 'Gaps in the Law'

If there is no precedent, the Supreme Court will create one, because the court only decides cases after leave of appeal/*certiorari* and precisely for the purpose of creating a precedent. Thus a 'yes' to *certiorari* usually means creating a precedent. If the Supreme Court gives *certiorari* and then, during proceedings, finds the case not to be suitable as a precedent, the case is not reported as a precedent but merely as a *'notisfall'* with only a notice and a short *per curiam* opinion.

Whether the opinion of the court is explicit or not depends on the circumstances. The court is not afraid of writing an explicit opinion, if it finds it necessary to help clarify the issue(s) (Cf. NJA 1984, s.693).

II   The Bindingness of Precedent

1   Kinds and Degrees of Normative Force

We may usefully differentiate bindingness, force, further support and illustrativeness or other value of a precedent as follows.

(1) *Formal bindingness*: a judgment not respecting a precedent's bindingness is not lawful and so is subject to reversal on appeal. Distinguish (a) formal bindingness not subject to overruling: (i) 'strictly binding' – must be applied in every case, (ii) defeasibly binding – must be applied in every case unless exceptions apply (exceptions may be well defined or not); (b) formal bindingness (with or without exceptions) that is subject to overruling or modification.

(2) *Not formally binding but having force*: a judgment not respecting a precedent's force, though lawful, is subject to criticism on this ground, and may be subject to reversal on this ground. Distinguish (a) defeasible force – should be applied unless exceptions come into play (exceptions may or may not be well defined) and (b) outweighable force – should be applied unless countervailing reasons apply.

(3) *Not formally binding and not having force (as defined in (2) above) but providing further support*: a judgment lacking this is still lawful and may still be justified, but not as well justified as it would be if the precedent were invoked, for example, to show that the decision being reached harmonizes with the precedent.

(4) *Mere illustrativeness or other value*. Although not strictly binding in the sense indicated in (1), precedents are regularly followed by Swedish courts, perhaps increasingly. The actual role of precedents in the Swedish law is significant. The decisions that have been rendered *in pleno* have an exceptionally large influence. The actual practice fits the concept used in the present work of 'not formally binding but having force'. This is clearly more than merely providing further support or having illustrative value. This is best seen in the Supreme Court's own use of its earlier precedents. The court refers explicitly to the precedents, using, for example, the phrase, 'see the earlier case such and such' or 'cf. this case'.

An interesting problem is whether we have to do with (a) defeasible (though not outweighable) force or (b) outweighable and defeasible force. The prevailing way to interpret precedents in Sweden is to regard them as outweighable. Although the Supreme Court avoids explicit statements declaring a precedent as outweighed in the considered case, it will tacitly depart from the precedent if the circumstances require it. The precedent thus weakened may still retain some force. A precedent may thus be outweighed in a single case only. Yet it also may happen – and indeed often does happen – that this new case originates a new precedent-based rule, defeating the old one. A clear-cut exception from the earlier established precedent can thus evolve, but this seldom happens in a dramatic manner, openly and in a single case. Rather, it requires a series of cases, each contributing to the change. Swedish case law is permeated with understatements and shadowy areas, tacitly but consciously preserved in order to facilitate reasonableness of future decision making.

Moreover, the ruling legal ideology evolves. In the periods of transition, the tendency to understatements may make it incoherent. In spite of the fact that the factual practice already at that time could have been characterized according to the idea of 'defeasible bindingness', the view that precedents are 'not binding' has been officially expressed in Sweden. The Parliamentary Commissioner for the Judiciary *(Justitieombudsman)*, in his annual report (1947), criticized a lower-court judge who had dealt with a legal question in conflict with a decision by the Supreme Court *in pleno*. In consequence of this, the parliament's First Standing Committee on Legislation declared that the lower instance is not bound by precedents and that 'only the weight of the reasons referred to by the Supreme Court in justification of its judgments should be determinative for the influence of the Supreme Court on the application of law in the lower instances'. This pronouncement provoked a lively discussion, in which Folke Schmidt (1955, p.109) expressed the following opinion: 'The Swedish judge follows precedents precisely because they derive from the Supreme Court. He does this even where he believes that a different decision would in itself have been more suitable. Only if there are strong reasons indicating that he ought to adjudicate... in a way different from that indicated by the precedent does the question arise of examining the *weight* of the reasons invoked by the Supreme Court.'

Today, the tendency to follow precedents, as pointed out by Schmidt, is even stronger. In the end, there is not a big difference between this practice and a system of formally binding precedents, even if precedents are not considered binding de jure. It has been argued (Strömholm, 1988, p.935) that the lower courts have a duty to follow precedents except when a precedent is created *per incuriam*. This would be a kind of a defeasible but not outweighable bindingness – precedents should be followed regardless of the weight of the counter-arguments, except when created per incuriam – but this is stretching it too far.

The degrees of bindingness are discussed in scholarly works, but not explicitly in judicial opinions. Not even the scholars use language as sophisticated as the analysis here suggests.

2   Law Concerning Precedent

In connection with the importance of precedents in Swedish legal practice, it is necessary to take into account the amendments of 1971 to the procedural law; see Section I.1, above. As stated earlier, Swedish precedents are not strictly binding and yet they are recognized as a source of the law which *should* be used in legal argumentation (cf. Peczenik, 1974, pp.48 ff and 121 ff). The difference between precedents interpreting and not interpreting statutes and so on is not recognized as relevant. Neither is the role of precedent as a pattern guiding future decisions restricted only to filling gaps in constitutions, codes or statutes. To be sure, Ch. 1, sec. 1, part 3 of the constitution (*Regeringsformen*) requires that 'the public power is to be executed under the laws'. This provision, however, is not regarded as implying an absolute demand for support in written statutes. Established custom may be sufficient (cf. Petrén and Ragnemalm, 1980, p.18). Moreover, the question whether a custom is established is most often answered on the basis of precedents.

The term 'source of law' is used very extensively in Sweden, not only in reference to the binding 'must' sources. Nothing prevents calling precedent such a 'source'.

There are areas within significant branches of law, for example the law of torts, which depend substantially on precedent and would be unintelligible, or ignored, if we failed to consider precedent.

The so-called 'legality principle' in penal law implies that no act may be regarded as a crime and no punishment may be imposed without statutory authorization (*nullum crimen sine lege, nulla poena sine lege*). Ch. 2 sec. 10 of the *Regeringsformen* requires that, for punishment to apply, the act in question must have been '*belagd med påföljd*' at the time of its commission. The Swedish expression cannot be translated properly; it can perhaps be read as implying that a statutory norm criminalizing the act must have been in force at this time. Before 1994, this constitutional provision had usually been interpreted as a prohibition of retroactive punishment, *not* as a prohibition of statutory analogy. In some (rare!) cases, the Supreme Court thus employed analogy to the disadvantage of the defendant. The new locution of Ch.1 Sec. 1 Penal Code (cf. law 1994:458) implies a prohibition of statutory analogy. Yet precedents still play a significant role in interpretation of criminal statutes. In NJA 1994, p.480, the Supreme Court thus interpreted a criminal provision rather extensively and stated that the principle of legality implies that a criminal provision may not be applied by analogy, but it does not prevent interpretation of a criminal provision according to established method. The court has also stated that no clear-cut borderline exists between analogy and interpretation.

3 Factors Determining Degrees of Normative Force

The factors in question II.3 of the Appendix which bear on the degree of bindingness of precedent will now be considered.

(a) Only precedents from the Supreme Court are 'defeasibly binding' in the indicated sense. Cases from the courts of appeal are only persuasive. They constitute arguments for a certain solution, unless weightier counter-arguments apply.

(b)   Among the Supreme Court's decisions the most important are those reached in *plenum*.

(c)   The reputation of the court or of the judge writing the opinion is not publicly considered as a factor affecting the authority of the precedent. Obviously, it may affect a 'private' motivational process of the future deciders, but it matters only in the 'context of discovery', not in the context of justification.

(d)   Changes in the political, economic or social background since the prior decision may decrease the degree of bindingness of a precedent. It may also encourage the Supreme Court to find new solutions. Justice Conradi (Conradi, 1993, pp.85 ff) has given some examples, such as new types of contracts (cf. NJA 1978, s. 147) or so-called 'factoring' (cf. NJA 1986, s. 217).

(e)   According to the dominating view, soundness of the supporting arguments in the opinion certainly affects the degree of bindingness of the precedent in question. If deemed unsound, the decision will be criticized. However, Heuman (1992, pp.226 ff) claims that the lower courts should 'follow both bad and good precedents provided that the legal opinion were expressed clearly... Rationality reasons have certainly obtained increased importance for the Supreme Court's manner of solving questions of principle, but they became less and less important for the interpretation and criticism of judicial decisions... This evolution has its ground in importance of a uniform and simple implementation of the law, the need of predictability and the increased importance of the efficiency argument.'

(f)   Old precedents, not confirmed by new ones, have as a rule less authority than do new precedents.

(g)   According to the common opinion, the value of a precedent is diminished if the bench was divided. However, some scholars disagree with this view (cf. Heuman, 1992, p.208). Heuman has also quoted cases (NJA 1987, s. 992 and NJA 1988, s. 521) that 'show that the Justices, for the cases of consequence, were not inclined to deviate from an established legal principle when the contrary opinion was to be preferred according to their personal views' (ibid., p.212).

(h)   The authority of a precedent is increased if a strong need exists for a legal regulation in an area, which, for example is not covered by sufficiently clear legislation.

(i)   An established practice, based on several decisions, has greater importance than a single precedent. The following of a precedent will thus be stronger if the precedent represents a trend. However, the importance of a precedent may also depend on the situation as a whole in the area in question. The following of a precedent will be less strong if the precedent has been severely criticized in a later precedent.

(j) The following of a precedent will also be less strong if the precedent has been severely criticized in the mainstream of academic writings.

(k) The following of a precedent will be less strong if a new statute is created dealing with the same question as the previous precedent.

(l) Cases fully reported in the NJA have more authority than cases summarily reported. No distinction is drawn between precedents dealing with statute law and precedents of other kinds.

4 Factors that Weaken Precedent

All the factors mentioned above in II.3, items (d), (e), (f), (g), (i), (j) and (k) may affect the weight of a previous decision in such an extremely negative way that it will no longer be considered a precedent. However, this is a borderline case, not a qualitatively distinct situation. (We do not mention here the easier case where a decision is defective in such a way that it may be nullified by extraordinary procedural means, for instance on the basis of a crime involved in decision making. Such a decision will be deemed invalid in general, and obviously it cannot be considered a precedent).

5 Vertical and Horizontal Bindingness

A lower court decides contrary to a precedent, established by a higher one, in principle only when wishing to give the latter a possibility to reconsider its practice, for example because the contested precedent conflicts with a statute, legislative preparatory materials or another precedent. (It is also possible that a lower court does not follow a precedent which depends on a mistake by the judge or a judgment given *per incuriam*).

If a lower court refuses to follow a precedent, its judgment will be reversed on appeal, but the judge refusing to follow a precedent cannot be sanctioned to do so in any other way than through reversing judgment on appeal.

The Supreme Court almost never states explicitly that a precedent-based rule it previously followed should no longer be applied. If it intends to change its practice, it usually restricts itself to pointing to some special circumstances of the new case, or simply pursues another line of reasoning than before. This makes it difficult to judge whether a total change of the precedent-based rule or a mere establishment of an exception from it has been intended (cf. Hellner, 1988, p.76).

Lower courts are rather reluctant to change their own practice, but they are not legally prevented from doing so.

6   *Analysis of Force, Support and Illustrative Role*

No legislation exists concerning the force of precedents in Sweden, except for the possibility of working in and deciding cases in the Supreme Court *in pleno.* Concerning the role of scholarly works and so on, see Section II.1 above.

III   The Rationale of Precedent

1   *General Rationales for Formal Bindingness*

Sweden does not recognize formal bindingness. (But see Sections II.1 and II.4.)

2   *Rationales for Force, Further Support and so on*

The main rationale for the existence of precedents with justifying force or the like is the uniformity of the legal order and legal decision making. The rule of law is promoted by precedents; that is, the parties can make predictions of how the courts will act in the future. Also pragmatic reasons are important, such as that the Supreme Court 'once and for all' decides a question after a painstaking and thorough deliberation process. After that, the lower courts have no need to reconsider the same question. This also saves time and money for the parties and their counsel.

The rationales of following precedents are taken for granted as tacit conditions and are not elaborated in the opinions when scope and weight may be discussed.

IV   Precedents: What They Stand for and How They Apply

1   *What Counts as Binding or Having Force?*

A precedent should be followed only in cases that *essentially* resemble the precedent case. However, to explain the judicial practice of deciding whether a certain similarity is or is not essential, Swedish literature in law often refers to the common law doctrine of *ratio decidendi.* The courts themselves seldom use this term, but their actual decisions seem roughly to follow this doctrine. The courts thus clearly distinguish essential and non-essential circumstances of the precedent. Another thing is that they quite freely judge which are which. No clear rules for establishing the *ratio* exist. This fact may explain why the practical role of the doctrine of *ratio decidendi* has been doubted by some legal scholars (Lars Heuman; cf. Bernitz *et al.*, 1985, p.137). The term *'obiter dictum'* (as opposed to *ratio decidendi*) is used frequently (cf., for example, NJA 1975, p.545; Hellner, 1988, p.84).

The *ratio* is a necessary condition of the decision which thus would have been different if the *ratio* had been different. In the theoretical literature (for example, Åke Frändberg), it is sometimes held that every use of a precedent as a pattern for future decisions is actually a generalization of the precedent into a precedent rule, stating that one must decide all cases with the same *ratio* in the same way. This is more a theoretical postulate than a statement of method actually applied by the courts. The court practice seems rather to be based on the model of particular analogy, where each case is treated as an illuminating example of a reasonable decision, given all its own facts, and hence a useful guide for decision in similar cases. Clear-cut statements of precedent rules exist, but only in exceptional cases. There is no significant discussion on whether the binding element of a precedent could be better characterized as a principle or a maxim.

What elements should one regard as essential, that is, as the *ratio decidendi*? This depends on a complex reasoning in the concrete case, involving weighing and balancing of two kinds of reasons. First, one may consider reasons set forth by the court in the precedent decision with the aim of justifying the decision and with the belief that they were necessary to justify it. Second, one may consider the reasons estimated as necessary to justify the decision, even though not set forth in the decision (constructed *ratio decidendi*; cf. Eckhoff, 1987, p.143). A good method of establishing the constructed *ratio decidendi* is to consider a set of precedents, at best extended in time.

In interpreting precedents, use is made of a number of reasons which in part resemble argument by analogy in statutory interpretation. Practice as a source of the law resembles a markedly casuistic statute, the application of which calls for conclusion by analogy on a large scale. The accepted technique in Sweden is to re-explain and rejustify the *ratio*. No simple criteria of *ratio* have been established. Though the courts realize that the use of precedent may require derivation from a precedent-based rule, they often fail to spell out the rule explicitly. This is the case for the following reasons. First, the judges may intuitively 'feel' what the right decision is and yet be unable to make clear which general value judgments and norms would, in combination with the statutory provision and the facts of the case, logically imply the decision. Second, a judge deciding the precedent case may be unable to predict all the cases the precedent will cover. Not even the best justification entirely prevents subsequent application of the precedent to cases that, for various reasons, ought to be decided differently. Third, the courts may consider their primary task to be deciding *individual* cases, and consider that only the legislator is empowered to enact general norms. Fourth, when a number of judges jointly decide the case, they often must find an acceptable compromise. In some cases, only a less extensive and less general justification can satisfy this demand. When unanimously accepted, a precedent may be stronger than an extensive and general majority opinion, accompanied by a dissenting opinion. A less coherent justification accompanied by consensus may be superior to a more coherent one without consensus. Fifth, in many cases, the judge has no *time* to prepare a general and extensive justification.

In a small number of cases, however, the Supreme Court has not hesitated to state explicitly a general principle. The majority of the Supreme Court in the case NJA 1977, p.176 thus expressed the following both important and highly controversial general principle of evidence.

> In torts, there is often a controversy about what caused the actual damage or injury... Many courses of events..., independently of one another, can constitute a possible cause... In such cases, full evidence ... can scarcely be given... If thus, in the light of all the circumstances of the case, it is clearly more probable that the actual course of events was that which the plaintiff has pointed out than that ... pointed out by the defendant, the statement of the plaintiff should form the basis for the decision.

In the case NJA 1976, p.458, a bicycle pump was changed so that it could be used for shooting a cork. The owner of the pump, A, a nine-year-old, permitted B, a six-year-old, to play with it. The cork got stuck. B asked D, a nine-year-old, to withdraw the cork. D tried to do it, accidentally 'shot' with the pump, and the cork hit B's eye. All instances ruled against B's claim for compensation from A. The majority of the Supreme Court did not consider A to be negligent, since the risk of injury had been minimal. Justice Nordenson dissented and made several subtle conceptual distinctions, *inter alia*, between the problems of negligence, remoteness of damage and the protection given by the law of torts. He also expressed a series of general principles.

But not even in the comparatively rare cases in which the decision explicitly formulates a general principle, is the degree of generality as great as it would be in the legal scholarship ('legal dogmatics'). More often, the Supreme Court argues in a very cautious manner. General arguments, which could support a wide rule, are often applied narrowly. For example, in the case of NJA 1993, p.41 I and II, the Supreme Court decided in *plenum* two cases concerning compensation for relatives of a murdered person. The compensation was granted unanimously, with a change of the earlier practice (cf. NJA

1979, p.620). Though a third party in principle does not receive damages according to the Swedish law, the court stated that this principle is no rule which 'in itself' would prevent compensation. Furthermore, mental problems of persons close (*närstående*) to the murdered one are 'typical and proximate' consequences of murder. The justification is, however, cautious (cf. Hellner, 1994, pp.96 and 119) since the duty to compensate has only been established as regards intentional murder: not, for example, rape; moreover, only the *närstående* can claim compensation. The court has stated that 'a radical extension of the discussed possibilities of compensation for a third party presupposes so profound a consideration of principled and practical character that it must be made by the legislator'. In NJA 1991, p.720, the Supreme Court developed policy reasoning to support strict liability of those who operate warm-water pipelines, 'The justification contains... a mixture of casuistic arguments, which apply only to warm-water pipelines, and general arguments, applicable to many others kinds of damage' (Hellner, 1992, p.101).

2 Reasoning about Applicability

The pragmatic and cautious way of justifying decisions makes the scope of a precedent a very difficult question. Judges tend to compare in detail the facts of the precedent and the facts of the case under consideration. This is sometimes seen in the opinions, but there is no accepted method for deciding scope and weight, or for the general use of precedents.

3 Juristic Discussion

Principled discussion is to be found in scholarly works, mostly textbooks and scholarly papers. No modern and profound treatise on this subject exists.

4 Illustrative or Analogical Precedent

The courts do not use precedents when not strictly in point. On the other hand, Swedish juristic literature is heavily precedent-oriented: cases are used to clarify, to harmonize and to demonstrate relevance often instead of more abstract reasoning.

5 Single Precedents or Lines of Decision?

If a number of precedents are relevant for the case, one of them is often discussed more extensively, others merely quoted. Sweden is a small country, and the number of precedents is restricted. The courts are seldom compelled to use precedents in a selective manner. When precedents are cited, they can be cited alone or with a number of other precedents, depending on the situation at hand. It is not uncommon for the Supreme Court to establish a new rule gradually through a series of precedents. The judges, now and then, discuss precedents openly in their opinions, but such 'discussions' tend to be dense and short. Conflicting lines of precedents do not occur. Another kind of a zigzag is, however, well known: a single line in which a new rule is slowly evolving by trial and error. Both the scope and the clarity of the rule evolve in subsequent cases according to the pattern 'two steps forward, one step back' and so on.

6   The Concept of a 'Leading Case'

Though there is no elaborate doctrine of leading cases, some cases have an exceptional influence and are quoted again and again. In NJA 1948, p.584, a general principle for criminal cases was established stating that only the facts explicitly proffered by prosecuting counsel could be used as material for the case and the conviction. This principle was then reasserted in NJA 1976, p.368. In NJA 1987, p.194, the same principle was stated and supported with a coherent set of explicit reasons. In NJA 1988, p.665, the reasons from NJA 1987, p.194 were stated again verbatim with reference to that case. The same happened once more in NJA 1990, p.361. (Cf. Bergholtz, 1992, pp.1 ff). No doubt, such cases may start a new line of precedents, but it is difficult to tell precisely when this is the case.

V   Distinguishing, Explaining, Modifying, Overruling

1   Distinguishing

As already mentioned, the Swedish courts do not feel a strong need to distinguish, but rather regard themselves as authorized to decide the new case on its merits. To be sure, such a decision implies either that the case under adjudication essentially differs from the precedent case, or that the latter had been decided incorrectly. The court may, however, prefer not to make such points explicit. The precedent case may be quoted in such a way that it is not clear to what extent the rule it expressed remains in force. For example, in the case NJA 1951, p.1, a customer claimed that a contractor had promised to perform the work in question at a lower price than later demanded. The contractor denied this. The Supreme Court (in *plenum*) decided that the contractor had the burden of proof. Then, in NJA 1975, p.280, the court confirmed this rule in a case in which a consumer contracted with a business establishment. The court emphasized the consumer relationship. The case from 1951 was quoted with the comment that there is no need to discuss the burden of proof in general. Finally, in NJA 1989, p.215, the burden of proof was reversed as regards a bookkeeping contract. The court mentioned the fact that an established practice was thus changed but the scope of the change remained unclear (cf. Heuman, 1992, pp.213 ff). See also the remarks concerning cautious justification of the Swedish decisions in general, in Section IV.1.

2 Juristic Commentary

The discussion of points of difference (distinguishing), both between reported precedents and in relation to hypothetical cases, plays a great role in the Swedish juristic literature. The courts certainly make use of such discussion, though in most cases implicitly. For example, the cautious use in the later cases of the rule established in NJA 1951, p.1 (see Section VI.1 above) is explainable by reference to such scholarly criticism (cf. Heuman, 1992, pp.213 ff).

3 Excessive Distinguishing?

Fine or unrealistic distinctions between cases do occur in the Swedish judicial practice but only in a very special manner. That is, if a later case is decided contrary to the precedent, it is often justified by a very detailed description of the case under adjudication; at the same time, the court leaves it unsaid whether it intends to establish a new rule for a thus restricted area only, or rather to make a more radical change of practice. This kind of cautiousness is often criticized in the scholarly literature (cf. Section IV.1 above). The literature itself explains change without fine distinctions. It is rather assumed that the change occurs because the later precedents simply take over the earlier ones. One might say jokingly: *praejudicatum posterior derogat priori*. Such is the case, except when very strong reasons justify criticizing (or sometimes ignoring) a later precedent.

4 Types of Overruling

Summarizing, one can say that the Swedish system has three types of overruling. The first is an explicit judicial act, with the Supreme Court deciding *in pleno*. This is used very seldom and the judges do not like it (*'horror pleni'*). Between 1983 and 1993, this procedure was used three times only (NJA 1985, p.802, NJA 1988, p.329; 1993, p.41). Silent overruling of a precedent is frequent and so is the explicit or implicit cutting down of scope. Whatever the type of overruling, the same types of arguments are used. Every court can be said to have the power to overrule a precedent, but this is seldom done except by the Supreme Court. The 'civil service' character of the Swedish judiciary may play a part here. The judge of the lower court may think that he should 'keep in line'.

5   Prospective Overruling

Swedish courts have no formal power to overrule precedents prospectively. The primary function of a court is always to decide the particular case, and the practice of precedents is merely a consequence of such decisions. Yet the Supreme Court may write its decision in a manner indicating that it is inclined to perform a more radical change of practice than it does in the case under adjudication. (See again Section IV.1 above on the cases NJA 1993, p.41 I and II and NJA 1991, p.720.) This is *not* a prospective overruling but it may be construed as an indication that overruling may happen in a future case.)

6   Anticipatory Overruling by Lower Courts

When a lower court (in rare cases) decides contrary to a precedent, it is mostly when wishing to give the upper court a possibility to reconsider its practice. This may be regarded as a case of anticipatory overruling.

7   Precedent and Legislative Practice

Changed judicial practice may be a reason for legislative change. As an example, one may quote the case of NJA 1956 C 187. A person who used a toy pistol to take money from a bank was sentenced for robbery. At this time, Ch. 8 Sec. 5 of the Criminal Code required for robbery that it 'involve acute danger'. The decision of the case was thus one of the (very rare) examples of statutory analogy disadvantaging the defendant. Subsequently, the statute was modified by addition of the locution 'or is regarded by the threatened as acute danger'. The legislator may modify a statute in order to reverse an interpretation of a statutory rule made by a precedent. The legislator may also use a precedent as a starting point for enacting a new rule, either to modify the precedent or in order to develop the law on the basis of the reasons given in the precedent. Mostly, such legislative practice deals with minor modifications of a technical nature. One may perhaps mention here a special situation, as well: in most cases when the European Court of Justice in Strasbourg condemns Sweden for abuse of human rights, a legislative change follows.

8   Conflicts of Precedents

A conflict between precedents arises when one precedent (or a series of precedents) supports a certain rule, whereas another supports another rule, logically, empirically or evaluatively incompatible with the first one. Two rules are *evaluatively* incompatible even if a person can, logically and empirically, observe (or apply) them simultaneously, when their simultaneous observance (or application) would lead to legally or morally objectionable effects, whereas each norm separately does not lead to such negative consequences. It is a common saying among lawyers that the unity of the legal order demands the following of precedents.

If conflicting precedents are at hand, there is no strong need to distinguish, but rather a choice for the judge. He has to choose the one or the other and in doing so declare the reasons for his choice. The usual practice is to follow the chosen precedent (or a line of precedents), to quote it and/or to repeat the reasons expressed in it. The precedents conflicting with this line are often not mentioned at all. A conflict of precedents may thus be resolved either by reinterpreting (and thus reconciling, harmonizing) the rules derived from them, or by arranging a priority order between these rules. If the judge finds that it is not reasonable to reconcile different precedents, he assumes that he should determine which are the most important. In so determining, all the factors named in question II.3 (Appendix) may be found relevant. However, no precise priority rules may be formulated. This may be a reflexion of the pragmatic Swedish attitude.

9   Hypothetical Cases

Hypothetical cases are used in scholarly works in a wide variety of ways, but they are unusual in judicial opinions. The opinions adhere closely to the real facts, without much abstract reasoning.

VI   Matters of General Perspective, Evaluation and Other

1   'Saying and Doing'

There is no real gap between saying and doing. Swedish courts are not bound by precedents, but they follow them regularly, and acknowledge this fact openly. Silent overruling is a well-known feature of the Swedish system. Since it is quite openly acknowledged by everybody concerned, you cannot say that it signifies a gap between saying and doing.

2   Recent Change or Evolution

The use of precedent is today more important than earlier. The precedents themselves have changed in style. The opinions are more discursive and open, like English or American precedents. Earlier, Swedish precedents were written more in the French style. This change has also indirectly brought about an increased use of them. In earlier times a type of older legal positivism (lagpositivism) was dominant (Bergholtz, 1987, pp.84–92). The courts were afraid to trespass on the territory of the legislator (the king and, later on, the parliament) and considered it outside their legitimate power to create general rules. This led to a gap between saying and doing. In saying only that the solution followed from this or that section of a statute, the courts created rules of a more or less general nature. This way of writing opinions was very long-lived because judges copied old opinions in style and form. Today this has changed, with the change starting 20–25 years ago. The younger generation of Supreme Court justices do not feel bound any more by the old ways (Bergholtz, 1987, pp.429–30 and Lind, himself a justice of the Supreme Court, 1994, p.594). Today there is not really a gap between saying and doing. The written opinions explain and justify the doing.

3   Changes in International Environment

The developments of transnational institutions have not yet changed the theory or practice of precedent. Another change is, however, coming gradually. The access of Sweden to the European Union may lead to a much weaker standing of legislative preparatory materials as an important source of law. Sweden will incorporate a lot of EU legislation and also in some ways change the legislative process and consequently legislative preparatory materials will lose their unique standing as a source of law (see, for example, Bratt and Tiberg, 1989, p.425). Instead, precedents will take that place. On the other hand, *travaux préparatoires* can retain a great role in those parts of the Swedish legal order which are not affected by the EU law (cf. Hellner, 1994, p.85). Moreover, nothing prevents the inclusion of *travaux préparatoires* in coherent legal argumentation which also pays increased attention to the EU legislation and so on. The only limit is that the *travaux préparatoires* will not any longer be recognized as a good legal reason, if they happen to collide with the practice of the European Court (cf. Abrahamsson, 1993, p.808).

4 *Juristic or Other Criticism*

The pragmatic Swedish attitude and some features of a civil law system may have impeded the systematic development of a precedent methodology in Sweden. The most important thing is to try to establish such a methodology. The uses of precedent in Sweden are certainly advancing the development of the law, but not without problems. Some critics, among them Heuman (1992, pp.232 ff), have pointed out that the scope and weight of older precedents is hard to judge in relation to new ones. The Supreme Court ought not to criticize an old precedent without making the relation between the old one and the new one clear. This could lead to 'a breaking down of precedents' and create confusion. Cf. Sections IV.1 and V.1 above. Heuman wants the Supreme Court to make clean breaks with past precedents when no longer following them, and wants the Supreme Court to adopt new principles in such cases *in pleno*.

5 *Similarities and Differences Compared to Other Systems*

In Sweden, precedents are not binding but are regularly followed. The striking difference between Sweden and, for example, common law countries is that Sweden does not have rules for bindingness (*stare decisis*) or distinguishing. This can mean that in Sweden precedents are followed more rigorously than in countries with rules of bindingness and distinguishing. In several respects Sweden is a civil law country, so legislation is the supreme source of law, and precedent can never be more than an important complement to legislation.

6 *General Explanatory or Critical Comment*

In Sweden, precedents support, clarify and supplement the legislation. Statutes with more or less general rules need precedents in order to work rationally. Precedents are used with caution, demanding close similarity between the precedent and the case at hand. This in turn may reflect the absence of a sophisticated method for the use of precedent and is rooted in Sweden's family resemblance with civil law countries. As far as we can judge, Sweden has a rational method of amending and changing the law. Speedy action is taken by the government and the parliament when a need is felt to amend or change the law. Therefore precedents are not always so badly needed as in countries with a less swift and orderly procedure for altering the law.

A critical remark may also be justified. As stated above, the Supreme Court argues in a very cautious manner. General arguments, which could support a wide rule, are often explicitly applied much more narrowly. Moreover, the precedent case may be quoted in such a way that it is not clear to what extent the rule it expresses remains valid. Obvious disadvantages of this judicial cautiousness are, however, counterbalanced by efficient legislative action continually modifying the law. An overall evaluation of this manner of changing the law must be based on a rather profound political theory, concerning legal certainty, justice, democracy, division of powers and so on.

References

Abrahamsson, A. 'Domstolsväsendets anpassning till EES och EG', *Svensk Juristtidning*, pp.805–11 (1993).

Bergholtz, G. (1987), *Ratio et Auctoritas*, Lund: Juridiska föreningen.

Bergholtz, G. (1992), 'Åtal och kontradiktion. Marginalanteckningar till några yngre rättsfall', in *Festskrift till Per Olof Bolding*, Stockholm: Juristförlaget.

Bergholtz, G. (1993), 'Alternative Dispute Resolution in Sweden', in *The International Symposium On Civil Justice In The Era of Globalization, Tokyo, August 1992*, Tokyo: Shinan Publishing Company.

Bernitz *et al.* (1985), *Finna rätt*, Stockholm: Juristförlaget.

Bratt, P. and Tiberg, H. (1989), 'Domare och lagmotiv', *Svensk Juristtidning*, pp. 707–16.

Conradi, E. (1993), 'Skapande dömande', in *Festskrift till Bertil Bengtsson*, Stockholm: Nerenius & Santérus förlag.

Eckhoff, T. (1987), *Rettskildelaere*, 2nd edn, Oslo: Tano.

Hellner, J. (1988), *Rättsteori*, Stockholm: Juristförlaget.

Hellner, J. 'Strikt ansvar för skada från fjärvärmeanläggning', *Juridisk Tidsskrift* 1991/92, 3, (1992).

Hellner, J. (1994), *Rättsteori*, 2nd edn, Stockholm: Juristförlaget.

Heuman, L. (1992), 'Högsta domstolens prejudikatnedbrytande verksamhet', in *Festskrift till Per Olof Bolding*, Stockholm: Juristförlaget.

Lind, T. in *Juridisk Tidskrift*, pp. 301–18, (1994).

Peczenik, A. (1974), *Juridikens metodproblem*, Stockholm: Almqvist & Wiksell.

Peczenik, A. *et al.* (1990), *Juridisk argumentation*, Stockholm: Norstedts.

Petrén, G. and Ragnemalm, H. (1980), *Sveriges grundlagar*, Stockholm: Liber Förlag.

Schmidt, F. (1955), 'Domaren som lagtolkare', in *Festskrift till Herlitz*, quoted from reprint in *Studiematerial i allmän rättslära*, 1971, Stockholm: Juridiska föreningen.

Strömholm, S. (1988), *Rätt, rättskällor och rättstillämpning*, 3rd edn, Stockholm: Norstedts.

10 Precedent in the United Kingdom

ZENON BANKOWSKI, *EDINBURGH,*
D. NEIL MacCORMICK, *EDINBURGH*
AND GEOFFREY MARSHALL, *OXFORD*

I Institutional and Systemic

1(a) Court Hierarchy

In the United Kingdom there are three jurisdictions: England and Wales, Northern Ireland and Scotland. The former two share what is substantially the same English common law, with a modern overlay of statute law. Despite a common substratum, there has been considerable divergence in statute law in modern times. Scots law is a 'mixed' system between civil and common law, owing much to the civilian traditions of Renaissance France and the post-reformation Netherlands, but subject to a considerable degree of convergence between Scottish and English substantive law in modern times through shared elements of statute law applicable throughout the UK and through the precedents of the highest court.

The House of Lords, technically the Upper Chamber of the UK parliament, is nowadays in its judicial function effectively a Supreme Court set apart from the legislature and staffed by the most senior judges ('Lords of Appeal in Ordinary'). It hears appeals from the lower courts of Northern Ireland and England and Wales on all matters, civil, public law and criminal; from Scotland, it has appellate jurisdiction only in civil matters (including public law). Technically, the three legal systems being distinct albeit sharing a single supreme legislature, precedents of the House of Lords from one jurisdiction are never strictly binding in relation to either of the others, and where specialized and distinctive subjects (such as land law) are in issue, the effect of this is clear. On many points, however, the convergence of the systems leads to a precedent from one jurisdiction being effectively decisive for the other two.

315

The level below the House of Lords is that of the Court of Appeal (England and Wales) and the Court of Appeal for Northern Ireland, each of which respectively has both a civil and a criminal division, normally sitting in panels of three judges; matters of public law normally come up through the civil division in each case.

In Scotland, the equivalent level in civil matters (including most matters of public law) is the Inner House of the Court of Session, which has two divisions, each of four judges. In criminal matters in Scotland, the only appellate level is that of the High Court of Justiciary sitting as a Court of Criminal Appeal (with no further appeal from this court to the House of Lords).

The first instance presents a patchwork in all jurisdictions. In England and Wales, the High Court (mainly centralized in London), has three divisions: the Chancery Division (dealing with matters chiefly of equity (including trusts and related matters) and of succession, the Family Division and the Queen's [King's] Bench Division dealing with general common law matters, and most issues in public law, and there are County Courts exercising a local jurisdiction in civil matters, with limits on the pecuniary value of the cases over which their jurisdiction is compulsory; for criminal law in serious crimes, there are Crown Courts sitting in main judicial centres throughout the country and, for less serious matters, there are magistrates' courts staffed by benches of lay magistrates. In the High Court and the Crown Court, judges sit singly, albeit with juries in indictable criminal offences; juries are now a rarity in civil cases, with the exception of cases of defamation. The pattern in Northern Ireland is similar, though in the criminal courts dealing with serious terrorist offences the right to trial by jury is in suspension, and judges sit alone to determine guilt or innocence as well as to pass sentence.

In Scotland, the Outer House of the Court of Session (single judges sitting usually alone, but still sometimes with a jury) shares civil and public law functions with the Sheriff Court, a localized court exercising a wide jurisdiction subject to geographical limits on the jurisdiction of the sheriffs; in criminal matters, sheriffs either sit with a jury for trials on indictment, or alone in summary trials, and there are also district courts staffed by lay magistrates dealing with minor offences. The High Court of Justiciary holds circuits around the country for criminal trials on indictment before a High Court judge with a jury.

In all three countries, there are many statutory tribunals of various kinds and compositions dealing with specialized issues of administrative law and tax law. Their decisions are subject to a variety of forms of appeal and review exercised within the 'ordinary' court hierarchies described above; nowadays, all jurisdictions have a special procedure for review of administrative decisions and other public law decisions.

Reported decisions concentrate fairly heavily on appellate decisions at the intermediate or ultimate level of appeal; but decisions at the level of the High Court or Outer House are reported when new points of law arise. Reports of the lower courts are fewer, but not unknown; and some specialized tribunals are reported in specialist series of reports.

All UK courts are nowadays subject to the procedure of reference to the Court of Justice of the European Community (CJEC) sitting in Luxembourg. Under Article 177, whenever there arises a point of law in any court of a member state of the EC requiring interpretation of the Rome and related Treaties or Community law made thereunder, the national court is required to refer this point to the CJEC. It can only proceed to judgment in the instant case on the footing of the CJEC's ruling on the material point of Community law.

1(b) Structural and Procedural Aspects

The House of Lords comprises the Lord Chancellor, 12 Lords of Appeal in Ordinary, and four other senior judges qualified to sit and regularly sitting in the Lords. Normally, they sit in panels of five, but a larger panel may exceptionally be convened for the purpose of reconsidering an established precedent or line of precedents.

The Court of Appeal (England and Wales) has the Master of the Rolls as president and 32 Lords Justices of Appeal; there are three Lords Justices in Northern Ireland; a normal panel for an appeal in these courts comprises three judges. In Scotland, the divisions of the Inner House of the Court of Session each have four judges sitting together on a regular basis, and presided over by the Lord President and the Lord Justice Clerk, respectively. In criminal appeals in all three jurisdictions, there is a somewhat larger total number of judges who regularly sit.

In Scotland, when problems of precedent arise, including the need to harmonize lines of precedent from different divisions, or to review and possibly overrule existing precedent(s), there is a practice of convening a 'Whole Court' of seven (or, in very exceptional cases more) judges to undertake this task in a specially authoritative way.

In all the British jurisdictions, the decisions of appellate courts are reached by majority decision, and each judge states his or her own opinion on the matter. There is always a leading opinion for the majority view and very frequently other members simply state their concurrence in that opinion; but in difficult or complex cases, or where there is agreement in outcome but not in reasoning for that outcome, appeal judges may and quite frequently do give concurring opinions offering their own analysis of the case and of the reasons in favour of the decision handed down. Dissenting opinions are also permitted, and quite frequent. Hence disagreements among the higher judiciary about the proper interpretation or development of the law are open and public. Over time, judicial opinion as to the desirability of working out a single opinion of the court, or of the majority, has varied. The matter remains one for the judges of each generation to settle for themselves – parliament has never legislated, or contemplated legislating, upon this.

Case loads per year (1995) are as follows: House of Lords, 72 appeals presented, 67 determined, 81 pending; Court of Appeal (England and Wales): Civil Division, 2504; Criminal Division, 2586 (1760 against sentence); Scotland: Court of Session, Inner House, 202; High Court of Justiciary (appeals) 3409.

1(c) Power to Select Cases

In general, appeals to the intermediate level are as of right. In criminal matters, there are some filters to cut out frivolous or legally inept appeals. At the highest level, the House of Lords, appeals must be by leave of the intermediate appeal court except in the case of the Court of Session (though there are some special cases where first instance courts can refer matters directly to the House of Lords), or by leave of a subcommittee of the House. Whoever gives leave to appeal, it should be on the ground of there being a point of difficulty in law which it would be advantageous to have settled by the highest tribunal, or which is only capable of being settled at that level. Examples of the latter would be a conflict of binding precedents from lower jurisdictions, or a need to produce a common doctrine for all parts of the UK in place of a divergence in the precedents observed in different countries.

2 Structure, Content and Style of Judgments

A typical judgment or opinion in a UK court has the following form. It will start off with a description of the facts which will in most instances be fairly detailed. After this will come a discussion of what the legal issues arising are, having regard to what the parties to the case want. In appellate judgments, there will usually be an outline account of the proceedings in the court(s) below. There will then follow discussion of these issues, arguing towards a conclusion about the binding law on those points on which it is deemed relevant or necessary to make a ruling. Where other points have been argued, there may be a statement that it is unnecessary to reach any conclusion on these, though it is not uncommon for judges to state an opinion on such a matter, though with disclaimer of any intention to settle that point authoritatively at this stage. In lower courts, where judges consider the matter capable of being settled by reference to only one or two points, they may nevertheless give findings of fact and opinions on law on other points so that, in the event of an appeal, the higher court will have adequate grounds to move to a final decision if it should disagree with the first instance judge(s) on the key points at issue. In difficult cases, it is usual for judges to acknowledge, even sometimes to summarize, arguments put forward by counsel and to indicate why these are rejected (or, as the case may be accepted) by the court. At the end there is a statement of the court's express judgment or decision of the matter(s) in issue between the parties, or upholding or reversing the decision of the court below.

The style of opinions in the higher courts of the UK is discursive rather than deductive, standing in marked contrast to, for example, the terse and quasi-syllogistic statement of 'visas' and 'motifs' in the arrêt of a French civil court. It has been pointed out, however, that the system of pleading in civil cases (that is, the system of setting out in formal terms the matters of fact and law that a party lays before a court for decision) has, especially in Scotland, an essentially syllogistic form, linking averments of fact and pleas in law to a conclusion that justifies the remedy claimed. Very occasionally, judges actually use the syllogistic form to set out the essence of counsel's argument on a point. It is a topic of current debate among legal scholars whether the discursive form of judicial opinion writing indicates a mode of reasoning that is essentially non-deductive and non-syllogistic, or whether such reasoning has a fundamentally deductive character that can be captured by a 'rational reconstruction' of the arguments stated by judges.

The reasoning involved is a mixture of the general and the formal, and particular and substantive. It can be said to be concrete and particular in that very often the reasoning starts from a detailed discussion of the facts of the instant case. This does not mean, however, that the reasoning is particularistic since the particular facts become generalized and universalized to enter the arena of legal reasoning which operates on both levels. The UK style is formalistic but not excessively so. Rules come first, but these are bedded in grounds of principle and, where appropriate, substantive elements of value or policy. Again the discursive nature of the opinions and often their length (though one might say that in general they are extended rather than elaborate) makes it difficult to separate out rules, principles and policies.

The style tends to be argumentative rather than magisterial. To this, two factors particularly contribute: first, the possibility and relative prevalence of concurring and dissenting opinions, demonstrating that many important issues of law are highly arguable, even among *collaborative) dialogical*

the highest decision-makers; second, the degree to which attention is explicitly given to arguments of counsel, indicating that law determination is a collaborative and dialogical activity involving bar as well as bench. Final authority, of course, rests with the latter.

3   Publication of Judgments

In all the jurisdictions of the UK, there is a plurality of published forms of law reports. In order of authority, these are as follows. First are the semi-official publications of judgments in a form checked by the judges, and containing an outline of the arguments put by counsel in these cases. These are (a) the Law Reports (England and Wales), which are divided into four series, respectively the Appeal Cases, the Queen's [King's] Bench Reports, the Chancery Division Reports and the Family Division Reports (formerly Probate, Divorce and Admiralty); (b) the Session Cases (Scotland); (c) the Northern Ireland Law Reports; and (d) the European Court Reports.

Second are the private or commercial series. Here we may find the All England Reports (chiefly for England and Wales) comparable to which are the Weekly Law Reports (in effect, a preliminary publication of material for the Law Reports) and the *Scots Law Times* (for Scotland). These series are all edited by barristers or advocates, and carry authority as law reports that may be cited before the courts. They lack, however, the final authoritativeness of having been checked by the judges themselves. Comparable to these in modern times are various specialist series of reports on particular branches of law, such as the tax cases, the *Scottish Criminal Law Review* and various series dealing with EU law.

Third are newspapers: the London *Times* has for many years maintained a series of Law Reports as part of its news coverage. These have been edited by barristers, and have been accepted by courts as valid sources for citation of precedent where other sources are unavailable. In recent years, other daily newspapers such as *The Independent* (England and Wales) and *The Scotsman* (Scotland) have adopted this practice.

Next are law journals, which sometimes include formal case reports alongside professional or scholarly articles about the law and legal questions (examples are the *New Law Journal* and the *Scots Law Times*). An important institution is that of the case note. This is a scholarly discussion, sometimes quite critical, of some recent reported case. Traditionally, in England and Wales, particular weight has attached to such notes when they appear in the *Law Quarterly Review*. This is particularly true of those by its long-term editor, Arthur Goodhart, but law journals in all jurisdictions contain case notes subscribed by many hands, and these all have some weight in developing precedents and accounting for their interpretation. By contrast with the notes published in French reports, they are printed separately in academic or professional journals rather than as attachments to the court's decision.

Finally, there are reports maintained through electronic media, of which Lexis currently has in effect the monopoly (Mead Data Corporation Inc, in association with Butterworths in the UK) . These have full-text reports of all reported judgments over several decades, and also contain unreported cases, ahead of formal publication in any of the printed series. The House of Lords has attempted to set restraints upon the citation of unreported cases from electronic media. (See *Roberts Petroleum Ltd* v. *Bernard Kenny Ltd* [1983] 2 A.C. 192, at 200–202, *per* LORD DIPLOCK.) These reports have a degree of immediacy which is more or less in inverse ratio to their authority. The last to appear in relation to any given case are the Law Reports and the Session Cases, often with quite a severe backlog awaiting final editing. The less official series are more immediately available. The essential question affecting the validity of material for citation before a court as a legal precedent is whether the report is certified to have been edited by a barrister or advocate, rather than by a person not learned in law.

The history of reporting was one in which initially all reports were unofficial, kept by individual lawyers for their own use. Then printed publication took place, with authority depending on the care and skill of an editor, and these became series signified by their editors' names. Finally councils of law reporting were set up to systematize reporting, and these acquired semi-official status, though not (yet) statutory authorization by parliament. There remain gaps to be supplemented, as noted above. The discretion as to what is reported remains an editorial rather than a judicial discretion at all levels.

The levels in the court hierarchy commonly reported are High Court and above (England and Wales, Northern Ireland); Sheriff Court (sparingly) and above (Scotland).

4   Contents of Reports

The Law Reports and Session Cases always contain the following:

(a)   Case name: that is, the names of the parties to the case.
(b)   The name of the deciding court, including the names of the sitting judges; also (at the end) the names of the lawyers who prepared and argued the case for the various parties.
(c)   (i) A rubric that indicates the main topics of the case; (ii) a Headnote that contains a summary account of the facts found in the case and the issues of law raised at first instance and on

appeal, and a statement (always prefixed 'Held') of the holdings of the court upon the points in issue. It is important to note that this statement is the editor's summary of the point of the case, and *not* a judicially approved statement of the *ratio* or *rationes* of the case

(d)   A statement of the facts of the case. In the case of reported first-instance decisions, the judge's findings of fact are stated by him or her as a part of his or her opinion en route to a decision. In the case of an appeal, the facts are summarized in the leading judgment, based on the findings of the court below. Often, this part of the judgment is excised from the text of the judicial opinion and printed as part of the introductory matter in the Law Report. The statement of facts is always quite detailed – sufficiently so to make it possible to read any legal rulings back into the factual context for which they were made.

(e)   There is always a discussion of the procedural background and at least a brief account of the prior phases of the case before the same or other courts.

(f)   Normally, the statement of legal issues is a prominent feature of the judges' opinions in the case, and especially of the leading opinion. This is the way in which judges signal the points on which they think it necessary to reach a decision in order to justify a decision of the particular case before them.

(g)   Wherever a statute or precedent is involved in such a way that its interpretation is essential to forming a view of the binding law relevant to a case, there is some explicit, often extensive, discussion in the reported opinion of the judge's view as to its correct interpretation.

(h)   There is often a quite clearly articulated ruling or holding on the legal issues, but sometimes this is left implicit rather than explicit. Only rarely do judges seek to lay down explicit propositions as express rulings or *rationes* (see Section IV.1 below), and there is no standard 'slot' in a judgment or a report for such a proposition.

(i)   There are, however, always elaborate reasons in favour of the judge's or court's view of the binding law and the way it justifies the particular decision of the particular case between the parties.

(j)   There is always a statement of the final decision between the parties, or upon the outcome of the appeal in hand.

(k)   Concurring opinions when given are always reported.

(l)   Dissenting opinions, likewise, are always reported.

(m)   A summary of arguments by counsel is included and, where judges have put questions to counsel, these, together with their answers, are sometimes recorded.

(n)   Normally, no other official views are recorded within a Law Report in relation to a case.

(o)   Juristic commentary on a decision is never printed as part of the report. Case notes in leading law journals are the accepted place for such commentaries.

(p)   Law reports contain lists of all the authorities (precedents and so on) cited by the judges in their opinions in the case, and also lists of the authorities cited by counsel to the court but not discussed in judicial opinions. This can be of importance in relation to the possibility (see Section II. 4 below) that a decision may be considered to have been reached *per incuriam*, if some relevant and binding authority were not considered by the court in coming to its decision.

5   Meaning of 'Precedent'

Our system is one of relatively strict application of precedent, and this applies even where a precedent is not binding in the narrow sense. A precedent is simply any prior decision of any court that bears a legally significant analogy to the case now before a court. If the prior decision is of a superior court in the same hierarchy, it will be a binding precedent that must be followed unless it can be distinguished on some point of significant fact or law. Otherwise, it will be a persuasive precedent, possibly a relevant analogy for decision of the present case; or it may illustrate an important legal dividing line between one class of cases and cases of the class now in issue.

There is, however, another usage, almost as significant, according to which 'a precedent' in the narrower sense is only a relevant case that is binding, and only that part of the case or opinion that actually binds. What that implies is that, once something is acknowledged to be a precedent, it has to be followed. The whole business of legal argumentation in respect of *stare decisis* is to show what must be followed and what does not count as a precedent. One may say that most judicial discussion of precedent and the whole discussion of departing or not from precedent implies the wider usage. Thus the narrower understanding of the term is contextually useful in some situations, but is not as useful as the wider when it comes to developing a theory of precedent. One might expand the wider sense by noting that on some occasions courts are mindful that the decision they make will be a precedent for future cases though it will not, strictly speaking, have been arrived at by the use of precedent. They will then talk of their decision as a 'precedent' (*MacLennan* v. *MacLennan* 1958 SC 105).

6   Mode of Citation and Discussion

Citation of precedents by counsel and by judges focuses on the detail of each precedent, both in respect of the facts and circumstances of the case cited and as to points of law and legal doctrine elaborated in judges' opinions. The degree of detail of the discussion will depend upon the importance of the precedent for the instant case – in particular, on the degree to which it is considered to be 'in point' and thus in some degree binding for the present case. Passages drawn from opinions will be quoted, sometimes quite extensively, especially if they purport to summarize or give a ruling on the law relevant to the class of cases under consideration.

Where a case has attracted discussion in periodical literature or in legal textbooks, especially where such doctrinal writing attempts to synthesize a body of legal doctrine and account for the precedent, or a set of precedents, in their whole legal context, this writing can be of considerable importance. Sometimes it will itself be explicitly cited, sometimes it will simply be tacitly adopted by counsel or judge in argument or opinion. The probability of express citation depends in part on the standing and prestige of the academic author.

Counsel are expected to explain and present argument upon relevant precedents in arguing cases before the courts. It is indeed the duty of counsel to draw to the court's attention all relevant precedents, and in particular to bring up all those that may seem unfavourable to their own clients. If not, counsel would be in breach of duty to the court if found suppressing relevant authority.

7   Overall Role of Precedent

As the above implies, precedents are of very great importance in the justification of legal claims or propositions, and legal decisions, in all the UK jurisdictions. In the absence of a single documentary constitution (as distinct from a body of statute law constitutional in character), the two main documentary sources of legal argumentation are statutes (together with subordinate legislation) and precedents. Even arguments from principle or from policy normally seek to ground statements of either in some previous dicta of judges, or to anchor principle or policy in some relevant statute. Certainly, scholarly writing can also be of considerable force in the elaboration of principles and policies, but usually these again are tied by the author onto some body of precedent or statute, or both. Even where a body of law is mainly drawn from statute, or where a branch of law has effectively been codified, as with income tax, or company law, or consumer credit law, the prior body of decisions about the various provisions of the statutes (quasi-codes, even) in question are of great importance in interpreting the statute in new situations.

8   Role of Precedent in Different Branches of Law

Some areas of law in all the jurisdictions remain predominantly matters of common law in the sense of case law. The law of torts (of 'delict' in Scotland) is still mainly built up out of case law, and so is the general part of the law of contract. In Scotland the major part of the criminal law, dealing with the most serious crimes, is largely to be gathered from case law. In all jurisdictions, the law governing judicial review of administrative action is in its main substance established through case law, though there have also been decisive legislative interventions (including subordinate legislation through rules of court) that have streamlined and improved the remedies available for challenging allegedly defective administrative action.

9   Precedent and 'Gaps in the Law'

In the widest sense of precedent (see Section 1.5) the judges do create precedent since a ruling is constructed by thinking what the decision might mean for the future: what sort of precedent it might make for future cases (see *MacLennan* v. *MacLennan* 1958 SC 105, where judges considered the precedent effects of a ruling that artificial insemination by donor (AID) was adultery). In a case-based system, part of the system of legal reasoning will be to relate present decisions to past cases. Thus part of the structure of justification will be to construct and discuss examples, however remote. This is seen all the time in judicial opinions. But it also means that there is less need to create precedent (in the narrow sense).

II   The Bindingness of Precedent

1   Kinds and Degrees of Normative Force

In the UK, the distinction between bindingness, force and illustrative value is made. Formal bindingness in the sense that judgments not respecting precedent's bindingness are not lawful and subject to reversal on appeal is found by virtue of court hierarchies. Each court is strictly bound to follow the precedents of the court above; a House of Lords precedent strictly binds the Court of Appeal while a precedent of the latter strictly binds the High Court. Decisions of High Court judges are only persuasive for other High Court judges and for inferior courts. *Mutatis mutandis*, the same goes for each of the other jurisdictions.

Defeasibly binding precedents are also to be found. An example is the Court of Appeal in England and Wales. It has a strict doctrine of the binding character of its own precedents as against later sittings of the same court. However, in *Young* v. *Bristol Aeroplane Co.* (1944) K.B. 7, the court held that it was bound by its own precedents except where these had been reached *per incuriam*, or when a case had been impliedly overruled by a later House of Lords decision, or where there was a conflict between two Court of Appeal judgments. This means that it will not be bound by decision reached in ignorance of relevant statute law, or relevant and binding prior precedent of the Court of Appeal or the House of Lords, or unless the precedent had been expressly or impliedly overruled by a subsequent House of Lords decision. (Cf. also *Duke* v. *Reliance Systems Ltd.* (1988) Q.B. 108, 113). This is perhaps the strictest version of defeasible bindingness to be found in British practice. The Court of Criminal Appeal has a slightly looser practice. (Cf. *R.* v. *Taylor* (1950) 2 K.B. 368, 371, where the court may depart from a previous decision in the interests of the accused.)

The bindingness of House of Lords decisions falls into a somewhat different category. They might be said to be formally binding but subject to overruling or modification. From 1898 to 1966, under the doctrine of *London Street Tramways* v. *LCC*, (1898) A.C. 37, the House of Lords was, at least in theory, strictly bound to follow its own precedents. But to avoid undue rigidity in law, the House developed ever more refined approaches to 'distinguishing' (see below) precedents it later found unsatisfactory. Finally, in 1966, a Practice Statement was issued by the Lord Chancellor, declaring that henceforward the House would hold itself free to depart from precedents in appropriate cases, while acknowledging the continuing importance for legal certainty of treating them as normally binding. By a steady accretion of cases over 30 years, the House has established a practice about overruling precedents when they are found unsatisfactory. A larger than normal committee of judges is usually convened for such cases, and argument is specifically addressed by counsel to whether or not sufficient reason exists to disturb or overrule settled precedent.

The above might appear to fit the category of defeasibly binding, as in the English Court of Appeal (above). But we can see the difference if we look at the divisions of the Inner House of the Court of Session which have a practice that resembles that of the House of Lords. When a precedent is to be considered for overruling, a 'Whole Court' of seven or more judges is convened. The same applies in criminal cases in Scotland, where the High Court of Justiciary sitting as an appeal court is the highest instance.

One may say that some judgments have force, though not the quality of bindingness. In general, they are those which have to be considered. Though it would not be unlawful not to follow them, this would be considered a matter of criticism and make the decision liable to reversal on appeal. It does not appear that this is a defeasible force in that they should be applied unless exceptions (well defined or not) come into play. Rather, they should be applied unless the reasoning behind them is clearly outweighed by stronger reasons for an opposite view on the matter under consideration. This 'persuasive' or 'weakly binding' character can be ascribed to all other precedents of higher courts in the UK, both in relation to courts at that level, and in regard to subsequent decisions by higher instances. Examples of this can be found in the Outer House in Scotland. In *Collins* v. *South of Scotland Electricity Board* (1977) SC 13, LORD GRIEVE refused to follow an earlier Outer House Decision (*M'Bay* v. *Hamlett* (1963) SC 282). He did not think it sufficient to express disagreement but gave reasons for his refusal.

Sometimes precedents of courts in Commonwealth jurisdictions, especially Australia or New Zealand, are considered as having almost as highly persuasive a quality as domestic precedents, but they would not justify a decision as well as use of the precedents above. They are, rather, supportive of a point.

Finally, there is still a practice of occasionally citing developments in US law; increasingly, membership of the EC (or now 'European Union') leads to an acceptance of citation of decisions from the European Court of Justice and even domestic courts in other European states. But it seems that such citations, except where a binding matter of EC law may be in issue, are only illustrative of a point.

2   Law Concerning Precedent

There is no statute law governing the use or citation of precedent in the UK. This is an aspect of common law which has developed itself purely by common law methodology. There is a substantial body of case law concerning the authority and bindingness of precedent, the degrees of bindingness and force as discussed above (though using somewhat different terminology), the exceptions to bindingness, and the rationale for following or not following precedent. There is also a substantial body of doctrinal discussion in journal articles, monographs and texts on legal reasoning or on legal system.

It is quite clear, as a matter of common law (hence, arguably, as dependent ultimately on the general custom of the realm), that precedent is binding de jure in all jurisdictions; hence precedent is properly deemed a source of law in its own right in them.

So far as the maxim *nulla poena sine lege* is concerned, it applies both to common law and to statutory crimes. In Scotland very extensively, but still for some significant and serious crimes (such as murder) in the other jurisdictions, the fundamental definitions of crimes are determined by common law, through precedent. Analogical development of common law rules to the detriment of the defence is held in the same disapprobation as analogical development of statute law. It is, however, controversial how far this goes. What is the difference between a new manifestation of an old principle (or an old crime committed in a new way) and the assertion of a new rule or principle based on the mere analogy of existing law? There is a body of opinion that the High Court in Scotland has on occasion stretched rather far the concept of an old crime committed in a new way, effectively applying the law by analogy in certain cases of public mischief. But it is acknowledged that merely analogical development of criminal law is an unacceptable infringement of the rule of law.

3   Factors Determining Degrees of Normative Force

The factors relevant to the formal bindingness of a precedent are the hierarchical rank of the court, whether a full bench took part in the decision or not (in Scotland), and whether or not a precedent can be said to have been decided *per incuriam*. In the House of Lords, the age of a precedent is material to the question of its being overruled. For example, the House has indicated that, in a question of recent interpretation of recent statute law, the question of overruling a precedent should not be raised. The other factors mentioned in this question are all of great importance in relation to the degree of force and persuasiveness attaching to a precedent, and all might be factors relevant to deciding whether or not to depart from or overrule a precedent where that course is technically open. But none goes strictly to the issue of bindingness as such.

4   Factors that Weaken Precedent

A precedent can lose its normal force if decided *per incuriam*; that is, while the court was in ignorance of relevant precedent or statute law. To check whether the court was not informed of relevant precedent, one can look at the lists of citations contained in the law report. This illustrates the very great importance attached in these systems to the duty of a lawyer to ensure that a court deciding a question of law is made fully aware of all the relevant law, even precedents (and so on) ostensibly unhelpful to the lawyer's own case.

A precedent can also be expressly or impliedly overruled by the decision of a higher court at a later date, thereby losing its force.

Statute law may also override case law on particular points, but, in England and Wales, is held not to be otherwise deprived of authority on points not dealt with by statute.

Precedents dealing with statute law are differentiated in the way noted above, but not otherwise. This is because parliament, on the initiative usually of the government, can revise statute law in the light of current judicial (mis)interpretations if it sees fit. One should also note that precedents on the meaning of statutory words will not be binding unless the same statute is in issue (cf. *R v. Evans-Jones and Jenkins* (1923) 17 Cr. App. Rep 121).

In Scotland the maxim *cessante ratione legis cessat lex ipsa* has on occasion been applied to justify departure from older case law where its main point has been made obsolete by later statute law, as in matters affecting the legal status of women.

5   Vertical and Horizontal Bindingness

'Vertical bindingness' is the general rule in the UK so far as concerns appellate jurisdictions. Horizontal bindingness also applies at the level of the intermediate appeals, though less strictly in Scotland than in the other jurisdictions.

The House of Lords applies a qualified doctrine of horizontal bindingness, treating its own previous decisions as formally binding but subject to overruling. The number of cases in which the House of Lords has reversed a precedent of its own over the three decades since the power to do so was asserted remains a small one, certainly less than one a year. But the power has been used in some very significant cases in both private and public law.

6   Analysis of Force, Support and Illustrative Role

The courts differentiate clearly between those precedents which are formally binding and those which (a) have justifying force, (b) provide further support or (c) are illustrative of some value. However, between (a), (b) and (c) they are less clear. In which category a precedent might be put is often something implicitly discovered from the practice of the judges. Thus the practice of giving reasons for departing from a decision of the Outer House in another Outer House case would seem to imply force. As to (a), one might find arguments that also occur in respect of bindingness which go towards distinguishing the precedent. In other cases, there appear to be no specific arguments for the categories and generally the arguments go to the precedent itself, utilizing the factors noted in Section II.3.

These factors are all discussed in scholarly works but not in the terms used here.

7   *Excess of Precedents?*

By and large, there is no feeling that there are too many precedents. With the rather strict nature of *stare decisis* that we have and the relatively small jurisdiction (as compared to the USA), the situation is not seen as overwhelming. However, problems might occur with the availability of cases not yet reported in electronic media; and, as we have seen, the House of Lords has attempted to set restrictions on their use. In some sense this implies an exception to *stare decisis* since those rules apply not to the actual case decision but the decision if reported.

III   The Rationale of Precedent

1   *General Rationales for Formal Bindingness*

(a)   Historically, there have been two principal rationales for precedents having the kind of status that they have in our system. These are the declaratory theory and the law-making theory of precedent. A third view discernible in modern times, but with ancient roots, might be called the 'determinative theory'.

The declaratory theory represents precedents as evidence of the law, rather than constitutive of it. The law is conceived as a body of principles about rights and duties and the like. It is implemented only partially in statutes, and carried into effect by judicial decisions. Judges as persons of great practical wisdom, experience and high legal learning are specially skilled in identifying and giving expression to the law. Hence their decisions have the status of precedents giving the strongest possible evidence of what the law is. This is especially so where there has grown up a line of decisions on similar topics in similar tenor. But the law itself is only evidenced and declared by, not made by, these decisions.

This doctrine of the independent existence of law presupposes an appropriate ontology for law, and this was supplied by either a theory of rationally evident natural law or a theory of law-as-custom, especially as 'learned custom'. Quite often, indeed, the natural law and the custom view were presented as mutually supportive and even logically linked. This view is put forward in the most authoritative early classical statements of both Scots and English law. Figures such as Sir William Blackstone (*Commentaries on the Laws of England*, 1st edn, 1765–9) or James Viscount Stair (*Institutions of the Law of Scotland*, 1st edn, 1681) subscribed to rationalistic versions of natural law theory and developed their accounts of English or, respectively, Scots law through this theoretical approach. Both take the theory of law-as-custom to be fully compatible with, and perhaps derivable from, their natural law premises, since they consider custom as itself evidence of the consensus of human reason wrestling over practical issues and confirming or overriding prior judgments in the light of later experience and maturer deliberation.

Later scholars such as Hayek have stressed the law-as-custom view without any conjoined assumption of rationalistic natural law. Here it is the distilled wisdom of the group which, having stood the test of time, is to be preferred as a way of organizing society rather than 'constructive rationalism' (Hayek, 1982).

What is important in the declaratory approach is that it is essentially custom that gives the rationale for precedent since this gives us a reason for doing 'what we have always done' as being evidence for some deeper truth (the will of God or the best way of going about things). There will, however, be less reason for departing from it in the latter than in the former.

Judicial law-making theories start from a denial of the natural law premises of the declaratory theory. A basic tenet of legal positivism is that all law derives from authoritative decision, hence all human law from authoritative human decision. There is no essence of law beyond or behind what is decided as law by some competent decision maker. From this it follows obviously that, if precedents are evidence of the law, they can be so only because judges are accorded authority to make law through their decisions. Conversely, the very recognition of precedent as evidence of the law amounts to recognition of the power of the courts to make law. The declaratory theory, and certain associated *façons de parler* used by judges to disguise any law-making activities, are at best polite fictions, at worst mischievous ideology disguising the real existence of judicial law making behind an elaborate pretence of law discovery. Jeremy Bentham, father of English legal positivism, was particularly strong in his denunciation of the declaratory theory as a form of mystification of law, hiding the power of 'Judge and Co', and insistent on recognition of the fact of 'judicial legislation' through precedent. His followers, from John Austin through to H.L.A. Hart, though less critical of judges and of the common law than Bentham, retain firmly the view that precedent is a 'source of law' in the sense that judicial decisions are constitutive rather than declaratory of law.

For all positivists, it is an almost inevitable corollary of this position on the nature of precedent that precedent has to be viewed as a subordinate source of law, subordinate to legislation enacted either by central sovereign parliaments or by local authorities or ministerial delegates. The space for judicial law making is only in the gaps of legislation properly so-called; judges do make law, but only 'interstitially'.

During the nineteenth century, and into the twentieth century, the positivistic view strongly predominated in the legal thought of the UK. This had considerable impact on the practice of the courts in relation to precedent, in two ways. First, there was a tendency to ever stricter doctrines of binding precedent, and to hierarchically ordered rankings of binding precedent, on the ground that this recognized the fact of judicial law making, but kept it to a minimum while establishing a rational hierarchy of interstitial legislative authority among the courts. Second, there was a considerable theoretical focus on trying to find exact ways of identifying the rules created by precedents, hence much focus on elucidations of the idea of the *ratio decidendi*.

The modern stress (cf. Dworkin, 1978; 1986) is on law as grounded in principles partly emergent from practice and custom, partly constructed out of moral or ideological elements that bring together practice and contemporary values in a coherent order (MacCormick, 1984). Legal rules and judicial rulings on points of law are then to be understood as 'determinations' (in the Thomistic sense) of background principles – neither simple deductions from them nor arbitrarily discretionary decisions about them, but partly discretionary decisions as to the best way of making the law determinate for a given (type of) case (Finnis, 1985). From this, the best present day rationale of precedent would seem to be what we would call a 'determinative theory', which can well account for the continuing role of judicial precedent as a 'source of law', but a defeasible one. Precedent is authoritative because each decision is a determination of law, but no decision is absolutely indefeasible. Precedents then bind defeasibly, the issue being what considerations can defeat an established precedent. This remains distinctively a doctrine of precedent, because the very fact of a point's having been previously determined is accepted as a special reason for continuing in that line of decision, even though another line might have been better had the matter first arisen for decision in the instant case.

However, theories about the general nature of law or the nature of the judicial process do not provide conclusive rationales for deciding how firm or rigid a doctrine of precedent should be. We thus have to distinguish between (1) theories that explain or provide a rationale for having a doctrine of precedent at all, (2) a rationale or justification for a fairly rigid doctrine of precedent and (3) a rationale or justification for an absolutely binding doctrine of precedent. The questions are, of course interrelated and, as we see below, it appears that (3) does not obtain in our system. The level of rigidity of *stare decisis* is best looked at in relation to lower-level theories or beliefs, which we discuss below.

(b)   Justificatory arguments for giving courts law-determining power are perhaps rare. Certainly, there has always been the 'default' argument. Judges have to make law where no one else will, and where there would otherwise be a gap in the law. The trouble about this, though, is that a 'gap' in this sense is almost inevitably a gap only given some value orientation. Mere silence of the law can be handled by appeal to the maxim that whatever is not prohibited is permitted. To go beyond that requires a view on how the law ought to be; the gap is a gap by virtue of there being no law where law (in a certain tenor) ought to be. Constitutionalism (separation of powers) and democratic theory militate against yielding to judges power to make law simply on the ground that, for some reason, law ought to be made. To a considerable extent, modern British judges have exercised self-restraint on the grounds of deference to parliament as the constitutional and the democratic law giver. Nevertheless, there are areas of technical law, of 'lawyer's law', and of relatively pure common law, where it is argued that, first, judges are technically more competent to settle the law and, second, parliament never has time to deal with such matters. Especially given the determinative theory (see above) or a Hayekian theory of the evolutionary character of the common law, this approach can justify judicial determination of law, but these very theoretical underpinnings also justify describing this process of determination as in its essence non-legislative.

(c)   Prescriptive or justificatory theories discuss how far precedents ought to be binding, and on what grounds. Approaches to the rationale of precedent and *stare decisis* affect views on the scope and weight of precedent in a variety of ways. The more that precedent is deemed a strict 'source of law' in the positivistic sense, the more constitutionalist doctrines preclude the relatively free practice of overruling and not following that the declaratory view can support. Then it becomes practically important to restrict quite severely the scope conceded to any particular precedent, both because political considerations restrict the extent to which it is desirable for judges to make law and because legal considerations make it undesirable for wide-ranging propositions to become settled unrevisably through single decisions.

On the other hand, the tendency to restrict the scope of precedents, with its allied practice of drawing fine distinctions, can lead to an excessively particularistic and fragmentary common law, a law which does resemble the poet's 'wilderness of single instances'. What Karl Llewellyn called the 'formal style' of legal reasoning is apt then to flourish. Atiyah and Summers (1987) largely corroborate on this point in their contrast of form and substance. But they warn of the opposite danger, of a simply free-wheeling response to the felt justice of particular cases if substance is wholly substituted for form, as excesses of 'American Realism' may have tended to do.

Contemporary (post-1966) developments in the theory and practice of precedent attempt to negotiate these two doctrinal mazes.

Doctrines like the 'determinative theory' which suggest a more holistic approach to legal systems or, more likely, to particular branches of law, favour the development of a strong sense of underlying principles proper to particular fields and branches of law, and the taking of a coherent view of legal doctrines as congeries of principles, values ('policies') and their determination through decision making which is truly sensitive to the full particularity of contexts of decision. See, for example, Dworkin (1986); Detmold (1984); MacCormick (1984); Bankowski (1991); Jackson (1988).

These approaches enable lawyers to differentiate the decisional force and scope of precedents (decisive within a quite narrow compass subject to tight explaining and distinguishing when appropriate, even overruling in extreme cases) from their weight or persuasiveness or 'gravitational force' (Dworkin, 1978) as sources of legal justification and legal development. The history of doctrinal development from such a case as *Donoghue* v. *Stevenson* (see Bankowski, 1991) provides a now almost legendary illustration of this. The scope of the decision in its original form was quite narrow, laying down a rule about the responsibilities of manufacturers of food and drink. But subsequent development of the doctrine of negligence liability have given all but legislative weight to Lord Atkin's 'neighbour principle' formulated in the original 1932 decision.

More particularly, further supporting arguments for following precedent have been adduced:

1   separation of powers – once the courts have settled a point, the legislature alone should have power to reconsider it;
2   constitutional propriety – since the highest court is also technically the Upper House of Parliament (albeit specially constituted for its appellate function), it ought not to be able to legislate on its own, as would happen if it could freely review its own precedents;
3   rule-of-law reasons, stressing the importance of the citizen's ability to rely on the durability of pre-announced decisions on matters of law;
4   formal justice reasons, captured with the slogan 'treat like cases alike';
5   reasons of legal expediency, deterring the expense of money and time involved in speculatively re-arguing points already determined by the highest judicial authority.

In general, one might say that considerations of legal certainty and predictability are generally acknowledged to back at least a presumption in favour of *stare decisis*. The more one can be sure that courts will follow their established decisions and lines of decisions, the more one can rely on similarity of decision in future. The more one can rely on such similarity of decision, the more confidence there will be in law as a secure guide to action. And the more confidence one reposes in the law, the stronger the argument from justice against unforeseen change.

The argument from certainty can, however, be countered by arguments from justice, from the general benefit and from *elegantia juris*. If a particular precedent is unjust in its substance, or gives rise to unforeseen ill consequences, or fits badly with the rest of the relevant body of law, there are obviously reasons for being ready to revise the law as explained (or as laid down) in the precedent. Admittedly, legal certainty is a part of formal justice, and legal certainty is generally beneficial; but one aspect of justice or utility can sometimes outweigh another, and where it does, surely precedent should not be followed?

The rationale of precedent is quite frequently discussed by judges, both judicially (in case opinions) and extrajudicially (in journal articles and the like). A *locus classicus* is the London Tramways decision ((1898) AC 375), where the 'disastrous inconvenience' of lack of finality in decision, and hence of prevailing lack of legal certainty, were argued to justify overriding even strong considerations of justice where reopening of a precedent was concerned; thus was laid down a rule of strictly binding force even for single precedents of the House of Lords.

In 1966, this rule was relaxed by the House of Lords, which announced its new resolution in a Practice Statement (1966) 3 All ER 77. Here again there is a terse statement of rationale. Precedent is an 'indispensable foundation' for law giving 'at least some degree of certainty' and a 'basis for orderly development of legal rules'. But precedent, if taken too rigidly, 'may lead to injustice ... and also unduly restrict the proper development of the law'. The relaxation of the rule should be one which guards against risks of retrospection in contractual and property matters, and which acknowledges 'the special need for certainty as to the criminal law'.

The new practice thus determined has in turn been elaborated in a series of cases which has explored the limits of binding precedent and the rationales for departing from precedent in particular cases and classes of case. These cases are further repositories for judicial theorizing about precedent.

2   Rationales for Force, Further Support, and so on

The rationales where precedents are recognized as having less than a binding force are not significantly different. Since our system is a common law one and has at base some idea of the value of case-by-case reasoning, the value of examples from similar circumstances even if not technically binding is always seen as important. The rationales above will apply and it will be the mixture and the weighing that will determine their effect. In *Donoghue,* LORD ATKIN said, 'It is always satisfaction to an English lawyer to be able to test his application of fundamental principles of the common law by the development of the same doctrines by the lawyers of the courts of the United States' (p.20). *MacPherson* v. *Buick Motor Co.* 111 N.E 1050 (1916) was cited in that case and in his dissent LORD BUCKMASTER said that 'such case can have no close application and no authority is clear, for though the source of law in the two countries may be the same, its current may well flow in different channels'; however, one may 'gain assistance by considering how similar cases are dealt with by eminent judges'. What is important to note is that rationale as to precedent in general will be the same but what will be different is the perception of the distance of that precedent from the vertical and binding structure of the legal system's rule of *stare decisis.*

IV   Precedents: What They Stand For and How They Apply

1   *What Counts as Binding or Having Force?*

The traditional doctrine of precedent in English common law has been that a precedent which is binding is binding only as to its *ratio decidendi,* that is, its 'rule of decision'. Only this is strictly authoritative for the future, and any explanatory or argumentative statements by the court or individual judges are deemed *'obiter dicta',* persuasive according to their cogency and relevancy, but not binding in law. The same applies in Northern Ireland. In Scots law, it has been argued on high authority (Smith, 1952) that the difference of legal tradition has generated both a broader conception of *ratio decidendi,* to include general principles rather than more particular rules of decision, and a somewhat less strict view of the binding quality of individual precedents. It seems a little doubtful if there survives any great present-day distinction in practice as regards precedents in the different jurisdictions of the UK (Maher and Smith, 1987).

That only the *ratio* is strictly binding, although true as a doctrinal statement, does not capture well the phenomena of case citation in legal argument in the UK. Good practice requires the citation in argument of all relevant reported precedents, absolutely so in the case of those precedents of higher courts which are binding on the instance in question. For the sake of making and supporting an argument, there are no actual or theoretical restraints on the use of elements in the precedents. General statements of law, judicial formulations of

general principle, arguments of policy or observations about fundamental values, analyses of factual situations and the discussion of
relevant actual or hypothetical analogies, and of course any careful
formulation of a ruling or holding on a point of law can be cited, and
can manifestly add to the weight of argument for or against a given
conclusion in law. This applies both to counsel arguing a case and to
judges stating their opinions in the judgment of a case. Precedents in
all their aspects can give support of variable strength to arguments
or decisions in subsequent cases, and this is well seen in the most
casual reading of any of the British series of law reports. But the
point of the doctrine that only the *ratio* is strictly binding in law is to
be able to isolate the binding part of the precedent. Counsel may
wish to present an argument, or a judge may wish to give a decision,
on a point on which there is binding precedent containing elements
adverse to that argument or decision. If the adverse elements can be
represented as *obiter dicta* only, not *ratio decidendi*, they are then persuasive only and can be outweighed by more persuasive or cogent
counter-reasons. But if the adverse element is the very *ratio* of the
binding precedent, then it settles the issue (but see Section IV.5 below). In principle, then, the matter is clear. Where a binding precedent
is relevant, its *ratio* binds in all cases to which it applies. But that
means that it does not bind (whatever persuasive force it may exercise) in those cases which are distinguishable on their facts, that is,
have facts to which the legal proposition contained in the binding
ratio does not strictly apply.

There can be acute problems about the interpretation of precedents
in difficult cases. The problem is that of identifying a *ratio decidendi* in
the precedent, and of interpreting the *ratio*, and debating the proper
qualification of the facts of the instant case on the issue whether they
do or do not count as facts of the type covered by the precedent's
ratio. That is an inquiry which necessarily involves scrutiny of the
facts of the precedent itself, whether conceived as raw facts, or as
facts qualified by the court in its descriptions or accounts of them
constructed en route to justifying its own decision.

Not surprisingly, although there has been much debate both judicial and scholarly on the question of the definition of the *ratio decidendi*
and of the proper method for ascertaining it, no unanimity exists. A.
L. Goodhart's suggestion that the *ratio* has to be ascertained by
taking the court's statement of the relevant facts of the case before it
together with the court's actual decision in the case has a certain
persuasive force. Professors Stone and Simpson have cast some doubt
on this, however, and the former suggests that the *ratio* belongs
among the categories of illusory reference, thus having a variable
meaning according to the values and policies bearing on particular
cases for decision. Sir Rupert Cross gave the following as a 'tolerably

accurate description' of the concept as used in UK and Common-wealth legal discourse: 'The *ratio decidendi* of a case is any rule of law expressly or impliedly treated by a judge as a necessary step in reaching his conclusion, having regard to the line of reasoning adopted by him, or a necessary part of his direction to the jury' (Cross, 1991, p.72). This carries great authority, but may need some amendment in a direction suggested by one of the present authors. As J.W. Harris notes in his latest edition of Cross's *Precedent*, MacCormick's relevant suggestion is:

> A ratio decidendi is a ruling expressly or impliedly given by a judge which is sufficient to settle a point of law put in issue by the parties' arguments in a case, being a point on which a ruling was necessary to his[/her] justification (or one of his[/her] alternative justifications) of the decision in the case. (N. MacCormick, 'Why Cases Have *Rationes* and What These Are', in Goldstein (1991, pp.155–82 at 170))

Anyway, in all views the point is that what has to be determined by a court is usually some proposition a great deal narrower than many of the statements made *arguendo* by a judge in justifying the decision he or she gives or supports in the case. When the decision is later cited as a precedent, the court to which the precedent is cited is free to have regard to dicta at any level in the precedent court's opinion(s); but that to which it must have regard is only the opinion on the point that had to be determined by the precedent court. However the later court formulates the proposition that it considers the earlier one had to determine, it is to that proposition that the later court will ascribe the status of *ratio decidendi*.

2   Reasoning about Applicability

In particular cases, where precedents are relevant either directly or analogically, it is the business of counsel to produce arguments for the applicability (or, respectively the inapplicability) of precedents ostensibly in point. In turn the judge(s) who must decide the case will give in their opinions reasons for preferring one to another line of precedent, showing why this or that precedent or line of authority is applicable and supports the decision given. This can in turn lead to scholarly discussions through 'case notes' or longer articles criticiz-ing, supporting or commenting on the case and the use of precedent in it. In textbooks and other legal monographs, commentators will construct explanations of authorities and lines of authority, discuss-ing their applicability or not to hypothetical cases devised by way of illustration. All such argumentation concerning the applicability of precedents is likely to involve close factual analysis, especially to discover how strong an analogy there is between precedent and instant case; and this frequently leads on into analysis of rules and principles stated in or implicit in the precedent case. For the purpose of ascertaining *ratio* or principles in a precedent, regard is properly had to any substantive reasons used by the prior court; but rarely if ever are such reasons reproduced as authoritative simply by virtue of their use in a precedent. The general rationales for following precedent are used in cases where the rational and just arguments seem to be against applying the precedent.

3 Juristic Discussion

There is a very considerable literature indeed on the question what precedents stand for. This has most characteristically taken the form of attempts to clarify either the concept *'ratio decidendi'* or some method for ascertaining the *ratio* of individual cases. There are also discussions of related topics such as the use and relevance of arguments from legal principles, the practice of explaining, distinguishing and overruling or not following precedents, and the use and abuse of arguments from analogy in law. The 'References' attached to this chapter gives a fair indication of this.

4 Illustrative or Analogical Precedent

Analogical arguments from precedents that are relevant in principle but not directly in point are very common in all the systems of the UK. They help clarify the law and harmonize it, as in the line of cases following *Rylands* v. *Fletcher* and *Donoghue* v. *Stevenson*. But they are mainly used to point out the relevance of certain arguments and thus move the law along. *Steel's* case gives a good illustration of this. In the law of delict or tort, it was established as early as the beginning of the twentieth century that a special rule applied in rescue cases, where one person, seeing another's imminent danger, rushes to give assistance and is injured. Where the first party's peril is imputable to the negligence of a third party, the question is whether the rescuer is entitled to compensation for injuries from the third party, or debarred from any remedy on the ground of voluntary assumption of risk and/or of being the substantial cause of his own injury. This problem was settled in favour of rescuers in several cases.

Subsequently, the question arose whether a person who went to salvage another's (or, indeed, her or his own) property was entitled to compensation if the danger to the property in question arose from a third party's culpable act. In the Scottish case of *Steel* v. *Glasgow Iron and Steel Co* (1944 SC 237) it was held that the analogy of the rescue cases gave sufficient ground for upholding the right to damages of the salvor of property, in at least a certain range of cases, and allowing for the fact that the analogy is incomplete, since the saving of life and limb justifies a greater degree of risk to oneself than does the saving of property.

5   Single Precedents or Lines of Decision?

There is no contemporary doctrine of *jurisprudence constante* as such in the UK, though historically in Scotland Stair and his contemporaries attached authority primarily to lines of concordant decisions rather than to particular cases. The US practice of comparing different lines of reasoning from different states or groups of states lacks any relevant parallel in the UK, partly because of the relative paucity of jurisdictions compared to the 50-plus jurisdictions of the USA. However, since the Practice Statement of 1966, it has become clear that, while the House of Lords now exercises freedom to depart from its own precedents, it is most unlikely to do so in cases other than those of relatively isolated precedents found unsatisfactory. To that extent, there is a difference of bindingness of single precedents by contrast with lines of authority, although it is probably most accurate to say that any precedent which belongs within and is fully compatible with a line or body of decisions is to that extent the less liable to be overruled or departed from.

There are many general concepts or doctrines within the common law that themselves are gathered from lines of precedent, without being directly laid down in any single one. Thus the English doctrine of consideration in contract, or of privity of contract, is to be gathered from many concordant decisions, as synthesized both in scholarly and doctrinal writing and in the case law itself. The same goes for such parallel or even converse doctrines of Scots law as that of the binding force of promises as such or the doctrine of *jus quaesitum tertio* (third party contractual rights). Sometimes there is confusion in law, where lines of cases do not add up to any single clear body of doctrine; problems of mistake or error in contract are a notorious instance. Here any effective synthesis has to start from a candid acknowledgment of irresoluble antinomies or conflicts between some of the precedents, with some resort to reasons of principle or other substantive reasons for preferring one line to another as constituting a satisfactory synthesis into a coherent legal doctrine. Sometimes identification of such problems can be used as a ground for judicial overruling of unsatisfactory precedents. A case in point is *Murphy* v. *Brentwood District Council* (1990) 2 All ER, reversing earlier decisions on 'economic loss' arising from faulty exercise of public powers by a local authority. It can therefore be said that review of synthesizing and of conflicting lines of authority is a feature of the UK systems in the senses indicated; but allusion to merely repetitive or confirmatory precedents is of little importance.

6 The Concept of a 'Leading Case'

There are doctrines of the kind discussed above which have come to be associated with particular decisions. The 'rule in *Rylands* v. *Fletcher'* is a complex body of law concerning strict civil liability for damage caused by escape of things from one person's property into another's, as when an artificially constructed reservoir bursts and causes a flood. The doctrine is evolved through a concordant line of authorities, but is always referred back to the leading case as its original source. More recent examples in the law of intellectual property are provided by so-called *Mareva* and *Anton Piller* injunctions, the names deriving from the leading cases from which the doctrine developed. One can also mention the doctrine in judicial review of 'Wednesbury unreasonableness' which relates back to the *Wednesbury Corporation* case.

However, 'leading cases' as such have really no special authority as precedents; they are features of the doctrinal evolution of law as much as of the doctrine of precedent itself.

V Distinguishing, Explaining, Modifying, Overruling

1 Distinguishing

Distinguishing ostensibly binding and applicable precedents is a most important feature of reasoning with precedent. In *Derry* v. *Peek* (1889) 14 App. Cas. 337, the directors of a company produced a prospectus which contained a material falsehood committed through negligence rather than wilful deceit. Investors who lost money after investing in the company sued the directors on the ground of 'equitable fraud'. Their case was rejected on the ground that there could be no fraud without intention to deceive, and no liability for loss arising from a false statement made without dishonesty and intent to deceive. Subsequently, some lawyers and judges argued that this case was distinguishable on the ground that it only really decided that fraud requires intent to deceive, without any necessary ruling on the question whether the independent tort of negligence extended to cover negligent words (see, for example, *Candler* v. *Crane Christmas* [1951] 2 K.B. 164). In cases involving financial loss, this distinction was denied (at least up to 1964), but where physical injury resulted from careless advice given, for example by an architect on a building site, the *Derry* ruling was clearly distinguishable, and was distinguished.

Liability was held to exist in favour of the injured party in such a case. Such examples can be multiplied endlessly. They illustrate an important rule of practice in the UK systems, whereby counsel are expected to cite all relevant authorities, even those apparently adverse to their client's case. In the case of the apparently unfavourable authorities, the issue is whether they can be successfully distinguished.

2   Juristic Commentary

The scholarly and juristic discussion of the difference between cases is an important part of UK practice. It is to be found particularly in the learned journals where articles and 'case notes' deal with this.

3   Excessive Distinguishing?

The case of *Steel* v. *Glasgow Iron and Steel Co* was discussed above (Section IV.4). There the salvor of property was held entitled to damages against the party who had negligently endangered it. In reaching this decision, the Court of Session confronted a precedent of its own. In this precedent a storekeeper had been injured trying to put out a fire in his store caused by mistaken delivery to him of drums of naphtha instead of the paraffin he had ordered. Despite the negligence of the shipping company, he was denied any right to damages for his injuries. Counsel for Steel suggested an explanation of the decision in the precedent (*MacDonald* v. *David MacBrayne*), namely that it was a case in which the salvor had himself acted unreasonably. The court agreed that it was 'a decision on its own special facts', thereby explaining and distinguishing it. It did this despite the fact that the earlier court had in no way spelled out any such special factor as that mentioned, and appears to have decided simply on the footing that a salvor has no remedy.

Wherever precedents are strictly binding, there is strong reason occasionally to resort to the practice of the rather far-fetched 'explanation' of the true doctrine of a case in order effectively to distinguish it. One can certainly see this practice in the scholarly and juristic commentaries.

4   Types of Overruling

There is no problem with overruling in the UK because of the system of *stare decisis*. A superior court with the power to overrule can do so and does explicitly. The *ratio* of the overruled case then ceases to have any authority. This form of explicit overruling is also practised by the House of Lords, and other courts which have the same power, to overrule their own decisions.

One can also see implicit overruling in the UK system. LORD GODDARD said, in *R* v. *Porter* [1949] 2 K.B. 128 at 132:

> When you find that a case, whether it has been expressly overruled or not by the final court of appeal, has been dealt with, or the facts, which were the governing facts in a particular case, have been regarded in a totally different manner by the final court of appeal, so that it is obvious in the opinion of a final court of appeal that the cause was wrongly decided, then whether they have in terms said they overrule the case or not, I think this court ought to treat the case as overruled.

Precedents which have force only are not explicitly overruled but would be taken account of.

One can see precedents whittled away to virtually nothing. In *Hillyer* v. *St. Bartholomew's Hospital* [1909] 2 K.B. 220, H was examined in the hospital by a doctor of his own choosing who did not have a contract of service with the hospital. While under anaesthetic with nurses and porters in attendance, he was severely burned. He failed in an action of damages. One judge held this on the broad ground that the hospital only had a duty to take reasonable care in the selection of nurses and porters and there was no evidence to show that that had been broken. Other judges concurred on the narrow grounds that (a) in the operating theatre, the nurses and porters were servants of the doctor and not the hospital and that (b) even if they were servants of the hospital it was not clear whether they or the doctor were negligent and the doctor was certainly not a servant of the hospital. In subsequent cases, the grounds for the decision were whittled away until in *Cassidy* v. *Minister of Health* [1951] 2 K.B. 343 LORD DENNING said: 'The result is that *Hillyer's* case can now only be supported on the narrow grounds on which FARWELL LJ explained it in *Smith* v. *Martin*, that the hospital authorities were not liable for the negligence of the consulting surgeon because he was not employed by them and no case of negligence had been proved against the nurses and carriers' (p.362). The implication of this is that *Hillyer* binds only in cases where facts are in all material respects the same.

It is now the practice of the House of Lords, as for a considerable time it has been a practice of the Inner House of the Court of Session, to convene a larger than normal panel of judges when the issue of overruling, or 'departing from', a precedent of the House is under consideration. There is a good practical reason for this, that it obviates the risk of one temporary majority of a part of the House overruling and then later being overruled by a temporary majority of a different part or division; the whole court forms a view, and this is the more firmly respected for the future.

5   Prospective Overruling

The before-mentioned case of *Derry* v. *Peek* was effectively departed from in the House of Lords in the 1964 case of *Hedley Byrne and Co* v. *Heller and Partners*. In that case, negligent misstatements were made by a bank to an advertising agency about the creditworthiness of an advertiser. When the advertising agency lost a large sum through the insolvency of the advertiser, it sued the bank. It was held that there was a non-contractual duty of care owed by the bank to the advertising agency. But, since the bank had issued its advice together with an explicit disclaimer of liability, it was in this case not liable for the consequences of its negligence. The advertising agency had relied on the advice given notwithstanding its full awareness of the disclaimer of liability.

Clearly, this decision effectively departs from *Derry's* case as discussed earlier. If there cannot be non-contractual liability for financial loss occasioned by careless statements, there is no need for any disclaimer, there being no possible liability to disclaim. Nevertheless, the actual effect of the decision is not to land the bankers with a liability they might have felt protected from by the rule in *Derry* as interpreted in a subsequent line of cases.

This draws attention to one of the objections of principle to a power of departure from precedent, and to most instances of its use, namely, the undermining of reasonable expectations that precedent will be followed. If it is possible in one case to indicate that in later cases a criticized precedent will be departed from, while not upsetting the present expectations of those at present relying on precedent, the objection is elided. That, in short, is the case for a practice of 'prospective overruling'. Yet many would hold that this practice smacks very noticeably of naked judicial legislation, and despite interesting arguments by R.H.S. Tur and others, the practice has not been formally adopted in the UK. *Hedley Byrne* perhaps shows that judges may be more willing to use the power of overruling when it can be used in a manner that has effects similar to, though a form different from, that of express 'prospective overruling'.

6   Anticipatory Overruling by Lower Courts

Lord Denning, Master of the Rolls and hence president of the Court of Appeal in England and Wales from the 1960s until the early 1980s, used his position in the Court of Appeal effectively to experiment with what amounted to 'anticipatory overruling'. But the practice was disapproved, and has not come to be accepted. Instead, in England and Wales, there is a practice in certain cases of 'leapfrogging' appeals, directly from the High Court to the House of Lords, where the whole outcome of the case depends on an overruling of precedent at either Court of Appeal or indeed House of Lords level.

7 Precedent and Legislative Practice

Legislation in the UK is usually drafted on a basis of careful attention to existing law, case law as much as statute law. Moreover, legislation is sometimes introduced and enacted expressly to reverse the effect of a precedent. The Directors' Liability Act of 1890 was passed to ensure that Directors of a Company could be held liable for false statements in the company's prospectus even when made non-fraudulently. But this was held to have no effect on the binding force of the precedent for purposes other than the special ones of company directors holding office under the Companies Acts. Except where, as in Scotland from time to time, the maxim *cessante ratione legis cessat lex ipsa* has been applied to deprive of effect precedents overtaken by legal change through reforming legislation (see, for example, *Beith's Trustees* v. *Beith* [1950] SC 66), precedents repealed as to the narrow rule may survive as respected statements of general common law principle.

8 Conflicts of Precedents

The orthodox approach to conflicting binding precedents is summed up by LORD SELBOURNE: 'It is your Lordships' duty to maintain as far as you possibly can the authority of all former decisions of this House, and although later decisions may have interpreted and limited the application of earlier, they ought not (without some unavoidable necessity) to be treated as conflicting' (*Caledonian Railway* v. *Walker's Trustees* (1882) 7 App. Cas. 259 at 275). The courts are now much more willing to recognize that precedents can conflict and will overrule (see Section V.6 above) where necessary and where they are able. What is a conflict is not an easy question and will still produce difficulties, for the ordinary way of reasoning in the system operates to deny the conflict through the process of distinguishing, constructing the *ratio* and so on.

9 Hypothetical Cases

The business of distinguishing between cases goes beyond simple comparisons of present argument with past decision. A noticeable feature of forensic argument in the UK is the use of the hypothetical example. The Scottish case of *White and Carter (Councils) Ltd* v. *McGregor* [1961] 3 All ER 1178 concerned an advertising agency, W, which had agreed a deal with a garage proprietor, M, to advertise the latter's business through publicly displayed notices. Very shortly after agreement was reached, M changed his mind and 'cancelled' the contract. W rejected this anticipatory breach of the contract, went ahead to display the advertisements as agreed, and sued for the whole contract price. M argued that W's only legitimate remedy was for damages for loss of profit on the deal as agreed. As LORD REID said in his opinion:

> An example was developed in argument. A company might engage an expert to go abroad and prepare an elaborate report and then repudiate the contract before anything was done. To allow such an expert then to waste thousands of pounds in preparing the report cannot be right if a much smaller sum of damages would give him full compensation for his loss. It would merely enable the expert to extort a settlement giving him far more than reasonable compensation.

But, holding against M, he distinguished the hypothetical example: 'It might be that the company could show that the expert had no legitimate interest in carrying out the work rather than accepting damages... . But that is not this case. Here [M] did not set out to prove that [W] had no legitimate interest in completing the contract and claiming the contract price.'

One illustration may again stand for many, many instances of a common form of argument. The 'expert' example was here adduced by counsel for M with a view to reducing to absurdity the proposition advanced for W that the innocent party in a case of contractual breach by repudiation is always entitled to carry on and complete his or her side of the contract regardless of the expressed wishes of the other party (see also *MacLennan* v. *MacLennan* (1958) SC 105 above, where the judges decided that AID without the husband's consent was not adultery partly because to hold it so would make adultery possible by a dead man). Again, this can be taken to be an example of an extreme or limiting hypothetical case, testing the proposition formulated by W. But what enabled LORD REID to distinguish it was exactly its extreme character, insofar as it was postulated as a case where there would be no legitimate interest of the innocent party in carrying out the contract.

In relation to developing paradigm cases of the applicability of a precedent, or for the purposes of testing limits to a precedent already established, both scholarly writers and judges will on occasion resort in a similar way to hypothetical examples.

VI Matters of General Perspective, Evaluation and Other

1 'Saying and Doing'

Judges in all courts in the United Kingdom except the House of Lords accept that they are bound by precedents set by higher courts and that the Court of Appeal is defeasibly bound by its own precedents (as is the House by its). To decide whether there is a gap between what is said and what is done it would be necessary to assess the degree to which courts fail to follow precedent by making inappropriate use of the many devices by which departures from what appear to be relevant precedents can be justified. To carry out such an assessment scientifically would be an impossible project. All reasoning from case to case is by analogy and selection of what are held to be relevant features of different fact situations. There is no easily available objective measure of plausibility that could be used to assess the number of occasions on which courts resort unjustifiably to the practice of distinguishing one case from another in order to avoid the necessity of following precedent. (See the examples of distinguishing, explaining and modifying cases given in Section V, above.) It seems quite likely that on some occasions a court, faced by what seems an unjust outcome if precedent is followed, may seek to avoid that result by distinguishing the case in issue from a previously decided and prima facie binding case. This may be done by picking out factual circumstances which differ between one case and the other; or it may be done by treating *rationes decidendi* as mere *obiter dicta*; or by stating the question of law that is in issue differently from the way in which it was formulated in the earlier case.

A simple example of factual and legal distinguishing may be seen in successive cases applying the rule set out in the Forfeiture Act 1982 to prevent financial gain accruing from inheritance by persons committing criminal acts. In *Re H* (Dec'd) (1990 1 FLR 441), P, who was severely depressed and on anti-depressant drugs, killed his wife and, as the sole beneficiary under his wife's will, was held entitled to inherit despite the forfeiture rule. But in *Jones v. Roberts* (1994 CLY 95) it was held that the forfeiture rule should apply to a potential beneficiary who had battered both his parents to death when he was suffering from paranoid schizophrenia and believed them to be KGB agents instructed to kill him. It might seem that the facts of each case were similar but it was held in *Jones v. Roberts* that *Re H.* was distinguishable. The forfeiture rule had been held to apply where there was deliberate, intentional and unlawful violence. The earlier case was explained as having been decided on the basis that the killer bore no responsibility at all for his crime, whereas in *Jones v. Roberts* there was diminished responsibility but nevertheless a deliberate act.

Comparison and distinction of relevant circumstances are the normal content of common law decisions and may lead to the legitimate avoidance of distinguishable precedents (as may have happened in the instance just cited). On the one hand, it would be impossible to deny that there are cases in which precedents are in some degree manipulated and their binding force loosened by distinctions that are less than compelling. On the other hand, many examples could be cited in which courts accept the fetters of precedent and concur with evident reluctance in the conclusion that earlier decisions cannot be displaced or differentiated. In *Williams* v. *Guest, Keen and Nettlefold* [1926] 1 K.B. 497 at 504, it was said that 'the appeal should be dismissed ... solely because I consider that this court is bound by the decision in *Steel* v. *Cammell Laird & Co.* which it is impossible to distinguish from the facts of this particular case' (*per* ATKIN LJ). It seems plausible also to assume that the constraining force of precedent is genuinely accepted in those cases in which the House of Lords, despite its power to overturn its own decisions, holds itself, nevertheless, not free to do so merely on the ground that an earlier decision is felt to be wrong. An example is the decision in *R.* v. *Knuller (Publishing, Printing and Promotions Ltd.)* [1973] A.C. 453. That case perhaps illustrates the fact that one feature of the British legal system (as against the American) that militates against a felt need to resort to the manipulation of precedents is the consciousness of potential remedial legislative action. It is of some importance that the judiciary is operating in a parliamentary system in which the legislature is recognized as the most legitimate agent of legal change. That is implied in LORD REID's remark in the *Knuller* case that, 'however wrong or anomalous the decision may be, it must stand and apply to future cases unless or until it is altered by parliament'. In recent years that clear conviction seems, however, to have declined and it is doubtful whether so high a degree of deference is felt by a majority of the present members of the House of Lords.

2   Recent Change or Evolution

Change or evolution in the use of precedent may be considered under two headings: (a) changes in the formal practice or procedure of the courts in relation to the application of precedent, and (b) changes in the willingness of the higher courts to develop the law by taking a liberal or expansive view of the judicial function and of the role of the courts as promoters of legal change despite the theoretical primacy of the legislature.

The main procedural evolution in the application of precedent in recent years has been the decision of the House of Lords to change the practice by which it regarded itself as bound by its own decisions (see Section II.1 above). There has been some difference of opinion as to the nature of the Practice Statement of 1966. When the House of Lords issued its statement, one of their lordships (Lord Simon of Glaisdale) referred to it as a constitutional convention having the force of law [1968] 2 Q.B. 118 at 135–6. However, this cannot be right since conventions have always been defined as rules that do not have the force of law. Some were also puzzled about the source of the validity of the new rule. One suggestion was that the Practice Statement owed its validity to the inherent power of any court to regulate its own procedure (Cross, 1977). That suggestion also presents some difficulties. If all courts had such a power, there would seem equally good grounds for the Court of Appeal to claim to regulate its own procedure. It might thus escape from its obligation to follow its own precedents so as to be able to decide what the exceptions to that practice should be. But the duties of the Court of Appeal in relation to precedent are matters of law and have been laid down by the House of Lords. It would seem that the House of Lords' own announcements that it is or is not bound by its own decisions are not conventions but special rules of common law and that the House's authority to make such statements is derived from the rules of recognition or the basic norms of the legal system, which are equally special and idiosyncratic rules of constitutional law.

Since the change of practice in the House of Lords, some efforts have been made by the Court of Appeal to assert its own freedom to depart from earlier precedents or to create additional exceptions to the cases in which departure is permitted under the rule in *Young* v. *Bristol Aeroplane Co.* (see *Davis* v. *Johnson* [1979] A.C. 264). But the House of Lords has held that, apart from the existing exceptions, the Court of Appeal remains bound to follow its own previous decisions. An attempt inspired by LORD DENNING (when in the Court of Appeal) to treat a decision of the House of Lords as having been made *per incuriam* was equally rejected and rebuked. In *Cassel & Co. Ltd.* v. *Broome* [1975] A.C. 1027, LORD HAILSHAM remarked, 'I hope that it will never be necessary to say ... again that in the hierarchical system of courts that exists in this country it is necessary for each lower tier, including the Court of Appeal, to accept loyally the decisions of the higher tiers' (at p.1054) (see Rickett, 1980; Aldridge, 1984).

Since the decision in *Pepper* v. *Hart* [1993] A.C. 593, which for the first time allowed parliamentary materials to be used as an aid to statutory construction (under certain limited conditions), there have been some attempts to use such legislative material to persuade the Court of Appeal not to follow earlier decisions of the House of Lords. In *Re Bishopgate Investment Management Ltd.* [1993] Ch. 452, it was argued that a decision of the House of Lords (*R.* v. *Director of Serious Fraud Office, ex parte Smith*) should not be followed on the ground that the speech of a minister in charge of the bill had shown that *Ex parte Smith* had been decided in ignorance of the intention of parliament and should be treated as having been made *per incuriam*. This attempt was rejected by the Court of Appeal, holding that they were bound by *Ex parte Smith* and that any reconsideration of that case must be made by the House of Lords.

It may be, however, that the licence given by *Pepper* v. *Hart* will persuade courts, including the House of Lords, that their own previous decisions should be reconsidered on the ground that previous statements of parliamentary intention were not cited to them.

It cannot be said that the House of Lords has made any lavish or free-wheeling use of its self-declared freedom to depart from precedent. Nor have the decisions in which precedents have been overruled led to any clear statement of the rationale for such departures (cf. Stone, 1972). The belief that a case has been wrongly decided is not thought to be in itself a sufficient ground for overruling. Some grounds for following the normal procedure of treating previous decisions as binding were mentioned in the Practice Statement. One was the danger of disturbing retrospectively the basis on which contracts, settlements of property and fiscal arrangements have been entered into and another was the special need for certainty as to the criminal law. It has sometimes been said that a typical case for reconsidering a decision is where some broad issue of justice or public policy is involved, but the construction of statutory provisions is not normally such a case. There are also arguments of expediency or public interest. The possibility of reconsideration of questions turning upon the interpretation of statutes might well, it has been said, encouraged frequent litigants, such as government departments or the commissioners of the Inland Revenue, to attempt to reopen arguments concluded against them (*Jones* v. *Secretary of State for Social Services* [1972] 1 A.C. 944).

Perhaps a greater measure of flexibility has been seen in public as compared with private law. Though in English law there is no doctrine of obsolescence, some areas of public law are characterized by changes in circumstances or tides in public opinion which may lead judges to espouse a degree of creativity in adapting or overruling precedents stemming from earlier times. On the question of marital rape, for example, there has clearly been a willingness simply to disregard earlier precedents as outdated and inappropriate to the present state of public sentiment (*R.* v. *R.* [1991] 4 A11 ER 481). Rejection of earlier precedents and conscious use of judicial law making is easier where there is a discernible public consensus. By contrast, in *Airedale NHS Trust* v. *Bland* [1993] 1 A11 ER 821 at 879, it was said by LORD BROWNE-WILKINSON that, 'where a case raises wholly new moral and social issues ... it is not for the judges to seek to develop new all-embracing principles of law in a way which reflects the individual judge's moral stance when society as a whole is substantially divided on the relevant moral issues'.

On the other hand, in constitutional and administrative law, there is a less divided moral consensus and on the major technical issues a more quiescent public opinion. Since the 1960s, changes in the personnel of the House of Lords and the initiatives of particular judges such as Lords Reid and Diplock have seen the overturning of many rules of law that appeared to be firmly based on precedents established in the 1930s, 1940s and 1950s. (See Paterson, 1982; Blom-Cooper and Drewry, 1972). Earlier decisions on governmental privileges in litigation, on the extent of the prerogatives of the Crown and on the availability of judicial review to quash discretionary decisions of ministers and civil servants have been overturned, distinguished or disregarded on a considerable scale.

3   Changes in International Environment

When the House of Lords relaxed its attitude to precedent it was said that the change would allow more attention to be paid to judicial decisions reached in the superior courts of the Commonwealth where they differ from earlier decisions of the House of Lords. It is noticeable that in recent years there has been a marked increase in the practice of citing decisions taken in Commonwealth courts and also – particularly in constitutional and civil liberty issues – decisions of the Supreme Court of the United States. In *Derbyshire County Council* v. *Times Newspapers Ltd.* [1993] 1 A11 ER 1011, reference was made to the decision in *New York Times v. Sullivan*, 376 U.S. 254 (1964) and to a Privy Council decision on the constitution of Antigua and Barbuda [1990] 2 A.C. 312 by way of illustrating the value of free speech considerations in defamation proceedings brought by governmental bodies. Recourse to such cases often enables new considerations to be injected into old precedents, so as to show them in a new light. Here the American distinction between private and public persons for defamation purposes stimulated the House of Lords to decide that a publicly elected body, which had previously been held capable of suing in defamation, should be placed in a different category from a private company. Similarly, although the European Declaration on Human Rights is not directly applicable in UK courts, frequent reference is now made to its provisions as a way of persuading a court either to resolve a statutory ambiguity in a way favourable to individual rights or as part of an argument that the common law already encompasses public policies that resemble those set out in the convention. In this way, new and previously unsuspected public policies have been discovered in or injected into the common law.

The effect of the imposition on UK law of the law of the European Community is harder to estimate. The duty to seek and apply a ruling of the European Court might in theory compel a UK court not to follow a decision of the House of Lords. The House of Lords now accepts a duty to apply decisions of the European Court even if they involve overturning its own well-established precedents and has, in one respect, changed a fundamental common law doctrine as the result of Community membership, since the manner in which it now applies Community law involves abandoning the firmly established doctrine that statutes inconsistent with earlier enactments implicitly repeal anything in the earlier statute that is inconsistent. That principle appears to have been abandoned where UK statutes passed since the European Communities Act of 1972 are inconsistent with European Community law that is directly applicable to the UK.

4   *Juristic or Other Criticism*

In 1930, Sir Arthur Goodhart in a comparison of case law in England and America (Goodhart, 1931) could observe, with some complacency, that there was no dissatisfaction with the working of precedent in England. 'The negative evidence,' he wrote, 'is overwhelming. A search through the English periodicals since 1900 does not show a single article or note by an English lawyer in which the system has been adversely criticised' (p.56).

Some 30 years later, Lord Denning in the Romanes Lecture, *From Precedent to Precedent* (1959), took a less sanguine view. The doctrine of precedent, he said, had in the past been hostile to liberty: 'To stand by precedents, however wrong they may be … does nothing to broaden the basis of freedom rather than to narrow it'. It might indeed be thought that, if *stare decisis* is defined as holding to decisions however wrong, the conclusion is plausible. If, on the other hand, the question is whether a judicial process unencumbered by precedent is likely to promote or hinder freedom, the question is less simple. A willingness to create new precedents may work in favour of government and against individual liberties, just as standing by precedent may fend off novel incursions against the rights of individuals.

In 1959, the burden of Lord Denning's plea was for the House of Lords to abandon its subjection to its own precedents and to accept responsibility for developing the law and acting as the fountain of justice. In some degree that responsibility has now been accepted, though it has operated unevenly in different fields and without the support of any clearly articulated judicial rationale. British judges remain cautious and reluctant shamelessly to assume the law makers' mantle. In 1995, LORD LOWRY advanced 'some tentative aids to navigation across an uncertainly chartered sea'. (*C. (a Minor)* v. *Director of Public Prosecutions, The Times,* 17 March 1995). Four suggested principles were the following:

1 Caution should prevail if parliament had rejected opportunities of clearing up a known difficulty or had legislated while leaving the difficulty untouched.
2 Disputed matters of social policy were less suitable areas for judicial intervention than purely legal areas.
3 Fundamental legal doctrines should not be lightly set aside.
4 Judges should not make a change unless they could achieve finality and certainty.

Academic writing about precedent and judicial method has tended to be analytical rather than subversive. A more philosophical turn in the character of British jurisprudence has brought a better understanding of the nature of legal rules and legal reasoning (see, for example, MacCormick, 1978; Twining and Miers, 1991; Goldstein, 1991; Schauer, 1991; Bell, 1983). One result has been to display the flexibility embodied in the combination of rules and principles that are involved in the application of precedent. Thus it is hardly necessary to unleash attacks on the supposedly unyielding citadel of precedent or to seek to undermine the superstitious worship of legal rules. In addition, the judges themselves proclaim their freedom from the delusion that the law is an Aladdin's Cave in which precedents and rules of law lie ready to be discovered (Lord Reid, 1972). But if we are all – up to a point – realists about precedent, there remains a variety of reasons to do with tradition, stability, predictability and deference to parliamentary authority that are probably sufficient to preserve the relative rigidity and formality within the common law world of the British model of precedent.

References

Aldridge, T. 'Precedent in the Court of Appeal: Another View', *M.L.R.*, 47, p.187 (1984).
Atiyah, P.S. 'Judges and Policy', *Israel Law Review*, 15, p. 346 (1980).
Atiyah, P.S. and Summers, R.S. (1987), *Form and Substance in Anglo-American Law*, Oxford: Clarendon Press; New York: Oxford University Press.
Bankowski, Z. (1991), 'Analogical Reasoning and Legal Institutions', in P. Nerhot (ed.), *Legal Knowledge and Analogy*, Dordrecht: Kluwer Academic Publishers, pp.198–216.
Bell, J. (1983), *Policy Arguments in Judicial Decisions*, Oxford: Clarendon Press/New York: Oxford University Press.
Blom-Cooper, L. and Drewry, G. (1972), *Final Appeal: A Study of the House of Lords in its Judicial Capacity*, Oxford: Clarendon Press.

Cross, R. (1977), 'The House of Lords and the Rules of Precedent' in Hacker, P.M.S. and Raz, J. (eds.), *Law, Morality and Society: Essays in Honour of H.L.A. Hart*, Oxford: Clarendon Press.

Cross, R. (1991), *Precedent in English Law*, 4th edn, by R. Cross and J.W. Harris, Oxford: Clarendon Press.

Denning, Lord (1959), *From Precedent to Precedent* (Romanes Lecture), Oxford: Clarendon Press.

Detmold, M.J. (1984), *The Unity of Law and Morality*, London: Routledge & Kegan Paul.

Devlin, P. (1979), *The Judge*, Oxford/New York: Oxford University Press.

Dworkin, R. (1978), *Taking Rights Seriously*, London: Duckworth/Cambridge MA: Harvard University Press.

Dworkin, R. (1986), *Law's Empire*, London: Fontana Books/Cambridge MA: Harvard University Press.

Finnis, J. 'On "The Critical Legal Studies Movement"', *American Journal of Jurisprudence*, 30, pp.21–42 at 23–5 (1985).

Freeman, M. 'Standards of Adjudication, Judicial Law Making and Prospective Overruling', *Current Legal Problems*, 26, p.166 (1973).

Goldstein, L. (1991), *Precedent in Law*, Oxford: Clarendon Press.

Goodhart, A.L. (1931), *Essays in Jurisprudence and the Common Law*, Cambridge: Cambridge University Press.

Goodhart, A.L., 'Precedent in English and Continental Law', *L.Q.R.*, 50, p.40 (1934).

Hayek, F.A. (1982), *Law, Legislation, and Liberty*, vol. 1 'Rules and Order', London: Routledge & Kegan Paul.

Jackson, B.S. (1988), *Law, Fact, and Narrative Coherence*, Roby: Deborah Charles.

Lester, A. 'English Judges as Lawmakers', *Public Law*, 38, p.269 (1993).

MacCormick, N. (1978), *Legal Reasoning and Legal Theory*, Oxford: Clarendon Press.

MacCormick, N. (1984), 'Coherence in Legal Justification' in W. Krawietz *et al.* (eds), *Theorie der Normen*, Berlin: Duncker & Humblot, pp.37–54.

Maher, G. and Smith, T.B. (1987), 'Judicial Precedent' in T.B. Smith *et al.* (eds), *The Laws of Scotland: Stair Memorial Enyclopaedia*, Edinburgh: The Law Society of Scotland/Butterworth, Vol. 22.

Paterson, A. (1982), *The Law Lords*, London: Macmillan Press.

Reid, Lord, 'The Judge as Law Maker', *J.S.P.T.L.*, 12, p.22 (1972).

Rickett, C.E.F., 'Precedent in the Court of Appeal', *M.L.R.*, 43, p.136 (1980).

Schauer, F. (1991), *Playing by the Rules*, Oxford: Clarendon Press.

Simpson, A.W.B. (1961), 'The *Ratio Decidendi* of a Case and the Doctrine of Binding Precedent' in A.G. Guest (ed.), *Oxford Essays in Jurisprudence*, Oxford: Clarendon Press.

Smith, T.B. (1952), *The Doctrines of Judicial Precedent in Scots Law*, Edinburgh: W. Green & Son.

Stone, J. 'On the Liberation of Appellant Judges: How Not to Do It', *M.L.R.*, 35, p.449 (1972).

Tur, R. 'Varieties of Overruling and Judicial Law-Making: Prospective Overruling in a Comparative Perspective', *Juridical Review*, pp. 37–44 (1978).

Twining W. and Miers, D.K. (1991), *How to do Things with the Rules* (3rd edn), London: Weidenfeld & Nicolson.

11 Precedent in the United States (New York State)

ROBERT S. SUMMERS, *ITHACA*

Introduction

Stare decisis, the principle that courts are to follow similar previous judicial decisions when deciding legal questions, has been a part of the American legal experience since before the time of the American Revolution in the late eighteenth century. Early American courts relied heavily on precedents derived from English common law, especially in decisions affecting traditional common law areas such as contracts, torts, property, and wills and trusts (Friedman, 1973, p.282). American courts soon extended the principle of *stare decisis* by following precedents interpreting statutes. After the federal and state constitutions were adopted, the federal and state courts began following precedents interpreting constitutions, too.

Contrary to an assumption frequently encountered in certain European countries, the United States does not consist of only two jurisdictions, one federal and one state, with the state jurisdiction consisting of an amalgamation of all the state-made common law created by the courts of all 50 states. Rather, the United States consists of 51 jurisdictions: one federal jurisdiction, to be explained later, and 50 state jurisdictions, each distinct and separate from each of the other 49 as well as distinct and separate from the federal jurisdiction. All of the state jurisdictions have court systems that, by now, have created what is a more or less self-sufficient body of common law. Thus, in most cases when an issue of common law arises within a given state, it can ordinarily be resolved primarily by invoking precedent created by the highest court of that state or by one of the intermediate appellate courts in that state. Of course, issues do sometimes arise which state courts resolve partly by reference to common law created by a sister state court.

Accordingly, this chapter merely treats adherence to precedent in the state court system of one particular American state, New York.

355

Moreover, it is confined mainly to the practice of following precedent in traditional common law fields such as contracts, torts, property, wills and trusts. Generally, precedents interpreting statutes are not treated here, nor are precedents interpreting constitutions. The US Supreme Court and the lower federal courts have little jurisdiction to create common law in traditional common law fields.

There are several reasons to focus on the New York state court system as a representative system of common law precedent. First, as just explained, there is simply no national system of common law precedent in the United States. Rather, each state is a separate legal jurisdiction in matters of common law. Second, in most important respects, the state court systems, as well as the rules, procedures and practices in following precedent in these state systems are quite similar to one another. Third, when states do borrow common law from other states, New York is one of the two or three most influential sources of such borrowed precedent. It may also be noted that the New York state court system is one of the two largest: the system has about 1150 judges, about 12 000 other employees and an annual budget approaching $1 billion (Lyall, 'Cuomo Nominates Judith Kaye to Top New York Judicial Post', *The New York Times*, 23 February 1993, A1).

I Institutional and Systemic

1(a)(b)(c)   Court Hierarchy; Structural and Procedural Aspects; Power to Select Cases

At the top of the New York state court system is the New York Court of Appeals. Below the Court of Appeals is the Supreme Court which is divided into two parts, the Appellate Division of the Supreme Court, which is made up of four geographically delineated intermediate appellate courts, and the Trial Term of the Supreme Court, which is made up of criminal and civil trial courts of general jurisdiction (*Waldo v. Schmidt*, 200 N.Y. 199, 202 (1910): 'There is but one Supreme Court... divided by the Constitution, the statutes and the rules of practice into two distinct parts'); N.Y. Const. art. VI, sec. 1(a): 'The state-wide courts shall consist of the court of appeals, the supreme court including the appellate divisions thereof...'). To reach the Court of Appeals, Supreme Court Trial Term cases must usually go through one of the intermediate appellate courts of the Appellate Division. Thus the hierarchy from top to bottom is Court of Appeals, Supreme Court Appellate Division and, finally, the trial courts of the Supreme Court. There are various other special lower courts. In New York, these include the individual county courts; the surrogate's court, which oversees all matters concerning the disposition of decedent's estates; the family court, exercising jurisdiction over a broad range of both civil and criminal family cases; the court of claims, which hears cases involving claims either by or against the state; and the city, village and town courts. These special lower courts will not be considered here. In this chapter, the intermediate appellate courts will sometimes simply be called the Appellate Division, and the trial courts 'Supreme Courts'.

What will sometimes be called Supreme Courts are, of course, not 'supreme', but are in fact two levels below the highest state court in New York State. (In other states, the words 'Supreme Court' usually mean the highest state court.) In these New York trial courts of general jurisdiction, most major state trials of disputed factual and legal issues take place. (The federal trial courts sitting in New York are treated briefly below.) These state trial courts do not, as such, create precedent binding on courts below; they are generally bound to follow the precedents of the New York state courts above them in the hierarchy; that is, the New York Court of Appeals and the four intermediate appellate courts within the New York 'Appellate Division'.

Immediately above the trial courts of general jurisdiction ('trial term' of the Supreme Court), then, is the Appellate Division, with its four intermediate appellate courts. New York State is geographically divided into four 'judicial departments', and each of these departments has a separate appellate court of the Appellate Division. The First and Second Departments have their own justices and have jurisdiction over the counties comprising and immediately surrounding New York City. The Third and Fourth Departments have their own justices and their jurisdiction extends over the northern and western portions of the state, respectively. Cases appealed to one of the Departments of the Appellate Division may be heard by a panel of justices with as few as three justices and as many as five. The jurisdiction of these intermediate-level courts is primarily appellate, with appeals heard from state courts of original jurisdiction, including the trial courts of general jurisdiction (that is, the Supreme Courts) and the other lower courts. The four intermediate appellate courts in the Appellate Division review questions of both law and fact.

The New York Court of Appeals is the state's highest court. The Court of Appeals is composed of seven judges, including a chief judge and six associate judges, each of whom is appointed for 14-year terms by the state governor, subject to confirmation by the state senate. Under the state constitution, five judges are needed for a quorum and four for a decision (NY Constitution, Art. VI, sec. 2). The New York constitution limits the jurisdiction of the Court of Appeals. It has appellate jurisdiction over both civil and criminal matters but has no original jurisdiction. The Court of Appeals reviews only questions of law decided by courts below, except for two situations in which the court may review facts. The first of these is an appeal from a criminal trial imposing the death penalty. The other is an appeal from an appellate court of the Appellate Division, that is, from one of the four intermediate appellate courts reversing or modifying a judgment, finding new facts, or directing that a final judgment be entered on new facts.

The bases for an appeal to the Appellate Division, that is, one of the four intermediate appellate courts, are very broad and virtually all decisions of the lower courts are appealable to the Appellate Division. Consequently, the state intermediate appellate courts in New York have very little power to select the cases they will decide. Section 5701(a)(1) of New York's McKinney's Civil Practice Law and Rules (CPLR) makes all judgments appealable to the Appellate Division, whether final or interlocutory. Appealability of orders as opposed to judgments is covered by 5701(a)(2) which in its language is quite generous to would-be appellants, making all orders, even intermediate orders without a final judgment, appealable.

Appealability from the four intermediate appellate courts of the Appellate Division to the New York Court of Appeals is more limited than appealability to the Appellate Division from the lower courts, such as the trial courts of general jurisdiction (Supreme Courts). There are two types of appeals to the Court of Appeals: those said to be as a matter 'of right' and those where permission is granted by the Court of Appeals or the relevant Appellate Division Court. Appeals as a matter of right are limited, and may be had in four situations: (a) from a decision where at least two justices dissent in the Appellate Division on a question of law in favour of the appellant; (b) from a final determination directly involving a state or federal constitutional question; (c) from an order of the Appellate Division granting or affirming the granting of a new trial or where the appellant stipulates that judgment absolute shall be rendered against him upon affirmance; and (d) from a final decision of a trial court, administrative agency or arbitrator, or from an order of the Appellate Division finally determining an appeal from such a decision where the Appellate Division has made an order on a prior appeal which necessarily affects the decision (CPLR section 5601(a–d)).

When and how do the Court of Appeals and the intermediate appellate courts of the Appellate Division grant permission for an appeal to be taken to the Court of Appeals? Under CPLR section 5602(a), whenever two judges of either the Appellate Division or the Court of Appeals vote in favour of permitting the appeal to advance to the New York Court of Appeals, the case will be heard by the Court of Appeals. An appellant may obtain permission to appeal in three ways: successful application to the Appellate Division, application to the Court of Appeals after unsuccessful application to the

Appellate Division, or direct application to the Court of Appeals (CPLR section 5602(a)(amended 1986)).

Separate and distinct from the state court system in New York just described is the federal court system. In each of the American states, there are federal as well as state courts. In New York, there are four federal trial courts of general jurisdiction. These are called Federal District Courts. Appeals are taken from these courts to the federal intermediate appellate court, which sits in New York City. This court is called the Court of Appeals for the Second Circuit. (This court also hears appeals from federal district courts of several other states besides New York, and it sits in these states as well.) In general, if the amount in controversy is greater than $50 000 and the parties involved are residents of different states (so-called 'diversity' cases), or the issue in the case involves a federal statute or the federal constitution, the federal court system has jurisdiction (U.S. Const. Art. III; 28 U.S.C. section 1332(a)). (The state courts often also usually have concurrent jurisdiction.)

The state court system and the federal court system in New York and elsewhere are essentially separate from one another. State courts generally follow the federal court of appeals cases interpreting federal statutes but less so cases interpreting the federal constitution. Conversely, federal courts defer to state court precedents under state common law, state statutes and under the state constitution. One impetus for the practice whereby federal courts follow state precedent springs from the 'Erie Doctrine', (*Erie R.R. Co. v. Tompkins*, 304 U.S. 64 (1938)). Under *Erie*, where state rather than federal law is applicable, a federal court in a particular state is generally charged with deciding cases just as the highest court in that state has or would decide them. As a result, much state court precedent is followed in the federal courts. (Similarly, with issues arising under federal law, state courts exercising concurrent jurisdiction are charged with deciding them as the federal courts have or would have decided them.)

In 1995, the New York Court of Appeals decided 340 cases. The four intermediate appellate courts of the New York Appellate Division together disposed of 18 831 appeals. Oral argument of counsel was heard in 5682 of these cases. Sometimes the judges of the Appellate Division sit in panels, and at other times they sit as one full court. The Court of Appeals usually sits as one full court. Except for 'memorandum' and '*per curiam*' opinions, the votes of individual judges are made public and are named in the opinions.

2   Structure, Content and Style of Judgments

Decisions of trial and appellate courts within the states are normally presented in the form of opinions or orders. These opinions and orders contain some common features and elements. A description of a typical New York appellate court opinion follows.

A typical decision in a full opinion rather than a memorandum or *per curiam* opinion will begin with the majority opinion, followed by a dissent if there is one. If the decision is unanimous, there will be a single opinion, unless there are separate concurring opinions. Concurring opinions follow after the majority opinion, and dissenting opinions follow after these. In a majority or unanimous opinion, the court will usually start by setting forth the facts and the prior decisions of the trial or intermediate appellate courts below. The court will then list or recite the issue or issues raised on appeal, noting any nuances or unusual elements in the facts that might make the resolution of the case particularly problematic. Thus, even at the appellate level, where the court is usually concerned solely with deciding issues of law, there will often be a fairly lengthy recital of the facts of the case.

After the facts are recited, the court will discuss the issue or issues raised on appeal. Opinions at the appellate level seldom contain a detailed statement of the various arguments of counsel, although a court will often directly or indirectly refer to one or more of these arguments in its opinion. In particular, the court will frequently refer to one or more precedents relied on by counsel in support of their respective arguments and will state whether or not the precedents are being followed or whether they are distinguishable from the case under consideration. Closely intertwined with the court's discussion of precedent will be the court's rationales or reasons for its ruling. A court might simply cite an applicable precedent, or line of precedents, and proceed without a discussion of specific reasons why the court thinks the precedent or line of precedents applies, or it may explain in detail why the precedent (or line of precedents) applies. In many cases where a decision is accompanied by an elaborate rationale, the court will be seeking either to modify, distinguish or overrule a prior precedent. In such cases, the court will often also give substantive reasons for decision.

In deciding the case, the court may address each issue raised on appeal, but the resolution of one issue will often enable the court to avoid resolving other issues. For example, if three issues are raised on appeal and the resolution of one of the issues is sufficient to resolve the entire dispute, courts often decline to engage in the academic exercise of resolving the remaining issues. See, for example, *Assets Realization Co. v. Howard*, 211 N.Y. 430 (1914); *Woodruff v. People*, 193 N.Y. 560 (1908).

At the end of the opinion, the court will normally issue a statement of its final decision. This often consists of one sentence concisely stating the court's overall ruling on the issues under consideration, but it may also be in the form of a directive that the judgment or order of the lower court be affirmed or reversed, or the matter remanded to the lower court for further consideration 'not inconsistent with this opinion'.

The length of opinions in common law cases varies according to a number of factors. Some opinions are quite lengthy – 50 printed pages or more. Among the factors which may tend to make an opinion more extended or elaborate are (1) the complexity of the facts of the case, (2) the number of issues brought on appeal, (3) whether the precedents to be applied are well settled or are conflicting, and (4) the importance of any issues of public policy involved.

In addition to the majority opinion of the court, which is the main portion of the decision that may become binding precedent, individual judges are free to draft concurring and dissenting opinions. While these are usually of little practical consequence to the parties in the case under consideration, they occasionally later lead to the overruling or modification of the very precedent announced in the majority opinion.

The prevailing style of higher state court opinions in the United States is discursive rather than deductive and subsumptive. The opinions set forth issues, resolve the issues and provide justification by citing and often discussing precedent. Most opinions tend to assume that only one right answer exists. Further, the style is often as substantive as it is legalistic. That is, the court will often give substantive reasons of policy or principle, as well as cite binding precedent (Summers, 1978, p.707). Finally, higher court opinions are argumentative and dialogic as opposed to merely magisterial and authoritative; the structure purports to be persuasive and to engage the reader in the court's reasoning process. (For more detailed discussion of these terms, see MacCormick and Summers, 1991, pp.496–501.)

3 Publication of Judgments

Today, there are over four million reported court decisions in the American system (Jacobstein, *et al.*, 1994, p.23). Of course, many of these are not in traditional common law fields. An extensive case-reporting system facilitates the use of precedents by lawyers and judges in the United States. The best known commercial reports are published by the West Publishing Company, founded in 1879 in St. Paul, Minnesota. Prior to 1879, most jurisdictions published 'official reports', but these were released in limited editions. The fact that nineteenth-century American courts regularly relied on precedent created a great demand for authentic reports of decided cases which in turn provided the impetus for companies to publish commercial reporters.

West Publishing Company flourished and soon dominated the commercial reporter field because of the remarkable system it developed to catalogue and index cases, a system which greatly eases the process of legal research. West first created a national system of reports, appropriately named the National Reporter System. This system reports cases from every state in the United States in a standard format. West then introduced a cataloguing system based on two essential features: 'headnotes' and the 'key number system'. West's headnotes summarize cases into select and distinct points of law, and these points are then assigned a key number under which all other cases dealing with the same matter are catalogued (Roalfe, 1957, p.51).

Currently, short of using the computerized databases discussed below, the West National Reporter system is the only means of access to the decisions of many of the state appellate court systems (Cohen, Berring and Olson, 1989, pp.49–51). West's National Reporter system organizes and catalogues the opinions of state appellate courts on the foregoing basis and collects the opinions into regional geographical groups. Thus New York appellate opinions are found in what is called the 'Atlantic Reporter'.

In New York, West also publishes a series of volumes entitled *New York Supplement*, which reports opinions of the New York Court of Appeals, the New York Appellate Division and the New York Supreme Courts, as well as selected opinions of all other New York courts. These volumes utilize the West 'headnote' and 'key number' systems.

New York is unusual in that a second publisher, Lawyer's Cooperative Publishing Company, also produces a series of volumes containing reports of legal decisions. These publications have their own particular key phrase system for facilitating research. They consist of three sets of volumes: *New York Court of Appeals Reports*, *Appellate Division Reports* and *Miscellaneous Reports*. The latter contains selected opinions decided in New York courts other than the Court of Appeals and the Appellate Division.

Unpublished opinions of New York courts are sometimes noted in the reporter volumes, but are only identified by the names of the parties to the case, and the date the case was heard. The opinions themselves are sometimes available on the computerized databases, Westlaw or Lexis, although it is clearly indicated that they are unpublished.

In the last decade, in addition to West's case reporters and the like, the use of computerized assisted legal research such as Westlaw and Lexis have made it even easier to find relevant precedent. Westlaw is a system offered by the West Publishing Company, and Lexis is provided by Mead Data Services. Both services are essentially case databases which provide ready access to an enormous body of case law with but a few keystrokes on a computer. Lawyers can literally have access to hundreds of cases on a particular set of facts or issues of law in a matter of seconds.

Westlaw provides computer access to cases through its already established 'headnote' and 'key number' system, discussed above. Lexis has an equivalent key words and phrases system. Both have general and specific topic databases. The search for applicable precedent can be still further expedited by selecting certain key phrases, words or facts and performing a 'word search'.

4 Contents of Reports

(a) The full case name is at the top of the opinion. The case name consists of the names of the parties involved.

(b) The name of the deciding court is below the name, and is followed by the date that the court rendered the decision.

(c) A brief paragraph provided by a publisher of the opinion comes after the court designation. It describes the disposition of the case. This precedes any headnote(s). The headnote(s) relate to specific legal subjects raised by the opinion, and they are provided by the publisher as part of its research system.

(d) The brief initial paragraph and the headnotes usually refer to some obviously relevant facts. Generally, the opinion itself will provide a much more detailed account of the facts. Some opinions do not recite the facts, but refer instead to the facts as set forth in the prior lower court opinion.

(e) The reports provide the procedural status of the case in the brief initial paragraph, and the opinion itself also contains a procedural statement.

(f) A statement of the legal issue or issues is to be found in the opinion itself. The headnotes indicate the questions addressed by the court.

(g) The opinion contains discussion of interpretational problems. The court also explains why it is affirming or reversing a lower court decision.

(h) The specific holdings or rulings on legal issues are described in the initial brief paragraph provided by the publisher. The opinion itself sets forth the holdings or rulings as part of the analysis of each issue.

(i) The reasons for the holdings or rulings are in the text of the opinion.

(j) The statement of a final decision may be found at the beginning or end of the opinion.

(k)   Concurring opinions follow the majority opinion.
(l)   Dissenting opinions follow the opinion and any concurring opinions.
(m)   Today, the reports do not contain a summary of arguments made by the lawyers (although older reports may). The court's opinion sometimes refers to the arguments, but only as part of the reasoning process, not as a separate section of the opinion.
(n)   Opinions by officials other than judges are not part of the report.
(o)   Juristic commentary on the decision is not included. The headnotes are merely part of the publisher's research system.

5   Meaning of 'Precedent'

In New York, the word 'precedent' is used in a variety of ways, but when used most strictly, precedent means binding decisions of *higher* courts of the same jurisdiction as well as decisions of the *same appellate court*. Courts generally accord such precedent decisive authoritative value, especially in common law areas, such as contract, torts, and property. See Farnsworth, 1983, pp.46–7.

6   Mode of Citation and Discussion

New York appellate judges and many trial court judges explicitly discuss precedents in opinions, often quoting at length from prior decisions and closely analysing the specific reasons for or against applying particular precedents to the facts of the case under consideration. *Waters v. New York City Housing Auth.*, 69 N.Y.2d 225 (1987), provides an example of judicial analysis of the applicability of precedents. In *Waters*, the Court of Appeals had to decide the extent of a landlord's civil liability under the common law of tort for crimes committed on his premises. There were several precedents which could have led to a finding of liability on the facts of the case, but the court did not follow their lead. JUDGE TITONE wrote for the court:

> Although plaintiff has made the necessary allegations of negligent security maintenance, notice of prior criminal intrusion and proximately caused injury, her case differs significantly from those in which the landowner's liability for inadequate security has previously been upheld. Unlike the tenant in *Miller v. State of New York*, [62 N.Y.2d 506,] and the business guest in *Nallan v. Helmsley-Spear, Inc.*, [50 N.Y.2d 507,] plaintiff had no connection whatsoever to the building in which her injuries ultimately occurred. Accordingly, we must look beyond *Nallan* and *Miller* to determine whether [a] landlord's duty should be extended to a person in plaintiff's position. (*Waters*, 69 N.Y.2d at 228.)

Where courts have addressed the issue on a number of prior occasions, the deciding court may cite a whole line of precedents. A court may also discuss precedents which are not in point or do not apply to the case being decided, but which have been cited to the court. Opposing counsel in an appellate case will file written briefs which often include numerous citations and discussions of precedent. Additionally, the appellate courts in New York have their own clerks and staffs who will often independently search for precedents bearing on the issues to be decided. Thus a court's opinion in a common law case may recite a precedent or a series of precedents employed by the court in support of its rationale for deciding the case, and also contrary precedents which are not applied but which the court takes the time to distinguish because they were cited by counsel or found by the court's staff. The case being decided may, in turn, become an important precedent even if it merely refines a prior precedent.

Scholarly treatises explain and synthesize precedents. Such treatises also provide analyses of particular precedents which aid lawyers and courts in arguing and deciding cases. In appellate briefs, lawyers often refer in detail to such treatises as support for their arguments. Lawyers appearing before courts cite and discuss relevant treatises in oral argument. Courts frequently refer to treatises for specific support of their decisions. In common law fields, treatises may have major influence. For example, *Farnsworth on Contracts* and *Prosser and Keeton on Torts* are influential. So is White and Summers, *The Uniform Commercial Code*.

7 Overall Role of Precedent

The relative overall role of precedent in the decision making of courts varies with the type of legal issue the case itself raises, and with the other authoritative materials that are relevant. For example, precedent in the New York courts is the primary source of decisive authority in common law subject areas such as contract, tort and property. In such areas, the New York courts decide many issues in accord with precedent. In other areas, the existence of relevant statutory text requires that the language of the statute in question be the primary point of analytical departure and, of course statute law prevails over any conflicting precedent. (So, too, the constitution prevails over statute and case law.) Also a precedent interpreting a statute becomes a binding interpretation for future cases. When there is no relevant precedent from New York or elsewhere, and no controlling statute, a scholarly treatise may have the most influence on the court. Also, in such cases, the court gives more than usual weight to purely substantive considerations of policy and principle.

8   *Role of Precedent in Different Branches of Law*

In the United States, the role of precedent-based law varies among the different branches of law. Some areas are largely statutory while others, such as contract, tort and property are made up primarily of common law precedents. There is also a vast body of precedents interpreting statutes. For example, the Uniform Commercial Code is a vast body of statute law, with many precedents interpreting it. There is also a vast body of precedents interpreting constitutions. The importance of precedent tends to vary among these different types of law, but it is important in all of them. (See Sections II.2 and II.3(h).)

9   *Precedent and 'Gaps in the Law'*

Sometimes the court will be unable to find any close precedent dealing with the issue at hand. In such cases, the court tends to acknowledge early and forthrightly in the opinion that it can find no applicable precedent and will frequently declare the issue to be one of 'first impression' for the court. Many, if not most, judges will then seek to settle the issue in accord with, as one court put it, 'the fundamental principles of our jurisprudence'. (*In re Leslie's estate*, 92 Misc. 663, 665 (1915).) Such considerations include policy, principle, justice and formal values, such as certainty and consistency. In one novel case, *Albala v. City of New York*, 54 N.Y.2d 269 (1981), the Court of Appeals considered whether an infant could sue for injuries caused by a tort against the mother prior to the infant plaintiff's conception. In holding that such a cause of action did not exist, the court recognized the potential impact of its decision on law and society. After acknowledging that the case presented a 'question of first impression', *Albala*, 54 N.Y.2d at 272, JUDGE WACHTLER concluded:

> While the temptation is always great to provide a form of relief to one who has suffered, it is well established that the law cannot provide a remedy for every injury incurred. In defining the common law, it is this court's duty to consider the consequences of recognizing a novel cause of action and to strike the delicate balance between the competing policy considerations which arise whenever tort liability is sought to be extended beyond traditional bounds. (*Albala*, 54 N.Y.2d at 274–5 (citation omitted))

Similarly, the Court of Appeals, in *Pulka v. Edelman*, 40 N.Y.2d 781 (1976), refused to extend liability in a novel case. The court stressed not only policy but the formal values of certainty and consistency in holding that a parking garage owner owes no duty to pedestrians struck by a car driven out of the garage by a customer of the garage owner:

> If a rule of law were established so that liability would be imposed in an instance such as this, it is difficult to conceive of the bounds to which liability logically would flow. The liability potential would be all but limitless and the outside boundaries of that liability ... would be difficult of definition. ... The burden cast on the operators of these parking establishments in order to discharge their responsibilities in respect to patron-operated vehicles beyond the confines of their properties would be an impractical and unbearable one. (*Pulka*, 40 N.Y.2d at 786)

New York courts, of course, are not unwilling to sustain a claim or cause of action which is 'novel in form or detail but sound in principle', as in *Shor v. Billingsley*, 158 N.Y.S.2d 476 (1957), even though there is no precedent at all:

> While no precedent is cited for such an action, it does not follow that there is no remedy for the wrong, because every form of action when brought for the first time must have been without a precedent to support it. Courts sometimes of necessity abandon their search for precedents and yet sustain a recovery upon legal principles clearly applicable to the new state of facts, although there was no direct precedent for it, because there had never been an occasion to make one. (*Kujek v. Goldman*, 150 N.Y. 176, 178 (1896))

The 1935 Report of the New York Law Revision Commission emphasized that a lack of precedent does not require that courts must necessarily await legislative action, stating: 'The common law does not go on the theory that a case of first impression presents a problem of legislative as opposed to judicial power' (Report of N.Y. Law Revision Commission, 465 (1935)). JUDGE RIPPEY sounded this same theme in *Rozell v. Rozell*, 281 N.Y. 106 (1939):

> It is also urged that the courts should wait until there is legislative sanction for such an action. ... It is not necessarily the function of a court to refuse to declare a rule of conduct until the economic and social order of the day forces its declaration by the State. The genius of the common law lies in its flexibility and in its adaptability to the changing nature of human affairs and in its ability to enunciate rights and to provide remedies for wrongs where previously none had been declared. (*Rozell*, 281 N.Y. at 112 (citation omitted))

However, the courts do generally observe the widely known limitation imposed by the principle, *nulla poena sine lege*. That is, the courts generally refuse to create precedent in a novel case which would extend the reach of a statutory criminal prohibition. This unwillingness is all the greater where the offence is a non-obvious, 'regulatory' type of offence (merely *'malum prohibitum'*):

> purely statutory offenses cannot be established by implication, and ... acts otherwise innocent and lawful do not become crimes, unless there is a clear and positive expression of the legislative intent to make them criminal. The citizen is entitled to an unequivocal warning before conduct on his part, which is not *malum in se*, can be made the occasion of a deprivation of his liberty or property. (*People v. Pestronk*, 157 N.Y.S.2d 492, 495 (1956))

II   The Bindingness of Precedent

In the common questions treated in this research project, it is said that 'we may usefully differentiate bindingness, force, further support and illustrativeness or other value of a precedent as follows:

(1)   *Formal bindingness*: a judgment not respecting a precedent's bindingness is not lawful and so is subject to reversal on appeal. Distinguish (a) formal bindingness not subject to overruling: (i) 'strictly binding' – must be applied in every case, (ii) 'defeasibly binding' – must be applied in every case unless exceptions apply (exceptions may be well defined or not); and (b) formal bindingness (with or without exceptions) that is subject to overruling or modification.

(2)   *Not formally binding but having force*: a judgment not respecting a precedent's force, though lawful, is subject to criticism on this ground, and may be subject to reversal on this ground. Distinguish (a) defeasible force – should be applied unless exceptions come into play (exceptions may or may not be well defined) and (b) outweighable force – should be applied unless countervailing reasons apply.

(3)   *Not formally binding and not having force (As defined in (2) above but providing further support*: a judgment lacking this is still lawful and may still be justified, but not as well justified as it would be if the precedent were invoked, for example, to show that the decision being reached harmonizes with the precedent.

(4)   *Mere illustrativeness or other value*.

1   *Kinds and Degrees of Normative Force*

The precedents generated by appellate courts such as the New York Court of Appeals and the intermediate appellate courts of the Appellate Division are generally considered to be *formally binding* on all courts within the state that are lower in the judicial hierarchy (New York Jurisprudence 2d, 29, § 483 (1983)). The Appellate Division courts, as the intermediate appellate courts below the Court of Appeals, are *formally bound* by the precedents set by the Court of Appeals, but the intermediate appellate courts are not formally bound by the precedents of each other that have not been ruled on by the Court of Appeals. The trial courts of general jurisdiction, that is, the New York 'Supreme Courts' (and other lower courts) are *formally bound* by the precedents of the Court of Appeals and at least by the precedents of the intermediate appellate court sitting in the geographical area in which the lower court sits. Although it may not be firmly settled that trial courts of general and special jurisdiction are *formally bound* by precedents set by intermediate appellate courts in other geographical areas, the cases strongly indicate that such is the case. See, for example, *People v. J.R. Cooperage Co.*, 485 N.Y.S.2d 438(Sup. Ct. 1985) (in absence of appellate ruling from that department, Supreme Court criminal term is formally required by *stare decisis* to follow precedents of another department); *Mountain View Coach Lines, Inc. v. Storms*, 476 N.Y.S.2d 918(App. Div. 2d Dep't 1984) (appellate division is single statewide court divided into departments for convenience, therefore trial courts are formally bound to follow precedents in another department); *Lee v. Consolidated Edison Co. of New York*, 413 N.Y.S.2d 826(App. Term 1978) (decisions of intermediate appellate courts should be followed by all lower courts). But see *Creagh v. Stilwell*, 489 N.Y.S.2d 690 (Civ. Ct. 1985) (refusing to follow *Mountain View*, lower courts only bound by own department). In those few instances where lower courts do not observe the clear precedents of any appellate courts higher in the hierarchy, they run the substantial risk of being reversed on appeal. These lower courts rarely overtly disregard the formally binding precedents of any courts higher in the hierarchy. Instead, they usually try to distinguish a case they do not follow.

To a somewhat lesser but still considerable extent, the New York State Court of Appeals will follow its own precedents. According to the definition of formal bindingness adopted for this comparative research project, the New York Court of Appeals cannot be said to be formally bound by its own decisions on issues of state law because such decisions are not reversible by a higher court. Yet the Court of Appeals accords its own decisions a high degree of respect, though it does sometimes overrule or modify them. See, for example, *People v. Westchester County National Bank*, 231 N.Y. 465 (1921); *Sternlieb v. Normandie National Securities Corp.*, 263 N.Y. 245, 251 (1934) (declining to overturn the common law rule that contracts were voidable if entered into by persons under the age of majority, even while noting that the rule often led to ridiculous results: 'Well, the law is as it is, and the *duty* of this court is to give force and effect to the decisions as we find them' (emphasis supplied).

The four intermediate appellate courts of the Appellate Division generally follow their own precedents as well, though these decisions are subject to overruling by these courts as well as the Court of Appeal. See, for example, *Dufel v. Green*, 603 N.Y.S.2d 624, 625 (App. Div. 3d Dep't 1993) ('Although [*stare decisis*] does not require unyielding adherence to even recent precedent, the mere existence of strong arguments to support a different result is not sufficient, in and of itself, to compel the court to overturn judicial precedent'); *DeAngelis v. Lutheran Medical Center*, 445 N.Y.S.2d 188, 194 (App. Div. 2d Dep't 1981) ('We are aware that courts should not shirk their duty to overturn unsound precedent and should strive to continually develop the common law in accordance with our changing society... Yet the mere potential ability to change the common law is not the same as the desirability of making a particular change').

Only the 'holding' in a precedent opinion can be formally binding. The holding is a ruling on a point of law put in issue by the parties and necessary to the decision. (See Section IV.1.)

Judicial opinions seldom explicitly discuss differences in degrees of normative force (formal bindingness, force, further support and so on) unless they are seeking to distinguish, overrule or state the relevancy of a precedent cited by advocates. But the New York courts do in fact recognize that a precedent of an upper court may not be overruled or modified by a lower court, though it may be overruled by an appropriate higher court. Also the power of higher courts to create exceptions to formally binding precedents is in fact recognized. The New York courts also in fact recognize that a precedent may have force yet not be formally binding. Courts often say such precedent is not binding but *persuasive*. For example, one intermediate appellate court may so regard a precedent of another intermediate appellate court. This approach can be seen in *Mountain View Coach Lines, Inc. v. Storms*, 476 N.Y.S.2d 918 (App. Div. 2d Dep't 1984). There the Second Department of the Appellate Division considered a case for which there was no precedent in the Second Department. There were, however, cases from the Third Department that the lower court had considered to be binding. In addressing the Third Department decisions in the Second Department, the court expressed itself as follows:

> the doctrine of *stare decisis* requires trial courts in this department to follow precedents set by the Appellate Division of another department until the Court of Appeals or this court pronounces a contrary rule. ...
> Such considerations do not, of course, pertain to this court. While we should accept the decisions of sister departments as *persuasive*, we

are free to reach a contrary result. ... We find the Third Department decisions [here] little more than a 'conclusory assertion of result', in conflict with settled principles, and decline to follow them. (*Mountain View Coach Lines*, 476 N.Y.S.2d at 920; emphasis supplied)

That decisions of other intermediate appellate courts are 'persuasive' in another such court places them in a similar category with decisions from other state courts, which are also treated merely as persuasive. Such precedent is not formally binding, yet has force. But the need for law to be consistent throughout the state gives the decisions of other coordinate appellate courts greater persuasive force than decisions from other states where the concern for consistency is not the same.

2 Law Concerning Precedent

There is no legislation in New York requiring or forbidding the use of precedent or otherwise regulating its formal bindingness or other normative bearing. But there is case law on this. See Section II.1, immediately above.

Common law precedent in such areas as contract, torts and property is, as a matter of court practice, considered to be formally binding, or to have force, or to provide support and so on, and thus generally qualifies as a genuinely independent 'source of law' in the American states. As such, it does not require an ultimate basis or foundation in statute law or custom or any other source. Prior statutory interpretations and previous constructions of constitutional provisions in litigated cases are likewise considered to be precedent, both for the courts lower in the hierarchy and for the court that decided the precedent.

At the appellate level, precedents concerning the interpretation of the state constitution seem to be somewhat less binding on appellate judges than are other precedents. See *In re Estate of Eckart*, 39 N.Y.2d 493, 499 (1976) ('In cases involving error in the construction of the Constitution or a statute, for sound reasons of policy and practicality, courts are generally more reluctant to change the statutory rule than the constitutional one'). By comparison, as a general matter, precedents dealing with areas of private law such as property, contracts, wills, trusts and commercial transactions are generally followed with greater regularity in appellate courts. See, for example, *Heyert v. Orange & Rockland Utilities, Inc.*, 17 N.Y.2d 352, 360–61 (1966); *In re Estate of Eckart*, 39 N.Y.2d 493; *Madfes v. Beverly Development Corp.*, 251 N.Y. 12 (1929). Moreover, precedents based upon the proper interpretation of a statute appear to have greater force in appellate courts than common law precedents dealing with areas of private law. See *People v. Hobson*, 39 N.Y.2d 479, 489 (1976) ('Precedents involving statutory interpretations are entitled to great stability. After all, in such cases courts are interpreting legislative intention and a sequential contradiction is a grossly arrogated legislative power').

Why these varying degrees of normative force of precedent springing from different sources of law – constitutional, statutory and common law? In particular, why do New York appellate courts treat precedent interpreting the New York constitution as having somewhat less normative force than, say, common law precedent? It is important to note that the legal issues involved are often closely interwoven with societal conceptions of justice, fairness and substantive rights, and that views on any of these may change. Perhaps courts interpreting constitutions intuit that the fundamental substantive policies and principles being served are more important than the stability and symmetry provided by continuity of precedent. Additionally, constitutions tend to be old documents, drafted in centuries past, which are extremely difficult to amend. Thus they must be reinterpreted by the courts from time to time. Contrast this state of affairs with precedents interpreting a statute. There American courts often adhere to a precedent construing a statute even while strongly criticizing the result, observing that, if a reading of the statute leads to an unjust result, it is the business of the legislature to modify the rule, a power of amendment it unquestionably has. In regard to constitutions, however, legislatures have no power of amendment.

In areas of judge-made common law not based on constitutions or statutes, such as contracts, torts and property, precedents are often based on well-established principles or venerable legal precepts. Moreover, people draft instruments of private law such as contracts, deeds and wills, and structure their commercial transactions with one another based partly on the assumption that courts will generally follow precedents. Further, at least legally counselled private parties tend to apportion the risk in their dealings with one another on the basis of precedents which delineate how the risk is to be allocated. The tendency of courts to follow precedents in contracts, torts and property is so pronounced that New York appellate courts routinely remark that, although they may not agree with an established precedent, they nonetheless feel constrained to follow it. For example, in a contract case decided in 1925, *Crowley v. Lewis*, 239 N.Y. 264, see also *Cammack v. J.B. Slattery & Bro., Inc.*, 241 N.Y. 39 (1925), the New York Court of Appeals declined to enforce a contract under seal against an undisclosed principal, and went back to 1876 for the applicable precedent. The Court of Appeals, while questioning the reasoning behind the precedent, nevertheless upheld it, saying, 'we do not feel at liberty to change a rule so well understood and so often enforced. If such a change is to be made it must be by legislative fiat' (*Crowley,* 239 N.Y. at 266). Similarly, in *Cullings v. Goetz,* 256 N.Y. 287 (1931), the Court of Appeals decided to follow a long-established rule for interpretation of a contract because it was well settled and frequently relied on by those entering into contracts. In this regard, the Court of Appeals said: 'The doctrine, wise or unwise in its origin, has worked itself by common acquiescence into the tissues of our law. It is too deeply imbedded to be superseded or ignored. Hardly a day goes by in our great centers of population but it is applied by judges and juries in cases great and small' (*Cullings,* 256 N.Y. at 291).

On the other hand, more recently JUDGE WACHTLER of the New York Court of Appeals, when comparing how far American courts and English courts adhere to the doctrine of *stare decisis,* observed that 'a more moderate view has always prevailed in our own country, particularly in the New York Court of Appeals' (Wachtler, 1985, pp.446–7). Several New York judges have emphasized what Wachtler called 'the flexibility aspect of the doctrine' (Wachtler, 1985, p.452). For example, in *Fleishman v. Eli Lilly & Co.,* 62 N.Y.2d 888 (1984), CHIEF JUDGE COOKE of the Court of Appeals noted that, although the principle of *stare decisis* deserves respect, 'the law is not and should not be so inflexible that it cannot correct itself from injustice and unfounded concerns espoused in prior decisions' (*Fleishman,* 62 N.Y.2d at 890). And in *Loschiavo v. Port Auth.,* 58 N.Y.2d 1040 (1983), JUDGE FUCHSBERG of the Court of Appeals pointed out that '*stare decisis* is no obstacle to ... self-correction', citing Holmes's warning against 'a rule which persists for no better reasons than that "it was laid down in the time of Henry IV."' (*Loschiavo,* 58 N.Y.2d at 1043 (FUCHSBERG, J, dissenting)). Finally, JUDGE FULD, in overruling the longstanding doctrine that charities are not liable for their torts, expressed the philosophy behind the 'flexibility aspect' of *stare decisis*:

> The rule of nonliability is out of tune with the life about us, at variance with modern-day needs and with concepts of justice and fair dealing. It should be discarded. To the suggestion that *stare decisis* compels us to perpetuate it until the legislature acts, a ready answer is at hand. It was intended not to effect a 'petrifying rigidity', but to assure the justice that flows from certainty and stability. If, instead, adherence to precedent offers not justice but unfairness, not certainty but doubt and confusion, it loses its right to survive, and no principle constrains us to follow it. (*Bing v. Thunig,* 2 N.Y.2d 656, 667 (1957))

3   Factors Determining Degrees of Normative Force

Various factors tend to affect the degree of normative force that a particular precedent will have.

(a)   The hierarchical rank of the deciding court affects this. Courts are formally bound to the highest degree by the prior decisions of higher courts of the same jurisdiction. But lower New York courts sometimes treat the precedents of the intermediate appellate courts somewhat less respectfully than the precedents of the Court of Appeals.

(b)   Decisions made by a panel are generally accorded as much precedential significance as those rendered by a full bench, but a full bench opinion certainly gets more attention.

(c)   The precedents of some courts are more influential than the precedents of other courts. A given prior New York Court of Appeals, because of its membership, may command more respect than a later New York Court of Appeals.

(d)   Changes in the political, economic or social background may influence how a court approaches the applicability of a prior decision. Such changes are often the primary motivation and justification for discarding an old precedent. See, for example, *People v. Westchester County National Bank*, 231 N.Y. 465 (1921), reversing 188 N.Y. Supp. 944 (1921) and *Sternlieb v. Normandie National Securities Corp.*, 263 N.Y. 245 (1934). As the answer to question II.2 (Appendix), above, indicates, such changes are, in fact, one of the very few legitimate reasons to stray from precedent. When the political, economic or social background changes, the higher courts, in order to maintain congruence between the legal and the social system, may adjust the law to conform to the new circumstances. Of course, such changes often directly diminish the force of a rule's original supporting arguments.

Some judges explicitly say that courts have a duty to re-examine precedents and bring them in line with current social realities. JUSTICE GIBBONS of the Second Department of the Appellate Division phrased his view of the judicial role in the face of changes in social factors as follows: 'The ever-changing demands of society have cast upon the courts an obligation to adjust the laws from time to time to such trends as may be necessary in order to achieve basic justice' (*Rakaric v. Croatian Cultural Club*, 430 N.Y.S.2d 829, 838 (App. Div. 2d Dep't 1980)). See also *DeAngelis v. Lutheran Medical Center*, 445 N.Y.S.2d 188, 194 (App. Div. 2d Dep't 1981).

An example of Gibbon's theory in action is found in *Woods v. Lancet*, 303 N.Y. 349 (1951). The question there, as the court stated it, was 'shall we follow *Drobner v. Peters*, or shall we bring the common law of this State, on this question, into accord with justice?' (*Woods*, 303 N.Y. at 351). The *Woods* court noted that *Drobner*, decided in 1921, 'must be examined against a background of history and of the legal thought of its time and of the thirty years that have passed since it was handed down' (*Woods*, 303 N.Y. at 352). JUDGE DESMOND pointed out that, at the time of decision, 'the practical difficulties of proof [of in utero damage to a foetus resulting in post-birth injuries] and the theoretical lack of separate human existence of an infant *in utero*' (*Woods*, 303 N.Y. at 353) led to adoption of a rule against recovery for an infant injured in utero. Asserting that 'it is the duty of the court to bring the law into accordance with present day standards of wisdom and justice' (*Woods*, 303 N.Y. at 355), the court recognized the cause of action of the infant plaintiff and held that recovery could be had with proper proof. In so doing, the court said it was acting 'in the finest common-law tradition' by 'adapt[ing] and alter[ing] decisional law to produce common-sense justice' (*Woods*, 303 N.Y. at 355). Thus it can be seen that a change in social attitudes and medical knowledge led to a change in precedent.

(e) If one of the advocates before the court overtly challenges the arguments which support the precedent, the court may be compelled to evaluate the soundness of the earlier arguments in determining whether to apply or distinguish a precedent. The attitude of the New York Court of Appeals in this regard is expressed in *People v. Bing*, 76 N.Y.2d 331 (1990) where the court said:

> Precedents remain precedents, however, not because they are established but because they serve the underlying 'nature and object of the law itself', reason and the power to advance justice. As Justice Frankfurter observed, '*stare decisis* is a principle of policy and not a mechanical formula of adherence to the latest decision, however recent and questionable'. Although a court should be slow to overrule its precedents, there is little reason to avoid doing so when persuaded by the 'lessons of experience and the force of better reasoning'. (*Bing*, 76 N.Y.2d at 338; citations omitted)

(f) Some precedents may be observed out of tradition. They have existed in the law for so long that they have become venerable, though no longer justified. Yet the fact that citizens have relied on the precedent may alone provide sufficient justification for following the precedent. (See, for example, *Dolphin Lane Assoc., Ltd. v. Southampton*, 37 N.Y.2d 292, 296 (1975) which rejected the more accurate formulation for determining high water mark because changing the traditional rule would introduce 'an element of uncertainty and unpredictability quite foreign to the law of conveyancing'.) But as the probability of unsound results increases, and in the face of mounting evidence that the rule no longer fits, courts do overturn precedent and create a new rule. *Battalla v. State*, 10 N.Y.2d 237 (1961), is just such a case. In *Battalla*, the Court of Appeals faced the question of whether negligent infliction of extreme emotional distress, with accompanying physical manifestations of injury, could be recognized as a tort even though there was no direct physical contact between the plaintiff and the harm-causing instrumentality. In New York, *Mitchell v. Rochester Ry. Co.*, 151 N.Y. 107 (1896), had held that there must be some physical contact; fright or emotional distress alone was insufficient. The *Battalla* court wrote, however, that 'It is our opinion that *Mitchell* should be overruled. It is undisputed that a rigorous application of its rule would be unjust, as well as opposed to experience and logic' (*Battalla*, 10 N.Y.2d at 239). Noting that 'it is fundamental to our common-law system that one may seek redress for every substantial wrong' (*Battalla*, 10 N.Y.2d at 240) and finding *Mitchell's* departure from this fundamental rule to be viable no longer, the court recognized the cause of action, thereby reversing a rule that had stood for nearly 70 years.

(g)   The presence or absence of dissent does not, as such, generally affect the degree of respect accorded a precedent. However, a dissent may provide arguments that will lead later judges to think that the precedent should be distinguished or overruled.

(h)   The degree of force of a precedent tends to vary among different branches of the law. In certain fields which may reasonably be assumed to give rise to a high degree of reliance on settled precedent, a fairly strict adherence to precedent is observed. For instance, the bindingness of precedent is particularly compelling in cases involving property and contractual rights – that is, 'wills, title to land, commercial transactions, and contracts' (Wachtler, 1985, pp.445, 449). In one case, the New York Court of Appeals went so far as to say that, in cases involving the transfer of property, where the settled rules are constantly being relied upon in everyday transactions, stability and adherence to precedent are more important than a better, or even the '"correct" rule of law' (*In re Estate of Eckart*, 39 N.Y.2d 493, 500 (1976)).

Courts tend to be more willing to re-examine and depart from common law rules they themselves have created. This is particularly true for tort liability cases, especially if there has been little or no reliance and justice seems to require an updated rule. See, for example, *People v. Hobson*, 39 N.Y.2d 479 (1976) and *MacPherson v. Buick Motor Co.*, 217 N.Y. 382 (1916). As indicated above, courts are also more willing to re-examine precedent in cases involving constitutional interpretation since the only alternative to change is through the extremely difficult process of constitutional amendment. Courts are perhaps most comfortable changing a purely procedural, rather than substantive, rule of law, because many of the formal values compelling a strict adherence to precedent are not implicated.

In the area of criminal law, the strong policy of protecting a defendant's rights has led to a general practice with regard to precedent. As JUDGE WACHTLER put it, 'any change in rule or statutory interpretation that would be detrimental to a defendant should be avoided, and may indeed violate due process, but changes favorable to a defendant should be, and frequently are, made' (Wachtler, 1985, p.453). (i) Moreover, courts are mindful of the precedents of other states and sometimes modify or overrule their own formally binding precedents when they perceive that their own precedents are contrary to a trend. See *Woods v. Lancet*, 303 N.Y. 349 (1951), discussed earlier. Here the court's decision to overrule the precedent was very much influenced by the weight of authority from other jurisdictions. (j) The formal bindingness or other degree of normative force of a precedent may be affected by academic writings. Such writings may provide support for adhering to or not adhering to precedent. (k) Legal change in related areas of the law may lead courts to examine the relevance of such change to the legal issues before them.

4 Factors that Weaken Precedent

A divided court issuing a majority and a dissenting opinion does not deprive a decision of precedential status; the law to be followed is that expressed in the majority opinion. But a precedent once laid down may fail to become settled law, and thus never acquire full status as a formally binding precedent in the first place. Such was true of *People v. Bartolomeo*, 53 N.Y.2d 225 (1981), where the Court of Appeals held that a 'suspect, represented by counsel on a prior pending charge, may not waive his rights in the absence of counsel and answer questions on new unrelated charges' (*People v. Bing*, 76 N.Y.2d 331, 335 (1990)). Although *Bartolomeo* stood until 1990 the *Bing* court noted the 'considerable difficulty in subsequent cases as the court tried to integrate… [*Bartolomeo*] into existing law' (*Bing*, 76 N.Y. 2d at 342). The court cited a litany of cases which limited or modified the rule, and declared: 'Manifestly, our many decisions in this area have failed to achieve the efficiency, consistency and uniformity in the application of the law which the doctrine of stare decisis seeks to promote' (*Bing*, 76 N.Y.2d at 348). In conclusion, the court stated: 'We find the *Bartolomeo* rule unworkable, and therefore overrule it' (*Bing*, 76 N.Y. 2d at 350), thus ending the confusion over a rule which never really became settled law.

As already noted, precedents involving statutory interpretation, particularly ones giving rise to a long line of precedent, are formally binding on courts below to a very high degree. Stability and reliability are thought to be crucial in cases construing statutes. See, for example, *Buffalo v. Cargill, Inc.*, 44 N.Y.2d 7 (1978) and *People v. Hobson*, 39 N.Y.2d 479 (1976). Additionally, it is generally assumed that the legislature is in a better position to rectify a misconstrued statute than is a court. For example, if a statute is misinterpreted by the courts, the legislature may easily step in and pass a new law, and do so prospectively (rather than retroactively, as commonly with courts).

5   *Vertical and Horizontal Bindingness*

See Section I.1.

6   *Analysis of Force, Support and Illustrative Role*

The New York Court of Appeals sometimes cites cases from another state as support for a decision in a case of first impression (where New York has no prior cases) or when overruling or modifying a precedent. The New York intermediate appellate courts do likewise. These latter courts also follow each other to some extent. In all such instances the cases cited are not formally binding yet are thought to have justifying force. (See Section II.1 above.)

The courts seldom explicitly discuss the distinction between formal bindingness and mere 'justifying force'. The latter is usually referred to merely as 'persuasive authority', rather than 'binding' authority. Nor is there much explicit discussion of any distinction between mere justifying force or 'persuasive authority' and 'further support'.

7   *Excess of Precedents?*

There is the view that in some fields there are far too many precedents. See, for example, Gilmore (1961, p.1037). Numerous conflicting precedents may undermine the overall formal bindingness, or force, of all of them. See Atiyah and Summers (1991, ch. 5).

III   The Rationale of Precedent

1 and 2   General Rationales for Formal Bindingness; for Force, Further Support, and so on

The power of common law courts in New York to create and follow precedents necessarily dates from earliest times and itself was a creature of necessity. For long periods in New York history, in many branches of law, the legislature was inactive. In many of these areas it continues to be so. Thus, if the courts were to decide cases in a law-like way, they would have to decide cases as instances of general rules and thereby set precedents to be followed by judges in future similar cases. This 'necessity' rationale continues to apply in many fields today, for the New York legislature has by no means codified the whole of the common law and, even if it had, there would still be gaps for the courts to fill with precedent, scope for precedent-setting interpretations and perhaps some need for judicial 'renovation' of highly obsolete statutes that the legislature has failed to amend.

American commentators have stated a variety of rationales for following precedent. Two common justifications for precedent are the stability it provides to the structure of society and the certainty that results when known rules are applied in a consistent and even-handed manner. One may call these formal values. Melvin Eisenberg has noted that a judicial system, through the use of the common law, 'should seek to satisfy three standards: social congruence, systemic consistency, and doctrinal stability' (Eisenberg, 1988, p.50). See also Summers (1982, pp.161–6). Others have remarked that precedent 'is necessary to preserve the certainty, stability and the symmetry of our jurisprudence' *Menge v. Madrid*, 40 F. 677, 679 (E.D. La. 1889). As one commentator has said:

> A decision of a court of last resort settles not only the principle of law involved in the case for the litigants themselves, but for all litigants coming into the same court with a case involving the same or substantially the same principles of law. As the precedent is applied again and again it becomes a principle of law upon which, in theory at least, everyone can rely in the regulation of his affairs and by which the law may be said to be defined and made certain. (Moore, 1958, p.4.)

Stability, certainty, judicial even-handedness and the rule of law seem to be the strongest formal values served by precedent. A court with power to overrule may instead follow a precedent and thus act on these rationales even though it would have decided the case differently were the matter one of first impression.

However, judges differ in the importance they accord to these rationales. For many judges, these rationales are simply to be weighed against policies or principles to be served by a new rule. For other judges, the rationales are so important that precedent is to be observed except under the most extraordinary circumstances. The New York Court of Appeals has had judges who have differed radically in their approach to precedent and in their regard for these rationales.

John T. Loughran, who served as Chief Judge of the New York Court of Appeals, placed great emphasis on adherence to precedent. Loughran believed, like Blackstone, that courts should follow precedent unless this would lead to a result 'flatly absurd or unjust' (Loughran, 1953, p.2):

> Nor is there any doubt that the basic tradition of the common law and sound considerations of policy demand that adherence to precedent shall be the rule and not the exception, and that departure

from that rule shall be sanctioned only where the justification and need are clear and cogent. The rule of stare decisis embodies a wise and important social policy. It at once provides the stability and fair measure of certainty which are prime requisites in any body of law. ... If judges were to be free, or indeed under the necessity, to decide cases without reference to principles and doctrines tested by experience and declared in prior decisions, there would be danger that each judge might become a law unto himself, with resultant chaos and utter uncertainty. ... Hence it is important to bear in mind that the overruling of a precedent may often cause more harm than good by the unsettling effect that it may have upon transactions concluded in reliance on the previously declared rules. (Loughran, 1953, pp.3–4)

Sol Wachtler, who also served as Chief Judge of the Court of Appeals, also stressed adherence to precedent, particularly in cases involving contract or property law. Like Judge Loughran, Judge Wachtler believed that precedent should be followed except in the most compelling circumstances. Consider, for example, the tenor of Judge Wachtler's comments in a dissent where the majority of the Court of Appeals chose to depart from a precedent dealing with a 'no-damage-for-delay clause' in a public construction contract:

A court is bound to follow precedent unless the need for a new rule of law far outweighs the need for stability, predictability, and uniform application of the settled rules. Indeed there are precedents which establish guidelines a court must follow in determining whether an existing precedent should be overruled. Primary among them is the rule that courts should be most reluctant to change the law affecting contractual rights and commercial dealings generally. Even those, like Justice William O. Douglas, who have urged that the doctrine of *stare decisis* has been too rigidly applied in some areas of the law recognize a greater need for 'uniformity and continuity' to preserve 'the integrity of contracts' and other matters dealing with commercial and property rights. (*Kalisch-Jarcho, Inc. v. City of New York*, 448 N.E.2d 413, 419 (N.Y. 1983), WACHTLER J, dissenting; citations omitted)

But some New York judges believe that, if courts adhere too strictly to precedent, erroneous principles of law will become 'embalmed' and the law will stagnate. For them it is unconscionable to rely on outdated legal principles which have come to be regarded as venerable merely because they have existed for so long, or were phrased in a manner easy to remember. As JUSTICE CARDOZO said, 'The repetition of a catchword can hold analysis in fetters for fifty years and more' (1931, p.689). Note the similar sentiment of JUSTICE HOLMES: 'But as precedents survive like the clavicle in the cat, long after the use they once served is at an end, and the reason for them has been forgotten, the result of following them must often be failure and confusion from the merely logical point of view' (Holmes, 1879, p.630).

The current Chief Judge of the New York Court of Appeals, Judith Kaye, has let it be known that in her view, adherence to precedent may manifest 'not judicial restraint but intellectual nonsense' (Kaye, 1988, p.1006). Moreover, in her view, because common law is by definition law made by judges, it is by the same token amenable to change by judges:

> The value judgments of appellate judges can hardly be alien to the development of the common law; they are essential to it. Choices among the precedents of another day – which to bring forward, which to leave behind, which to extend to meet some new condition, which to limit or overrule – mark the progress of the law. This process breathes life into our law; it gives relevance and rationality in the year 1988 to rules fashioned for another day, so that they command acceptance as principles by which we live. (Kaye, 1988, pp.1009–10)

For other judges, certainty, stability and other formal values are just further variables to be weighed against other important variables such as flexibility and individual justice in the particular case. For example, writing in dissent in *Higby v. Mahoney*, 48 N.Y.2d 15 (1979), JUDGE FUCHSBERG expressed his approach to *stare decisis*:

> *Stare decisis*, to its credit, is a far more subtle and flexible concept than some of those who would give it slavish adherence suggest. Its limitations are inherent, for the stability it espouses must coexist with both the dynamics of an evolving society and the accruing wisdom born of the repeated injustices which a particular ruling has wrought. To that end, its temper partakes more of the malleability of gold than of the rigidity of steel. (*Higby*, 48 N.Y.2d at p.22)

JUDGE FUCHSBERG was reacting to a majority which followed an interpretation of the election laws firmly established by prior decision, but which in application tended to work injustices. The majority in *Higby* had said:

> Whether it is appropriate for the courts to overturn judicial precedent must depend on several factors. Among them will be the nature of the · rights and interests at stake and the extent and degree to which action may justifiably have been taken in reliance on the precedent. In addition to such familiar considerations but apart therefrom, weight may properly be attached to the relative ease or difficulty of modification or change in the precedent. Invitations to judicial reconsideration carry more weight when addressed to constitutional issues because of the very great difficulty of effecting change by constitutional amendment. By contrast the courts show greater restraint in stepping in to under-

take correction of what may be perceived as erroneous determinations with respect to questions arising under legislative enactment. In addition to the relative ease of accomplishing statutory change, this hesitancy may be grounded in either or both of two additional considerations. First, the Legislature has far greater capabilities to gather relevant data and ... its members are properly politically responsive to the electorate. Second, and of greater significance, under our polity of government and distribution of powers, responsibility for making the policy decisions inherent in the adoption of the original legislative provision was, by its very nature, vested in the legislative branch. (*Higby*, 48 N.Y.2d at 18-19; citations omitted)

Later, JUDGE WACHTLER echoed sentiments expressed in *Higby* when he wrote that courts 'cannot fail to take into account considerations of institutional stability and the mandates of *stare decisis*. An appellate court should not depart from its prior holdings "unless impelled by the most cogent reasons"' (*Donawitz v. Danek*, 42 N.Y.2d 138, 142 (quoting *Baker v. Lorillard*, 4 N.Y. 257, 261, cited in *In re Estate of Eckart*, 39 N.Y.2d 493, 499)); internal quotes and citation omitted).

While the New York judges seem to regard principles of certainty and stability as the most important formal values served by precedent, there are other important rationales as well, many of which are mentioned by judges from time to time. A fuller account (Summers, 1982, pp.163–4) is as follows:

The use of precedent promotes judicial economy and efficiency and conserves the resources of judges, lawyers and parties. Once an issue has been thoroughly examined by a court and resolved, it becomes 'settled' and does not have to be examined anew in subsequent similar cases.

The practice of following precedent facilitates private dispute settlement and discourages litigiousness, thus serving the values of self-rule, party autonomy and conservation of private as well as judicial resources. Relatedly, precedents provide a pre-existing and independent external framework within which the issues between disputing parties may be defined. This enables those parties, with the help of lawyers, to determine on their own what evidence and arguments are legally relevant and likely to be decisive if the dispute goes to court. As a result, many disputants decide to settle out of court in light of the precedents they think a court would apply if called upon.

The practice of following precedent 'depersonalizes' decisions and thus renders it more likely that losing parties will adhere to the decision without the winning party having to resort to coercive measures (with attendant friction and waste). Losers will see that the decision is not merely 'against' them, ad hoc, but 'against all others similarly situated'.

The practice of following precedent accords with the maxim: 'Treat like cases alike.' Official evenhandedness may itself be a valuable form of fairness, especially when the issue is one on which there is no clear balance of reason favouring one side. The practice of following precedent diminishes the scope for partiality.

In a new case for which there is no precedent, the prospect that any decision the court reaches will be regarded by future judges as a precedent imposes special standards of rigour on the deciding court and calls for it to try to think through the implications for future cases of alternative decisions and possible reasons for them. Among other things, a deciding judge must, before deciding the case at hand, consider what the reasons supporting alternative decisions in the case at hand would commit him or his successors to in deciding future cases ('universalizability'). Also to adopt a general approach to a class of cases rather than decide a single instance is ordinarily to set general priorities between conflicting reasons (and therefore between competing values).

A practice of following precedent makes for more coherence and intelligibility in the law than would ad hoc and patternless exercises of power. This coherence and intelligibility is desirable on two grounds: it renders the law more 'followable' and also more susceptible to rational evaluation and criticism.

IV   Precedents: What They Stand for and How They Apply

1   What Counts as Binding or Having Force?

In New York, the formal bindingness, force or other support that a precedent has may vary significantly. The only part of the opinion which can be formally binding or have high normative force is the 'holding' or 'holdings'. This is the portion of an opinion in which the court rules on the issue (or issues) necessary to the decision. A holding is a specific ruling on a specific issue before the court. In order to determine the scope of a holding, it is always necessary to formulate the issue before the court (MacCormick, 1978, pp.155–82).

Sometimes the court will *explicitly state* the holding on an issue quite broadly. For example, in *Montgomery v. Daniels*, 38 N.Y.2d 41, 45 (1975) a case dealing with the New York No-Fault Insurance Act, the Court of Appeals began the opinion with this sentence: 'We hold that the New York no-fault automobile accident compensation law is not unconstitutional.' Here the holding is quite explicit, unambiguous and easy to identify. It is also stated without reference to any particular set of facts, and so is quite broad.

On other occasions, a court will declare a more narrow holding in fact-specific language. For instance, in *Simpson v. Phoenix Mutual Life Ins. Co.*, 24 N.Y.2d 262, 266 (1969), a case dealing with the construction of the terms of a life insurance policy, the Court of Appeals announced its holding only 'after a fairly lengthy recital of the facts. The court then *couched its holding in factual terms* as follows: 'We conclude that employment, as defined in this group policy, is a condition of insurance and, therefore, since the insurer did not contest the employee's eligibility within the period of contestability, it is barred from raising it as a defense to the beneficiary's action.' Note that the *Simpson* court here identified specific facts and circumstances to which its stated holding would apply in future cases. In both *Montgomery* and *Simpson*, the holding is explicitly stated.

Sometimes, however, courts face the task of extracting a holding from a case in which the holding is left more or less implicit. This can be done by trying 'to ascertain which aspect of the opinion engaged the first court's most careful judgment' Greenawalt (1989, pp.439–42). For example, if a court devotes most of its opinion to a discussion of a particular legal principle, the subsequent court is more likely to construe the holding to be an application of that principle. If, on the other hand, the focus of the opinion is on certain specific facts of the case, it is more likely the holding is narrowly confined to those particular facts.

A narrow view of the *scope* of a holding is that it is limited to the bare decision on the facts of the case. A broader view extends the scope of the holding to the facts that the prior court expressly stated were necessary to the decision, but a later court may determine what the facts necessary to the prior decision were. The reasoning of the precedent may also extend the scope of the holding. The full scope of the holding may be unknown until later courts interpret and apply the decision. The full scope of a precedent may be unknown until later courts act. Such precedential uncertainty occurs as a result of cases like *Garrett v. Holiday Inns, Inc.*, 58 N.Y.2d 253 (1983) (holding a town proportionately liable to hotel owner third party plaintiffs although not liable to motel guests as original plaintiffs) and *O'Connor v. City of New York*, 58 N.Y.2d 184 (1983) (holding a city not liable for inspector's failure to discover a gas leak, resulting in building damage and personal injury). These cases were handed down on the same day, with the dissenting and majority opinion writers switching roles. If the municipality did not owe a duty to the directly injured party, how could it logically be responsible for a share of the award to that party? Future cases were left to cope with the anomalous results.

Some parts of an opinion are not formally binding as precedent. This is true of the views or opinions of the court which are *not necessary* to the resolution of the specific issue before the court. This language is called 'dicta' and it is generally not binding. As indicated, dicta are usually defined simply as statements in the opinion 'not necessary' to the court's decision on the issue or issues. The most common type of dicta consists of general statements of the court about issues the court is not really deciding or called on to decide. The main rationales for disregarding such dicta are twofold: (1) judges preparing or signing the opinion in which dicta appears are not likely to give as careful consideration to dicta as to holdings, and (2) judges are not as likely to be well informed in regard to dicta because the opposing parties will usually have concentrated their briefs and arguments on the issue on which the case really turns.

In multiple issue cases, however, a statement by a court may be regarded as an 'alternative holding' even though it is not strictly necessary to the decision. For example, if a court's resolution of 'issue 2' is unnecessary because the court's resolution of 'issue 1' decides the outcome, it might seem logical that the court's resolution of 'issue 2' should be regarded as dicta and thus not binding. Nonetheless, a subsequent court may consider the court's ruling on 'issue 2' to be an alternative holding even though the ruling was actually not necessary to resolve the case. For instance, JUDGE BREITEL, in *Highland Falls v. State*, 44 N.Y.2d 505 (1978), upheld a determination that the state need not compensate a property owner for the unfulfilled possibility that the state, while holding a temporary easement on the property, might interfere with the owner's use of his property. He wrote:

> It has been held by this court, albeit in a case where the issue was but one among many, that compensation need not be paid for the State's taking of a temporary easement when there is no actual interference with the property owner's use of his property. In this case,… there is insufficient reason for abandoning that precedent. (*Highland Falls*, 44 N.Y.2d at 507 (citing *Great Atlantic & Pacific Tea Co. v. State*, 22 N.Y.2d 75, 87 (1968))

Moreover, a court may accord some weight to dicta when there is evidence that the higher court gave particularly serious consideration to the matter. Dicta may also offer a clue as to how a particular judge or court thinks in regard to issues that have not yet been squarely ruled on by the court. In general, however, lower courts often construe language cited by counsel which was not necessary to the resolution of a prior case as mere 'dicta' and consider this language to be without any bindingness whatsoever.

Furthermore, 'Questions which merely lurk in the record, neither brought to the attention of the court nor ruled upon, are not to be considered as having been so decided as to constitute precedents' (*Webster v. Fall*, 266 U.S. 507, 511 (1925); see also *Bard-Parker Co. v. Commissioner*, 218 F.2d 52, 57 (2d Cir. 1954)).

Whether a court is applying a common law precedent or interpreting a statute may have an impact on how the holding or that part of the opinion developing the rule or precedent is phrased. For example, consider again the language of the Court of Appeals' holding in *Montgomery v. Daniels*, 38 N.Y.2d 41 (1975). See discussion above. In interpreting the New York No-Fault Insurance Act, the court used very broad and general language: 'We hold that the New York no-fault automobile accident compensation law is not unconstitutional.' The language here is fairly inclusive and leaves hardly any room for subsequent attempts to distinguish factually the rule by other courts or by counsel in later cases. Compare again *Montgomery* with the opinion of the court in *Simpson v. Phoenix Mutual Life Ins. Co.*, 24 N.Y.2d 262 (1969), discussed above, in which the common law issue was whether an insurer should be estopped from denying coverage to a policyholder on the basis of his employment status. The holding in *Simpson* was much more fact-specific than in *Montgomery*, where a statute was being interpreted.

A precedent interpreting a constitution or statute will normally be phrased in broad and general terms. Loughran (1953 p.7) says: 'A large number of the cases in which the doctrine of stare decisis has been held to immunize challenged rules or doctrines against judicial alteration have involved the construction of statutes.' If by chance the court's interpretation of a statute leads to an absurd or unjust result in a later case, then this may be the fault of the legislature for failing to take into consideration this circumstance. Moreover, courts which attempt to second guess the legislature, by creatively interpreting the language of statutes to cover circumstances not envisioned by the legislature, run the real risk of being accused of 'legislating from the bench'. See, for example, the remarks of former Chief Judge Sol Wachtler of the New York Court of Appeals:

> It is the legislature and not the judiciary that is possessed of resources by which to understand general circumstances, and it is that body which is designed to make law in the abstract. Thus judicial lawmaking outside of the context of a concrete dispute not only risks erroneous determinations, it is nothing more than simple arrogation of legislative power, without the safeguards that allow a legislature to make law in the abstract. This is true 'judicial legislation'. (Wachtler, 1990, p.21)

The holding of a case is not only different from the rationale (or justification), but is also distinct from any general rule or principle derivable from the holding. Whereas a holding is a specific resolution of a specific issue, a rule or principle is a generalization which may be derived from the holding. The process of derivation may yield a rule or principle of varying degrees of breadth. The appropriate degree of breadth will be determined by several related factors: (1) how wide or narrow the issue is, (2) how wide or narrow the rationale for resolving the issue is, and (3) how 'generalizable' the facts are.

2   Reasoning about Applicability

The judicial, scholarly and juristic practice of arguing for or against the applicability of precedent regularly takes the form of close analysis of material facts. Judges carefully examine the material facts to ascertain degrees of relevant similarity. Scholars use similarity or lack thereof as support for argument. Advocates stress factual similarity or dissimilarity as a major structural component of the position they take in their presentation to the court (see Section I.6). In the case of *United States ex rel. Susi Contracting Co. v. Zara Contracting Co.*, 146 F.2d 606 (2d Cir. 1944), the defendants attempted to apply the holding of two cases. The two cases were *T.J.W. Corp. v. Bd. of Higher Educ. of City of New York*, 296 N.Y.S. 693 (1937) and *Niewenhous Co. v. State*, 288 N.Y.S. 22 (1936). But the court ruled that the facts of those cases differed from the situation in *Zara*. The court's statements indicating that it was distinguishing these cases based on differences of material facts were as follows: 'these cases are limited to. ... The situation is quite otherwise... here. ...' (*Zara*, 146 F.2d at 610). While this language is not necessary to distinguish a case based on the facts, the statements effectively convey the message.

Argumentation over the applicability of precedent also involves isolating rules and principles. In so doing, courts, scholars and advocates will argue that a rule or principle explicit or implicit in the holding does or does not apply to the case at hand. Further, courts sometimes determine the applicability of a precedent by considering whether the next case falls within the substantive reasoning underlying the precedent.

3   Juristic Discussion

The main ideas discussed in this literature are to be found in such references as the following: Eisenberg (1988); Farnsworth (1983); Goldstein (1991); Jones *et al.* (1980); Levi (1962); Llewellyn, (1951, 1960); MacCormick (1978).

4   Illustrative or Analogical Precedent

Precedents which are not strictly in point may be used as illustrative examples or analogies to clarify a court's conclusion. Such precedents may raise similar considerations as those before the court. As a result, such precedents may also generate an overall harmonization argument favouring one outcome rather than another. Such clarification and harmonization is illustrated by *Albala v. City of New York*, 54 N.Y.2d 269 (1981). *Albala* was acknowledged to be a case of 'first impression', but JUDGE WACHTLER noted the bearing of *Park v. Chessin*, 46 N.Y.2d 401 (1978), saying that case, 'although instructive, is ... distinguishable from the case at bar' (*Albala*, 54 N.Y.2d at 272 (1981)). After illuminating the distinction between the cases, WACHTLER continued, 'the teaching of *Park* is not altogether inapposite, for in that case we isolated the central concern which inevitably brings us to the difficult conclusion we reach today' (*Albala*, 54 N.Y.2d at 273). The concern was for designing a rule that assigned liability, if any, in a way that was neither artificial nor arbitrary (*Albala*, 54 N.Y.2d at 273). The conclusion was that there could be no recovery for a child who suffered from birth defects caused by a preconception tort to the mother. Thus *Park*, although distinguishable and distinguished, clarified the 'central concern' upon which the decision in *Albala* was based.

Another example of indirect reliance on precedent is found in *Scott Eden Management v. Kavovit*, 563 N.Y.S.2d 1001 (1990), decided by the Supreme Court of Westchester County, New York. The case was one of first impression, in which the court faced the question of whether an infant actor could, by disaffirming his contract, avoid payment of commissions due in the future to his agent for contracts already obtained by the agent. In holding that the commissions must be paid, the court relied on a general analogy to *Mutual Milk & Cream Co. v. Prigge*, 98 N.Y.S. 458 (App. Div. 1st Dep't 1906). There a defendant minor entered an employment contract to deliver milk which included a restrictive covenant prohibiting him from soliciting the plaintiff's customers for three years after leaving plaintiff's employ. The defendant disaffirmed the contract and started working for a competitor, breaching the no-solicitation provision. Although the contract was disaffirmed, the court granted an injunction enforcing the no-solicitation obligation on the principle that a minor should not be able to disaffirm and also escape such a contractual obligation. Despite the differences in the contracts, the *Kavovit* court found 'The rationale of the *Mutual Milk* case ... applicable to this case... In each case, the infant consumed the fruits of the contract and refused to pay for that fruit, to the clear prejudice of the other party' (*Scott Eden Management*, 563 N.Y.S.2d at 1003).

5   Single Precedents or Lines of Decision?

Although a single precedent of a higher court is technically formally binding, a long line of precedent will generally have more normative force: that is, be less subject to overruling or other modification.

American juristic commentators and courts regularly engage in the practice of synthesizing a group of related precedents. The practice of synthesis may reveal not only what was 'in' the various precedents from early on, though not explicitly set forth, but also how the case law has changed over time (Jones *et al.*, 1980, p.132). The rule or rules of law that emerge from a sound synthesis of a body of precedents articulate standards that individuals may rely on, and thus serve the goals of 'social congruence, systemic consistency, and doctrinal stability' (Eisenberg, 1988, p.50).

Sometimes what is called a 'synthesis' is really a radical transformation of existing law, as in JUDGE CARDOZO's opinion in *MacPherson v. Buick Motor Co.*, discussed in Section VI.1, below.

6   The Concept of a 'Leading Case'

The concept of a 'leading case' plays a distinctive role. A 'leading case' establishes the law on a major point and is recognized for this. Courts and advocates cite such cases as dispositive, and may even cite them as the sole justification for the decision. If a 'leading case' is in a party's favour, that party has a powerful advantage, both strategically and legally. Such a party has a better chance of negotiating a favourable settlement or prevailing in court. Further, a 'leading case' guides courts and advocates by setting the parameters of the conflict and therefore makes for more expeditious resolution of disputes. A leading case also 'radiates' influence outwards beyond its facts. *Palsgraf v. Long Island R.R. Co.*, 248 N.Y. 339 (1928), decided by the New York Court of Appeals in 1928, is just such a case. A search on a computerized database yielded over 1500 case and periodical sources in which the case has been mentioned, a quantitative indication of the impact *Palsgraf* has had on the legal system. Using Westlaw, this search consisting only of 'Palsgraf' in the databases covering federal and state cases, as well as law reviews and legal periodicals, produced the result. It should be noted that coverage of law review articles on Westlaw generally goes back not more than 20 years, so the search result is highly understated. In terms of qualitative impact, there is not a law student in the United States who has made it through his or her first year torts course without struggling over the implications of Cardozo's 'eye of reasonable vigilance' (*Palsgraf*, 248 N.Y. at 343). With *Palsgraf*, Cardozo changed the face of negligence law in New York and generated significant national debate, as the many references to the case demonstrate. No longer was the existence of duty to the plaintiff, a legal predicate to recovery in negligence for breach thereof, to be decided by the often unpredictable jury. The existence of a duty to the plaintiff, as disclosed by the 'eye of reasonable vigilance' (*Palsgraf*, 248 N.Y. at 343), became a matter for the judge to decide, thereby fundamentally altering the dynamic of negligence actions. Without a legally recognized duty owed by the defendant to the plaintiff, there can be no recovery, regardless of the foreseeability of harm or blameworthiness of the defendant. Moreover, as is demonstrated by reading any one of the innumerable cases citing *Palsgraf*, the case continues to provide key elements of the legal framework for negligence recovery in New York today (more than 60 years later).

V   Distinguishing, Explaining, Modifying, Overruling

1   *Distinguishing*

A lawyer confronted by an unfavourable precedent will frequently attempt to distinguish the precedent, arguing either that the material facts were different or that the substantive rationale for the ruling does not apply to the facts of the case under consideration. The principle enunciated by Llewellyn in *The Bramble Bush*, 'the rule follows where its reason leads; where the reason stops, there stops the rule' (Llewellyn, 1951, pp.157–8), is applied with vigour by many American lawyers and judges. See, for example, *Donawitz v. Danek*, 42 N.Y.2d 138 (1977), holding that a precedent was still valid, but not controlling because *stare decisis* did not require the extension of the rule and reason did not support an extension. But some courts are less 'substantive rationale-minded' when applying precedent and, if they think a precedent includes a holding that is strictly relevant to the issue, they will follow the precedent even though the substantive rationale in the earlier opinion is not clearly applicable. This can be seen in *In re Estate of Eckart*, in which the court wrote, 'our affirmance in *Cairo*, without opinion, does not constitute an indorsement of that rationale. It is the result [on the material facts] that counts, and in our view it cannot be said that the result is clearly erroneous' (39 N.Y.2d at 502 (1976); citation omitted).

The opinion in *Roberson v. Rochester Folding Box Co.*, 171 N.Y. 538 (1902), reveals various methods for distinguishing precedents. In considering whether a right of privacy existed giving rise to a cause of action for unauthorized use of a person's likeness, the court distinguished numerous cases which might logically lead to the recognition of such a right. *Prince Albert v. Strange*, 1 Macn. & G. 25, cited at 171 N.Y. 547–48, in which an injunction against unauthorized use was granted, was said to deal with property rights, not personal privacy as in *Roberson*. Thus the material facts were quite different. *Pollard v. Photographic Co.*, L.R. 40 Ch. Div. 345, cited at 171 N.Y. 548–49, was distinguished as based on breach of an implied contract, not 'threatened injury to the feelings' of the plaintiff as in a true privacy case. The *Roberson* court noted that, on the facts of the *Roberson* case, a photographer hired by a woman to take her picture and make a specified number of copies, made copies for himself and sold them, so that the contract rationale applied in *Pollard* was inapplicable to the case under consideration. Finally, *Schuyler v. Curtis*, 147 N.Y. 434, cited at 171 N.Y. 550–52, a case heavily relied upon by the plaintiff, was determined not to control on institutional grounds. It was a lower court opinion reversed by the Court of Appeals. Further, the expressions by the Court of Appeals in reversing the lower court which were claimed to indicate recognition of a right to privacy were dismissed as dicta. These are but a few of the cases treated in *Roberson* demonstrating various judicial techniques for distinguishing cases or demonstrating their lack of force for the case at hand. See further, the discussion of bindingness in Section II.3, and of distinguishing on the ground that the material facts differ, in Section IV.2.

This practice of distinguishing prior cases often leads to further refinement of the scope of the original precedent, that is, the rule generalized from its holding in light of its underpinning reasoning or rationale. For example, a ruling by a court that resolves a particular dispute fairly and equitably may lead to an unjust or absurd result when applied to a set of facts only marginally different from the facts of the case that created the rule. By examining the reasoning behind the original rule, and noting the underlying values and principles exemplified in the rule, the court will be able to see if the same principles and values are served through the application of the old rule to the new case with only marginally different facts. If these principles are not served, or if applying the rule will lead to an unjust or absurd result, then a later court will usually decline to apply the original rule. Of course, this does not necessarily mean that the later court is ignoring or overruling the original rule.

New precedent is often created through the process of examining the rationales for prior decisions (without necessarily questioning the validity of the prior rule) and adapting the original rule to fit the issue posed by new facts. In other words, the original rule stands alongside the new rule as legitimate precedent, but it may have been limited or extended to some extent by the creation of the new rule.

Thus courts will often examine closely the facts or rationale of a prior decision to ensure that a rule, which seems superficially relevant to resolving a dispute, is not applied to the facts of a case that would not be well resolved under the prior decision. An example is the New York Court of Appeals opinion in *Tobin v. Grossman*, 24 N.Y.2d 609 (1969). In *Tobin*, a mother who had witnessed injuries caused to her two-year-old child in an automobile accident sought to recover against the tort-feasor for mental and emotional injuries arising from her shock and fear at witnessing the accident. The Court of Appeals cited several prior holdings, including *Battalla v. State*, 10

N.Y.2d 237 (1961), in which the court had held that 'one may have a cause of action for injuries sustained although precipitated by a negligently induced mental trauma without physical impact' (*Tobin*, 24 N.Y.2d at 613). The court also cited its holding in *Woods v. Lancet*, 303 N.Y. 349 (1951), in which it had permitted the plaintiff to recover against a third party for injuries sustained to the plaintiff as a foetus in utero resulting from an impact to her mother. Although permitting the plaintiff in *Tobin* to recover might seem to be a logical extension of the holdings of these two cases, the court nevertheless declined so to extend the holdings of *Battalla* and *Woods* to permit the mother to recover against the tort-feasor for her emotional harm:

> Beyond practical difficulties there is a limit to attaining essential justice in this area. While it may seem that there should be a remedy for every wrong, this is an ideal limited perforce by the realities of this world. Every injury has ramifying consequences, like the ripplings of the waters, without end. The problem for the law is to limit the legal consequences of wrongs to a controllable degree. ... It is enough that the law establishes liability in favor of those *directly or intentionally harmed*. (*Tobin*, 24 N.Y.2d at 619; emphasis supplied)

2   Juristic Commentary

Scholarly commentators frequently make similarities and differences between reported precedents a major part of their academic writing. These academic writings usually appear in legal periodicals and treatises. Courts, in turn, may make extensive use of such writings. For example, courts often cite scholarly analyses and syntheses of precedent. Or a court may overrule a precedent for social, political or economic reasons, and may cite academic writings in support of this.

3   Excessive Distinguishing?

Sometimes judges exercise their power to distinguish a precedent to draw excessively fine or unreal distinctions, thereby eroding the precedent without expressly overruling it. Courts may also create 'exceptions' to the rule that are really hostile to it (Eisenberg, 1988, pp.70–74). This is a technique whereby courts 'draw distinctions, in the form of exceptions, that seem plausible in form but are in substance either inconsistent with the announced rule, given the social propositions that support the rule, or impossible to administer in such a way that cases are treated in a consistent fashion' (ibid., p.71). For example, in contract law, one version of the pre-existing legal duty rule provided that 'a bargain is unenforceable if one party's performance consists only of an act he had already contracted to perform' (ibid., p.71). This general rule was increasingly eroded, however, as courts began creating exceptions, or 'distinguishing' it. One exception held the rule 'inapplicable if the duty under the prior contract was owed to a party other than the promisor' (ibid., pp.71–2). Another exception deemed the rule 'inapplicable if the duty is to pay a debt whose total amount is disputed, even though the performance consists of paying the part that is admittedly due' (ibid., p.72). In *Schwartzreich v. Bauman-Basch, Inc.*, 231 N.Y. 196 (1921), the New York Court of Appeals evaded the legal duty rule through the fictional distinction that 'in this case we have an express rescission and a new contract' (*Schwartzreich*, 231 N.Y. at 205). Of course, this fictional 'distinction' could easily be drawn in any case in which the court wished to avoid the rule (Eisenberg, 1988, pp.71–2).

Exceptions and distinctions are often created in cases laying down broad rules without proper consideration of the consequences. Courts then pare the rule back to avoid absurd or inconsistent results, but retain it to the extent that the results it yields seem proper. Eventually, the precedent may be overruled. The line of cases emanating from *People v. Bartolomeo*, 53 N.Y.2d 225 (1981), as explained in *People v. Bing*, 76 N.Y.2d 331 (1990), also demonstrates this dynamic. The rule from *Bartolomeo*, as stated by the *Bing* court, is:

> a suspect, represented by counsel on a prior pending charge, may not waive his rights in the absence of counsel and answer questions on new unrelated charges. If the police are chargeable with knowledge of the prior representation, any statements the suspect makes, not only about the prior charges but also about the new charges, must be suppressed. (*Bing*, 76 N.Y.2d at 335)

After stating the rule, the court immediately noted that, 'Since the rule was announced nine years ago, scarcely a term of court has passed without a *Bartolomeo* issue being presented to us in one form or another' (*Bing*, 76 N.Y.2d at 335). Moreover, the cases which followed *Bartolomeo* 'failed to achieve the efficiency, consistency and uniformity in the application of the law which the doctrine of stare decisis seeks to promote' (ibid., at 348). Citing a number of post-*Bartolomeo* decisions, the court generalized that the trend in the cases represented an 'effort to limit the rule to better balance the benefits of evenhanded administration of the criminal law with the cost the rule exacted from effective law enforcement' (ibid., at 342–3). Accordingly, the court revised the rule. The police were no longer held to a 'know-or-should-have-known' standard regarding representation on a prior outstanding charge, but had to possess 'actual knowledge' of such representation before the right to counsel was violated by police taking statements from a suspect (*Bing*, 76 N.Y.2d at 343, citing *People v. Bertolo*, 65 N.Y.2d 111, 112

(1985)). The burden of proof regarding this knowledge was placed on the defendant (*Bing*, 76 N.Y.2d at 343, citing *People v. Rosa*, 65 N.Y.2d 380, 384 (1985)). Further limitations on the *Bartolomeo* rule included an exception for placing a defendant, already represented on a prior unrelated charge, in a line-up without his attorney present (*Bing*, 76 N.Y.2d at 343, citing *People v. Hawkins*, 55 N.Y.2d 474, 485 (1982)), permission for police to 'eavesdrop on conversations between an informer and a suspect who has counsel on a pending charge' (*Bing*, 76 N.Y.2d at 343, citing *People v. Hauswirth*, 60 N.Y.2d 904 (1983)) and refusal to suppress statements made about a new crime when the prior crime was being appealed (*Bing*, 76 N.Y.2d at 343, citing *People v. Colwell*, 65 N.Y.2d 883, 885 (1985)).

These exceptions to and modifications of the *Bartolomeo* rule derived from a 'failure to elaborate the basis for the rule, and the questionable policy behind it' (*Bing*, 76 N.Y.2d at 342). The failure of reason and policy, compounded by erosion through exceptions, led the court in *Bing* finally to put to rest the much maligned rule and overturn *Bartolomeo*. Thus *Bing* demonstrates that courts may and do create exceptions undermining bad precedent which eventually lead to the overturning or radical reformulation of that precedent.

Courts do sometimes 'explain' or restate what precedents stand for and thereby reconcile ostensibly unfavourable precedent with the present decision. In *MacPherson v. Buick Motor Co.*, 217 N.Y. 382 (1916), JUDGE CARDOZO did just this where he 'explained' that cases such as *Thomas v. Winchester*, 6 N.Y. 381 (1852) were not limited to liability for harm caused by poison, explosives and other dangerous things for which a seller may be liable to a remote (non-privity) buyer. Thus, according to CARDOZO, this case could be reconciled with holding a seller liable in negligence to a remote buyer. (See Section VI.1, below.)

Scholars may uniformly condemn (or nearly so) a given precedent or line of precedent. When this happens, the life span of the precedent tends to be shortened.

4   Types of Overruling

On those relatively infrequent occasions when the New York Court of Appeals explicitly overrules a binding common law precedent, it has sometimes been met with resounding criticism for failing to recognize the widespread and unforeseen consequences of abandoning the old rule by judicial decision. Often when an American court alters a long-standing precedent that has come to be relied upon, the court is criticized for undermining the stability of relationships between private parties and for usurping legislative power.

One well-known example in which the New York Court of Appeals overruled precedent is *Boomer v. Atlantic Cement Co.*, 26 N.Y.2d

219 (1970). The defendant was the operator of a large cement plant who was sued by neighbouring landowners seeking to enjoin the plant from operating because of vibrations and dust emanating from the plant. The plaintiffs contended that the cement plant was a tortious wrong called a 'nuisance' and sought to close the plant. On appeal to the Court of Appeals, it was not disputed that the cement plant constituted a tortious 'nuisance' and had damaged the plaintiffs property. At issue was whether the court should enjoin the nuisance, that is, order the plant to close down or otherwise abate the harm. But 'The total damage to plaintiffs property [was] ... relatively small in comparison with the value of defendant s operation' (*Boomer*, 26 N.Y.2d at 223). The defendants had invested $45 million in the plant and employed more than 300 people. Nevertheless, prior to *Boomer*, the settled common law precedent in New York had been to the effect that a nuisance would be enjoined even though the injunction would impose a substantial economic hardship on the defendant and there would only be slight harm to the plaintiff if the nuisance were not enjoined. A prior precedent, *Whalen v. Union Bag & Paper Co.*, 208 N.Y. 1 (1913), had been so decided on remarkably similar facts. A unanimous Court in *Whalen* had issued an injunction halting the defendant's relatively minor pollution of a creek, apparently unimpressed by the $1 million that the defendant had invested in his pulp mill and his 500 employees. The court in *Whalen* had stressed, 'Although the damage to the plaintiff may be slight as compared with the defendant's expense of abating the condition, that is not a good reason for refusing an injunction' (*Whalen*, 208 N.Y. at 5). The Court of Appeals in *Whalen* thus decided that private property rights, protected by long-standing precedent, had to be upheld.

In *Boomer*, notwithstanding the precedent of *Whalen* and the long-standing rule that such a nuisance would be enjoined regardless of the cost to the defendant, the Court of Appeals declined to follow the precedent and refused to enjoin the nuisance. Instead, the court merely awarded damages to the plaintiffs. The dissent in *Boomer* sternly rebuked the majority for breaking with the prior rule, noting that, 'It has long been the rule in this State, as the majority acknowledges, that a nuisance which results in substantial continuing damage to neighbors must be enjoined' (*Boomer*, 26 N.Y.2d at 229, JASEN J, dissenting). Moreover, the dissent noted that the majority decision contradicted other long-standing precedents as well; saying that it is not 'constitutionally permissible to impose servitude on land, without consent of the owner, by payment of permanent damages where the continuing impairment of the land is for a private use. (See *Fifth Ave. Coach Lines v. City of New York*, 11 N.Y.2d 342, 347; *Walker v. City of Hutchinson*, 352 U.S. 112.)' (*Boomer*, 26 N.Y.2d at 231, JASEN J, dissenting).

The Court of Appeals decision in *Boomer* was criticized by various scholars for failing to follow precedent, for making a judicial change in the law and for legitimizing and sanctioning what the court admitted to be the defendant's wrongful act. It was said that the Court of Appeals did not sufficiently defer to precedent, and thus undercut the image of the Court of Appeals as a body that applies reason in developing precedent. But some scholars believed the *Boomer* decision was justified on policy grounds.

Of course, an artistic opinion writer may overrule in a way that is made to seem only a logical extension or reformulation of prior precedent. For example, in *MacPherson v. Buick Motor Co.*, 217 N.Y. 382 (1916), JUDGE CARDOZO, writing for the New York Court of Appeals, rejected a long-standing line of precedent beginning with the English case of *Winterbottom v. Wright*, 152 Eng. Rep. 402 (1842), which had held that an original seller of goods was not liable for damages caused by defects in the goods to anyone except his immediate buyer or one in privity with him. The Court of Appeals purported to base its holding of liability in negligence on the New York case of *Thomas v. Winchester*, 6 N.Y. 397 (1852), a case that had been confined to inherently dangerous goods. See, further, the discussion of the case in Sections V.3 and VI.1.

There are at least three major types of justified overruling of precedent. The first type occurs in instances when technological innovations or improvements make the precedent obsolete. Because of the rapid influx of manufactured products into the market-place in the early twentieth century and the growing number of individuals being harmed by these products, the *MacPherson* opinion, dispensing with the requirement of privity in a negligence action against the manufacturer, recognized the transformation of American society through technological innovation. Or, as CARDOZO stated in *MacPherson*, 'the things subject to the principles do change', as 'the needs of life in a developing civilization require' (*MacPherson*, 217 N.Y. at 391).

A second major type of overruling of precedent occurs when the change or abandonment of precedent is necessary to bring the common law into line with growing social or moral enlightenment; that is, when the substantive values upon which the precedent was based are no longer tolerable. An example of this second type of justified overruling can be found in the New York case of *Woods v. Lancet*, 303 N.Y. 349 (1951). The rule prior to this decision, established by the Court of Appeals in *Drobner v. Peters*, 232 N.Y. 220 (1921), had been that an infant could not recover against a defendent who caused it prenatal injuries in the ninth month of the mother's pregnancy. The Court of Appeals in *Woods* found that the rationale for the prior decision was no longer supportable and that the court was justified in overruling *Drobner* in order to 'adapt and alter [the] decisional law to produce common-sense justice' (*Woods*, 303 N.Y. at 355). The Court of Appeals then went on to sustain the plaintiff's right of action. A new view of moral rightness may have explained this case, and perhaps the *Boomer* case, above, too.

A third type of justified overruling is in those instances where subsequent experience with a precedent shows that it was substantively quite erroneous or ill-conceived *from the beginning*. An example of the Court of Appeals recognizing original error in a prior decision and overruling the precedent is *People v. Nixon*, 248 N.Y. 182 (1928). In *Nixon*, the Court of Appeals rejected settled precedent which had required a defendant in a criminal case tried without a jury to make a formal motion to dismiss in order to preserve on appeal his contention that the evidence was legally insufficient to warrant a conviction. In its overruling of a line of cases, the Court of Appeals in *Nixon* described the unfairness of the precedent: 'It is right that this court should hesitate to overrule a previous decision, but when convinced that an artificial rule of practice, created by it, is erroneous and hampers the administration of justice, it is its duty to refuse to perpetuate previous error' (*Nixon*, 248 N.Y. at 192).

It is important to stress that, in the absence of one of the three types of unusual circumstances discussed above, the New York Court of Appeals generally follows precedent, at least when it is not distinguishable. New York judges seeking to disavow prior settled common law face an uphill battle. The position discussed in 1850 by JUDGE HARRIS in *Baker v. Lorillard*, 4 N.Y. 257 (1850), is relevant today:

This court ... may, and undoubtedly ought, when satisfied that either itself, or its predecessor, has fallen into a mistake, to overrule its own error. I... hold it to be the duty of every judge and every court to examine its own decisions, and the decisions of other courts without fear, and to revise them without reluctance. But when a question has been well considered and deliberately determined, whatever might have been the views of the court before which the question is again brought, had it been *res nova*, it is not at liberty to disturb or unsettle such decision, unless impelled by 'the most cogent reasons'. (*Baker*, 4 N.Y. at 261).

Indeed, it may be that the New York Court of Appeals today is even less likely to overrule precedent than in 1850.

5   Prospective Overruling

Retroactive application of an overruling decision may upset substantial reliance on the overruled precedent and will treat parties similarly situated quite differently. At minimum, the 'victim' of the overruling decision will be treated differently from those who come after and who thus benefit from the new rule. As a result, courts have invented the practice of overruling in some cases only prospectively. That is, the new rule is to apply only *after* the overruling decision so that the old rule is still, in effect, applied to all prior parties similarly situated except the litigants before the court (thereby preserving incentives to seek change).

Although it is common practice that a rule will be applied retroactively, New York courts do have the power prospectively to overrule in certain limited circumstances. According to one court, *Ceres Partners v. Gel Assocs.*, 714 F. Supp. 679 (S.D.N.Y. 1989), a new rule will generally be applied retroactively, unless three types of factors converge to favour prospective overruling:

1   the holding must establish a new principle of law, either by overruling clear past precedent on which litigants may have relied or by deciding an issue of first impression whose resolution was not clearly foreshadowed;
2   the merits and demerits in each case must be weighed by looking to the history of the rule in dispute, its purpose and effect, and whether retroactive operation will further or retard the rule's operation;
3   retrospective application must create the risk of producing substantially inequitable results.

6   *Anticipatory Overruling by Lower Courts*

In the New York State court system, the trial courts of general jurisdiction have no power to anticipatorily overrule precedent set by intermediate appellate court decisions, even though the Court of Appeals has not passed upon the question, the soundness of the intermediate court's decision is in doubt, and the precedent appears to be unsound. A fortiori, the trial courts may not anticipatorily overrule Court of Appeals decisions. Precedent can only be overturned through legislative action or appellate court decision: see *Cannon v. Cannon*, 20 N.Y.S.2d 605 (1940). Trial courts are always bound to follow the law as laid down by the appellate courts whose pronouncements control in their jurisdiction: see *Meisel Tire Co. v. Ralph*, 1 N.Y.S.2d 143 (1937). Likewise, the four intermediate appellate courts, that is, the Appellate Division, being lower in the judicial hierarchy, do not have the power to anticipatorily overrule Court of Appeals decisions. However, the fact that this power is said not to exist does not mean that such Appellate Division activity never occurs.

By contrast, in the federal court system, anticipatory overruling was not uncommon prior to 1989, when the majority view was that 'lower courts should disregard [federal] Supreme Court decisions when they are reasonably sure that the Supreme Court would overrule them given the opportunity' (Bradford, 1990, p.41). In the 1989 case of *Rodriguez de Quijas v. Shearson- / American Express, Inc.*, 490 U.S. 477 (1989), however, the Supreme Court spoke for the first time on the appropriateness of the doctrine and strongly condemned it: 'If a precedent of this Court has direct application in a case, yet appears to rest on reasons rejected in some other line of decisions, the Court of Appeals should follow the case which directly controls, leaving to this Court the prerogative of overruling its own decisions' (*Rodriguez*, 490 U.S. at 484).

It might be argued that 'Anticipatory overruling makes the law more responsive to change, it ensures litigants fair and equal treatment, it enhances the predictability of the law and it promotes judicial efficiency' (Bradford, 1990, p.42). Another scholar has argued that the power to overrule anticipatorily is appropriate, particularly in the federal court context (Eisenberg, 1988, p.191, n.43). Because the United States Supreme Court reviews very few cases each year, the federal courts of appeal are generally the court of last resort for the vast majority of litigants. Such limited possibilities for review by the Supreme Court mean that, if the federal courts of appeal have no power to overrule anticipatorily, outdated Supreme Court precedent may nonetheless stay in effect for a very long time, until the Supreme Court finally decides to review a case raising the issue. Thus this scholar argues that 'both fairness and institutional considerations suggest that in determining whether a case should be anticipatorily overruled, the lower federal courts should replicate the reasoning the Supreme Court uses to determine whether a case should be actually overruled' (ibid., p. 191). Of course, the 1989 ruling of the Supreme Court, above, remains law in the federal system: no anticipatory overruling of US Supreme court precedents.

7   *Precedent and Legislative Practice*

Drafters of legislation are often strongly influenced by prior case law and precedent. For instance, sometimes a legislature will simply pass a statute adopting, in whole or in part, the rule developed in the case law. This process in common law countries is sometimes called 'codifying' the case law. Even if the legislature does not follow the case law to this extent, it will often draft the statute in light of the common law. According to one commentator, the influence of the common law in drafting statutes 'is most pervasive in the definition of terms used in statutes' (Maltz, 1988, p.386). Moreover:

Common-law doctrine also influences the interpretation of statutes in some cases in which the language of the written law seems on its face to displace that doctrine. Judges at times strain to preserve precedents that they believe establish just rules. This tendency is readily discernible in the maxim that 'statutes which are in derogation of the common law are to be strictly construed'. (Ibid., p.386)

The New York case of *Kaiser v. Kaiser*, 402 N.Y.S.2d 171 (Fam. Ct. 1978), provides an example. In *Kaiser*, the issue was how to construe a statute making parents, as well as step-parents, responsible for the support of children under the age of 21 who are receiving public assistance. The petitioner sought to receive support under this statute from her stepmother, despite the fact that the stepmother's husband, the petitioner's natural father, had died. The petitioner argued that, under New York law, the death of the natural father did not terminate the stepchild relationship. The language of the statute clearly seemed to make the stepmother liable for support. The court, however, denied the petition. One explanation is as follows:

Noting that the relevant provision was in derogation of the common law and thus should be strictly construed, the court relied on the absence of specific language that would extend the obligation of the stepparent beyond the death of the natural parent. In so doing the court placed the statute in the context of existing common law rather than reaching the result that, in isolation, the clear statutory language seemed to require. (Maltz, 1988, p.387; citation omitted)

8   Conflicts of Precedents

Sometimes one finds lines of cases or individual precedents that conflict when applied to a particular set of facts. Courts have a variety of methods for resolving such conflicts. First, the court should determine whether one precedent comes from a court higher in the judicial hierarchy than the other precedent. If such is the case, the court will usually follow the precedent set by the higher court. Another approach is to examine whether one line of precedents is based on facts distinguishable from the case under consideration. If this is so, then the precedent or precedents which are determined not to be in point are disregarded. Yet another method is for the court to take note of which of the precedents in conflict is more recent. Alternatively, the court may choose the precedent that seems best justified in substantive policy. Or a court may follow the precedent that seems to 'do justice' in the particular case under consideration.

9   Hypothetical Cases

Scholarly commentators frequently present precedents in relation to hypothetical cases in their writings in order to explain or develop a thesis. Professor Eisenberg usefully discusses two uses of hypotheticals in common law reasoning. In the first type, the hypothetical functions to help justify extending a rule. Here, the reasoner imagines a hypothetical to which it would be justified to extend the rule. The reasoner then argues that the facts of the hypothetical cannot be distinguished from the facts of the case before the court for decision. Hence the rule should be extended to decide that case. In the second type, the hypothetical helps justify rejecting a proposed rule in the case at hand because the rule would be unsuitable when extended to the hypothetical, which itself cannot be distinguished from the case at hand. These two uses of hypotheticals are common. See Eisenberg (1988, pp.99–103), where examples are elaborated.

There are still other important uses of hypotheticals in common law reasoning. Thus a hypothetical case may be used to demonstrate that a proposed formulation of a possible rule would be too wide because, in the hypothetical case to which such formulation would apply, the result would be absurd, or 'a parade of horribles' or the like. Or, to demonstrate the justificatory basis of a given rule, a paradigm hypothetical case may be imagined to which the rule, by its terms, squarely applies. By inference and explication, a policy rationale for this rule as so applied can then be robustly articulated. In light of this, the rule can then be evaluated more intelligently, or its scope can be delineated with more assurance, or the extent of its consistency or harmony with related rules be more effectively determined.

VI   Matters of General Perspective, Evaluation and Other

1   'Saying and Doing'

Most often, judges say and do the same thing. But judges sometimes actually say one thing and yet do another. Thus judges might declare their freedom to depart from precedent yet follow the precedent in the case under consideration. Without more, this cannot be objectionable. But a court may also declare it is following precedent, yet in reality not be.

Sometimes judges say they are following a precedent, yet disregard the holding and follow only dicta because the judges misclassify dicta as holding. Sometimes judges say they are following a precedent, yet misconstrue the holding of the precedent and decide the case at hand inconsistently with what the precedent stands for. Sometimes judges say they are following a precedent when the precedent is really distinguishable. Sometimes a judge will radically reformulate the rule of a line of precedent, effectively overturning the rule yet still say he or she is following precedent. JUDGE CARDOZO's opinion in *MacPherson v. Buick Motor Co.*, 217 N.Y. 382 (1916), provides a good example of such transformation in the law of products liability. As noted earlier, in *MacPherson*, the New York Court of Appeals rejected a long-standing line of precedent beginning with the English case of *Winterbottom v. Wright*, 152 Eng. Rep. 402 (1842), which had established the general rule that a 'negligent manufacturer of a defective product was ordinarily liable only to the immediate buyer' (Eisenberg, 1988, p.58). Claiming that *MacPherson* fell within the *Thomas v. Winchester* exception to the requirement that the plaintiff be in privity of contract with the defendant, JUDGE CARDOZO went on to find the manufacturer liable and, without explicitly overruling the line of precedent, effectively adopted a new approach to the law of negligence.

MacPherson involved a claim for damages against Buick Motor Company by the buyer of a new Buick automobile who had suffered injuries when a defectively made wheel on the car collapsed, causing an accident. Buick had manufactured the car. However, Buick had not made the wheel, but had purchased it from another manufacturer. Moreover, the plaintiff had not purchased the car directly from Buick, but from a dealer who had purchased the car from Buick. Clearly, the buyer was not in direct privity of contract with the manufacturer of the wheel. A line of precedent in New York beginning with the 1852 case of *Thomas v. Winchester*, 6 N.Y. 397 (1852), however, had carved out an exception to the general rule, such that a plaintiff other than the immediate buyer of goods may be able to recover in cases that involved an 'inherently' or 'imminently' dangerous instrument, such as a jar of poison. CARDOZO claimed that Buick was liable under the *Thomas* reasoning, despite the fact that a car would not seem to fall under the category of an *inherently* dangerous instrument. Even as CARDOZO was radically transforming the law of negligence, however, he couched his opinion under 'the cloak of the old rule':

> We hold, then, that the principle of *Thomas v. Winchester* is not limited to poisons, explosives, and things of like nature, to things which in their normal operation are implements of destruction. If the nature of a thing is such that it is reasonably certain to place life and limb in peril when negligently made, it is then a thing of danger... If to the element of danger there is added knowledge that the thing will be used by persons other than the purchaser, and used without new

tests, then, irrespective of contract, the manufacturer of this thing of danger is under a duty to make it carefully. (*MacPherson*, 217 N.Y. at 389)

Thus CARDOZO radically transformed the law of products liability, allowing recovery in tort by a plaintiff not in contractual privity with the defendant on the basis of negligence, and discarding the contract-based requirement of privity, while not expressly overruling a single case and, indeed, purporting to follow a body of precedent.

2   Recent Change or Evolution

In New York there have been no major changes in the main aspects of the doctrine of precedent itself in recent times. The New York Court of Appeals has overruled precedent from time to time, but this has long been recognized to be within the court's authority. For discussion of the court's exercise of its power to overrule, see Section V.4, above.

3   Changes in International Environment

Changes in the international environment generally are only for the federal government of the United States. The states are precluded by the federal constitution from conducting foreign affairs. Thus New York state courts do not have a major role in dealing with the impact of international treaties and conventions.

4   Juristic or Other Criticism

There are no recent systematic and comprehensive critical essays or other publications devoted to the way precedents are created and used in the courts of the state of New York. However, there are at least three general currents of criticism in the periodical and other literature addressed in whole or in part to common law precedent generally in the United States.

First, it is frequently said that there are simply too many precedents on many questions that arise (see Gilmore, 1961, pp.1042–3). This view is difficult to counter. Today there are over four million reported common law precedents. Sometimes this means that in the same state there will be as many as a half-dozen precedents on a point of law, and many more if precedents from other states are cited to the court by the lawyers. In such circumstances, it may be difficult to know what the law on a given point really is, even when the cases are not conflicting. But not infrequently, some of the cases will be in conflict, especially when precedents from other states are taken into account. One result of this is that the judges may feel free, or at least freer, just to pick and choose in order to find support for whatever they wish personally to decide. To my knowledge, no American court considers itself bound by the English appellate court practice of writing opinions which purport to take account of all the precedent cited to the court, explaining away the cases not followed (see Tunc, 1984, p.150). The problem of a surfeit of precedent may eventually lead to the overthrow of the common law and the substitution of codes, though it cannot be said that this is likely in the near future. The undue freedom of decision and consequent uncertainty that a surfeit of precedent can bring is not the only objection. A surfeit of precedent is costly. Litigants must pay for lawyers to chase down numerous cases at billing rates often at or above $250 per hour!

A second current criticism of precedent to be found in the American system is that many judges on the highest state courts are simply not bold enough or not creative enough to overrule precedent that is outdated or otherwise unsound. Indeed, sometimes this criticism is even made of lower courts for not readily revising precedents of the courts above! See, for example, Caminker (1994, p.817). Yet American appellate judges expressly overrule precedents at least two or three times each year in almost every state (see Atiyah and Summers, 1991, ch. 5). Sometimes courts are even the major agencies of reform in a given field. For example, in the 1950s and 1960s, many American highest state courts made numerous major changes in the common law of tort (see, for example, Keeton, 1969). Not only is the criticism that courts are not creative enough overstated, one could also say that some state supreme courts have been too ready to change the common law and have not only departed from precedent, but also created new rules that are of dubious quality. The deficiencies of quality are partly attributable to the limitations of courts themselves. Frequently, these courts could not be well informed as to the relevant 'legislative facts' on which the new precedents had to be based. Two state supreme courts whose revisionist decisions in the decades of the 1960s and 1970s were notoriously subject to this criticism were those of California and New Jersey.

A third current of criticism is that American judges in common law cases sometimes 'manipulate' precedents to their own ends to 'support' decisions they are really making on other (often 'policy') grounds (see Atiyah and Summers, 1991, pp.124–5). This is a valid criticism of certain decisions in the highest state courts every year. But to determine how widespread this practice is would require an elaborate study beyond the scope of the present one. Yet, at the very least, we could have more candour from certain courts.

Bibliography

Atiyah, P.S. and Summers, R.S. (1991), *Form and Substance in Anglo American Law*, Oxford: Oxford University Press.

Blackstone, W. (1765–9), *Commentaries on the Laws of England*, Oxford: Clarendon Press.

Bradford, C. 'Following Dead Precedent: The Supreme Court's Ill-Advised Rejection of Anticipatory Overruling', *Fordham Law Review*, 59, p.39 (1990).

Brenner, S. (1992), *Precedent Inflation*, New Brunswick, NJ: Transaction Publishers.

Caminker, E., 'Why Must Inferior Courts Obey Superior Court Precedents?', *Stanford Law Review*, 46, p.817 (1994).

Cardozo, B. (1928), *Paradoxes of Legal Science*, New York: Columbia University Press.

Cardozo, B. 'Mr. Justice Holmes', *Harvard Law Review*, 44, p.682 (1931).

Cohen, M., Berring, R. and Olson, K. (1989), *How to Find the Law*, 9th edn, St. Paul, MN: West Publishing Co.

Eisenberg, M. (1988), *The Nature of the Common Law*, Cambridge, MA: Harvard University Press.

Farnsworth, E. (1983), *Introduction to the Legal System of the United States*, Dobbs Ferry, NY: Oceana Publications.

Friedman, L. (1973), *A History of American Law*, 1st edn., New York, Simon & Schuster.

Gilmore, G., 'Legal Realism: Its Cause and Cure', *Yale L.J.*, 70, p.1037 (1961).

Goldstein, L. (ed.) (1991), *Precedent in Law*, New York: Oxford University Press.

Greenawalt, K., 'Reflections on Holding and Dictum', *Journal of Legal Education*, 39, p.431 (1989).

Hand, L. (1958), *The Bill of Rights*, Cambridge, MA: Harvard University Press.

Holmes, O., 'Common Careers and Common Law', *American Law Review*, 13, p.608 (1879).

Hopkins, J., 'The Role of an Intermediate Appellate Court', *Brooklyn Law Review*, 41, p.459 (1975).

Jacobstein, J., Mersky, R. and Dunn, D. (1994), *Fundamentals of Legal Research*, 6th edn, Westbury, N.Y.: Foundation Press.

Jones, H., Kernochan, J. and Murphy, A. (1980), *Cases and Materials on Legal Method*, Mineola, NY: Foundation Press.

Kaye, J., 'The Human Dimension in Appellate Judging: A Brief Reflection on a Timeless Concern', *Cornell Law Review*, 73, p.1004 (1988).

Keeton, R. (1969), *Venturing to Do Justice*, Cambridge, MA: Harvard University Press.

Kraut, J. (ed.) (1983), *New York Jurisprudence*, 2nd edn, vol. 29, Rochester, NY: The Laywers Co-operative Publishing Co.

Levi, E. (1962), *An Introduction to Legal Reasoning*, rev. edn, Chicago: University of Chicago Press.

Llewellyn, K. (1951), *The Bramble Bush*, Dobbs Ferry, NY: Oceana Publications.

Llewellyn, K. (1960), *The Common Law Tradition: Deciding Appeals*, Boston: Little, Brown.

Loughran, J., 'Some Reflections on the Role of Judicial Precedent', *Fordham Law Review*, 22, p.1 (1953).

MacCormick, D.N. (1978), *Legal Reasoning and Legal Theory*, Oxford: Oxford University Press.

MacCormick, D.N. and Summers, R.S. (eds) (1991), *Interpreting Statutes – A Comparative Study*, Aldershot: Dartmouth.

Maltz, E., 'The Nature of Precedent', *North Carolina Law Review*, 66, p.367 (1988).

Moore, R. (1958), *Stare Decisis: Some Trends in British and American Application of the Doctrine*, New York: Simmons-Boardman.

Roalfe, W. (1957), *How to Find the Law*, 5th edn, St. Paul, MN: West Publishing Co.

Schranger, D. and Frost, E. (1986), *The Quotable Lawyer*, New York: Facts on File Publications.

Summers, R., 'Two Types of Substantive Reasons – The Core of a Theory of Common Law Justification,' Cornell Law Review, 63, p.707 (1978).

Summers, R. (1982), *Instrumentalism and American Legal Theory*, Ithaca, NY: Cornell University Press.

Surrency, E., 'Law Reports in the United States', *American Journal of Legal History*, 25, p.61 (1981).

Tunc, A., 'The Not So Common Law of England and the United States, Or, Precedent in England and in the United States, A Field Study by an Outsider', *Modern Law Review*, 47, p.150 (1984).

Wachtler, S., 'Stare Decisis and a Changing New York Court of Appeals', *St. John's Law Review*, 59, p.445 (1985).

Wachtler, S., 'Judicial Lawmaking', *New York University Law Review*, 65, p.1 (1990).

Williams, G. (1982), *Learning the Law*, 11th edn, London: Stevens.

12 Precedent in European Community Law

JOHN J. BARCELÓ, *ITHACA*

Introduction

Rather than one 'European Community', there are actually three different European Communities created by three separate treaties: (1) the European Coal and Steel Community (ECSC) (formed by the Paris Treaty of 1951), (2) the European Economic Community (EEC) (formed by the Rome Treaty of 1957), and (3) the European Atomic Energy Community (EAEC) (formed by the Euratom Treaty of 1957). This chapter focuses on the European Economic Community (EEC), which came into existence in 1958 and was always the most important of the three. The Maastricht Treaty, which took effect on 1 November 1993, created a 'European Union' based on all three communities. It also amended the EEC treaty (Rome Treaty) to establish 'the European Community' in place of 'the European Economic Community'. Thus, when this chapter speaks of 'European Community' law, it refers to the law under the original EEC treaty (Rome Treaty), as now amended and renamed the 'European Community' treaty.

I Institutional and Systemic

1(a) (b) (c)   Court Hierarchy; Structural and Procedural Aspects; Power to Select Cases

In formal structure there are only two courts in the European Community legal system – the Court of Justice of the European Communities and the Court of First Instance. As will be explained later, however, in legal effect all the courts in each of the 15 member states are part of the Community legal order.

The Court of Justice of the European Communities (ECJ)   The Court of Justice, which sits in Luxembourg, is the highest court for European Community law. It has 15 judges, one from each member state. (See Council Decision 95/1, Art. 10(1), O.J. L 1/1, at 4 (1 Jan. 1995).) It also has eight advocates general, who function as quasi-judges, following French procedure. (For transitional purposes there will be nine advocates general until 6 October 2000 – see Decision of the Representatives of the Governments of the Member States of the European Communities, Art. 4, O.J. L 1/223 (1 Jan. 1995).) After the case is assigned either to the full court or to a smaller panel of judges for decision but before the court or panel meets to deliberate, the advocate general for the case prepares a thorough and often lengthy opinion explaining how he would decide it. The advocate general does not participate in the court's deliberations or vote. Two scholars have described the advocate general as a kind of 'institutionalized *amicus curiae*' (see Brown and Kennedy, 1994, p.62.)

Cases come to the EC in several ways. First, and most commonly, when a court in any member state confronts a question of European Community law bearing on the case before it, it may request a 'preliminary ruling' from the ECJ on the relevant point(s) of Community law, for example the proper interpretation of the EC Treaty or of some part of the Community's secondary legislation. This is known as an Article 177 reference. A member state's lower courts have the option to refer a Community law question, but Article 177 *requires* a member state's court of last instance to do so.

Second, under Article 173 any act of a Community institution (such as Commission decision, Council regulation or directive) may be challenged by another Community institution, a member state or a private person or entity directly affected. The claimant in such a case brings the claim directly to the ECJ seeking to annul the act in question. Under Article 175, a claim to establish that a Community institution has *failed to act* when it has an obligation to do so can be brought to the ECJ in a similar manner.

Third, under Articles 178 and 215(2) a claimant, typically a private party, may bring an action in the court against the Community for the wrongful acts of a Community institution or servant that causes injury. The action is for damages.

Fourth, under Articles 169 and 170 the Commission or a member state may bring an action in the ECJ against another member state to establish that the latter has failed to fulfil an obligation under Community law.

The ECJ sits either in plenary session or in smaller three-judge or five-judge panels. The panels are formed each year in October at the beginning of the jurisdictional year. The decision whether to assign a case initially to the full court or to one of the panels is taken by the full court. Important cases – those involving important legal issues or the subject of widespread public interest – are reserved for the full court. A case of lesser importance but still involving some legal difficulty is assigned to a five-judge panel. A case primarily of interest only to the immediate parties is assigned to a three-judge panel. A panel considering a case may decide, because of the case's importance, to refer it to the full court.

European Community law is limited to questions that arise from the principles and rules of economic and social integration contained in the Rome Treaty creating the European Economic Community, now called simply the European Community. It consists largely of obligations imposed on the member states not to obstruct the free flow throughout the EC of goods, services, persons and capital (the 'four freedoms') and to adhere to certain common policies in areas like antitrust, environmental protection, consumer protection, agricultural policy and transport policy.

The ECJ's role is in many ways similar to that of an administrative law court in a continental civil law country. Its cases often involve a private party challenging government action that burdens one of the four freedoms, or one EC institution challenging the action or inaction of another. The cases before the court do not normally involve disputes between private parties – on a contract, tort or property question, for example. (A question of treaty, or secondary legislation, interpretation referred to the court under Article 177 may, of course, involve an underlying private law dispute between private parties in a national court.) It may be that the character of the court's jurisdiction influences the way precedent operates as a source of law in the Community legal system. In France, for example, administrative law is the domain in which court judgments play the most important law-making role. See Koopmans (1982, pp.12–13); see also Merryman (1996, p.111).

Speaking of the ordinary civil law courts, Cappelletti has argued that the reduced 'authority' of court judgments in civil law countries is attributable to three factors. First, in these countries the higher civil law courts tend to sit in panels, rather than *en banc*, and their opinions are anonymous. Second, these courts normally must decide large numbers of cases with no control over their dockets. Third, civil law judges tend to be career civil servants who are generally most comfortable with narrow or 'technical' opinions, rather than more discursive, policy-oriented judgments (see Cappelletti, 1981, p.381). He also contrasts the civil law courts with the special constitutional courts set up, for example, in Germany and Italy. These constitutional courts take fewer cases, and their judges are generally distinguished jurists who are more comfortable with policy-oriented issues and judgments. Constitutional court judgments, like those of the highest administrative courts, are generally considered more authoritative.

Under this form of analysis, one would expect ECJ judgments to be treated with considerable respect – as in fact they are. Although ECJ decisions are anonymous, with no indication of disagreement, and the court may sit in panels, it hears important cases in plenary session, the judges are all distinguished jurists and the court seems to have a reasonable case load, especially since the creation of the Court of First Instance. The ECJ is also much more like an administrative or constitutional court in the continental European tradition than a civil law court. It deals with administrative–constitutional issues, such as the consistency of member state measures with Community law, the powers of EC institutions, the validity of EC legislation and the consistency of EC measures and those of member states with the 'fundamental rights' of citizens.

The Court of First Instance (CFI)   The Single European Act of 1987 amended the Community treaties to permit creation of a Court of First Instance. This new court was established in 1989, largely to ease the case load burden on the ECJ. The CFI was given jurisdiction over actions brought by natural or juristic persons, but not those brought by the EC institutions or a member state. Article 177 references are also excluded. The CFI is confined in subject matter to antitrust questions, staff complaints, antidumping cases and certain issues under the European Coal and Steel Community Treaty. (See Brown and Kennedy, 1994, pp.74–6.) Appeals on questions of law can be taken from the CFI to the Court of Justice.

The CFI has 15 judges, presumably one judge from each member state. The judges generally sit in panels of three or five. If an advocate general is used, which does not happen in every case, he is chosen from among the judges (ibid., 1994, p.77). In 1990, the CFI dealt with 52 cases. In that same year the ECJ dealt with 380 cases, but it rendered 225 judgments (see The Council of Europe, 1990).

Courts of the member states   For two reasons, the European Community legal system could be said to include all the courts in each of the member states. First, under the Article 177 reference procedure, any court in any member state can refer a question of European Community law to the ECJ for a ruling on a question of Community law. Second, and more important for present purposes, Community law is in most instances directly applicable within the member state legal systems and, where it is so, it is superior to member state law, even member state constitutional law. Community law frequently grants rights, which are to be protected, and imposes duties, which are to be enforced, by actions in member

state courts. Thus the member state courts are the front-line enforcers of Community law.

2 Structure, Content and Style of Judgments

When a case comes to the ECJ, the president of the court chooses one
judge to be the *juge rapporteur* and assigns an advocate general to the
case. The *juge rapporteur* writes a preliminary report stating the facts
and summarizing the issues and the arguments of the parties. On the
basis of this report, the full court decides whether to assign the case
to one of the panels or the full court and whether to seek more
information concerning the facts or member state law. Thereafter, a
public hearing is held, at which the parties present arguments and
answer questions. After the public hearing, the advocate general
presents his written opinion on how he believes the case should be
decided. The court, having the advocate general's opinion before it,
then deliberates and renders a decision.

The ECJ renders a single composite opinion and judgment, un-
signed by any judge; there are no dissenting or concurring opinions.
ECJ opinions are decidedly deductive, legalistic and magisterial. (For
discussion of these terms, see MacCormick and Summers, 1991,
pp.496–501.) After a brief statement of the facts and the procedural
posture of the case, the opinion continues syllogistically with the
statement of general principles and logical deduction from these
principles to elements of the final conclusion. The principles or rules
cited may come from the treaty articles or secondary legislation, but
increasingly over the last one or two decades the court has cited its
own prior cases as the source of the asserted principles. Generally,
however, the court does not discuss the facts of prior cases and
makes no attempt to justify the asserted rules and principles. It mentions policy considerations only rarely and more or less obliquely.

The advocate general's opinion is quite different. It is usually much
longer and more thorough than the court's decision. It is also more
discursive, substantive and argumentative. The advocate general ex-
plores arguments and discusses the consequences of different
approaches to the case, although, it seems to this author, not quite in
as full and thorough a way as one would typically find, for example,
in a US Supreme Court opinion. Perhaps this comparative point
could be made better by saying that the advocate general's opinion,
while it will often mention policy considerations that could affect the
judgment, is less likely than an American Supreme Court opinion to
dwell on these considerations or to treat them as decisive. Instead,
the advocate general is more likely to concentrate on defining legal
concepts, explaining their elements, deciding their scope and then
deducing from this analysis his proposed resolution of the case.

3   Publication of Judgments

The decisions of the ECJ are published officially in the European Court Reports (ECR). These reports appear in the official languages of the Community: Danish, Dutch, English, Finnish, French, German, Greek, Italian, Portuguese, Spanish and Swedish. There is also an unofficial series, the Common Market Law Reports (CMLR). Both sources publish opinions of the ECJ and, in a separate section of the same volume, those of the CFI.

The published ECJ cases include the case name, the report of the *juge rapporteur* (facts, procedural history, issues and party arguments), the opinion of the advocate general and finally the decision of the court. As of January 1994, the published reports no longer include the report of the *juge rapporteur* (also called the report of the hearing).

The full ECJ case report, as it appears in the official reporter, is also available on the Lexis database in both English and French. It appears in French on Lexis within about a month of the judgment. This is because French is the court's working language. The judges draft and agree upon the final opinion in French. The opinion is then translated into what is known as the 'language of the case'. The language of the case is indicated at the bottom of the first page in the published official reports. In all Article 177 preliminary ruling cases, the language of the case is that of the referring member state court. In direct actions against member states, or against legal entities or private persons having the nationality of a member state, the language of the case is that of the member state. In direct actions against the Community or Community institutions, the claimant chooses the language of the case. Translation of the opinion into languages other than French and the language of the case can take six months or longer. Thus most cases are available on Lexis in French a long time before they appear in English (see Hartley, 1994, pp.78–80). CFI opinions are also included on the Lexis database.

The Westlaw database coverage of ECJ and CFI cases is less thorough than that of Lexis. Westlaw contains only English language cases, and it sometimes gives only a summary of the case.

4   Contents of Reports

The following discussion concerns ECJ opinions. CFI opinions will be described at the end of this discussion.

(a)   The case name, consisting of the parties involved, is included at the beginning of the report. The case identification number (or docket number) is also included. ECJ cases are usually identified by name and docket number.

(b) Because only ECJ cases are reported in the first section of each volume of reports, the name of the court is not given. The names of the judges on the panel deciding the case or the full court, as the case may be, are given later in the report of the decision.

(c) After the case name, the report includes a parenthetical description of the basic legal issues involved and the nature of the action, if the latter is not clear from the parties. For example, if the case involves two private parties, the parenthetical rubric may explain that the case involves a reference for a preliminary ruling from a certain named national court, and it will state the basic legal issue. On the other hand, if the claimant is the Commission and the respondent a member state, the case name reveals that the Commission is proceeding against the member state for violation of a Community obligation. The parenthetical rubric will then simply indicate the nature of the legal issues raised. A summary of the judgment then follows the parenthetical rubric.

(d) As noted above, for each case the president of the court appoints a single judge to be the *juge rapporteur*. That judge prepares a 'report for the hearing' prior to the first hearing in which the parties present their arguments orally. This 'report' contains a full statement of the facts, the procedural history, the issues and the party arguments. Prior to January 1994, the court published the 'report for the hearing' in full as the fourth element of a reported case, following (1) the case name, (2) the parenthetical rubric and (3) a summary of the judgment. Since January 1994, the published reports no longer contain the report for the hearing (though it is available on demand from the registrar of the court). The facts of the case are also recounted, however, in the advocate general's opinion and in the opinion of the court.

(e) The report for the hearing, again only before January 1994, gives the procedural background of the case and its procedural posture before the ECJ. This information is also contained in the advocate general's opinion and in the opinion of the court.

(f) The parenthetical rubric gives a very general and summary statement of the issue or issues. The advocate general's opinion, which follows the 'report for the hearing' (prior to January 1994) and is the fifth element of the report, gives a much more thorough statement and examination of the issues.

(g) The advocate general's opinion gives a full discussion of interpretational problems concerning the EC Treaty, regulations, directives and precedents, but the court's opinion does *not*. The court's opinion, which is the sixth element of the report and follows the advocate general's opinion, usually begins with a statement of the formal nature of the proceeding, the parties and the basic issues. The court then generally states the legal rules or principles it finds relevant, gives a cursory explanation of the authority for each rule or principle, and then gives the consequences for the case that derive from the rules and principles.

(h)   The specific holding or ruling on legal issues is given in two places. First, a 'summary of the judgment' appears, usually beginning on the first page of the report, following the parenthetical rubric. This is the third element of the report. It begins with a statement of the legal points decided, listed in 'headnote' form. This headnote list is then followed by a one or two paragraph statement for each headnote giving the judgment or holding of the court corresponding to each headnote. An editorial note on the inside front cover of the published official reports states that these summaries 'have no binding force and are in no way to be regarded as an authentic interpretation of the decisions summarized therein'. Second, at the end of its opinion, the court itself restates its holding (or ruling) on the major issues in the case.

(i)   As mentioned in point (g) above, the court's reasoning is given in its opinion printed immediately after the advocate general's opinion. Again as mentioned in point (g), the court's opinion does not give a full discussion of interpretational problems concerning the treaty or regulations and directives and does not discuss policy issues fully. The advocate general's opinion gives a much fuller discussion of these matters, but that opinion is solely the view of the advocate general (who does not participate in the decision) and is not an explanation of the judgment.

(j)   At the very end of its opinion, the court gives a statement of its specific ruling or rulings in the case.

(k)   The court's opinion and rulings are given as the ruling of the entire court or panel considering the case. No concurring or dissenting opinions are given. Of course the opinion of the advocate general, who is not a decision-making judge, may constitute a quasi-concurring or dissenting opinion, but it will never be so labelled. Indeed, it is delivered before the court reaches its own decision and is usually the starting point for the court's deliberations.

(l)   With regard to question I.4(l) of the Appendix see (k) above.

(m)   A summary of the written views of the parties and of any intervening parties – for example, interested member states or the Commission – is given in the 'report for the hearing', the fourth element of the reported case. As mentioned, this element appears in the published reports only prior to January 1994.

(n)   With reference to question I.4(n) (Appendix), see the discussion of the advocate general's opinion in (g) and (i) above.

(o)   No judicial or other commentary is included in the reported case. Legal journals and treatises in all member states and in many non-member states contain extensive discussion and analysis of the court's major decisions.

CFI Decisions   Reports of CFI decisions follow a slightly different format. A reported decision includes (1) the case name, (2) a parenthetical rubric similar to that used for ECJ cases, (3) the name of the court ('Court of First Instance') and the chamber (for example, 'Second Chamber'), (4) a summary of the judgment, and (5) the opinion of the court (including at the beginning the names of the judges sitting). The opinion of the court includes a thorough statement of the facts, the procedural background and the arguments of the parties. It then gives the court's reasoning and at the very end the court's specific order or judgment.

5   Meaning of 'Precedent'

Both the advocates general and scholars use the concept of 'precedent' in discussing the court's past decisions, but they are rarely explicit about the meaning they attach to the term. Clearly, the usage sometimes refers only to a past decision of the ECJ, which the writer may view as having only persuasive, not binding, authority. (See Toth, 1985, pp.19–20.)

Scholarly writers plainly disagree about whether the concept of a binding 'precedent' or the rule of *stare decisis* exits in Community law. Toth has shown that there is a range of scholarly opinion on this issue (see ibid., pp.2–3). At one end of the spectrum, scholars maintain that ECJ case law is not binding and hence not a formal source of law. See, for example, Bebr (1981, p.9): 'the case law of the Court does not constitute a formally binding precedent, as understood in a technical sense under the Anglo-American legal system'; and Toth (1984, p.81): 'Since "precedents" in Community law have only a persuasive authority but no binding force ... the case-law of the European Court of Justice cannot, strictly speaking, be regarded as a formal source of Community law'. The middle ground view is that the case law is at least de facto binding because the court is so consistent in following its past decisions. See, for example, Slynn, 1984, p.423: 'The Court may never refer to *stare decisis* or the doctrine of precedent, or be strictly bound by its own decisions, yet in general it clearly does follow them ... There are passages in the judgements where the weight and the number of the previous decisions seem almost to be felt to be such as to make them binding in fact, if not in theory.' The view at the opposite end of the spectrum is that ECJ decisions are binding on all European courts except the ECJ itself, just as could be said of House of Lords' decisions within England. See Mackenzie Stuart and Warner (1981, p.276): 'the European Court is not bound by its own decisions in the way that the English Court of Appeal is ... [however] all Courts throughout the Community [with the exception of the ECJ itself] are bound by the *ratio decidendi* of a judgment of [the ECJ]'; Koopmans (1982, pp.21–24): 'When the Court relies on its own judgments, it appears to consider them as binding authority ... . Its case-law on Article 177 seems to imply that it thinks national courts should do the same ... national courts are bound by the *ratio* of the earlier judgment'. It is interesting to note that the writers who express this last view include two former ECJ judges, Lord Mackenzie Stuart and T. Koopmans, and a former advocate general, J.-P. Warner. For a fuller discussion distinguishing among the ECJ itself, the CFI and member state courts on the question of the bindingness of ECJ decisions, see below, pp.420–24.

The ECJ itself cites its former decisions, in recent years with increasing frequency. The reference, however, is usually just a means of giving a source for a stated principle of law. The court does not discuss the facts of the prior case or the *ratio decidendi* to demonstrate that the holding is truly in point. The ECJ is well known for having handed down decisions inconsistent with prior cases, without even mentioning the latter. See Dine (1991, p.78): 'It has long been notorious that the European Court of Justice does not state directly when it is not following its earlier case law'; see also, Brown and Kennedy (1994, p.345). This practice appears to be dying out, however – if it exists at all any longer.

There are examples of decisions which distinguish prior cases or even overrule them, especially in the opinions of the advocates general, but also in those of the court itself. (See the discussion below, in Section V.) These decisions are the best evidence for the proposition that the Community legal system has a concept of *stare decisis* or at least is developing one. It is certainly clear that, at its current state of development, Community law does not contain an elaborate system of rules defining the force and binding character of past decisions, such as exists in England. (For an authoritative discussion of the English rules, see Cross, 1977.)

6 Mode of Citation and Discussion

Refer to Section 1.5 above. Scholars frequently discuss the decided cases of the ECJ in considerable detail, approving, criticizing or commenting on them. Scholars play an important role in synthesizing and analysing bodies of decided cases. However, as just discussed, scholars are not in agreement about whether ECJ cases should be viewed as formally binding precedent, as having de facto precedential force, or as having merely persuasive authority if well reasoned and correctly decided. The ECJ judges never refer to past decisions as 'precedents', but they do use the cases as justification for stated rules or principles. Usually the court cites a line of cases concerning a firmly established point. Thus an ECJ opinion might say: 'in accordance with settled case law' and then cite a string of cases. The opinion would then state an abstract principle, often using language identical to that used in the prior cited cases themselves.

Advocates general sometimes discuss conflicts in existing lines of decision and the need to resolve the conflict. (See Advocate General Lenz's opinion in *Faccini Dori v. Recreb Srl*, Case C-91/92, [1994] ECR I-3325.1.) As mentioned in Section I.5 above, two former ECJ judges and one advocate general seem to accept the notion that ECJ decisions have binding, precedential force. Lawyers who appear before the ECJ would almost always refer to past ECJ decisions in making written and oral arguments to the court.

7 Overall Role of Precedent

The ECJ relies primarily upon two main justificatory sources: 'legislation', in the form of the EC Treaty and secondary 'legislation' of the EC institutions (regulations, directives and decisions) and case law (the ECJ's own past decisions). Thus one would have to say that 'case law' plays a major justificatory role. The ECJ itself never cites academic writings or other professional commentary.

Nor, as a general rule, does the court discuss policy factors in any detail or with any degree of discursiveness. On the other hand, policy justifications do spring up in opinions, though usually in the barest terms. An example can be found in the well-known *Keck and Mithouard* case (Cases C-267 & 268/91, [1993] ECR I-6097; [1995] Com. Mkt. Law Rep. 101). A major issue in the case was how broadly to define the concept of a 'measure with equivalent effect' to a quantitative restriction. EC Treaty Article 30 prohibits member states from employing quantitative restrictions on the free flow of goods within the Community and measures with equivalent effect. In an early landmark case, *Procureur du Roi v. Dassonville*, Case 8/74, [1974] ECR 837, the court defined the concept of 'measure with equivalent effect' very broadly to include any government measure which actually or potentially, directly or indirectly, hindered the flow of trade between member states. Thus internal regulations of all kinds, whether discriminating against imports or not, were caught by this broad definition. In *Keck and Mithouard*, the court consciously and expressly retreated from this definition for a specific subset of cases, those involving 'national provisions restricting or prohibiting certain selling arrangements' [1993] ECR at para. 16; [1995] Com. Mkt. Law Rep. at p.124). This vague terminology refers to such measures as Sunday closing laws, rules against certain types of advertising potentially taking advantage of vulnerable consumers, prohibitions on resale below purchase price, and so on. The court explained its decision to change course in part because of a policy consideration:

> In view of the increasing tendency of traders to invoke Article 30 of the Treaty as a means of challenging any rules whose effect is to limit their commercial freedom even where such rules are not aimed at products from other Member States, the Court considers it necessary to re-examine and clarify its case-law on this matter. (*Keck and Mithouard*, Cases C-267 & 268/91, [1993] ECR I–6097, at [para. 14]; [1995] Com. Mkt. Law Rep. at 124)

In other words, the court had found that the breadth of the former rule had allowed businessmen to launch judicial challenges against virtually all member state regulations affecting trade in goods, even where there was no real protectionism (disguised or de facto) at play. Both the explicitness of this reference to a policy consideration and the court's express overruling of a prior line of cases, especially one so firmly entrenched as the *Dassonville* line, are unusual. The overruling of *Dassonville* will be discussed further below, in Section V. The policy reference in *Keck* appears only in the barest terms. In that sense the decision is typical. The court does not normally anchor decisions in expressly articulated policy grounds. Moreover, even when policy is acknowledged, it does not march 'front and centre' as a primary justificatory factor. By contrast, the court clearly does use its own past decisions as a primary source of justification.

As discussed above in Section I.2, the advocate general's opinion is different. It is much more discursive and may openly discuss scholarly views and policy considerations, along with legislative texts and past ECJ decisions. On the issue of relative justificatory force, the advocate general, like the court, treats past decisions as belonging in the first rank of importance.

8   Role of Precedent in Different Branches of Law

As explained above, European Community law cannot be divided into the traditional branches of law found in a national legal system. It is all essentially administrative–constitutional law.

9   Precedent and 'Gaps in the Law'

Given the nature of European Community law, it is difficult to imagine a case that does not involve interpretation of the European Community Treaty or the secondary legislation of the Community institutions. Nevertheless, unanswered interpretive questions of Community law constantly arise. In answering those questions, and hence in creating new law, the court itself does not generally speak explicitly or in a methodologically self-conscious way about the creation of new precedent.

There is one important exception to this general rule. On several occasions the court has included in its ruling a discussion of whether the ruling would apply retroactively or not. This has occurred specifically with respect to Article 177 interpretive rulings. Some such rulings have been limited to prospective application only. In these instances the court is clearly methodologically conscious of creating new precedent, even if the term 'precedent' is not used. For a detailed discussion of prospective rulings, with examples, see the discussion below in Section V.

Although theoretically, at least, the court is always interpreting the Community Treaty or secondary legislation and although it is generally not explicit about creating new precedent, a former member of the court, Judge T. Koopmans, has noted that it is precisely in areas in which the Treaty is almost silent that the court's case law has been the most prominent. The burden of his argument is that a form of *stare decisis* does exist in Community law and that one of the preconditions for its existence is that some of the main rules are unwritten:

> From this point of view, European law is comparable to French administrative law. There is legislation galore, in the treaties and in the thousands of regulations and directives. ... Nevertheless, the main rules for judicial activities are unwritten: the treaties are practically silent on the relationship between Community law and national legislations, and criteria for assessing the legality of Community decisions are expressed in a way which, though recalling the grounds for review known to French administrative law, leaves much room for interpretation, precision and further elaboration. (Koopmans, 1982, p.15)

II   The Bindingness of Precedent

1   Kinds and Degrees of Normative Force;
2   Law Concerning Precedent;
3   Factors Determining Degrees of Normative Force;
4   Factors that Weaken Precedent;
5   'Vertical' and 'Horizontal' Bindingness;
6   Analysis of Force, Support and Illustrative Role.

Although many of the distinctions raised in the above heads of discussion do not arise in European Community law, some discussion of the nature of the bindingness or justifying force of European Community case law may nevertheless be useful.

Given the structure of the Community court system, the question of the bindingness of precedent arises at several different levels. First, is the Court of Justice bound by its own decisions? Second, is the Court of First Instance bound, either by its own decisions or by those of the ECJ? Third, are the member state courts bound by decisions of the ECJ or CFI? Where bindingness or justifying force is attached to European Community case law, what is its nature? Although many of the distinctions raised in the above questions do not arise in European Community law, some discussion of the nature of the bindingness or justifying force of European Community case law may nevertheless be useful.

Is the ECJ bound by its own decisions?   There seems to be broad agreement among legal scholars that the ECJ is not bound by its own decisions. As mentioned already, the ECJ frequently cites its own prior decisions, but in doing so it never explains its action as in any sense compelled. That the court does not recognize an obligation to follow its own past decisions seems especially evident in its practice – which is perhaps less common now than in the past – of reaching a result inconsistent with a prior decision without even citing the prior case. There are only very few instances, as will be discussed later, in which the ECJ has expressly explained that it is departing from a prior case. There appear to be no decisions in which the ECJ has expressed any sense of obligation to follow one of its previous decisions, except in the weak sense just mentioned that it felt an obligation to explain a departure from a prior decision. On the other hand, commentators are also in agreement that the court has a good record, as a de facto matter, of following its own decisions.

Is the CFI bound by ECJ decisions?   T. Millett, principal administrator of the ECJ, points out, as noted above, that the ECJ has never regarded itself as bound by its previous decisions. Thus he concludes that the CFI will probably also not consider itself formally bound by its own decisions (Millett, 1990, p.74). One commentator considers that there can be little doubt about this point, noting that there is no written rule requiring the CFI to adhere to its past decisions and that the vast majority of CFI judges come from civilian systems in which courts are not bound by their previous decisions (Arnull, 1993, p.262). As a practical matter, however, the CFI adheres closely to its previous decisions, as does the ECJ with respect to its own decisions.

There are two situations in which the CFI is formally bound by an ECJ decision, both provided for in the Statute of the Court of Justice, which was amended in 1988 to create the CFI. First, under Article 47 of the statute, if the ECJ decides that a case falls within the jurisdiction of the CFI and remands the case to it, the CFI must take jurisdiction. Second, Article 54 of the statute expressly states that the CFI is bound by the ECJ's decision on points of law in an appeal from the CFI whenever the ECJ refers a case back to the CFI.

There is no comparable legislation on whether the CFI is bound in general by other ECJ decisions. One commentator, Marc van der Woude, asserts: 'The CFI is, in principle, not bound by judgments of the Court of Justice' (Van der Woude, 1992–3, p.459). This view is shared by Arnull (1993, pp.262–3). On the other hand, both van der Woude and Millett speculate that, as a practical matter, the CFI will consider itself bound by ECJ decisions, at least where they are clear and unambiguous. (See Millett, 1990, p.74.) Otherwise the CFI could expect to be reversed.

Millett also adds the interesting observation that he would expect the same result 'even where the ECJ had reached its decision against the views of its Advocate General' (Millett, 1990, p.74). The implication here is that such decisions of the ECJ somehow carry less authoritative weight, yet still sufficient weight to control the CFI. But this comment should not be misunderstood. Neither decisions nor scholarly comment can be found supporting the view that individual ECJ decisions vary in their degree of formal bindingness. What Millett seems to mean is that the CFI is always free to decide contrary to a previous ECJ decision as a way of urging the ECJ to change its mind. One might expect that the CFI would be more likely to do so where a 'dissenting' advocate general's opinion signified particular controversy surrounding a decision. Yet, even in these cases, Millett believes that the CFI will normally follow the ECJ, unless the circumstances are truly exceptional. See also Arnull (1993, p.263).

Are member state courts bound by ECJ decisions?   The question whether member state courts are bound by ECJ decisions has arisen mostly in the context of Article 177 references from a member state court seeking an interpretation on a point of Community law. Obviously, a referring court is bound by the ECJ's answer to a 177 reference, but are other member state courts also bound? Recall that Article 177 requires the court of last instance in a member state to refer to the ECJ any questions of Community law. In *Da Costa v. Nederlandse Belastingadministratie*, Cases 28–30/62, [1963] ECR 31, the court held that a member state's court of last instance was not obligated to refer a question of Community law that had previously been decided by the ECJ. The court also said, however, that the member state court in question would be permitted to refer the question if it chose to do so. Brown and Kennedy thus reason from this decision that member state courts are bound by prior ECJ decisions: they must either apply the previous decision or refer the question for a new ruling (Brown and Kennedy, 1994, pp.352–3). This reasoning seems persuasive. The ECJ seems to regard its decisions as directly applicable sources of law binding on member state courts unless and until the ECJ itself alters the decision.

This view is not shared, however, by A.G. Toth, even when commenting on the *International Chemical Corporation* case, Case 66/80, [1981] ECR 1191, which to the ordinary reader's eye would seem to establish that the ECJ regards its decisions under Article 177 as binding on all member state courts. In the *ICC* case, the plaintiff had previously forfeited the security he had posted in connection with various imports, as required by a Council regulation. The ECJ had declared the regulation null and void in a previous Article 177 proceeding involving different parties. In the *ICC* case the plaintiff sought the return of the forfeited security, relying on the declared illegality of the relevant regulation. Again in an Article 177 proceeding the ECJ ruled as follows:

> Although a judgment of the Court given under Article 177 of the Treaty declaring an act of an institution, in particular a Council or Commission regulation, to be void is directly addressed only to the national court which brought the matter before the Court, *it is sufficient reason for any other national court to regard that act as void* for the purposes of a judgment which it has to give. That assertion does not however mean that national courts are deprived of the power given to them by Article 177 of the Treaty and it rests with those courts to decide whether there is a need to raise once again a question which has already been settled by the Court where the Court has previously declared an act of a Community institution to be void. There may be such a need especially if questions arise as to the grounds, the scope and possibly the consequences of the nullity established earlier. (*International Chemical Corp.*, Case 66/80, [1981] ECR at 1223; emphasis added)

Toth regards this language of the court, especially the language emphasized above, as not saying that member state courts are bound by the court's previous decision, but rather that they are *permitted* to rely on it. He also stresses the national court's right, expressly mentioned by the ECJ, to resubmit the question under a 177 proceeding (Toth, 1985, pp.65–9).

But the Toth analysis seems unpersuasive. It seems that the court uses permissive language ('it is sufficient reason ...') in order to hold open the alternative of a further 177 reference. And, even as to that option, the court seems to have mostly in mind a reference to clarify the meaning and scope of a prior decision, rather than a request that the court change its mind – although this last possibility is not ruled out, especially because the court does not regard itself as technically bound by its own past decisions. Still, that a litigant in England may be able to ask the House of Lords to overturn one of its prior decisions would not be regarded as showing that the *stare decisis* doctrine does not apply in England. The better view would seem to be that the ECJ does consider its Article 177 decisions as binding on courts in all member states, unless the ECJ itself alters the precedent. A well-reasoned commentary and the opinions of several advocates general support this view. See Brown and Kennedy (1994, pp.352–3) and, in particular, the opinions of Advocate General Reischl in *International Chemical Corp.*, Case 66/80, [1981] ECR at 1224 and of Advocate General Warner in *Manzoni v. FNROM*, Case 112/76, [1977] ECR 1647 at 1657.

The binding force of ECJ decisions on member state courts is also supported by the decision in *Firma Foto-Frost v. Haupzollamt Lübeck-Ost*, Case 314/85, [1987] ECR 4199. That case holds that member state courts may not themselves declare a Community 'act' invalid on the ground that it violates superior Community law. When the validity of a Community 'act' is questioned in a proceeding before a member state court, the court must either find the act valid and apply it or refer the question of invalidity to the ECJ under Article 177. In *Firma Foto-Frost*, the Community 'act' in question was a decision of the Commission. It would thus seem to follow, a fortiori, that a member state court is not permitted itself to decide that a previous ECJ decision is invalid, incorrect or mistaken. It must either apply the previous ECJ decision or refer the question of its correctness or proper interpretation to the ECJ. Again, member state courts seem bound by previous ECJ decisions.

Toth argues further that an ECJ decision is not to be regarded as a 'source of law', by which he means, drawing on Cross, 'that from which a rule derives its validity as rule of law' (Cross, 1977, p.155). Toth (1984, p.69) claims that 'no rule of Community law ... derives its validity from the Court's judgments'. Rather, he says, 'All such rules, including the judgments themselves, derive their validity, directly or indirectly, from the basic Treaties' (ibid., p. 69). In a similar vein, Toth asserts: 'While judicial decisions do not make the law, they contain authoritative statements of what the law is on a given point at a given time. It may therefore be concluded that the judgments of the European Court are *not sources* but *authoritative evidences* of Community law' (ibid., p.70; emphasis in original). But one could say something similar about judgments of the US Supreme Court. They derive their validity from the US Constitution. But that does not prevent them from being sources of law and binding precedents. Thus, again, these assertions by Toth seem unconvincing. If Article 177 decisions by the ECJ are binding on member state courts, as in the alternative view they seem to be, then it is difficult to see why at the same time they are not also legitimate 'sources of law'.

III   The Rationale of Precedent

1   *General Rationales for Formal Bindingness*

2   *Rationales for Force, Further Support, and so on*

To our knowledge, *stare decisis* has not been discussed in any ECJ opinion, but Advocate General Warner has addressed the topic both in one of his opinions and in scholarly writing. Warner's opinion in the *Manzoni* case, Case 112/76, [1977] ECR at 1657, is one of the clearest statements in support of the role of *stare decisis* in Community law, at least in Article 177 preliminary rulings on questions referred to the ECJ by a member state court. He stresses *uniformity* as the major purpose underlying the Article 177 procedure and the *stare decisis* doctrine:

> ... to hold that a ruling of the Court under Article 177 had no binding effect at all except in the case in which it was given would be to defeat the very purpose for which Article 177 exists, which is to secure uniformity in the interpretation and application of Community law throughout the Member States. ... This, it seems to me, is where the doctrine of *stare decisis* must come into play. (*Manzoni*, Case 112/76, [1977] ECR at 1662)

In a scholarly piece, Warner and his co-author, Lord Mackenzie Stuart, a former judge of the ECJ, discuss the role of *stare decisis* in Community law more generally. In addition to the uniformity rationale, the authors note that the doctrine serves the goal of efficiency in avoiding an undue volume of litigation and the goal of certainty in the law, which allows lawyers to rely on past decisions in advising clients (Mackenzie Stuart and Warner, 1981, pp.273, 275). They implicitly make a further point: they argue that the presence of *stare decisis* in English law and its absence in French law derive paradoxically from the same purpose – the desire of a central government to strengthen and consolidate its authority. In England historically the doctrine of precedent assisted the royal courts in gaining authority over the decentralized customary courts. Had the royal courts failed to follow their own decisions, they would have created uncertainty as to what the 'common law' was and thus undercut the common law's authority. In France the French kings of the *ancien régime* sought to consolidate power over the local law-giving bodies by claiming exclusive legislative power for themselves. The leaders of the French Revolution apparently followed the same purpose in forbidding judges to lay down the law. (See Mackenzie Stuart and Warner, 1981, p. 276.) The authors' implicit point seems to be that the Community institutions are also concerned about establishing a strong central authority for Community law and that *stare decisis*, or something close to it, can be important in promoting the authority of ECJ decisions and hence the centralizing and unifying role of Community law.

Another former judge of the European Court, Judge Koopmans, has also analysed the role of *stare decisis* in European Community law. He asserts that a system of precedent, to be truly functional, must meet three 'conditions' and that all are present in the Community legal system. The first condition, the prevalence of unwritten rules, was discussed above in Section I.9. The second condition, the need for courts to impose uniformity in the service of a centralizing political authority, was discussed immediately above.

Koopmans says that his third condition 'is more difficult to formulate: it is something like the necessity of resorting to principles' (Koopmans, 1982, p.16). He says judges will more readily follow previous decisions if those decisions are based on or frame a 'general proposition of law'. Whereas in a common law system judges start with an individual case and inductively extract a principle from it, in the continental approach judges prefer to start with the principle. Subsequent decisions then either expand or narrow the principle (see Koopmans, 1982, pp.16–17). This discussion accurately describes the ECJ's methodology. The court begins its analysis by stating a general principle, which it attributes to a case or a line of cases. The decision at hand may then simply apply the principle or go on to give a broader or narrower interpretation of it.

There is an embedded rationale for *stare decisis* in this discussion. *Stare decisis* can be seen as a mechanism for generating principles needed for deciding cases and giving guidance to lawyers and clients. Principles, by their nature, must maintain reasonable consistency over time. Of course the need for this mechanism is greater if there is no code to provide the principles and the major rules are unwritten. Both conditions apply for Community law (as well as for French administrative law). Of course the EC Treaty provides written rules and principles, but it is not a code, and many of the major rules of Community law are not based directly on treaty language: as with, for example, the rules on direct effect of the treaty and Community directives in member state law and on the role of 'fundamental rights' in limiting both secondary Community legislation and member state measures within the field in which Community law applies.

Concerning the ECJ's not being bound by its own decisions, Brown and Kennedy make the important point that the ECJ functions like a constitutional court, in the sense that its decisions are final and can be overridden only by an amendment of the EC Treaty, which can only rarely be accomplished. Thus, to preserve some level of flexibility in the face of changing conditions, the court has found it necessary occasionally to change direction, though mostly by narrowing or broadening existing decisions. See Brown and Kennedy (1994, p.347).

The uniformity and centralizing role of ECJ opinions would be undercut if the practice of dividing the court into panels or chambers were to lead to conflicting panel decisions. This has generally not been a problem in Community law. Important cases and cases likely to involve conflicting panel views are assigned to the full court. Moreover, a panel may at any time (for example, at the first appearance of a potential panel conflict) refer a case before it to the full court. See Brown and Kennedy (1994, p.347).

The notion of a precedent having influence only on the basis of persuasiveness arises in EC law in connection with advocate general opinions, which are not binding. There are two situations in which an attorney may rely on these opinions as persuasive. First, if the advocate general discusses a legal point that the court's opinion does not touch upon, the advocate general's views represent the only authoritative voice on the issue. The force of that voice depends, though, on its persuasiveness. Second, if the court decides contrary to the advocate general's opinion, lawyers may cite the advocate general's opinion in later cases only for the purpose of persuading the court to change course and adopt the advocate general's view. In this second case, the advocate general's opinion plays the role of a dissenting opinion. See Brown and Kennedy (1994, p.348).

IV   Precedents: What They Stand For and How They Apply

Although many of the distinctions raised in Section IV heads of discussion do not arise in European Community law, the case law is used and does have a kind of binding force.

The Binding Element in a Precedent

The most characteristic use the ECJ makes of its past decisions is to cite them as the source for a stated principle of Community law, usually formulated in broad language. The court then reasons from the principle thus isolated and articulated to deduce the solution for the case pending before it. Frequently, the court repeats almost the exact language used in a prior case in stating the principle, but often with a subtle variation that may narrow or extend the meaning of the principle slightly. The court's attention focuses upon the principle derived from the cases and not upon the cases themselves.

The Importance of Ratio Decidendi

While the court does not openly discuss the concept of *ratio decidendi* or deal directly with it by some other name, one scholar, former ECJ Judge Koopmans, has concluded that in practice the concept is recognized and followed in Community case law (Koopmans, 1982, pp.22–4). In support of his conclusion, Koopmans cites an example first identified by Mackenzie Stuart and Warner, the case of *Express Dairy Foods Ltd. v. Intervention Board for Agricultural Produce*, Case 130/79, [1980] ECR 1887.

In *Express Dairy Foods*, the ECJ acted very much like a common law court in isolating the *ratio decidendi* of a previous decision in order to apply the rule of the precedent to the case pending before it. The case is striking because the advocate general had urged the court to side-step the issue of the precedential value of its prior decision and simply repeat the reasoning of the previous case. Thus the ECJ's reliance on previous *ratio decidendi* seems deliberate.

In *Express Dairy Foods*, the plaintiff had exported large quantities of powdered whey. According to a Commission regulation, itself authorized by a Council regulation, the plaintiff was required to pay certain monetary compensatory amounts even though intervention prices had not been fixed for powdered whey. Under the Council regulation, this was proper only if the price of powdered whey were dependent upon the price of a product for which intervention arrangements were in force. In this case the reference product would have been powdered milk. But in a previous Article 177 decision, also involving compensatory payments for the export in member state trade of powdered whey, the Court had ruled that the Commission regulation imposing the compensatory payments was invalid because the price of powdered whey was not dependent upon the price of powdered milk (see *Milac v. Hauptzollamt Saarbrücken*, Case 131/77, [1978] ECR 1041). The Commission regulation struck down in *Milac* was not, however, the same regulation that governed the *Express Dairy Foods* case, although the provisions of the two Commission regulations were essentially the same and both depended for validity on the same Council regulation. Relying on the *Milac* judgment, the plaintiff in *Express Dairy Foods* sought reimbursement for the illegal compensatory payments.

Although Advocate General Capotorti acknowledged in his opinion that the Commission agreed with the plaintiff's argument that 'all national courts will be bound to apply the *ratio decidendi* of the said *Milac* judgment in accordance with the essential aim of Article 177 [uniformity]' (*Express Dairy Foods*, Case 130/79, [1980] ECR at 1904), he suggested that the court did not have to reach that question because it could simply rule for the plaintiff by repeating the grounds given in the *Milac* judgment (*Express Dairy Foods*, Case 130/79, [1980] ECR at 1905). The court refused. Instead, it explained the *ratio decidendi* of *Milac* (that the price of powdered whey did not depend on the price of powdered milk) and concluded:

> In the light of the judgment delivered by the Court in Case 131/77 [*Milac*] the conclusion should therefore be drawn that the Commission regulations [challenged in this case] must be regarded as invalid in so far as they fix monetary compensatory amounts in respect of trade in powdered whey. (*Express Dairy Foods*, Case 130/79, [1980] ECR at 1899, para. 8)

In further illustrating the influence of *ratio decidendi* analysis in Community law, Koopmans gives examples in which the court seems to conclude that member state courts are bound only by the *ratio decidendi* of its earlier decisions and in which the member state courts themselves follow a similar analysis. (Koopmans, 1982, pp.23–4). It seems significant, however, that these results are more implicit than explicit. Commentators and former judges see the rudiments of a *stare decisis* system in Community case law, but the court does not openly and expressly mention these ideas.

Jurisprudence Constante and Leading Cases

Even though under the better view a single decision of the ECJ under the Article 177 preliminary ruling procedure is binding on member state courts, several commentators claim that the court gives extra weight to a consistent series of holdings in a line of cases – similar to the notion in French law of the precedential value of *jurisprudence constante*. (See, for example, Bengoetxea, 1993, p.69.)

Certainly, the Court frequently refers to a string of cases as establishing a legal principle and, without actually saying so, gives the impression that the presence of a string of decisions is significant. At the same time the court also seems to give 'leading case' status to certain decisions that are cited again and again, and that may be the only case cited as evidence of a consistent line of decisions.

One can see these patterns in the well-known 'German Beer' case in which the ECJ held incompatible with the EC Treaty Germany's prohibition of the use of the word 'bier' on beverages not brewed according to the German purity law. (See *Commission v. Germany*, Case 178/84, [1987] ECR 1227.) The EC treaty prohibits, as to trade between member states, all quantitative restrictions, such as quotas, and 'all measures having equivalent effect'. In the well-known *Dassonville* case, a leading decision, the ECJ gave a very broad definition to that concept (*Procureur du Roi v. Dassonville*, Case 8/74, [1974] ECR 837). Here is the court's language in the 'German Beer' decision, which gives the *Dassonville* definition in inverted commas:

> *According to a consistent line of decisions of the Court* (above all, the judgment of 11 July 1974 in Case 8/74 *Procureur du Roi v. Dassonville* [1974] ECR 837) the prohibition of measures having an effect equivalent to quantitative restrictions under Article 30 of the EEC Treaty covers 'all trading rules enacted by Member States which are capable of hindering, directly or indirectly, actually or potentially, intra-Community trade'. *Commission v. Germany*, Case 178/84, [1987] ECR at 1269, para. 27; (emphasis added)

The court seems to give weight here to the consistency of a line of decisions and also singles out the *Dassonville* decision (the first to use the quoted language) as a leading case.

Again in the 'German Beer' case, the same pattern occurs concerning one of the best known of all ECJ decisions, the *Cassis de Dijon* case (*Rewe-Zentral AG v. Bundesmonopolverwaltung für Branntwein*, Case 120/78, [1979] ECR 649). In *Cassis de Dijon*, the court held that, despite the prohibition of Article 30, a member state regulatory rule which hindered the flow of trade could nevertheless be valid, but only if it applied alike to domestic and imported goods, served a fundamental public purpose (such as consumer protection) and was 'proportionate' or 'reasonable' – meaning that the means chosen were appropriate to the end sought and were not excessively burdensome to trade. Here is the relevant language from the 'German Beer' case:

The Court has also consistently held (in particular in the judgment of 20 February 1979 in Case 120/78 ... [the *Cassis de Dijon* case] ... that 'in the absence of common rules relating to the marketing of the products concerned, obstacles to free movement within the Community resulting from disparities between the national laws must be accepted in so far as such rules, applicable to domestic and to imported products without distinction, may be recognized as being necessary in order to satisfy mandatory requirements relating *inter alia* to consumer protection. It is also necessary for such rules to be proportionate to the aim in view. If a Member State has a choice between various measures to attain the same objective it should choose the means which least restricts the free movement of goods'. *Commission v. Germany*, Case 178/84, [1987] ECR at 1270; (emphasis added)

V   Distinguishing, Explaining, Modifying, Overruling

Perhaps some of the strongest evidence for the proposition that ECJ decisions are regarded as having considerable weight (even as being sources of law) can be found in the opinions of advocates general and the ECJ itself in which prior decisions are explicitly distinguished or overruled. Such opinions exist, although they are not plentiful. The discussion above has already noted the ECJ's earlier practice of departing from prior decisions without even acknowledging the prior case law. In recent times it seems that the court has been increasingly willing to acknowledge openly when it departs from a prior decision.

One prominent example occurred in the *Hag II* case, *CNL Sucal SA v. Hag GF AG*, Case C-10/89, [1990] ECR I-3711. The court had previously decided in *Hag I* that a trademark owner could not use its trademark to block goods from another member state, where the infringing trademark on the imports had a common origin with the complainant's trademark. (See *Van Zuylen v. HAG*, Case 192/73, [1974] ECR 731.) In *Hag II*, the ECJ openly reversed itself on essentially the same facts. It concluded that the common origin concept would not apply where the infringing trademark had not been voluntarily transferred by the original trademark owner. In both *Hag I* and *Hag II*, the transfer had resulted from the seizure in Belgium of enemy property during the war. Thus, in *Hag II*, the German owner of the German trademark was allowed to block entry into Germany of decaffeinated coffee from Belgium bearing the 'Hag' trademark.

An even more prominent example, because of the significance of the decision, occurred in 1993 in the *Keck and Mithouard* case, discussed above in Section I.7. The case concerned whether a French law prohibiting retailers in France from reselling below their purchase price violated EC Treaty Article 30's prohibition on measures with equivalent effect to a quantitative restriction. Previous case law, beginning with the leading *Dassonville* case, *Procureur du Roi v. Dassonville*, Case 8/74, [1974] ECR 837, had defined 'measures having equivalent effect' to include all measures that directly or indirectly, actually or potentially restrained trade in goods between member states. It was not necessary that the measure in question discriminate against imports. Because of this broad definition, the court had faced a series of difficult decisions in which litigants had challenged member state regulations on business hours, advertising and promotional techniques for increased sales. None of the regulations in these cases had seemed to involve disguised or even de facto discrimination against imports. Nevertheless, the court was forced to scrutinize the regulations involved and sometimes even struck them down as inconsistent with the EC Treaty. Some commentators saw these decisions as confusing and as intruding unnecessarily into member state affairs.

Although the case had originally been assigned to a single chamber, that chamber referred the case to the full court, which decided that it was time to depart from the broad *Dassonville* definition. The court did so in the following language:

> ... contrary to what has previously been decided, the application to products from other Member States of national provisions restricting or prohibiting certain selling arrangements is not such as to hinder directly or indirectly, actually or potentially, trade between Member States within the meaning of DASSONVILLE ... so long as those provisions apply to all relevant traders operating within the national territory and so long as they affect in the same manner, in law and in fact, the marketing of domestic products and of those from other Member States. (*Keck and Mithouard*, [1993] ECR I–6097 at para. 16 [1995] Com. Mkt Law Rep. at p.124)

Thus the Court in *Keck* did not reject *Dassonville* in its entirety. It did so only for a subset of cases, those involving 'national provisions restricting or prohibiting certain selling arrangements', and only insofar as they were truly non-discriminatory. Characteristically, the court worked with the principle derived from and stated in *Dassonville* and not so much with *Dassonville* itself or the facts underlying it. Indeed, the court does not even make clear in the passage quoted that it is the *Dassonville* case that the court is partially overruling. *Dassonville* had said that 'all trading rules' that 'are capable of hindering, directly or indirectly, actually or potentially, intra-Community trade' were 'measures with equivalent effect'. ([1974] ECR at para. 5). *Keck* redefined the category 'measures with equivalent effect' to exclude from it 'national provisions restricting or prohibiting certain selling arrangements'. Though different in style, *Keck* is the equivalent of a common law court's partial overruling of a previous leading decision. See generally Brown and Kennedy (1994, pp.345–7).

Prospective Overruling

While in ECJ case law we have found no examples of prospective overruling of a prior decision, there is an example of limiting an Article 177 interpretive ruling to prospective application only. The case in point is *Defrenne v. Société Anonyme Belge de Navigation Aérienne Sabena*, Case 43/75, [1976] 1 ECR 455.

In *Defrenne*, the court held that Article 119 (equal pay for men and women for equal work) had direct effect within member state legal systems. Thus a female 'air hostess' was able to rely on the article for a complaint against Sabena Airlines that she was paid less than male 'air stewards' who did the same work. Article 119 is addressed only to member states and instructs them to ensure the application of the 'principle that men and women should receive equal pay for equal work' during the first transition stage: that is, before 1 January 1962. For member states, like Belgium, that had failed to fulfil this obligation through appropriate legislation, the court held that Article 119 would have 'direct effect'. Although Sabena Airlines is arguably a public entity, the court made clear that the 'direct effect' was to be both 'horizontal' (applicable between private parties) and 'vertical' (applicable in a suit by a private party against a member state).

Theoretically, the direct effect should have been triggered on 1 January 1962. The concept in prior decisions had allowed direct effect to become operative from the moment that a member state had failed to take the appropriate national action to protect the right involved. (See, for example, *Pubblico Ministero v. Ratti*, Case 148/78, [1979] ECR 1629.) Here that moment came at the end of the first transition stage (1 January 1962), but the court expressly held that its judgment would only be applicable to claims already filed for past discrimination and for any future pay discrimination that arose after the judgment (see *Defrenne*, Case 43/75, [1976] 1 ECR at 481, para. 75). Clearly, the court understood that its judgments make law.

The reasons the court gave for this outcome were pragmatic and principled. The pragmatic rationale related to the potential existence of a very large number of claims dating back from the time of the judgment in 1976 to the theoretical beginning of direct effect, 1 January 1962. The court noted that dating the effectiveness of its judgment from 1 January 1962 could spell bankruptcy for some undertakings. (See *Defrenne*, Case 43/75, [1976] 1 ECR at 480–1.)

The court also invoked the principles of reliance by private parties on the prior state of the law and 'legal certainty'. It asserted that undertakings could not have foreseen a legal outcome dating a right to equal pay for women and men from 1 January 1962. It also reasoned that the member states, who did nothing to bring the principle of equal pay for equal work into existence, and the Commission, which had threatened legal action against recalcitrant member states without following up the threats, had misled the undertakings affected. So in effect these undertakings were entitled to rely on the absence of a right to equal pay in those member states that had not passed appropriate legislation.

VI   Matters of General Perspective, Evaluation and Other

When the ECJ was created it was modelled on the French *Conseil d'Etat*, the court of last resort in the administrative court system in France. Some of the ECJ's earliest decisions were written in the style of a French decision, comprised of a string of 'whereas' clauses punctuated at the end by a single declarative clause stating the ruling. Its origin still explains much of the style of ECJ opinions. Indeed, French is still the working language of the court. At the same time, the court has evolved over almost 40 years into a different institution.

The case law of the ECJ has been and remains of fundamental importance to the development of the Community. The court has pushed forward the cause of European integration and unity through many imaginative rulings that were not clearly foretold in the constitutive treaties. The court found large portions of Community law to have direct effect in the member states, creating rights and even obligations for ordinary citizens. That caused member state courts to be the frontline enforcers of Community law (not the distant officials and magistrates in Brussels or Luxembourg). Almost in the teeth of the treaty language, the court found some parts of directives also to have limited direct effect. Not surprisingly, it also ruled that Community law is supreme over member state law. And almost out of whole cloth the court fashioned the doctrine of fundamental rights, that incorporated into Community law the constitutional traditions of all member states and the European Convention on Human Rights. All of these rulings have become accepted parts of Community law, in some cases having been expressly ratified by subsequent changes in the EC Treaty. These were rulings of fundamental importance, created by an activist court, clearly making law.

The court's decision-making style and treatment of precedent has seemingly evolved over the last two decades somewhat in the direction of common law methodology. It appears to be developing, at least in a de facto sense, a doctrine of *stare decisis*, although employing a continental methodology and style that focuses on the rules and principles articulated in the cases, rather than on the cases themselves in their factual settings. Although the court generally refers to the consistency of repeated decisions in referring to its case law – a point reminiscent of the French doctrine of *jurisprudence constante* – it is clear that a single decision, such as *Keck*, can have law-making significance. (See the discussion above, in Section V.)

Whereas in its earlier decisions the court was content to reach results inconsistent with prior decisions without even mentioning them, much less justifying the departure, in some of its more recent decisions, such as *Hag II* and *Keck*, it was explicit about overruling a prior precedent. In a trend that seemed to accelerate after the admission into membership of two common law jurisdictions, the United Kingdom and Ireland, the court can be counted on to cite a significant number of its own decisions in crafting its opinions and to pay much more attention to consistency in its case law and the requirements of a system of precedent. At least one sitting ECJ judge, Judge Mancini, believes this change is directly attributable to the presence of common law judges and advocates general on the court. (See Mancini and Keeling, 1995, p.402.)

Still, the court has retained its basic syllogistic style of opinion writing without much in the way of substantive reasoning. The opinions of the advocates general, which are more substantive and discursive, are at the same time more informative and explanatory, even when written by an advocate general from a continental tradition. Of course the court's style may be dictated by the need to produce a collegiate opinion that will command a majority out of sometimes as many as 15 judges. That is at least an explanation favoured by Mancini (Mancini and Keeling, 1995, p.402).

One is tempted to ask what would be sacrificed, were the court to allow signed opinions, including dissents and concurrences. Perhaps at the beginning the court may have worried that the appearance of division would undercut its authority. That motive may also explain why for most of its history the ECJ has chosen to ignore departures from past decisions – that and the continental tradition common to all the judges until the United Kingdom and Ireland became members in 1973. But the court is well established now. A more substantive decision style would not reduce respect for its rulings. It would, however, lead to more informed critiques and analyses of court decisions by jurists and commentators, and thus would bring to bear on the court's decision making a wider range of opinion and informed analysis. It would allow the court to write more substantive opinions, taking better and more precise account of past decisions. Presumably, these changes would lead not only to better decisions but also to a more frank and open decision-making process and to more guidance for lawyers and their clients.

But there is another consideration, which would almost certainly block any reform in the direction just suggested. The court consists of 15 judges, one from each member state, appointed for six-year renewable terms. Thus a single collegiate judgment seems necessary to ensure the absence of national bias, or the appearance of bias, in the court's work and to insulate the judges from the political pressures that would otherwise build up.

Under a different system for selecting judges, more substantive decision making, including signed opinions and dissenting and concurring views, would be conceivable. The court itself is on record as not opposing a reform which would lengthen the term of appointment and make it non-renewable. (See Court of Justice of the European Communities, 1995, p.11.) This would strengthen the independence of the judges and allow more substantive opinions. Both changes seem desirable to this author. Whether either will come about remains to be seen.

References

Arnull, R., 'Owning Up To Fallibility: Precedent and the Court of Justice', *Common Market Law Review*, 30, (1993).

Bebr, G. (1981), *Development of Judicial Control of the European Communities*, The Hague: Martinus Nijhoff Publishers.

Bengoetxea, J. (1993), *The Legal Reasoning of the European Court of Justice*, Oxford: Clarendon Press.

Brown, L.N. and Kennedy, T. (1994), *The Court of Justice of the European Communities*, 4th edn, London: Sweet & Maxwell.

Cappelletti, M. (1981), 'The Doctrine of Stare Decisis and the Civil Law: A Fundamental Difference – or No Difference at All?', in Bernstein, H., Drobnig, V. and Kötz, H. (eds), *Festschrift Für Konrad Zweigert*, Tübingen: Mohr, p.381.

The Council of Europe (1990), *European Yearbook*, vol. 38.

Court of Justice of the European Communities (1995), 'Report of the Court of Justice on Certain Aspects of the Application of the Treaty on European Union', *The Proceedings of the Court of Justice and Court of First Instance of the European Communities*, 22 to 26 May, no. 15/95.

Cross, R. (1977), *Precedent in English Law*, 3rd edn, Oxford: Clarendon Press.

Dine, J. (1991), *Procedure and the European Court*, London: Chancery Law Publishing.

Hartley, T.C. (1994), *The European Court and the Court of Auditors*, 3rd edn, Oxford: Clarendon Press.

Koopmans, T. (1982), 'Stare Decisis in European Law', in O'Keeffe, D. and Schermers, H. (eds), *Essays in European Law and Integration*, 11, Boston: Kluwer Law and Taxation Publishers.

Koopmans, T. 'The Birth of European Law at the Crossroads of Legal Traditions', *American Journal of Comparative Law*, 39, p.493 (1991).

MacCormick, D.N. and Summers, R.S. (eds) (1991), *Interpreting Statutes – A Comparative Study*, Aldershot: Dartmouth.

Mackenzie Stuart, A.I. and Warner J.-P. (1981), 'Judicial Decision as a Source of Community Law', in Grewe, W., Rupp, H. and Schneider, H. (eds), *Europäische Gerichtsbarkeit und Nationale Verfassungsgerichtsbarkeit*, Baden-Baden: Nomos.

Mancini and Keeling, 'From *CILFIT* to *ERT*: the Constitutional Challenge Facing the European Court,' *Yearbook of European Law*, 11, p.1 (1991).

Mancini and Keeling, 'Language, Culture and Politics in the Life of the European Court of Justice', *Columbia Journal of European Law*, 1, p.397 (1995).

Merryman, 'The French Deviation', *American Journal of Comparative Law*, 44, p.109 (1996).

Millett, T. (1990), *the Court of First Instance of the European Communities*, London: Butterworths.

Slynn, 'The Court of Justice of European Communities', *International & Comparative Law Quarterly*, 33, p.409 (1984).

Toth, 'The Authority of Judgments of the European Court of Justice: Binding Force and Legal Effects,' *Yearbook of European Law*, 1984, 4, p.1 (1985).

Van der Woude, 'The Court of First Instance: The First 3 Years', *Fordham International Law Journal*, 16, p.412 (1992–3).

13 Institutional Factors Influencing Precedents

MICHELE TARUFFO, *PAVIA*

1 Organization of Courts

In every legal system the organization of courts influences the nature and the use of precedents at least in two ways: (a) it determines which courts may create precedents, how precedents are created and what is a precedent; (b) it determines how precedents are used by courts and by other people, particularly by practising lawyers. Therefore the content and the force of a precedent are connected with the structure of the judiciary, the place of the various courts within this structure and with the functions performed by supreme courts, and by other courts as well, in the several legal systems.

1.1

Hierarchy of courts is the organizational feature that seems to be common to every modern system of justice. The fundamental model includes three levels of ordinary courts: courts of first instance or trial courts, intermediate appellate courts and a supreme court at the top. Such a model may be taken as a general reference in order to have a basic idea of the hierarchical organization of courts. Moreover, it is a reliable description of many actual systems, the organization of which has the form of a three-layered pyramid. *Within* this model there may be, however, some variations. For instance, sometimes the first instance level is subdivided into different courts with different venues (distinguished by matter and/or by amount of the case, as well as territorial jurisdiction). Sometimes among first instance courts there is a distinction concerning the kind of personnel involved, as in the case when there are justices of the peace (as in the UK and now in Italy) or when the court is a mixed panel with professional judges and lay assessors (as in Poland or in some labour courts) or when a lay jury rather than a judge finds the facts (still general in the USA for civil and criminal matters; now almost solely criminal in the UK). Another variation within the model occurs in special instances in which there are only two levels instead of three. The most important case of this is that of EC courts. Some other instances exist in some systems where a case is considered at only two levels. This happens in several systems of administrative justice (for instance in Italy) where the highest administrative court is actually an appellate court of second instance, and in some systems of tax courts (as in Germany). Moreover, a two-level jurisdiction exists when a direct appeal from a first instance court may be brought *omisso medio* to a supreme court. On the other hand, a jurisdiction may have four levels (as, for instance, in the German system of ordinary civil courts).

Of course systems are not identical: there are in fact many differences concerning the composition of courts, their roles and functions and their organization. The three-layered pyramid is, however, a useful conceptual model for the analysis of the most important modern systems. Such an analysis may be significant in order to understand the complex phenomenon of precedent in at least three ways.

First, a hierarchical structure means that the greatest authority is placed at the highest level, and that some degree of subordination characterizes the lower courts. Such a subordination increases passing from higher to lower courts in a multi-layered system. This means that hierarchy may explain some important features of the so-called *vertical* dimension of precedents in which lower courts follow upper court precedents. First of all, precedents of highest or supreme courts are the most important and the most authoritative, *inter alia* just because they stem from the apex of the judicial system. Such courts are vested with the greatest authority within the system also because they are courts of last resort. At least in principle, they may control and revise what happened at the levels below. By deciding appeals they are also able to impose their own opinions.

Intermediate appellate courts are under the authority of supreme courts, but they are also higher courts from the viewpoint of trial courts. Then they are supposed to follow the precedents of supreme courts, but trial courts should follow precedents not only of the supreme court but also of the intermediate level courts. Moreover, in several systems (and mainly when supreme courts have power to select the cases they decide: see Section 2.2 below) decisions made by appellate courts are virtually final. Their authority is strengthened because their decision may be the last one on a given legal issue. Therefore precedents of appellate courts are substantially authoritative, depending upon their institutional role in the system.

Because they are located at the lowest level, trial courts must generally follow both the precedents of supreme and intermediate appellate courts, and decisions of such lowest level courts are not precedents.

Second, a hierarchical structure shows also which courts are at the same level. This may affect how far a court at a given level must follow its own precedents ('horizontal' precedent) and how far a court may be bound to follow precedent of another court at the same level (also a 'horizontal' matter).

A precedent of another court situated at the same level may be cited, but its function is to provide further support or to be illustrative. A very special case is that of precedents *of the same court*. Whether a court must or should or need not generally follow its own precedents is one of the main features of the system of precedent. The topic of departures from precedent (Chapter 17) is closely related to this. Law courts (including supreme courts) in civil law countries do not consider themselves bound by their own precedents, although they cite and quote such precedents rather frequently. The consistency of a court in following its own precedents is considered, however, to be a significant value. The same is true for common law courts: see, for instance, the famous Practice Statement delivered by the House of Lords in 1966. The House stated that, from that moment, it would not consider itself bound by its own precedents, but in fact it still adheres closely to its own precedents, departing only occasionally. According to guidelines set by the House of Lords in 1995, there are considerable restrictions on the circumstances in which precedents will be reviewed for possible departure (see Chapter 10).

Third, an organized structure defines both what it includes and what it excludes, that is which courts properly belong to the system. It may affect the problem of precedent because a precedent of the system is the one that is set forth by a court that is inside the system. Judgments by courts not belonging to the system may be cited and quoted and so still have some force. Some distinctions should be made, however. External precedents from foreign courts are quoted very infrequently, but a relevant exception is the use of 'regional' precedents by Scandinavian courts. Another exception, the importance of which is growing in European countries, is the reference to precedents of EC courts in cases in which those precedents are not directly binding.

A precedent may be external also because it comes from a court which belongs to a different branch of the same system. Thus, for instance, decisions of an administrative court may be quoted by a civil court, or vice versa. These are not precedents in a proper sense, but they may be significant examples of the application of a rule.

Finally, a precedent may be external because it comes from a court that belongs to the same jurisdiction but is not placed hierarchically over the court that quotes it (for instance, a precedent of an appellate court that has no jurisdiction on the case). In such cases, a precedent may have only an illustrative function, but its role may be considerable when it is delivered by a court having scientific or cultural authority. A quite special case of external precedents, with peculiar features, is that of judgments delivered by constitutional courts (see Section 1.3 below).

However, what happens inside a system is not necessarily uniform and consistent from the point of view of precedent. Divergences about the existence and the force of precedents may occur, in fact, even within the same jurisdiction. It may happen, for instance, that higher courts emphasize the binding force of their precedents but such a force is not acknowledged by lower courts (see Chapter 17 on departures from precedent). Or it may happen, as for instance in Germany, that a constitutional court does not recognize that ordinary courts must be consistent in their decisions, but the force of precedents is acknowledged in other ways by these courts.

1.2

Besides the variations existing within the hierarchical basic model, some other diversifying factors deserve consideration. One of these factors is the federal structure of the state, insofar as it influences the organization of courts. The USA and Germany are significant (albeit substantially different) instances of systems in which there are a federal and several state jurisdictions. The distinction between federal and state jurisdictions is too complex to be analysed here. It has to be stressed, however, that in a federal system such as that of the USA the federal supreme court is considered to be the highest court in the system in matters of federal law, while the state higher courts are 'supreme' only in a relative sense, that is within the single state organization of courts in respect to matters of state, not federal, law. From the point of view of precedent, this entails a significant complexity. The vertical dimension of precedent is complicated by the double dimension of the organization of courts. Moreover, judgments of federal courts in the USA are commonly treated as relevant precedents by state courts, at least where the state courts have concurrent jurisdiction in federal matters, while the judgments of state supreme courts are proper precedents for intermediate and lower courts of the state in matters of state law, but not for courts of a different state. In such a federal system, therefore, the allocation of authority among courts follows very complex patterns influencing the use and the force of precedents. Thus, in the USA each of the 50 states has its own judicial organization with a supreme court at the top. Within each state system (as in the case of New York described in Chapter 11) there are precedents on state law issues according with the structure of state courts, and the most important precedents are the ones delivered by state supreme courts. Then one might speak of '50 common laws' at the state level. The federal system is in a sense 'superior to' and in another sense 'different from' the state systems, so that the federal law is in a limited sense the fifty-first 'common law' jurisdiction in the USA in matters of federal law. State lower courts follow 'their own' state supreme court precedents, state intermediate court precedents and their own precedents. They also follow federal precedents when they have concurrent jurisdiction in matters of federal law.

Germany seems to be an example of a federal system in which federal courts perform a significant unifying role even in regard to state courts, by means of federal precedents that are considered directly authoritative by state courts. This does not happen, however, in matters belonging exclusively to state jurisdiction in which state courts follow different patterns also because there are no federal appeals.

Things are much simpler in non-federal systems, where courts are organized only on a single dimension. Even among these systems, however, an important distinction has to be drawn between 'compact' and 'diversified' organizations. A system of courts may be defined as 'compact' when it includes only ordinary courts with general jurisdiction about all kinds of matter (civil, criminal, administrative, commercial, labour, tax and so forth). The system of EC courts is compact in this sense; Norway is another example. The Spanish system is partly compact at the level of the supreme court, which is unique, but it is diversified at the lower levels where courts are diversified in several branches with different jurisdictions.

A system is 'diversified' when it is divided vertically into several branches. The most common vertical division is between ordinary courts with civil and criminal jurisdiction and administrative courts with special administrative jurisdiction. This division is fundamental in many civil law systems such as France, Italy, Finland, Sweden and Poland. The historical model that influenced all these systems was the French model based upon the *Conseil d'Etat*. According to this model, the autonomous system of administrative justice is usually organized with two instances, with a supreme administrative court.

There are also important countries, such as Germany, in which the vertical division among courts is even more complex and may include no fewer than five branches of courts (civil and criminal, administrative, labour, tax and social matters). Each of these is autonomous and includes from two to four, but mainly three levels, with its own supreme court at the top. There are then five supreme courts with different jurisdictions. As already mentioned, the Spanish system is partly similar: the ordinary lower courts are differentiated according to five different jurisdictions. The supreme court is unique, but it is divided into five chambers, each dealing with different matters corresponding to the jurisdictions of the branches below.

The vertical division within the system of courts is important since each single branch has its own precedents, mainly represented by judgments of its own supreme court. A judgment of the supreme court of a branch is usually not considered a proper precedent by courts belonging to a different branch, although it may be cited and quoted.

A further variation is that in some countries, as for instance in France, there are courts of special jurisdictions dealing with very special matters such as labour (*conseils de prud'hommes*), commerce (*tribunaux de commerce*) and leases of land (*tribunaux des baux ruraux*). Such courts are often composed totally or partially of lay members, who sometimes are representative of classes of people involved in the specific kind of litigation. They produce a case law that is often important and interesting, but their precedents are effective only within the particular areas they are concerned with.

1.3

A further structural factor that has to be taken into account is whether there is a special constitutional court or whether ordinary courts perform also the task of a 'diffuse' constitutional review. The first situation is rather frequent in civil law systems, as for instance Italy, Spain, Germany and Poland. France has a peculiar system in which the *Conseil Constitutionnel* has to be considered a court from many points of view, although it only has powers of pre-enactment review of the constitutional legitimacy of statutes. Constitutional courts deal specifically and exclusively with constitutional matters and may be activated in various ways by several subjects according to the specific regulations existing in each system. As a rule their judgments are legally binding when the court finds that a statute or an act is in conflict with a constitutional provision, and the act or statute is in some way nullified by the court's judgment. Moreover, a constitutional court's judgment is usually considered a persuasive and sometimes authoritative precedent by ordinary courts dealing with the same or similar subject matter. The effect of precedent is typical of constitutional courts' judgments independently of their specific content. They are used as persuasive precedents also when the court finds that a statute is not unconstitutional.

Things are somewhat different when ordinary courts are vested with the power to perform the function of constitutional review of the statutes or acts they should enforce. This happens typically in common law systems such as in the USA, but also in some civil law countries such as Norway and Sweden, and now also in Finland. There are, however, important differences concerning the degree and scope of constitutional review performed by ordinary courts. Such a review seems to be frequent and thorough in the USA, but it is infrequent and minimal in other countries, as for instance in Sweden. In such systems the interpretation of ordinary statutes or of the common law is always done 'in the light' of constitutional principles, since they are applied, more or less directly or explicitly, in the daily administration of justice. Thus the interpretation of constitutional provisions is not made *in abstracto* or in general terms, because such provisions are invoked in order to decide single and concrete cases. In these systems the supreme courts are at the same time courts of last resort *and* constitutional courts. Their judgments have a double effect: they decide the merits of the single case with a binding legal effect on that case; they also have the force of a precedent influencing future decisions on the same or similar matters. This effect may be especially broad and intense when important constitutional principles are involved. This effect may even be far more important than the decision of the single case. It is, however, a typical effect of precedent which works on a 'case-to-case' basis without being formally binding. In such systems, in many cases, constitutional precedent is structurally identical with the non-constitutional precedent.

The difference between the two systems of constitutional review is less striking, however, if one considers that, even when constitutional courts exist, as in Italy, Germany, Spain and Poland, constitutional provisions are directly applied by ordinary courts in their daily practice. They take into account and tend to prefer the 'constitutional interpretation' of statutes when they apply the law. Therefore, constitutional precedents become more and more important and pervasive in the current administration of justice performed by ordinary courts, since the areas covered by constitutional interpretation are growing in number, importance and extension. (A peculiar case of 'diffuse' review made by ordinary courts exists in some countries, as for instance in France, in which all courts review statutes by reference to European treaties.)

2   Functions and Structures of Supreme Courts

A structural and functional typology of supreme courts in the various legal systems cannot be presented here because it would be exceedingly complex. Comparative analysis of the various models of court organization shows that there are several types of supreme courts, sometimes even inside the same legal systems, and that such courts perform different functions. Sometimes different functions are performed by the same court, even while deciding the same case. In this complicated landscape, some factors seem especially relevant in order to understand the phenomenon of precedent. These factors deserve some attention.

2.1

A very important factor is whether a supreme court, while deciding a case, adopts a *prospective* or a *retrospective* orientation. A prospective orientation requires, according to the definition in Chapter 3, a decision concerning whether the judgment on that single case will possibly be a precedent, or not. This is to say that the court looks to the future, to the forthcoming cases concerning identical or similar matters, and has the intention of guiding or determining their decision. Then the court consciously performs the function of stating rules that should be effective in future cases. Sometimes, as for instance in Finland, this attitude influences the form and the style of the judgment: it tends to be shaped in more abstract and general terms when it is aimed at stating rules for subsequent decisions. Such prospective orientation is more or less present in all the systems in which a court has the power to select those cases that the court will decide on the merits (see Section 2.2). This selection is made according to several criteria and courts usually do not justify their choices. However, one may guess that a prospective orientation, in the sense of setting forth a new precedent or overruling an old one, may determine or influence the choice of deciding a case on its merits. This may be true of supreme courts with extensive power of selection such as the US Supreme Court, the New York Court of Appeals and the UK House of Lords, but probably also is true of courts selecting cases for decision merely according to the 'importance of the legal issue involved' or anything similar, as in the German system, or in other courts following similar patterns, as in Norway and Sweden. It is rather clear, in fact, that the 'decision to decide' a case may be influenced by the choice (albeit implicit) of establishing a precedent. At least the decision not to decide a case is clearly based on the choice not to set a precedent on that matter.

A prospective orientation is obviously present when the court itself chooses the judgments that will be reported (see Section 4.2 below) since obviously the court will select the precedents that in its opinion should be followed in future cases.

A very peculiar form of prospective orientation exists in Poland, where it is the basis for a unique type of judgment that is delivered by the Supreme Court. Such a judgment sets forth a resolution concerning a 'legal principle' that may be stated under specific conditions regulated by the law. In most important cases, the 'legal principles' stated by special panels of the Polish Supreme Court are legally binding for all the chambers or panels of the court, since they are aimed at solving doubts or at explaining a legal rule. Of course these very special judgments are oriented to determining the decision of future cases.

A retrospective orientation is present when a court concentrates its attention only or mainly on solving the specific issues raised in the concrete single case. This generally occurs in courts that do not select cases for decision, but must decide all the cases that are brought to them by the parties (as for instance in Italy and Spain). More generally, a retrospective attitude is typical of supreme courts interpreting their own function as that of a third instance in the single case. Correspondingly, these courts tend to deal only with the specific and peculiar issues of that case. Legal rules are interpreted in order to formulate a criterion for the decision of the specific case, rather than with the aim of eliciting a standard that could be valid for future decision making as well. Such an attitude seems to prevail in systems such as those of Italy, Spain and France, in which the supreme court is conceived essentially as the last instance of decision of cases by way of ordinary appeals.

Both the prospective and the retrospective orientations may be present in the same court and even in the same particular judgment. The matter, then, is which of the two attitudes actually prevails, depending on the content and the style of the judgment and the institutional role that the court wants to play.

2.2

As already indicated, one of the most important differences among supreme courts is whether the court has the power to select the cases deserving a decision on the merits, or is required to deal with all the appeals filed.

In several European systems, supreme courts have no power of selection: this is the case in Italy, Spain and Poland. Italy is a sort of extreme case from this point of view, since a constitutional provision (Article 111, al.2) vests any party with the right to bring an appeal to the supreme court and to obtain from the court a judgment on the case. Spain has a rather peculiar situation because the ordinary supreme court has no power of selection, but the constitutional court recently created has the possibility of not judging the merits of a case when, according to the unanimous opinion of a panel of the court, there is a precedent that would ground the dismissal of the appeal. This is a very interesting instance of precedents used as criteria for the selection of cases deserving decision, or at least for excluding decision of cases already 'covered' by precedent.

In other civil law systems, various devices have been introduced in the last decades, providing for the selection of cases for decision by supreme courts. Leaves to appeal by the court *a quo* and/or by the supreme court itself are sometimes required, according to different standards and procedures. Sometimes, as in Germany, the selection is aimed at letting 'important issues' be decided by supreme courts. Only a few apparently unfounded or non-important cases are not decided on the merits. In some other civil law systems, the supreme courts have a broader discretionary power to select cases deserving a decision, as happens in Scandinavian countries.

At the other extreme of the scale, there are the common law systems, where *certiorari* (or something similar) is often available to select for decision only some dozens or a few hundred cases a year. Total discretion without any justification is the basic rule for such courts.

The purposes served by the selection of cases are various in the different systems. Correspondingly, the legal devices used and the standards applied in the selection change from case to case. Moreover, the reasons for the selection are almost never explained, so that a direct analysis of such reasons is actually impossible. At any rate, among these purposes is the need to manage the workload of the supreme court and the opportunity to avoid the waste of time required to deal with frivolous or clearly ungrounded appeals. However, a relevant purpose relates to the problem of precedent. When a court selects a case for decision, a good reason for doing it may be the opportunity to set forth a new precedent, to overrule an old one or to solve a conflict or overcome an inconsistency among precedents. This may not be the only reason for the selection, but it may often be a sufficient reason to 'decide to decide' a case. At least, it may often be a good concurring reason for such a decision. On the other hand, a judgment concerning a case that has been selected by a supreme court because of the importance of the legal issues involved will probably be referred to by later decisions concerning such issues. Precedents and selection of cases may then be connected in a double way: the opportunity to establish a precedent may justify the selection of a case for decision; a decision of a case selected because of its importance will probably become a precedent.

2.3

Other relevant variations may concern the size and the composition of supreme courts, and some procedures by which they perform their task. As to the size, the range goes from one-panel courts composed of a few judges, as for instance the US Supreme Court with its nine members, and the New York Court of Appeals with its seven members, to huge courts including several hundred judges sitting in many panels, as for instance in the Italian *Corte di Cassazione*. Most courts of countries belonging to the civil law world, such as Spain, France, Sweden, Finland and Poland, are composed of numerous judges. They are usually divided into panels dealing with different matters such as civil or criminal cases (and sometimes also labour and administrative cases).

The format of compact and small supreme courts, existing for instance in US and EC courts, and in some constitutional courts, is extremely important from the point of view of precedent. These courts usually do not divide into panels and chambers; the whole court decides all the cases. In some instances, the court itself has chosen the cases for decision. This means that, within a reasonable period of time (depending on the turnover of judges), all decisions are referable to the same group of people, or at least to a relatively stable group of people inside the court. Then the choice, attitudes and orientations of the court are referable to these people. Correspondingly, the 'source' of precedents is a relatively compact, stable and identifiable group of judges. This means that judgments delivered by such courts may be relatively coherent and consistent. The UK House of Lords is rather atypical since it is formally a unique body but actually it works by means of unofficial and informal panels, and cases are assigned to single members for analysis and for the writing of opinions.

Things are obviously different when courts are composed of 80 or 90 judges and work by panels or chambers of five, seven or nine judges each. In these cases 'the court' is a sort of fiction, since many people, divided into small groups, actually decide cases. Obviously, there is the possibility of confusion and inconsistency due to the number of people involved and to organizational problems. When a court is divided into sections or chambers, each dealing with a specific area of legal issues (as in Spain), there may be some degree of consistency in the attitudes of the single section or chamber. The same goes for Germany, with five supreme courts, each one dealing with its own specific matters. Therefore a significant degree of consistency and continuity of precedents might be expected in these courts. Consider, however, that these supreme courts deal with a relatively high number of cases each year (from one thousand to three or four thousand) and that the variety of cases is higher, so that consistency and continuity become difficult to achieve. This difficulty may be greater when a section or chamber works by several panels with a changing composition.

All these problems and difficulties are magnified when a supreme court is composed of hundreds of judges and delivers many thousands of judgments a year, as happens in Italy, France and, to some extent, in Spain. These courts are divided into several chambers and each chamber works by panels with a possibly changing composition. This means that the same legal issue may be decided, even in a short time, several times by different people, with possibly different outcomes. Consistency and continuity in the court's orientations are practically impossible to achieve. Variations, changes, conflicts and inconsistencies are then the typical features of the body of precedent produced by courts of this type.

When a court is composed of sections or chambers, and when they or some of them may deal with the same legal issues, the problem of solving conflicts among judgments delivered by different chambers arises. The usual device to deal with these is to defer the decision to a special chamber or panel composed of a higher number of judges, or in extreme cases (and in some countries) to the *plenum* of the court. It is also possible to refer a case to a special panel or to the *plenum* when there is no conflict, but the case involves especially important legal issues.

This procedural device is very important from the point of view of precedent. Solving a conflict within the case law of single panels or between panels, or preventing conflicts by giving an especially authoritative interpretation of a rule concerning an important legal issue, is necessary or useful insofar as it is acknowledged that the court's function is to set forth interpretive guidelines that should be followed in forthcoming cases by the single chambers of the court and by lower courts. Among the precedents of a supreme court, the ones delivered by special panels or by the *plenum* in order to solve conflicts or because of the importance of the legal issues involved are especially influential. Even when they are not formally binding, they have nonetheless a special authority for the single chambers of the supreme court.

3   Styles of Opinions

Since precedents are judgments and are essentially based upon the *ratio decidendi* of cases, the way in which judgments are structured and opinions are written exerts influence upon their force and content. Moreover, the style of judicial decisions influences how they are used as precedents by judges of subsequent cases.

Looking at a possible typology of judicial styles, a distinction may be made between two ideal (and extreme) models. One model is that of a *legalistic, deductive* and *magisterial* style, in which the final ruling is presented as the last and necessary outcome of a legal and logical set of arguments that is formally structured as a demonstration. Arguments are expressed in a neutral, official and authoritative language and often have a deductive or syllogistic form. The other model, at the opposite extreme, is that of a *substantive, discursive* and *personalized* style. The decision is supported by several and even competing or converging arguments, including value judgments and personal opinions of the judge. It deals with the specific merits of the case and arguments are expressed in common language and in a discursive form.

A comparative analysis of these models and of their variations cannot be presented here (see MacCormick and Summers, 1991, Chapter 12). However, they may be useful in order to emphasize significant features of precedents in the various systems.

3.1

The legalistic and deductive style is typical of traditional European courts and especially of supreme courts because they deal mainly or essentially with issues of law. It has been generally and still is extremely influential in continental Europe. The specific function performed by the highest courts in those systems following the French model (*Cour de Cassation*) such as Italy and Spain is not to establish facts or review fact findings in light of the weight of the evidence. Such courts take the facts as found in courts below and decide only issues of substantive and procedural law. Matters are different in the intermediate appellate courts where fact findings of the lower courts can be reviewed and reconsidered, sometimes even on the basis of new and fresh evidence.

At present the judicial style which is nearest to a legalistic and deductive model is the French *phrase unique*, especially in the *Cour de Cassation*. In such a judgment all the justificatory reasoning is expressed by a brief and synthetic unique statement clearly and strongly structured as a chain of logical steps having the final dictum as the last necessary outcome. In other European supreme courts, legalistic and deductive style is somehow less rigid, but still to a certain degree dominates. It is evident in Germany, Italy, Poland, Spain, Finland and also to an extent in EC courts. The judgments of these supreme courts tend to be written in a formal and technical language, to be structured according to legal standards of validity and to follow logical patterns of reasoning. Every system has of course its own peculiarities in its concrete approximation to the model. Specific features are due to different legal cultures and traditions. However, the legal–deductive style has for a long time been the typical 'European style'.

Things are changing even within the civil law systems, however, because of two major factors. One is the general transformation occurring in the European legal culture since the beginning of the twentieth century. This transformation accelerated after the Second World War because of the influence of comparative law and legal sociology, of new constitutions, and of new political and ethical ideals. In many civil law countries the legal culture became less rigid and formalistic, more open to moral values and more sensitive to social problems, political issues, principles of equality and substantive justice. This trend is now reflected in the style of judicial opinions, despite the fact that changes in judicial styles are usually very slow.

The other factor is the influence of constitutional courts and their decisions. Dealing by definition with fundamental principles having a broad social, moral and political relevancy, constitutional courts necessarily invoke value arguments and substantive considerations in their judgments. Their opinions tend to be less formal and to include discussion of policy issues. Insofar as constitutional court decisions become influential precedents, they are influential also for their style, which is a new model for ordinary courts as well.

Correspondingly, the prevailing judicial style is now changing in several civil law countries. Changes are occurring, for instance, in Finland, Poland, Sweden and Italy. Moreover, some countries, such as Germany, Sweden and Norway, may now be located somewhere in the middle between the two ideal styles sketched above.

On the side of the substantive, discursive and personalized judicial style, we find opinions of common law courts. There is not a lot to say about this, since American and English courts are traditionally ones in which this style is used. The willingness to deal frontally with the real substance of the case and with the values and policies involved, the tendency of judges to impose their own personal style, and the habit of expressing directly the arguments supporting the decision, have long been understood as peculiar features of the style of common law courts. It is worth emphasizing that here things are not changing: common law opinions still are discursive, personalized, open to the discussion of issues of value and policy and justified by well developed arguments.

3.2

A further important factor of variation among the different court practices is the use of dissenting and concurring opinions. Traditionally, this was an important divide between civil and common law systems. The former excluded dissenting and concurring opinions, while the latter admitted them. The usual form of a civil law judgment was the final ruling supported by a single formal opinion written in the name of the whole court, without any information concerning the votes of the single judges. In the usual common law judgment, the decision is not secret. Even when the judgment is no longer delivered *singulatim*, the rule is that any judge may express his or her own personal opinion, even by way of explicit dissent.

The foregoing difference is still substantially present, but there are some interesting changes now occurring in some civil law countries. They concern some constitutional courts in which concurring and dissenting opinions are now admitted, as in Germany and Spain, and also in some ordinary supreme courts, such as in Norway (where each judge states his own decision separately). Moreover, there are some countries in which a *votum separatum* is generally admitted and disclosed: this is the case in Poland, Finland and Sweden. In Spain, dissents have recently appeared in ordinary court decisions under the influence of the practice of the constitutional courts. On the other hand, some civil law countries, such as France and Italy, still do not allow concurring or dissenting opinions, even in constitutional courts, and still keep to the rule that authorship of opinions is not disclosed. Also EC courts do not use dissenting opinions, mainly with the aim of performing a unifying function in the interpretation of EC law.

4   Reporting

A judgment may actually become a precedent only when it is known not only by the parties to the single case but also to other courts, to lawyers and virtually to the general public. Therefore the devices aimed at publishing judgments in order to make them known are essential to any system of precedent. If only a published judgment may be a precedent, the ways in which judgments are reported substantially determines the nature and the use of precedents.

There are usually two basic kinds of reports: official and private. Sometimes, however, the enterprise of reporting judgments is mainly managed by semi-official or private organizations (see, for example, the West Publishing system in the USA, the private system in Norway, and the semi-official systems in Sweden and Italy). More often both systems exist: an official reporting system is organized in several countries (for instance, Germany, France, Spain, Poland, Finland and the EU) in which judgments are published in official records or series. Moreover, a significant number of judgments is published by legal reviews, often with notes and comments written by scholars and judges.

Judgments delivered by constitutional courts are regularly reported in official reporters, except in Germany, where only decisions declaring a statute unconstitutional are officially recorded. Decisions of supreme courts are usually officially reported as well. Lower courts' decisions in nearly all countries in our study are not regularly reported. They are sometimes published by legal journals, but only when they deal with especially important legal issues. Judgments delivered by intermediate appellate courts are sometimes published; publication of decisions by trial courts is rather unfrequent.

More or less efficient systems of electronic storage of data concerning precedents, and of access to these data, are now available in most countries. Of course, computer informatics applied to the collection of, and access to, judgments makes the use of precedents much easier and faster than in the recent past. Any legal operator may have quick access to a huge amount of virtual precedents. This is a double-edged tool, however: legal informatics facilitates the use of precedents, but at the same time it opens the way to overuse, abuse and misuse of precedents. Some signs of this are already clear in several countries. Quoting lists of precedents requires less and less time since one finds them ready just by using computerized systems of research. On the other hand, a careful and thorough analysis of the single precedent is discouraged by the high number of precedents that may be found quickly. Quantity of references, therefore, tends to take the place of proper and specific use of relevant precedents.

4.1

An important factor influencing the use of precedents is *what* is actually reported. In several countries, both in common and in civil law, the whole judgment is published, including the final ruling, the justificatory opinion and also any concurring and dissenting opinions, if any. This is the case in the USA, UK, France, Spain, Germany, Norway, Sweden, Poland and the EC courts. This means that, so to speak, the whole decision may be used as a precedent. The judge of a subsequent decision may consider the facts of the case (insofar as reported), appreciate the whole content of the judgment and take into account the arguments supporting (or even criticizing) the judgment. Of course, in highest courts of most countries in our study except the UK and the USA, the facts are not fully reported in the published opinion.

There are cases in which the court's report does not include the whole judgment. Only a short statement of the legal issues decided, sometimes with an extremely synthetic reference to the reasons supporting the decision, is actually published. Besides Finland, the main instance of such a system is Italy. Judgments delivered by the Italian *Corte di Cassazione* are reported and published only in the form of the so-called *massima*, that is a short abstract (of three to ten lines usually) of the decision concerning a legal issue. A *massima* does not include (except in very rare cases) any reference to the facts of the case, nor does it express the arguments supporting the decision, nor does it reproduce the logical and legal structure of the opinion. It is only a short sentence stating a legal principle, which is picked up from the original judgment. A special office of the supreme court, composed of judges who are not necessarily members of the court, performs the task of extracting the *massime* from the judgments. Needless to say, in this case a precedent is a very peculiar thing, much more similar to a statement of a legal rule than to a decision of a case. Something quite similar also occurs in France in the *Cour de Cassation*.

It is worth stressing, however, that even where the whole judgments are reported, the main way to use them is not to read and discuss the full text of the judgment. Mere abstracts drawn from the original judgments are rather frequently used. They are sometimes published by legal journals. There are also books, casebooks and commentaries in which such abstracts are collected and published by private authors, with a more or less systematic editing. Collections of cases in short form and with synthetic comments are often published by legal journals. In the daily practice of judges and lawyers, these sources of information are widely used. Only when an especially important judgment is found is it fully analysed. The differences between the systems in which the whole judgments are published and the systems in which they are not may, then, be less dramatic when actual common practice is considered. The really important difference is that when the whole precedent is reported it is easily accessible to anyone at any moment. This is not so with a mere abstract; when a mere abstract is published, a full copy of the judgment has to be specially requested from the clerk of the court.

4.2

A further relevant factor is *which judgments* are reported. As a rule all the judgments of constitutional courts are reported (in their full text, even in Italy). The same happens with the judgments of EC courts. Different systems exist for decisions delivered by supreme courts. In some countries all the decisions of supreme courts are reported: this is true, for instance, in the cases of Spain and Norway (where the whole judgment is reported) and Italy (where only the *massime* of almost all cases are reported).

The most interesting method of reporting precedents is where only a selection is reported, especially when the court itself makes the choice. In France, for instance, a large proportion of highest courts' judgments are published in official journals reproducing the full text of judgments, but it is up to the court to select the cases for the report. A similar system exists in Germany, where a broad selection of federal courts' decisions is published in official series edited by members of the courts. This is also the case in Sweden, where judges select and edit decisions in semi-official series, and Finland, where the supreme court makes a restrictive selection of decisions to be published, corresponding roughly to one in ten of the appeals filed, and to about 50 per cent of those for which a leave is granted. A very peculiar system of selection exists in Poland: the selection is made first by the judge who writes the opinion, then by other members of the chamber of the court, and finally by a special 'Office of Judicial Decisions' including judges, scholars and a representative of the Ministry of Justice.

Among these systems the standards of selection may vary, for instance from the broad selection of France and Germany to the strict selection of Finland. The methods of selection are different as well. In all the systems where cases are selected for publication, the important feature is, however, the exclusive or prominent role that is played by the judges of the same court that delivers the judgments. Their selection is obviously precedent-oriented: judges select for publication just the cases that in their opinion are significant and worth following in subsequent cases. In a word: courts select prospective precedents, in some cases emphasizing the value of the precedents selected either by using narrow standards of selection, as in Finland, or by using special methods of selection, as in Poland.

5 Uses of Precedents

Precedents are commonly used, with few exceptions, by courts and lawyers. However, even a general look at the actual use of precedents in the judicial practice of the various systems reveals that there are different attitudes towards precedents and different ways of using them.

5.1

Significant differences exist as to the number and frequency of references to precedents. At one extreme of the scale there is the case of France, where no precedent is ever quoted by the judgments of the *Cour de Cassation*. Of course this does not mean that precedents are not actually used. On the contrary, it is clear that in practice French judges use precedents no less than their colleagues in other European countries. But the 'French style' is aimed at showing that the decision is no more than a logical consequence of statutory premises, and of nothing else except legal logic. So, at least officially, precedent cannot be explicitly used.

At the other extreme of the scale, one may find American courts using precedents frequently and with explicit references. The 'American style' seems to be oriented, in fact, towards a regular and effective reference to precedent as a basis for the justificatory arguments which are set forth in judicial opinions.

The practices of the other countries vary as between these two extremes. The use of precedents is a common device for interpreting the law in all systems. Sometimes, as for instance in Finland and in EC courts, only a few precedents, carefully selected, are used. Sometimes, on the contrary, strings or lists of precedents are frequently quoted, as happens, for instance, in Italy and Spain. A frequent but controlled use of precedents seems to be the common practice in Germany and in other countries as well. However, the frequency and quality of the references to precedents may vary substantially from case to case, even within the same system and in the judgments of the same court.

5.2

Relevant differences exist also as to the ways of using precedents. The practice of common law both in US and UK courts is characterized by broad discussions of precedents. The *ratio decidendi* of a case is often analysed in all its relevant aspects. This way of using precedents is rather infrequent in civil law systems. Only occasionally and in important cases are precedents thoroughly discussed. Instead, the prevailing practice in Italy, Spain, Norway, Sweden, Germany, Poland and in EC courts seems to be one of merely quoting a precedent or a list of precedents as supporting materials, without considering them individually and analytically. Not infrequently, precedents are quoted just as examples without developing any real argument based upon them. The decision is presented as implicitly supported by the bare quotation of precedents, with formulas such as 'in the same sense see also...'. In these systems, the relatively high frequency of references to precedents is somehow counterbalanced by the fact that precedents are quickly quoted and used merely as supporting materials, almost without due attention to their specific content. The use of precedents is almost never justified by ad hoc arguments, and their relevancy and usefulness are tacitly assumed.

5.3

The importance of precedents in the context of justificatory arguments is commonly defined as remarkable or very high. At least, the importance of precedents is comparable with that of other legal sources, such as statutes or other regulations.

The role of the reference to precedents seems to be especially significant in judgments delivered by constitutional courts, as in Spain, Italy, Germany and Poland, since their function is a step-by-step concretization of general principles and guarantees. The same happens in judgments on constitutional matters delivered by the other supreme courts, for just the same reasons. It seems that deciding constitutional matters requires in any case an intensive use of precedents, probably because of the generality and openness of constitutional provisions. From this point of view, the differences concerning the nature and the structure of courts deciding constitutional matters seem to be relatively less important.

However, the role of precedents is relevant and growing also in the ordinary courts of all systems. Even in France, where precedents are not explicitly cited, their importance is considerable in the development of the law by means of judicial interpretation. If compared with other legal sources, the role of precedents is generally important. Nowhere do precedents prevail over other legal sources or arguments, but in several systems (such as in Norway, Italy, France and the EC) they may be ranked at the same level as other legal grounds of decision.

The role of precedents varies substantially in the different areas of the law. The prominent importance of precedents in constitutional matters has already been stressed. At the level of ordinary law, some extremely important areas are almost completely 'covered' by precedents in several systems. This is often the case of commercial law, torts and product liability, and generally of new and rapidly emerging legal issues such as environmental protection, computer law, and so forth. In other areas, such as in criminal law and tax law, the role of precedents may be narrower, mainly because of the existence of more complete and detailed statutory regulation, and of accented principles of strict interpretation of statutes (*nullum crimen sine lege*). Scotland is an exception from this point of view, since its criminal law is customary and case-based, and not codified. Administrative law is a domain in which experiences are diverging in the different systems. In some countries, as for instance in the USA, it is often covered mainly by detailed regulations leaving less room for precedents. In other countries, such as Italy and Spain, the role of precedents in administrative law is far more important.

The interaction between precedents and statutory law is extremely complex and varying also in historical perspective. In some areas, such as torts, few very general principles are applied to a multitude of cases and courts refine these into a number of more concrete and detailed rules. Then precedents are extremely important as a development and an integration of basic legal rules. Elsewhere in the legal systems, precedents are used in order to interpret detailed and complex statutory regulations. Then the function and role of precedents is connected and changing in correspondence with the developments and changes occurring in the status of other legal sources. Sometimes precedents anticipate statutes because the courts are the first in developing new legal issues and then the legislature intervenes, 'absorbing' precedents into new statutes, or using statutes to reject precedents in favour of different solutions. Sometimes precedents interpret statutes, modifying, extending or updating their meaning. Sometimes precedents just 'apply' a statute, adapting it to specific facts.

5.4

The growing practice of using precedents is present also in the work of lawyers. In the pleadings, mainly in proceedings before supreme courts, precedents are usually quoted and discussed. Even in France, where precedents are not cited or quoted by the highest courts themselves, they are normally used and quoted by counsel. The knowledge and the analysis of precedents is fundamental for any practising lawyer. From this point of view, no significant differences exist in modern systems.

A further important factor influencing the use of precedents is the role played by law professors, and generally by legal writers. Insofar as precedents are concerned, legal writers may perform different tasks, and often such tasks are performed at the same time. First of all, precedents are collected, analysed and discussed. Often the definition of the *ratio decidendi* of a case is made by the legal literature before being used by a court. Legal writers also connect, reconstruct, rationalize and compare precedents. Sometimes their work is limited to collecting precedents and putting them into some order. Sometimes their work goes deeper and includes the tracing of the historical development of precedents or a reinterpretation of precedents showing their consistency. On the other hand, the scientific analysis of precedents may be based upon the critique of precedents or of the way in which they are used by courts. Such an analysis may emphasize inconsistencies, gaps and errors in decisions made by courts while creating and/or using precedents. Legal writers may argue that a precedent is legally wrong or obsolete or no longer congruent with the current legal or social conditions, and so forth. Thus they may urge departures from precedents or overruling of precedents. The legal literature, therefore, may be a relevant factor in the change and development of precedents. It may even be a factor of deviation or manipulation in the use of precedents. This happens when the analysis or reconstruction of a precedent or a line of precedents is biased, uninformed, incomplete or incorrect. It also happens when the panorama of precedents is distorted, for instance giving the impression that only a few 'hard cases' are worth considering, without quoting dozens or hundreds of 'easy cases' constantly decided in the same way.

6   Precedents and the Role of Courts

In every system, the role of courts is usually defined as that of 'declaring' or 'establishing' the law. Then decisions are assumed to 'apply' the law to the facts of concrete cases, after interpreting a pre-existing legal rule. Theoretically this conception of the role of courts is in conflict with an effective use of precedents. When this theory is strictly adhered to, as it still is in France, the consequence is that courts do not make any explicit reference to precedents as a basis for interpretive arguments, although they actually make an intensive use of precedents. However, these are the terms in which the role of courts is presented by traditional general theories. The actual practice of the use of precedent is quite different, since precedents are commonly used everywhere as important points of reference in the justification of judicial decisions and, as far as it may be guessed, in the decision making as well. Independently of whether precedents are defined as 'legal sources' or not, they are commonly used by courts. This is the case in many civil law systems such as Italy, Germany, Spain, Poland, Norway, Finland and Sweden. This is also the case in EC courts. Of course, this is also the case in common law systems.

Therefore, if the 'declarative' theory of decision making is to be maintained (and several decisive arguments may be invoked for the opposite theoretical position), it should be at least recognized that in all systems courts find and declare the law by means and on the basis of precedents.

On the other hand, the growing use of precedents even by civil law courts, and even in areas of the law that are regulated by statutes, suggests that the actual current role of courts in modern developed systems is much more complex, flexible and varying than the one once defined, as it was in the middle of the eighteenth century, by Montesquieu. Also because of the extremely important experience of constitutional adjudication, the role of courts needs to be redefined in much more sophisticated terms. In such a redefinition, the use of precedents in decision making plays a crucial role.

There are, however, some significant variations in the functions ascribed to courts when they use precedents. In some countries, any power of courts to create new precedents is denied: courts may use precedents but, at least in principle, they are not allowed to create new ones. In other countries, a creative role is admitted, at least in exceptional and infrequent cases, as in Spain and Italy. Generally, the function of precedents is defined as that of interpretive devices which may be used in order to elicit the meaning of the existing law (as in Germany, for instance). Sometimes the interpretive function of precedents is extended to solving interpretive doubts arising in the application of the law (as in Poland and the EC) or to filling gaps in the law in order to solve cases not explicitly regulated by the law (as in Finland, the EC, Poland and Italy). A tendency to deny the existence of an unlimited creative power of the courts, and therefore to maintain a somewhat restrictive conception of precedents, is present even in common law countries, notwithstanding the tremendously important role that 'creative' precedents have, especially in the American judicial practice. Once again, however, the gap between theoretical reconstructions and definitions of what courts do or should do and the reality of their work may be wide and difficult to overcome. At any rate, this problem is not exclusively peculiar to the use of precedents. In a sense, precedent in continental systems is just one of the problems (albeit a very important one) concerning the role and powers of courts in the interpretation of the law.

The degree of 'manifest consciousness' of courts in the creation of precedents is very different from case to case. New precedents are usually created in several systems, but this often happens tacitly, probably in order not to raise conflicts with the idea of an interpretive role of courts. The express creation of a precedent occurs in civil law systems, but a new precedent is most often presented as a new interpretation of a pre-existing law, rather than as the creation of new law.

The degree of consciousness of courts in using precedents is also different from case to case. In many civil law countries, where precedents are just quoted without detailed arguments (see Section 5.2 above), they are used almost automatically, that is with a low degree of explicit consciousness. Things are different in constitutional courts because of the special institutional role they play, although some tendencies towards a standardized use of precedents may be detected even in these courts. The situation may be different, of course, in common law systems, since precedents are usually discussed and analysed in some detail.

At any rate, the general growth in the use of precedents in every system and the essential role that precedents achieve in the judicial practice of all countries are important factors of change. This is not to say that courts have an unlimited power to create new law. Rather, it should be acknowledged that, even in civil law systems, the interpretation of codes and statutes is now based largely upon precedents already interpreting these codes and statutes. Precedents have become unavoidable means for the 'concretization' of legal rules and principles. Many relevant situations are 'legalized' or 'jurified' by courts according to precedents, and many legal issues are decided on the basis of precedents. The idea of a true conflict between precedents as such and law as such has lost any actual meaning even in civil law systems. On the contrary, precedents are a constant and omnipresent factor in the judicial interpretation of law.

The differences and variations sketched above reflect the influence of different institutional settings upon the ways in which courts make and use precedents. Beyond these differences, and notwithstanding their importance, the massive and intensive use of precedents is a general and growing trend in all the modern systems of justice.

References

Kötz, H., 'Taking Civil Codes Less Seriously', *Modern Law Review*, p.1 (1987).

MacCormick, D.N. and Summers, R.S. (eds) (1991), *Interpreting Statutes – A Comparative Study*, Aldershot: Dartmouth.

Wells, M., 'French and American Judicial Opinions', *Yale Journal of International Law*, 19, p.81 (1994).

14 The Binding Force of Precedent

ALEKSANDER PECZENIK, *LUND**

1 Introductory Remarks

All students of comparative law know that historically common law (in the UK, USA and so on) is to a great extent based on precedents, whereas the Roman–Germanic (continental, 'civil') law has been mostly based on statutes. They also know that precedents are formally binding in the common law countries on all courts below the highest courts. That is, it is legal error not to follow upper court precedent and such failure will ordinarily be reversed on appeal. In the highest courts, the precedents set by those courts also have strong normative force, even though there is no possibility of reversal on appeal. But in countries of the European continent, precedent is not thus formally binding, yet it is a fact that precedents are regularly followed by the courts. This fact also explains why some jurists say that precedents in the continental legal systems are binding de facto, but not de jure.

Only very special kinds of precedents in a few continental systems are binding de jure. Thus, in Germany, precedents established by the Federal Constitutional Court are recognized as formally binding on the courts below. Ordinary precedents established by the Federal Court of Justice are not formally binding but they have to be followed except where special reasons can be shown to the contrary. In Poland, the situation is similar. The resolutions of the Constitutional Tribunal, establishing generally binding interpretations of statutes, are the only candidates for the role of formally (legally) binding precedents for the courts below. Legal principles established by the Polish Supreme Court do not formally bind the courts but have normative force. This concerns particularly those of the Supreme

* I am grateful to Aulis Aarnio and Robert Alexy for all the help and inspiration I received during our discussions about the topics dealt with in the present chapter.

461

Court resolutions which have gained the status of legal principles. Where a legal principle has been established, the Supreme Court cannot depart from that principle simply by passing a judgment contradictory to it, but can only do so if it states an adequate justification for an alternative view of the law. Thus ordinary judgments of the Polish Supreme Court and Supreme Administrative Court are precedents in the sense that they have force in later analogous cases, or provide 'further support' in the sense of adding weight to other legally relevant arguments for the decision handed down. In Spain, too, precedents of the Constitutional Court can be considered as formally binding for all other courts. They must also be followed by the Constitutional Court itself except if it offers some sufficient reason for changing its own prior ruling(s). Prior judgements of the Spanish Supreme Court only have force or provide further support.

Decisions of the Court of Appeals in New York, by contrast, are formally binding – binding as a matter of law – on intermediate appellate courts and on the trial courts of general jurisdiction within New York State, and so are decisions of the House of Lords in relation to the Court of Appeal and the lower courts of the relevant jurisdictions within the United Kingdom. Thus decisions to the contrary by courts below are not lawful, and will be reversed on appeal. These highest-level courts can, indeed, reconsider their own prior decisions and do occasionally depart from or overrule them on the ground of carefully weighed and argued reasons, but, in the concepts and terminology of this study, these are not formally binding on the highest courts, for no appeal lies to a higher court. All the same, the highest courts treat their own decisions as having strong normative force. So far as concerns courts lower in the hierarchy, the precedents set by these lower tribunals provide examples of 'vertical' formally binding precedents. And in relation to their own earlier decisions, they have the power to depart from or overrule their own precedents on a restricted range of grounds, and for strong reasons, but must otherwise accept them as binding in law.

2   The Normativity of Following Precedent

As the introductory remarks indicate, this chapter mainly addresses a number of distinctions concerning the nature of the force that can be ascribed to precedents. It does so in the light of responses in the country-by-country chapters prompted by question II.1 submitted to authors and co-authors of the country chapters (see Appendix). It is material to repeat the key concepts and terminology of the question in full here.

II.1   We may usefully differentiate bindingness, force, further support, and illustrativeness or other value of a precedent as follows:

(1)   *Formal bindingness*: a judgment not respecting a precedent's bindingness is not lawful and so is subject to reversal on appeal. Distinguish

   (a)   formal bindingness not subject to overruling: (i) 'Strictly binding' – must be applied in every case; (ii) defeasibly binding – must be applied in every case unless exceptions apply (exceptions may be well defined or not);

   (b)   formal bindingness (with or without exceptions) that is subject to overruling or modification.

(2)   *Not formally binding but having force*: a judgment not respecting a precedent's force, though lawful, is subject to criticism on this ground, and may be subject to reversal on this ground. Distinguish

   (a)   defeasible force – should be applied unless exceptions come into play (exceptions may or may not be well defined);

   (b)   outweighable force – should be applied unless countervailing reasons apply.

(3)   *Not formally binding and not having force (as defined in 2) but providing further support*: a judgment lacking this is still lawful and may still be justified, but not as well justified as it would be if the precedent were invoked, for example, to show that the decision being reached harmonizes with the precedent.

(4)   *Mere illustrativeness or other value.*

A critic of the present project could legitimately ask whether the foregoing draws distinctions that are too sophisticated. Would these distinctions even be understood by the very judges whose practice they are supposed to help us analyse? Are any of these distinctions actually expressed in so many words by courts or by scholars?

Setting aside the question of their being understood, we can readily concede that some of the terms and perhaps even some of the concepts set forth above are not used in judicial or scholarly discussions of precedent. Not even in the UK, where perhaps there is the richest practice of analysis of precedent internally in the judicial process, are these distinctions drawn explicitly by the courts. Therefore categorizing a decision in the stipulated terms depends on interpreting the practice of the judges in the light of a conceptual framework independently established. In the United States (here represented by New York) judicial language seems to be even less explicit in this respect. There is seldom any explicit judicial discussion of the distinction between formal bindingness and mere normative force of a lower order. Moreover, to the extent there is, the latter is usually referred to merely as 'persuasive authority', rather than 'binding' authority. Nor is there much explicit discussion of any distinction between mere 'force' and 'further support'. By analogy, the distinction between 'defeasible' and 'outweighable' force is not explicitly discussed by the judges either.

In other systems, the courts are even less explicit. European Community law does not contain these sorts of distinctions concerning the case law. Not even scholars discuss the ECJ's decisions in these terms. In France and in Spain such distinctions are not made either. The only discussion in Spain, by no means an extensive discussion, has been basically theoretical, dealing with the traditional question of the character of judicial precedent as a source of law. In Italy it is uncommon for the degree of force or bindingness of a precedent to be explicitly discussed in judicial opinions. The courts in continental systems do not differentiate clearly, as far as precedents are concerned, between (a) having force, (b) providing further support and (c) merely illustrative value. In Germany, otherwise well known for a very theoretical approach to the law, the situation is similar: differing degrees of normative bearing of precedent are seldom explicitly discussed in judicial decisions. Normally, judges do not even make any general remarks on this. In Nordic countries the actual practice generally fits the definition stipulated for 'not formally binding but having force'. In Poland neither the law nor doctrine uses the fine distinctions between precedents 'having force', 'providing further support' and being 'merely illustrative'. Not even scholars use such language.

The critic's objection must be rejected, however. Even though the present distinctions are not explicitly or at all used by judges or scholars, this does not make them useless, though it does require us to justify the worth we hold them to have. Even though they clearly transcend judicial or other self-understanding in any single system, they are a valuable tool for rationally reconstructing practices of decision making. This is especially so in the context of an attempt to tease out and to understand differences as well as similarities between diverse systems and traditions of law. It must be said clearly that the comparisons we draw are not confined to, or mainly addressed to, comparing the judicial use of language (indeed, of the various natural languages in use in the systems we study). Rather, our concern is with practices of precedent. A useful language of comparison has to be a kind of 'metalanguage', containing terms and distinctions not present, or not articulated, in any of the particular object languages of judicial practice and scholarly doctrine internal to particular systems in their ordinary functioning. Thus some such rational reconstruction of practices, in some such concepts, is a necessity.

3   Binding De Facto?

The fact is that the authors of the country-by-country chapters in our study have generally attempted to use these distinctions under as nearly as possible a common understanding of them. In order to understand these chapters properly, some further conceptual clarifications may be helpful.

All main varieties of normative bearing here – formal bindingness, force and support – are normative in the sense that they are taken to indicate degrees of justificatoriness of the reasons generated by precedent. The very expression 'non-normative force' seems to be problematic, in some contexts even self-contradictory. This also poses problems for what is a quite commonly used expression in a number of countries, namely 'binding de facto' an expression that is, in such countries, also contrasted with 'formally binding', or binding de jure. The expression 'binding de facto' seems to imply that the precedents have no normative force, no justificatoriness, but have to be followed to the extent at least that they are in fact usually followed. Such a view may be theoretically naive or it may be accompanied by some sophisticated theories. For example, a theorist may adopt an external point of view with regard to legal practice. A theorist may thus interpret the expression 'de facto bindingness' as referring to some statistical regularity, supposing it to be established empirically that judges regularly follow certain (types of) precedents. A theorist may also state that the 'de facto force' of the precedents means that the precedent is (a part of) the motivational basis of the judge. This was, for instance, Alf Ross's idea, in his theory about the normative ideology of the judge. Thus Ross's theory was an external description of the internal point of view of the judges. In this perspective, respect for precedent has only a 'psychological force' in the decision making.

However, any non-normative interpretation of 'binding de facto' is contrary to the lawyers' internal understanding of legal practice in some countries. There are at least some contexts in which it is self-contradictory; for most others it is theoretically uninteresting. It is contrary to the fact that the highest courts in several systems may issue guidelines with some normative force, recommending that subsequent courts follow a precedent or class of precedents, perhaps on the basis of statutory authorization. In such cases, normative force is prospective. The court is trying to affect the future practice. Here only a normative conception of bindingness, force or support is possible. There is no statistical or other regularity to be referred to.

To be sure, the situation may be the other way around. A judge deciding a subsequent case looks back, into the past, and follows a pattern established in a previous decision, regardless of the issue whether or not the prior court issued any command or recommendation addressed to lower or subsequent courts. Here, from the point of view of the later court, the precedent may either be conceived as having normative force or may be conceived merely as a factually available model of decision, in some way influential as such. But even if the latter is the case, the expression 'binding de facto' is self-contradictory, because the very word 'binding' indicates a normative force, which is something more than the mere fact of following the precedent. Indeed, it indicates that what is going on is taken to be justificatory.

The non-normative conception of bindingness de facto is also theoretically uninteresting because it leaves out the reasons for following precedents. If a practice is followed for certain reasons, these reasons must have some normative character. And surely courts that follow precedents must be presumed to have some reason for doing so. Otherwise, the practice of following precedents would appear to be irrational and incomprehensible. No doubt, the judges often follow precedents and feel motivated to do so, but it is difficult to believe that they do not also consider this motivation, explicitly or implicitly, to be right on account of some statable, even if not stated, normative grounds. If so, precedents have a kind of normative force. A merely explanatory approach such as that of Ross cannot provide any hint as to the nature of this force.

Any of the following might be offered as a justifying reason for following precedent: the practice of the precedent-making court; the practice of the precedent-applying court; the common opinion of legal scholars; the expectations of the parties; and of course all the various rationales for following precedent recited in the various country chapters and discussed in detail in Chapter 15. So-called 'bindingness de facto' may thus explicitly or implicitly derive its normative character from various practices and general rationales, none itself a formally established legal norm such as is in issue where constitutional or statutory provisions provide that precedents are to be followed in certain conditions.

As an example of implicitly normative character in the bindingness of precedents, one may refer to the Swedish situation. Swedish precedents are not formally binding yet, according to the Code of Judicial Procedure, the Swedish Supreme Court must grant *certiorari* to enable appeals to be brought before it in cases where it is important that a general ruling be given by way of precedent for judicial practice. This statutory provision would be meaningless if such general ruling lacked any kind of normativity. Thus one may conclude that the Code implies this normativity, without explicitly providing for it.

From all this it follows that the expression 'binding de facto' as used in various countries must not be interpreted literally. On any reasonable interpretation, it does not indicate lack of normativity. It only indicates that the normative reasons for following precedents are different from, and in some sense somewhat weaker than, the reasons for following or complying with other legal provisions such as legislation, subordinate legislation or articles of a constitution, all of which we may suppose to be 'formally binding' in any contemporary legal system.

4   Non-formal Legal Normativity

In my view, one simple way to express the various kinds of normativity involved in formal 'bindingness', 'force' and 'further support' is this: precedents that are formally binding, or binding de jure, must be regarded as authoritative reasons for decision in legal argumentation. Precedents which are not formally binding but which have force or provide further support are still ones which should be used as authoritative reasons in legal argumentation. Reasons which merely generate force, or provide further support, are important, but they are not formally binding. That is, failure to decide in accord with such precedent-based reasons will not usually yield decisions that are unlawful and which, if appealed, will be reversed. Indeed, most precedents in continental systems are of this kind. The same is true of the availability of precedents from foreign but cognate legal systems, as when a Danish precedent might be taken into account by a Swedish court, or an Australian by an English.

Thus precedents which are binding in a weaker sense than formal or de jure should still be regarded as having the character of legally authoritative reasons. They are reasons which should be applied, and this 'should' is legal in character, albeit not in the strict sense of binding de jure: that which in the present usage we characterize as a reason that must be applied as a matter of strict legal requirement such that departure is not lawful and will be reversed on appeal. The normative force of all precedents, even those which are not binding de jure, has to be distinguished from that of so-called 'substantive reasons', whose force is dependent merely on their content, not their form or origin (or 'pedigree'). On the contrary, it is a legally authoritative force. Both legal norms which are formally binding de jure and those which merely 'should' be regarded as authoritative reasons are also explanatory factors in the law: one can, for example, explain the content of a judicial decision by the fact that it has statutory support – and one can explain it by the fact that it follows a precedent.

All this has interesting consequences for the structure of legal systems in general. One may say that a legal system may consist of two layers: norms which *must* be regarded as authoritative reasons in legal argumentation, that is formally binding or binding de jure, and norms which merely *should* be regarded as authoritative reasons in legal argumentation. Most types of precedents in continental systems belong to the latter category. In common law systems, much precedent is formally binding (de jure) and some has lesser normative force.

Statutes and custom had a special position in the classical continental doctrine of the sources of law in the nineteenth century. They had the power to create rights and duties of private persons; they also determined the limits of legal, that is authoritative, argumentation (cf. Malt, 1992, pp.55 ff). The classical doctrine also recognized a number of secondary sources of the law (argumentative auxiliary tools) such as 'the nature of things', legal practice, *travaux préparatoires* and foreign law (ibid., p.52).

Consequently, those legal sources which *must* be regarded as authoritative reasons are more important than those which merely *should* be thus regarded. The concept 'more important' implies the following.

1   A more important source is legally a stronger reason than a less important one. For example, statute is a stronger legal reason than a precedent in continental law. Some counter-arguments that are sufficient to outweigh a precedent are not sufficient to outweigh a statute.
2   The hierarchy of legal sources in this sense is merely provisional, prima facie. If a collision occurs between a more important source and a less important one, the former has priority, if no outweighing reasons exist which reverse the priority order. If one assigns priority to a less important legal source above a more important one, one has the burden of argumentation for this priority. Outweighing reasons are thus required to follow a precedent contrary to the plain meaning of a statute.
3   In some legal systems, these differences of weight have institutional consequences. In Sweden and Finland (but not, for example, in Denmark) a judge who ignores a binding statute can be prosecuted (cf. Ch. 20 of Criminal Code). This is not true of a judge who ignores a precedent. (These institutional consequences may be perceived as intrinsic to the very sense of 'bindingness de jure'. From this point of view, it may be an anomaly to have a legal system which recognizes formal bindingness, that is bindingness de jure of a norm, and yet does not contain any sanction for the breach of such a norm. In this perspective, the Swedish and Finnish solution appears natural, while the Danish one is a kind of *lex imperfecta*. But, on the other hand, this view is controversial because criminal liability of a judge for having neglected a binding norm is extremely narrow in legal systems.

In the UK, where precedents are unquestionably binding de jure, the prevailing conception of judicial independence precludes any possibility of civil or criminal sanctions being imposed on a judge on account of errors, however gross, committed in a judicial capacity.)

4 A prima facie more important legal source can, however, have less weight than a number of less important ones, in cumulation. In some systems, a number of precedents can thus jointly weigh more than some statutes read according to their literal meaning. This point deserves further elaboration. It is possible to say that the sound interpretation of the statute is that which has already taken fully into account the bearing of precedents on it. The statute so interpreted then retains its priority over precedents. However, this way of interpreting the situation leads to a number of problems which cannot be discussed in this chapter. For example, one has to answer the ontological question, 'In what sense can the interpreted meaning be regarded as existing prior to the judicial act of interpretation?' (This pre-existence would be possible, if the act of interpretation were purely cognitive. On the other hand, it would be impossible, if interpretative reasoning is constitutive, not merely cognitive.)

5 A counter-argument which 'wins' against a stronger source of law must be stronger than a counter-argument which is sufficient to win against a weaker one.

5 More about the Legal Character of the Normative Bearing of Precedent 'Having Force' or Providing 'Further Support'

The legal character of precedent that is not formally binding yet has force or provides further support can be seen in a number of ways. First and foremost, such precedent-based reasons, simply by virtue of judicial and other practices within the system, come to be taken as authoritative reasons for decision: as having justificatory status within the system. A second way to grasp the legal character of the normative bearing of precedents 'having force' or providing 'further support' is to consider how precedents share an important property of all legal reasons, namely that they help to exclude some reasons from the universe of legal determinativeness. It is obvious that a formally binding, and so undoubtedly legal, precedent excludes at least some conflicting reasons for decision. Thus it excludes contrary substantive reasons, for example. But even non-formally binding precedent, such as a precedent in a civil law country that merely has force or provides further support, also shares the characteristic of legal reasons generally, namely that such precedent operates to exclude contrary reasons from consideration by the decision maker. This will now be treated in more detail.

All kinds of practical reasoning, legal and moral, involve weighing and balancing of several factors at the same time. Yet the law imposes some restrictions on this process of weighing. One way to achieve this result is to enact rules. The existence of a rule precludes recourse to certain kinds of relevant background reasons, including (usually) the very reasons that led to the introduction of the rule itself. A legal rule may thus work as a second-order reason which may justify in some cases not doing what ought to be done in the light of the totality of all moral reasons (cf. Peczenik, 1989, p.240, claiming that this view is a paraphrase of Joseph Raz's theory of exclusionary reasons in the law; see Raz 1979, pp.18, 27 and 33).

The same can be said about precedents. Precedents can be regarded as prima facie reasons for excluding many other reasons from legal argumentation. This point may be difficult to grasp, because the use of precedents not only excludes some reasons from the process of weighing and balancing, but also adds some new reasons to it, or at least shifts the weight of the reasons involved. In the application of a precedent, weighing and balancing implies an effort to achieve a 'reflective equilibrium' between the precedent norm taken as the starting point for argumentation and the other admissible reasons bearing on one's decision. This reflective equilibrium is a kind of coherence. But there is no algorithm, no finite and unambiguous set of rules deciding what is more and what is less coherent.

Jurists usually aim at presenting the law as a coherent system, but the concept of coherence is difficult to define precisely. According to Neil MacCormick's theory of normative coherence (1984, pp.235 ff), legal principles support and explain a number of legal rules and make them coherent. But such legal principles are often implicit, accessible as a result of weighing and balancing of other principles and particular judgments. Moreover, discovery and justification of an implicit precedent-based rule is an intellectual activity involving the weighing and balancing of several criteria of coherence. Among other things, a deeper and broader support makes a theory about the content of the precedent rule in question more coherent. *Ceteris paribus*, the degree of coherence of such a theory depends on the number of supported statements that belong to it, the length of the chains of reasons that belong to it, the number of the connections that exist between various supportive chains belonging to the theory and how many statements belonging to the theory are relevant in the type of reasoning the theory uses (cf. Alexy and Peczenik 1991, pp.130 ff).

The role of weighing and balancing reasons is particularly clear when one considers the fact that the process of applying precedents involves an effort to achieve diachronic coherence (cf. Peczenik, 1995, pp.603 ff) of the law. The law changes continually. A new interpretation of a precedent must have support of the legal tradition, yet it implies a change of the tradition (cf. Krygier, 1986, pp.237 ff; Bankowski, 1991, p.208). Ronald Dworkin's theory of 'integrity' (1986, pp.225 ff) is an example of a kind of coherence in time, often called 'narrative' (see, for example, Jackson, 1988, pp.155–6). *Ceteris paribus*, the degree of diachronic coherence achieved through the practice of following precedent depends on how many of its actual components (rules, principles, particular judgments, data, theories and so on) are justified and explained by the legal tradition, how long a time the tradition covers and how much this justification approximates to the best balance of the criteria of synchronic coherence.

Now the point is that the precedent-applying judge assigns relatively more weight to the reasons weighed and balanced in the context of establishing the precedent-based rule than to non-legal reasons. A judge may thus follow precedents which derive from the highest court, even where he believes that a different decision would have been more suitable on the balance of all moral and other reasons, had the court not decided previous cases in the way it did. Following the precedents involves weighing and balancing, too, but it is simpler than weighing all the moral reasons would be. Only if there are particularly strong reasons indicating that the judge ought to give judgment in a way different from that indicated by the precedent(s) does the question arise of deviating from the precedent.

The phenomenon of excluding some reasons within the law, even if these reasons are good outside of the law, is particularly complex due to the fact that it occurs at several levels, often confused with each other. For example, not only do precedents themselves exclude some reasons from legal discourse, there are also some recognized rules concerning the use of precedents, and these rules exclude some reasons from 'meta-legal' discourse about the force of precedents.

Whenever a practice of respecting precedents exists, there also evolve some rules for the use of precedents. In particular, a legal system may thus regard precedents as formally binding. This means, among other things, that deviation from a precedent is regulated by a set of rules, requiring some special kind of reasoning (a technique of distinguishing, for example; see Chapter 17). To be sure, all such rules have a somewhat uncertain scope ('open texture': see, for example, Hart, 1961, p.124), yet they decrease the overall uncertainty of the application of precedents. A legal system may also assign a weaker kind of normative force to a precedent. Even this force can be characterized by means of a set of rules, mostly implicit, yet possessing a legal character.

The law may thus impose rules, precedents and again rules about the use of precedents, all of them restricting the number of factors to be taken into account in the justification of coherence judgments determining analogies between cases. Such a restriction decreases coherence between the law and morality. On the other hand, it often increases the internal coherence of the law itself. This is perhaps the point of all law: a Hercules or archangel can make holistic judgments of coherence of all morally relevant factors, but a human being needs the help of social institutions; among other things, she or he needs legal rules and precedents, binding de jure or not.

In sum, many precedent-based reasons, even though not formally binding, that is not binding de jure, are still legal in character. They are accepted in the law as having force or as providing further support, and thus as types of authoritative reasons for legal decisions. They also share a leading characteristic of legal reasons, namely that they exclude other reasons.

6   Not Formally Binding but Having Force, or Providing Further Support – Degrees of Normativity

The conceptual framework devised through common debate and consensus for our study, and reflected in our various questions, includes question II (see Appendix) which provides that a formal binding precedent is one that must in later similar cases be respected, that is, followed by courts below the precedent-setting court, so that a judgment not respecting a precedent's bindingness is not lawful and so will be reversed on appeal. However, a precedent not formally binding yet 'having force' or providing further support is, in our conceptual framework, one that courts below the precedent-setting court in later similar cases should also respect, that is, follow. The only differences between the degrees of normativity or authoritativeness of the two types of precedent-based reasons are that the failure to follow precedent merely having force is subject to criticism on this ground (as something that should have been done) and *may* be subject to reversal, whereas the failure to follow formally binding precedent 'is not lawful' and so 'is subject to reversal on appeal'. These, then, represent, in our view, a major difference of degree in the normative bearing that the two types of precedent-based reasons have. Of course, our conceptual framework also recognizes the possibilities that, in a given system, a formally binding precedent or one having force may be subject to overruling or modification by an appropriate higher court.

The conceptual framework of this study recognizes a further and lesser degree of normative bearing, too, one in which a precedent is not formally binding and does not have force (as here defined), yet which nevertheless provides 'further support'. Here it is merely true that the failure of the later court to invoke the precedent in a similar case signifies simply that the decision of the court is not as well justified as it would be if the precedent were invoked, for example, to show that the decision being reached harmonizes with the precedent.

These, then, represent three degrees of normative bearing that precedent may have in a later case. It is not claimed that these exhaust all the possible degrees that may be identified in a given system, but this is a sufficient variation in degrees to enable all systems in our study to be plotted at some point on a kind of common continuum. Thus it is clear that formal bindingness of precedent is widely recognized in common law systems and also to a limited extent (mainly in the constitutional courts) in civil law systems. It is also plain from the various national studies here that one or both of the two foregoing lesser degrees of normative bearing of precedent are widely recognized in the civilian systems.

With respect to precedents not formally binding but having force, the participants in this project deemed it important to differentiate between precedents having 'defeasible force' and precedents having 'outweighable force'. The concept of defeasibility utilized in the conceptual framework of the study applies to two types of situations, the first far more common than the second. In the first type of defeasibility, the precedent should be applied to the similar subsequent cases 'unless exceptions come into play'. Here the exceptions are exceptions *to the rule or principle of law derivable from the precedent case*, and it is a commonplace that such exceptions exist to many rules and principles in precedent-based law in modern systems of the kind in our study. Of course, such exceptions are usually created over time rather than on the occasion the precedent itself is created. Moreover, when such exceptions are created, the precedent-based rule or principle typically itself remains in the system, although there are instances when a series of exceptions ultimately swallows up the rule itself, so that it may be said no longer to exist.

Secondly, it is also true that some systems do recognize basic exceptions *to the general doctrine of precedent itself*, that is, the version of the doctrine (formally binding, force, further support, and so on) applicable in the system (as distinguished from exceptions to some particular legal rule). One type of such exception recognized in some common law systems is that, when a precedent-setting court decides a case *'per incuriam'*, that is in ignorance of relevant binding authority, the case has no normative bearing as a precedent whatsoever. In a sense, it is eliminated from the system and thus is defeasible in this more drastic sense.

Of course, questions can arise also as to exactly what it is that has normative bearing in a precedent. Let us return to some distinctions, made in question II of the Appendix. As regards a precedent, we may thus distinguish (a) defeasible force – should be applied unless exceptions come into play (exceptions may or may not be well defined) and (b) outweighable force – should be applied unless countervailing reasons apply. First of all, what is it that has the defeasible and/or outweighable binding force? Three possibilities must be considered: the precedent case itself, a rule based on the case and, finally, a principle based on the case.

An important point in this context is that the force and rationale of a precedent is the force of analogy between the cases. Analogous cases should be decided in a similar manner. This sounds plausible, but invokes very difficult theoretical problems. One can logically reconstruct the principle of analogy between cases as demanding the creation of a precedent-based norm (a rule or a principle). If one assumes that the case itself has binding force, one must mean that this precedent-based norm is not determined by the 'law itself' and thus must be created by the person who interprets the precedent. For, surely, one cannot make sense of the idea that (a) two cases (the precedent case and the subsequent case) are analogous to each other, although (b) no norm can be discovered, or at least created, which tells us what makes these cases analogous. Analogy between cases requires a link between them, and this link cannot be anything other than a norm under which the cases can be subsumed. Such a norm can be either pre-existent or created by the interpreter, but it must be thinkable.

On the other hand, even if the pre-existent precedent-based norm is discernible, the scope of such a norm is inevitably uncertain (see, for example, Hart, 1961, pp.121 ff). Only relevant similarities between cases constitute a sufficient reason for conclusion by analogy. But what is relevant? Judgments of relevance are justifiable by weighing and balancing of various reasons, often principles.

Relevant resemblance can concern many different things, such as persons, things, documents, rights, duties, circumstances concerning space and time, social effects of the application of the law to different cases and, finally, the place of the cases in respective 'stories' ('narratives' – see, for example, Jackson, 1988, pp.155–6). In any case, one needs a 'key of relevance' (cf. Aarnio, 1987, pp.104 ff), a conception by which rational weighing and balancing is possible. Yet there appears to be no algorithm of weighing, no finite set of unambiguous criteria. Secondly, relevance of similarities is a matter of degree. The degree of relevance decreases with the increasing 'distance' from the precedent case. (The logical side of this fact is the following: the relation of analogy between cases is not transitive; a case, C_1, can be analogous to the case C in question, another case, C_2, analogous to C_1, without C_2 necessarily being analogous to C. (See Frändberg, 1973, pp.150 ff.)

Following precedents is seldom a mechanical process of following pre-existing rules. It is rather like weighing and balancing of reasons, *inter alia* pre-existent precedent rules (or principles) in order to make new rules. A reason for deciding the new case like the old one is to be considered. Counter-arguments can prevail in some cases, and it is not known in advance in which ones, albeit the result will almost always be not only to solve the case, but also to confirm or modify the precedent rule.

7   Defeasible and Outweighable Force of Precedent-based Rules or Principles: Four Possibilities

The participants in this study agreed on the following conceptualization of precedent not formally binding but having force:

Not formally binding but having force: a judgment not respecting a precedent's force, though lawful, is subject to criticism on this ground, and may be subject to reversal on this ground. Distinguish
   (a)   defeasible force – should be applied unless exceptions come into play (exceptions may or may not be well defined);
   (b)   outweighable force – should be applied unless countervailing reasons apply.

In addition, in regard to formally binding precedent, the participants in this study recognized the possibility that formally binding precedent might not only be defeasible but might also be outweighable when they recognized 'formal bindingness (with or without exceptions, that is subject to overruling or modification)', for such overruling or modification occurs in the face of considerations that outweigh the precedent overruled or modified.

The relations between the concepts 'outweighable' and 'defeasible' can now be summarized. There are four logical possibilities.

1   A given precedent-based rule or principle may be both outweighable and defeasible. Thus, we say it is to be respected, that is, followed, in all future cases to which it is applicable, unless outweighed by countervailing reasons. The precedent-based rule or principle may also be defeasible in the ordinary sense that its application is subject to exceptions already recognized or yet to be recognized. It may also be defeasible in a much more drastic sense, namely that it may be eliminated entirely from the system by operation of some general exception to the doctrine of precedent itself, as in the case of a *per incuriam* decision (although it might be better to say that such a precedent never achieves valid-

ity as a precedent in the first place). A new case which brings about an ordinary exception or restriction to an existing precedent-based rule or principle changes the legal situation. After judicial legal weighing and deliberation about the matter and eventual decision, the result of the departure from the precedent-based rule or principle will be the creation of a new rule or principle which includes an exception to the old one. In the terminology proposed by Dworkin and Alexy, only principles (hence not cases and not rules) have the dimension of weight. In their terminology, therefore, that which outweighs and that which is outweighed is strictly the principle behind, respectively, the defeating and the defeated rule. An 'outweighing reason' has thus to be conceptualized as being like a principle, not like a rule. The result of outweighing is, on the other hand, always a rule, that is, an exception laid down in a new precedent-based rule that derogates from the scope of the old precedent-based rule. Thus the creation of the exception is the same as the creation of a rule.

2   A precedent-based rule or principle may be defeasible although not outweighable. This is the case when it may be eliminated from the system by a process other than by being outweighed (and, say, overruled). According to a plausible theory, at least one such process (and a relatively infrequent one) is one that is not a matter of interpretation of the substantive content of the precedent but rather concerns the way the precedent has been created. For example, defeasible (but not outweighable) precedents can be found in the Court of Appeal in England and Wales, which is formally bound by its own precedents except where these have been reached *per incuriam*. By contrast, the decisions of the House of Lords are formally binding on the Court of Appeals and lower courts, but outweighable, that is, subject to overruling or modification on the basis of outweighing reasons as discussed above. Of course, this is not to say that no precedent of the Court of Appeals could ever be both defeasible and outweighable. For example, on a new point not theretofore ruled on by the House of Lords, the Court of Appeal might decide, after weighing the reasons on both sides, in favour of a given rule. On later appeal to the House of Lords, that court might then reweigh the reasons and reverse. In other countries, such as Norway, lower courts treat the previous decisions of the Supreme Court as binding, strictly or at least non-outweighably (though defeasibly).

3   A precedent-based rule or principle may be neither outweighable nor defeasible. It is not outweighable because it cannot be outweighed by counter-arguments. Neither is it defeasible, because it cannot be defeated in part or in whole by a subsequent practice. The only lawful way to depart from it is by new legislation.

Absolutely binding precedents in these senses are no longer to be found in any of the systems discussed in the present work. A judgment of a constitutional court setting aside a statute because of contrast with a constitutional provision is neither outweighable nor defeasible. But it is not a precedent in a proper sense, if this 'formal' effect is considered.

4   A precedent-based rule or principle may be outweighable but not defeasible in the drastic sense of elimination from the system. It is outweighable because it is a principle, to be followed in all future cases to which it is applicable, unless outweighed by counter-arguments. Depending on the circumstances, even if it has been outweighed in a case, it may not be eliminated from the system and, if so, should be followed in a still later case, unless outweighed by counter-arguments which occur in that case. Such a principle is not defeasible in the sense that it can be eliminated from the system by the courts, though it may be defeasible in the sense that exceptions can be created to it. The only way to put it out of the system is by legislation.

The only example of outweighing in a single case only, which does not establish an exception from the precedent-based rule or principle, is outweighing by a lower instance. In some countries, for example Germany, Italy, France and Spain, lower courts exercise the freedom to depart from precedents set by highest instance on the ground of their being outweighed by relevant considerations in the given case. Even if the precedent had thus been outweighed in a particular case, it stays in the system, and should be followed in a still later case, unless outweighed by counter-arguments which occur then. Only the higher instance, which had created the precedent rule, has power to make a decision that defeats it. The lower instance may only hold it outweighed in a particular case.

8   Degrees of Bindingness

The conceptual framework of our study contains (question 11.3, Appendix) the following list of factors which may be treated as relevant to determining the degree of bindingness (normative bearing) of a precedent.

a   The hierarchical rank of the court.
b   Whether the decision is merely of a panel or by a full bench.
c   The reputation of the court or of the judge writing the opinion.
d   Changes in the political, economic or social background since the prior decision.

e   Soundness of the supporting arguments in the opinion.
f   The age of the precedent.
g   The presence or absence of dissent.
h   The branch of law involved (for example, precedent being more weighty in property law than in the law of tort).
i   Whether the precedent represents a trend.
j   How well the precedent is accepted in academic writings.
k   The effects of legal change in related areas.

Interpreted in a certain way, the expression 'the degree of bindingness' (normative bearing) is applicable both to formal bindingness and to the other, lesser, degrees of normative bearing that a precedent may have: 'force', 'further support', 'illustrative value' and so on.

No doubt, formal bindingness may be regarded as a non-graded concept, like 'pregnant': a precedent is formally binding or not, and it cannot be binding to a degree. However, in the common conceptual framework of our study, formal bindingness is treated, not as one side of a dichotomy, but as merely one type of bindingness on a continuum that also includes 'having force', 'providing further support' and so on.

As explained in Section 2 above, the analysis which determines the existence of formal bindingness in the conceptual framework of our study, and which differentiates it from the lesser degrees of normative bearing that precedent may have, is that failure of a subsequent court below to respect the precedent and so not follow it signifies that the decision so made is 'not lawful and so is subject to reversal on appeal'. But it does not follow that the determination of whether a given precedent of a highest court in, say, the UK or New York is to be treated as formally binding in a system recognizing such formal bindingness is a mechanical one without any scope for exercise of any judgment by the court below (even assuming that the material facts of the higher court precedent are relevantly similar to the case at hand). For example, where there is only one precedent, it cannot be denied that, for instance, a decision of the highest court is likely to be taken somewhat more seriously than would be a single decision of the intermediate appellate court; so, too, a decision by the full bench of the upper court, rather than by merely a panel. The age of a precedent may be a factor too. And a decision *per incuriam* of the highest court may in a given system not be treated as a precedent at all. But systems differ precisely in the range of such factors that may enter a determination of unlawfulness and thus the likelihood of reversal of a decision not following an upper court precedent.

As regards various degrees of non-formal normative bearing, for example having force or providing further support, it appears that almost all the various factors set forth above influence it, one way or another, in all the systems. In particular, this can be said about the hierarchical rank of the court, the composition of the court (full bench or not), changes in the political, economic and social background, soundness of the supporting arguments in the opinion, age of the precedent and whether the precedent represents a trend. However, there are also some differences between systems. In Poland, the date of a decision (before or after the fall of communism) plays a particular role in this context. In Sweden, appeal to the authority of the Supreme Court seems to weigh much more than the substantive reasons uttered by it. The system seems to evolve towards a greater degree of 'formality'. An interesting complication occurs in Germany, France and Italy: since it is not made public which judge wrote the opinion, his or her reputation is generally not relevant. The age of a precedent is of minor weight as such. The branch of law involved seems not to be of importance. Even these exclusions may be understood as showing a trend towards a certain 'formality' in the system.

Bibliography

Aarnio, A. (1987), *The Rational as Reasonable*, Dordrecht: Kluwer.

Aarnio, A. (1989), *Laintulkinnan teoria*. Helsinki: WSOY.

Alexy and Peczenik, 'The Concept of Coherence and its Significance for Discursive Rationality', *Ratio Iuris*, 3, pp.130–47 (1991).

Bankowski, Z. (1991), 'Analogical Reasoning and Legal Institutions', in Nerhot, Patrick (ed.), *Legal Knowledge and Analogy*, Dordrecht/Boston/London: Kluwer.

Dworkin, R. (1986), *Law's Empire*, London: Fontana Press.

Frändberg, Å. (1973), *Om analog användning av rättsnormer* (with a summary in English: On Analogical Use of Legal Norms), Stockholm: Norstedts.

Hart, H.L.A. (1961), *The Concept of Law*, Oxford: Clarendon Press.

Heuman, L. (1992), 'Högsta domstolens prejudikatnedbrytande verksamhet', *Festskrift till Per Olof Bolding*, Stockholm: Juristförlaget.

Jackson, B. (1988), *Law, Fact and Narrative Coherence*, Roby: Deborah Charles Publications.

Krygier, M. 'Law as Tradition', *Law and Philosophy*, 5, pp.237–62 (1986).

MacCormick, D.N. (1984), 'Coherence in Legal Justification', in Peczenik, A., Lindahl, L. and Roermund, B. (eds), *Theory of Legal Science*, Dordrecht/Boston/Lancaster: Reidel Publishing Company, pp.235–51.

Malt, Gert-Fredrik (1992), 'To glemte linjer i tradisjonell rettsfinningslaere', *Tidsskrift for Rettsvitenskap*, pp.48–83.

Nerhot, Patrick (ed.) (1991), 'Legal Knowledge and Analogy Between Cases', *Fragments of Legal Epistemology, Hermeneutics and Linguistics*, Dordrecht/Boston/London: Kluwer.

Peczenik, A. (1989), *On Law and Reason*, Dordrecht/Boston/London: Kluwer.

Peczenik, A. (1995), *Vad är rätt?*, Stockholm: Norstedts.

Raz, J. (1979), *The Authority of Law*, Oxford: Clarendon Press.

15 Rationales for Precedent

ZENON BANKOWSKI, *EDINBURGH,*
D. NEIL MacCORMICK, *EDINBURGH,*
LECH MORAWSKI, *TORUN* AND
ALFONSO RUIZ MIGUEL, *MADRID*

1 Law Making or Interpretation?

There is a fundamental distinction to be drawn at the outset of any comparative discussion of the rationale for respecting precedents. This concerns the power of the courts to create law: does a given legal system formally acknowledge the existence of judge-made law or not? If so, two further questions that arise are how extensively does this judge-made law create precedents, and what sort or degree of normative force have these precedents for judges and courts other than the original decision maker? We might say that we are dealing on the one hand with the way case-based reasoning generates norms and on the other hand with the status of those norms within the system.

The common law systems studied in the present volume, those of the United States as exemplified by New York and of the United Kingdom, all share the feature that, for them, a substantial but always diminishing part of the contemporary law is acknowledged to have no source other than the precedents of the superior courts and, arguably, the long-standing customs and usages that these enshrine. In standard accounts of such legal systems, doctrines concerning 'the sources of law' therefore accord to judicial precedent a place, albeit one subordinate to the constitution (where relevant) and enacted statute law, among the criteria of validity or 'formal sources' of law.

This way of understanding precedent represents a 'positivization' of practices that were originally rationalized on quite different grounds. Seventeenth- and eighteenth-century institutional writings, such as those of Blackstone in England (and, for many purposes, the

481

USA) or Stair in Scotland, were decisively important in giving the common law an intelligible form and substance for rapidly modernizing and commercializing societies. But they justified the citation of precedent by reference to what they considered to be its evidentiary weight, the common law being the embodiment for local purposes of the law of nature and reason, worked out through the general customs of the realm. This is a 'declaratory' theory, according to which precedents declare law but do not make it. With the demise of rationalistic jusnaturalism in the nineteenth century, a positivistic rationale supervened, and every law was represented as depending on some human act of will, the judges being envisaged more as subordinate legislators than as discoverers or formulators of a pre-existing law grounded in the nature and reason of things. Jeremy Bentham, the father of English positivism, was particularly strong in his criticism of the power of 'Judge and Co', and insistent that the fact of judicial legislation through precedent had to be acknowledged and, if possible, reformed. This had considerable impact on the system of precedent in the UK in two ways. First, one can say that positivist theories of precedent heralded the development of and move to a system of stricter *stare decisis* and, concomitant with that, a greater theoretical focus on the rules that created precedents and the elements in precedents that were actually binding (hence much work on the idea of *ratio decidendi*; compare Chapter 16).

In relation to the civilian systems, a substantially similar movement in thought from a rationalistic to a voluntaristic conception of law took place, but yielded different doctrinal conclusions, both as a cause and as a consequence of the movement towards codification. In revolutionary and post-revolutionary France, regard for Montesquieu's insistence on a strict separation of powers that precludes overconcentration of state powers in the hands of particular agencies or individuals was married to a Rousseauian vision of statute as expressing the *volonté générale* of the French nation. Such a conception of the division between legislative and judicial power precluded and to this day is conceived as precluding, at least in theory, recognition of the judges as even subordinate law makers, depicting the judicial function as a purely law-applying, not in any measure law-making, function. This view acquired a certain credibility in the context of codification, for here the legislature has at least in theory addressed and provided for every legal contingency through a coherent overall scheme of rights, obligations and remedies. Either the code leaves no gaps or, if it were to, it would be for legislators, not judges, to fill them. (Not all codifiers have been so categorical, however. The Swiss Civil Code expressly gives judges a last resort power to fill gaps in the Code by enunciating the norm that in their view would be most appropriately enacted by the legislature, in any case in which all other resources for filling the gap have failed.)

Germany followed a somewhat different path from France. Though the movement towards codification started relatively early and was driven by absolute monarchs with ideas for codification inspired by natural law, the movement towards codification was checked in the post-Napoleonic era by the massively influential opposition of Carl von Savigny. He treated law as dependent more on custom than enactment, arguing that law resides ultimately in the spirit of a people and has to be elaborated for them by their jurists. This law of jurists originates in two ways: first, by finding the guiding principles of the law and deducing consequences from them – thus producing 'new' norms by elaborating the latent content of positive law; second, by establishing leading scholarly opinions (*communis opinio doctorum*) and firm adjudications (*usus fori, Gerichtsgebrauch*). A single precedent, based on norms the court has arrived at in the first way, owes its binding force exclusively to its 'inner truth', that is, its being a correct elaboration of the law. The same holds true for leading opinions and lines of judicial precedent, up to the point at which these qualify as customary law. So the theory of precedent presented by the Historical School is a classical form of a declaratory theory. The underlying concept is that law comprises a body of convictions and principles, embedded in legal relationships and institutions, prior to statutory, customary and established scholarly law. The Savigny theory was greatly influential in the Germanic countries, but for perhaps obvious reasons it also had considerable appeal in common law jurisdictions, where it was to a degree matched, if in less high-romantic terms, by the work of scholars such as Maine, Bryce, Holmes and Carter. In the nineteenth and early twentieth centuries historical jurisprudence was a prominent rival to positivism in common law thinking.

Nevertheless, the French conception cast a long shadow over most civilian systems other than the German. It extended in influence even to the self-understanding of the Nordic systems, though these never achieved full codification, and today retain some appearances similar to the mixed case law and statute-based systems of the common law countries. In its classical form, the French conception is one that mandates a rejection of precedent as a formal source of law, and in France itself has even gone so far as to discourage formal acknowledgment of precedents in the *motivation* of court decisions; that is, in the statement of the formal opinion of the court as distinct from the reasoning and argumentation that precedes the formal enunciation of the judicial opinion, stated anonymously for the whole court.

It does not follow, of course, that a reasonable or realistic representation of contemporary civilian systems does or could ignore the significance of judicial precedent within these systems, and the present volume is eloquent testimony to this fact. The official rationale within the systems still strongly influenced by the classical French conception, however, has to be other than by way of a direct acknowledgment of precedent as yielding legal norms that have normative force in themselves, simply in virtue of the authority of the deciding court. In one form or another, the account offered is essentially in terms of the interpretative function of judicial decision making, and the interpretative rather than law-making character of the precedents it establishes.

Thus, in the French system, precedent may not be cited as the sole ground of a judgment, since this does not constitute a *motivation* (justification) according to law *(loi)*. The authors of Chapter 4 therefore present a dichotomy concerning precedent, dividing between 'precedent of solution' and 'precedent of interpretation'. The latter is a precedent envisaged, not as presenting a rule for the solution of future cases, but as determining an appropriate interpretation of written law or of legal principles for cases of the type in question; hence, when reference is made to such a precedent, what is done under its guidance is a matter of applying the relevant law in its best interpretation, not deferring to what would be an illegitimate regulatory role assumed by the precedent court. Thus, even if it is in a universalized or generalized form that the 'precedent of interpretation' operates for later courts, this can be seen as the recognition of the law's principle(s), not the ascription of law-making power to the courts.

Notwithstanding the early hopes of revolutionary codifiers, all codified systems have for long fully acknowledged the need for interpretation, for it is necessary to resolve emerging ambiguities, obscurities and indeterminacies in the provisions of the codes. Resolving these in a rational and responsible way, however, proves to be both a matter of elucidating the law through expounding its underlying principles in a way that reveals and preserves or even constitutes it as a rationally coherent body of law and a matter – an increasingly urgent one – of ensuring that legal rules and principles march in reasonable time with evolving or developing societal needs. This interpretational role has been at its most expansive where the written law is most skeletal and, not surprisingly, has become particularly evident (and urgent) in the development of public law, first through administrative tribunals in the nineteenth and earlier twentieth centuries, and then additionally and yet more fundamentally through constitutional tribunals and courts in the post-1945 period.

In Germany, where the courts are by the constitution stated to be 'bound to statute and to law' (*'Gesetz und Recht'*), the reference to a body of law wider than the written statute law has been interpreted as requiring the courts to expound fundamental principles implicit in the law, sometimes even in preference to the letter of the law. The constitutional court has a duty to implement the principles of the constitution, including the requirements for democracy and the 'social *Rechtsstaat*'; this is a strikingly wide and highly important power to shape the fundamentals of law. Germany is not alone; wherever constitutional courts, tribunals or councils have been created as watchdogs on constitutionality, they have necessarily exercised a fundamental role in developing the basic elements of the constitutional order and legal system, and laying down precedents, often formally binding ones, on these matters. The present chapters on Italy, France, Spain and Poland all bear witness to this, and it is notorious that the constitutional jurisprudence of the Supreme Court of the United States has exercised unparalleled influence in the period since 1945.

Comparable with the role of constitutional tribunals in national jurisdictions has been the role of the European Court of Justice in working out a coherent corpus of quasi-constitutional law for the European Community from the allusive and fragmentary norms laid down in the foundational treaties and their subsequent amendments. The *Manzoni* case, discussed in Chapter 12, is of importance in enunciating this.

In turn, the decisions of the ECJ have functioned as precedents in relation to the courts of member states, including the constitutional courts, sometimes requiring the non-application even of parliamentary enactments, as well as bringing about changes in the settled jurisprudence of the courts themselves. Decisions of the European Court of Human Rights have had a comparable effect within that court's sphere of responsibility. This has, as in the case of national constitutional adjudication and adjudication in relation to general clauses in codes and statutes, frequently involved giving concrete meaning to quite vague concepts and texts. Here, where the judicial contribution operates by way of working out the underlying principles and giving them concrete effect in series of landmark decisions, it seems almost artificial or even fictional to draw a line between interpretative and law-making precedents. The interpretation is so far-reaching, and guided by such flimsy fragments of written law, that the 'law-making' rationale seems at least as credible as the 'interpretative' one. On the other hand, a growing and powerful body of contemporary thought in the common law world, associated particularly with the work of Ronald Dworkin (1986), is engaged in arguing against the positivistic view of precedent and putting in its place a declaredly 'interpretivist' approach to understanding the common law and its processes of reasoning, thereby reinstating a declaratory theory in a modern form. So there may in fact be a two-way convergence of approaches.

2   Why Follow Precedent? *Stare Decisis* and Juridical Uniformity

Further elements of similarity, or even of convergence, can be seen when we turn to considering the reasons offered in support of following precedents. In considering the systems of codified law, one striking aspect of the rationale for following 'precedents of interpretation' is that of unity or uniformity in law and in decision making throughout the whole legal order – it is not sufficient that nominally the same body of written law be observed throughout the different judicial regions, but it should be in force in the same interpretation in all parts. The very institution of *pourvoi en cassation* and its equivalents originates in an understood need to secure the lawfulness of decisions throughout a state; and this almost inevitably implies their lawfulness under a common interpretation of the law. As the *Manzoni* case shows, this is of like importance in European Community law, especially in those domains in which the implementation of Community law is largely in the hands of judges in the courts of the member states, with the ECJ exercising an interpretative supervision under the provision of Article 177.

In Finland, the Supreme Court has in the recent past become more explicitly a court whose function it is to preserve uniformity. In Sweden, this role is even more strongly emphasized, having been introduced by statute in the Code of Procedure of 1972. This is also the case in the Italian Supreme Court, where the task of ensuring uniformity is laid down by Article 65 of the law concerning the organization of courts, though the multiplicity of panels of the Supreme Court and the great number of references to the court make this perhaps more an aspiration than a perfected achievement. Perhaps the introduction of a system requiring leave to appeal to the highest court would have the effect of enabling the Supreme Court to pick out strands from the various regional appeal courts that it wants to develop and enforce over the country as a whole. Express powers of constitutional courts to make rulings on the constitutionality of statutes and their proper interpretation, with binding force for all courts, are striking examples of the same essential point.

New York exhibits, and the United States taken as a whole exhibits yet more, one of the features of concern in the European civilian systems, namely a plurality of courts exercising coordinate or parallel jurisdiction in a geographically defined area, even at the penultimate level of appeals. In such contexts, a court with highest-level appellate jurisdiction, such as the New York Court of Appeals, has a special responsibility for sustaining the unity of state law. This is somewhat less urgently a feature of the systems of the United Kingdom, though it may have played an important role in the historic development of an English common law through the deliberations of the Inns of Court and the Royal Courts in London. In the contemporary UK, certainly, the maintenance of a coherent body of common law in each of the several jurisdictions is of great acknowledged importance, as well as a common and coherent interpretation of those bodies of statute law, and indeed some bodies of case law, that are common to the several jurisdictions within the UK, in each of which there is a unitary instance of intermediate appellate jurisdiction.

Given that (or so far as) we are here dealing with societies characterized by an adherence to the ideology and the practice of 'rational' legal order in the sense proposed by Max Weber (1967), we can indeed say that coherence in interpretation of particular provisions over many cases, and interpretative practices aimed at securing an overall coherence of the legal system, are absolutely fundamental to them. Coherence in both senses is of the very essence of rational legal order, just as it is definitive for the idea of a rational legal discourse. It is not surprising that, in all the systems studied, the value of coherence of law is one key element in the locally understood rationale for the practice of treating precedent as binding in whatever is the particular sense or senses locally ascribed to its bindingness (or, more generally, its normative force). This is understandable as an independent rationale for precedent, rooted in the very character of the rational argumentation essential for rational legal order.

From a different point of view, the unifying role of precedent can also be seen as simply an aspect of the unitary character of the legal system of a well-ordered state, one which it is the particular role of courts to sustain. Legal coherence, together with uniformity of decision, is indeed an everywhere acknowledged value served by respect for the force of argument from precedent, and one which it is the particular function of courts in their interpretative role to achieve. The value of uniformity can be deemed a technical–legal desideratum, just as coherence may be considered an aspect of *elegantia juris;* but both also go to the overall integrity of the state as guarantor of a single legal system. Again we should note, in the vein of 'integrity', how persuasively it has been argued that the ECJ's role as a precedent setter in the courts of the member states has played a decisive part until now in the promotion of European integration (see Weiler, 1991).

3 *Stare Decisis,* Equality and the Rule of Law

A similar rationale for the normative force of precedent concerns fundamental constitutional and politico-moral values. That courts maintain uniformity in law and in its interpretation and application from case to case can be considered a requirement for securing the rule of law or *Rechtsstaat*; for these are ideals that demand the equal treatment of individuals in the sense of formal equality before the law. This would be a sham if the law were subject to varying interpretation from case to case, for it would only be nominally the same law that applied to different cases with essentially similar features among themselves. Thus uniformity of law is an essential part of equality of treatment of essentially similar cases, that is, cases which qualify as similar under a given (and stable) interpretation of the law. This is fully acknowledged in all the civilian reports, and likewise in the common law ones. Nevertheless, there are aspects of equality that go beyond uniformity of law, as the Italian constitutional provisions about equality show. The German and Spanish constitutional courts have likewise held that equality before the law cannot be supposed to mandate an absolute bindingness of precedent.

Closely related values, also often subsumed under the rule of law ideal, are those of legal certainty, legal stability and the predictability by citizens of the probable mode of application of legal norms. These well-established *rechtsstaatlich* values uphold a practice of following precedents and, particularly, of following settled lines of precedent whether these are deemed merely 'precedents of interpretation' in the French sense or are considered 'precedents of solution' under the common lawyers' conception of precedent. Clearly, in any legal system, a readiness of the courts to give some weight to the very existence of a precedent, independently of the intrinsic merits of the decision contained in the precedent, can be strongly justified by the needs for stability and predictability both of the law and of the courts' decisions handed down in the name of the law. And all this is of the very essence of giving citizens a tolerable measure of legal security and confidence in their enjoyment of whatever rights the law confers on them.

As the French and Italian reports indicate, however, the interpretative conception of precedent also lays special stress on the determination of legal principles, and indeed conceptualizes these as principles implicit in the codes or in the general conception of law settled under the constitution and codes and having regard to binding international treaties, including the European Union Treaties and, therefore, the precedents of the ECJ and the European Court of Human Rights. Especially in Italy, the system of reporting is one that extracts statements of principle and divorces them from the factual setting of particular cases. Whether this relatively broad-brush use of precedent is as helpful as other approaches to the value of certainty in law might be questioned.

Certainly, it is possible to draw at least a partial contrast with the common law – and also the Nordic – understanding of precedent, where styles of reasoning both in relation to the issues in hand and in respect of the precedents cited and applied (whether followed or distinguished in the given case) focus quite closely on the facts of the particular case in their often considerable complexity. This facilitates two special aspects of reasoning that may be of less importance in other settings. First, a step-by-step development of law by working from analogy to analogy allows principles to be worked out experimentally over a series of cases without the risk of crystallizing an overbroad proposition of law in an untimely way. Secondly, there is a ready escape from prematurely being bound by overbroad generalizations, because decisions read closely in line with their factual particularities are more readily distinguishable than those that are enunciated as bare generalizations enunciating a broad rule or principle without reference to the facts of the cases from which they are derived, as in the case of Italian *massime*.

Thus common law systems with their case-by-case way of arguing (however one might rationally reconstruct particular analogies into general principles) put a particularly strong focus on the facts and the reasoning about facts and law in each precedent, since the style of the judgments deals with the detailed articulation of cases that appear similar. Sometimes the process even presents the appearance of a form of iterative storytelling and story-matching. Once we move into the terrain of analogical extrapolation from one story to the next, we face questions as to the nature and strength of the 'gravitational force' that other stories might have on the instant one. Civilian systems which do not focus as closely on the particularity of cases as common law systems do, but which concentrate on precedents as interpretations of code provisions or of general principles, clearly do not raise this question in the same way.

Differences here are real, but should not be exaggerated; for instance, in France, a genuine element of factual specificity enters the case reports whenever there is discussion of the legal qualification of the facts, and even in the most abstract and magisterial pronouncements of the *Cour de Cassation*, the facts material to the decision are summarized with masterly brevity in the stated judgment; in Germany, Italy and the ECJ, statements of principle boldly announced may be subsequently limited by the elaboration of exceptions and limiting conditions. Indeed, wherever there is stress on the line of authority, the *jurisprudence constante* or *ständige Rechtssprechung*, rather than the authoritative law-making character even of the single highest-court precedent, a step-by-step character is built into the development of legal principle by devices different from the particularistic, analogizing and distinguishing, style of common law development with its especially close attention to facts of cases. In Sweden, however, the stress on particularity without the elaboration of grounds of distinguishing appears to have somewhat weakened the contribution of the courts to the confident or even bold development of legal principles; but a countervailing factor there is perhaps the practice of using judicial conferences to determine the areas of law needing development through case law.

Equality before law, security under law, and legal certainty or predictability, can all be interpreted as matters of intrinsic rightness, even as fundamental rights. But it is important to remember that they have also an instrumental aspect. In the present work, the authors of Chapters 11 and 12, on the USA (New York) and the European Community respectively, draw particular attention to the instrumental value of strong respect for precedent. But the arguments they put have clearly a quite general relevance. Whatever may be the problem-specific individual policies towards which given decisions are instrumentally effective, the practice of respecting precedents once they have been laid down include at least the following:

1   efficiency in the sense of economy of judicial effort – the same point should not be too often re-argued;
2   efficiency in the interest of private parties, who can more reliably reach out-of-court settlements of points in dispute if they regard the law as clearly decided and unlikely to be upset; and
3   avoidance of pointless litigation, if a lower court decides against the standing jurisprudence of courts higher in the same hierarchy of jurisdiction, and is time and again reversed on appeal.

Rule-utilitarian considerations of this kind have very great importance as rationales for the practice of precedent, and have to be considered alongside deontological interpretations of legal certainty and security. Indeed, there is a well-understood standpoint in practical philosophy that represents the rule-utilitarian argument as the fundamental basis for the rule of law, not as either coordinate with or subordinate to some conception of rightness in the conduct of government. This is not the place, however, to enter into, far less purport to adjudicate upon, that long-running and deep philosophical controversy.

4   Limits to *Stare Decisis*

In favour of respecting precedents, as we see, it is possible to line up a series of weighty considerations, and these are indeed advanced in practice to justify usages of binding precedent in all the systemic variations here studied. It is important, however, not to give a wholly one-sided representation of this. There is at least a sense in which all the reasons supporting recourse to binding precedent are formal in character, and they can all find themselves opposed by considerations of a more subtantive kind. In summary:

1   Overstressing uniformity in law or in governmental practice is the enemy of a sensible responsiveness to local variability of conditions and sociopolitical attitudes; uniformity needs to be balanced by subsidiarity – a concept now recognized explicitly for the EU in the preamble to and third article of the Maastricht Treaty. Albeit in different terminology, the same debate has had long currency in the USA around the issue of states' discretion versus commonality of rights for all Americans.
2   Coherent elaboration of unfair legal norms, or norms that have outlived their social usefulness or been bypassed by new social understandings, may lead to conflict with a more fundamentally coherent moral understanding of social relations.
3   Formal equality before the law can coexist with extreme and strongly contested ('substantive') inequality of treatment – for example, in the case of fairly and equally applied laws that allow racial segregation of schools, exclusion of women from voting, or denial to homosexuals of competence to adopt children.
4   Stability and certainty in law can be the enemies of adaptability of law to changing technological, economic and social circumstances, and to changing ideas of good order and fair law. Complete stability must necessarily stifle even such change as is imperatively demanded by progress (according to any given understanding of 'progress').

Thus, to put it simply, there are both social–functional and ultimate-value grounds in all systems for resisting the ascription of any absolute weight or indefeasibility even to long-settled precedents. Changes in technology, commerce and industry, and evolving social attitudes to gender, generational and familial relationships, and a multitude of similar considerations, can give rise to a sense of legal rules and doctrines being 'out of step with' needs and aspirations widely felt in society. Moreover, new appreciations of basic rights and of essential human liberties can give rise to a strong sense that, instead of representing the wisdom of the past, respect for precedents becomes a dead weight on social progress, the entrenchment of substantive unfairness or injustice in the guise of a formal justice of treating 'like cases alike'.

A classical example of the need for precedents creating radical changes at least in the interpretation of established law is provided by countries like Spain or Poland, where the courts, in particular the constitutional tribunals, had to take over the task of adjusting the 'old' law (respectively Francoist and communist) to a new democratic reality. Moreover, in Poland, with the changeover to a market system, much legislation has had to be changed and much still needs to be changed. The Polish Supreme Court has quite understandably said that uniformity should not be made into a fetish, and in the transitional stage between a command and market economy in Poland, precedents must sometimes provide new law even at the cost of some momentary incoherence or lack of uniformity in the system as a whole.

More generally, when there is a perceived paralysis of the legislature or a low probability of effective parliamentary legislation, it appears that in any system the courts will take upon themselves the role of developing new directions of legal or at least of interpretational change. Again, there have been remarkable transformations in styles of legislative drafting, even in the structure of legal languages, which become more and more abstract, increasingly subject to 'open texture', hence there seems always to be an increasing necessity for courts to give abstract provisions some suitable concrete meaning for particular cases and contexts.

Additionally, it is worth stressing that present-day societies, in comparison to their predecessors, are far more complex. This growing complexity results in the growing fallibility of our norms and decisions, including those posed by the courts. Accordingly, it strengthens our readiness to open legal systems to the possibility of corrections or modifications of mistaken decisions so as to avoid or to compensate for possible harms and costs. This amounts to a rejection of juridical fundamentalism, and leads to what we might call a progressive instrumentalization of legal systems. By this we mean the development of an approach to law which assumes that law serves primarily as an instrument for the pursuit of substantive social policies and therefore must be effective in realizing its tasks and goals. The need to ensure the effectiveness of legal regulation forces not only legislators but courts as well to adopt procedures facilitating correction of those decisions which turn out to be erroneous. At any rate, the idea of law as instrumental in this sense is incompatible with any kind of absolutely strict doctrine of precedent that treats even manifestly unsatisfactory precedents as binding until abrogated by new legislation.

Functional and substantive-value arguments are thus always available, at least to justify a restrictive interpretation of settled precedents, and ultimately, usually after a set of 'distinguishing' or 'whittling down' interpretations, a simple reversal or overruling of established precedent. In all jurisdictions there is a measure of concern about the legitimacy of this process, exposed as it is to adverse comment from the standpoint of the twin doctrines of rule of law and separation of powers. But, in the systems under review, the issue is nowhere whether precedent should be indefeasibly binding; everywhere, it is a difficult and discussed question when and how far sufficient reason exists to disturb or vary settled precedent, but the trend is towards an approach that gives substantial weight to established precedent while allowing departure from precedent, or even overruling of it, when the case has become strong enough to cancel the claims of the formal values supporting adherence to precedent.

Finally, none of the foregoing discussion settles the question how far precedents that are either formally binding or endowed with strong normative force may be treated as bases for innovative development of the law. One cannot conflate arguments for saying that precedents ought to be respected on account of uniformity and integrity or rule of law values with arguments concerning the 'gravitational force' (see Dworkin, 1978) to be ascribed to particular precedents or lines of precedent. It is one thing to ask what is the minimal proposition for which a precedent must be followed, another to consider the extent to which, for the sake of the principles or values it encapsulates, it can properly be taken as having justificatory force in relation to cases that might seem only imperfectly or even loosely analogous. The fact that judicial decisions do have gravitational force does not go so much to the question in what cases they must be followed, but rather the question – highlighted in the Italian report – how far they may be followed; the issue is of the right to follow the precedent rather than of the duty not to ignore or undercut it.

This reminds us again of an apparent convergence in self-understanding of different systems. The most recent thought in relation to the common law systems lays stress on an interpretative rather than a subordinate–legislative understanding of precedent (compare Chapter 10, 'United Kingdom', Section III); and while the civilian systems edge towards recognizing the real overlap between interpretation and determination of law, they remain doctrinally resistant to accepting any full-blooded 'formal source of law' account. Indeed, we have to record the still sometimes prevalent interpretation of constitutionalism and legality by the Spanish and Italian judiciary according to which this requires an acknowledgment of the independence not only of the judiciary considered collegially, but of each individual judge; so the normative grounds in favour of uniformity of interpretation and respect for precedents are not accepted as generating a strong obligation on the judge in favour of fidelity to precedents, either vertically or horizontally. (This is subject to the important exception, in Spain, concerning the legal obligation of the judge to follow constitutional interpretations, including interpretations of statutes for conformity with the constitution, as these are laid down by the constitutional court.)

5   Deeper Scepticisms

So far, so good; it is reasonable to acknowledge certain well-under-stood ways of rationalizing precedent, but at the same time one must also accept that no rationale can be carried too far; in the end, a non-absolute approach to precedent seems the appropriate one, striking a balance between the values secured by precedent and the counter-values that oppose undue deference to it. Hence the systems we study seem rightly to converge towards a principle of limited *stare decisis*. In the common law world, the House of Lords' renunciation of strictly binding precedent in 1966 represented a retreat from the high classical doctrine (and in New York, successor chief judges still debate the extent to which the Court of Appeals ought to be bound by its own prior determinations). In the countries of codified law, variably 'civilian' in inspiration, precedent is acknowledged to play an ever-growing role in the determination of the law and in the practice of decision making. Certainly, this is very variably acknowl-edged in the official pronouncement of court judgments and nowhere involves the careful and detailed analysis of precedent so markedly characteristic of the non-codified legal systems, and even of such a system as Scots law, which is still quite largely civilian in fundamen-tal doctrines while being entirely of the common law camp in judicial methodology.

Convergence and consensus are the very stuff of complacency, of the mutual self-congratulation of lawyers coming together from dif-ferent traditions. Complacency invites critique and, indeed, all that has been said about precedent and its rationale has been the target of withering critique, from at least two distinct angles, that of Legal Realism and Critical Legal Studies in the common law world, and that of traditional separation of powers doctrine in the civilian. We shall consider these in that order.

Scepticism about the determinacy of precedent has a long history, especially but not only in the United States. At least, the idea that precedents add up to clear rules directly applicable in successor cases has been under hostile scrutiny since long ago. The 'Realist Movement' in the American law schools of the 1920s–1950s was deeply sceptical of the idea that case law is a set of easily determined rules, perhaps even of 'rules' at all, and this encouraged an approach to precedent that directed students and lawyers (also judges) ever more towards a detailed appreciation of the full complexity of fac-tual backgrounds in cases, coupled with caution as to the ease of extrapolating from one or several cases to a new case of first impres-sion. The successor scepticism of 'Critical Legal Studies' has gone a good deal farther, and has attacked the notion that there can be any doctrinally based certainty whatsoever in law. On this view, for every legal principle there is a readily statable counter-principle (our study of the values and counter-values in the rationale of precedent might be considered a copybook case of this); consensus about the values in issue and their reasonable balancing is a merely ideological mask, hiding the true motor of politicoeconomic interest that drives decision making forward under the guise rather than the reality of reasonably constrained law finding.

To the extent that the present work is concerned with the rational reconstruction of prevailing doctrines, it does not have a direct reply to this. For our project is not sociologically empirical, not directed at testing the asserted certainties of precedent against revealed uncertainties in 'real life'. Yet, even if the ideals of equality before law and certainty in law or security before it were illusory, it would remain to be asked whether we have here accurately reconstructed the dominant ideology, however at variance that may be with the underlying facts of sociolegal experience. Further, we are entitled to add, and do add, that a conception of legal discourse rooted in the possibility of rational practical argumentation has its own resources to counter the most radical scepticisms.

An approach to legal reasoning that is open and articulate about its grounds of argumentation, and that does its weighing and balancing of reason and counter-reason under public scrutiny, does indeed show that there is no deductive paradigm of absolute certainty which can certify the incontestable correctness of every decision made in lawcourts. But it also gives grounds for believing that, between the extremes of absolute certainty and total arbitrariness, there is a range of reasonable decision making, genuinely guided by principles, enacted rules and precedents, which admits of tolerable certainty and predictability, and which gives real substance but not absolute weight to the ideal, or if you will ideology, of equality before the law and the rule of law.

Defence against the first critique exposes one to a pincer-thrust from the second, associated perhaps with a charge of undue common law bias in the discussion up to this point. The second critique argues that too little weight has been given to the classical paradigm of the judicial role developed in France and later adopted by certain other civil law countries. Should we not take more seriously than we have done the idea that the courts perform a specific, decidedly non-legislative, function of the state? Are they not charged with receiving the law in the form of legislated general norms and applying them to concrete disputes with whatever interpretative reasoning is necessary to transform general norm into adequate ground for particular decision?

Moreover, warned by various excesses of judicial conformism seen in many unfortunate places in Europe's past, often tragic, century, should we not attend carefully to those doctrines of judicial independence that entitle, even obligate, the lower court to decide according to law in the light of its own best interpretation, not blindly following precedent, but considering each issue on its legal merits? Of course this will not be lightly done, for courts must and do bear in mind that the hierarchy of courts makes it easy for the higher court to reverse the independent-minded decision on appeal, at needless expense to parties, if indeed an appeal takes place. The doctrines of separation of powers and of judicial independence are not univocal, indeed they belong to the family of essentially contested concepts, and the civilian systems share conceptions of these concepts that deserve serious attention in their own right.

Whereas proponents of Critical Legal Studies express scepticism about the possibility of *stare decisis* as anything other than an ideological device, the traditional paradigm of the judicial power broadly shared among France, Italy and Poland has, as we saw, tended to reject it as an unacceptable ideology, and to propose a different approach altogether, declaring firmly against any law-making activity of courts, and thus against any acknowledgement of precedent as a legally justifying ground of decision, or as a binding constraint upon decision, such as would presuppose the existence of a power of judicial law making. Still, the chapters written by experts from these countries show that in reality, even there, courts do regularly create, and sometimes are even forced to create, law. But the prevailing ideology generally leads them to present their decisions either as following from statutes or as merely acts of interpretation that disclose the 'true' meaning of the statutory prescription in issue. In this case, then, a gap opens up between what the legal system officially permits and what the courts necessarily do. This is a real gap between what is said and what is done. The balance of opinion among the present authors is that it would be better to adopt a greater candour in legal practice than has prevailed in relation to this. The point is put with particular force in the Polish chapter (Chapter 7) of this book. Sustaining a gap between official ideology and inevitable practice, between 'saying' and 'doing', seems to favour neither the good functioning of the legal system, which may have become unworkable in some areas owing to legislative inaction, nor its prestige.

In fact, this has clearly been the modern direction of evolution of judicial practice in Scandinavian countries, in Germany and, to some extent, in Spain and Italy. Courts in these countries are gradually abandoning the old model of the judicial role and have increasingly accepted openly their active role in law-developing, even law-making, processes. Hence they do not have to conceal what they really do. One remarkable sign of this shift of paradigm is, for instance, the decisions of the German Constitutional Tribunal and German Federal Supreme Court that permit the courts in exceptional circumstances 'very carefully and in accordance with established legal values' to create rules even contrary to the wording of statutes.

6 Pluralism about Precedent

One upshot of the foregoing discussion might be to suggest the need for a decidedly non-monolithic approach to the concepts of precedent and of *stare decisis*. Just as the 'binding' quality of precedents is subject to a variety of interpretations, so may there be more than one way of using past decisions to guide the present and future. The whole tenor of the discussion so far rejects the very idea that there is but one single and uniform use of precedent. Indeed, there is a case for differentiating at least three models of reasoning from precedent:

1 The *model of particular analogy*, where each case is simply treated as an illuminating example of a correct (or reasonable) decision given all its own facts, and hence a useful guide for decision in similar cases. Here, the issue is which are similar cases – in what level of detail must one compare and contrast the instant case and the proposed precedent?

2 The *rule-stating model*, where some rule (*'ratio decidendi'*) is ascribed to the precedent as one which it is appropriate for later courts to apply unless they can distinguish or overrule it. Here, a court deciding a case should ascertain whether any precedent has a *ratio* relevant to the instant case, and should then apply it unless some material point of distinction between the instant case and the precedent can be identified, or unless some other valid reason exists for not applying it.

3 The *principle-exemplifying model*, where the precedent, in relation to its own factual context, can be seen as exhibiting, and giving support to, some legal principle or principles that may be relevant for deciding future cases, and perhaps contributing to new legal developments. In the instant case, one looks to the precedents to see whether they contain or represent principles useful for justifying the currently preferred decision.

For each of these models, we can differentiate formally binding versions of the model from ones which attract only normative force in some degree short of the formally binding. In common law systems, where precedents are clearly accepted as formally binding in some contexts, depending on court hierarchies and the like, it is a matter of discussion whether cases are binding only according to their particular facts, as in the model of analogy, or also as to the *ratio decidendi* envisaged as a strict rule embodied in the precedent, or perhaps even in respect of more general principles expressed or implied in the judge's opinion. It is probably more common, though, to treat broader statements of principle as technically *obiter dicta*, and thus only persuasive, perhaps highly persuasive, in their normative force. And, of course, precedents which are not formally binding may be in greater or less degree persuasive and available in the fashion of model (1) or (2) as stating a persuasive analogy or a possible rule of decision that gives a legal grounding for the present decision, even though not making obligatory the handing down of a decision conforming to the precedent.

Where precedent is not recognized as formally binding, yet where it has the kind of less than formally binding normative force discussed in Chapter 14, it is probable that models (1) and (3) will predominate over (2); for there is little point in laboriously spelling out the specific rule or ruling in law for which a precedent stands if no such rule can in any event be acknowledged formally as binding or as in itself an adequate legal motivation ('justification') for a decision. Indeed, Chapter 16 on the binding element in precedents confirms that close and detailed discussion of the *ratio decidendi* and its differentiation from *obiter dicta* is confined to the common law countries, except to the extent that, within the EU, common lawyers have extended the discussion into the analysis of precedents in Community law. Whether it will transplant from there into the juristic consciousness of civilian member states remains to be seen.

Accordingly, in a legal system in which precedents play any part, legal reasoning will instantiate at least one of these models in the justification of decisions. But more than one of the models may be in use. Acknowledgment of precedent as formally binding does not preclude a broader use of precedents as helpful particular analogies or as sources that exemplify and help to formulate legal principles. Equally, that precedents are discountenanced as formally binding sources of law does not mean that they cannot be used, at least in legal dogmatics and perhaps even in judicial opinions, as useful analogies or as illustrations of legal principles.

So long as legal rules or constitutional doctrines preclude reference to precedent as a source or form of law, as in France, this will doubtless sustain a continuing practice of formally ignoring precedent in the judicial statement of reasons ('*motifs*') for the legal decisions of the courts. But juristic doctrine and learned commentaries on law and on individual decisions of importance will continue to indicate the real importance of precedent in the mode of model (3) as exemplifying principles and thereby unifying interpretation of the codes. Perhaps under the influence of the Realist movement, the legal systems of the USA have differed from those of other common law countries by the fact that they have placed much more emphasis on (1), precedent as particular analogy, and (3), precedent as exemplifying principles, than on (2), precedent as stating strict rules. By contrast, in the UK and in Commonwealth countries, although the development of law owes much to (1) and (3), the (nowadays somewhat diminishing) weight placed on a relatively strict approach to formally binding precedent has given model (2) a particularly prominent role in the theory of precedent and the practice of law.

One source of the difference of the USA from other common law jurisdictions is obvious: in a federal system like that of the USA, the only formally binding precedents are those of courts within a particular state or other special jurisdiction, being decisions of a level higher in the given hierarchy than that of the deciding court. But the practice of citing precedents is by no means restricted to the local jurisdiction, and precedents from courts throughout the USA and (less frequently nowadays) from other common law countries are freely cited in arguments of counsel and in opinions of judges in some cases. Such precedents being only persuasive, never formally binding, they normally function only in the manner of model (1) or model (3). But it should not be forgotten that, when we focus on the particular common law of a particular state, especially a large, powerful and historically self-confident state such as New York, we see (as Chapter 11 very forcefully shows) that there may be a strong attachment to formally binding precedent in respect of the decisions of the highest state court whenever relevantly applicable in all the lower courts of the state.

Unacknowledged precedent in certain continental systems owes its origin to the deliberate rejection of precedent as a formal source in any way coordinate with legislation. As we saw, the reasons for this rejection in France lie in the legal theory of the Revolutionary period, both negatively, in respect of the revolutionaries' desire to do away with the perceivedly illegitimate law-making role of the old *Parlements*, and also positively, in the context of a particular theory of separation of powers that assigned to the judiciary only a law-applying, not a law-making, role. One may fully sympathize with the desire to secure legislative supremacy, especially in the context of democratic answerability of legislators, but one must nevertheless acknowledge that a measure of overall coherence in the interpretation of legislation, even in the context of a code, requires regard to what French scholars now call 'precedents of interpretation' at least in the sense of model (3), if not possibly also (1). The danger of any too strong denial of any legal quality of precedent could lie in this leading also to rejection of precedent as an acceptable basis for rationally satisfying legal argumentation that shows a due regard for coherence in the body of the law administered by the courts. In fact, the models of particular analogy and principle exemplification, (1) and (3) above, do not require or entail treating precedent as a formal source of law at all. It is clear that, in France, the stress given to the idea of precedent as 'precedent of interpretation', that is, to the idea that precedents work out the guiding principles inherent in written law, and thus guide towards the proper (and uniform) application of the law, saves legal practice from this criticism, while leaving alive the earlier stated concern about the gap between saying and doing.

Even when precedent is formally binding, the same considerations generate an ever-present temptation to pay mere lip-service to awkward precedents while engaging in implausible feats of 'explaining' and 'distinguishing' them; for it may seem urgent that law should develop in new ways despite the authority of settled precedent. Here let us not forget the extent to which, under other models, precedent is also enabling. A regime that allows for the use of precedent as analogy or as exemplifying principles is one that acknowledges the legitimate power of courts to contribute to development of the law in an incremental way quite distinct from the modern model of parliamentary, governmentally directed, statutory enactment. In this way, precedent can be a dynamic force whereby higher courts, in particular, can take a deliberate role in developing the law, even where they develop it solely in the guise of offering new interpretations of codes, constitutions or statutes – or, for that matter, of precedents and doctrines of the common law, or fundamental principles of law.

In any event, reflection on the models reveals the extent to which the role of precedent in law is Janus-faced. On the one hand, the rule of *stare decisis* is in its very essence conservative. It restricts judges from embarking on new ventures and ties them to following the wisdom (or folly) of the past. On the other hand, it constitutes a formidable power to direct the future decision making of the courts along determined pathways; for whatever decision a court is free to give within the leeways of interpretation of previously binding statutes and precedents, that decision becomes in its own turn a binding precedent for the future. To relax the bindingness of the precedents already in being gives present-day courts more of a free hand to develop new law in ways sensitive to contemporary needs and gathering trends. At the same time, it weakens somewhat the power to lay down effectually binding norms towards these very ends. To conclude: a decently pluralistic approach to models of precedent and to their rationales may be a sound base from which to respond to the scepticisms noted in the preceding section of this chapter.

References

Dworkin, R. (1978), *Taking Rights Seriously*, London: Duckworth/Cambridge, MA: Harvard University Press.

Dworkin, R. (1986), Law's Empire, London: Fontana/Cambridge, MA: Harvard University Press.

Weber, Max (1967), *On Law in Economy and Society*, ed. Rheinstein M. and Shils, E., New York: Simon & Schuster.

Weiler, J., 'The Transformation of Europe', *Yale Law Journal*, 100, p.2403–83 (1991).

16 What is Binding in a Precedent

GEOFFREY MARSHALL, *OXFORD*

1 Introduction

The idea of following precedent is a complex one. It involves a mixture of conceptual and practical difficulties. What are to count as precedents? How are the events that constitute precedents to be described? And once we know what are to count as precedents, how and for what are precedents to be counted? (See Appendix, question IV.)

These questions have historically been of more significance in common law than in civilian systems. But even in jurisdictions in which no strict doctrine of *stare decisis* prevails, and in which lower courts are not strictly bound by the decision of higher courts, judges, advocates and legal advisers select and distinguish precedents (more particularly, and increasingly, in public law litigation). Some importance must therefore attach to the alternative ways in which relevant, material or authoritative elements are extracted from judicial decisions and to the ways in which manipulation of the boundary between those elements and any less authoritative elements affects (and in some degree infects) the practice of precedent.

2 'Precedent'

The term 'precedent' itself has a number of applications. In the first place, it is sometimes applied without further thought or analysis to a body of allegedly relevant prior decisions (typically gathered together and cited by counsel on both sides in a common law case). Secondly, 'precedent' can be used as a description of the result or outcome of a particular decision that is thought to be of some significance. Thirdly, the term may be used to state a wider rule that the decision in a particular case is alleged to instantiate or illustrate.

These three usages might be called the advocate's sense, the judge's sense and the scholar's or critic's sense. Discussion of the binding nature of precedent has focused primarily on the second and third of these usages.

3   Selecting Facts and Describing Rules

Even the selection of precedents (in the first sense) as relevant, let alone binding, requires the extraction of some material element. There is no unique or agreed way of describing the result of any legal decision. The difficulty is similar to that which arises outside the law in recording constitutional precedents for the purpose of identifying the conventions of a political system. The question, 'What happened?' can be answered in an indefinite number of ways – briefly or at length; at varying levels of generality and with varying amounts of detail. The head of state, let us suppose, refused to allow the prime minister to hold a general election. But what happened when this episode occurred? A politician whose name was X, aged 65, with grey hair, made the request in person on a Wednesday evening at 11 pm. Some features of the episode are almost certainly irrelevant for purposes of describing the event as one to be termed a precedent for future behaviour. The name and hair colour are almost certainly not essential elements. But frequently we cannot at the time of observing the event know for certain what features should be included in the description. Does it matter what day of the week it was? Or whether the request had been made before? Or whether it had been made without prior consultation with the cabinet? The answers to some of these questions may become clearer if we are considering a series of episodes with similar features. We may then feel able to specify more clearly which features of the event it is essential to include in its description.

The same difficulty is notoriously present in setting out the facts which become the basis for a legal decision. To give but one vivid and frequently discussed example, a particularly famous case from the United Kingdom, determinative of the development of tort liability for negligence throughout the Commonwealth, was *Donoghue* v. *Stevenson* [1932] A.C. 532. Mrs Donoghue, a widow, visited the Wellmeadow Café in Paisley, Scotland, with a friend who bought for her an 'iced drink', provided by the proprietor, Mr Minghella, who put ice cream in a glass and poured over it part of the contents of an opaque bottle of ginger beer; later, at a table in the café, Mrs Donoghue poured the remainder of the contents of the bottle into her glass, only then discovering that the bottle had also contained the decomposing remains of a snail. She suffered shock and gastroenteritis, and sued the manufacturers of the ginger beer, Stevenson & Co. It was argued for the manufacturers that there was no contract between them and Mrs Donoghue, and that they were therefore not liable to her for any defect in their product, but the House of Lords held that they did owe a duty to her to take reasonable care in the preparation and packaging of the ginger beer, and hence were liable if they could be shown to have failed in this duty.

Nowadays, this case is commonly understood to be authority for the proposition that a manufacturer of goods owes a duty of care to the ultimate consumer to take reasonable care to avoid causing harm to the safety and health of the consumer. But could it have been argued that it only applied to manufactured drinks? To manufactured drinks in opaque bottles? To manufactured drinks in opaque bottles consumed in public places of refreshment? Or could it have been confined to food and drink? Or must it go so far as to cover all manufactured articles? How material is the question of the ultimate user's opportunity to inspect and check the safety and suitability for use of the article in question? Does it cover the case of repairing as well as the case of manufacturing an article? Most such questions emerged for decision in later cases, and it is difficult to argue that the subsequently deciding courts could not have 'distinguished' the *Donoghue* case in some or all of these, on the ground of genuine factual distinctions such that the precedent did not apply to the cases at hand. As it happened, they did not, and this case is the first of a long line in which liability for negligence was gradually broadened out to the point of becoming the main body of doctrine in the modern law of torts (or of 'delict' in Scotland).

There is no unique way of saying what has happened in a particular case, and to describe it is to select features of it that seem relevant for the purpose in hand. In comparing any two cases or situations, a distinction will necessarily have to be made between the material and immaterial features of the two episodes. It follows that, in any legal system in which attention is paid to case law, some distinction must be made between the legally relevant and irrelevant features of earlier decisions or precedents, and that where any degree of authority is allotted to them the force or authority in question cannot attach to the decision or precedent as such but only to some description of what has occurred and what has been decided that is extracted from the decision. It seems probable that the need to define with some degree of accuracy and precision what this extracted element (usually called the '*ratio decidendi*') is and by what means it is extracted will be greatest in legal systems that embody a theory of binding precedent. So it seems hardly surprising that in common law systems a very large part of the discussion of the workings of precedent has historically been concerned with the problem of what is meant by the *ratio decidendi* of a case and how the *ratio decidendi* is to be established. This will involve differentiating the binding element from other statements made in judges' reported opinions on the case, usually called '*obiter dicta*'. In civil law systems, where statute or code is the primary source of private law, little attention has been given to this issue. It has, however, acquired some significance in public law areas and, according to some commentators, in the jurisprudence of the European Court of Justice (see Chapter 12, Section IV; also Koopmans, 1982, pp.23–4).

4 The Binding Element

Out of the considerable body of common law literature devoted to this subject over the past century, and from the less structured remarks to be found in judicial opinions, a number of theses, not all compatible, have emerged as to the proper characterization of the *ratio decidendi* of the case. Given that a *ratio decidendi* is a legal statement or ruling, whose relationship to the facts of the case in question remains to be established, there are at least three possibilities. The *ratio decidendi* might be:

1 a rule of law or a ruling in the light of material facts that a prior court explicitly declares or believes itself to be laying down or following; or
2 a ruling in the light of material facts that a prior court (when the decision is analysed) is, as a matter of fact, laying down or following; or
3 a ruling in the light of material facts that a prior court ought properly (in view of the existing law, facts and precedents) to be laying down or following.

Some authorities (possibly moved by the instincts of legal realism) have attempted to attach the notion of *ratio decidendi* solely to the perceptions of later courts called upon to apply earlier decisions. 'For precedential purposes,' wrote Jerome Frank, 'a case means only what a judge in a later case says it means' (Frank, 1949, p.274). That being so, there remain two, or perhaps three, further possibilities, namely that the *ratio decidendi* might be:

4 a ruling that a subsequent court or courts say that an earlier court believed itself to be laying down in the light of material facts; or
5 a ruling that a subsequent court or courts say that an earlier court was laying down or following in the light of material facts; or even

6   a ruling that a later court or courts ought (on a proper analysis by
legal scholars) to have said that an earlier court was laying down
or following in the light of material facts.

Outside the common law framework of *stare decisis*, these questions
do not have the same salience. In some jurisdictions there may be no
judicial or doctrinal attempts to distinguish *rationes* from *dicta* and
courts may regard themselves as free to cite any part of earlier judgments (see Chapter 7, Section IV). If, as in France, precedents have in
principle no formally binding authority, there will be little need to
pursue distinctions between binding and non-binding elements in a
precedent. Nevertheless, insofar as courts and commentators pay
attention to earlier decisions or regard them as persuasive or useful
when deciding and criticizing cases, it must be to some extracted or
putatively relevant or significant element in the decisions and not to
every element in the decisions that attention is paid. The element
could perhaps best be described by saying that it is an imputed rule
or principle that is discerned in the decision in question.

To discover the correct formulation or extension of the principle
one must examine the reasons given by superior courts to justify
upholding or overruling the decisions of inferior courts. For example,
in one French case (see Rudden, 1974, p.1021) a bystander tried to
help a moped rider involved in a collision by applying a fire-
extinguisher to put out flames lapping around the engine.
Unfortunately, there was an explosion and the helpful bystander was
injured. If there was a 'rescue contract' between the rider and his
helper, the helper could be compensated. There was no finding that
the rider had expressly accepted the helper's implied offer of help.
But, said the *Cour de Cassation*, 'the court of appeal did not have to
find the express consent of the victim since, when an offer is made in
his exclusive interest, the offeree is presumed to have accepted it'.
Accordingly, it rejected an appeal against the holding that the rider
(or his insurance company, we may suppose) should compensate the
helper (*Cour de Cassation* 1.12.69, D.S. 1970.422). It is not hard to
discern here what might be taken as a governing principle about the
presumed acceptance of offers, though one might wonder whether
the doctrine will be confined to rescue cases, or given a broader
scope in later decisions.

There is an observable similarity between the idea of a *ratio decidendi* as the ruling in the light of material facts that a court ought
properly to be laying down (possibility (3) above) and the proposition that in France 'the obligation of the court is to apply not the
precedent but the rule behind the precedent' (see Chapter 4, Section
IV). Indeed, that notion is not far removed from what was said in
common law courts before the development of strict rules of *stare*

decisis: the law was not to be found in particular cases, but in the principles for which they stood. Even after the development of clearer hierarchical rules of binding precedent, achieved by the reorganization of the English courts into substantially their present pyramidal structure in 1875, that idea persisted. 'In the last analysis, the judge follows "binding" authority only because *it is a correct statement of the law* ... . When it is plainly and admittedly founded on error his obligation disappears. He owes a higher obligation to his mistress, the law' (Allen, 1958, p.281; emphasis in original).

There would seem to be no necessary or simple connection between beliefs about what constitutes *ratio decidendi* or the authoritative element in a decision and the existence or non-existence in a legal system of a theory of *stare decisis* or binding precedent. But where there is, for whatever institutional reason, no theory of binding precedent, the force or persuasiveness that is accorded to a precedent clearly will not be thought to derive merely from its having been explicitly enunciated by a higher court or in an earlier decision. So in Germany, according to the classical theory (Chapter 2, Section IV), the authority of a precedent in the Federal Constitutional Courts is said to depend exclusively on its being a correct interpretation of the law. A legal system would not, however, be precluded by that belief from having a system of binding precedent, since the question of what constitutes a precedent can be separated from the question as to who is to decide (and with what authority) what precedents there are to be. The German system, nevertheless, illustrates the lower priority that in the absence of a firm principle of *stare decisis* is likely to attach to the question of separating the *ratio decidendi* from *obiter dicta* that have less authority. On occasion, and exceptionally in the German Federal Constitutional Court, binding force has been said to attach to *all* legal arguments contained in a decision. (That is, we must presume, to all the reasons for the decision stated in each of the arguments put by the court; see Chapter 2, Section IV.) Other decisions and the opinions of some scholars suggest that force or authority is limited to the *grounds* for the decision. If the authority of the decision in question rests upon its correctness and not on its temporal or hierarchical priority, the 'grounds' of the decision could best be understood as meaning the judicial case norm (*Fallnorm*) which on a correct analysis of the law ought to have been laid down by the precedent in question and not the legal ruling in fact propounded by the court (though the two may of course be held to coincide in a particular case). This would be equivalent to the third rather than the first or second senses of *ratio decidendi* distinguished above.

Whether this is acknowledged may depend, however, on the form in which a decision is promulgated. Where there is an explicit and succinct formulation of the rule that a court believes to be the rule it laid down in the decision – as with the judicial *massima* in Italy – there may be a strong tendency to treat that as the *ratio decidendi*. If *massime* are extended to include other legal statements (see Chapter 5, Section IV) there becomes scope for debate as to which elements of a *massima* are essential grounds or *rationes* and whether the *massima* correctly states the ground or *ratio decidendi* of a particular case – especially when that case is held to be an exception from a rule or principle already established or generally valid. (Is the *ratio* the general principle or the reasons given for its non-applicability?)

An unwillingness to envisage strict distinctions between *rationes decidendi* and *obiter dicta* may also be favoured by theories about the sources of law in general. The thesis that jurisprudence or case law is in principle not a source of law in various continental countries implies that none of the legal assertions made by the court, whether of a central or peripheral character, carries authority in its own right. If, therefore, a rule for future cases has to be inferred or constructed from the decision by a later court, there is less reason to exclude any class of statements on the ground that they are *dicta*, not central or necessary to a particular decision. Such *dicta* may represent legal evaluations or paraphrases of constitutional or statutory rules to which weight may be attached. Thus, in Spain, according to a decision of the constitutional court, 'reasons cited by the constitutional court as *obiter dicta* may be considered as authorised criteria ... and are sometimes used as judicial and doctrinal arguments'(see Chapter 8, Section IV). Here, it is added, a distinction may be made between 'a simple *dictum* or "assertion *en passant*" and an argumentative dictum that is connected with, if not central to, the ruling in the particular case'. In Spain the use of precedent in single cases is restricted. The appeal of *casación* for infraction of jurisprudence must involve two or more precedents. In Finland *dicta* may contribute to the construction of lines or clusters of cases, which may be used by scholars or commentators who are concerned to construct a principle for general or future application rather than to provide a sufficient ground for the resolution of a particular dispute (see Chapter 3, Section IV).

A legal system may stand somewhere between the civil law jurisdictions that have no formal theory of binding precedent and the common law jurisdictions that embody a fairly strict *stare decisis* doctrine. In Norway the courts have allotted authority to precedents without reasoning in an explicit way about their theory or practice (see Chapter 6, Section IV). Even a flexible system of binding authority, however, is committed to some search for the essential or material elements in a decision, but, like the common law systems, is likely to find itself balanced between different senses and means of ascertaining the *ratio* or binding element. Thus, there are three alternative ways that current legal theory enumerates, when stating how the Norwegian courts identify the binding part of a previous judicial decision. – First, to search for a rule both expressly stated in the opinion of the previous decision and necessary for the outcome of the decision. – Second, to construct a rule that one thinks the previous decision 'must' be seen as an instance of ... And third, to compare the facts of the previous case with the facts of the case at hand. (Eng, 1994, at Section 2.4.3.1.)

In Sweden, too, the courts in practice apply a distinction between the *ratio decidendi* of a decision and *obiter dicta*, but there are, as elsewhere, rival theories about the derivation of a *ratio*. 'First, one may consider reasons *adduced* by the court in the precedent decision ... Second, one may consider the reasons estimated as necessary to justify the decision even if not adduced in the decision' (see Chapter 9, Section IV).

5   The Common Law History: A Confusion of Definitions

Within the common law the differentiation of binding and non-binding elements within a decision has been historically connected with the existence of a formal practice of *stare decisis* and hierarchical subordination. Though precedents were commonly cited in the seventeenth century, and though Blackstone held that 'precedents and rules must be followed unless flatly absurd or unjust' (*Commentaries*, I, p.70), it was only when the firmer theory of binding precedent developed with the structural change of the hierarchy and organization of the courts in the later nineteenth century that the elaboration of theories about the character of the *ratio decidendi* began. Perhaps the process was assisted by the distinction insisted upon by Lord Mansfield between the 'reason and spirit of cases' and the mere 'letter of particular precedents' (*Fisher* v. *Prince*, 1762, 3 Burr 1363).

Some of the subsequent lack of clarity about the characterization of the principle laid down in cases may have reflected the widespread historical ambivalence as to whether the law is to be thought of as contained in the decision of the judges. For Blackstone and for the common lawyers, amongst whom the doctrine of precedent achieved recognition, the decisions of courts of justice were *evidence* of the rules of common law, but the law and the opinions of the judges were not always convertible terms (*Commentaries* I, p.71). That view, as we have seen, has been asserted by English jurists even in the twentieth century. Thus C.K. Allen could write that it is 'as true today as it was in the eighteenth century' that 'every precedent is and can only be "an illustration of principle" ... It is what we really mean when we say that the only part of a precedent which is authoritative is its *ratio decidendi'* (Allen, 1958, p.213).

The phrase *'ratio decidendi'* had been used by John Austin (1869) in his lectures on jurisprudence in the 1830s: 'Law made judicially must be found in the general grounds or reasons of judicial decisions. The general reasons or principles of a judicial decision (as thus abstracted from any peculiarities of the case) are commonly styled by writers on jurisprudence the *ratio decidendi.'* Seventy years later, Sir John Salmond's *Jurisprudence* concluded similarly that the *ratio decidendi* was 'the underlying principle (of a decision) which ... forms its authoritative element'. John Chipman Gray (1909) said that such a principle was to be discovered in an opinion of a judge, the formation of which was *necessary* for the decision of a particular case. Another American jurist, Eugene Wambaugh (1894), suggested also that, when a case turns only on one point, the doctrine or *ratio* must be a general rule without which the case must have been decided otherwise. He added that the doctrine of the case must be one that is in the mind of the court.

Subsequent debates in common law systems on the nature of the *ratio* of the case have produced varying and inconsistent views as to how the *ratio* is to be described and how it is to be determined. If a *ratio* is a general principle, it must in some sense flow from and be consistent with the past. 'A case is only authority for what it actually decides. I entirely deny that it can be quoted for a proposition that may seem to flow logically from it' (*Quinn* v. *Leathem* [1901] A.C. 459, 506). But if *rationes* are principles established by particular cases, they must flow logically from them and Lord Halsbury's remark must be either false or an empty tautology.

Arthur Goodhart (1931) appeared to agree that the *ratio* was a principle, but his discussion raises the question whether the principle is one that is ascertainable entirely from what is laid down or stated by the court, as distinct from what is properly to be inferred from the facts of the case. Goodhart argued that a case might lay down a binding precedent, although the reasons given for his decision by the judge might all be wrong. The principle of the case was to be discovered, he said, by deciding what facts were held to be material by the judge. He added that all facts that are stated by him to be material must be considered material. But it seems unclear why, in assessing what principle is instantiated by the holding in a case, the judge's reasons or analysis of prior cases should not be conclusive but his assessment of the relevance or materiality of facts should be so treated.

Goodhart's discussion is perhaps the first of many in which attention is shifted implicitly away from the deciding court towards the judgments made by a later court (see Stone, 1959). A question about the *ratio* of a case can of course be raised by commentators at the time of the decision, or it may even be – though rarely – referred to in the decision itself. But it is also true that the most usual and important occasion on which a question is posed about the *ratio decidendi* of a case is when it falls to be considered on a later occasion whether the decision in the earlier case is binding and should be followed.

Perhaps, for this reason, many recent commentators have underlined the ambivalence of *'ratio decidendi'* as between (a) the rule that a judge who decided the case intended to lay down and apply to the facts or (b) the rule that a later court concedes him to have had the power to lay down (see Williams, 1982; Montrose, 1957). To define the *ratio* as a rule constructed by a later court does, however, have inconvenient consequences. One would be that it would then be impossible to say that a court had misunderstood an earlier court's *ratio*, and analysis of cases not yet considered by another court would have to be framed merely as prophecies as to what in the future would be the *ratio* of a case already decided (see Simpson, 1961).

In his standard work on *Precedent in English Law* (1961), Sir Rupert Cross defined the *ratio* as 'any rule of law expressly or implicitly treated by the judge as a necessary step in reaching his conclusion, having regard to the line of reasoning adopted by him, or a necessary part of his direction to the jury'. This definition (focusing on the opinion of the deciding court) has attracted some criticism. Simpson noted that 'It is difficult to see the force of any logical necessity which would guide the judge in deciding what precise rule *was* necessary' (Simpson, 1961). MacCormick has suggested that Cross's definition contains too much. A *ratio* has to relate to a point on which a decision is necessary for a justification of the holding in the case, but the ruling need only be *sufficient* to settle it. MacCormick's suggestion is that a *ratio decidendi* is:

> a ruling expressly or implicitly given by a judge which is sufficient to settle a point of law put in issue by the parties' arguments in a case, being a point on which a ruling was necessary to his justification (or one of his alternative justifications) of the decision in the case. (MacCormick, 1987)

This definition clearly pictures the *ratio* as an actual element in the decision of the court, whose ruling is in question, rather than as the formulation of a later court considering the application of the earlier decision. Cross's definition also would appear to treat the judge's beliefs as conclusive in deciding what is necessary in the decision.

Juristic discussions, involving both judges and scholars, do thus exhibit a certain confusion, a difficulty in capturing or conceptualizing in clear terms some central elements of practice. The *ratio* is perhaps to be considered an essentially contested concept, because it is not purely descriptive but also evaluative or normative in force. The difficulty, perhaps impossibility, of achieving consensus in definition should not be thought to mirror a like confusion in practice; for on the whole experienced lawyers and judges are able, with a relatively high degree of common understanding, to operate effectively in practice with a system of precedent in its application case-by-case, as distinct from its abstract description. The beginning of wisdom here may be to recognize the variety of problems that arise in common law systems concerning application of precedents. This has to do, *inter alia*, with the absence of standardization in the opinions that come under consideration. Sometimes, in justifying a decision, a court will lay down a rather broad proposition of law; later courts, while acknowledging the decision as binding, may find good grounds in new fact situations to restrict the operation of the proposition to some narrower category compatible with the material facts of the precedent, either as the original court expressed them or as the later court reassesses them in the light of new situations that have come under view and seem to require different treatment. Again, a court may reach a decision and account for it without making explicit any governing proposition of law, but indicating clearly enough the precedent or precedents that govern or provide guidance by analogy. A later court may then seek to make explicit its understanding of the ruling (or 'holding', to use the term more common in the USA) implicit in the earlier case, either in order to distinguish it, or in order to confirm its applicability to the facts of the instant case. Further, especially where multiple judgments have been issued in the earlier case, there may be a set of alternative rulings or holdings expressly or impliedly available when it comes to later decisions in analogous circumstances; here the process is one of weighing and selecting, so that over one or several cases a governing proposition or principle comes to be settled, while on first consideration of the original precedent the later court has inevitably discretion to choose among available alternatives. Experienced lawyers, both practitioners and academics, are perfectly able to handle all these situations, and the many variants on them that may arise, and to implement a coherent system of precedent, though it is perhaps asking too much to find any single definition of the term *'ratio decidendi'* that will do all the work that is called for in the practical setting.

6   *Rationes* as Positive or Critical Norms

Some of this ambivalence may be resolved if we consider that the conceptual problem of defining the *ratio decidendi* of a case has often been run together with the practical problem of deciding where the evidence for it can most usefully be sought. Whilst it would be absurd to *define* the *ratio* of a case as being the ruling of a future court, it may be plausible to say that what the *ratio* of a particular case turns out to be can sometimes be settled only after a number of similar cases have received judicial consideration and when rulings that are too broad or too restrictive have been corrected by subsequent reconsideration in the context of a series of similar decisions.

There remains, however, a second reason for confusion which is analogous to the ambiguity found outside the law in the discussion of conventions founded upon constitutional precedents. Some authorities treat these as the positive morality of the constitution: namely, the rules which the leading political actors believe themselves to be bound to follow. Others treat conventions as the critical morality of the constitutional system: namely, as those rules which political actors *ought* to consider themselves bound to follow when the relevant precedents are properly analysed (Marshall, 1984).

In the same way, the binding elements in legal precedents may be treated as either positive or critical norms. The critical view of precedent implies that what is binding is the ruling that is required on a proper assessment of the law and the facts of the case – as compared with a positive attitude that merely reports what as a matter of fact a judge believes himself (perhaps confusedly or shortsightedly) to be laying down. The adoption of a critical normative standpoint may be thought to some degree to be subversive of the values of the hierarchical system of precedent whose rationale includes the idea of following rulings in fact laid down by higher courts, even when they may be held to be confused or wrong. Where lower courts are bound by higher court rulings, their view of precedent is inevitably a positive one or at least one that embodies a stipulation that the views of superior courts in the judicial hierarchy should normally be treated as constituting more or less irrebuttable evidence as to what the proper assessment of the law and the related facts should be held to be. That presumption is in fact what a system of hierarchically binding precedent in practice requires.

Much present-day Anglo-American discussion of the *ratio decidendi* of cases tends to adopt a positive standpoint in debates about the decisions of appellate courts with a number of different judgments (on which see Cross and Harris, 1991, chap. II, s.9). Here, in contrast to the problem encountered in dealing with the single decision, attention tends to focus on reconciling or distinguishing propositions that were as a matter of fact set out by different judges. Problems obviously arise as to the conclusion to be drawn if there is no discernible common proposition shared by all of the judges. It was once said in the House of Lords by Lord Dunedin that, if the *ratio* is not clear, 'I do not think it is part of the tribunal's duty to spell out with great difficulty a *ratio decidendi* in order to be bound by it' (*Great Western Railway Company* v. *Owners of SS Mostyn* [1928] A.C. 57 at 73). Multiple judgments and the discursive character of judicial reasoning in Anglo-American courts increase the difficulty of finding a common *ratio* as they do the problem of distinguishing the *ratio decidendi* from *obiter dicta*. From the positive standpoint, some appellate decisions may simply have no discernible *ratio decidendi*.

7 Obiter Dicta

There is in one sense no problem in defining the character of *obiter dicta*, since they consist in all propositions of law contained in the decision that are not part of the *ratio*. But that negative assertion masks a number of different ways in which judicial *dicta* may be related to the holding in a particular case. An opinion as to a point of law may be:

1 irrelevant to the disposition of a case or to any other important legal issue;
2 relevant to the disposition of the case but not necessary to the holding;
3 relevant to some collateral issue in the case in question;
4 relevant to the disposition of other important issues that may arise in other cases.

Thus the concept of *obiter dicta* may include remarks on a point raised but not decided in the case, or remarks based on hypothetical facts, remarks on a point not raised in the instant case, or general statements about law or practice, particularly those made on appeal.

The importance that may be attached to *dicta* will obviously differ depending on whether it is one or the other of the above four. Depending upon the authority of the court, a *dictum* may often be treated as authoritative in subsequent cases both by lower courts and by commentators, particularly if a higher court has devoted time or attention to it (see Chapter 11, Section IV) or if it relates to a matter of some generality (see Greenawalt, 1989, pp.439–42). A good example in the United Kingdom is provided by the pronouncements about the independent status of chief police officers in *R.* v. *Metropolitan Police Commissioner, ex parte Blackburn* [1968] 2 Q.B. 118, which are constantly cited (for want of any better authority) though the case in which they occurred involved quite another issue. Similarly, remarks made in dissenting judgments, which by definition could form no part of the judicial holding, may later, after the law has changed, either by subsequent overruling or by legislation, come to be treated as important pronouncements on points of law. LORD ATKIN's dissenting judgment in *Liversidge* v. *Anderson* [1942] A.C. 206 on the interpretation of discretionary powers conferred on ministers by statute is a clear example. So, also, are some of the dissenting opinions of LORD DENNING, for example on the subject of sovereign immunity in *Rahimtoola* v. *Nizam of Hyderabad* [1958] A.C. 379.

There is another form of *obiter dictum* which is in effect a putative *ratio decidendi* reduced in rank by subsequent judicial reasoning. It may be held that a principle apparently laid down as the reason for a particular decision was too widely stated or in some other way inappropriate. This observation about the possible relationship between the two concepts illustrates the importance that attaches to the notion of an *obiter dictum* in the common law systems of precedent. In those systems the rigidity of a system of *stare decisis* and of hierarchical rules as to bindingness may be moderated in a number of ways. One form of flexibility is introduced by the recognition of types of circumstances in which decisions which are otherwise binding need not be followed: for example, if they are taken *per incuriam*, that is, in ignorance of applicable precedent or statute. Another avenue of flexibility is opened by the ever-present possibility of distinguishing otherwise binding cases. Amongst the variety of ways in which precedents may be avoided, however, is the ability to conclude that what has been alleged to be a binding *ratio* falls into the category of *obiter dictum*. That is why the category is important. 'Obiter-ing' a precedent is one way in which a precedent may be confined, outflanked, loosened, avoided, reviewed or reconsidered. The general principle and the incidental facts of particular cases may be manipulated in either of two directions. It may be said that (a) although there is an alleged rule or principle that covers the instant and earlier cases, the facts are sufficiently different (specify some, of many, differences) to conclude that the rule or *ratio* does not apply to the present case. Alternatively, it may be found that (b), although the facts of this case allegedly differ from those in earlier cases, they are sufficiently similar (mention some, of many, similarities) to conclude that the rule or *ratio* should apply to the present case. Thus the demotion of *rationes* and the promotion of *dicta* also constitute a special case of the general activity of departure from, and distinguishing of, precedents (considered in Chapter 17) that characteristically moderates the rigidity of a system of binding precedent.

References

Allen, C.K. (1958), *Law in the Making*, 6th edn, Oxford: Clarendon Press.

Austin, J. (1869), *Lectures on Jurisprudence*, Lecture XXXVII ('Statute and Judiciary Law'), London: J. Murray/New York: Cockcroft and Co.

Blackstone, Sir W. (1769), *Commentaries on the Laws of England* (Section 3 of the Laws of England), Oxford: Clarendon Press.

Cross, R. (1961), *Precedent in English Law*, Oxford: Clarendon Press.

Cross, R. and Harris, J.W. (1991), *Precedent in English Law*, 4th edn, Oxford: Clarendon Press.

Eng, S., 'The Doctrine of Precedent in English and Norwegian Law -- Some Command Specific Features' *Scandinavian Studies in Law* (1994).

Frank, J. (1949), *Courts on Trial: Myth and Reality in American Justice*, Princeton: Princeton University Press.

Goodhart, A.L. (1931), 'Determining the *Ratio Decidendi* of a Case', *Essays in Jurisprudence and the Common Law*, Cambridge: Cambridge University Press.

Gray, J.C. (1909), *On the Nature and Sources of Law*, Boston: Beacon Press.

Greenawalt, K., 'Reflections on Holding and *Dictum*', *Journal of Legal Education*, 39, p.431 (1989).

Koopmans, T. (1982), *'Stare Decisis* in European Law', in O'Keefe, D. and Schermers, H. (eds), *Essays in European Law and Integration*, Deventer/Boston: Kluwer.

MacCormick, N. (1987), 'Why Cases Have *Rationes* and What These Are', in Goldstein, L. (ed.), *Precedent in Law*, Oxford: Oxford University Press.

Marshall, G. (1984), *Constitutional Conventions*, Oxford: Clarendon Press.

Montrose, J., 'The Ratio Decidendi of a Case', *Modern Law Review*, 20, p.124 (1957).

Rudden, B., 'Courts and Codes in England, France and Russia', *Tulane Law Review*, 48, pp.1010–28 (1974).

Simpson, A.W.B. (1961), 'The *Ratio Decidendi* of a Case and the Doctrine of Binding Precedent', in Guest, A. (ed.), *Oxford Essays in Jurisprudence*, Oxford: Oxford University Press.

Stone, L., 'The *Ratio* of the *Ratio Decidendi*', *Modern Law Review*, 22, p.597.

Wambaugh, E. (1894), *The Study of Cases*, 2nd edn, Boston: Little, Brown.

Williams, Glanville (1982), *Learning the Law*, 11th edn, London: Stevens & Co.

17 Departures from Precedent

ROBERT S. SUMMERS, *ITHACA* AND
SVEIN ENG, *OSLO*

This chapter addresses a variety of theoretical and comparative issues relating to judicial departures from precedent under code, under statute, or under mere common law, but not under constitutions. The chapter is inspired by and based partly on the answers in the 10 national chapters to the set of questions on 'distinguishing, explaining, modifying and overruling' precedents (question V in the Appendix). This chapter does not, however, purport to provide a comprehensive analysis of all features of practice treated in those answers.

1 The Importance of Departures

The subject of departures from formally binding precedent or from precedent not formally binding but yet having force or providing other support is worthy of separate focus for two quite different reasons, both fundamental in character. First, if a legal system were to make no provision for 'remedying' judicial departures from precedent at least in the lower courts, or only to make quite inadequate provision, or if a system were to take no critical notice whatsoever of departures, then it would simply not be true that precedent is formally binding, or has any force, or provides any support, in that system. As a result, judges within the system would, in varying degrees, decide the same cases differently, and the decisional law might in some areas even become a wilderness of single instances. This would be true not only in common law systems. It would even be true in a civil law system, especially in areas governed by open-ended code or statutory language. The occasions for, and the pressures on, judges to decide similar cases differently at the same, or at different, times are intense and incessant in any legal system. This is so not only in similar cases before the same judges but also in similar cases before different judges. Every litigant tends to think of his or her or its case as somehow special. Every litigant naturally lacks some objectivity, and tends to be a kind of biased judge in his or her or its own cause, all the more so when free of the constraints of consistency of decision.

If a system does not remedy or otherwise take account of inappropriate departures from precedent, the judges will not interpret and apply codes, statutes and precedents in rule-like fashion, and will thereby sacrifice such formal 'rule of law' values as legitimacy, objectivity, certainty, equality before the law, dispute avoidance and private dispute settlement. Such a system would not only lack formal unity, it would also lack substantive unity in the sense that substantively similar cases would frequently be decided differently, without coherent implementation of the substantive policy and principle embedded in precedent. Moreover, such an inconsistent system would be highly inefficient. Judges would be constantly called upon to reinterpret, and to reweigh and rebalance the same arguments, ad hoc, even in substantially similar cases, thereby forfeiting the efficiencies of a precedent system in which initial decisions settle points of law for subsequent cases, points which generally cannot thereafter be reconsidered, at least not until significant time has elapsed. Such a system would also be costly. More litigation, more judges and more lawyers would be required. (On rationales for following precedent, see Chapter 15.)

Thus the first reason why the general subject of departures from precedent is important is that some provision must be made in any legal system to secure general consistency of decision in like cases. But the subject of departures is worthy of special focus for a second, similarly fundamental reason. In a rationally designed legal order, some types of departures, even by judges, may, in limited circumstances, actually be justifiable despite the force of the foregoing general rationales for following precedent. It is a special and important challenge for any legal system to provide appropriately for the recognition of limited types of justified departures, and to do so in ways that do not unduly undermine whatever practice of following precedent exists in the system.

2   Departures Defined

For purposes of this discussion, it is necessary to remind the reader of what counts as a 'judicial departure' from precedent in the present study. The precedent decision (or decisions) must first of all be 'in point'. That is, the precedent decision must be appropriately similar to the subsequent case. (See Chapter 16.) At the very least, the precedent case and the case to be decided must pose the same legal issue, and the precedent case must have resolved that issue. In at least the common law systems, such 'sameness of issue' can always be further refined in terms of sameness of material facts. But in the highest courts in several non-common law systems in our study, officially published judicial opinions commonly do not include any, or at least not any detailed, statement of facts (at least in non-constitutional cases). This is generally true of officially published case law of the highest courts (non-constitutional) in Norway, France, Germany, Italy and Spain. In such systems, 'sameness of issue' often cannot be further refined through a systematic analysis of 'similarities in the *material* facts' in the official opinions of the highest courts without requesting from these courts copies of the original opinions or procuring from some other official a statement of facts that is fuller than what appears in the original opinions of these highest courts. In the opinion of intermediate appellate courts, however, a fuller statement of facts usually appears. (See Chapter 16.) Of course, in common law systems such as the United Kingdom and the states of the United States, sameness of issue can always be further refined in terms of similarities in the material facts of the precedent case and the material facts of the subsequent case to be decided, for in those countries the facts of each case are fully and carefully reported in opinions both of the intermediate appellate courts and the highest courts.

It follows that, in common law countries, a departure from precedent by a subsequent court can usually be readily identified as a different ruling on an issue posed by material facts relevantly similar to the material facts of the precedent decision. In most non-common law countries in our study, what constitutes a departure cannot be so readily identified. As indicated, in some of those countries, the existence of a departure by a highest court can sometimes be determined in the foregoing manner by procuring a full opinion from the court, or from another official which does provide a full statement of facts. But in the absence of this, the existence in most of these countries of a departure by the highest appellate court from an earlier decision of that court can generally be identified solely in terms of a different ruling on an abstract legal question ruled on by the prior court, and not in terms of a different ruling on an issue posed by similar material facts. It follows, too, that the same is true with respect to whether a subsequent intermediate appellate court has departed from a ruling of the highest court. Of course, where the new ruling is merely a different ruling on a narrow issue of code or statutory interpretation, it can usually be readily identified as a departure.

But it is not only a subsequent highest court or intermediate appellate court that may depart from a precedent of a prior appellate

court. In fact, a departure may occur initially in some civilian systems at the trial court level: that is, in the court of first instance.
When this occurs, the departure may become the subject of an appeal, and the same question as that discussed above may arise. That
is, without more, the issue on appeal may be definable only in terms
of whether the trial judge ruled on an issue as required by a highest
court precedent itself consisting mainly of a ruling on an abstract
issue. Again this issue cannot be refined in terms of sameness of
ruling on an issue posed by relevantly similar material facts, for the
highest court precedent will consist only of a ruling on an abstract
question.

How well a precedent system can really work, especially in fields
governed mainly by case law, without ready access to officially published material facts of prior and subsequent cases in the highest
courts posing the relevant legal issues is an important question on
which it is only possible to speculate, given the limited scope of the
present study. Practitioners and theorists in the common law tradition are likely to be sceptical of mere similarity of abstract formulations
of rulings, and to trust only similarity of material facts with respect
to issues ruled on. Common law practitioners and theorists would
defend this partly on the ground that similarity of material facts
guarantees a similarity of relevant considerations more effectively
than mere similarity of abstract issue formulations.

3   Non-overt Departures

A departure from precedent may or may not be overt. Explicit overruling is the most overt type of departure. Departures that are not
overt but merely implicit may occur in trial courts, in intermediate
appellate courts and in the highest courts. Departures that are not
overt may take a wide variety of forms, and their accurate identification and characterization may require rational reconstruction. In all
systems in our study, departures occur, although they are not formally presented as such. For example, a subsequent court may
consciously ignore a precedent. Or a subsequent court may, in good
faith, think a precedent is not appropriately similar when in fact it is.
(In common law countries, it would be said that such a court considered the precedent distinguishable when in fact it was not.) Or a
subsequent court may depart from precedent because it reconcep-
tualizes or reformulates the 'holding' or *ratio decidendi* in the precedent
in terms not really faithful to its true thrust. Or a subsequent court
may recharacterize the facts of a precedent, or revise the facts of the
very case being decided (or both), thereby appearing to escape the
true bearing of the precedent. Or the subsequent court may simply

'pour new wine into old bottles' and thus rely on fictions. Or the subsequent court may reinterpret a series of precedents to mean something different from what they truly stand for. Or the subsequent court may 'explain and distinguish' ostensibly conflicting precedent that really should be determinative. In all such instances (and still others), the result is a departure from precedent by the subsequent court, even though the subsequent court does not itself expressly so view matters and may even be entirely silent about what is clearly a decision that departs from precedent.

On the basis of the type of research in the present study, it is not possible to generalize about the overall frequency of departures that are not overt within any given system, and for this reason it is not possible to generalize about the frequency of non-overt departures across systems. It may seem likely that non-overt, that is implicit, departures occur more often in those systems in which the official opinions that are published lack detailed statements of facts, as, for example, in Italy and France. On the other hand, the full statements of facts in common law precedents also may serve as invitations to subsequent courts to find ways of distinguishing that are not really justified.

4 Overt Departures

Overt forms of departure in all systems include decisions in which courts explicitly overrule, explicitly modify or explicitly 'whittle away' a precedent (as by creating an exception internally at war with the rationale of the precedent itself). Another form of overt departure may consist of a purported synthesis or reconstruction of a line of cases such that the cases come to stand for a new point. Still another form of overt departure occurs when an intermediate-level court or a still lower court openly refuses to follow a precedent, with or without a stated reason.

What opinions are expressed in the national chapters on the overtness of departures? When the intermediate appellate courts and the highest courts do overrule or modify precedent, do they usually do this overtly, that is, by specifically stating that this is what they are doing? Constitutional cases aside, it appears from the national chapters that, in several civil law systems in our study, when the higher courts do depart from precedent, they often do not do this overtly. This is true of Sweden, Italy, Spain and France. In Germany and Poland, however, it appears that the usual practice is for the higher courts to overrule or modify overtly. In Finland wholesale overruling is done overtly, but modifying tends not to be overt. Explicit overruling is not unusual in Norway.

In most of the civil law systems in which the higher courts depart from precedent, but often do not depart overtly, there is an exception. Most such systems allow for certain special types of departures to be made only after some special judicial procedure such as a hearing before a full court of judges. Such special procedures apply, for example, when there is need to resolve a conflict between precedents, or to resolve some especially important issue of policy or principle. When such procedures are invoked, any resulting departure is, of course, overt.

In common law countries, when the highest courts and the intermediate appellate courts overrule or modify their own precedent, is it the usual practice for this to be done overtly? In general, yes. But non-overt departures occur, too, and in this study we have no way of knowing how often this occurs.

The lower courts – the trial courts of general jurisdiction – do not, in any of the systems in our study, appear to have the power to overrule or modify a precedent in anticipation that upper courts will agree. That is, the institutional act of voiding a precedent or of officially revising a precedent is simply not within their authority. But this is not to say that they never depart from, or alter the effect of, a precedent set by an upper court. Let us consider first the position in the civil law countries. According to the views set forth in the national chapters, the trial courts of general jurisdiction in France, Italy, Poland and Germany do depart from upper court precedents with some frequency. In some of these countries, the trial judge who departs does so openly, and states what is supposed to be a good reason, such as the need to adhere more closely to the code or statutory text, or to serve justice or policy in the particular case more fully than prior interpretations. It is said that in Finland, Spain and Sweden the lower courts rarely depart, but, when they do, they tend to be explicit about what they are doing.

In the common law countries, the trial courts of general jurisdiction are not supposed to depart from binding upper court precedent. They do sometimes depart, but we have no way of knowing how often. When they do depart, they are, of course, seldom explicit about it. Such non-explicit departures may take a variety of forms, including 'specious' distinguishing, and also 'overdistinguishing' whereby judges ignore the truth that there must be some limits to distinguishing if precedent is to be recognized as binding at all. Of course, such forms of distinguishing are not the only ways a court may depart from precedent without being explicit about it. (See Section 3, above.) And courts may simply be in a hurry, or counsel may do a poor job of arguing the bearing of precedent, and departure occur.

In most civil law countries, the distinguishing of precedents at all court levels occurs far less frequently than in common law countries.

This is partly because precedent is simply not formally binding in most of these countries. As already noted, however, matters could not be otherwise in some of these countries, or at least not conveniently otherwise, anyway, for judicial opinions of the highest courts do not include sufficiently detailed statements of facts to make distinguishing a viable justificatory course of action for the deciding court.

In the common law countries, the trial courts of general jurisdiction generally do not have power overtly to depart from binding precedent of an upper court, even for a so-called 'good reason'. This is a striking difference between the common law countries and several of the civil law countries. This topic is the subject of further discussion in the concluding chapter, where an attempt is made to set forth the possible rationales that may justify such a radically different practice, including the rationale that it exerts pressure on upper courts to change the law or its interpretation.

5 Justifying Grounds for Departures

In all systems at the highest court levels, some power explicitly to overrule, modify or otherwise depart from precedent is recognized. But, at least in some systems, it is generally not sufficient for the departing court merely to demonstrate that, if it had decided the precedent originally, it would have decided differently. The following justifying grounds for departures from precedent play especially important roles in the upper courts of civil law countries in fields covered by code or statute. Thus that a precedent is a plainly incorrect *interpretation* of a code or statute in the first place, or that a precedent has been subsequently reversed by statute, or that there is other clear evidence that the legislature disapproves of the precedent, or that the prospective departing court has itself already in prior cases been veering away from the precedent are all considered to be justifications for departure. Of course, all such justifying grounds would have force in common law countries, too, though all but the last would not be as frequently in play, given that code and statute law are relatively less common in common law countries.

At the same time, in common law countries, there are general grounds that at least contribute to the justification for departures that, it appears, are far more often in play than in civil law countries. Some of these grounds are negative in nature, others more affirmative. Thus one type of ground contributing to a justification for departure may simply be that the general rationales for following common law precedent are themselves not so strongly engaged in the type of case at hand. (On the nature of such rationales, see Chapter 15.) For example, a departure may be of a type that does not upset reliance on precedent because the field of human conduct involved is generally not one where citizens typically rely on precedents (with or without legal advice). Or a departure may not pose other 'rule of law' issues, or issues of desired unity, in the system overall. A similar type of contributing ground is simply that the departure would not put the court on a 'slippery slope.' Another type of contributing ground in common law jurisdictions may simply be that the relevant precedent is, on close analysis, factually rather remote from the case at hand, even if not, strictly speaking, distinguishable. In such event, the precedential argument for following precedent is merely in the nature of a general harmonization argument rather than one of formal bindingness or strong normative force. Of course, all the foregoing types of justifications are merely 'contributing' grounds for departures and they usually presuppose an additional, more affirmative, justifying ground for departure.

There are various affirmatively justifying grounds for departing from precedent. Thus a departure may be affirmatively justified because the precedent is somehow obsolete, given changes in social or other conditions. Obsolescence in the common law is familiar enough, but a precedent in the form of an interpretation of a suitably open-ended statute may become obsolete too, and might justify a departure from the precedent even though the language of the statute is not itself amended. Further, new moral or social enlightenment since the date the precedent was decided may similarly justify a departure from a precedent, even one under a general statutory or code provision. Then, too, a precedent may have been misconceived as to means or as to ends from the very beginning, and the highest court of a system may simply undertake to remedy what has come to be viewed as 'original error'. All of the foregoing may be compelling grounds for departures in civil law countries, too, especially where the code or statute is open-ended. But the very existence of code or statute makes some of the foregoing inappropriate as grounds for departure, given that only legislatures have formal power to amend a code or statute, and a proposed departure may be of a kind that rather plainly calls for legislative amendment.

6   Factors Affecting the Frequency of Departures

In this study, no attempt has been made to quantify departures from precedent in the various systems and to compare their frequency, were this possible. But, on rational grounds, it is possible at least to identify factors that presumably affect the frequency of departures from precedent by the courts in the different systems. First, the convenient accessibility of precedent is essential to following precedent in the first place. The bodies of precedent in each field must be organized into coherent frameworks and be well indexed. Without this, judges, practitioners and scholars cannot find precedent, and more departures will occur at all levels. Second, the volume of precedent is a factor. The more reported precedents on the same or similar points, the greater the risk of conflict and thus the impossibility of avoiding departures. A third factor is the frequency of appeals. If, for whatever reason, appeals are generally infrequent, or happen to be infrequent in a given area of the law, there will simply be less opportunity to reverse lower court departures and more will occur. A fourth factor relates to the composition of appellate courts. The more they are divided into separate panels, the more the chance that variant lines of precedent will develop, at least one of which may consist of a series of departures. Fifth, the legislature may be active or it may be passive. If highly active, and consistent, it is the legislature that will generally renovate precedent, and the occasions for judicial departures in the name of reform will lessen. Sixth, the willingness of the highest courts (always affected by case loads) to grant hearings to litigants who wish to argue that precedents should be overruled, modified or otherwise changed obviously affects the frequency of departures. Seventh, the adoption or non-adoption of a practice of recording and publishing dissenting opinions will also affect the ultimate frequency of departures. For example, some published dissents will ultimately come to command a majority, and thus lead to departures. Eighth, the existence or non-existence of a tradition of vigorous academic criticism of 'bad' precedents is likely to affect the willingness of courts to depart from precedent. Ninth, it may be that judges recruited from independent legal and political careers are, other things equal, more likely to be receptive to judicial renovation of the law than judges with a civil service background. Finally, academic writings may be a factor, a topic to be treated as part of the next section.

7   The Roles of Academics in Regard to Departures

Professors of law and other academics in universities and in research institutes can play major roles in the working of a system of precedent within their country. They may organize a body of precedents under a given code or statutory provision or within a discrete common law field and test this case law for coherence. Such systematization and rationalization makes precedents more accessible to the judiciary and to the lawyers acting on behalf of litigants. These scholarly efforts also identify departures, including old cases that conflict with each other, and new cases that conflict both with earlier cases and with still other new cases. Authors of academic treatises and journal articles perform an especially important function within the legal order when they devote close analysis to cases and identify such conflicts. (In so doing, they may also criticize attempts by courts to distinguish precedents that should have been treated as controlling.) This overall function is all the more important if the official system for reporting decided cases is itself not very comprehensive or coherently organized (as in some countries in our study). Academics in all systems in our study perform the foregoing tasks of systematization and rationalization, in varying degrees.

A further task for academics is that of identifying precedents that should be overruled, modified or the like, and marshalling the arguments in support of such actions. In some systems in the study, academics carry out this task admirably. In a few systems, academics are not so willing to engage in criticism of the judges in this way. There are various possible explanations. One is that no general tradition of academic criticism of the judiciary may have developed in the legal culture of the country. Another is that the very academics who might offer criticism are sometimes themselves engaged as counsel or as experts before the very courts that could be objects of such criticism.

In performing their roles as organizers, rationalizers and critics of precedent, academics in some systems in the study make extensive use of hypothetical cases in their work, a matter that merits further comment. Indeed, this is a major technique used in the United Kingdom and in the United States, and also in most civil law countries. This important mode of reasoning seems to play only a very minor role in Poland and in Spain, however.

In those systems where hypothetical case reasoning is frequent, academics and practitioners deploy such reasoning for a wide variety of purposes, including the construction of clear cases to which a code section, statute or doctrine must apply if it is to have any rational application; the construction of *reductio ad absurdum* arguments demonstrating the unsoundness of proposed applications of code sections, statutes or doctrinal formulations; the elaboration of coherent patterns of applications of authoritative language and demonstrations of how proposed or possible applications would not be coherent, the formulation of paradigm cases so as to display a policy rationale in its clearest application; the articulation of distinctions between paradigm cases and borderline cases and the creation of conceptual bridges between cases along a continuum. Also a scholar can use a well-designed hypothetical case to help justify extending a rule. Here the scholar imagines a hypothetical case to which it would be justified to extend the application of the rule in a precedent. The scholar then argues that the facts of the hypothetical cannot be rationally distinguished from another case the court has just decided (or is about to decide) and concludes that it is therefore justified to so extend the rule. In another type of analysis, the hypothetical case functions to help justify rejecting the application of a rule in a precedent to the case just decided (or about to be decided) because the rule can be shown to be unsuitable when applied to the hypothetical, yet the hypothetical cannot be rationally distinguished from the case involved.

8   Techniques for Limiting and Circumscribing Departures

All systems in the study deploy various techniques to limit and circumscribe, in varying degrees, departures from precedent. The possible techniques or devices include the following:

1   full and readily accessible official reporting of all decisions of higher courts that are formally binding or have force, or provide further support;
2   facilitation of immediate appellate review of any case in which there is a claimed departure from precedent by lower courts, and reversal, as appropriate, of those decisions that depart;
3   a provision that only the highest court in the system having jurisdiction over the matter may explicitly depart from precedent, with corresponding denial of any power to intermediate-level and lower courts to overrule or modify in anticipation that the highest court will do so;
4   requiring that highest courts with power expressly to overrule or modify precedent follow special procedures when they do so, for example, empanel a full court, and requiring that this court satisfy a high burden of justification;
5   facilitation of identification of departures through publication of dissents and the like, and facilitation of academic evaluation.

It appears that no system in the study adopts all of these, and today no system relies solely on the legislature to reform unsatisfactory precedents. After 1966, the United Kingdom has no longer purported to adhere to a practice in which its highest court, the House of Lords, was to leave all major renovation of precedent entirely to the legislature and thus (officially) did not even dare to depart from one of its own prior decisions, however unsound.

On the other hand, nearly all countries in the study limit the power explicitly to overrule or modify, or the like, to the highest appellate court or intermediate appellate court of the system having jurisdiction over the matter. Intermediate appellate courts may not anticipatorily overrule precedents of the highest court. The trial courts of general jurisdiction in common law jurisdictions generally may not anticipatorily overrule or modify even precedents that they believe the highest court or intermediate court would no longer follow. Indeed, these lower common law courts generally have no official power to depart from precedent explicitly or otherwise. They are required to follow even outmoded or unjust precedent, unless, of course, this precedent is distinguishable. Again, this is not to say that they never depart from precedent.

Similarly, the trial courts of general jurisdiction in most civil law countries in the study do not have or exercise formal power to overrule or modify precedents expressly. That is, these trial courts are not empowered formally to void precedents or similarly modify them. However, in some civil law countries, such as France, Italy and Poland, these trial courts not infrequently decline to follow precedent. In some countries, Germany being a prime example, while it appears that trial court judges seldom decline to follow precedent, when they do depart, they are expected to give a good reason for doing so.

A number of systems, unlike the United Kingdom and the United States, do not permit judges to write and publish dissenting opinions. It is difficult to assess the affect of this on departures. On the one hand, a dissenting opinion may have as its objective that of demonstrating that a given majority decision is a departure, and this very prospect of such a dissent inside a court may deter a departure. On the other hand, a dissenting opinion may attack the substantive soundness of the majority opinion, itself admittedly consistent with precedent, and this dissenting opinion may eventually be adopted by the same court, differently composed, thereby leading to a departure.

Bibliography

Atiyah, P.S. and Summers, R.S. (1991), *Form and Substance in Anglo American Law*, Oxford: Oxford University Press.

Eisenberg, M. (1988), *The Nature of the Common Law*, Cambridge, MA: Harvard University Press.

Summers, 'How Law Is Formal and Why It Matters', *Cornell Law Review*, 85 (Issue no. 5, forthcoming) 1997.

18 Further General Reflections and Conclusions

D. NEIL MacCORMICK, *EDINBURGH* AND
ROBERT S. SUMMERS, *ITHACA*

A single closing chapter cannot by any means summarize the entire fruits of the ambitious comparative and theoretical venture to which this book is dedicated. It can only select and reflect upon several main ideas opened up by the work. As written, the chapter is the responsibility solely of its named authors; but its origin was in discussions among the whole group of authors that took place at the final conference of project members held in Tampere, Finland in August of 1996. That meeting revealed a very considerable emerging consensus about some overall conclusions towards which our studies pointed, and about some of the questions that remained open after the project was complete. Themes that were prominent in the discussion concerned (a) the evident convergence of the legal systems in our study in their use of precedent, (b) the importance, despite this convergence, of certain surviving differences, and (c) implications of the foregoing for legal theory. Then (d) we are, as a group, conscious that our venture has left a number of open questions. Among these are the desirability, and the possibility, of further change, even of deliberate reform of practice; the background concerns in political and constitutional theory posed by the very idea of judicial law-making power; and various points of empirical inquiry that could and should be pursued in the future, even if not by any of the present writers.

1 Convergences in the Treatment of Precedent

Two major similarities should be stressed. The first major similarity is that precedent now plays a significant part in legal decision mak-

ing and the development of law in all the countries and legal traditions that we have reviewed. This is so whether or not precedent is
officially recognized as formally binding or merely as having other
normative force to some degree. For historic reasons, certain legal
systems formally discourage or even discountenance the open citation of precedent in judgments at the highest level. But even in these
cases, precedent in fact plays a crucial role. The present-day law in
France, for example, would be incomprehensible without reference
to the precedents of higher courts filling gaps in or otherwise supplementing the codes and other formal legal sources. And in France
even precedent closely interpreting statutes and codes still has normative significance. The second major similarity is that all systems
also accommodate change and evolution in precedent through judicial action. We will now discuss each of these major similarities in
turn.

   In the common law systems, precedent set by the highest courts is
formally binding on lower courts, including the intermediate appellate courts. And consistent precedents set by the intermediate appellate
courts are formally binding on lower courts. That is, lower courts
must follow precedents set by courts higher up in the same hierarchy
and, when they do not do so, their judgments are not lawful and will
generally be reversed on appeal. This is so not only in so-called
'common law' fields such as contract, tort, property and the like; it is
also true in areas regulated by statute, for, in these, precedent often
adds important interpretative glosses that bind subsequent courts.
But 'formally binding' does not mean 'strictly binding'. Bindingness
in the common law in all fields is subject to exceptions, that is, it is
defeasible, and at least the highest courts have some power to depart
from, or even to overrule their own precedents, though acknowledging them to have normative force of a high order.

   The caricature picture of civil law systems free from the shackles of
precedent in contrast to the common law enslaved to its own past (or
'preserving the good old order') is certainly no longer remotely accurate, if ever it was. There is in fact no sharp dichotomy here, but a
continuum. In the civil law systems, although courts seldom explicitly acknowledge this, precedents are in practice generally recognized
at least as providing strong (but defeasible or outweighable) force,
and can also be cited as providing further support for decisions for
which there are other legally justifying grounds of a kind that might
seem somewhat shaky but for the support afforded by reference to
precedent(s). There has been a tradition in some civil law countries
of describing normative force in terms of a precedent's being merely
' binding de facto', and it is sometimes assumed that this characterization can preserve the traditional theory that, in the civil law,
precedent generally has no important normative role. But the present

study shows that this characterization is at least highly misleading and at most quite fictional. The normative force that precedents in practice have in all the systems here studied, variable as that force may be from system to system, is, in our common view, normative force as a matter of law, that is normative force de jure.

Thus there can be 'bindingness as a matter of law' or 'legal normative force' whether or not precedent is explicitly recognized in constitutions, codes or other statute law, or subject to reversal on appeal to a higher court. The normativity of precedent has evolved as a matter of judicial practice and marks the emergence of a new type of accepted legal authority in civil law countries beyond constitution, code, statute and administrative regulation or decree, and even beyond hierarchical reversibility. Precedent is now everywhere cited and accepted – even called for – in legal argumentation as essential to making a legally satisfactory case. In all countries save France (at *Cour de Cassation* level) this is further mirrored in the citation by courts of precedents in their judicial opinions. Precedents so cited at least have force or provide further support, even for judicial decisions rather closely governed by general code or particular statute. It is no longer true that a well-justified judicial decision in a civil law country must always include a citation to the nearest applicable statute or code provision, no matter how remote or otherwise problematic the citation (again, France aside). Of course, it has long been true that precedents play an important justificatory (and, indeed, law-making) role in nearly all civil law countries in areas where code and statute are less comprehensive than normal, or are stated in vague or general terms (as in 'general clauses').

In all legal systems, it appears that there are some fields of law in which legal development has been particularly a matter of precedent, much less of explicit or detailed statute law (with none at all, in some cases). Public law, especially administrative law, is a case in point, as is the law of civil reparation for injuries, the law of torts. Interestingly, there is some parallelism between civilian and common law jurisdictions in the areas which have been nearest to purely precedent-based, rather than depending on a close interaction of statute and precedent. Accordingly, it might for some purposes be as significant to conduct comparisons between the role of precedent in specific branches of law considered across different legal systems as to make holistic comparisons between different systems in their entirety.

Common law countries recognize as fully as do civil law countries that, apart from formally binding precedent, there may be many gradations of normative force, from the mildly persuasive upwards. Among the highest varieties of normative force short of formal bindingness itself is that degree of force recognized by the highest common law courts when they make it a general practice to follow their own precedents even though this action is not subject to reversal, there being no higher court of appeal. Various other degrees of normative force or support fall between this and the lowest gradations. Thus, for example, though precedents of one common law jurisdiction are not formally binding in another jurisdiction, they still may be recognized as providing further support for an independently justifiable decision, or as sufficient to legitimize quite bold new developments in law. In all systems in our study, precedents are not only recognized as having force in some degree, they are also recognized as having varying weight, weight that depends on a range of factors which appear to exhibit a great degree of commonality across systems, for reasons that are brought out clearly enough in the earlier chapter on rationales for precedent (Chapter 15).

The foregoing fundamental similarity is part of a secular convergence between major contemporary legal systems of the 'Western' world. We believe this convergence is not confined to precedent. There is also an ever-greater reliance in all systems on statute law. Vast areas of law in 'common law' systems are now statutory, and statutes have an almost codifying effect in certain spheres, as one may be reminded by the vast body of law in the 'Uniform Commercial Code', adopted by all states in the USA, with certain minor variations from state to state. Certainly, there remains in the common law countries a substratum of fundamental legal concepts and institutions which have so far escaped capture in statutory formulations. Of course, in the civil law countries, partial obsolescence of codes has led to the growth of specialist supplementary legislation on various topics that overlay the law of the code much as specialist statutes may overlay common law in the USA or the UK. In all cases, it is often argued that social needs march faster than the legislature can move; and the intervention of piecemeal statute law in fields once ruled by the settled harmony of common law or code leaves problems of potential incoherence in the law that the courts have to cure in default of any other public agency available to do so. Sometimes this calls for harmonizing interpretation, sometimes for 'filling the gaps', sometimes even (though never openly in common law countries) for interpretation against the strict terms of a statute ('interpretation *contra legem*').

But in the upshot, just as common law systems now place greater reliance on codes and statute law, various trends in legal life lead civilian systems to place greater reliance on precedent, and to be ever more open in acknowledging this. Most civil law systems in our study are still in various stages of transition, with, in some respects, France, Italy, Poland and Spain still somewhat more wedded to traditional paradigms than others. This trend cannot be explained empirically on the basis of research of the type done in our study, but it is possible to offer rational speculation. Major factors in the movement of civil law systems towards the recognition of precedents set by upper courts are those noted in Chapter 15 above on rationales for precedent. Here we merely stress that coherence in law and equality before the law can readily be understood as especially lawlike and authoritative. Another factor is the value of unity in the national legal order. And various 'rule of law' or *rechtsstaatlich* rationales apply everywhere.

The second major similarity between common law and civil law systems is that all these systems accommodate justified legal change and evolution through *judicial* as well as legislative action, that is, through precedent. *Stare decisis* does not signify stasis in law, conceptually or otherwise. Common law and civil law practice, each in like fashion to the other, likewise admit of justified departures from precedent, though we believe this tends to be conducted more openly in common law systems than in most civilian ones. And in both types of systems, new precedents are set which take the place of the precedents set aside or modified, though in civil law systems this is done less overtly. Moreover, what common law judges call 'cases of first impression' – cases calling for a fresh interpretation of statute law or calling for case law on which no precedent has hitherto been set – arise with some frequency in all systems, and decisions here frequently set important precedents, even ones commencing whole new lines of decision. Further, various types of conflicts between precedent emerge and are resolved. In all these ways, common law courts and civil law courts set aside or renovate old precedents and create new precedents with formally binding or other force, thereby contributing to the overall evolution and development of the law.

Systems of precedent thus not only secure stability but do so without necessarily inhibiting desirable change. What balance it is appropriate to strike between stability and change is essentially a political question, albeit one particularly of the politics of the law, and as such lies beyond the proper concern of the present work. But it is worth remembering that the courts creating and administering precedent are not the only custodians of this balance. In some branches of law in most systems in our study, legislatures appear to be quite active in renovating the law, though in others less so. Administrative agencies also have law-making functions in all systems.

2   Significant Remaining Differences in the Treatment of Precedent

Despite the two major tendencies to convergence just discussed, there remain differences in the treatment of precedent of a highly important kind. Several of these are deeply engrained in the different textures of the systems and especially in their styles of reasoning, of opinion stating and of law reporting. Some of these are well known, and some not.

First, there are differences between common law and civil law systems in the very nature of the officially (or semi-officially) published judicial opinions of higher and highest courts in the two types of systems. And what is reported substantially determines what is readily available to be used as a basis for argumentation in later cases. Unlike typical common law opinions, most officially published civil law opinions of the highest courts (constitutional courts aside) in most countries in our study do not include what common law observers, at least, would consider to be detailed statements of facts, although it is true that a detailed statement of facts may be available on request from the court or other sources (including the lower court opinion). Moreover, unlike many common law opinions (and unlike virtually all such opinions overtly overruling or modifying precedent), the typical officially published civil law opinion of the higher or highest courts (constitutional courts aside) in most countries includes no or very little purely substantive reasoning appealing to policy, although arguments from principle (sometimes quite elliptically stated) have a greater prominence. Moreover, the typical opinion in most civil law countries says relatively little about the procedural posture below of the case on appeal (whether, for example, it arises on an objection to evidence or a ruling on a point of law, and so on).

Second, in the civil law systems, the treatment of precedents in judicial opinions differs markedly from that of the common law systems. There is usually none of the detailed analysis and in-depth discussion of the point and purport of rulings on issues in prior cases, none of the careful teasing-out of points of distinction, both at the factual and at the legal level, that so markedly characterizes most common law reasoning and opinion writing. This, we suggest, reveals a crucial difference in the very concept of what constitutes a precedent as between civil and common law systems, or perhaps, as suggested in Chapter 15, Section 6, what is at issue is a different emphasis among commonly available models of precedent. In any event, the concept, or balance of emphasis among models, varies somewhat from civil law system to civil law system. To generalize, however, precedents are commonly conceived as loci of relatively abstract rules or (perhaps even more) principles, and it is generally to the stated rule or principle of law espoused by the court as an interpretation of code or statute that normative force attaches for the subsequent court, even where code or statute does not closely govern. There is usually not, as in common law systems, a restriction of the binding element to a ruling on an issue of law considered in the special light of the material facts of the case. Thus what we call the model of particular analogy plays far less part here. (See Chapter 15.) Of course, in common law systems, courts frequently essay formulations of a relevant rule of law or general principle, but such a formulation will usually be accepted as binding only insofar as it constitutes a relevant ruling on the issue of law posed by the material facts of the case. (See Chapter 16.)

Third, and related to the immediately preceding point, as a matter of civilian methodology, there is almost no tradition of differentiating systematically in regard to a precedent opinion between *ratio decidendi* and *obiter dicta* – between holding and dictum – as in the common law, and this is true of civilian methodology, again even for fields of law not closely controlled by code or statute. On the other hand, at least in German and in EU law, we do find a common practice of embarking at the outset of an opinion on a bold and wide statement of governing principle, usually with reference to, but not detailed discussion of, relevant precedents; then in the body of the opinion the principle is narrowed down and rendered more precise or subjected to relevant exceptions that finally are concretized in the particular decision of the case, or the holding on the issue of interpretation referred to the court. Though structurally in contrast with common law method at the surface level, this seems to be an approach with considerable functional similarity from the viewpoint of a deeper theory of argumentation.

Fourth, and related to the two preceding points, rules in the common law are contextualized within and emerge from fact situations and fact patterns. These fact situations and fact patterns, as well as the verbal formulations of the rules, play a major role in shaping the scope of common law rules, as applied by subsequent courts. This is far less true in most civil law systems in our study, where the verbal formulations of general rules (statutory and other) and any relevant interpretive methodology are usually the primary determinants of their ultimate scope (always, of course, in conjunction with whatever article of statute or code may require interpretation in the decision). This, of course, is partly so of necessity, because the fact patterns involved may only appear in a relatively formulaic and unanalysed recitation of material facts, or may not appear at all, in the officially published opinion of the civil law court.

Fifth, and related to the three preceding points, no sophisticated methodology of distinguishing precedents otherwise arguably applicable has developed in any of the civil law countries (again, constitutional cases aside), yet distinguishing has long been something of a high art among practitioners and judges in the common law countries. In civil law countries, perhaps because precedents lack the formally binding character or explicitly legal normative force ascribed to them by common lawyers, a process of tacit overruling or other departure appears to be deemed sufficient. While this lightens the load of burdensome detail in law reports, it can give rise to subsequent obscurity as to the line that ought to be drawn between closely analogical precedents that point in different directions. And again, at least at the level of published opinions, the ground for preferring one line to another in any subsequent case is frequently left rather inexplicit.

Sixth, in most cases in most of the civil law countries, a single precedent is usually not on its own sufficient to count as authoritatively settling a point of law (again, constitutional cases aside). Several precedents, that is, a 'line' of precedents, are usually required, and in some countries many precedents may be mentioned on a point. On the other hand, in common law countries, a single precedent of a highest court is frequently enough to settle a point of law (unless serious questions arise later as to its substantive soundness). Here the relative narrowness and 'fact-boundness' of the common law conception of *ratio* is important; in fact, and when the initial *ratio* is relatively wide, it may take a series of decisions to settle points of principle with final clarity, so there may be some functional similarity between superficially contrasting approaches here.

Seventh, a vital difference concerns the liberty of even lower courts to depart from a single higher-court precedent, or even from a line of several precedents. Doctrines of judicial independence, coupled with non-recognition of 'case law' as strict law rather than legally relevant material for argumentation, give to lower courts in several civil law countries competence to hold – for stated reasons – that they find the law or the 'true' law to be other than as laid down from above, and to decide accordingly, of course with the risk of being reversed on appeal, and perhaps with the risk of blighting the career of a judge who might otherwise hope for promotion to higher courts. In Italy, Germany, Finland, France and Spain at least, apparently settled points can be reopened even by trial courts of general jurisdiction on their own judgment as to what is the law, or good law. A purportedly different or new interpretation of code or statute is the usual justification for such departures, at all court levels. This can even lead to the same contested point of law being relitigated many times, before it is taken to be finally settled. (Chapter 2, section II (5), gives a striking example from the law of asylum in Germany.) This historically understandable stress on the need for every judge and court to exercise independent judgment rather than risk injustice under a kind of 'cloak of superior orders' may in some settings lead to confusion, if literally dozens of precedents can be cited for the same point, especially if different appellate tribunals or panels of a supreme court have to pronounce, perhaps in somewhat different terms, on such iterative rejections of precedent. Chapter 5, on Italy, gives some indication of such a problem.

Eighth, in five of the civil law systems in our study, Sweden, Italy, Spain, France and Norway, the higher and highest courts consciously, and with some regularity, depart from precedent without even mentioning this fact. (In the French *Cour de Cassation*, this follows naturally because there the court does not even cite precedent when it does follow it; at the same time, some departures from precedent are expressly noted in the annual report of the *Cour de Cassation* to parliament.) Certainly, departures will come more easily to judges if they need not depart overtly and so need not explicitly justify their changes. Departures may also come more easily to judges where precedents take only the form of abstract interpretations that may seem more flexible or particularistic and so more readily defeasible or outweighable. And departures no doubt come more easily to courts which view themselves as essentially concerned to interpret code or statute as the formal source of law.

Finally, in summary and perhaps extension of the foregoing points, we should note the following features of civil law reasoning that contrast sharply and significantly with common law practice: precedents can be treated as applicable, and applied, without any explicit consideration of their aptness for application to the instant case in the light of its material facts; precedents may be followed, confirmed even, by courts of final instance without express citation or mention, far less express confirmation; likewise, precedents may be tacitly departed from or set aside by such a court, the court leaving it to commentators to draw the legal community's attention to this. In the view of the authors of this chapter, these features (which are common, though not universal, in the civilian systems) are symptomatic of a conception of precedent that deems it something other than or less than a full-dress formal source of law and which, accordingly, has somewhat lower normative force. Also, because courts see themselves bound to do justice according to law, they may confine themselves to citation of code or statute in their opinions, and in their view need not, even ought not to, go into excessive detail in their treatment of materials that are often viewed more as aids to good interpretation than as part of the very fabric of the law.

For all the reality of convergence that we have noted, the foregoing differences are real and sharply visible. Some are likely to continue, even if we may see some prospect of their tending to diminish over time. It is by no means clear that these differences add up to radical differences in the results concretely adjudicated by the different legal systems, and there is some reason to suspect that, in a time of 'globalization' of law, at least some differences of technique may mask an underlying functional similarity in terms of results standardly produced to solve similar problems in countries with similar economic and political systems and values. Although the differences mentioned are very striking, and although they account well for the radically different 'feel' or 'look' of case reports between different types of system, we think it would be easy, especially for common law lawyers, to read too much into differences most of which may be mainly of outward appearance. We believe these differences do not entail as radical a difference in outcomes, or in the total quality of the practice of lawyers and courts in different systems, as appearance might suggest. As often in comparative legal studies, there may be substantial functional equivalence despite considerable difference in the forms in which law and legal reasoning are presented. From the standpoint of the present work, however, focused as it is on legal method, namely on the method of handling and interpreting precedent, the differences are of great interest, perhaps even the more so if our hypothesis of functional similarity or even of equivalence does hold good.

The prior chapters on institutions and on the rationales for precedent (Chapters 13 and 15) go a fair way to accounting for the differences that we find continuing even in a context of secular convergence. We have already remarked in relation to convergences that juristic opinion in all our countries acknowledges substantially common reasons in favour of some principle of *stare decisis*, albeit there are differences in conception of the principle and perhaps in strength of commitment to it. As for the differences, we believe that these ultimately have their primary roots in differences of history and of institutions.

It may be too easy in good times to forget how hard-won the independence of the judiciary has been, and how many situations of authoritarian or downright dictatorial government have chilled or crushed it. But when we remind ourselves of it, it is at once easy to sympathize with rather stringent doctrines of separation of powers, and with practices of at least superficially strict legalism, coupled with the anonymity of the individual judge participating in a collegiate and magisterially stated, often ostensibly deductive, opinion, purporting to derive an ineluctably determined conclusion from a preannounced law for which a quite different state institution has responsibility. (Our Finland chapter, Chapter 3, reminds us of the exigencies under which Finnish judges had to operate during subjection to Imperial Russia, and other more recently problematic situations

in other of the mainland European countries need no explicit remark.) In the historical reality of such a context, it may be that an
acknowledgment of the existence of judge-made precedent as a distinct legal source – an open endorsement of judge-made law – is
what cannot be accepted. The 'precedent of interpretation' is thus
exalted above the 'precedent of solution'. To go beyond this may be
viewed in other quarters as usurpation, and lead to reactions that
threaten judicial independence. Even in better times and happier
circumstances, it remains at least tempting to keep as clear a line as
reasonably possible between the sphere of democratic law making
by elected legislators and the sphere of professional law applying by
appointed judges.

There is a vital historical contrast with a common law tradition in
which at the crucial periods for the development of representative
government (long before any kind of full-scale democracy was even
thinkable) the courts and the legal profession were a part of the
vanguard of resistance to royal power or the tyranny of the executive, and not a subservient force. If in the end there was a politicization
of the judiciary, the long-term tendency was towards politicization
on the side of fundamentally democratic values. Here an openly, if
interstitially, precedent-making judiciary and legal profession, subject to the doctrine of last-resort legislative supremacy, has been
acceptable (though often under withering criticism – the Critical
Legal Studies movement has had many major antecedents, to mention
only Benthamite utilitarianism and American Legal Realism). Where
legislative supremacy, as in the United States, has been subject to
justiciable constitutional restraints, the power of the judiciary has
clearly been massive, and not always received with equanimity from
the standpoint of democratic politics. But in both common and civil
law jurisdictions the marked trend of the times is towards rather
than away from ever more deep-going constitutional adjudication.

However that may be, existing legal systems have their own institutional histories and institutional structures; their own systems of
and approaches to legal education, professional training, appointment of judges and judicial training or lack of it. Built deeply into all
these are similar but diverging understandings of and rationales for,
and different practices in relation to, the use, citation and recording
of judicial precedents. This is so despite tendencies to convergence
arising from commonly acknowledged reasons for some conception
of *stare decisis*.

One hypothesis might be hazarded with a view to supplying a
potentially available test for the foregoing argument: where new
institutions, however brought into being, have scope for an organic
development, this may lead to changes of the kind that we would
otherwise suggest to be improbably achievable by deliberate contriv-

ance. Thus the development of a new style of adjudication through the European Court of Justice, and the likelihood that it will generate far-reaching effects in the legal practice of member states, is worth taking specially into account. One could speculate that over time it may contribute to a 'Europeanization' of approaches, far-reaching in relation both to statute law and to precedent, with the long-run effect that we shall end up thinking it as natural to differentiate the European from the American as we at present do to differentiate the civilian from the common law styles of reasoning with precedent. One important point of difference between the present work and its predecessor, *Interpreting Statutes*, is that there is included here a chapter specifically on European Community law.

3   Some Implications for Legal Theory

The present study has implications for legal theory, in particular for the critique of what we will call voluntaristic theories of law, as well as simplistic conceptions of legal validity and the doctrine of 'sources of law'. These implications also follow from the main findings of our collective work. The historical tendency towards convergence (even with highly significant surviving differences) between the civil law systems and the common law systems in their recognition of precedent as an independently grounded type of authoritative reason for decision with distinctive justificatory force of its own strongly reinforces the proposition that any concept of law that cannot felicitously accommodate among genuine propositions of law those that are precedent-based must be untenable. The countries represented in the study here are themselves highly varied and include, not only two continents, but nine languages (and many other material differences). Moreover, the civil law countries that are in transition to more full-fledged precedent systems include several that, for historical and other reasons, have had periods of past hostility to, or at least scepticism towards, the recognition of precedent as an independent basis for law. It would, therefore, seem likely that any system of law that has a hierarchical court system and publishes the courts' decisions to any appreciable extent, and that exists for any significant period, will eventually come to recognize precedent as a major source of authoritative reasons for decision.

In addition, the convergence with respect to precedent recorded in this study demonstrates and so further confirms a general truth that some would claim to be already implicit in the legal cultures of the common law, namely the conceptual inadequacy of narrowly voluntarist theories of the nature of law (among these, we might include the theories of Jeremy Bentham and the later Hans Kelsen).

Such theories conceive of laws as the contents of discrete acts of will on the part of officials occurring at particular moments of time (except for the case of custom, which differs in several ways). For these voluntarist theories, the paradigmatic forms of law are statutes, administrative regulations and official decrees.

Precedents are not like these, though they do depend on judicial decisions issued in final form at discrete moments. For decisions, even judicial decisions, in their particular, individual person-addressing character are not, as such, general or universal. The decision, when conceived as a precedent, is general or universal because in this conception it is the justifying opinion of the judge or court, not the bare act of deciding, that really counts. Decisions can be precedents only to the extent that they are conceived to rest upon justifying grounds; for these justifying grounds, according to a model of rational and discursive justification, cannot be confined to the single case. They must be available for like application in like cases, whether by some simply intuitive leap of analogical reasoning or (more plausibly) by a more reflective process that universalizes justifying grounds and tests them against similar facts in later cases. So, even with the single case, it is features of decision making other than the particularly volitional, namely the rationally deliberative and discursive features, that account for the exemplary character of the case *qua* precedent. All the plainer is this when several precedents accumulate, for then what they together come to mean for new cases is a matter of reasoned analysis and synthesis that is quite at odds with 'act of will' theory. Again, when we consider the precedent or line of precedents in the broader context of a legal system comprising statutes, constitution and accumulations of interpretation of these, making sense of what lies before us on an assumption of rational legal order requires an assessment of more or less coherent ways of conceptualizing the whole matter. This is not a process of voluntaristic free choice, thus of volition; but it is by no means a process of arbitrary decision either. Thus the law becomes something that takes on a force of its own, and over time becomes something that is not so much 'laid down' from above as something that 'grows up'. Indeed, it emerges from a great patchwork of choices articulated through many deliberations and discourses, and at each time of its application has to be rethought in however partial a way.

In the long history of legal theory, few distinctions have played as prominent a role as the distinction between valid and invalid law. This distinction is at home in relation to certain kinds of procedurally formal acts – legislation, subordinate legislation, issuing court orders and executing private deeds and instruments. That law in its contemporary forms within states and multi-state unions essentially includes such acts and the norms that issue from them is both true and a fundamentally important feature of the legal scene. The voluntaristic fallacy is that which treats such norms as characteristic and thus as the exclusive body of valid law. Systems of law in which precedent plays a considerable part, that is, all the systems here studied, and all the other like systems of the present day, reveal the fallacy. Precedents do not have validity in the all-or-nothing way characteristic of acts performed under requirements of procedural formality. The validity, it might be better to say the 'soundness', indeed, the 'bindingness' or 'force' of precedent is not an all-or-nothing matter. This is a truth already understood in some quarters within common law systems, but the partial convergence of civil law systems recounted here requires us to face up to it frontally.

To begin with, in mature systems in which common law is recognized as valid, there are discrete acts by judges handing down opinions which do not ever yield anything in the way of settled law, and so never achieve any validity beyond the binding effect of the concrete decision on the parties immediately affected. To become settled law at all, and so valid law in general, precedents in many such common law fields must at least pass a minimum threshold test both of substantive acceptability and of reasonable coherence with the pre-established legal context. If a precedent does not do this, it is likely to sink out of sight. That is, it will be ignored, 'confined to its facts', distinguished away on formal grounds, eventually overruled if not simply permitted to wither away in unsung obscurity.

It is not possible to specify in the abstract just what the required threshold of substantive acceptability and coherence that a new precedent must meet to be valid law really is, and in any event, that threshold occupies a point or a series of points on a continuum and may vary from field to field. It is not an all-or-nothing matter. It is not sharply 'on–off', as the valid–invalid distinction normally implies, if we insist on importing it misleadingly into this context. The farther from the threshold, the less normative weight a precedent carries, the nearer to the threshold, or the further over it, the more. (Alternatively, we may, of course, reconstruct the concept of validity to make it a matter of 'more or less'.)

The very scheme of degrees of normative force discussed and applied throughout this book lies outside the all-or-nothing conception of the valid–invalid distinction. Precedent is formally, even if sometimes defeasibly or outweighably, binding or has persuasive normative force to some extent in all systems covered by this study. Propositions of law formulated on the authority of such precedents hence have a provisional, a tentative and a defeasible quality, and they may have to be weighed against, or adjusted in the light of, other propositions similarly founded. If we call them valid in the wider sense, we acknowledge them as valid provisionally, only insofar as certain circumstances hold, for a time, and not if confronted by better derived or farther over-threshold propositions.

A further matter of general theoretical interest is this. H.L.A. Hart and others have described one traditional task of legal theory as that of providing adequate concepts for the representation of general features characteristic of law in modern systems. We believe that the critical points we have made here about the concepts 'act of will' and 'valid–invalid' are in this spirit. But there is more to be said in this spirit which also draws on the fruits of our common research. We believe that, for example, the very concept of bindingness as a continuum rather than as a dichotomy that we deploy here and in our questions is an advance because it enables us to capture the true normative-cum-valuational reality of the practices of following precedent in the various countries. Further, by introducing and deploying the concept of departures from precedent, this project has been able to focus analysis and evaluation on an important element in rational legal deliberation and discourse variously exemplified in many systems (see Chapter 17).

Finally, we are forced to rethink a further concept which recurs throughout this book, and in much legal thought, namely that of a 'source of law'. We have variously stated and implied that it is an important difference between legal systems whether precedent is a 'formal source of law' or not. In terms of the self-characterization of legal systems, achieved under dominant paradigms of legal thought, this is quite accurate and unobjectionable. Common law systems do differ from the systems of codified law in what they characterize as their own 'formal sources'. However, once we draw clear attention to the difference between procedurally formal norm-creating acts, which do admit of all-or-nothing validity, and discursive or deliberative procedures of elaborating legal justifying grounds for decisions and the like, and once we ascribe legal normative force to a greater or lesser degree to the importantly varying products of this process, we see that there is a hopeless ambiguity in applying the term 'source' to both these cases. At that rate, we should 'side' with the civilian approach that refuses to classify precedent as a 'formal source'; but we should also 'side' with the common law in holding that nevertheless the propositions that are elaborated in this process have a genuinely legal quality, though having more or less soundness, greater or less weight.

4 Some Open Questions on Reform of Practice and Other Matters

Finally, it behoves us to acknowledge that a study of this kind leaves open in the end at least as many questions as it may hope to have answered on the way through. A first set of questions to be approached very tentatively concerns desirable future developments. Systems of the different types represented in our study are now significantly convergent in their treatment of precedent, yet noteworthy differences remain, and these pose an interesting question: should the civil law systems contemplate assimilating themselves to the common law as it is today, or should the common law systems contemplate accelerating convergence towards the present situation of the civilian? And are there still other general issues of reform in precedent systems for which our study may have implications? Our study did not specifically address proposals for reform, but we believe that the foregoing issues merit tentative articulation and treatment of a kind that might serve as a useful background for consideration of specific reform proposals in particular systems within our study. We will not attempt to be comprehensive, and we will not offer any specific proposals for reform for any particular country.

An initial question is whether the published official opinions of the judges in those civil law systems in which such opinions are rather sketchy should be more comprehensive. In some systems, most notably France, the opinions do not include full statements of facts and are generally devoid of substantive reasoning. In other systems, the proportion of detailed facts and the proportion of substantive reasoning falls below, often well below, those proportions in opinions in common law countries. It might be thought that the civil law systems should, here, continue their movement towards the common law systems. After all, material facts may be thought to be a firmer basis for circumscribing the scope of a precedent as applied to later cases than mere abstract statements of law. Moreover, a fuller statement of the substantive reasons that actually influence decisions would seem preferable on grounds of candour, predictability and limitation of judicial power. On the other hand, it may be asked whether the full facts in common law opinions actually free subsequent judges far more than the abstract propositions of law in many civilian precedents. It is notorious that common law judges can distinguish prior cases on specious factual grounds and that they sometimes 'overdistinguish', that is, differentiate prior cases on grounds that fail to respect the threshold of similarity that must be accepted if any system of precedent is to survive at all. Furthermore, the elaboration of numerous substantive reasons that one often finds in common law opinions may or may not serve candour or operate to limit judicial power, especially when these reasons serve only as 'make-weights' or the issues are ones (not infrequent) on which substantive reasoning can be just as easily made up for both sides of the issue in question.

At the heart of the civil law movement towards a system in which precedent plays a larger justificatory role is simply the notion that a precedent comes to be taken as an authoritative reason for the decision of a subsequent case, a reason that enhances the justificatory force of the overall opinion. If this be so, then it would seem to follow that, when civilian judges do rely on precedent, they should always do so quite openly, and it would also seem to follow that they should not merely cite the relevant precedents but also explain why they apply, especially when their applicability has been contested. These proposals are already in course of implementation in most systems, though more in some than in others.

It is plain from the present study that even what seem to be settled points of law, points settled by lines of precedent, are nevertheless often relitigated in some civil law countries, so that on a given point of law there may be dozens of superfluous precedents that uphold the point in question. There are obvious objections to relitigation on this scale, not least the costs involved and the consumption of court time which might be better spent writing more extended judicial opinions in the cases that are appropriately appealed. It may be that the remedy is to impose some limits on rights of appeal, or number of instances available for appeal, rather than to continue asserting it as almost a God-given right to appeal, no matter what. This does seem to be a problem in some civil law countries. When litigants have such a right of appeal, this inevitably restricts the role of appellate courts. In addition to having little time to write opinions dealing with issues of law, these courts have no time to deal with issues of fact, matters over which trial judges can easily become petty tyrants. Yet the rule of law requires rule over fact, too. Moreover, the multiplicity of appeals generates numerous conflicts, given that numerous judges are required who sit in appellate panels which always seem not to know what other panels are doing or have done.

The fact that a court may easily and consciously depart tacitly, and without any statement of justifying reasons, from a precedent having force (or providing possible support) requires observers to guess at what is going on, disserves predictability, frees judges from most of the constraints of precedent, and more. Yet such non-overt departures are not uncommon in several civil law countries. The problem, however, is common to both civilian and common law systems. The existence of a non-overt departure is often a matter of controversy and can usually be demonstrated only by rational reconstruction or something like it. A statistical basis for assertions as to frequency would be impractical to construct. It is obvious that non-overt departures through specious distinguishing and the like occur with some frequency in the common law systems. Indeed, they may be more frequent. In this respect, both types of systems display a common deficiency. But the remedy is not obvious. No one, in the long history of the common law, has discovered how to make judges stick to precedent, or how to make them explicitly own up to their departures. And unacknowledged departures in civil law countries may somehow be attributable to the generality and opacity of the precedents.

Where should the power to take the initiative to depart lie? With trial judges? With intermediate appellate courts? With the highest court having jurisdiction? Several civil law countries allow trial judges of general jurisdiction (courts of first instance) to depart, but, at least in Germany, trial judges may depart only if they provide a 'good reason'. The lower courts in Sweden, Finland and Norway have no such power to depart. In the common law countries in our study, courts of first instance generally may not depart from precedent. Rather, departure is a matter for the higher courts, and frequently only for the highest courts. Which way should the systems go? It might be said that granting a trial judge power to depart from generally binding precedent only reinforces the already existing tendency in some places of some trial judges to become petty tyrants. Also such a power would signify that upper court precedent in the trial courts cannot be relied upon, either for out-of-court planning or for purposes of preparation for the trial of disputed facts. On the other hand, it could be argued that trial judges are closer to the facts and the parties, and thus are in a better position to feel the force of arguments in favour of departures, so to do justice or serve policy better. Moreover, it may be that allocation of initial power to depart to trial judges may ease the burden on the poor litigant. Obviously, this matter requires more intensive study than we can give it here.

There is a major point to be made about opinions in the common law systems, especially in the highest courts. These are now plainly becoming overlong. This affects the extent to which they can be effectively used and greatly increases the costs to citizens in and out of litigation who must retain lawyers. Here the terseness of many civil law opinions may be seen to have a special merit of its own.

Finally, we observe that, while the convergence of systems with respect to the recognition and use of precedents is to an extent a welcome development, it has not been confined to interpretive precedents, to precedents filling gaps or otherwise supplementing statutes and codes, and to traditional common law precedents. In nearly all countries, there is also a rapidly growing, and, in some countries, a vast body of, constitutional case law. This extension of precedent-based reasoning to constitutional matters can also lead to the displacement of other bodies of law and to what is sometimes called overconstitutionalization. The fact that many project members have expressed serious reservations about increasing overconstitutionalization of their law does not mean that the authors of this final chapter have any solutions to offer here. Certainly, the subject would seem an apt one for further cooperative study.

5 *Rechtsstaat* or *Justizstaat*

Any reform of or improvement in the practice of precedent in any of our countries leaves open a deep question, that concerning the legitimate power of courts and judges in a contemporary society. In most countries, judges are appointed rather than elected, and the experiments that there have been in the election of judges, chiefly to state courts in various of the United States, have not encouraged or at any rate led to importation of the idea of an elective (and recallable) judiciary elsewhere.

In this context there is reason for some concern about 'judge-made law' in countries which purport to have constitutional government under a separation of powers and democratic government, with law-making power primarily vested in the people or their representatives in a parliament, congress or national assembly. The problem is enhanced wherever democratic institutions are held to presuppose an entrenchment of basic human rights to guarantee the security and dignity of every person, hence to secure citizens in the ability to take a full and proper part in democratic deliberation. If entrenched rights are not justiciable, or are freely alterable by the decision of parliamentary assemblies or popular referenda, they may prove ineffectual, mere paper guarantees. If they are justiciable, the judges of the constitutional tribunal, whatever be its name and composition, necessarily exercise formidable powers, and they are powers in certain matters to second-guess the ordinary democratic process. If the idea of the state under law, the 'law-state' or (in its original language) the *Rechtsstaat*, is to be taken as entailing, not only a governance of state officials under the rule of law, but also the justiciable guaranteeing of some Bill or Charter of Rights, or indeed some international convention of like purport, we face a paradox. Must the *Rechtsstaat* after all turn into a *Justizstaat*, the law-state into a justiciary state or the rule of law nothing better than a rule of judges rather than parliamentarians?

We have recounted in several other places how sharply different approaches to political and constitutional theory have divided over particular implications of the idea of separation of powers. Similarly, it has always been in question how far the sovereignty of elected parliaments, or of the people voting in referenda, is compatible with the rule of law, as A.V. Dicey so confidently asserted it to be, at least in the context of the doctrine of parliamentary sovereignty put forward in his account of the British constitution.

We regard it as question posed, not answered, by our study to show how all these antinomies and tensions can be reconciled or kept in due balance, or shown to be unreal. We record here only that there is convergence despite differences in understanding of key doctrines. We add a brief conjecture: democratic government, as distinct from – usually momentary – popular tyranny cannot indeed endure in mass societies without robust institutions of private and public law. The possibility of continuing and free public debate of a kind that allows for democratic will-formation, almost inevitably through the competition of parties marshalled by professional politicians, is absolutely conditional on legal and constitutional stability. But there cannot be legal and constitutional stability without a trusted judiciary genuinely independent of partisan involvement and political favour. That judiciary must have interpretative power of a far-reaching kind. The best check on its use of power is the fullest publicity in what it does, including a serious level of pressure for consistency of decision over time, yet without inflexibility in face of changing social, political, technological, and economic circumstances. To say this is perhaps not to answer the question, but at least to focus it somewhat. In the spirit of the present endeavour, that is as far as it is proper to go.

Appendix: *Final* Version of the Common Questions, Comparative Legal Precedent Study, September 1994

Introduction and Guidelines

These are the final questions as agreed to be revised during our Bologna and Florence meetings in June 1994. Our next meeting will be in Bologna on 21–22 June 1995. Please revise your answers in light of the new questions below. The new questions below are the *same* as the previous (Ithaca, 1993) draft *except* insofar as specifically indicated below by asterisk or parenthesis. *Much* of what you have already prepared will continue to be usable as answers, but some changes and additions will be necessary.

The questions are grouped under six general headings, guided by the following hypotheses:

I The use of precedent varies from system to system by reference to institutional factors such as court system, style and content of reporting decisions, etc.

II The normative effect given to precedents (bindingness, force, further support, etc.) is likely to be a matter of degree, variable according to type of legal system, with factors of various kinds determining or contributing to the degree of bindingness or force or further support etc. of the precedent.

III Any system will tend to have some understood rationale (or rationales) for its use of precedent, and these will have a bearing on the effects precedents have and on how they are handled.

IV Where precedents are binding, have force, or provide further support etc., they tend to be considered only in respect of some element or elements in the case as reported, and different systems may have different approaches to determining what this element (or elements) is.

V   Precedents can sometimes be distinguished, modified or even overruled and each system may have a distinctive approach to this.

VI   There is always scope for reflection on and criticism of practice in relation to precedents, and changes may be made in response to criticism, to changes in the international environment, and other factors.

Each section below contains a list of detailed questions set out in what we hope is a thematically rational order. So far as possible, please answer in the order indicated; but above all please aim to produce in each section a coherent account of your system in the relevant aspect.

To avoid overlap between sections, be guided by a sense of relevance in each section to the hypothesis underlying the section suggested above.

I   Institutional and Systemic

1(a)   What is the basic hierarchy of courts in your system, that is, beginning with your basic trial courts of general jurisdiction and moving upward, to what higher courts are there appeals? Alternatively, describe the hierarchy from the top down if this is a more convenient method of description. List only the *main* levels of courts. Distinguish in your answer between civil and criminal, and/or administrative, if this affects the hierarchy importantly. Mention any special courts that may be of particular significance for the discussion of precedent. Insofar as your system is a federal system, explain how this affects the hierarchy.

1(b)   How many judges are there in your higher courts producing possible precedents? How many cases do they decide each year? Do the judges sit as one court or in sections or panels? How are votes cast in decision making? Are differences confidential to the court or are they made public? Are any other aspects of court structure or procedure significant in relation to precedent?

1(c)   What power do your higher courts producing possible precedents have to select the cases they will decide? By what criteria? Can the power of selection be used specifically in order to review precedents or to set new ones?

2   What is the normal structure and content of higher court judgments? Is the prevailing style (a) deductive or discursive; (b) legalistic or substantive; (c) magisterial or argumentative? (For the sense of these terms, see *Interpreting Statutes*, Ch.12, pp.496–501.)

3 How are judgments of the higher courts published? In official series? Semi-official series? Commercial or private series? Academic journals? Newspapers? Are any such reports authenticated by judges? Who selects what cases are to be reported? How accessible are reports? Are electronic media used for storage and access? How many levels in the court hierarchy are regularly reported?

4 What do your best available reports of court judgments characteristically contain? Describe, explain and consider:

a	Case name and any other identification?
b	Name of the deciding court?
c	Headnote or rubric?
d	Statement of facts (how detailed)?
e	Discussion of procedural background and prior decisions in this very case?
f	Statement of legal issue or issues?
g	Discussion of interpretational problems as to statutes and as to precedents?
h	Specific holding or ruling on legal issues?
i	Reason or reasons for the ruling?
j	Statement of final decision?
k	Concurring opinions?
l	Dissenting opinions?
m	Summary of arguments by counsel?
n	Opinion by legal officials other than judges, e.g., secretary of court?
o	Juristic commentary on decision?

If the report does not contain one or more of the above, are these generally discoverable from other sources? Explain.

5 'Precedent' is sometimes taken to mean (a) any prior decision possibly relevant to a present case to be decided, or (b) sometimes to mean only such a prior decision when it is in some measure formally binding, or (c) sometimes only to mean a decision which the deciding court expressly adopts or formulates to guide future decision making. Explain what is true in your system. (Do not overlap your answer with II below.)

6 When judges or practitioners or scholars refer to precedent, do they refer in detail to reported published texts and their contents as detailed in (4) above? Is detailed discussion of precedents found in judicial opinions and/or in juristic legal writing, or neither? How important a role do scholarly or other juristic treatises and other writings have in explaining and synthesizing bodies of precedent law? Are lawyers who argue cases before the courts expected to cite and discuss precedents in written or in oral argument?

7   Compared to other justificatory materials and types of arguments including codes, statutes, constitutions, authorized types of interpretive arguments, policy, principle, substantive reasoning, and academic writings or other professional commentary that courts in your country use to decide cases, what is the relative overall role of precedent? Major? Minor? Discuss and explain. (Do not overlap your answer with (8) below.)

8   Does the importance of precedent-based law ('case law', '*jurisprudence*' in the French sense, etc.) in your system differ as between different branches of law, e.g., private law, commercial law, administrative law, constitutional law? Explain.

9   Sometimes on the issue before the court there is no statute and no precedent or at least no close precedent. In such cases, do judges frequently create precedent? Discuss. When judges do create precedent, how explicit and methodologically self-conscious are they about it in their written opinions? Explain.*

II   The Formal Bindingness of Precedent or Other Justifying Force, etc.

Precedents when used at all are generally used only when relevant or 'in point'. We explore this matter of relevance (being in point) in Section III below. Here we concentrate on the formal bindingness, force, etc. of a relevant precedent and on the factors with which this varies.

1   We may usefully differentiate bindingness, force, further support and illustrativeness or other value of a precedent as follows:**

(1)   *Formal bindingness*: a judgment not respecting a precedent's bindingness is not lawful and so is subject to reversal on appeal. Distinguish:

  (a)   formal bindingness not subject to overruling: (i) 'strictly binding' – must be applied in every case, (ii) defeasibly binding – must be applied in every case unless exceptions apply (exceptions may be well defined or not);

  (b)   formal bindingness (with or without exceptions) that is subject to overruling or modification.

(2)   *Not formally binding but having force*: a judgment not respecting a precedent's force, though lawful, is subject to criticism on

---

*This question I.9 is a new question added at Bologna–Florence.
**Question II.1 was substantially revised in Bologna–Florence. The footnote in the Ithaca questions at p.8 thereof is omitted.

this ground, and may be subject to reversal on this ground.*
Distinguish:
  (a) defeasible force – should be applied unless exceptions come
       into play (exceptions may or may not be well defined);
  (b) outweighable force – should be applied unless counter-
       vailing reasons apply.
(3) *Not formally binding and not having force (as defined in (2)) but
providing further support*: a judgment lacking this is still lawful and
may still be justified, but not as well justified as it would be if the
precedent were invoked, for example, to show that the decision
being reached harmonizes with the precedent.
(4) *Mere illustrativeness or other value.*

Are precedents in your systems recognized in any of these degrees?
Are these degrees, or similar degrees, explicitly discussed within
judicial opinions? In scholarly or other juristic commentaries? Explain.
2 Is there any legislation in your system requiring or forbidding the
use of precedent or otherwise regulating its formal bindingness? Is
there any case law about the formally binding character of precedent?
  Is it common, in your system, to differentiate precedent as binding
de jure or only de facto, and if so in what sense of these terms? Is
precedent deemed a source of law independent of statute or custom,
or does precedent have status as law only in conjunction with statute
or custom? Are there areas or branches of your system of law in
which the main substance of the contemporary governing law derives from precedent? Where this is so, is there still a requirement of
an ultimate basis or foundation in statute law or custom, or is the use
of precedent alone legally sufficient? Is pre-existing statutory law
(rather than mere precedent) generally required for lawfulness of a
decision insofar as the maxim *nulla poena sine lege* applies?
3 What factors are treated as relevant to determining the degree of
formal bindingness of a precedent? Consider such possible factors
as:

a   The hierarchical rank of the court.
b   Whether the decision is merely of a panel or by a full bench.
c   The reputation of the court or of the judge writing the opinion.

*An example of precedent not binding in common law systems but sometimes
having force would be a precedent of another appellate court in the same system
where that court is not a higher court but one of the same level. In most civil law
systems, precedent almost never has formally binding effect. But precedents of the
highest courts in such systems usually have 'defeasible force' (and sometimes they
have only 'outweighable' force).

d   Changes in the political, economic or social background since the prior decision.
e   Soundness of the supporting arguments in the opinion.
f   The age of the precedent.
g   The presence or absence of dissent.
h   The branch of law involved (for example, precedent having more force in property law than in the law of tort).
i   Whether the precedent represents a trend.
j   How well the precedent is accepted in academic writings.
k   The effect of legal change in related areas.
l   Other?

4   Are there any types of factors which may deprive a precedent of the formal bindingness it would normally have? Can decisions be held defective in some way so as never to achieve the status of formally binding precedent? Is any distinction drawn in the degree of formal bindingness between precedents dealing with statute law and precedents of other kinds?
5   Must lower courts generally follow precedents set by higher courts ('vertical formal bindingness')? Are decisions of courts of the same level binding on each other ('horizontal formal bindingness')? Must the highest court (or courts) in your system generally follow its own precedent? Does it do so in practice?
6   To the extent that your system recognizes that precedents have (a) justifying force, (b) provide further support, or (c) merely have illustrative value (and for definitions of these terms, see II(1) above), discuss:

(1)   how clearly the courts differentiate between these possibilities, and
(2)   the major factors that contribute to the weight of (a), (b) and (c) individually.

If there is any legislation in your system about the matters in (6) above, discuss. If there is discussion of these matters in treatises or other scholarly works, discuss their influence.*
7   Is there any view that there are too many precedents in some fields? Explain. How does the presence of numerous precedents affect the bindingness, force, etc. of precedent? (This question is new from Bologna–Florence.)

*This entire question II.6 is newly added here in Bologna–Florence.

III The Rationale of Precedent

1   If your system accords formal bindingness to precedent as indicated in Section II.1(1) above, are there generally recognized rationales for treating precedents in this way? Consider and discuss, e.g.:

a   theories of the authoritative or declaratory status of precedent as a source of law, form of law making, or the like;

b   justificatory grounds for giving courts power to create and develop law through precedent, e.g., gaps, indeterminacy of other types of legal materials, responsiveness to particular needs for precedent, limitations of legislatures as where they fail to amend obsolete statutes so that courts must sometimes do so in light of policy and principle;*

c   justificatory theories for requiring courts to follow precedent, e.g., predictability, certainty, uniformity, reduction in litigation;

d   other.

In your system, are such rationales ever discussed in judicial opinions and, if so, how are they considered relevant to the degree of formal bindingness of a precedent?

2   To the extent your system recognizes that precedents have justifying force, provide further support or have mere illustrative value, describe and discuss the recognized rationales for these. Consider, as relevant, the items in III.1(a), (b) and (c) above.

IV Precedents: What They Stand for and How They Apply

This section deals with what precedents may stand for, and with how a precedent is determined to be relevant or in point.

1   What in your system does a judge find or reconstruct from the prior decision that is binding or has force or provides other support? Consider and discuss the following:

a   relevant facts as decided on;

b   explicit or constructed 'holding' on an issue of law, or '*ratio decidendi*';

c   explicitly formulated (or implicit) rule;

d   explicitly formulated (or implicit) principle;

e   substantive reasons stated for (a) or (b) or (c) or (d);

*The order of (b) and (c) was reversed in Bologna–Florence and (b) has been slightly revised.

f   carefully formulated *obiter dicta* dealing authoritatively with a point of law not ultimately resolved by the court;

g   other.*

2   Is there a judicial, scholarly or other juristic practice of giving arguments for and against the *applicability* of a precedent to the state of facts before the court? If yes, please explain the nature of the types of argument in terms of whether they:

a   take the form of close factual analysis or characterization of facts;

b   take the form of isolating rules, or principles, in the precedent and reasoning from the language of those;

c   take the form of argument in terms of the applicability of substantive reasons in the precedent to the case at hand;

d   take the form of reasoning from general rationales for following precedent;

e   other.

3   Is there a body of judicial or scholarly or other juristic discussion of *methods* for defining and finding what a precedent stands for? Describe and discuss.

4   Are precedents used as illustrative examples or analogies even when not strictly in point? Explain. Consider whether such examples are:

a   merely to clarify,

b   to harmonize,

c   to show relevance and/or non-relevance,

d   other.**

5 Does your system draw any distinction between the bindingness or force or further support of single precedents on the one hand and lines of precedents on the other hand?*** Explain. Do your courts more commonly rely on one or a few precedents or do they more commonly rely on lines of precedent (if available) when they follow precedent? Explain. Do precedents belonging to a line have a different bindingness, force or other normative importance than a single precedent? Explain. Do the following lines of precedents exist in your system and, if so, describe anything distinctive about their character and their bindingness, force, etc., as appropriate:

*A few relatively minor changes were made in question IV.1 in Bologna and Florence. Question IV.2(d) was also added.
**This question was expanded at Bologna and Florence.
***Questions 5 and 6 (below) were substantially revised at Bologna and Florence.

a   Lines consisting of 'merely repetitive' precedents.
b   Explicit confirmation of lines of precedents.
c   'Synthesizing' or reconstructive lines (the precedents are taken to stand for a legal point not explicitly formulated in the prior precedents considered individually).
d   'Conflicting' (zigzag) lines of precedents. What roles do scholars and other juristic commentators play here? How far do they organize and synthesize or reconstruct such lines of precedents? Reconcile such lines of precedents? Are these efforts influential in the courts?

6   In the light of (5), or otherwise, has the concept of a 'leading case' (leading precedent) any distinctive part in your system's approach to precedent? Explain. Do such precedents sometimes start a line of precedents? When? Explain.

V   Distinguishing, Explaining, Modifying, Overruling

1   Sometimes a precedent which is ostensibly or arguably applicable may on analysis be seen to stand for a point other than the point at issue in the present case. In this situation, do courts have a practice of expressly 'distinguishing' the precedent (to show why it is *not* binding in *this* case) or are precedents simply ignored by courts when considered not it point? Explain.
2   Do scholarly or other juristic commentators discuss points of difference (distinguish) between reported precedents? (A reference to hypothetical cases in the Ithaca version of this question was omitted at Bologna–Florence.)
3   Is the judicial power to distinguish a precedent sometimes used in such a way as to draw excessively fine or unreal distinctions? Is there a practice of 'explaining' or restating precedent either as to their facts or the characterization of facts or as to the legal holding or *ratio*, and thereby reconciling an ostensibly unfavourable precedent with the present decision? Are there other ways in which subsequent decisions can lead to or involve modification or revising of precedents? Does any of this occur in or through scholarly or other juristic commentaries in addition to judicial practice? (At Bologna–Florence the last line of this question was changed.)
4   What types of overruling exist in your system:*

*Ithaca question (4) was deleted at Bologna–Florence, and Ithaca question (5) became (4) here, but it was substantially revised in Bologna–Florence.

a　　Overruling in the strict sense – an explicit judicial act of overturning a *binding* precedent or a line of precedent?

b　　Overruling in a broader sense – an explicit judicial act of rejecting a precedent (or line of precedent) having only *force,* or other possible support?

c　　Silent overruling – not following a precedent (or line of precedent) and not explicitly acknowledging this?

d　　Overruling whereby a precedent is explicitly or implicitly cut down so severely in scope that it no longer exists as a precedent, e.g., is 'confined to its facts', as common law judges say.

When a precedent or line of precedent is explicitly overruled, are special procedures followed (e.g. convening a larger number of judges)? Must special reasons be given? Describe. Are there variations as between overruling precedent dealing with a constitution, or a code, or a non-codified statute, or mere case law area? Are there variations between overruling a single precedent and overruling a line of precedent? Can only the highest court overrule a precedent?

5　Is there any power in courts to prospectively overrule precedent? (By 'prospectively overruling' of a precedent we mean overruling a precedent with effect only on future cases and therefore no effect on the case being decided which is still decided in accord with the precedent being overruled.) Is there a practice of prospective overruling? On what grounds and within what limits is prospective overruling deemed appropriate?*

6　Is anticipatory overruling by lower courts permitted? (By 'anticipatory overruling' of a precedent we refer to a lower court refusing to follow a precedent in anticipation of the likelihood that a higher court will overrule it.) Is it much in use?

7　In legislative practice, do drafters of legislation or members of government or the legislature take account of case law and precedent as well as prior statute law when reforming the law by legislation? Does apparent legislative confirmation or reversal of case law through statute count as a reason for or against the bindingness of precedent?

8　When precedents conflict, how are such conflicts resolved? Note that conflicts of precedent include open contradiction, or inconsistency of result and reasoning, implicit such contradiction and also major differences in reasoning yet sameness of result. Also explain the likely effects of resolutions of such conflicts.**

9　How do scholarly or other juristic commentators, and how do judges and lawyers, utilize hypothetical cases in reasoning about the

*Questions (5), (6) and (7) here were formerly (6), (7) and (8) in the Ithaca draft.
**This question and question (9) below are new in this final Bologna–Florence draft.

creation and application of precedent? Are the following uses recognized? Explain.

a   The use of hypothetical cases in *reductio ad absurdum* argumentation when creating or applying precedent.

b   The use of hypothetical cases as paradigms of the applicability of a rule or principle in a precedent.

c   The use of extreme hypothetical cases to test the appropriateness of formulations of a rule or principle in a precedent.

d   The use of extreme hypothetical cases to test the limits of the scope of a precedent.

e   Other.

VI   Matters of General Perspective, Evaluation and Other

1   Is there any general opinion that the real justificatory use of precedent in your system fails to be reflected in the reported decisions? Thus: Do judges *say* they are 'free', yet de facto follow precedent? Do judges *say* they are bound by precedent, yet decline *in fact* to follow it? Is there no real gap between *saying* and *doing*?*

2   Has there been recent change or evolution in the creation or use of precedent in your country? If so, discuss and explain.

3   Have changes in the external legal environment, e.g., the development of transnational institutions such as the EC, EFTA, human rights agencies, or the like contributed to new approaches in either the theory or practice of precedent? If so, explain.

4   Are there any currents of academic or other criticism of how precedents are created and used in your country? If so, describe and give your own view.

*This question was newly revised at Bologna–Florence.

About the Authors

Aulis Aarnio is Professor of Law, Director of the Research Institute for Social Sciences at the University of Tampere, Finland. He was educated at the University of Helsinki. His books include: *Perspectives in Jurisprudence* (Helsinki: Acta Philosophica Fennica, 1983), *The Rational as Reasonable* (Dordrecht: Reidel, 1987) and *Reason and Authority* (Dartmouth, 1997).

Robert Alexy is Professor of Public Law and Legal Philosophy at the University of Kiel, Germany. He received his degrees from the University of Göttingen, and is the author of *A Theory of Legal Argumentation* (Oxford: Oxford University Press, 1989) a translation of: *Theorie der juristischen Argumentation* (Frankfurt/M.: Suhrkamp, 1978/1991) and author of *Theorie der Grundrechte*, Baden-Baden 1985: Nomos (Frankfurt/M.: Suhrkamp, 1994).

Zenon Bankowski is Professor of Legal Theory at the University of Edinburgh. He was educated at the universities of Dundee and Glasgow. His books include: (as co-author) *Lay Justice?* (Edinburgh: T. & T. Clark, 1987) and (as co-editor) *Informatics and the Foundations of Legal Reasoning* (Dordrecht: Kluwer, 1995).

John J. Barceló is William Nelson Cromwell Professor of International and Comparative Law, Cornell University. He is also Elizabeth and Arthur Reich Director of the Berger International Legal Studies Program at Cornell. He was educated at Tulane University, Tulane Law School and Harvard Law School. His scholarship focuses on international trade and transactions law and European Community law.

Gunnar Bergholtz is Professor of Procedural Law at the University of Lund, Sweden. He is a former district court judge and justice of appeal. He is author of *Ratio and Auctoritas* (Lund, 1987) and other works in the field of procedural law.

Ralf Dreier is Professor of General Legal Theory at the University of Göttingen. He was educated at the universities of Hamburg, Freiburg/ Br. and Münster. His books include: *Recht-Moral-Ideologie* (Frankfurt: Suhrkamp, 1981) and *Recht-Staat-Vernunft* (Frankfurt: Suhrkamp, 1991).

Svein Eng is Associate Professor of Law at the University of Oslo, Norway. He was educated at the University of Oslo. He is the author of *Analysis of dis/agreement – with particular reference to law and legal theory* (forthcoming in Norwegian by Universitetsforlaget, Oslo; to be translated into English and published by Kluwer, Dordrecht). His other writings include a series of studies of basic legal concepts and methodology, including studies of the concepts of 'competence', 'in/ validity' and 'juristic act' and studies in the doctrine of precedent.

Christophe Grzegorczyk is Professor of Law at the University of Paris X (Nanterre) and Professor of Legal Theory and Philosophy at two Swiss universities: Neuchâtel and Fribourg. He was educated at the Jagellonian University of Cracow (Poland) and he received his degrees from the University of Paris II. He is the author of *Théorie générale des valeurs et le droit* (Paris: LGDJ, 1982) and the co-author of *Positivisme juridique* (Paris: Economica, 1990).

Francisco J. Laporta is Professor of Philosophy of Law at the University of Madrid (Autonoma). He is former Director of the Centre of Constitutional Studies and of the Spanish Council of State. His books include: *Entre el Derecho y la Moral*, 2nd edn (Mexico City: Intamara, 1995).

Massimo La Torre is Professor of Legal Philosophy at the European University Institute in Florence. He was educated at the University of Messina, and received a LLD degree from the European University Institute in Florence. He is the author of *La 'lotta contro il diritto soggettivo'* (Milan: Giuffre, 1988), and the editor of N. MacCormick and O. Weinberger, *Il diritto come istituzione* (Milan, Giuffrè, 1990). He is also Assistant Editor of 'Ratio Juris'. An International Journal of Jurisprudence and Philosophy of Law', published by Basil Blackwell, Oxford/Cambridge (MA).

D. Neil MacCormick is Regius Professor of Public Law, the law of Nature and Nations at the University of Edinburgh. He was educated at Glasgow and Oxford universities and holds an honorary doctorate of the Universities of Uppsala and of the Saarland and Queens University Western Ontario. His books include: *Legal Reasoning and Legal Theory* (Oxford: Oxford University Press, 1978) and (as co-author with Ota Weinberger) *An Institutional Theory of Law* (Dordrecht: D. Reidel, 1986).

Geoffrey Marshall is Provost of Queen's College Oxford. His books include: *Constitutional Theory* (Oxford: Clarendon Press, 1975) and *Constitutional Conventions* (Oxford: Clarendon Press, 1986).

Alfonso Ruiz Miguel is Professor of Philosophy of Law at the Universidad Autónoma of Madrid. He was educated in the same university. His books include: *Philosophy and Law in Norberto Bobbio* (Madrid: Centro de Estudios Constitucionales, 1983), *Justice of War and Peace* (idem, 1988) and *Abortion: Constitutional Problems* (idem, 1990).

Lech Morawski is Professor of Legal Theory at the University of Torun. His books include *Legal Presumptions* (Torun, 1980) and *Legal Argumentation, Rationality and the Law of Evidence* (Torun, 1980).

Aleksander Peczenik is Professor of Legal Theory at the University of Lund. He was educated in Poland and in Sweden. His books include: *The Basis of Legal Justification* (Lund: University Press, 1983) and *On Law and Reason* (Dordrecht/Boston/London: Kluwer, 1989).

Robert S. Summers is McRoberts Research Professor of Law, Cornell University, and during 1991–2, was Arthur L. Goodhart Visiting Professor of Legal Science, University of Cambridge. He was educated at the University of Oregon and Harvard Law School and holds honorary degrees from the University of Helsinki and the University of Göttingen. His books include: *Form and Substance in Anglo-American Law* (with P.S. Atiyah) (Oxford: Oxford University Press, 1987) and *Instrumentalism and American Legal Theory* (Ithaca: Cornell University Press, 1982).

Michele Taruffo is Professor of Law at the University of Pavia. He was educated at the University of Pavia. His books include: *American Civil Procedure An Introduction* (New Haven: Yale University Press, 1993) (with G.C. Hazard) and *The Proof of Legal Facts* (Milan: Giuffrè, 1992).

Michel Troper is Professor of Law at the University of Paris X (Nanterre). He received diplomas or degrees from the Institute of Political Studies in Paris and from the University of Paris. His books include: *The Separation of Powers in French Constitutional History* 2nd edn (Paris: LGDJ, 1980) and the co-author of *Legal Positivism* (Paris: LGDJ, 1991).

Marek Zirk-Sadowski is Professor of the Theory and Philosophy of Law at the University of Lodz in which he also served terms of office as Dean of the Law Faculty and as the Vice-Rector of the University. His books include: *The Understanding of Evaluations in the Legal Language* (Lodz, 1984) and *Law and Participation in Culture* (Lodz, 1996).

Index

N.B. Page references to tables are in italics.